ELECTRONIC MEDIA
LAW

ELECTRONIC MEDIA
LAW

ROGER L. SADLER
Western Illinois University

SAGE Publications
Thousand Oaks ▪ London ▪ New Delhi

For information:

Sage Publications, Inc.
2455 Teller Road
Thousand Oaks, California 91320
E-mail: order@sagepub.com

Sage Publications Ltd.
1 Oliver's Yard
55 City Road
London EC1Y 1SP
United Kingdom

Sage Publications India Pvt. Ltd.
B-42, Panchsheel Enclave
Post Box 4109
New Delhi 110 017 India

Printed in the United States of America on acid-free paper.

"Academy Award" is a registered trademark of the Academy of Motion Pictures Arts and Sciences.

Library of Congress Cataloging-in-Publication Data

Sadler, Roger L.
Electronic media law / Roger L. Sadler.
p. cm.
Includes bibliographical references and index.
ISBN 1-4129-0588-5 (pbk. : alk. paper)
1. Telecommunication—Law and legislation—United States. 2. Broadcasting—Law and legislation—United States. 3. Digital media—United States. I. Title.
KF2765.S23 2005
343.7309'94—dc22

2004026097

05 06 07 08 09 10 9 8 7 6 5 4 3 2 1

Acquiring Editor:	Margaret H. Seawell
Editorial Assistant:	Jill Meyers
Project Editor:	Claudia A. Hoffman
Copy Editor:	Catherine M. Chilton
Typesetter:	C&M Digitals (P) Ltd.

CONTENTS

Preface   xvii

Acknowledgments   xix

1. The American Legal System   1
   The American Legal System   1
       Constitutional Law   2
       Amending the Constitution   2
       Statutory Law   3
       Administrative Law   3
       Common Law   4
       Equity Law   4
       Executive Powers   4
   The Courts   5
       Trial Courts and District Courts   5
       Appeals Courts   6
       The U.S. Supreme Court   7
       How a Case Makes Its Way to the Supreme Court   7
       State Courts   9
       Criminal and Civil Law   9
       The Civil Lawsuit Process   11
       Names and Citations of Cases   12
   Legal Research Online   13
       Key Government Web Sites   15
   Summary   15

2. Understanding the First Amendment   16
   Roots of American Law   16
   Sedition in the United States   17
       The Alien and Sedition Acts of 1798   18
       Sedition Laws Resurface in World War I   18
       The Clear and Present Danger Test   19
   States and the First Amendment   20
       World War II: The Smith Act   21
   Fighting Words   23
       Are These Fighting Words?   23
   Hate Speech   25
       Cross Burning and Swastikas   25
       Campus Speech Codes   26

Flag Desecration   27
Prior Restraint   28
   Near v. Minnesota   28
   The Pentagon Papers   29
   The H-Bomb Case   31
Time, Place, and Manner Restrictions   31
   Criteria for Time, Place, and Manner Restrictions   32
   Krishnas and a State Fair   32
   Rock Concerts and Volume   33
Summary   34

3.   Applying the Principles of Broadcast Regulation   35
   The Federal Communications Commission   36
   The Communications Act of 1934   36
      FCC Commissioners   37
      Drafting New Regulations   38
      Important FCC Terminology   38
      FCC Bureaus   39
      FCC Licensing   39
      Broadcast Stations and Minority Employees   40
      FCC Licenses and Minority Preferences   41
      TV and Radio License Renewals   41
   Political Broadcasting Rules   43
      The "Equal Time" or "Equal Opportunity" Rule   44
   Section 315 Analyzed   45
      "Equal Time" Really Means "Equal Opportunities"   45
      Deadlines   45
      Legally Qualified Candidates   46
      Ads Without a Candidate's Voice or Picture   46
      Other "Uses"   47
      Celebrity Candidates   47
      Section 315 and Primaries   49
      No Censorship of Political Ads   50
      Lowest Unit Rate   52
   Section 315 and News Exemptions   54
      Debates and the Aspen Rule   54
      Section 315 and Talk Shows   57
      Sponsorship Identification   58
   BCRA (FECA)   58
      Federal Candidate Ads and BCRA   58
      BCRA and Lowest Unit Rate   60
      Third-Party Restrictions Under BCRA   60
      Political File   62
   Section 315 Violations   62
   Section 315 and Ballot Issues   62
   Section 315 and Newspapers   63
   Reasonable Access: Section 312(a)(7)   63
      Important Rules Regarding Reasonable Access   66
   Political Editorial and Personal Attack Rules   66
      Personal Attack and Political Editorial Rules Thrown Out   67
   Fairness Doctrine   67
   Summary   69

4.	Cable and Satellite Regulation	70
	Early Cable Regulation	71
	Leapfrogging	72
	The FCC Is Allowed to Regulate Cable	72
	Cable and "Public Interest"	73
	The 1972 Cable Television Report and Order	74
	Antisiphoning Rule Struck Down	74
	The Cable Communications Policy Act of 1984 (The 1984 Cable Act)	75
	Franchises	76
	Access Channel Rules	77
	PEG Channels No Longer Mandatory	78
	The KKK and Public Access	80
	Mandatory Leased Access	81
	Privacy	81
	Cable TV and Copyright Law	81
	Compulsory Licensing	82
	"Must-Carry" Rules	83
	The Cable Television Consumer Protection and Competition Act of 1992	84
	"Must-Carry" and "May-Carry"	84
	Rate Regulations . . . for a Time	86
	Rate Rollbacks	87
	Proportional Rates	87
	Channel Repositioning	87
	Service Standards	87
	Syndicated Exclusivity ("Syndex")	88
	Syndex Reborn	89
	Network Nonduplication Rules	89
	Cable Descramblers	89
	Public Inspection Files	90
	Cable System Fines	90
	Satellite Radio and TV	90
	Satellite Radio	91
	Satellite Radio Regulations	92
	Satellite TV	93
	Satellite TV Regulations	93
	High Definition Television (HDTV)	95
	A Brief History	95
	2009 Target Date	96
	Missed Deadlines	96
	Manufacturer Deadlines	96
	Overall, a Slow Start but Gaining Momentum	98
	Digital Radio	98
	Developing a DAB Standard (IBOC)	99
	Digital Radio: Advantages for Listeners	99
	Digital Radio: Advantages for Stations	100
	Summary	101
5.	Media Ownership Rules	101
	History of Broadcast Ownership Rules	102
	1940: The Duopoly Rule	102
	1943: The Supreme Court Limits Broadcast Network Powers	102
	Broadcast Station Ownership Limits: 7–7–7, 12–12–12, and Beyond	104

Cross-Ownership Rules   105
   Independent Voices   106
   TV-Newspaper Cross-Ownership Liberalized   107
   Satellite TV–Cable Cross-Ownership   107
The Telecommunications Act of 1996   108
   Radio Ownership Limits   108
   Other Major Changes From the Telecomm Act of 1996   112
TV Duopoly Rules Updated   113
The New 2003 TV and Cross-Media Rules   113
   1. Proposed 45% National TV Ownership Limit   114
   2. Local TV Multiple Ownership Limits   114
   3. Cross-Media Limits Rule   115
   4. Dual Network Ownership Prohibition   116
   5. Defining Radio Markets   116
2003 Ownership Changes Harshly Criticized   116
   Court Blocks New Ownership Rules   117
National Cable Ownership Rules   117
Antitrust Laws and Media Mergers   118
Low-Power FM Stations   119
   Opposition to LPFM   121
Low-Power Television (LPTV)   122
Local Marketing Agreements (LMA)   122
Summary   123

6. Broadcast Station Regulations   124
Broadcast Identifications   124
   Station Identification (or Legal Identification)   124
   Content   125
Important Station Paperwork   126
   Logs   126
Power Readings   127
Main Studio Rules   127
The Emergency Alert System   128
   Basic EAS Rules for Stations   128
   EAS and the "Amber Alert"   130
Chief Operators and Logs   131
   Guidelines for Chief Operators   131
Public Inspection File   132
The Station Copy of FCC Rules and Regulations   134
Telephone Rules   134
The "Live" Rule   135
   Live Newscasts and Teasers   136
   Live News Reports   136
Broadcast Hoaxes   136
   Volcano in Connecticut?   137
   Fake Nuclear Attack   137
   "Confess Your Crime" Hoax   137
   Dead Radio Host Hoax   138
   FCC Creates Broadcast Hoax Rule   139
Broadcast Content   139
   News Content   139
   Drug Lyrics   140
   Contests   140

Payola and Plugola 143
    Payola 143
    Plugola 143
Other Legal Issues 145
    Sponsor Identification 145
    Subliminal Advertising 145
    Soliciting Funds 146
    Unattended or Automated Radio Stations 146
    Telephone Access 146
Non-FCC Legal Issues 147
    Radio Traffic Jam 147
    Radio Traffic Jam II 147
    It Pays to Read 148
    Prank Phone Call to the White House 148
    Animal Cruelty Case 148
    Wedding Announcement Prank 148
    "Worthless Money" Prank 149
    Honk If You Want a Lawsuit 149
    Radio "Terrorist" 149
Summary 150

7. Libel 151
  Libel and Slander 151
    Six Elements of Libel 151
    Direct and Indirect Libel 151
    Media Defenses Against Libel 152
  Defining Truth 152
    The Actual Malice Standard 156
  Public Figures and Private Citizens 157
    Rosenbloom Rethought 158
    Time v. Firestone 158
    Wolston v. Reader's Digest 158
    The "Chicken Butt" Case 159
  Reckless Disregard for the Truth 159
    Attempted Assassinations Lead to a Radio Libel Suit 159
    Deadline Pressure 160
  Defining *Privilege* 162
    Neutral Reportage 162
  Fair Comment and Criticism 164
    Marxist Professor? 164
    The Wrestling Coach and Alleged Perjury 165
    Radio Call-in Show Leads to Defamation Suit 166
    Veggie Libel 166
    Oprah Winfrey Versus the Beef Industry 167
  Intentional Infliction of Emotional Distress 167
    Ugliest Bride 168
  Taking Liberties With Quotations 168
  Libel and Statutes of Limitations 169
    Libel and Jurisdiction 170
  Libel and Large Groups 171
    The Guns of Autumn 171
  Some Good Tips to Keep You Away From Libel Cases 172
  Summary 173

8. Privacy 174
    History of Privacy Law 174
    Privacy Law Torts 175
        Four Basic Torts of Privacy Law 176
    Intrusion and the Media 176
        TV Camera on a Sidewalk 177
        Journalists Airing Recorded Phone Conversations 178
        Crime and Disaster Scenes 179
        Jails and Prisons 180
    Public Figures and Privacy Rights 181
        Antipaparazzi Law Passed 182
        Actress Sues Tabloids Over Topless Photos 183
    Sexual Assault Victims 183
        Publishing or Broadcasting Rape Victims' Names 183
        Media Coverage of Rape Trials 185
    Publishing the Names of Juveniles 185
    Disclosure of Embarrassing Private Facts 186
        Video Voyeurism 186
        Accidental Public Exposures 187
        Sex Change Revealed 188
        Newspaper "Outing" 188
    False Light 189
        Pictures and False Light 189
        News Reporter Embellishes a Story 190
        TV News Video and Herpes 191
        TV News Video and Drugs 191
        Man Harassed After Radio Station
            Airs His Phone Number 192
        An Expensive Lesson From a "Sexy Teacher" 192
    Misappropriation 193
        Baseball Cards and Baseball Players 194
        Misappropriation and the News Media 194
        Endorsement Claims 195
        Striking a "Careful Balance" 196
        A Right of Publicity Test 197
        Misappropriate of an Identifying Characteristic 198
        Celebrity Sound-Alikes 199
    General Tips About Privacy 200
        Danger Areas 200
        Safe Areas 201
    Summary 201

9. Intrusive Newsgathering Methods: Hidden Cameras,
Media Ride-Alongs, Ambush Interviews 202
    Mixed Rulings on Hidden Cameras and Microphones 202
        "Crackdown on Quackery" 202
        Privacy, Car Accidents, and Ambulances 203
        Some Workplaces Are "Private" 205
        Is the Outside of Your Home Private? 209
        Summary on Hidden Cameras and Microphones 210

Media Ride-Alongs 211
    Media Ride-Alongs With Paramedics 211
    Courts Limit Media Ride-Alongs With Police 212
Ambushing 216
    The Le Mistral Case 217
    Inside Edition Gets Too Close 217
Summary 218

10. Media Liability Lawsuits 219
Common Criteria in Copycat Cases 220
    America's First Media Copycat Claim? 221
    Radio Station "Mad Scramble" 221
Stimulus Versus Encouragement 222
    The Mickey Mouse Club Case—"One Out of 16 Million" 223
    "We Warned You. . . ." 224
    "TV Intoxication" 225
    Advertisements and "Foreseeable Harm" 226
Tabloid Talk Shows 227
    TV Talk Show Topic Leads to Murder 227
MTV Pushes the Envelope 228
    Jackass 228
Movies 229
    Natural Born Killers 229
    Paducah School Shooting Lawsuit 230
Music and Suicide 231
    "Suicide Solution" 231
    "The Music Made Me 'Do It'" 232
The Internet 233
    Antiabortion Web Site 233
Summary 234

11. Obscenity 235
Obscenity Laws: A Brief History 236
    "What Is Only Fit for Children. . . ." 237
    The Roth Test 237
    Is It Legal to Own Obscene Material? 239
    Transporting Obscene Material 240
    Congress Calls for Study on Pornography 240
The Landmark Miller Decision 241
    The Miller Test 241
    Local Standards, Not National 242
Time, Place, and Manner Restrictions and Pornography 243
    Zoning Ordinances 243
Obscenity and Disclaimers 245
The Meese Commission 245
Children and Obscenity 246
    Protecting Children From Accessing Pornography 246
Child Pornography 247
    1977 Protection of Children Against Exploitation Act 248
    1996 Child Pornography Prevention Act (CPPA) 249

	Obscenity and Popular Music	250
	The Internet: A New Battleground in Obscenity Law	252
	Summary	253
12.	Indecency and Violence	255
	A History of Broadcast Indecency Regulation	255
	"Topless Radio"	256
	FCC v. Pacifica	257
	The Safe Harbor: 10:00 p.m. to 6:00 a.m.	258
	Shock Radio	259
	The Rules Start to Change	259
	A Smaller Harbor?	260
	Howard Stern Strikes Again—and the FCC Strikes Back	260
	2001: The FCC Issues New Guidelines on Indecency Regulation	261
	Eminem and "The [Edited] Real Slim Shady"	263
	A Song Denouncing "Indecent" Hip-Hop Lyrics Is Called Indecent	263
	2003: Public Outrage Builds Over Indecent Broadcasts—and FCC Rulings	264
	New Crackdown on Indecency	266
	The 2004 Super Bowl "Wardrobe Malfunction"	266
	Bono Ruling Overturned	268
	Congress Reacts With Tough New Fines	268
	Fining Individuals?	268
	Another Record Indecency Fine	269
	Indecency and Other Electronic Media	270
	Cable TV	270
	Renewed Efforts to Regulate Indecency on Cable	271
	Cable Access Channels	272
	Leased Access Channel "Lists"	273
	Indecency Regulations on "Pay-per-View"	273
	Indecent Phone Services	274
	Congress Tries to Ban "Dial-a-Porn" and Fails	274
	Congress Passes Another "Dial-a-Porn" Law	274
	Indecency and the Internet	275
	Communications Decency Act	275
	Child Online Protection Act (CDA Part II?)	277
	Children's Internet Protection Act	278
	Violence	280
	Violent Music Lyrics Spark Controversy	280
	The V-Chip and the TV Rating System	281
	Broadcast TV and Children's Programming Rules	284
	Children's TV in the 1980s	284
	The Children's Television Act of 1990	284
	Music Warning Labels	285
	1984: The Music Industry Takes Some Heat	285
	Summary	287
13.	Copyright: The Basics	288
	The Six Basic Rights of Copyright Holders	289
	First Sale Doctrine	290
	Works for Hire	290
	Obtaining a Copyright	291

	Duration of Copyright	292
	Public Domain	292
	Confusion About Public Domain	293
	Music Licensing	293
	The Three Basic Rights	295
	Public Performance	295
	Mechanical Rights	297
	Synchronization Rights	299
	Fairness in Music Licensing Act	302
	Special Exemption for Music Stores	303
	Live Bands and Jukeboxes in Businesses	304
	Compulsory Licensing	304
	Music Plagiarism	304
	Subconscious Copyright Violation	304
	Summary	306
14.	Copyright: Fair Use	307
	Fair Use and the VCR	308
	Fair Use and Sampling	309
	Fair Use and Broadcast News	310
	Using Movie Clips in Broadcast News Stories	310
	Movie Sound Clips in Radio	311
	Using "Newsworthy" Video in a TV New Story	312
	Writing Broadcast News Stories From Newspaper Articles	314
	Copyright and Sports Scores	315
	Parodies	316
	Saturday Night Live Parody	317
	The Rap on "(Oh) Pretty Woman"	318
	Satire	319
	Movie Poster Cases	319
	Copyright and the Internet	320
	Digital Millennium Copyright Act (DMCA)	320
	MP3s	321
	Napster	322
	The Recording Industry Strikes Back	323
	Radio Station Webcasting	324
	Movie Bootlegs, the Internet, and CSS	325
	File-Sharing Software Ruled Legal	326
	DVD-Copying Software Faces Legal Challenges	326
	BBS Sites	327
	Trademarks	328
	Trademarks in News Stories	328
	Abandoned Trademarks	329
	Radio Station Trademarks	329
	TV Show Trademarks	330
	The Federal Trademark Dilution Act of 1995	330
	Summary	331
15.	Advertising Law	332
	Early Advertising Law	332
	No First Amendment Protection for Advertising?	332
	Other Early Advertising Cases	333
	The Courts Give Commercial Speech More Protection	334

The Landmark Central Hudson Case 335
False Advertising 336
    Federal Agencies Overseeing Advertising 336
    Important Terms 337
    Some Famous False Advertising Cases 338
    Puffery 342
    Testimonial 344
    Mock-Ups 345
Regulating Ads for Harmful Products 346
    Gambling 346
    Cigarettes 349
    Alcohol 353
Underwriting Rules 355
    What to Avoid 355
    Examples of Unacceptable Underwriting 356
    Promoting Nonprofit Events 357
Regulating Telemarketing 357
Regulating "Spam" E-Mail 357
Summary 358

16.   Media and the Courts 359
Cameras in the Courtroom 359
    Cameras No Longer "Intrusive" 360
    Canon 3A (7) Challenged 360
TV News and Videotaped Confessions 360
The Famous Sam Sheppard Murder Trial 361
    Problems With the Sheppard Guidelines 362
Right of Access to Trials 363
    Trials Should Be Open to the Public 364
    Closing Trials Involving Young Sex Victims 364
    Federal Courts and Cameras 365
    States and Cameras in Court 366
Gag Orders 367
    Media Gag Orders Struck Down 370
    Media Gag Orders Upheld 372
Opening Pretrial Proceedings 372
    Jury Selection Process 373
    Press-Enterprise Test for Closing Pretrial Proceedings . . 373
    Pretrial Hearings 373
Civil Trials and Cameras 374
    Court Documents 374
    Access to Audio and Video Evidence 375
    When Broadcast Would Damage Fair Trial 376
Summary 377

17.   News Sources 378
Confidential Sources 378
    The Landmark *Branzburg v. Hayes* Case 378
    State Shield Laws 381
Civil Contempt 381
Important Post-*Branzburg* Cases 382
    Reporters' Sources Protected 382
    Reporters' Sources Not Protected 386

	Nonconfidential Materials	386
	The Leggett Shield Law Case	389
	Defining *Journalist*	389
	Journalists as Eyewitnesses to Crime	390
	Newsroom Searches	391
	Promises of Confidentiality—Keep Your Promises!	392
	Indirect Contempt	393
	Summary	394
18.	Media Access to Government Sources	395
	Access to Government Records and Documents	395
	The Freedom of Information Act	395
	The Vaughn Index	399
	The Electronic Freedom of Information Act of 1996	400
	Exemptions	400
	FOIA and September 11 Detainees	404
	Access to Government Meetings	405
	The Sunshine Act	405
	Media Credentials	406
	State FOI Laws and Sunshine Laws	407
	State Sunshine Laws: Some Common Principles	407
	State FOI Laws: Some Common Principles	407
	Sunshine Laws and Sensitive Information	408
	Prisons	410
	The News Media and Access to Prisons	410
	Court Reaffirms Prison Restrictions for the Media	410
	Access to Rap Sheets	411
	Important Federal Privacy Statutes	412
	Privacy Act of 1974	412
	Access to School and University Records	412
	Access to Driving Records	414
	Access to Government or Public Property	415
	1. Traditional Public Forums	415
	2. Limited Public Forums	415
	3. Nonpublic Forums	416
	Public Access to Executions	416
	Access to Military Information	417
	World War I	417
	World War II	417
	The Vietnam War	417
	Grenada and Press Pools	418
	The 1991 Persian Gulf War	418
	The War in Afghanistan	420
	The War in Iraq: Historic Media Access	420
	The Media and Military Bases	421
	Summary	422
	Table of Cases and FCC Rulings	423
	Appendix: The FCC Inspection	433
	Index	439
	About the Author	447

PREFACE

This first edition of *Electronic Media Law* was written to provide a comprehensive, up-to-date textbook on the constantly changing and often complex world of electronic media law. This text is designed primarily for use in undergraduate media law classes and emphasizes case law and regulations related to broadcasting, cable TV, satellite services, and the Internet. At the same time, though, cases from the print media and general First Amendment law are also covered because they often contain important concepts that are relevant to the electronic media. For example, *New York Times v. Sullivan* is obviously an important case to cover when discussing libel.

It must be stressed that this text is written for mass media students, not future lawyers. The author is a broadcasting professor, working TV news reporter, and radio personality who saw a need for a more "user friendly" media law textbook. The result is a book that uses down-to-earth language and explanations of "legalese" when necessary. Each chapter is broken down into numerous categories and sections, and each section is captioned clearly to make it easier to research specific topics. This text makes frequent use of bullet points and FAQs to highlight important points from cases. As a result, the text will appear less intimidating than some textbooks and make it easier for students to study and remember main points. This will be an easy-to-use reference guide as well as a textbook. It includes all of the most current cases and regulations affecting the industry.

Even though this text explains complex legal concepts in more basic terms, it still challenges the students. There is a wealth of information in this text. It begins with chapters on the American legal system and the meaning of the First Amendment to provide students with a necessary foundation for understanding principles discussed in later chapters. The text then takes students directly into the regulations of the FCC and devotes entire chapters to such topics as political broadcasting rules, regulations for station operations, cable regulation, media ownership rules, "copycat" cases, media liability lawsuits, and indecency regulation. Other issues, such as intrusive newsgathering methods, media restrictions during wartime, and FCC station inspections are also given special attention in this text.

The text provides chapters on libel, privacy, copyright, advertising, freedom of information, cameras in the court, obscenity, and privilege. Whenever possible, pertinent broadcasting cases are included in the discussion of these issues. Of course, major print media cases are included when pertinent.

The result is a textbook that provides a firm understanding of the First Amendment and the American legal system, with an emphasis on electronic media. It is a text that broadcasting professors and students will find to be most helpful in their understanding of the laws and regulations affecting the electronic media in the United States.

ACKNOWLEDGMENTS

To my parents, Martin and Elizabeth Sadler, who taught me the value of hard work and a good education: I would not be where I am today without them.

To my wife, Connie, who has been so supportive during the writing of this book. To my daughters, Lauren and Sarah, who simply fill my life with joy.

To my brother, Chris, who has always inspired me to do my best.

To Al Montanaro, my educational mentor: Thank you for your steadfast dedication to teaching and learning. It rubbed off on me.

I thank God for all of you.

Special thanks to the following persons, who provided valuable commentary and suggestions during the writing of this textbook: Robert Bellamy, Associate Professor of Media Communication at Duquesne University; Greg Lisby, Professor in the Department of Communication at Georgia State University; Anthony L. Fargo, Assistant Professor, School of Journalism, Indiana University; Christine Corcos, Associate Professor of Law of the Paul M. Hebert Law Center, Louisiana State University; and Ronald G. Garay, Associate Dean and Lockett Professor, Manship School of Mass Communication, Louisiana State University–Baton Rouge.

1

THE AMERICAN LEGAL SYSTEM

This thing—this Constitution—is the most important thing in the life of every person living in the United States.

—Floyd C. Cullop[1]

The U.S. Constitution. It guarantees us numerous freedoms, including freedom of speech and freedom of the press, both found in the First Amendment. Those of us studying or working in the electronic media often talk about our "Constitutional rights" or our "First Amendment rights." However, as we will see throughout this book, these rights are not absolute rights. The government and the courts often place limits on these freedoms.

Laws and regulations governing the electronic media are frequently evolving. That is because the electronic media are ever changing. As a result, it is often a challenge for those in electronic media to keep pace with new laws and regulations. However, before we can discuss these laws, it is important to get a basic grounding in how our entire legal system operates.

This text is not written for lawyers or for students in law school. It is designed for students studying electronic media, specifically broadcasting and cable. It is also designed for professionals who work in the broadcasting and cable industries. A prior knowledge of law and broadcast regulation is not assumed.

THE AMERICAN LEGAL SYSTEM

Like any civilized country, the United States is a nation governed by laws. Before looking at the setup of the American court system, we must first gain a basic understanding of the various types of law that are fundamental to our legal system. Let's start at the top with that "thing" called the U.S. Constitution.

---

[1]Cullop, F. G. (1984). *The Constitution of the United States.* New York: Mentor. p. vi.

Constitutional Law

On March 4, 1789, the U.S. Constitution became the cornerstone of the American legal system. It is the oldest written constitution still in use in the world.[2] It includes an introduction called the "Preamble," a main body of text, and 26 amendments. The Constitution outlines the basic structure for the federal government (the executive, legislative, judicial branches). It lays out what powers are given to state and local governments and what powers fall under federal jurisdiction. If any law conflicts with the Constitution, that law is invalid.

However, interpreting the Constitution's meaning can be a challenge for the courts. Look at the wording of the First Amendment. The language is absolute: *Congress shall make NO law . . . abridging freedom of speech*. The courts, though, often do not take an absolutist view of the First Amendment. There are many types of speech that the courts say are *not* protected by the Constitution—shouting "Fire!" in a crowded theater, libel, obscenity, perjury, threats of violence—and the list goes on.

The courts say they are simply striking a balance and that the Constitution must be applied with other concerns in mind. For example, shouting "Fire!" in a crowded theater could lead to panic, and the person who shouted "Fire!" may be held liable for any resulting deaths or injuries. In this instance, the courts have ruled that public safety concerns outweigh the First Amendment rights of the speaker. This demonstrates that the principles outlined in the Constitution are flexible. The Founding Fathers knew that the Constitution would be useless if it were too rigid.

That is why the Constitution is considered one of the finest governmental doctrines ever written. It was designed to be "easily understood and leave no room for mistaken ideas about what it contained. It is no accident that our Constitution has been amended (added to or changed) only 26 times in . . . 200 years."[2] It has stood the test of time.

Amending the Constitution

The first ten amendments are called the Bill of Rights. These amendments were added in 1791, when the states noticed that the Constitution did not address many individual rights and liberties, such as freedom of speech and religion, the right to a speedy and public trial, the right to bear arms, and prohibitions against cruel and unusual punishment.

Passing amendments is difficult.

1. It takes a *two thirds vote in both the House and Senate* just to *propose* an amendment. (The Constitution also says amendments may be proposed by special conventions called by Congress at the request of two thirds of the state legislatures. This has never happened, though.)

2. The proposed amendment must be approved or ratified *by three fourths of the state legislatures*. This is how amendments are usually passed. However, amendments may also be approved by *special conventions in three fourths of the states*. Special conventions have only been used once. In 1919, the 18th Amendment ushered in the era of prohibition, during which time alcohol was outlawed. Then, in 1933, state conventions ratified the 21st Amendment, which repealed the 18th Amendment, and alcohol was once again legal.

---

[2]*Ibid.*, p. 24

It is the U.S. Supreme Court that makes the final determination about whether a law violates the U.S. Constitution. However, lower courts may also make determinations about the constitutionality of laws. Our nation's highest court rules on any conflicts that arise between state constitutions and the U.S. Constitution. As will be seen throughout this text, decisions handed down by courts determine constitutional law.

All 50 states also have constitutions, and they operate on the same basic principle as the federal constitution. No state law can stand if it violates that state's constitution, and state supreme courts ultimately determine whether a law is unconstitutional for that state. It is also easier to amend a state constitution, which is often done through a direct public vote.

Statutory Law

Members of the U.S. Congress, state legislatures, and local legislative bodies are called lawmakers. They write laws. A law passed by such elected officials is also called a *statute*. Laws or statutes are passed to maintain order within a society. There are laws against everything from murder to jaywalking.

In Article 1, section 8, the U.S. Constitution grants the House and Senate the "Power to make any laws necessary and proper for seeing that the powers given to Congress, to the United States government, and to any department or officer of the United States government are carried out." State constitutions give the same power to state legislatures. However, federal laws always have precedence over state laws. (This concept comes from the "supremacy clause" in Article VI of the U.S. Constitution.) If you need to find the text of a federal statute, it can be found in either *Statutes at Large* or the *United States Code*.

Legislative bodies are not the sole caretakers of the law. At the federal level, Congress may pass a law, but the president may choose to veto it. Even if the president signs a bill into law, the courts can still step in and declare the law unconstitutional. If Congress is unhappy with the court's ruling, lawmakers may pass another law in an attempt to override the court decision. It is all a part of the system of "checks and balances" that the Founding Fathers incorporated into our Constitution.

Administrative Law

This type of law comes from regulations and rules passed by administrative bureaus and agencies known as *independent regulatory agencies*. At the federal level, this includes the Federal Communications Commission (FCC) and the Federal Trade Commission (FTC). The texts of these rulings can be found in the *Code of Federal Regulations* and the *Federal Register*. The rulings may also be found in specific agency publications, such as the *FCC Record*.

Although regulations passed by such agencies are not considered laws in the truest sense, these regulations still carry the power of law. Consider the Federal Communications Commission. Like other federal agencies, it has the power of *rule making*. It also has the power to enforce its rules through various forms of punishment, including monetary fines. However, the FCC does not always have the final say. As will be seen throughout this text, the FCC is sometimes taken to court over its rulings. To expedite matters, such appeals are taken directly to the U.S. Court of Appeals in Washington, DC, and sometimes all the way to the U.S. Supreme Court. It is important to note here that legal matters involving non-regulatory but broadcast-related matters may be decided in federal courts other than the Washington, DC, Court of Appeals.

Agencies such as the FCC also have the power to *adjudicate*. This means federal agencies are given the legal authority to settle disputes between parties involving matters directly related to that agency's authority.

Common Law

Common law involves rules and principles of law that are developed and modified through court decisions and not by legislatures. Common law is often called "case law" or "judge-made" law.[3] It is law that is developed through an accumulation of court decisions over time. Therefore, it is not the type of law that you can find in one place or in one case. It evolves. It is law that often can be traced through hundreds of court cases. It has its roots in English law and is considered the oldest form of law.

Most common law is state law, not federal. The Supreme Court, in fact, has declared that common law does not exist at the federal level. Instead, common law is developed and established in the various state courts.

In common law, judges follow *precedents* established in previous court cases. This concept is known as *stare decisis* or "let previous decisions stand." As a result, each new court ruling adds another concept or nuance to the common law established in previous rulings. Judges rarely overturn precedents. In fact, higher courts will often overturn a judge's ruling if it includes the breaking of a precedent.

It is important to remember that statutory law and constitutional law have more power than common law. Common law applies only when there is no applicable statute or constitutional law on a given matter.

Equity Law

Historically, equity law has its roots in common law. Equity law is a means of settling disputes between parties. However, this is not the same as civil lawsuits in which some people sue others for monetary damages. Such civil cases are heard by juries. In equity cases, a judge settles disputes between parties based on equity or "fairness." Examples include divorce proceedings and disputes over child custody.

In equity cases, a judge may order an *injunction* to prevent injury or harm. A good example is when a court orders a magazine not to publish information that could be damaging to national security. In essence, the judge in such cases is looking for the fairest solution to a problem.

Executive Powers

Along with legislatures and government agencies, executive officers, such as presidents and governors, are important in the lawmaking process. Article II, Section 3 of the Constitution says the president is responsible for making sure that "laws be faithfully executed." Much of the president's power in lawmaking comes through the power to nominate justices to the U.S. Supreme Court as well as nominating judges for federal courts. The president also makes appointments to several important federal agencies, including the

---

[3]Wren, C. G., & Wren, J. R. (1986). *The legal research manual* (2nd ed.). Madison, WI: Adams and Ambrose. pp. 221-222.

Federal Communications Commission and the Federal Trade Commission. This can give a president the ability to "stack" the courts and federal agencies with judges and commissioners who reflect the president's legal and political philosophies. For example, in the 1980s, President Reagan appointed commissioners to the FCC who championed Reagan's philosophy of broadcast deregulation.

THE COURTS

There are more than 50 judicial systems in America. Each state and the District of Columbia have individual court systems, as do the territories of Puerto Rico, the U.S. Virgin Islands, and Guam. There is also the federal court system, which is made up of district courts, appellate courts, and the U.S. Supreme Court. The federal setup is very similar to court systems at the state level (see Figure 1.1).

The judiciary is the third branch of government, along with the legislative and executive branches. The hierarchy and the roles of the different courts are established by the U.S. Constitution and the various state constitutions. Each branch of government has its own important role in the lawmaking process: The *legislative branch* writes the laws; the *executive branch* enforces the laws; the *judicial branch* interprets the laws.

Trial Courts and District Courts

The job of a trial court at both the state and federal level is to "find the facts" and determine the major issues in a case. Most cases start in trial courts.

At the federal level, a district court can be thought of as a federal trial court. There is at least one U.S. district court in each state, each U.S. territory, and the District of Columbia. Larger states may have several district courts. Our most populous state, California, has four district courts; smaller states, such as Rhode Island, have one. District courts include a judge and jury who hear testimony from witnesses. The jury then hands down a verdict based on the facts and on testimony.

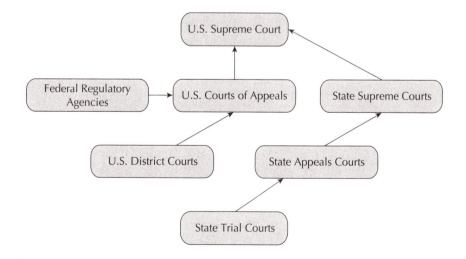

Figure 1.1   Court Hierarchy

Sometimes trials result in *hung juries* or *mistrials.* A hung jury is a situation in which jury members cannot reach a unanimous verdict. The judge will then declare a mistrial, which means the proceedings are canceled. A mistrial may also be declared when a judge determines that there are "prejudicial" factors that may prevent one or both sides from receiving a fair trial. In either case, another trial may be ordered.

Appeals Courts

The law provides that each party that loses a case in a trial court has the right to appeal that decision. The person bringing the appeal is called the *appellant* and the other person is the *respondent.* It is the role of appeals courts to hear these appeals. Appeals courts are called *appellate courts* and, at the federal level, *circuit courts.* Unlike district courts, appeals courts do not usually analyze the facts in the case. Instead, appeals courts analyze whether the trial court or district court applied the law properly in the case and whether proper procedures were followed in reaching the verdict. There are no juries at the appeals court level. Federal district courts must follow all decisions handed down by federal appellate courts that are within their jurisdiction. There are 13 federal appeals courts in the United States that serve different *circuits* or geographic areas. The first 11 circuits cover the 50 states and U.S. territories:

First Circuit: Maine, Massachusetts, New Hampshire, Puerto Rico, Rhode Island

Second Circuit: Connecticut, New York, Vermont

Third Circuit: Delaware, New Jersey, Pennsylvania, Virgin Islands

Fourth Circuit: Maryland, North Carolina, South Carolina, Virginia, West Virginia

Fifth Circuit: Louisiana, Mississippi, Texas

Sixth Circuit: Kentucky, Michigan, Ohio, Tennessee

Seventh Circuit: Illinois, Indiana, Wisconsin

Eighth Circuit: Arkansas, Iowa, Minnesota, Missouri, Nebraska, North Dakota, South Dakota

Ninth Circuit: Alaska, Arizona, California, Guam, Hawaii, Idaho, Montana, Nevada, Northern Mariana Islands, Oregon, Washington

Tenth Circuit: Colorado, Kansas, New Mexico, Utah, Oklahoma, Wyoming

Eleventh Circuit: Alabama, Florida, Georgia

Each of these circuit courts rules independently, and no circuit court is obligated to follow rulings from appeals courts in other circuits. The number of judges in each circuit varies and is established in Title 28 of the U.S. Code, Section 44. For example, the First Circuit is the smallest, with six judgeships, and the Ninth Circuit has 28. Usually a panel of only three judges will hear each case. When a case is of major legal significance, a court will sit *en banc:* This usually means that all judges in the circuit will participate in the proceedings. (There are exceptions for larger circuits. For example, the Ninth Circuit, with its 28 judges, will have an en banc panel of 11 judges.)

The 12th and 13th circuits are not known by numbers. The "12th" is the U.S. Court of Appeals for the District of Columbia (or the DC Circuit Court of Appeals). The DC court hears appeals involving federal regulatory agencies such as the FCC and FTC.

Congress created a "13th circuit" in 1982, which became the court of appeals for the federal circuit. It handles specialized areas of law, including appeals from district courts on such issues as trademarks and patents. It also hears appeals from specialized federal agencies, such as the U.S. Court of International Trade and the U.S. Claims Court.

The U.S. Supreme Court

This is the highest court in the United States. It is the oldest federal court, established by the Constitution in 1789. There are nine justices that preside on the Supreme Court, and a chief justice is chosen by the president. (The official title for this position is Chief Justice of the United States, not Chief Justice of the Supreme Court.) All justices serve on the court for life or until retirement. This court has the final say for all cases, and all lower courts must abide by the rulings handed down by the Supreme Court. A lower court cannot overturn a Supreme Court decision.

It is very difficult to reverse a Supreme Court decision. Future Supreme Court rulings can overturn a previous ruling, or Congress and the states can pass a constitutional amendment. In the 1803 case of *Marbury v. Madison*,[4] the Supreme Court granted itself a great deal of power by ruling that it had the authority to overturn laws passed by Congress.

Supreme Court justices are nominated by the president and approved by the Senate.

Politics often plays a key role because presidents often appoint potential justices based on "judicial philosophy." In recent decades, some Senate confirmation hearings of Supreme Court nominees have shown just how political the process can become. In 1991, President George H. W. Bush nominated Clarence Thomas to replace Justice Thurgood Marshall. The confirmation hearings became a media spectacle when Anita Hill appeared before the Senate and testified that Thomas had sexually harassed her a decade earlier when the two worked together in a government office. Also, liberals in the Senate opposed Thomas because of his conservative views on issues such as abortion and civil rights. However, the Senate went on to confirm Thomas by a narrow margin.

In 1987, the Senate rejected President Reagan's nomination of Robert Bork to the high court. Senate liberals garnered enough votes to reject Bork's nomination, mainly because of Bork's conservative views on legal and social issues. Conservatives have not forgotten Bork's rejection. Today, if a conservative judge is rejected for nomination based on his political views, conservatives will say that judge has been "Borked."

The Supreme Court hears roughly 100 cases per year. The court will usually only hear cases for three reasons: when there are significant legal or constitutional issues involved, when the case deals with new areas of law, or when a lower court erred in issuing a ruling. The Supreme Court usually hears cases that come from a federal appellate court or from a state supreme court that ruled a federal law unconstitutional.

How a Case Makes Its Way to the Supreme Court

The Petition

The Supreme Court frequently hears cases based on a *writ of certiorari*. Certiorari is a Latin word that means a court is willing to review a case. Usually an attorney will file a written argument with the court asking for a review of a ruling by a state supreme court or

---

[4]*Marbury v. Madison*, 5 U.S. 137 (1803)

a federal court. This is known as a *petition of certiorari.* All nine justices will review the petition, and four justices must then vote to approve this request to grant a writ of certiorari (commonly called "granting cert"), thus placing the case on the court's calendar. When the court grants cert to a case, the lower court must send all records from that case to the Supreme Court. However, the Supreme Court rejects the vast majority of petitions of certiorari. This is also known as "denying cert."

If the Supreme Court denies cert and refuses to hear a case, the lower court decision stands. There are no legal options left. It is important to note that denying cert does not mean that the Supreme Court has upheld a lower court's opinion. It just means that the Supreme Court could not find a legitimate legal reason for hearing the case. Still, the lower court decision will stand.

Preparing the Case

Once the Supreme Court has agreed to accept a case, a date is set for oral arguments to take place before it. Lawyers on both sides will then submit their legal arguments, known as *legal briefs,* to the court so the justices may analyze each side's case before oral arguments begin.

The Oral Arguments

Lawyers on each side are given time limits—often no longer than an hour—when presenting their arguments. For cases dealing with substantial constitutional issues, the lawyers may solicit the help of "friends" to help argue the case. This is known as *amicus curiae,* or "friend of the court," briefs. For example, in major broadcasting cases, groups such as the National Association of Broadcasters may be allowed to submit amicus curiae briefs and present arguments to protect their interests in a matter before the court.

Making a Ruling

Within a few days after oral arguments, the nine justices gather in seclusion to discuss the case. No one else is allowed in the room during these deliberations. The chief justice determines the key issues to be discussed in each case and may limit discussion time for each justice. The discussion is followed by a secret ballot vote so each justice's decision will be based on his or her own legal reasoning and not by the "peer pressure" of how other justices are voting. The votes are then tallied.

Writing the Court's Opinion

If the chief justice voted with the majority, he or she will then appoint a justice who voted with the majority to write the *court's opinion.* This opinion will explain why the court ruled the way it did. If the chief justice is in the minority, then the most senior justice in the majority makes the appointment. Of course, the chief justice or senior justice can always appoint him- or herself to write the opinion.

Once the opinion is written, all justices are then allowed to review it. The opinion is then usually rewritten to reflect comments or concerns of fellow justices.

Justices in the majority may also write *concurring opinions.* This is done when a justice agrees in general with the ruling but wants to make important points or arguments not mentioned in the court's opinion.

Concurring opinions may also result in something called a *plurality opinion.* A plurality opinion is one that has the most justices "signed on," but it does not have a majority of justices. For example, consider a 6-3 ruling for which the chief justice writes the court's opinion but only three other justices agree to sign it. The two other majority justices write separate concurring opinions. Thus, the court's opinion written by the chief justice is called a plurality opinion.

Justices in the minority may also write *dissenting opinions.* Here, justices present arguments for their belief that the majority opinion is wrong. Dissenting opinions play a valuable role in our legal system. Throughout this text, you will see examples in which dissenting opinions helped to establish important legal precedents for future cases.

State Courts

All 50 states have court systems that are, often, similar to the federal system. There are trial courts, which can be at the county or state level. Like federal district courts, these trial courts have juries. Most states also have one or two levels of appeals courts.

Each state also has its own "supreme court" or highest court. These state supreme courts have the final say unless the U.S. Supreme Court accepts an appeal of one of their rulings and overturns it. However, the state supreme court has the ultimate power to interpret that state's constitution. The U.S. Supreme Court cannot tell a state supreme court how to interpret its own state's constitution.

Although judges for federal courts are appointed, many judges at state levels are elected. Many states also use a system in which judges are nominated by the governor and approved by a judicial commission, or vice versa. The approved judges then serve for an appointed term and go up for reelection by the public during the next general election.

Criminal and Civil Law

Criminal Law

Criminal law involves an offense against society, such as murder, robbery, or assault. For example, in the famous O. J. Simpson case, the former National Football League (NFL) star faced criminal charges for murder and was found not guilty by a jury. In a criminal case, a state or federal government brings formal charges against the accused person, who is also called the *defendant.* Such formal charges are known as *indictments.*

In the federal courts, a *grand jury* (typically containing 23 people) is responsible for bringing indictments. If indicted, a defendant must then appear at an *arraignment,* at which the charges are read publicly and the defendant is advised of his or her constitutional right to a court or jury trial. The defendant at this time may enter a plea of guilty or not guilty. If the plea is *guilty*, the court formally accepts the plea and announces the verdict. The judge may issue a sentence at that time or set a future date for sentencing.

If the plea is *not guilty*, a trial date is set. If the defendant cannot afford an attorney, the court will appoint a *public defender* to represent the defendant at trial. The judge may order the defendant to be held in jail until the trial is concluded. The judge may also allow the defendant to be released on *bail*. Bail means that the defendant pays money to the court in lieu of being placed in jail. (Bail may also be paid by a defendant's friends or family.) Bail is designed as an "insurance policy" that the defendant will show up for the trial. If the defendant fails to appear for trial, the court keeps the bail money. Such a failure to appear is also known as *jumping bail*. As a result, bail amounts vary and are much higher for more serious crimes or where there is likelihood the defendant might jump bail. However, for crimes such as murder, bail is often not even an option.

Before the trial begins, though, there is something called a *preliminary hearing* ("prelim") or *probable cause hearing.* The prosecutor presents evidence or witnesses to convince a judge that there is adequate evidence to go to trial. The defendant may also bring forth witnesses and evidence. The burden of proof, though, is much less than it would be for an actual trial. If probable cause is determined, then the defendant is "bound over" for trial. However, if probable cause is not established, the judge may reduce the charges to a misdemeanor or dismiss the charges altogether.

Civil Law

A civil lawsuit is also called a *tort.* Tort law is personal injury law. Simply put, civil law involves *lawsuits,* or disputes between two parties. This may include a citizen suing another citizen, a citizen suing the government, or the government suing a corporation. In any of these instances, one party sues another for monetary damages. Unlike criminal law, however, civil law does not involve "crimes against society." As a result, the burden of proof in a civil trial is much lower. In criminal cases, a person must be found guilty *beyond a reasonable doubt.* In civil cases, a person must prove his or her case by a *preponderance of the evidence.*

Lawsuits have become an increasingly popular form of litigation in the United States. One of the more famous civil lawsuits in recent memory was settled in 1994 after a 79-year-old Albuquerque woman spilled a cup of hot McDonald's coffee in her lap and suffered third-degree burns. She sued the restaurant chain and won, arguing that McDonald's was knowingly distributing a dangerous product by making its coffee too hot.

In this case, the woman was the *plaintiff,* or the one bringing the charges. A good way to remember this is that the *plaint*iff is the person who has a com*plaint.* McDonald's was the *defendant,* or the party that has to *defend* itself against the charges.

Keep in mind that civil law is very different from criminal law. The O. J. Simpson case provides a good contrast. As mentioned, Simpson was acquitted of *criminal* murder charges, for which he could have spent time in prison. However, he still had to face a *civil* trial, in which the families of the victims sued him for the "wrongful deaths" of their loved ones. The families won the case, and the court ordered Simpson to pay millions of dollars in damages to the families. In a civil trial, a defendant is not found guilty or not guilty, as in a criminal trial, and there is no threat of imprisonment. Instead, the court holds the person "legally responsible"—and financially responsible—for his or her actions.

Civil damages or awards come in two forms, and the McDonald's case provides good examples of both. A court awarded the woman *compensatory damages* in the amount of $160,000 to *compensate* her for such things as medical expenses, as well as pain and suffering. A court or jury may also award *punitive damages,* which are meant to *punish* the defendants for their actions and to encourage the defendants to correct bad behaviors. In the McDonald's coffee case, the court eventually awarded the woman $480,000 in punitive damages. Did McDonald's correct its behavior? After the verdict, various news media discovered that McDonald's restaurants in Albuquerque had lowered the temperature of their coffee to 158°F. Before the lawsuit, McDonald's had served their coffee at between 180° and 190°.[5]

---

[5]Consumer Attorneys of California. (2004). Know the facts: The McDonald's coffee case. *Consumer Resources: Know the Facts.* Retrieved November 10, 2004, from http://caoc.com/facts.htm

This text deals with civil or tort law in many areas, including libel, invasion of privacy, negligence, and infliction of emotional distress. You will see that most communication cases involve civil law, not criminal law.

The Civil Lawsuit Process

How the Process Works. A plaintiff contacts a lawyer and files a *legal complaint* against a defendant. This complaint includes a demand for a specific amount of money for damages. Once this has been done, a court then issues a *summons,* which requires the defendant to appear in the court. Failure to appear can result in contempt of court charges. It also can result in the judge ruling in favor of the plaintiff by default. The judge can also award damages at this time.

If the defendant responds to the summons, the court will set a *hearing* date. At the hearing, each side presents its arguments, which are also known as *pleadings*. At this point, there are several *pretrial motions* that can result in a case being dismissed without a trial: (a) A plaintiff or defendant may wish to avoid a potentially costly and lengthy trial and *settle out of court.* In such an instance, each side agrees on a money settlement, and the case is over. (b) Each side may also ask the judge to issue a *summary judgment.* This is when the judge determines that there are no disputes about the facts in a case, and the judge then makes a ruling for one side or the other. The case does not proceed to trial. (Note: A summary judgment cannot be granted if there are any disputes about facts that are material [or vital] to the case.) (c) Defendants may also ask the judge for a *motion to dismiss,* or a *demurrer.* In such an instance, the defendant argues that although all of the facts in the complaint may be true, the defendant did not actually break any law. If the judge agrees, the case is dismissed or dropped.

If the case proceeds, each side engages in *discovery* before the trial. Discovery is the gathering of information about the other side's arguments and evidence. Each side may also request that the judge issue a *subpoena,* which requires that a particular person testify in court or hand over evidence essential to the trial. Later in this text, you will read about journalists receiving subpoenas that require them to divulge the names of confidential sources from news stories. Failure to obey a subpoena can result in contempt of court charges and even jail time.

A *jury trial* then begins. Evidence is presented from both sides, and the jury reaches a verdict. The jury may also assess damages. However, the judge may overturn a verdict if the jury did not apply the law properly in reaching its decision. A judge may also lessen or throw out jury damages if the judge finds those damages to be excessive.

The losing side has a right to *appeal.* The person who appeals is the *petitioner,* or *appellant,* and the person contesting the appeal is the *respondent.* On appeal, a court may overturn the ruling or lessen jury damages. Damages are never paid out until all appeals have been exhausted.

At this point, it is important to discuss the concept of *double jeopardy*, which is found in the Fifth Amendment. It says that no person may be put on trial two times for the "same offense." The two O. J. Simpson trials may appear to be an instance of double jeopardy, but they are not. Simpson faced criminal charges of murder in the first trial, and he faced civil charges of wrongful death in the second trial. In such cases, courts have ruled that these separate charges constitute separate offenses, and double jeopardy does not apply.

In a criminal proceeding, once a jury finds a person not guilty, prosecutors may not put that person on trial again for that crime. This is meant to protect people from overzealous prosecutors and to keep the courts from being overwhelmed with repeat cases.

However, double jeopardy sometimes seems grossly unfair, such as in one famous Kentucky murder case. Mel Ignatow had been acquitted in 1991 of the sexual torture and murder of Brenda Schaefer. In 1992, a person who had bought Ignatow's house found film hidden under some floorboards. The photographs clearly showed Ignatow torturing and killing Schaefer. Ignatow later confessed to the crime. Even with this overwhelming evidence, the commonwealth of Kentucky could not retry Ignatow for Schaefer's murder because of double jeopardy. However, the commonwealth did successfully prosecute Ignatow for perjury for lies he told federal investigators about Schaefer's disappearance.[6] The Kentucky Court of Appeals in 2003 upheld the perjury conviction. The court ruled the perjury was considered a separate offense and did not constitute double jeopardy.

Names and Citations of Cases

The Name

Whoever initiates a case or an appeal is named first. Therefore, in a civil case called *Smith v. Jones,* it is Smith who is suing Jones. If Jones loses the case and appeals, it is Jones bringing an action against Smith, and the case is called *Jones v. Smith.*

In a criminal case, it is the government that is bringing charges against a person. For example, if a man named Brown had been on trial for killing a federal law officer, the federal government would have filed murder charges against Brown, so the case name would be *U.S. v. Brown (2000).* The date signifies the year a ruling was handed down. If Brown lost and appealed, the appeals case would be *Brown v. U.S. (2002).* If Brown had won that appeal, the federal government might have appealed that decision to the U.S. Supreme Court. If the case was accepted by the high court, the case would have become *U.S. v. Brown (2004).*

In state criminal proceedings, the case name might be something such as *State of Montana v. Johnson* or *Commonwealth of Kentucky v. Brown.*

The Citation

All cases are given names and numbers, which are known as *citations.* Citations also include other information to make it easier to find and research cases.

Consider the following citations:

UMG Recordings, Inc. v. MP3.com, Inc., 92 F. Supp. 2d 349 (S.D.N.Y. 2000)

First, in italics, is the name of the case. "F. Supp." refers to the *Federal Supplement.* This is a collection of volumes containing copies of case decisions from U.S. District Courts. The *Federal Supplement* is an example of a *case reporter.* The number 92 is the volume number. In a library, the *Federal Supplement* is arranged in order according to volume numbers. The subsequent "2d" means this case can be found in the second edition of the *Federal Supplement* series. If the citation has no reference to an edition, such as in 105 F. Supp. 325 (S.D.N.Y. 1952), it means the case can be found in the first edition of the series. The number "349" refers to the page number on which the case begins. Thus, to find this case,

---

[6]See *Melvin Henry Ignatow v. Commonwealth of Kentucky,* Court of Appeals of Kentucky, No. 1999-CA-0077-OA

you would take volume 92 of the second edition of the *Federal Supplement* and turn to page 349. "S.D.N.Y. 2000" means the case was decided in the year 2000 in the U.S. District Court for the Southern District of New York.

United States v. A.D., 28 F. 3d 1353 (3d Cir. 1994)

"F." refers to the *Federal Reporter,* the case reporter for cases from U.S. Courts of Appeal. The following "3d" means the third edition. (The *Federal Reporter* may also contain some decisions from U.S. District Courts.) After that comes "3d Cir. 1994," which means that this case was decided by the Third Circuit Court of Appeals in 1994. Therefore, this case can be found in volume 28 of the third edition of the *Federal Reporter* on page 1353.

Craig v. Harney, 331 U.S. 367 (1947)

"U.S." refers to *U.S. Reports,* a case reporter for decisions from the U.S. Supreme Court. The case can be found in volume 331 of *U.S. Reports* on page 367. The case was handed down in 1947. Note that in the parentheses here, there is a date but no reference to the court issuing the decision. There is no need for such a reference because only one court's decisions can be found in these volumes—the U.S. Supreme Court.

Parallel Citations

Melon v. Capital City Press, 407 So.2d 85, 8 Media L. Rep. 1165 (La. Ct. App. 1981)

This is a parallel citation, which means this case can be found in two places: volume 407 of the second edition of the *Southern Reporter,* on page 85, and also in volume 8 of the *Media Law Reporter,* on page 1165. This decision was handed down in 1981 by the Louisiana Court of Appeals.

Extra Numbers in Citations

Zamora v. CBS, 480 F. Supp. 199, 201-202 (S.D. Fla. 1979)

This case is in volume 480 of the *Federal Supplement,* on page 199. The extra numbers "201-202" are used in footnotes when the writer is indicating the specific pages from which certain information or quotations were obtained.

Table 1.1 is a brief guide to citations for various types of court cases and the case reporters in which these cases can be found. The guide also includes citations for laws and regulations passed by Congress and independent regulatory agencies.

LEGAL RESEARCH ONLINE

Much legal research today is done online. No longer do researchers have to wade through stacks of case reporters to find material. The Internet has provided a much faster and easier way to access court cases and other legal writings. In fact, many university libraries now make online legal research tools available to their students. There are a number of legal sites on the Web that allow you to find cases from local, state, and federal courts. LexisNexis®,

Table 1.1   Legal Reference Guide

Courts	Example of Citation
Supreme Court	
U.S. Reports (official)	438 U.S. 726 (1978)
Supreme Court Reporter	104 S. Ct. 2199 (1987)
Supreme Court Reports (Lawyer's Edition)	86 L. Ed.2d 593 (1984)
U.S. Courts of Appeal	
Federal Reporter	563 F.2d 343 (7th Cir. 1977)
Federal Cases (older cases)	16 F. Cas. 471 (1848)
U.S. District Courts	
Federal Supplement	348 F. Supp. 954 (M.D. Pa. 1972)
Federal Rules Decisions	166 F.R.D. 268 (1996)
Federal Reporter/Federal Cases	See *Federal Reporter* citation, above
Regional court reporters (Compilations of state court decisions from specific geographic areas)	
Atlantic Reporter	441 A.2d 966 (Md. Ct. App. 1984)
Northeastern Reporter	446 N.E.2d 428
Northwestern Reporter	304 N.W.2d 814
Pacific Reporter	653 P.2d 511 (Ct. App.)
Southeastern Reporter	320 S.E.2d 70
Southern Reporter	421 So.2d 92 (Ala. 1982)
Southwestern Reporter	779 S.W.2d 557
State court reporters (Each state has a case reporter for its highest court. Some states also have reporters for lower courts. These are just two examples.)	
California Reporter	25 Cal.3d 763
New York Supplement	46 N.Y.S.2d 304
U.S. Congress	
Statutes	
U.S. Code	18 U.S.C. 1464
U.S. Code Annotated	18 U.S.C.A. 1464
U.S. Code Service	18 U.S.C.S. 1464
U.S. Statutes at Large	77 Stat. 49 (1974)
Regulatory agencies (federal)	
Code of Federal Regulations	84 C.F.R. 319
FCC Record	2 F.C.C.R. 2705 (1987)
FCC Reports	41 F.C.C.2d 777 (1977)
Federal Register	47 Fed. Reg. 40, 443 (1982)
Broadcasting references	
Media Law Reporter	18 Med. L. Rep. 1953 (1991) or 18 M.L.R. 1953 (1991)
Fischer's Radio Regulation	40 R.R.2d 1577

VersusLaw®, and FindLaw® are some of the more popular sites available for online legal research. These sites may also provide searches for other legal materials, including articles from legal newspapers and law journals. Searches may be done by case name, citation, topic area, and key words. Be aware that some sites are free, but others may charge for their search services. Many university libraries provide free access to such sites, but some do require students to pay for their use.

Key Government Web Sites

(Note: These Web site addresses are correct as of this text's publication date.)

Code of Federal Regulations: http://www.gopaccess.gov/cfr/index.html

Federal Communications Commission: http://www.fcc.gov

Federal Register: http://www.gpoaccess.gov/fr/index.html

Federal Trade Commission: http://www.ftc.gov

Statutes at Large: http://memory.loc.gov/ammem/amlaw/lwsl.html

U.S. Code: http://www.gpoaccess.gov/uscode/index.html

U.S. Supreme Court: http://www.supremecourtus.gov

Summary

The U.S. Constitution is the oldest living constitution in the world. It is the bedrock of the American legal system. There are five basic sources of law: constitutional law, common law, equity law, administrative law, and statutory law. The executive branch may also issue executive decrees, which some consider a sixth source of law.

The courts are an integral part of our legal system. The highest court in the land is the U.S. Supreme Court. The second-highest courts in the federal system are appeals courts, which often hear cases appealed from federal district courts. Each state also has its own court system, which is similar to the federal system.

Criminal law punishes people for crimes against society, such as murder; civil law involves the settling of disputes between private parties. Criminal law often involves jail time or fines; civil law usually results in monetary settlements between parties. Most communications cases are civil cases.

2

UNDERSTANDING THE FIRST AMENDMENT

*Congress shall make no law respecting an establishment of religion, or prohibiting
the free exercise thereof; or abridging the freedom of speech or of the press; or the
right of the people peaceably to assemble, and to petition the government for a
redress of grievances.*

—The First Amendment to the U.S. Constitution

The most cherished part of the Constitution for those in the field of communications
is the First Amendment. Before going into detail about broadcasting regulations,
though, it is important to have a firm understanding of the First Amendment, its
history, and how it has been applied by the courts in communication cases and related
areas of law.

ROOTS OF AMERICAN LAW

Much of American law has its foundation in English law. Freedoms of press, speech, and
religion evolved in colonial America from legal traditions established in England. However,
the English did not see free speech as an absolute right.

One thing the government of England would not tolerate was *seditious libel* or *sedition*.
Sedition is when a person speaks out against the government or its leaders. England
began enforcing sedition laws in the 13th century. It did not matter if the sedition were
true or not because the government said such dissent might undermine the foundations
of the government.

A few centuries later, in 1585, the king of England wanted even more government control over free expression and introduced the infamous Star Chamber. This body required
that all English publishers had to obtain government licenses and could only publish material that had been preapproved by the government. The Star Chamber was abolished in
1641, but the government maintained its licensing of the press. English authorities continued to use licensing as a means of punishing any "offensive" speech. These British Licensing

Acts allowed for the imprisonment, torture, and execution of any person found guilty of publishing "obnoxious works."[1]

Such heavy-handedness by the government outraged John Milton, which led him in 1644 to write a historic plea for free expression, *Areopagitica.* He said the government should drop its licensing scheme altogether because it inhibited free expression of ideas. He believed that people should discover for themselves whether ideas were good or bad. It is important to note that even Milton, a devout Puritan, felt there should be some limitations on speech: He did not support free and open debate on important religious matters.

Another important voice for free expression in the 1600s was John Locke, with his "social contract" theory. He said that every human being has personal or natural rights, including the right to life, liberty, and property. This concept later became part of the Declaration of Independence, when Thomas Jefferson wrote:

> We hold these truths to be self evident: that all Men are created equal; that they are endowed by their Creator with certain unalienable Rights; that among these are Life, Liberty and the Pursuit of Happiness.

In 1694, Locke argued against the renewal of the British Licensing Acts, saying the Acts violated people's personal liberty by not allowing them to express themselves. Locke's arguments apparently had some impact because the British Parliament allowed the Licensing Acts to expire in 1695. However, British sedition laws were still in place, and these laws were applicable to colonial America, which was under British rule. Americans, though, soon showed their disdain for such restrictions on speech.

SEDITION IN THE UNITED STATES

Sedition made headlines in colonial America in 1734 when colonial governor William Cosby threw publisher John Peter Zenger in jail. Zenger's crime? He used his publication the *New York Weekly Journal* to criticize Cosby. The colonies were still under British authority, and Zenger's criticisms violated England's sedition laws. Zenger's lawyer was Alexander Hamilton, and he argued that what Zenger wrote in his paper was simply the truth. The jury then basically thumbed its nose at British sedition laws and found Zenger not guilty. The Zenger case set an important precedent, and Americans after this case felt more comfortable criticizing colonial authorities.

Later in the century, in 1791, the states ratified the Bill of Rights, including the First Amendment, which guaranteed American citizens freedom of speech, press, and religion. However, citizens soon discovered that this First Amendment was no guarantee against the American government enacting its own sedition laws. These first laws did not last long. However, sedition laws would resurface in 20th century America.

---

[1] Gillmor, D. M., & Barron, J. A. (1984). *Mass communication law* (4th ed.). St. Paul, MN: West. p. 738.

The Alien and Sedition Acts of 1798

When the United States was fearing a possible war with France, Congress rushed through several acts that outlawed any speech or publication that was "false, scandalous and malicious"[2] against the president, Congress, or the U.S. government in general and any speech or publication that brought these three entities "into contempt or disrepute."[9]

These acts were in effect during the presidency of John Adams and resulted in roughly 25 arrests and 15 prosecutions. Thomas Jefferson was vice president but belonged to a different party. Adams belonged to the Federalist Party, as did the majority of Congress, so lawmakers used the sedition laws mostly to target supporters of Thomas Jefferson. Jefferson's supporters in Congress had opposed passage of the sedition laws.

In *U.S. v. Cooper*,[9] a jury convicted Thomas Cooper for printing publications critical of President Adams' policies. It did not help Cooper that the judge overseeing this trial was a member of Adams' Federalist Party. The judge told the jury that anyone who criticized the government as Cooper did "effectually saps the foundation of the government."

The public, however, did not like the sedition laws, and Jefferson capitalized on that discontent in 1800 when he ran for president and won. Then, shortly into his presidency, Jefferson pardoned everyone who had been prosecuted under the Sedition Act before 1801. The Sedition Act expired in 1801. More than 100 years later, a world war would lead Congress to bring back sedition laws.

Sedition Laws Resurface in World War I

The U.S. entered World War I in 1917, and the government passed several acts to punish any speech that was seen as harming the war effort. For the first time in the country's history, the Supreme Court handed down rulings that dealt with the very essence of First Amendment freedoms.

The Espionage Act of 1917

The first part of this act provided punishments for people who willfully communicated national defense information to our enemies. Section 3 of the Espionage Act made it illegal to use false reports to damage the war effort. Section 3 was amended in 1918 and became known as:

The Sedition Act of 1918

The amendment made the language a little more specific, banning "any disloyal, profane, scurrilous or abusive language about the form of the government of the United States or the Constitution . . . or military or naval forces . . . or the flag . . . or the uniform."

FAQ

Aren't words such as disloyal and scurrilous rather vague? How did the government define such words?

---

[2]25 F. 631 (1800)

It did not define them. The government purposefully used such words to give it the right to punish a wide range of speech and activities. For example, the Sedition Act made it a crime to do any of the following "disloyal" activities: obstruct the sale of U.S. bonds, obstruct the recruitment efforts of the U.S. military, willfully display the flag of a foreign enemy, impede the efforts of U.S. industry in producing materials needed for war, give any speech or publish any work supporting the cause of a foreign enemy. Violators faced fines of up to $10,000 and prison terms of up to 20 years. Roughly 1000 people were convicted under these acts.

The "Clear and Present Danger" Test

In two major cases, the Supreme Court ruled that it was constitutional for the government to punish sedition, saying that the First Amendment did not give blanket protection to all forms of speech. In *Schenck v. U.S.,*[3] Charles Schenck had been prosecuted under the Espionage Act for giving military recruits and draftees about 15,000 leaflets that denounced the draft and urged the men not to serve in the armed forces.

The U.S. Supreme Court in 1919 upheld Schenck's conviction, saying that his speech created a "clear and present danger" of bringing about "substantive evils that Congress has a right to prevent." The Court compared Schenck's speech to a person crying "fire" in a crowded theater and creating an unnecessary panic.

A short time later in 1919, the court once again upheld the Espionage Act in *Abrams v. U.S.*[4] Jacob Abrams and four other persons were prosecuted for publishing antiwar leaflets. The court said the leaflets presented a "clear and present danger" because their purpose was to "excite, at the supreme crisis of the war, disaffection, sedition, riots, and . . . revolution in this country."

FAQ

The Supreme Court really considered leaflets from one man to be a great danger?

Yes. However, the *Abrams* case is well known for a famous dissent by Justice Oliver Wendell Holmes, Jr. Holmes had written the majority opinion in *Schenck,* but then he had a change of heart. In this case, he said he considered the Espionage Act a violation of the First Amendment and that the act was punishing mostly harmless speech:

> The best test of truth is the power of the thought to get itself accepted in the competition of the market.

> Now nobody can suppose that the surreptitious publishing of *a silly leaflet by an unknown man,* without more, would present any immediate danger that its opinions would hinder the success of the government aims or have any appreciable tendency to do so. (Italics added)

---

[3]249 U.S. 47 (1919)

[4]250 U.S. 616 (1919)

Holmes's opinions did not take root in the court for several more decades. Within the next few years, though, the court would uphold state laws that banned activities and speech considered "dangerous" to the government. It would also establish a landmark ruling regarding states' obligations to follow the First Amendment.

STATES AND THE FIRST AMENDMENT

Radical political groups had become more vocal in many parts of America in the early 20th century, so numerous states passed laws prohibiting speech or activities that encouraged "political radicalism." The states said the laws were necessary because many of these political groups preached overthrow of the government through force.

In 1925, the high court heard its first case dealing with state political radicalism laws.

In *Gitlow v. New York*,[5] Benjamin Gitlow had been prosecuted under a New York State criminal anarchy law. Gitlow was a socialist who helped print and distribute a publication called *The Left Wing Manifesto*, which called for the overthrow of the government. Gitlow appealed his conviction to the U.S. Supreme Court, saying the state law violated his First Amendment rights. Gitlow faced a problem with this approach, though. In 1833, in *Barron v. Baltimore*,[6] the Supreme Court had ruled that the Bill of Rights (including the First Amendment) only protected persons prosecuted under federal laws, not state laws. Therefore, the court said that states were free to pass laws that restricted free expression. Gitlow was asking the court to overturn this precedent and rule that the First Amendment should protect speech at the state level as well.

Instead of asking the court to overturn a precedent, Gitlow's lawyers argued that their client also had protection under the 14th Amendment, which says that no *state* shall "deprive any person of life, liberty or property, without due process of the law." This is also known as the *due process clause*. Gitlow said free speech guaranteed under the First Amendment was also a basic "liberty" protected by the 14th Amendment. The Supreme Court agreed, saying the 14th Amendment protected all of the "liberties" enshrined in the First Amendment and that states must also protect these liberties.

The court established an important constitutional doctrine in *Gitlow:*

> States may not pass laws that violate the First Amendment rights of their citizens because these rights are included in the "liberties" guaranteed to each individual in the 14th Amendment. States must abide by the First Amendment as well.

Strangely enough, this ruling did not help Gitlow. The Supreme Court upheld his conviction under state law, saying the First Amendment still did not protect his "radical" activities.

Two years later, in 1927, the court upheld California's criminal syndicalism law. This statute prohibited membership in any group that advocated violence to achieve political or social change. The case of *Whitney v. California*[7] involved Charlotte Whitney, who was prosecuted for attending a meeting of the Communist Labor Party. Actually, Whitney spoke out against the party's violent policies at the meeting, but the state still prosecuted her for being involved in criminal syndicalism.

---

[5] 268 U.S. 652 (1925)

[6] 32 U.S. 243 (1833)

[7] 274 U.S. 357 (1927)

The U.S. Supreme Court upheld the conviction. Justice Brandeis voted with the majority for technical reasons, but his concurring opinion (he was joined by Justice Holmes) strongly criticized the court's restrictions on free speech. Brandeis wrote that there is no danger from speech such as what was being punished in the *Whitney* case. He said, "The remedy to be applied is more speech, not enforced silence."

FAQ

What exactly did Brandeis mean by "more speech"?

He meant that the best way to combat "offensive" speech is to respond to it with opposing viewpoints. In this case, for example, he would have suggested that people debate the Communist Labor Party on its beliefs instead of punishing the group for its beliefs. He argued that the government should only restrict freedom of expression in the most extreme circumstances. Forty years later, the court adopted the Brandeis philosophy, but not before upholding more sedition laws from the World War II era.

World War II: The Smith Act

In 1940, America had not yet entered World War II, but many members of Congress were concerned about "unpatriotic" speech or activities that might undermine the American government during this unstable time in world history. These concerns led to the Smith Act, which was added onto the Alien Registration Act of 1940. The Smith Act prohibited several types of speech that involved advocating a violent overthrow of the government or belonging to a group that advocated toppling a government by force.

The Smith Act was enforced mostly after World War II, during the period known as the "Cold War," when there was widespread fear about communism taking hold in America. As a result, the Communist Party in the United States became a primary target. The federal government used the Smith Act to prosecute close to a dozen party members for advocating a violent overthrow of the U.S. government. In 1951, in *Dennis v. U.S.*,[8] the Supreme Court ruled that the Smith Act was constitutional, and the court upheld the convictions. The court said the men's free speech rights were outweighed by national security interests and argued that the men represented "a highly organized conspiracy with rigidly disciplined members" who were very likely to respond to a "call to action" from their leaders. At the same time, though, a plurality of justices said the men did not represent an immediate clear and present danger of *actually carrying out* their plans. Still, the court felt their beliefs presented a possible future threat to the country, even if it was unlikely that these people had the ability to carry out their plans. In essence, the court reflected the American public's fears about communism.

The *Dennis* ruling gave the Smith Act more legitimacy, and the federal government in the next few years prosecuted hundreds of citizens for violating the act. These prosecutions came during the "Red scare" of the 1950s, which included the notorious Senator Joseph McCarthy's crusade to rid the country of communism. The House Committee on Un-American Activities targeted persons believed to be "anti-American," and this resulted in countless persons losing their jobs through the infamous "blacklists."

---

[8]341 U.S. 494 (1951)

The Smith Act was severely curtailed by the Supreme Court in 1957 in *Yates v. U.S.*[9] The court had a new chief justice in Earl Warren, who would take the court in a more liberal direction on many issues, including free speech. *Yates* involved 14 people convicted of participating in communist activities. The court overturned the convictions, saying these people should not be convicted solely on the basis of their beliefs. Instead, the court ruled that there had to be evidence that showed that these people's speech presented a *clear and present danger* that was likely to result in illegal *action*. Only then would the government be justified in curtailing the speech. The Smith Act was rarely used after this decision because it was much more difficult now for the government to prove the *likelihood* of speech leading to illegal and violent activities.

FAQ

Was there any proof the Smith Act had been weakened?

Yes. For example, the Smith Act was never used against Vietnam War protesters in the 1960s and 1970s, demonstrating that the *Yates* decision had definitely taken the teeth out of the act.

In 1969, the court continued to weaken sedition laws in *Brandenburg v. Ohio*.[10] The case involved a Ku Klux Klan (KKK) member named Brandenburg who spoke at a KKK rally. Brandenburg told a small crowd that Jews should be sent back to Israel and that "niggers" should be returned to Africa. He threatened "revengeance" if whites continued to be suppressed and that 400,000 people would march on Washington, DC, on July 4th to support the KKK's political goals. His speech was filmed and later broadcast on national television. Ohio convicted Brandenburg under a state criminal syndicalism law that banned advocating political reform through illegal means. The state said Brandenburg's speech was an illegal "call to action."

The U.S. Supreme Court overturned the conviction. The justices said Brandenburg's call to action was protected by the First Amendment because it was not *likely* to "incit[e] or produc[e] imminent lawless action." There was no clear and present danger that Brandenburg would or could actually follow through on these threats. (For example, the march on Washington never materialized and Jews were not shipped back to Israel.) The court had decided to adopt the view of Justice Brandeis from the *Whitney* case in 1927: Only speech likely to produce immediate illegal action should be restricted. A government may only punish speech when that speech "is directed to inciting or producing imminent lawless action and is likely to incite or produce such actions."

The court reaffirmed this new clear and present danger test 4 years later in *Hess v. Indiana*.[11] A demonstrator had been convicted for shouting "We'll take the fucking street later" at a college antiwar rally. The court ruled that such words were protected speech because they were unlikely to result in immediate lawless actions.

---

[9]354 U.S. 298 (1957)

[10]395 U.S. 444 (1969)

[11]414 U.S. 105 (1973)

FIGHTING WORDS

Fighting words are different from sedition because they do not have to involve encouragement to overthrow the government by force. Fighting words are words that are likely to result in immediate violence. The legal question becomes: Should the words themselves be illegal, or should we just punish the actions that result from those words?

The fighting words doctrine was established in 1942 in *Chaplinsky v. New Hampshire.*[12] A New Hampshire man named Chaplinsky was arrested after confronting a local marshal on the street and calling him "a goddamned racketeer and a damned fascist." A New Hampshire law prohibited the use of "offensive, derisive or annoying" words directed at others in public. There was no physical confrontation between the two men, but the U.S. Supreme Court upheld Chaplinsky's conviction and the New Hampshire law because (a) the words were *likely* to inflict injury or immediately provoke the average person to violence, (b) fighting words have "no essential part of any exposition of ideas," and (c) banning fighting words helps to protect "the social interest in order and morality."

FAQ

Were Chaplinsky's words really that "dangerous"? After all, his words didn't lead to a fight.

The Supreme Court was concerned that such words *could* lead to violence in similar situations. Also note that the court brought up the issue of "morality" as part of the justification for the ruling here. However, the courts would address this issue in numerous cases in the years to come, and the fighting words doctrine would be weakened. In 1972, in *Gooding v. Wilson,*[13] the Supreme Court struck down a Georgia law that banned "abusive language tending to breach the peace." The court said that any laws banning fighting words must be restricted to messages that have "a *direct* tendency to cause acts of violence by the person to whom, individually, the remark is addressed." Therefore, fighting words cannot be banned simply because they may offend someone. They may be prohibited only if the words are likely to result in a breach of peace.

Are These Fighting Words?

In 1971, the Supreme Court ruled that Paul Cohen could not be punished for walking around a Los Angeles courthouse wearing a jacket with the words "Fuck the Draft" on the back. The court said in *Cohen v. California:*[14]

▣ "One man's vulgarity is another man's lyric." The court said it could not punish the speech simply because other people might be offended by it.

---

[12]315 U.S. 568 (1942)

[13]405 U.S. 518 (1972)

[14]403 U.S. 15 (1971)

- ▣ Cohen was using the vulgarity to make a political statement, and the court said the government should always be extremely cautious about censoring political speech.
- ▣ The message on the jacket did not constitute fighting words because it was not likely to provoke a physical confrontation or to breach the peace.

The Famous Skokie Case

Concerns about breach of peace are heightened when inflammatory speech involves larger groups with larger potential audiences. Such was the case in 1977 in Skokie, IL, when the town denied a parade permit to the American Nazi Party. Many Jews lived in Skokie, and town officials feared that violence might erupt between the marchers and local residents, especially if the marchers displayed the Nazi swastika symbol and wore Nazi uniforms. The town would later argue that the march itself would be a form of fighting words. It was, after all, the Nazis who exterminated 6 million Jews during World War II, and the group picked Skokie because of its Jewish population.

The town then required that the Nazis obtain liability insurance for the parade. The Nazis refused, and the town got a judge to block the march. Skokie lawmakers passed several ordinances placing restrictions on parades and protests such as banning any material (including swastikas) meant to incite racial hatred. The town also made it illegal for a member of a political party to wear any military clothing in a public demonstration. In 1978, in *Village of Skokie v. National Socialist Party*,[15] the Illinois Supreme Court said the town's restrictions were a violation of the Nazis' free speech rights: (a) The fighting words doctrine could not be used here because it would place a "prior restraint" on the Nazis' speech; (b) the court said the swastika was "abhorrent" to many, but it was still protected as "symbolic political speech"; (c) the court also said that "those engaged in peaceful demonstrations cannot be totally precluded because that display may provoke a violent reaction by those who view it"; and (d) the marchers gave prior notice of their intent to march, and therefore people who might be offended by the swastikas and Nazi uniforms were "forewarned and need not view them. A speaker who gives prior notice of his message has not compelled a confrontation with those who voluntarily listen."

The Nazis wound up canceling their march out of fear of counterdemonstrations brought on by all of the publicity.

FAQ

Isn't this what Justice Brandeis was talking about when he wrote about "more speech" being preferable to enforced silence?

It is a perfect example. Notice how the threat of censorship emboldened the Nazis to fight and take their case to court. However, when confronted with the prospect of "more speech" from counterdemonstrators, the Nazis did not even show up.

Still, the Nazis' victory in this case showed clearly that the courts are willing to protect people's free speech rights, no matter how offensive that speech may be to others.

---

[15]373 N.E.2d 21 (Ill. 1978)

In recent years, governments and universities used elements of "fighting words" laws to try to ban "hate speech." Such laws were designed, in part, as a means of maintaining public peace. Hate speech laws also present special constitutional problems because these laws are often targeted at speech that is "offensive" or "racist," as in the *Skokie* case. Are such laws a violation of the First Amendment? Should "hateful" words be banned because they might also be fighting words? In recent years, the courts have often rejected the comparison, applying the same reasoning that was used in *Skokie* and *Cohen*.

HATE SPEECH

Cross Burning and Swastikas

In 1992, the Supreme Court wrestled with a St. Paul, MN, city ordinance that prohibited anyone from expressing racial or religious hatred through methods such as painting swastikas on buildings or burning crosses in people's yards. Under this ordinance, officials convicted a 17-year-old white male of a misdemeanor for placing a burning cross in the fenced yard of an African American couple.

In *R.A.V. v. St. Paul*[16] (R.A.V. were the white male's initials), the court used the same reasoning it had applied in *Cohen* and overturned the young man's conviction. People have a right to express offensive or unpopular thoughts, the court reasoned, and the city ordinance unlawfully punished the expression of ideas. The court said, "The First Amendment does not permit St. Paul to impose special prohibitions on those speakers who express views on disfavored subjects." The court did not approve of the city's punishing the boy for his speech. This was wrong. The city *would* have been justified in punishing the boy for trespassing or arson.

FAQ

Couldn't cross burning be considered a form of illegal "fighting words"?

No. The Supreme Court said that expressing hatred toward certain groups (racial, religious, etc.) must be protected under the First Amendment, no matter how offensive or intimidating the speech might be to some people.

Cross Burning as Illegal "Intimidation"

However, in 2003, the court narrowed the scope of protection for cross burning in *Virginia v. Black*.[17] The court now said that states might ban symbolic speech, such as cross burning, if the main intent of the speech was intimidation. The case concerned a Virginia law that made it a felony for anyone to burn a cross on another person's property or in a public area with the "intent of intimidating any person or group." Virginia authorities had

---

[16]505 U.S. 377 (1992)

[17]123 S.Ct. 1536 (2003)

used the law to prosecute two persons who tried to burn a cross on an African American neighbor's yard. Authorities also arrested and convicted a man for allowing a cross to be burned on his property during a KKK rally.

The persons appealed their convictions, saying the Virginia law violated their constitutional right to freedom of expression. The Supreme Court, however, ruled that the law was constitutional because of the historical context of cross burning. Justice Sandra Day O'Connor wrote the court's opinion, saying that states have the right to protect their citizens from certain types of intimidation. In this case, the court said the Virginia law was justified because of "cross burning's long and pernicious history as a signal of impending violence." O'Connor cited *Brandenburg* and *Chaplinsky,* stating that the First Amendment did not protect speech that incited violence or presented a genuine threat to the peace.

However, the court in the next case would argue that even though hateful words themselves were protected, persons might still be punished for the illegal actions resulting from those words.

African Americans Attack White Youth

The case of *Wisconsin v. Mitchell*[18] involved a group of African American youths who were upset about scenes they had just watched in the movie *Mississippi Burning*, a film about the murders of three civil rights workers in the 1960s. After seeing the movie, 19-year-old Todd Mitchell and several of his African American friends were walking down the street when they saw a 14-year-old white youth. Mitchell asked his friends, "Do you feel all hyped up to move on some white people?" He added, "There goes a white boy. Go get him." The African American youths beat the white youth, who lapsed into a coma for several days.

Wisconsin had a hate crimes law that increased the sentences of offenders whose crimes were committed because of racial or religious hatred, among other things. The state convicted Mitchell of aggravated battery and then made his sentence longer under the hate crimes law. Mitchell had obviously instigated the attack on the 14-year-old boy because the boy was white.

Mitchell appealed the increase in his sentence, saying he should not get extra punishment because of his speech. However, the U.S. Supreme Court upheld Mitchell's stiffer sentence. The court said the State of Wisconsin was justified in increasing the sentence based on Mitchell's *motivation.* The court said motivation is frequently a factor in determining prison sentences. In murder cases, for example, people get stiffer sentences based on motivation. If a murder was planned (first-degree murder), the sentence is often more severe than it would be for someone who killed a person in a spontaneous argument (second-degree murder). The court then emphasized that Mitchell was not being punished for his speech but for the actions that resulted from the speech: "A physical assault is not by any stretch of the imagination expressive conduct protected by the First Amendment."

Campus Speech Codes

In the late 1980s, universities across the country began developing and enforcing speech codes that prohibited students from using "hate speech." Universities claimed the codes were necessary to create a friendlier campus environment that would be more favorable to students' academic pursuits, but critics charged the codes were meant to censor the free expression of "politically incorrect" ideas.

---

[18]508 U.S. 476 (1993)

A federal district court addressed the issue of campus speech codes in 1989 in *Doe v. University of Michigan.*[19] The University of Michigan had become concerned about some recent incidents on campus, including the distribution of fliers which called African Americans "saucer lips, porch monkeys, and jigaboos." In response to this and other incidents, the university adopted a speech code prohibiting any speech or activity that "stigmatizes or victimizes an individual on the basis of race, ethnicity, religion, sex, sexual orientation, creed, national origin, ancestry, age, marital status, handicap, or Vietnam-era veteran status."

FAQ

Isn't this another type of speech restriction with vague wording? What is meant by stigmatize and victimize?

Those were concerns brought up by a psychology graduate student ("John Doe"). He said the speech code prohibited him from discussing psychological theories that suggested certain personality and cognitive differences between men and women and between racial groups. He challenged the speech code in court, and a federal district agreed that the speech code violated the First Amendment. Specifically, the speech code banned a "significant amount of 'verbal conduct' and 'verbal behavior' which is unquestionably protected speech." Speech cannot be banned simply because it may offend some people. Although the court recognized that the university had noble intentions in trying to create a friendly campus, "such efforts must not be at the expense of free speech." The court also considered that the speech code was vague and created a "chilling effect" on student speech: Students "were forced to guess at whether a comment about a controversial issue would later be found to be sanctionable under the Policy." The university provided no proof that such speech would interfere with any student's academic pursuits.

Flag Desecration

In the 1960s, it happened at protest rallies of all kinds. An activist wanted to make a powerful political statement and get on the TV news, and burning an American flag would often achieve both of those goals. Some activists desecrated the flag in other ways, such as tearing it or urinating on it. These practices especially upset military veterans who had fought in wars to protect America, and they said the flag was a powerful symbol of the freedoms for which they fought. By the 1980s, public opinion polls consistently showed that a large majority of Americans supported laws to protect the flag. Politicians soon "rallied around the flag" and called for a constitutional amendment to ban its desecration. Still, protesters and civil liberties groups argued that desecrating the flag needed to be protected as "symbolic speech" even though it was highly offensive to many people. Protesters said they had a right to express their anger at America through flag burning.

The Supreme Court agreed, in two cases that upheld the rights of protesters to use flag desecration as a form of symbolic speech. In 1989 in *Texas v. Johnson,*[20] a man named

---

[19]721 F. Supp. 852 (E.D. Mich. 1989)

[20]491 U.S. 397 (1989)

Gregory Johnson had burned an American flag as a form of protest during the 1984 Republican National Convention in Dallas. In a narrow 5-4 ruling, the court said the State of Texas could not punish Johnson for engaging in this form of "speech." The court said Johnson's "speech" had even more protection because he was trying to make a political point with his flag burning.

FAQ

Was there ever any action on a Constitutional amendment against flag desecration?

Not really. However, Congress responded soon after the *Johnson* ruling with the Flag Protection Act of 1989, which mandated jail time and fines for people who desecrated the American flag. In 1990 in *U.S. v. Eichman*,[21] the Supreme Court overturned the Flag Protection Act in another 5-4 ruling. The majority opinion provides a good summary of the court's feelings on this issue, as well as its feelings about laws restricting fighting words and hate speech: "The government may not prohibit the expression of an idea simply because society finds the idea itself offensive or disagreeable."

PRIOR RESTRAINT

Near v. Minnesota

Prior restraint is a condition in which the government forbids a party to publish or broadcast specific material. The government's goal in such cases is to keep the information from ever reaching the public. Prior restraint is also called "prepublication censorship."

FAQ

What are some examples of prior restraint?

Example 1: The government suspects a newspaper is going to publish an article that contains top secret military information, and the government orders the newspaper not to publish it. The government has "restrained" the speech "prior" to publication.

Example 2: The government demands that a publication submit "controversial material" for approval before the government will allow publication, just like the British Star Chamber used to do.

The landmark American prior restraint case is from 1931, *Near v. Minnesota*.[22] The case involved a Minnesota law that prohibited the publication of any material that was "obscene, lewd, and lascivious" or "malicious, scandalous and defamatory." People could be

---

[21]496 U.S. 310 (1990)

[22]283 U.S. 697 (1931)

found guilty of a "nuisance" not only for publishing such material, but for distributing it, selling it, possessing it, or giving it away.

Jay Near and Howard Guilford were publishers of *The Saturday Press*. In 1927, local officials accused the newspaper of violating the law for printing numerous articles that were "malicious, scandalous and defamatory." The articles had accused the Minneapolis Chief of Police of having "illicit relations with gangsters" and that he was guilty of "gross neglect of duty." The articles accused Minneapolis law enforcement officials of "going easy" on a Jewish gangster who was involved in bootlegging and racketeering. The articles also accused the mayor, county attorney, and a grand jury member of being "in sympathy with the gangsters."

A district court ruled the newspaper was a "nuisance" and prohibited the newspaper from publishing any articles unless the publishers were able to convince the courts that the newspaper would avoid printing any further offending material. The Minnesota Supreme Court upheld the lower court ruling, saying the state had a right to regulate public nuisances such as the articles in *The Saturday Press*.

However, the U.S. Supreme Court ruled 5-4 that the Minnesota nuisance law was unconstitutional. The court also criticized the Minnesota courts for shutting down the newspaper. Censoring a newspaper before it is even published, said the court, is prior restraint and violates the First Amendment. The government should only punish publishers *after* publication of unlawful material. If publishers have to seek government permission before they print even one word, "it would be but a step to a complete system of censorship."

The Supreme Court also pointed out that the Minnesota law was too vague in its definitions. It provided no clear-cut definitions for words such as *scandalous* or *malicious*. As a result, officials could make up the rules as they went along to punish newspapers or publications they simply did not like. The Minnesota law was also dangerous because it allowed censorship of publications that criticized public officials. The court said the media play an important role in holding public officials accountable.

The government may only exercise prior restraint on a publisher if there are exceptional circumstances (national security, incitements to violence).

FAQ

Are there any cases in which the government has been successful with such prior restraint arguments?

The government has on several occasions used national security concerns as a reason for imposing prior restraints on the press. The courts, though, say these concerns must be legitimate and substantial, as in the next two cases.

The Pentagon Papers

On June 13, 1971, the *New York Times* published a story about secret Pentagon studies on the Vietnam War, which became known as the "Pentagon Papers." The actual title of this 47-volume study was "History of the United States' Decision-Making Process on Vietnam Policy." A man named Daniel Ellsberg had written some portions of the Pentagon Papers, and he was the one who leaked the papers to the *Times*. Several other major newspapers soon picked up on the *Times* story. The papers basically told the story of how the federal government had lied to the public about the objectives of the war in Vietnam.

President Nixon said the release of information from the papers created a threat to national security and would prolong the war, and he asked the Justice Department to seek an injunction to bar the *Times* from further publication. A federal appeals court in New York enforced the Justice Department's injunction against the *Times* and prohibited further publication. However, the federal appeals court in Washington, DC, refused to grant a similar injunction against the *Washington Post*, which was also reporting on the Pentagon Papers.

The U.S. Supreme Court stepped in quickly. It overturned the DC appeals court ruling and ordered the *Post* to cease publication of the story until the court had time to decide whether the Pentagon Papers contained any information that threatened national security.

This Supreme Court ruling was highly unusual because of the speed of the legal process. The story had appeared in the *Times* on June 13. The Supreme Court agreed on June 25 to hear an "expedited review" of the cases. The court then delivered its opinion a week later. It often takes years for cases to reach the U.S. Supreme Court, and then it is often many more months before the court releases its decision. In this case, there was a vital national security issue involved, and the court felt a need to issue a ruling quickly. (The court used similar speed in 2000 when ruling on the Florida election dispute that eventually led to George W. Bush being declared the winner over Al Gore.)

In *New York Times v. U.S.*,[23] the court voted 6-3 in favor of the *Times* and the *Post*. The court ruled that the government did not meet its "heavy burden" to justify suppressing the information:

- ▣ *"Secrecy in government is fundamentally anti-democratic."* This statement from Justice Douglas's opinion is the probably the most famous quotation from the ruling. Douglas said the government must always strive for openness over secrecy.
- ▣ *The papers were no longer secret.* The papers were not "under any controlled custody" and there were numerous sets available. Justice Douglas said the material was "destined for publicity, not secrecy."
- ▣ *The material was outdated and no longer a threat to national security.* Again, Justice Douglas: "It is all history, not future events. None of it is more recent than 1968." (The court heard the case in June 1971.) The information in the papers was anywhere from 3 to 20 years old.

FAQ

Did this case provide clearer guidelines about what kinds of prior restraint are permissible?

This aspect of the case disturbed many journalists. The Supreme Court did not say the government was prohibited from using a similar "prior restraint" in the future. The court also gave no guidelines about what conditions might permit the government to do so. Also, the three dissenting justices expressed their disgust that the case was "rushed" through the

---

[23]403 U.S. 713 (1971)

legal process. They said national security issues need more prolonged and thoughtful scrutiny. Eight years later, national security and the "right to live" convinced a court to uphold a prior restraint that prevented the publication of information about nuclear weapons. The ruling was short lived, though.

The H-Bomb Case

In 1979, a Wisconsin publication, *The Progressive,* was ready to go to print with an article titled "The H-Bomb Secret: How We Got It, Why We're Telling It." The article provided the details about the construction of a hydrogen bomb, and concerns were immediately raised about national security. Government officials were fearful that sensitive information about a very deadly weapon would be readily available to enemies of America. The magazine argued that the article would provide much-needed public discussion about the dangers of nuclear weapons. The government took the magazine to court to stop publication of the article. In *U.S. v. Progressive,*[24] federal district court judge Robert Warren ruled that prior restraint by the government was justified in this instance. The information in the article would "give an advantage to a foreign enemy" and represented the likelihood of "immediate, direct, irreparable harm to the United States."

Warren cited Section 2014 of the Atomic Energy Act, which prohibits the release of all information concerning "the design, manufacture or utilization of atomic weapons." The court said there was "no plausible reason why the public needs to know the technical details about hydrogen bomb construction to carry on an informed debate on this issue."

This was a debate about freedom of speech versus freedom to live. The judge said freedom to live had to be more important. There could be no valid comparison to the *Pentagon Papers* case, the judge said; that case was about outdated information, and this case was about current information that posed a genuine threat to national security.

The *Progressive* claimed that the majority of the information in the article was taken from public sources, and it was information that any citizen could find. The magazine also claimed that other nations already possessed the H-bomb data. Still, the judge issued an injunction against the magazine to prevent it from publishing the article.

However, the case became *moot* (pointless) when a newspaper in Madison, WI, in September 1979 published a story with much of the same H-bomb information as the *Progressive* article. Now the government no longer had a reason to try to suppress the *Progressive* article because the information had been released through another publication, and the government was powerless to stop its further dissemination. As a result, a federal appeals court dismissed the government's case in October 1979.[25]

TIME, PLACE, AND MANNER RESTRICTIONS

These are restrictions that are placed on *how* speech is delivered and not on the content of the speech itself. As will be seen in the following cases, the government is allowed to regulate the time, place, and manner of some speech as long as the goal is not to censor a particular message.

[24]467 F. Supp. 990 (W.D. Wis. 1979)

[25]610 F.2d 819 (7th Cir. 1979)

FAQ

What are some examples of restrictions based on time, place, and manner?

▣ Time restriction: *Noise laws.* You have a right to mow your yard, but you may not have a right to mow it at midnight, when the noise might wake your neighbors. Some communities have passed ordinances regulating the time a person can engage in noisy activities such as lawn mowing.

▣ Manner restriction: *Public nuisance laws.* People have a right to listen to music on a stereo in their cars. However, many towns have laws about the manner in which a person can play this music. For example, communities have laws that limit the volume at which people may play music in their vehicles, or they may require that drivers have the car windows up when playing music.

▣ Place restriction: *Parade permits.* Persons have a right to protest a war, for example. However, those persons do not have a right to engage in such protests in the middle of a busy public street. Cities have the power to issue or not to issue parade permits based on concerns such as safety and traffic flow.

Criteria for Time, Place, and Manner Restrictions

Historically, the courts have considered four basic issues when ruling on the legality of a time, place, or manner (TPM) restriction: (a) The regulation must be "content-neutral," which means the regulation is not meant to censor the content of a message; (b) the regulation must not ban the speech entirely; (c) there must be a "substantial state interest" served by the regulation, and (d) the regulation must be narrowly tailored.

These four criteria are applied and explained in the analyses of these next rulings.

Krishnas and a State Fair

The 1981 Supreme Court case of *Heffron v. Krishna*[26] is a landmark ruling regarding TPM restrictions. The case involved the 1977 Minnesota State Fair, which had rules stating that people distributing literature during the fair "could do so only from fixed locations on the fairgrounds." The International Society for Krishna Consciousness religious group said the rules violated their rights to distribute their message in the way they desired. The Krishnas preferred to greet people one on one. They said being restricted to a "fixed location" such as a booth prevented them from practicing their religion in their own way.

The Supreme Court ruled that the fair's rules were indeed fair. The court applied the four criteria:

▣ The fair's rules were *content neutral.* The fair did not single out the Krishnas because of their message. All groups at the fair had to abide by the same rules.

▣ The rules *did not ban* the Krishnas from speaking. They could still deliver their messages, but they had to do so from a booth.

▣ There was a *substantial state interest* here: safety and convenience for the crowds. The fair restricted groups to booths to ensure better traffic flow on the fairgrounds. The fair attracted very

---

[26]452 U.S. 640 (1981)

large crowds, and the court said, "the State's interest in the orderly movement and control of such an assembly of persons is a substantial consideration."

▣ The fair's rules were *"narrowly tailored."* In other words, this rule was "narrow" and focused on the issue it was supposed to address—crowd control. The rule did not wind up restricting the rights of anyone to deliver a message. The rules were reasonable and not overly restrictive.

Rock Concerts and Volume

The 1989 case of *Ward v. Rock Against Racism*[27] dealt with some loud rock concerts in New York City's Central Park. A group called Rock Against Racism (RAR) organized annual concerts, but local residents complained about the "noise pollution" created by the loud rock bands. The city said the concerts could continue but the rock bands could not play above a certain volume level. The city placed devices behind audience areas to make sure the bands did not exceed the volume limits.

During one concert, RAR ignored officials' demands to turn down the volume several times. Officials got fed up and cut off electricity to the concert stage. The city then banned RAR from sponsoring future concerts in the park. RAR sued the city, saying the noise ordinance violated the First Amendment rights of the musicians.

The U.S. Supreme Court ruled for the city, saying that limits on noise were a reasonable TPM restriction.

1. *Was the regulation "content neutral"?* Yes. The city was not trying to censor the lyrics or any other messages from the musicians. The city was simply regulating the *manner* of the speech, not the content.

2. *Did the city ordinance ban the speech entirely?* No. The city allowed the music to be played, just not louder than a reasonable volume.

3. *Was there a "substantial state interest" here?* Yes, said the court. The state (or in this case, the city) had an interest in protecting nearby residents from excessive noise.

4. *Was the regulation "narrowly tailored"?* In other words, did the regulation fix the intended problem (noise) without unnecessarily limiting protected speech? The court said yes. The ordinance focused specifically and narrowly on the noise issue.

FAQ

What would be an example of an ordinance that was not narrowly tailored?

If the city had responded to the noise complaints with an ordinance that banned *all* rock concerts in Central Park, such an ordinance would not be considered "narrowly tailored."

In March 2004, the city council in Hamtramck, MI, stirred controversy when it amended a noise ordinance, voting unanimously to allow a mosque to use public loudspeakers to broadcast Muslim calls to prayer five times a day. The council, however, ruled the calls

---

[27]491 U.S. 781 (1989)

to prayer could only be done between 6:00 a.m. and 10:00 p.m. Many local residents complained about the potential noise, but Muslims argued that the calls were no different than church bells ringing. By May, local residents gathered enough signatures on petitions to force the city council either to rescind the amendment or to put the matter to a citywide vote. The council voted to keep the amendment, and Hamtramck residents voted in 2004 in favor of it.

TPM restrictions are often a source of contention in society and in communications cases. More TPM cases will be discussed in other chapters of this book, particularly in the chapter on obscenity.

SUMMARY

Understanding the history of freedom of expression is vital to any student studying communication law. Britain enacted sedition laws and licensing schemes to control what people said and what people published. Proponents of free expression, including Milton and Locke, said that such restrictions violated people's rights to express themselves freely.

In the late 1700s, America crafted its own sedition laws during the war with France. Those laws punished anyone who criticized the U.S. government or its leaders. Those laws soon expired, but sedition laws reappeared in America during both world wars. Although they were upheld by the Supreme Court for decades, the court eventually whittled away at sedition laws. The "clear and present danger" test evolved and now requires that the government can only restrict "seditious" speech if it is likely to result in "imminent lawless action."

The courts have struck down many hate speech laws as violations of free speech.

The courts are also reluctant to allow governmental prior restraints on speech unless there are substantial, provable dangers involved, such as national security. Time, place, and manner restrictions are permissible as long as the restrictions are reasonable and are not meant to punish the content of the speech.

3

Applying the Principles of Broadcast Regulation

[Broadcast licensees must operate] in the public interest, convenience and necessity.

—Radio Act of 1927

B roadcasting is a form of communication and speech that is subject to numerous government regulations. As soon as radio began to develop in the early part of the 20th century, the federal government realized the great potential for broadcasting as a communications medium. The government also recognized a need to place various controls on this rapidly growing industry. One of the first controls came in 1910, when Congress required all U.S. passenger ships to have a radio. However, the sinking of the Titanic in 1912 revealed a flaw in the system. Titanic sent out radio distress signals to nearby ships, but many did not receive the message because it was late at night and many ships had no one monitoring their radios.

The Radio Act of 1912 amended this problem by requiring that all ship radios should be monitored 24 hours a day and that a separate frequency be set aside for distress calls. The act also required that all radio operators had to have broadcasting licenses from the federal government. All radio transmitters were required to be licensed as well, and the Secretary of Commerce was placed in charge of all licensing. However, anyone who applied for a license could get one. The secretary had limited powers, such as making determinations about specific time periods when persons could broadcast or on what kind of radio wavelength. As would soon be discovered, such a system was ripe for abuse.

By the 1920s, people rapidly discovered the convenience and immediacy of radio, and the medium began to grow quickly. There soon were too many stations on the limited radio spectrum. There were, after all, only so many frequencies allocated on the AM dial (FM had not been established yet). There was no government agency to assign frequencies to broadcast stations, so many stations went on the air on whichever frequency they desired. As a result, the airwaves became cluttered with stations overlapping other stations' signals. In the early 1920s, Secretary of Commerce Herbert Hoover held a number of national "radio conferences" to try to get radio broadcasters to work out these problems on their own.

However, more radio stations went on the air each year, and interference problems only seemed to get worse. In fact, by 1926, there were nearly 1000 unlicensed radio stations broadcasting across the nation.

It was a licensed broadcaster in 1926 who tested the limits of Hoover's power. WJAZ radio in Chicago was licensed to operate at 930 AM. However, several other stations also broadcast on 930 AM in that area, so WJAZ's license only permitted the station to broadcast for 2 hours each week on that frequency. WJAZ's owner, Zenith Corporation, applied for a license to broadcast at 910 AM, but Hoover denied the request because only Canadian stations were permitted to use that frequency. Zenith ignored Hoover's denial and began broadcasting WJAZ on 910 AM. Zenith and Hoover took their dispute to court, and in *U.S. v. Zenith Radio Corporation,*[1] a federal appeals court ruled against Hoover. The court said, "There is no express grant of power in the [Radio Act of 1912] to the secretary of commerce to establish regulations."

The *Zenith* case and radio interference concerns led to the Radio Act of 1927. Congress passed this act to create a five-member panel called the Federal Radio Commission (FRC), to bring some order to the burgeoning radio industry. The FRC was granted numerous powers, including the assigning of frequencies to radio stations to alleviate possible interference problems between radio stations. The FRC could also deny broadcasting licenses if there was no more room on the spectrum. The commission said its goal was to make sure that each American could receive at least one radio station and, when possible, a diverse number of radio stations. The FRC also demanded that radio stations' programming serve in the "public interest, convenience, and necessity."

With these guidelines in place, the Radio Act of 1927 helped to end the problems of radio station interference. However, other federal agencies still were given control over other aspects of broadcasting and other forms of electronic communication. Seven years later, though, power over all electronic media would be given to the Federal Communications Commission.

THE FEDERAL COMMUNICATIONS COMMISSION

The Communications Act of 1934

The Communications Act of 1934 replaced the Radio Act of 1927 and remains the foundation for broadcasting regulation today. The Communications Act also replaced the FRC with the Federal Communications Commission. You can find the text for the Communications Act (and all of the amendments since 1934) in Title 47 of the *United States Code,* which can be found in the *Federal Register.* There you will find the government's purpose for establishing the FCC. The commission was designed to oversee "all of the channels of interstate and foreign radio transmission." The FCC was also given jurisdiction over the telephone industry.

The act established certain principles and rules for the FCC, which follow.

The "Public Airwaves" and the "Public Interest, Convenience and Necessity." These concepts had their birth in the Radio Act of 1927. The government was announcing it would not

---

[1]12 F.2d 614 (N.D. Ill. 1926)

treat the broadcast airwaves like other media, such as newspapers or magazines. Instead, the airwaves would be regulated more like a public street. For example, private citizens are allowed to use a public street, but the street still belongs to the government. Therefore, the government has the right to pass certain laws about the use of this street (speed limits, parking regulations, etc.). The government said the public airwaves are similar to a public street and the government has some authority to regulate the "traffic" on that street. However, defining the "public interest" is a fairly subjective process. As a result, broadcasters frequently wage battles with the FCC and the courts over the exact parameters of "public interest."

Scarcity Rationale. This concept says the public airwaves are a "scarce" resource. There are a limited number of channels made available for broadcast radio and TV, and confusion results if the government does not step in as a "traffic cop." This provides another rationale for allowing the government to regulate broadcasting.

Licensing. The FCC handles the licensing for all stations and broadcasters and may reject applicants who do not meet FCC standards. Licenses are granted for specified time periods.

Allocation of Frequencies. Like the FRC before it, the FCC assigns frequencies to broadcasters. Broadcasters do not *own* their frequencies. The FCC controls all channels of interstate and foreign radio transmission.

Fines. The FCC has the power to levy fines on broadcasters who violate rules.

No Government Censorship. The FCC is not allowed to "interfere with the right of free speech by the means of radio communication." However, as we will see throughout this book, the courts treat this part of the act with great flexibility!

No Local or State Regulation of the Airwaves. Even if a radio station signal does not cross state lines and is not an "interstate" signal, the FCC still has the sole power to regulate that station. The Supreme Court upheld this FCC doctrine in 1933 in *U.S. v. Nelson Brothers.*[2] Local and state governments have no jurisdiction in broadcast regulation.

Regulations. The FCC has the power to pass rules and regulations affecting broadcasters. Of course, those regulations may be overturned in court cases or changed through laws passed by Congress.

FCC Commissioners

Today the FCC is made up of five commissioners appointed by the president of the United States and approved by the Senate (until 1982, there were seven commissioners). The president is responsible for choosing the FCC's chairperson, who establishes the commission's agenda. As a result, the chairperson has great power in setting the tone for commission actions. In 1981, President Reagan appointed Mark Fowler FCC chair, and he led the fight for deregulation in many areas of broadcasting. President Clinton placed Reed

---

[2]289 U.S. 266 (1933)

Hundt at the helm in 1993, and Hundt focused on issues such as cable regulation and the Internet. President George W. Bush appointed Michael Powell chair in 2001, and Powell has pushed the commission toward more liberal ownership rules and stricter indecency enforcement.

There can be no more than three commissioners from one political party. Commissioners serve 5-year terms, and those terms are "staggered" so there is never more than one term expiring each year. This helps to maintain a level of consistency within the agency. Commissioners are also prohibited from having financial interests in any FCC matters.

Drafting New Regulations

If the commission wants to draft new rules or amend existing ones, commissioners must follow certain procedures.

First, there is a Notice of Proposed Rule Making. This is a public notice that the FCC or other regulatory agency must issue when it is considering a new regulation. Interested parties may submit comments to the FCC supporting or opposing a proposed regulation. After having received written comments for a specified time period, the FCC will hold a hearing at which interested parties may present their points in person before the commission.

If the FCC or other regulatory agency wants more information on a certain subject or controversy, the agency issues a Notice of Inquiry. For example, if the FCC needs more information about a new technology, the commission must issue a Notice of Inquiry seeking input from broadcasters and the public. This helps to ensure that the FCC is getting valuable and up-to-date information and commentary on important matters. The FCC will then have a public hearing on the issue.

After considering comments received through a Notice of Inquiry or Notice of Proposed Rule Making, the FCC votes on a ruling and issues a Report and Order. This document is published in the *Federal Register*. It explains new rules or how rules have been changed. The Report and Order may also be used to explain why a rule was not changed.

Important FCC Terminology

Comparative hearings: The FCC used to have these hearings to "compare" applicants who were applying for the same specific broadcast station license and then choose one applicant. The FCC no longer holds comparative hearings. It is mentioned here because comparative hearings are mentioned later in this text.

Auctions: Today, instead of comparative hearings, the FCC usually just auctions off a new license to the highest bidder.

Licensee: The person or company granted a broadcast license by the FCC.

Title 47: This is the section of the *Federal Register* that contains the Communications Act of 1934 and related broadcasting regulations. The *Federal Register* is a series of volumes that contain federal laws and regulations. You can find a wealth of information about FCC regulations at the FCC Web site, http://www.fcc.org, or through Title 47 on the *Code of Federal Regulation*, which is available through the Government Printing Office Web site, http://www.gpo.gov.

Common carrier: The most common example is a telephone system. A common carrier is a message delivery system that anyone can use for a fee. The government is not supposed to interfere with the content of the messages. The FCC has the right to regulate some aspects of common carriers, though, such as rates charged for interstate services.

FCC Bureaus

The FCC is broken down into six bureaus to handle the various responsibilities of the commission. Very briefly, here are the names and duties of each bureau.

Media Bureau: This bureau handles licensing and the subsequent paperwork for commercial TV and radio stations, as well as cable companies. It also oversees issues related to direct broadcast satellite services and other services.

Enforcement Bureau: This bureau is in charge of handling complaints, levying fines, and enforcing punishments for broadcasters who violate the rules.

Wireline Competition Bureau: This bureau mostly handles issues dealing with common carriers, such as the interstate telephone industry. States regulate telephone services within their borders.

Consumer and Governmental Affairs Bureau: This bureau is the public affairs office for the FCC, providing information to the public about FCC matters.

Wireless Telecommunications Bureau: This bureau oversees radio services not on the public airwaves. These include amateur "ham" radio, CB (citizens band) radio, two-way radio systems used by fire and police departments, and marine radio services.

International Bureau: This bureau regulates satellite transmissions that cross international borders. It also oversees and licenses shortwave radio stations that have signals reaching into other countries.

FCC Licensing

A person or party may apply for a broadcast license for a new station or, in most cases, for an existing station. The person must fill out the necessary FCC forms and file them with the Mass Media Bureau to obtain a construction permit. Because this can be complicated, many persons hire communication law attorneys to handle this process. The FCC will not consider applications that are incomplete or filled out improperly.

FAQ
What if more than one person applies for the same license?

The FCC will conduct hearings if there are multiple applications for the same license.

Potential licensees must detail how their station would serve the public interest. They must also hire someone to conduct an engineering study, which provides detailed technical information about such things as the station's signal reach and tower height and ensures that the new station will not interfere with existing stations.

Once that is done, the FCC will grant the construction permit, and the person may begin construction on the broadcast facilities. Stations then have 3 years from the issuance of the permit to complete construction and file the application for a license (see 47 CFR §73.3598). If the facilities meet FCC standards, the commission will grant the license.

Before a station can begin broadcasting, though, the applicant must meet qualifications in five areas: legal, financial, technical, character, and equal employment opportunity (EEO) rules.

- ▣ *Legal:* Must be a U.S. citizen or company with less than 25% foreign ownership. Licenses may be denied or not renewed for violations of FCC rules or U.S. laws.
- ▣ *Financial:* Must have enough money to construct and run the station for 3 months (this cannot include any potential revenues from advertising).
- ▣ *Technical:* Must have the technical expertise required by FCC rules to run a broadcast station or have employees with such expertise.
- ▣ *Character:* Must be of good character. Licenses may be denied to an applicant who has a record of lying to the FCC, has engaged in anticompetitive activities, or has been convicted of a felony.
- ▣ *EEO Rules:* The FCC requires that all licensees prove they do not engage in discrimination in their hiring practices. A more detailed discussion follows.

Broadcast Stations and Minority Employees

The FCC used to require that stations meet certain EEO percentages. Every broadcast station was required to have employees who reflected the population in their community. To achieve this, the FCC required stations to achieve 50% "parity." This meant if the community was 30% Hispanic, then 15% of employees at the broadcast station had to be Hispanic. Many broadcasters complained about these rules, saying it forced them to hire employees based almost entirely on race instead of on experience or qualifications.

FCC's Old EEO Rules Struck Down

In 1998 in *Lutheran Church–Missouri Synod v. FCC,*[3] the DC Circuit Court of Appeals tossed out the EEO requirements. The case involved two church-run radio stations that objected to the FCC's requirement that the stations hire "non-religious" employees for non-air jobs for the sake of diversity. The church argued that the First Amendment's freedom of religion clause meant the stations should not have to hire people who did not support the church's beliefs, even if those people were not on the air (secretaries, sales staff, etc.). The appeals court said the church was right, and the FCC's EEO guidelines were found to be unconstitutional because they mandated hiring quotas.

In 2000, the FCC tried to enforce new EEO guidelines that said broadcasters and cable companies were required to engage in "broad outreach" efforts to ensure a "diverse" workplace. The rules were somewhat vague, and many broadcasters were not sure what types of "outreach" would make the FCC happy. The DC appeals court once again struck down the FCC's EEO rules in 2001 in *MD/DC/DE Broadcasters Association v. FCC.*[4] The court said the new EEO rules created a "race-based classification" that did not serve any important government interest.

Current EEO Rules

In 2002, the FCC adopted new EEO rules with a three-prong approach. *Prong 1:* Licensees must widely distribute notices about full-time job openings ("full-time" being at

---

[3]141 F.3d 344 (D.C. Cir. 1998)

[4]236 F.3d 13 (D.C. Cir. 2001)

least 30 hours per week). This requirement may be waived if there are unusual or "exigent" circumstances, but the FCC does not clearly define exigent and says it will analyze exceptions on a case-by-case basis. *Prong 2:* Licensees must provide information about job openings to employment agencies upon request. *Prong 3:* Licensees should engage in recruitment initiatives, such as job fairs and internship programs, or develop their own outreach methods.

Broadcasters must keep records of their EEO compliance. Each year on the anniversary date of the station's license renewal, the station must place an EEO report in the public file describing recruitment activities for the previous year. This EEO report is required during the license renewal process. For radio stations with at least ten full-time employees and TV stations with at least five, the EEO report is required during a midterm review process. Religious broadcasters may be exempt from EEO rules and hire based on an applicant's religious beliefs. However, these broadcasters must prove they are not discriminating in areas such as sex, race, or nationality.

FCC Licenses and Minority Preferences

Historically, in comparative licensing processes, the FCC would often give preference to women and minorities over white males for broadcast licenses. That is because there were few women and minorities in broadcast ownership positions.

White males began to take the FCC to court over the matter, saying that the minority preference policy discriminated against white males who may have been better qualified than minority candidates. In 1990 in *Metro Broadcasting v. FCC,*[5] the Supreme Court voted 5-4 to uphold the minority preference rules, but this did not last long.

Minority and Women Preferences Struck Down

In 1995, the court reversed itself and struck down FCC minority preferences in *Adarand v. Pena.*[6] The court ruled that minority preferences were illegal. The court added that the preferences were a "highly suspect tool" because they ultimately led to discrimination against another group (in this instance, white males).

Several years earlier, in 1992, a federal appeals court had also struck down the FCC's women's preferences in *Lamprecht v. FCC.*[7] The court ruled 2-1 that the FCC did not prove that such preferences would lead to "diversity" on the public airwaves. Therefore, the court said, the rules proved to have no other real purpose than to discriminate.

TV and Radio License Renewals

The Telecommunications Act of 1996 extended TV and radio license terms to 8 years. This lessens paperwork and hassle for stations as well as for the FCC. Stations will basically be guaranteed license renewal if they meet three criteria: (a) The station can prove it served the public interest, convenience, and necessity; (b) the station had no "serious violations" of FCC rules or of the Communications Act; and (c) the station has no "pattern of abuse" of FCC rules or of the Communications Act.

---

[5]497 U.S. 547 (1990)

[6]515 U.S. 200 (1995)

[7]958 F.2d 382 (D.C. Cir. 1992)

If the station satisfies the FCC in these three areas, the commission will not even consider any competing applications that may have been filed for that station's license. Competing applications would only be considered if a station's license renewal is denied.

(For both commercial and noncommercial TV stations, each renewal application must include a summary of comments and suggestions regarding violent programming.)

Seven months before a station's license expires, the FCC will send a reminder notice on a postcard to the station. Stations must file renewal paperwork no later than 4 months before their license expiration date. The FCC also requires stations to air four "prefiling" and six "postfiling" announcements provided by the FCC. These must air on the 1st and 16th days of the month.

Sample Timeline If a Station's License Expires on December 1

May 1: FCC sends postcard renewal reminder to the station.

June 1 and 16 and July 1 and 16: Station is required to air prefiling announcements.

August 1: Deadline to file for license renewal.

August 1 and 16, September 1 and 16, and October 1 and 16: Station is required to air postfiling announcements.

Prefiling Announcement Guidelines. For radio stations, at least two of the announcements need to be made between 7:00 a.m. and 9:00 a.m. or between 4:00 p.m. and 6:00 p.m. (If a station for some reason is not broadcasting between these times, it is required to air the announcements within the first 2 hours of that day's broadcasting.)

For commercial TV stations, at least two of the announcements must be made between 5:00 p.m. and 10:00 p.m. for the Central and Mountain time zones and between 6:00 p.m. and 11:00 p.m. for the Eastern and Pacific time zones.

Postfiling Announcement Guidelines: At least three of the announcements must be broadcast between 7:00 a.m. and 9:00 a.m. or between 4:00 p.m. and 6:00 p.m., at least one between 9:00 a.m. and noon, at least one between noon and 4:00 p.m., and at least one between 7:00 p.m. and midnight.

After the last postfiling announcement, the station must place a written record of compliance in its public file within 7 days. This record should list the dates and times of the announcements. If the station could not follow the announcement guidelines for certain dates or times, the station needs to provide legitimate explanations in writing.

As TV stations are broadcasting these announcements, they must also place the FCC's and station's addresses on screen. If for some reason the station cannot broadcast the announcement during a required time (because of an emergency situation), the station must broadcast the announcement the following day during the scheduled time. See Figure 3.1 for examples of how the announcements are worded.

FAQ

What about a college radio station that might not be on the air during some of these dates?

Prefiling Renewal Announcement

On [*date of last license renewal*] Station [*call letters*] was granted a license by the Federal Communications Commission to serve the public interest as a public trustee until [*license expiration date*]. Our license will expire on [*repeat expiration date*]. We must file an application for license renewal with the FCC by [*first day of fourth full calendar month before expiration date*]. When filed, a copy of the application will be available for public inspection during our regular business hours. The renewal application will contain information concerning the station's performance during the last 8 years. Individuals who wish to advise the FCC of facts relating to our renewal application and of whether the station has operated in the public interest should file comments and petitions with the FCC by [*first day of last full calendar month before the month of expiration*]. Further information concerning the FCC's broadcast license renewal process is available at [*insert address for public inspection file*] or may be obtained from the FCC, Washington, DC 20554.

Postfiling Renewal Announcement

On [*date of last license renewal*], Station [*call letters*] was granted a license by the Federal Communications Commission to serve the public interest as a public trustee until [*expiration date*]. Our license will expire on [*repeat expiration date*]. We have filed an application for license renewal with the FCC. A copy of this application is available for public inspection during our regular business hours. It contains information concerning the station's performance during the last 8 years. Individuals who wish to advise the FCC of facts relating to our renewal application and of whether this station has operated in the public interest should file comments and petitions with the FCC by [*first day of last full calendar month before the month of expiration*]. Further information concerning the FCC's broadcast license renewal process is available at [*insert address of public inspection file*] or may be obtained from the FCC, Washington, DC 20554.

Figure 3.1   Examples of Prefiling and Postfiling Announcements

Noncommercial stations are required to follow these rules only if they are regularly scheduled to be on the air on the specified dates.

POLITICAL BROADCASTING RULES

Because of such concepts as the scarcity rationale and the "public airwaves," the courts have ruled that various broadcast content regulations are constitutional. For example, the courts have upheld the FCC's right to regulate "indecent" or sexually explicit material on the airwaves. Children have easy access to broadcasting, and the courts say that restricting indecent broadcast programming is a way to protect children from what are considered unwholesome messages and images. The courts have ruled this all of part of serving the broader "public interest."

The courts have also upheld other content regulations for broadcasters. When it comes to political broadcast content, there are rules to ensure that broadcasters do not use the power of the airwaves to favor one candidate over another.

The "Equal Time" or "Equal Opportunity" Rule

This rule originated in the Radio Act of 1927 and was made part of the Communications Act of 1934. It is known as Section 315 because the rule is included in that section of the Communications Act (for exact wording, see box). The rule applies to radio and TV stations, both broadcast and satellite, as well as community cable systems that originate their own programming. In simple terms: "If a station gives or sells air time to a legally qualified political candidate, that station must also give or sell a comparable amount of time to every other legally qualified candidate running for that office."

One congressman, at the time the Communications Act was being written, said Section 315 was necessary or else "American politics will be largely at the mercy of those who operate these stations." Politicians know the power of broadcasting. Hundreds of millions of dollars are now spent every 4 years on the U.S. presidential race alone, and most dollars from candidates' advertising budgets go to broadcast advertising.

Section 315: The "Equal Time" Rule

(a) If any licensee shall permit any person who is a legally qualified candidate for any public office to use a broadcasting station, he shall afford *equal opportunities* to all other such candidates for that office in the use of such broadcasting station:

Provided. That such licensee shall have no power of censorship over the material broadcast under the provisions of this section. No obligation is hereby imposed under this subsection upon any licensee to allow the use of its station by any such candidate. Appearance by a legally qualified candidate on any:

(1) bona fide newscast,

(2) bona fide news interview,

(3) bona fide news documentary (if the appearance of the candidate is incidental to the presentation of the subject or subjects covered by the news documentary), or

(4) on-the-spot coverage of bona fide news events (including but not limited to political conventions and activities incidental thereto), shall not be deemed to be a use of a broadcasting station within the meaning of this subsection. Nothing in the foregoing sentence shall be construed as relieving broadcasters in connection with the presentation of newscasts, news interviews, news documentaries, and on-the-spot coverage of news events, from the obligation imposed upon them under this chapter to operate in the public interest and to afford reasonable opportunity for the discussion of conflicting views on issues of public importance.

(b) The charges made for the *use* of any broadcasting station by any person who is a legally qualified candidate for any public office in connection with his campaign for nomination for election, or election, to such office shall not exceed—

(1) during the 45 days preceding the date of a primary or primary runoff election and during the 60 days preceding the date of general or special election in which such person is a candidate, the lowest unit charge of the station for the same class and amount of time for the same period; and

(2) at any other time, the charges made for comparable use of such station by other users thereof.

(c) For purposes of this section—

(1) the term "broadcasting station" includes a community antenna television system [CATV, or cable]; and

(2) the terms "licensee" and "station licensee" when used with respect to a community antenna television system mean the operator of such system.

[In 1993, the FCC ruled that direct broadcast satellite services—satellite TV providers—must also abide by Section 315 and Section 312 (a) (7). In 1997, the FCC said satellite radio providers also have to abide by these rules.]

(d) The Commission shall prescribe appropriate rules and regulations to carry out the provisions of this section.

SECTION 315 ANALYZED

"Equal Time" Really Means "Equal Opportunities"

Even though Section 315 is frequently called the "Equal Time" rule, it is actually more practical to think of it as the "Equal Opportunities" rule. In Section 315, the FCC explains what it means by *equal opportunities:* If a broadcast station or local cable operator accepts advertising or programming from a legally qualified candidate, it must all allow "equal opportunities" for opposing candidates. This means that a station or cable system operator must give all candidates an equal opportunity to reach the same *potential* audience. For example, it would be unfair for a radio station to offer one candidate ads during the afternoon, when there are many listeners, and offer another candidate ads only late at night, when there are fewer listeners.

This rule applies to all candidates at all levels—federal, state, and local. In all of its practices, the station must not give the appearance that it is favoring one candidate over another.

Deadlines

FAQ

Must a candidate make an "equal time" request within a certain time frame?

A candidate has *7 days* to request equal opportunity from a station or cable system. The candidate must make the request directly to the station within 7 days after an opponent's ad or program has aired. After the 7th day, that candidate no longer can demand equal time for those spots already aired by an opponent.

This rule was put in place so candidates could not come to a station to demand equal time for ads or programs that aired weeks or months earlier. A broadcast station is under no obligation to notify candidates about the airing of an opponent's material. The candidate is ultimately responsible.

Legally Qualified Candidates

The FCC says a person is a legally qualified candidate if he or she publicly announces candidacy for nomination or election to a local, state, or federal office; meets the legal qualifications for that particular office (age, residency requirements, U.S. citizenship, etc.); qualifies to be placed on the ballot or is eligible for legal votes by another method, such as write-in or sticker; *and* has made a substantial showing as a bona fide candidate—*or* has been officially nominated by an established or well-known political party.

A station is not responsible for verifying whether a person is a legally qualified candidate. The burden of proof falls on the candidate.

FAQ

What qualifies as a "use"?

Section 315 is supposed to apply only to broadcast ads or other material that constitute a legitimate "use" by a candidate. The FCC says a "use" occurs when a recognizable voice or picture of the candidate appears in an ad or other broadcast campaign appearance.

Ads Without a Candidate's Voice or Picture

FAQ

What about ads that don't use the candidate's voice or picture?

In such instances, something called the Zapple Doctrine or Zapple Rule applies. This rule came about in 1972 to address the issue of candidates using spokespersons in their ads to avoid "uses" and subsequent Section 315 obligations.

The Zapple Rule says if a *spokesperson* for a candidate appears in an ad, the station must provide equal access to an *opposing candidate's spokesperson.* The Zapple Rule applies only during campaign periods and only to spokespersons of major political party candidates.

FAQ

Can a candidate demand "equal time" to respond to an opposing candidate's spokesperson?

No. The Zapple Rule only allows spokespersons to respond to other spokespersons. The station would *not* be required to offer airtime to the actual opposing candidate in such a situation.

Other "Uses"

To try to alleviate confusion, the FCC in 1978 issued a report to detail instances it considers broadcast "uses" by candidates: (a) any time a candidate secures air time, even when not discussing his or her candidacy; (b) an incumbent politician's "weekly reports" broadcast on radio or TV; (c) a candidate's appearance on a variety program, no matter how brief; (d) any on-air appearances by actors or broadcast station employees who are also running for public office.

Celebrity Candidates

FAQ

So any "celebrity" who's running for public office puts Section 315 into effect?

Yes. Much to the dismay of many who work in broadcasting, Section 315 does apply to such people as a radio disc jockey, TV weather announcer, or actor who is running for public office. That was not always the case, though.

The 1960 case *Brigham v. FCC*[8] concerned radio and TV weatherman Jack Woods, who had decided to run for the Texas legislature. Woods' opponent William Brigham said Woods' radio and TV weather reports were a use under Section 315, and Brigham demanded equal time on the air. A federal appeals court upheld an FCC ruling that Woods' broadcasts were part of his regular job and not "something arising out of the election campaign." Thus, Section 315 did not apply to Woods' weather report.

However, the FCC and the courts changed their minds on this matter more than 10 years later, saying that such "uses" result in a kind of free advertising for a candidate.

Paulsen v. FCC

In January 1972, Pat Paulsen was a legally qualified candidate for the Republican presidential nomination. Paulsen was also a professional entertainer who would soon be appearing on television in Disney's *The Mouse Factory*. The producer of the show contacted the FCC to see if Paulsen's appearance would count as a use under Section 315. The FCC said stations airing *The Mouse Factory* would be obligated to provide Paulsen's Republican opponents with equal time if those candidates requested it.

In *Paulsen v. FCC*,[9] a federal appeals court upheld the FCC ruling. Even nonpolitical uses of airtime constitute use of a broadcast station because they are free public relations for a candidate, the court said. "A candidate who becomes well-known to the public as a personable and popular individual through 'non-political' appearances certainly holds an advantage when he or she does formally discuss political issues to the same public over the same media." Section 315 needs to apply here because a station could subtly endorse

---

[8]276 F.2d 828 (5th Cir. 1960)

[9]491 F.2d 887 (9th Cir. 1974)

one candidate by inviting him or her to appear on numerous "entertainment" shows and not inviting other candidates.

Also in 1972, NBC broadcast an old Doris Day movie in which Paulsen was seen for 30 seconds. This also qualified as a use, and two of Paulsen's Republican opponents were given 30 seconds of equal time on NBC in that same time slot.

FAQ

Did Section 315 apply in 2003 when movie actor Arnold Schwarzenegger was running for governor of California?

Yes. In fact, the National Association of Broadcasters (NAB) alerted its member stations in California and neighboring states about potential Section 315 problems. The NAB warned broadcast stations that airing old Schwarzenegger movies such as *Total Recall* or *Conan the Barbarian* would have triggered Section 315. It was, potentially, a huge problem because this was a special recall election, with more than 100 legally qualified candidates, all of whom could have demanded equal time. Also, Section 315 applied to stations in adjacent states that broadcast to large numbers of California voters.

FAQ

What about cable channels airing Schwarzenegger movies? Did they have to abide by Section 315?

No. Remember, Section 315 applies only to broadcasters and *local* cable system operators. Therefore, *national* cable channels could have aired these movies without worrying about equal time requests. By the way, there were other celebrities running for governor of California in 2003, including Gary Coleman, who starred in the 1980s sitcom *Different Strokes,* and Don Novello, who played Father Guido Sarducci on *Saturday Night Live*. Local stations were advised to avoid airing reruns of these shows, but national cable channels continued to air them.

Section 315 also applies to local TV celebrities, such as newscasters.

Branch v. FCC

William Branch was an on-air news reporter for KOVR-TV in Sacramento, CA. He would appear in newscasts roughly 3 minutes each day. In 1984, Branch decided to run for the town council in nearby Loomis. Under Section 315 (a), Branch knew that his on-air reports were a "use of the station by a legally qualified candidate." As a result, his station determined it would have to give Branch's opponents 33 hours of response time, even though Branch would not be using his reports for political purposes. Branch's news reports would still count as a use.

KOVR told Branch to take an unpaid leave of absence during the campaign, with no guarantee his reporting job would still be available if he lost the election. Branch decided to keep his TV job and drop out of the race. He still took his case to the FCC, feeling it was unfair that his TV job kept him from running for political office. He also argued that he was part of a "bona fide newscast," and he should be exempt from Section 315. In *Branch v. FCC*,[10] a federal appeals court ruled that Section 315 does apply to on-air personalities and performers and that newscasters get no special exemption. The court said that newscasters must *not* be exempt from Section 315 and that this ruling would help prevent "unfair and unequal use of the broadcast media." The court's response to Branch's argument that he had to choose between his TV job and political office was, "Nobody has ever thought that a candidate has a right to run for office and at the same time to avoid all personal sacrifice."

FAQ

So, for example, if a local radio disc jockey decides to run for city council, that disc jockey's time on the air would count as a use?

Yes. If a broadcaster who is running for office chooses to keep a broadcasting job during a campaign, it can create headaches for the broadcast station. The station will have to keep track of how many minutes that broadcaster is on the air each day, including his or her voice work on any commercials and promotions, and then offer comparable time *for free* to all opponents for that political office. It would be free because the candidate-broadcaster is not paying the station to be on the air during these times, and therefore opposing candidates cannot be required to pay either.

FAQ

Does this apply to the primaries as well as to the general election?

Yes, but there are some important differences to keep in mind regarding how Section 315 works during primaries and during general elections.

Section 315 and Primaries

Primaries. Let's say Bob Smith is a Republican running for city council, and there are three other Republicans running against him in the primary. There are three Democrats vying for that party's nomination as well. If Smith buys ads on a station, only his Republican opponents would be allowed to request equal time under Section 315 in response to

---

[10]824 F.2d 37 (D.C. Cir. 1987)

Smith's ads. The Democrats are not his opponents at that time, so they would not be allowed to request equal time based on Smith's ad. The Democrats *would* be allowed to request equal time if a Democratic primary opponent was given air time.

General Elections. By this time, the parties have chosen their candidates. Now the party lines are gone, and Section 315 applies to all candidates from all parties for a particular office.

No Censorship of Political Ads

Stations are not allowed to censor a use by any political candidate for any reason. Even if the ad is poorly produced, is extremely negative, or is from a radical political party, the station must run the ad as is.

FAQ

What if the ad contains libel? Can't the station get in trouble for running a political ad that is libelous?

Libel in Political Ads

Libel involves untrue statements made about a person that damage that person's reputation or harm that person in other ways. Stations are not legally responsible for any libel in political ads that are considered uses. In *Farmers Educational and Cooperative Union of America v. WDAY*,[11] the Supreme Court ruled in 1959 that a broadcast station did not have a right to remove libelous or defamatory material from a political ad that is a use. The court said it did not want broadcast stations to "set themselves up as the sole arbiter of what is true and what is false." Again, those stations cannot be sued if the ad does indeed contain libelous material. However, candidates can be held liable for any defamatory statements made in political ads or programs.

FAQ

Can a station be held responsible for libelous statements in non-use ads?

Yes. That is why stations are allowed to censor an ad by *spokespersons* for a candidate because this type of ad is not considered a use.

FAQ

Isn't such an ad considered a use when equal time is invoked?

---

[11]360 U.S. 525 (1959)

No. Equal time is given because of the Zapple Rule, but that does not make it a use.

Stations are expected to edit any potentially libelous material from such non-use ads. This is important—*stations can be held responsible for airing libelous ads from supporters of candidates.*

FAQ

Are stations allowed to edit ads that may be distasteful or indecent?

No. The following case is a good example.

Aborted Fetuses in Political Ads

In the early 1990s, numerous politicians across the United States used pictures of aborted fetuses in their TV ads. The visuals were graphic, including pictures of fetuses with severed limbs or fetuses with skin that had been blackened by a process called "saline abortion." The politicians running the ads said they were showing the pictures to make people aware of what abortion does to a fetus. These politicians were also aware of the "no censorship" clause in Section 315. They knew stations would have to run the ads uncensored.

One such ad by congressional candidate Daniel Becker ran on WAGA-TV in Atlanta early one evening. The station received complaints from viewers, who said the ads were too graphic for broadcast, especially at that time of day. Becker dismissed the complaints and asked the TV station to give him 30 minutes of airtime for a video called *Abortion in America: The Real Story*, which contained more graphic images of aborted fetuses. Becker wanted the video to air late on a Sunday afternoon after an NFL broadcast. The station said the material was too graphic for that time of day and said it would only air the video after midnight, when there would be fewer children in the audience. Becker argued that the station simply did not like his message and was trying to censor his speech.

The FCC agreed that the ad was disturbing and would be harmful to children. Therefore, the FCC gave WAGA the right to air the ad only during late-night hours, from 10:00 p.m. to 6:00 a.m. A district court later upheld the FCC ruling.[12]

However, in 1996, a federal appeals court overturned that ruling in *Becker v. FCC*.[13] The court pointed out that the images in the ads were not indecent. The FCC's definition of indecency includes only material that has graphic depictions of "sexual or excretory activities and organs." This was not sexual material, the court said.

Channeling Becker's ads to late at night deprived him of reaching "particular categories of adult viewers whom he may be especially anxious to reach." Thus, Becker was deprived of the equal opportunities allowed him in Section 315. The FCC was allowing the station to channel the ads "based entirely on a subjective judgment that a particular ad *might* prove harmful to children." If stations are allowed to channel graphic ads for abortion, the court said, the FCC would have to allow stations to channel graphic political ads about the death penalty, gun control, and animal rights. The court feared this would lead to "content-based

---

[12]*Gillett Communications of Atlanta, Inc., v. Becker,* 807 F. Supp. 757 (D.C. Cir. 1992)

[13]95 F.3d 75 (D.C. Cir. 1996)

channeling." Allowing channeling of such ads might make candidates avoid certain controversial issues. The court concluded that channeling the ads violated Becker's "reasonable access" to the airwaves.

This ruling upheld the principle that government attempts to censor "unpopular" messages run head-on into the First Amendment.

Lowest Unit Rate

This is also known as the *lowest unit charge.* You will also hear broadcasters referring to this as LUR or LUC. All candidates—federal, state, and local—are eligible for the LUR. Lowest unit rates for broadcast uses apply only during certain time periods: 45 days before a primary and 60 days before a general election.

FAQ

What exactly does lowest unit rate mean?

LUR requires that stations give candidates the cheapest available ad rates. Therefore, a station is not allowed to inflate ad prices for "uses" by political candidates. Stations must charge candidates the lowest unit (per second, per 15-second block, or however that station charges) rate that the station would charge to its most favored advertisers for the same type or class of advertisement, for the same length of commercial, and for the same time of day. Stations need to provide candidates with as much information as they can about classes of ads, rates, terms, conditions, and discounts that are offered to favored advertisers.

Stations should draw up *political rate cards* for politicians so that it is very clear what the station is charging for political ads and for a particular class of advertisement.

FAQ

What is meant by "class of advertisement"?

Broadcast stations sell different types of ads at different rates. For example, sponsoring a newscast (a "fixed position" ad) will cost an advertiser more money than just running an ad at random times of the day ("run-of-schedule"). Politicians must be made aware of these various classes and the rates that are charged. Politicians will wind up paying different prices for different types of ads during different times of the day, but they must always be given the best possible rate.

FAQ

I work at a radio station. We sometimes have "fire sales" on ads, where we give advertisers some great bargain ad rates, near the end of the month. Do we have to include these rates in the LUR calculations?

The FCC says such "fire sale" ad rates and other "specials" must be included in LUR. In 1992, the FCC tried to alleviate confusion about LUR by issuing these guidelines:

- The commission recognizes four classes of advertising time: nonpreemptible, preemptible with notice, immediately preemptible, and run-of-schedule.
- Stations may create subclasses for each of these four areas as long as the subclasses are clearly defined.
- All classes must be fully disclosed and made available to candidates.
- Stations may not have a separate "premium period" class of time made available only to candidates.
- Stations may increase ad rates during an election season only if they have good reason, such as an increase in ratings or seasonal program changes.
- LUR may be calculated as often as every week.
- Prices for "bonus spots" given to commercial advertisers must be made available to candidates as well.

FAQ

Our station also does a lot of barters, or trade-outs, with businesses. Do we have to calculate the values of these arrangements when calculating LUR?

No, as long as the barter or trade-out did not involve any cash payments from the advertiser. If any cash does exchange hands, then the station must calculate the value of such transactions and include it in the LUC.

FAQ

A candidate purchases ads at a certain rate in July. In August, our station offers an ad rate to another client that is lower than the rate given to the candidate. Must our station give this new rate to the candidate?

Yes. First, the station must apply this rate to future ads by the candidate. Second, for ads that have already aired, the station must calculate the cost of those ads at the new rate and refund the candidate the difference (a "rebate"). That candidate also has the option to use the difference as "credit" and apply it to future ads. It is the responsibility of the station to alert candidates to any new rates, and it must be done in a timely fashion.

FAQ

Does the Zapple Rule apply to LUR? Can a candidate's supporters get the LUR for their ads?

No. LUR applies only for "uses" (ads containing the candidate's voice or image). Ads from supporters of a candidate do not qualify for LUR.

> **FAQ**
>
> What if a candidate can't afford to buy ads? In the spirit of fairness, shouldn't the station give that candidate some free time?

Political broadcasting rules do not require stations to give free airtime to any candidate. However, as mentioned, if a station gives one candidate free time for some reason, the station must then grant equal free time to opposing candidates.

Stations may also protect themselves from politicians who try to buy advertising time on "credit" and then never pay their bills. A broadcast station can demand that a *federal* candidate pay for airtime up to 7 days before an ad airs. For state and local candidates, those politicians must follow each station's rule regarding credit or payments in advance. These policies must be reasonable, however, and not unfairly keep a candidate from taking advantage of his or her rights under Section 315.

> **FAQ**
>
> For local races, does a station have to honor Section 315 obligations for candidates who are from districts outside of the station's main listening area?

No. Candidates who represent districts outside of a station's "principle service area" may not demand equal opportunities under Section 315.

Section 315 and News Exemptions

When a candidate appears in a "bona fide" news story or any other type of broadcast news event, the station is not required to give opposing candidates equal time in present or future news stories and programs. In other words, a news reporter is under no *legal* obligation to grant equal or comparable time to candidates in legitimate news stories.

Debates and the Aspen Rule

> **FAQ**
>
> In 2004, presidential debates on TV only had George Bush and John Kerry. Shouldn't Green Party candidate Ralph Nader and others have been included in these debates under Section 315?

There has been heated debate about whether debates should qualify as "bona fide news events" and thus be exempt from Section 315.

This issue first came up in 1960, with the first televised presidential debate between John F. Kennedy and Richard Nixon. Producers of the debate felt the public was much more interested in hearing from Nixon and Kennedy than from any of the other presidential candidates, who were largely unknown, and Congress agreed. Congress suspended Section 315 for the debates and said the TV and radio networks did not have to include candidates from "smaller" parties. The debates could be treated as "news events" and be exempted from Section 315. There were no presidential broadcast debates in 1964, 1968, and 1972. Then in 1975, the FCC echoed the 1960 congressional ruling in the Aspen Rule: Broadcast debates are bona fide news events and are exempt from Section 315.[14]

However, at the time, the FCC said the debates had to be sponsored by a non–broadcast entity such as the League of Women Voters. In 1983, though, the FCC dropped that requirement and said that broadcasters could directly sponsor and organize the debates and still be exempt from Section 315.

FAQ

Isn't the Aspen Rule unfair to candidates from smaller parties?

Those candidates certainly think so. In 1976, one small-party presidential candidate named Shirley Chisholm took the FCC to court over the Aspen Rule, but a federal appeals court in *Chisholm v. FCC*[15] ruled that the FCC was justified in exempting broadcast debates from Section 315.

Broadcasters tend to like the Aspen Rule for logistical reasons. For example, there are usually about 25 legally qualified candidates who run for president every 4 years. Broadcasters argue that it would be extremely difficult to have a meaningful debate between 25 people and that such an event would attract fewer viewers than a debate featuring the main candidates. In the next case, the court said the Aspen Rule also helps to avoid a "chilling effect" on broadcasters.

FAQ

What about state and local races? Does the Aspen Rule apply?

Yes. The Supreme Court addressed such concerns in 1998 in *Arkansas Educational Television Commission v. Forbes*.[16] A public TV station aired a debate between the Republican and Democrat running for Congress in Arkansas' Third District. An independent candidate, Ralph Forbes, argued that he should have been included in the debate, and an appeals court ruled for Forbes. That appeals court caused a public station in Nebraska to cancel a

---

[14]See *In re Aspen Institute and CBS*, 55 F.C.C.2d 697 (1975)

[15]538 F.2d 349 (D.C. Cir. 1976)

[16]523 U.S. 666 (1998)

candidate debate in 1996. The station said it would prefer to have no debate at all rather than be forced to invite all candidates to participate.

But in 1998, the U.S. Supreme Court said the Aspen Rule applied in this situation as well. It said TV stations, even public stations supported by tax dollars, do not have to include certain candidates. The court reasoned that (a) a broadcast debate is a "nonpublic forum." It is not a public forum like a park, and candidates do not have an automatic right of access. (b) Broadcasters may exclude candidates based on judgments of newsworthiness (i.e., the candidate is trailing badly in the polls). However, candidates may not be exempt because of their beliefs or stands on issues. (c) Placing such rules on broadcasters creates a "chilling effect." The court specifically mentioned the Nebraska station canceling a debate after the appeals court's ruling in favor of Forbes. Justice Anthony Kennedy said such a ruling "does not promote speech but represses it."

FAQ

What about press conferences? If an incumbent politician holds a press conference, is this a bona fide news event? Wouldn't this give the incumbent an unfair advantage to use the news media for free publicity?

Incumbent politicians will often hold numerous press conferences in the months before an election. If the news media cover the press conferences, it can be like free advertising for the incumbent candidate. Many nonincumbent politicians say such press conferences create an unfair advantage for incumbents.

A federal appeals court addressed this issue in 1980 in *Kennedy for President Committee v. FCC.*[17] Earlier in 1980, Senator Edward Kennedy of Massachusetts had challenged President Jimmy Carter for the Democratic presidential nomination. Just before the important New Hampshire primary, President Carter appeared on national TV for a presidential news conference, and he used part of the time to attack the views of Kennedy on several issues. Kennedy said such press conferences were inherently unfair because the president can use "the power of incumbency" to get more media attention.

Kennedy's campaign committee demanded equal time under Section 315 because "millions of viewers were misinformed about Senator Kennedy's views on national and international issues critical to voters in the campaign for the presidential nomination." The Kennedy campaign pointed to a 1964 FCC ruling[18] that said news conferences were a use under Section 315. However, in the 1975 *Aspen* ruling, the FCC had reversed course and decided press conferences were not a use.

Thus, in this case, the FCC ruled that the Carter press conference was a "bona fide on-the-spot coverage of bona fide news events" and would not be considered a use. An appeals court agreed and denied Kennedy's request for equal time under Section 315. Broadcasting the press conference was not an endorsement, the court said. There was not "even so much as a whisper of network bias in favor of the president." The networks were simply covering a bona fide news event and "had exercised good faith journalistic

---

[17]636 F.2d 417, 432 (D.C. Cir. 1980)

[18]See *CBS, Inc.*, 40 FCC 395 (1964)

judgment in concluding the event was newsworthy." Kennedy could not use Section 312(a)(7) to demand "reasonable access" for free; he should have held his own press conference to respond to Carter.

The court said also that a ruling in favor of Kennedy would create a chilling effect: "Broadcasters could never be sure that coverage of any given event would not later result in equal-opportunity obligations to all other candidates: resultantly, broadcaster discretion to carry or not to carry would be seriously if not fatally crippled."

Section 315 and Talk Shows

FAQ

What about candidates who are guests on radio and TV talk shows? More politicians are using such programs as part of their campaigns these days. Do these appearances count as "bona fide news interviews?"

This issue was first addressed in 1959. Congress said the FCC should give exemptions to more types of programs and not only to "standard" news programs. Congress said this would provide the public with more outlets for political discourse.

Eventually, the FCC developed three criteria to determine if a program should be exempt from Section 315:

- Whether the program is regularly scheduled
- Whether the program is controlled by the broadcaster or an independent producer (programs controlled by the broadcaster are often more likely to be exempt)
- Whether producers of the show choose the format, content, and participants based on newsworthiness and not to help or harm any candidate

By the 1990s, presidential candidates had begun to circumvent the national news media by doing interviews on talk shows such as the *Oprah Winfrey Show* and *Larry King Live*. In many instances, these types of interviews qualify as "news interviews," and Section 315 does not apply. However, it depends on the content and character of the show. If the host of a show is endorsing or "cheerleading" for a candidate, the FCC may rule that Section 315 applies. The FCC has been more lenient in giving exemptions to nontraditional news programs since 1988 and since an appeals court ruling in *King Broadcasting Co. v. FCC*.[19]

King Broadcasting wanted to air two pretaped programs highlighting George Bush and Michael Dukakis, the major party presidential candidates that year. The first program was an hour and gave each candidate 30 minutes to "state his case" to the public. One program was to air at the start of the campaign season and another would air just before the election. King also wanted to air an interview show with both candidates being asked questions by a journalist, and the candidates were allowed rebuttal time.

The FCC ruled the programs did not qualify as legitimate news events because King showed bias by not inviting presidential candidates from smaller parties and because the

---

[19]860 F.2d 465 (D.C. Cir. 1988)

programs were not regularly scheduled. The FCC also said the format of the programs was more like advertising because it allowed the candidate to make "stump speeches."

The appeals court overturned the FCC ruling and said the King programs should be exempt as bona fide news interview programs. The court pointed out that the FCC had not applied the "newsworthiness test" to King. (The court remanded the case to the FCC, and the commission then determined that the King programs were indeed newsworthy.) The court felt that the King programs were not "ads" or "stump speeches," as the FCC claimed, and that the FCC must consider exemptions for "hybrid formats" such as the King format. (The programs were called *hybrid* because they were not just straight news interviews or news stories. The programs contained a combination of candidate speeches, news interviews, and rebuttals.) The court added that the decision in *Aspen* allowed King to treat its programs like debates and invite only the major party candidates.

In 2003, the FCC ruled that even "shock radio" programs, such as the *Howard Stern Show,* were hybrids and qualified as bona fide news interview shows. Using similar criteria, the FCC has determined that the following programs can qualify as "news" interviews and be exempt from Section 315 obligations:

- "Entertainment talk" shows, such as the *Phil Donahue Show*, the *Oprah Winfrey Show*, the *Rosie O'Donnell Show*
- "Entertainment news" shows, such as *Entertainment Tonight, Access Hollywood*
- Cable documentary programs, such as A&E's *Biography*
- News magazine candidate profiles, such as a *Nightline* special "Who is Ross Perot?"
- TV political talk shows that include host commentary, such as *Politically Incorrect*
- Network and cable news interview shows, such as *Meet the Press, Face the Nation,* the *Larry King Show*
- Radio talk shows that include listener calls and candidate interviews, such as Rush Limbaugh and Howard Stern's

Sponsorship Identification

The following are the basic rules for *local and state races.*

All political ads and programs must be clearly labeled as such with "disclaimers." For radio ads, there must be a verbal statement indicating that the spot is a political ad. For TV, there must be a visual or audio statement, and it may be placed anywhere in the ad. The ads should contain a phrase such as "sponsored by," "paid for by," or "furnished by." These statements are usually pretty basic: "The preceding [following] ad was paid for by the Jane Jones for Mayor Committee." Make sure all local and state political ads at your station contain these sponsorship identifications and that the complete name of the sponsoring candidate or organization is accurate.

The rules for federal races are a little more complicated.

BCRA (FECA)

Federal Candidate Ads and BCRA

Many members of Congress argued that the FCC's sponsorship rules were too vague, especially for TV ads. One problem concerned special interest groups that ran "attack ads" against candidates. These "third-party" ads would often contain only a visual disclaimer at the end of the ad, a disclaimer that was often flashed on the screen very quickly or written in very small print. As a result, many voters did not see the disclaimers and assumed the ads were paid for by opposing candidates or parties, creating confusion about who was delivering these messages.

The Bipartisan Campaign Reform Act of 2002 (BCRA) was a response to such third-party ads, as well as other concerns. The act also is known as the Federal Election Campaign Act (FECA), and it was the outgrowth of legislation sponsored by senators John McCain and Russ Feingold. The act was challenged in court as a violation of the First Amendment, but the U.S. Supreme Court upheld most of the act's provisions in 2003 in *McConnell v. FEC.*[20]

The BCRA provides specific guidelines for disclaimers that must be included in political broadcast spots for federal candidates. The act covers all "public communications" paid for by federal candidates or by any person or group advocating the election or defeat of a federal candidate. It also includes all public communications that solicit funding for political purposes. Public communications include spots or programs on radio, TV, cable, and satellite, as well as articles and advertisements in newspapers, magazines, outdoor advertising, mass mailings, telephone banks, and public political advertising. The Federal Elections Commission (FEC) enforces BCRA.

"Stand by Your Ad" disclaimer

For federal candidates, BCRA mandates that certain disclaimers be included in all radio and TV ads that are authorized or paid for by the candidate. The FEC provides two examples:

- ▣ "I am *[name]*, a candidate for *[title of federal office]*, and I approved this advertisement."
- ▣ "My name is *[name]*. I am running for *[title of federal office]*, and I approved this message."

For radio, either of the above statements (or statements with reasonable variations of this wording) must be delivered clearly *in the candidate's own voice.*

For TV, the candidate has two options. The candidate may appear in a clear, full-screen shot while personally delivering one of the above disclaimers, *or* the candidate may use a recognizable picture or video of him- or herself that fills at least 80% of the screen and is accompanied by a voiceover of the candidate delivering the disclaimer.

Also, TV ads (whether broadcast, cable, or satellite) must have the candidate's name and approval statement *in writing at the end of the ad.* The writing must take up at least 4% of the vertical picture height and be on screen for at least 4 seconds. The wording should also be easy to read with a "reasonable degree of color contrast" between the lettering and the background.

FAQ

Does the BCRA require disclaimers for political Web pages or e-mails?

No. The Internet is exempt from these disclaimer rules.

---

[20]124 S. Ct. 619 (2003)

BCRA and Lowest Unit Rate

Federal candidate ads *that have direct references to an opponent* must contain certain disclaimers to qualify for LUR. TV ads must mention the office being sought and contain an identifiable candidate image at the end of the ad. The image must last at least 4 seconds and must display in writing an approval statement from the candidate. The wording must also tell what authorized committee paid for the ad. Radio ads must also tell the office being sought, along with an audio identification of the candidate. The audio must also contain a statement of approval from the candidate.

If a candidate runs ads that directly refer to an opponent, the candidate's ads will not qualify for LUR if the ads lack disclaimers.

FAQ

What are the rules for political ads that are not authorized or paid for directly by the candidate?

Such third-party ads are often produced by "527 groups," so named because of rules established in Section 527 of the Internal Revenue Code. These 527 groups can accept unlimited donations from unions, corporations, and individuals but cannot coordinate ads with presidential campaigns.

Third-party ads must have disclaimers. For radio, an announcer must clearly say a disclaimer such as "_____ is responsible for this advertising." The blank should be filled with the name of the person or political group paying for the ad. The ad must also clearly state that the message has not been authorized by the candidate or the candidate's election committee.

For TV, the disclaimer may be read as a voiceover by a representative of the ad's sponsor. The representative is not required to appear on screen. The other option is that the disclaimer be delivered through "an unobscured full-screen view of a representative of the political committee or other person making the statement." Such TV ads must also place the disclaimer in writing at the end of the ad, with the lettering filling at least 4% of the vertical picture height and being visible for at least 4 seconds, with good color contrast.

Within 24 hours of the broadcast, a 527 group must provide the FEC with donor names, amount spent, and the names of the broadcast stations or networks that aired the ads.

Third-Party Restrictions Under BCRA

Third parties are prohibited from running radio or TV ads 30 days before a primary and 60 days before a general election, if the ad names a federal candidate, if the ad is aimed at the candidate's district or voters, and if the ad is paid for with unlimited union or corporate contributions.

FAQ

What about third-party ads that are funded by unlimited individual contributions?

These ads do not have the 30-day or 60-day restrictions. A 527 group that is funded entirely by unlimited individual contributions may run ads opposing or supporting a candidate up through election day, which happened in the 2004 election campaign. Two 527 groups that gained national attention were the Swift Boat Veterans for Truth, who ran ads critical of Democratic candidate John Kerry, and MoveOn.org, which advertised against President George W. Bush.

FAQ

Are nonprofit groups bound by these restrictions as well?

No. In 2002, the FEC ruled that these restrictions do not apply to tax-exempt religious, educational, and charitable organizations. Groups such as the Sierra Club had fought for the exemption, saying they should be allowed to run ads prior to an election to inform voters about important issues. The ads can still name a federal candidate but are not permitted to endorse election or defeat of the candidate. However, supporters of the law argued that misleading issue ads by some tax-exempt groups were part of the reason for passing BCRA in the first place. The FEC argued, though, that tax laws already prohibited such groups from directly endorsing or attacking candidates, and the groups risk losing their tax-exempt status if they do so.

FAQ

Are there exemptions for newscasts?

Yes. News reports, editorials, and commentaries are all exempt.

FAQ

What about movies or TV shows that mention political candidates?

In 2002, the FEC ruled that late-night comedy monologues and talk shows that discuss or feature federal candidates would be exempt from BCRA guidelines, although the FEC said it would judge such matters on a case-by-case basis. The FEC added that public service announcements featuring candidates would also be exempt.

Controversy erupted over BCRA in June 2004 when filmmaker Michael Moore released his movie *Fahrenheit 9/11*. The film was extremely critical of George W. Bush's presidency and his handling of the war on terrorism. A Republican group, Citizens United, filed a complaint with the FEC, arguing that ads for the film constituted "electioneering communications" that were designed to alter the outcome of the election. In August 2004, the FEC voted unanimously to dismiss the complaint, ruling that the movie ads did not violate BCRA.

Political File

Stations must keep track of ALL requests made for political ads or programs and place them in a "political file." This file should be kept with other papers included in the general "public file" and must be composed of information about how requests were handled, including rates charged to each politician, including discounts or package deals given to candidates or organizations; the date and time the ads or programs aired; classes of time bought; number of spots purchased by each candidate or organization; and amount of free time (if any) given to candidates.

The FCC says all of this information should be placed in the political file "as soon as possible." What does that mean? The FCC elaborates: "As soon as possible means *immediately* absent unusual circumstances." In other words, as soon as you have the paperwork completed on political ads, place it immediately in the political file.

The station must keep this file for 2 years.

Section 315 Violations

Failure to follow the FCC political broadcasting rules can result in fines as high as $25,000 per day for each day violations occur. Stations that are unsure about certain aspects of political broadcasting rules should consult an attorney. It just might be worth the money.

In 1998, for example, the FCC fined WFXD-FM in Marquette, MI, for failing to maintain an accurate political file and for questionable sales practices regarding political ads.[21] The FCC said that the station did not provide adequate details about how it determined the LUR for the 1994 and 1995 primaries and general election. The FCC said the station's "political rate card did not appear to contain even the most rudimentary elements of [its] sales practices." The station tried to argue that the problems were because of "employee error," but the FCC said the licensee is ultimately responsible for the actions of its employees. Someone should have double-checked to make sure the station was compliant with FCC rules.

The station's political file was also lacking necessary information, such as the dates of advertising purchased by candidates or the rates charged to some candidates. The FCC fined WFXD $6000 for three distinct violations ($2000 each): failure to inform candidates about ad rates and classes, inaccurate calculations of lowest unit rate, and failure to maintain a proper political file.

This is just one example. The FCC frequently hands out fines to stations for violations of political broadcasting rules. Politicians know the rules, and they are often very eager to file a complaint with the FCC about a station that does not follow these rules.

Section 315 and Ballot Issues

FAQ

Are ballot issues covered under Section 315 or Section 312(a)(7)?

---

[21]DA #98-447, released March 6, 1998

No. Stations do not have to accept advertising for ballot issues if they do not want to. The lowest unit rate does not apply to ads supporting or opposing ballot issues. Stations may charge their standard rates for such ads. The "no censorship" clause also does *not* apply. A station may edit or reject issue ads if the station fears the ads are libelous or indecent (a station can be sued for airing issue ads that are false or defamatory). In fact, a station can reject an issue ad for any reason, just as it is free to reject commercial ads. However, ballot issue ads must have clear sponsorship identification, just like other political ads.

Section 315 and Newspapers

In 1913, the State of Florida passed a law that was basically a Section 315 for newspapers. It mandated that if a political candidate was attacked in a newspaper editorial or story, the newspaper was required to give that candidate a chance to respond. That law remained unchallenged until 1972.

The challenge concerned Pat Tornillo, a candidate for the state legislature. The *Miami Herald* had printed two editorials in September 1972 criticizing Tornillo, including accusations that he had orchestrated an illegal teachers' strike several years earlier. Under the 1913 Florida law, Tornillo demanded space in the *Herald* to reply to the attacks, but the newspaper refused. Tornillo took the newspaper to court, saying many large cities had only one major newspaper, and it was unfair that a major information source such as a newspaper did not provide opportunities for response. Eventually, the Florida Supreme Court ruled for Tornillo, saying the state law enhanced free speech.

However, in 1974, the U.S. Supreme Court ruled that the Florida law was unconstitutional. In *Miami Herald v. Tornillo,*[22] the court said that press responsibility or fairness "is not mandated by the Constitution." The law made newspapers avoid controversy, said the court: "Government-enforced right of access inescapably dampens the vigor and limits the variety of public debate." Newspaper editors, not the government, must be the ones to decide what opinions and news appear on their pages.

The Florida law imposed *fines* for papers that did not follow the rules. The Supreme Court said this was a "penalty on the basis of the content of a newspaper." Such content restrictions and penalties are unconstitutional. Broadcasters use the public airwaves and are subject to content regulations. Newspapers are "private," and government may not regulate their content.

Reasonable Access: Section 312(a)(7)

FAQ

Section 315 says "if a station offers time." So, can a station choose to air no political ads? If a station doesn't provide time for any political ads, then it won't have to worry about providing "responses" from opposing candidates.

---

[22]418 U.S. 241 (1974)

In 1971, any confusion about this wording in Section 315 was clarified for federal candidates. Congress amended the Communications Act with Section 312(a)(7), which is also called the "reasonable access" rule (see box).

Section 312(a)(7): The "Reasonable Access" Rule

(a) The Commission may revoke any station license or construction permit—. . . (7) for willful or repeated failure to allow *reasonable access* to or to permit purchase of *reasonable amounts of time* for the use of a broadcasting station by a legally qualified candidate for *Federal* elective office on behalf of his candidacy. (Italics added)

FAQ

What is considered "reasonable access" or "reasonable amounts of time?"

Rules like this tend to frustrate broadcasters because words like "reasonable" are vague. The Supreme Court attempted to define "reasonable" in a landmark ruling on Section 312(a)(7) in the case of *CBS Inc. v. FCC*.[23]

In 1979, President Jimmy Carter and Vice President Walter Mondale announced they were running for reelection. The Carter-Mondale campaign committee, on October 11, 1979, made what it thought was a "reasonable" request of the three major TV networks. The committee wanted to run a 30-minute political ad between 8:00 p.m. and 10:30 p.m. on any day from December 4 through 7, 1979, and it was giving the networks 2 months advance notice to get ready.

The networks were not eager to accommodate the request. NBC said no, arguing that December was too early to air political ads. ABC said it would not start taking sales for political ads until January 1980. CBS said 30 minutes was too much, but it did offer the Carter campaign two 5-minute segments—one at 10:55 p.m. on December 8 and one in the daytime.

In general, the networks said the request for a 30-minute ad was not reasonable because (a) a 30-minute political ad during "prime time" would greatly disrupt their programming schedules; (b) network news shows were already doing a good job of covering the presidential candidates and keeping the public informed on the major issues; (c) there were numerous candidates for president, and the networks were worried about having to provide "response time" under Section 315; (d) it was 11 months before the 1980 election, which, the networks said, was "too early in the political season" for ads. Should the networks have to follow Section 312(a)(7) before the campaign had even started?

The Carter campaign said the presidential campaign was indeed underway, and the networks were not granting reasonable access as mandated by Section 312(a)(7). The Supreme Court later ruled in *CBS Inc. v. FCC*[56] that the broadcast networks should have

---

[23]453 U.S. 367 (1981)

given the requested time to the Carter campaign. The Carter campaign gave the networks 2 months advance notice. The campaign was being reasonable in this regard. The rights of viewers and listeners are more important than the rights of broadcasters, the court said. Section 312(a)(7) "makes a significant contribution to freedom of expression by enhancing the ability of candidates to present, and the public to receive, information necessary for the effective operation of the democratic process."

The reasonable access rule does not take effect until the start of the "campaign season," but the court said that the presidential campaign was "in full swing" by December 1979. How is this determined? The court provided guidelines:

Signs That a Campaign Season Has Begun Include: (a) *Announcements of candidacy.* Twelve candidates had already formally announced intentions to run for the Republican and Democratic nominations. (b) *Dates of major political events.* The very important Iowa caucuses were in January, so of course candidates would be campaigning in December. (c) *State delegate selections.* Many states had already begun selecting delegates to the national party conventions. (d) *Fundraising activities.* Most candidates were already actively raising campaign funds. (e) *Media coverage.* Newspapers across the country had been covering the campaign for roughly 2 months. (f) *Campaign organizations.* At the time, many of the candidates had already formed active organizations. (g) *Endorsements.* Candidates were already beginning to get endorsements from various groups and other politicians.

However, many broadcasters were angered by the ruling, saying the Carter campaign's request for 30 minutes of prime time television was disruptive to TV scheduling and was therefore not "reasonable." For example, stations could make more money from advertising during a scheduled program than they would make from the Carter ad. In a dissent, Justice Byron White agreed with broadcasters' arguments, saying, "There is no basis in the statute for this very broad and unworkable scheme of access."

Section 312(a)(7) does not give candidates an *automatic* right of access to the airwaves, but it appears to be a pretty strong right. The Supreme Court said that broadcasters must show compelling reasons for rejecting a candidate's request for time, such as a large amount of time already sold to the candidate, a major impact on broadcast scheduling or programming, or the likelihood of a large amount of equal time requests from other candidates.

Important note: Section 312(a)(7) applies only to *federal candidates*—any person running for the U.S. House of Representatives, the U.S. Senate, or the presidency. *State and local candidates are not covered by this rule.*

FAQ

So stations must accept advertising from federal candidates, but they can choose not to accept any ads from local and state candidates?

That is correct. Section 312(a)(7) applies only to federal candidates, and stations are not required to provide reasonable access—or *any* access, for that matter—to local and state candidates. However, once a station *has* accepted advertising from a candidate for local or state office, Section 315 kicks in. The station must then give equal opportunities for airtime to other legally qualified candidates running for that same office.

Important Rules Regarding Reasonable Access

These rules apply only to candidates for federal office.

- ▣ A station may not limit the length of a political program or ad.
- ▣ Candidates are allowed to choose whatever format they want. The station may not demand that a candidate use a specific format.
- ▣ A candidate is allowed to choose any time of day for ads.
- ▣ However, a station does not have to honor *extremely specific* requests for time (for example, if a candidate asks for an ad to be run at 5 minutes and 35 minutes past the hour and your standard advertising times are at 20 and 50 minutes past the hour, the candidate will have to settle for those times).
- ▣ Stations are allowed to restrict political ads during newscasts so as not to give the appearance of favoring a candidate during an "objective" newscast.
- ▣ Because of Section 312(a)(7), a station may not place any unreasonable limits on ads for federal candidates. For example, you cannot tell a federal candidate that he or she is limited to six ads per day. There must be reasonable access.

FAQ

Section 312(a)(7) talks about advertising. How does this rule apply to noncommercial stations?

In 2000, Congress voted to amend the Communications Act to exempt public broadcast stations from Section 312(a)(7). Therefore, public stations have no obligation to provide airtime to federal candidates. However, public stations must still abide by Section 315.

Also, public stations are prohibited from endorsing or opposing any candidate or public office.

POLITICAL EDITORIAL AND PERSONAL ATTACK RULES

These two rules were codified by the FCC in 1967.

The Political Editorial Rule. This rule stated that if a licensee aired an editorial that endorsed or opposed a legally qualified candidate, the station had to notify opposing candidates for the same office within 24 hours. Stations then had to provide a script or tape of the editorial and a "reasonable opportunity" for opposing candidates to respond on air.

The Personal Attack Rule. Similarly, this rule mandated that stations provide reasonable response time for persons whose character or integrity have been "attacked" on the air during discussions of controversial public issues.

Broadcasters argued that the rules created a chilling effect and that they avoided airing editorials or controversial discussions to avoid having these rules kick in. Broadcasters said dropping the rules would actually lead to more political discussion on the airwaves.

Personal Attack and Political Editorial Rules Thrown Out

In 1999, the NAB and the Radio-Television News Directors Association (RTNDA) took the FCC to court over the rules. The DC Circuit Court of Appeals said the FCC had not given good reasons for keeping these two rules. The court asked the FCC for better justifications, and the FCC suspended the rules for 2 months to study the rules and get comments from broadcasters.

A month before election day 2000, the appeals court ruled that the FCC had not provided valid reasons for keeping the two rules. In *RTNDA v. FCC*,[24] the court threw out the personal attack and political editorial rules. The court said the rules were "unsupported by reasoning that would demonstrate to the court that they are in the public interest."

The courts used similar reasoning in the 1980s when they allowed the FCC to dissolve the Fairness Doctrine.

Fairness Doctrine

The history of the Fairness Doctrine (FD) gives valuable insight into how FCC regulations can evolve and the pivotal roles of the judicial, legislative, and executive branches in formulating FCC rules. The FCC enforced the FD from 1949 to 1987. The doctrine was written to ensure that broadcasters served the public interest by allowing for discussion of both sides of controversial issues. The FD required that broadcasters "provide coverage of vitally important controversial issues of interest in the community served by the licensees" and "provide a reasonable opportunity for the presentation of contrasting viewpoints on such issues."

Broadcasters in general did not like the FD and, as with the political editorial and personal attack rules, said they actually avoided controversial issues so they would not have to worry about airing "contrasting viewpoints." In 1969, in *Red Lion Broadcasting v. FCC*,[25] the Supreme Court ruled that the FD was constitutional because of the scarcity of airwaves. As a result, the court said the FD did not violate broadcasters' rights.

By the 1980s, the FCC (under President Reagan) wanted fewer regulations, and the Fairness Doctrine became one target. By 1984, the FCC was arguing that the ruling in *Red Lion* was outdated because there was no longer "scarcity." Cable and other technologies were allowing more voices to be heard via the electronic media. However, the FCC was not sure it had the regulatory authority to get rid of the FD. In 1986, in *Telecommunications Research Action Committee v. FCC*,[26] a federal appeals court ruled that the FCC had the power to repeal the FD. The FCC just needed a test case.

The FCC got its chance in *Meredith Corporation v. FCC*.[27] The case focused on WTVH-TV (owned by Meredith Corporation) in Syracuse, NY, and the broadcast of several ads supporting construction of a nuclear power plant. The Syracuse Peace Council demanded time under the FD to respond to the nuclear plant ads. When the station refused the request, the Peace Council took the matter to the FCC.

---

[24]229 F.3d 269 (D.C. Cir. 2000)

[25]395 U.S. 367 (1969)

[26]801 F.2d 501 (D.C. Cir. 1986)

[27]809 F.2d 863 (D.C. Cir. 1987)

The commission had just completed a study on the FD, a study it had started in 1985. The FCC said that their study showed the Fairness Doctrine did not serve the public interest and should no longer be enforced. However, the commission said the matter needed further clarification from the courts and Congress. It was apparent, though, that the FCC was anxious to get rid of the FD and was hoping to use the *Meredith* case to do that.

In January 1987, in *Meredith,* the court gave the FCC permission to drop the FD if the commission felt that the doctrine was "contrary to the public interest." However, in the spring of 1987, the House and Senate passed a bill to override the FCC and make the Fairness Doctrine a law, but President Reagan vetoed it. There were not enough votes to override the veto, and the commission stopped enforcing the FD in August 1987.

Eventually, in 1989, in *Syracuse Peace Council v. FCC,*[28] a federal appeals court solidified the deal and ruled again that the FCC did have the power to get rid of the Fairness Doctrine. However, the court left the door open for future congressional action. The court did not say that the Fairness Doctrine violated the First Amendment rights of broadcasters. As a result, Congress once again tried to get involved, and the House in 1989 passed a bill to make the Fairness Doctrine a *law.* However, President Bush threatened to veto the bill, and the legislation stalled.

As it stands now, the Fairness Doctrine is dead and has *been* dead since 1987.

FAQ

Radio talk show host Rush Limbaugh says that if the Fairness Doctrine came back, political talk radio would suffer significantly. Is that true?

In 1993, Congress once again began talking about passing a Fairness Doctrine law (Bill Clinton had just been elected president, and he hinted that he would sign such a law). Limbaugh called the new attempt at legislation "The Hush Rush Law." The conservative talk show host argued that if radio stations aired 3 hours of Limbaugh, the Fairness Doctrine would require the stations to air 3 hours of "liberal programs." He said that stations might wind up dropping Limbaugh's show just to avoid the hassle of meeting Fairness Doctrine requirements.

It is hard to ignore the evidence that talk radio shows began to flourish in the late 1980s, after the FCC dissolved the Fairness Doctrine. Stations no longer had to worry about providing "response time" to opinionated talk radio hosts. In 1985, there were roughly 100 talk radio stations in the United States. By 1992, five years after the repeal of the Fairness Doctrine, there were 500. That number ballooned to 1350 by 1998.[29] Also, "News/Talk" has, in recent years, been the number one radio format in the Arbitron ratings. It is hard to believe that this would be the case if the Fairness Doctrine were still around.

---

[28]867 F.2d 654 (D.C. Cir. 1989)

[29]The talk radio research project. (2004). *Talkers Magazine Online.* Retrieved November 10, 2004, from http://www.talkers.com/talkaud.html

Summary

The federal government regulates the electronic media through the Federal Communications Commission. This five-member panel has the power to pass regulations, but Congress and the courts can always overturn those regulations. The FCC mandates that all broadcasters operate within the "public interest, convenience, and necessity," a concept that is sometimes difficult to define.

Political broadcasting rules are designed to ensure that candidates have fair and equal access to the broadcast airwaves and cable. Section 315 says that if a station offers time to one candidate for political office, it must make time available to opposing candidates.

However, stations are only required to grant reasonable access to federal candidates under Section 312(a)(7). (These rules do not apply to print media.) Stations are under no obligation to grant any access to state and local candidates.

Political broadcasting rules can be very confusing when one is attempting to determine what counts as a "use." News broadcasters, disc jockeys, and other broadcast personalities often give up broadcasting careers when running for public office to avoid conflicts with Section 315.

Many rules designed to promote "equal access" to the airwaves are no longer in effect, including the fairness doctrine, the political editorial rule, and the personal attack rule. The rules were found to be outdated and were no longer considered to be serving the public interest.

4

CABLE AND SATELLITE REGULATION

Regulation of emerging video technologies requires a delicate balancing act of competing interests.

—*Quincy Cable TV, Inc., v. FCC*[1]

Because of its nature, cable television presents a unique regulatory problem. Cable TV, also known as CATV or Community Antenna Television, got its start in the United States in the late 1940s. As the name indicates, CATV involves a community or business erecting a large antenna to receive television station signals more clearly. These clearer TV signals are then sent to individual homes via cable. At first, most CATV systems were located in smaller, more remote communities where it was difficult to pick up TV stations with just an antenna on a TV set or a roof. People could pick up TV signals with an antenna very easily in larger cities, so cable TV did not grow as quickly in metro areas. At that time, cable systems mostly retransmitted the signals of broadcast stations.

The Communications Act of 1934 gave the FCC the power to regulate "all interstate communication by wire or radio." The government soon had to determine how it would regulate this emerging technology, but cable TV presented interesting regulatory issues:

- *Is it "interstate"?* Most cable systems' wires do not cross state lines, so they technically are not "interstate communication." However, cable systems do retransmit TV signals from other states, so they are interstate in that regard.
- *Is it broadcasting?* CATV is technically not a broadcast medium because the signals are carried over wires. At the same time, though, cable operators do retransmit broadcast station programming.
- *Is it a common carrier?* CATV is transmitted over wires, so it is similar to a common carrier such as a telephone company. However, CATV does not fit into that category because cable companies choose what material goes over their wires, and common carriers do not.

These were just some of the issues considered as the government tried to determine how cable needed to be regulated. Cable TV does not use the public airwaves, and the courts do not consider it "pervasive," like broadcasting. Broadcast airwaves come into a

---

[1]*Quincy Cable TV, Inc., v. FCC*, 768 F.2d 1434 (D.C. Cir. 1985)

home uninvited, but consumers must choose to invite cable into the home. As a result, the FCC does not have the same kinds of regulations for cable systems as it does for broadcast stations.

EARLY CABLE REGULATION

In 1959, there were only 550 cable systems nationwide, and the FCC said it had no plans to regulate cable TV. In 1960, a bill to give the FCC authority over the cable industry died in a congressional committee. Still, the FCC would soon make some rules to try to regulate the cable industry. One of the main concerns was the economic effect that cable systems could have on local broadcasters, and this highlighted the FCC's concept of *localism*. Localism is directly related to the "public interest" standard and says that broadcast stations must air programming to serve the needs and interests of their communities. Therefore, the FCC will take steps to ensure that other media do not hinder broadcast stations' ability to serve the public interest or hinder the public's access to broadcast station programming.

This concept of localism was tested in 1962. The FCC ruled that cable systems could use microwave relay systems to bring in broadcast signals from distant cities, but the cable companies had to prove that this signal importation would not economically damage broadcasters and hinder localism. Still, broadcasters complained. These distant stations from larger cities often carried more movies and better overall programming than smaller local stations did, and cable companies soon found that the big city stations were popular with cable subscribers. As a result, local broadcasters feared they would go out of business as a result of lost viewers and reduced advertising revenue. Most of the population (especially in rural areas) did not have access to cable at this time. Therefore, if these small broadcasters went off the air, localism would be severely damaged because many citizens would have no access to a local broadcast station.

These were the kinds of concerns that arose later that year in Wyoming. The FCC had given permission to the Carter Mountain Transmission Corporation to use microwave links to provide distant TV station signals to cable companies in the towns of Riverton and Thermopolis. KWRB-TV in Riverton fought the FCC decision and, after a hearing, the FCC reversed itself and ruled in favor of KWRB. The commission decided that the microwave relays did indeed pose a genuine economic threat to KWRB and could result in the loss of TV service to a large rural population that did not have access to cable TV. The FCC said it would reconsider the ruling if Carter could guarantee the cable companies would carry KWRB and would not carry distant stations that duplicated KWRB's programming. Carter decided not to appeal to the commission and instead took the FCC to court. A federal appeals court upheld the FCC's decision in 1963 in *Carter Mountain Transmission Corporation v. FCC*.[2] The court reaffirmed the FCC's doctrine of *localism* by ruling that the commission's decision in this matter was a "legitimate measure of protection for the local station and the public interest."

By 1965, the number of cable systems had grown to 1847, more than tripling in just 6 years, and the FCC was seeing a greater need to regulate the rapidly growing industry. The commission was also becoming more concerned about cable's effects on local broadcast

---

[2]321 F.2d 359 (D.C. Cir. 1963)

stations. In its *First Report and Order*[3] on CATV in 1965, the FCC used the *Carter Mountain* ruling as a justification for giving itself more power to regulate cable TV, and it did so with two rules:

- ▣ "Must-carry": The FCC said cable systems must carry the signals of local broadcast stations if the cable system is within the "A" contour of the station. (The A contour is the area in which a broadcast station's signal provides quality reception the majority of the time.)
- ▣ "Nonduplication": Cable systems could not carry distant stations that duplicated programming on a local station. Cable systems were allowed to carry duplicated programming on distant stations as long as it did not air within 15 days of the local station airing that same programming. (This would later be called the *network nonduplication rule*.)

With these rules, the FCC further demonstrated its commitment to localism by protecting the interests of local broadcast stations. It was becoming clear that the FCC was viewing cable systems as supplements to local stations and not as substitutes.

In the *Second Report and Order*[4] in 1966, the FCC said its regulations would now apply to all cable systems. It also decided to give more protection to fledgling UHF stations by prohibiting cable systems in the top 100 markets from importing distant signals. The commission also wanted to have more control over telephone companies entering the cable business. In 1968, the commission required that telephone companies obtain a Certificate of Public Convenience before building a cable system. Two years later in 1970, the FCC further greatly restricted telephone companies' entrance into the cable industry by prohibiting phone companies from owning a cable system within their telephone service areas.

Leapfrogging

Many cable systems up until 1968 had been carrying distant stations on their systems without the permission of those stations. The FCC instituted an "antileapfrogging" rule in the top 100 markets that required cable systems to get permission from distant stations before placing those stations on their systems. This rule was eliminated in 1976.

The FCC Is Allowed to Regulate Cable

Some cable operators were becoming increasingly uncomfortable with the FCC's cable rules, but broadcasters appreciated the FCC's protection of their economic interests. One broadcasting company, Midwest Television, used these rules to its advantage. The company complained to the FCC, saying that Southwestern Cable Company in San Diego was carrying TV stations from Los Angeles and that this was having a negative impact on Midwest's station in San Diego, KFMB-TV.

In 1968 in *U.S. v. Southwestern Cable*,[5] the U.S. Supreme Court upheld the FCC's concept of localism and said the San Diego cable system's actions were "disrupting Commission-licensed broadcasting in the San Diego market." The court upheld the FCC's cable regulations

---

[3]FCC First Report and Order, 38 F.C.C. 683 (1965)

[4]FCC Second Report and Order, 2 F.C.C.2d 725 (1966)

[5]392 U.S. 157 (1968)

and indicated that the FCC had authority to regulate cable TV. The Telecommunications Act of 1934 granted the FCC the right to regulate "all interstate communication by wire or radio," the court said; the FCC's "regulatory authority over CATV is imperative if it is to perform with appropriate effectiveness certain of its other responsibilities."

As for the extent of the FCC's power to regulate cable, the court said that question would be answered in the future: "There is no need here to determine in detail the limits of the Commission's authority to regulate CATV."

FAQ

What impact did the Southwestern Cable case really have on cable regulation?

Even though the Supreme Court did not provide explicit detail about the extent of the FCC's power to regulate cable, the justices had upheld the FCC's basic right to regulate cable. The court had also reiterated the doctrine of "localism," ruling that local broadcast stations needed to be protected to serve the public interest. That protection, if necessary, could come in the form of certain restrictions on cable providers.

CABLE AND "PUBLIC INTEREST"

As cable became more popular in the late 1960s, the FCC decided that cable systems had to serve the public interest in some way. In 1969, the commission required cable systems with more than 3500 subscribers to provide locally originated programming, as well as facilities for production. Many cable operators did not like the government mandating that certain types of programs be provided on cable systems, and in *U.S. v. Midwest Video*,[6] a cable company took the FCC to court over these local programming rules. In a 5-4 ruling, the Supreme Court in 1972 upheld the FCC's right to regulate cable. The court said that FCC could require cable companies to serve the public interest in some ways as long as the rules are "not inconsistent with law, and as the public interest, convenience, or necessity requires." Local programming rules were not a great burden, the justices said: These larger cable systems were capable of producing local programs "without impairing their financial stability, raising rates, or reducing the quality of service." The court said that providing facilities for original local programming was usually simple, requiring only a camera and a videotape recorder.

The Supreme Court agreed with the FCC's argument that the "unregulated explosive growth of CATV," as well as cable practices such as leapfrogging, threatened to "deprive the public of the various benefits" of local broadcasting stations. Therefore, cable regulation was necessary in this regard. Cable is part of the "broadcasting system," the court said. "CATV is dependent totally on broadcast signals and is a significant link in the system as a whole and therefore must be seen as within the jurisdiction of the [Communications Act of 1934]."

---

[6]406 U.S. 649 (1972)

The four dissenting justices believed so. Justice Douglas argued that these FCC cable regulations gave the commission too much power and were a violation of cable operators' First Amendment rights. Douglas said cable operators, not the government, should be the ones to decide what programs are placed on their systems.

The dissenters brought up arguments that continue to be made today by opponents of cable regulation. Douglas wrote that the majority ruling allowed for "no limits short of complete domination of the field of communications by the Commission." Regarding cable regulations in general, Douglas wrote that "Congress is the agency to make the decision," not the FCC. CATV should not be regulated like broadcasting because "CATV systems do not in fact broadcast or rebroadcast. Broadcasters select the programs to be viewed; CATV systems simply carry, without editing, whatever programs they receive." As for the majority argument about CATV being "dependent totally on broadcast signals," Douglas argued that the court could apply the same reasoning and regulations to manufacturers of TV sets.

That same year, the FCC, under the leadership of Dean Burch, put even more emphasis on local cable programming and mandated other rules for the cable industry.

The 1972 *Cable Television Report and Order*[7]

As the number of cable systems exploded, the FCC realized it could not "license" cable companies, but the commission needed some means of record keeping. In its 1972 *Report and Order*,[6,7] the commission required all cable companies to get a *certificate of compliance* from the FCC to operate a cable system or to add a TV broadcast signal.

The FCC also mandated that all cable systems be built with the capacity to handle at least 20 channels. The FCC then imposed some "broadcasting rules" on many cable systems. Any cable operator who originated local programming had to abide by such rules as sponsorship identification, the Fairness Doctrine, and Section 315. The FCC required that cable operators file annual reports with the commission and maintain employment and financial records.

The 1972 *Report and Order* also instituted a wide range of rules that included cross-ownership, technical standards, access channels, franchise rules, and syndicated program exclusivity. Many of these rules would be modified or eliminated in the years to come, as will be discussed shortly.

Antisiphoning Rule Struck Down

In 1975, the FCC was concerned that popular movies were being "siphoned" away from broadcasters by cable television. It was simple economics. Filmmakers could usually make more money by placing their movies on pay cable channels than on advertiser-supported broadcast television. Fearing that the cable industry was again threatening local broadcast

[7]36 F.C.C.2d 143 (1972)

stations, the FCC established rules that prohibited cable companies from offering pay movie channels with feature films less than 3 years old. The rules also prohibited cable channels from offering paid access to certain major sporting events (such as the World Series) if these events had been shown on broadcast TV within the previous 5 years. The FCC said the siphoning of such programs away from broadcast stations would limit the public's ability to access such programs on "free TV." Also, the FCC said that pay programming involving sports programs and feature films could not make up more than 90% of total cable pay operations.

FAQ

Didn't the cable industry find the antisiphoning rules unfair?

Yes, and HBO took the commission to court over the rules and won. The DC Circuit Court of Appeals invalidated the antisiphoning rules in 1978 in *Home Box Office (HBO) v. FCC*.[8] The court ruled that the FCC exceeded its authority and provided "no evidence to support the need for regulation of pay cable television." The court said the commission did not prove that broadcasters were actually being harmed by "siphoning." The court basically said that the FCC was trying to solve a problem that did not exist.

FAQ

Didn't the HBO ruling signal a change in how the courts viewed FCC regulation of cable?

Yes. The *HBO* case was important because the court demanded that the FCC provide concrete rationale for its cable regulations. The FCC was forced to recognize that cable operators had the right to make independent programming choices free of FCC interference. Subsequently, the ruling also opened the doors for other cable pay channels, which would soon result in a rapid growth of the cable industry.

The Cable Communications Policy Act of 1984 (The 1984 Cable Act)

This act is credited with spurring the rapid growth of cable in the late 1980s. It was designed to "encourage the growth and development of cable systems," and in it, Congress amended the Communications Act of 1934 to give the FCC official authority to regulate cable television. Cable regulations established in the 1960s became law under this act, and this gave the FCC more freedom in passing regulations affecting cable television. At the same time, the 1984 Cable Act would lead to a substantial deregulation of cable at the federal level and shift more power to local authorities.

Before 1984, many local governments and cable operators were confused about how much power they had in the cable regulation arena. Congress helped to clarify some of

---

[8]567 F.2d 9 (D.C. Cir. 1978)

their concerns in the 1984 Cable Act, which was negotiated between cable industry and broadcasting groups. Congress ruled as follows.

- ▣ Cable operators must obtain *franchises* granted by local governments, which act as *local franchising authorities* (LFAs).
- ▣ Franchise fees could not exceed 5% of the cable system's gross revenues.
- ▣ Local governments may establish technical requirements for the cable system.
- ▣ The franchise renewal process must be orderly and not unfairly deny renewals to existing cable operators. LFAs may deny renewal to a cable operator for reasons such as violations of a franchise agreement, providing inferior service to the community, and being technically unqualified.
- ▣ The local government is not allowed to dictate cable system programming.
- ▣ The local government may request that cable systems set aside channels for educational, governmental, or public access use.
- ▣ Cable operators must run wires in the entire franchise area. (Some companies had a practice of not stringing wires in "less profitable" neighborhoods.)
- ▣ The FCC is allowed to establish certain technical standards for cable system equipment and facilities.
- ▣ In general, neither the local government nor the FCC may regulate rates. However, the act allowed the FCC to regulate basic cable rates for systems in places where there was no effective competition in the market. Later, the FCC would define *competition* very broadly so that most cable systems wound up being exempt from FCC rate regulation of basic cable service.
- ▣ Cable systems were not allowed to own a TV station within the same market. (This rule was later dropped. See chapter 5.)
- ▣ Local governments may award more than one cable franchise in the community.

FAQ

Don't most communities, though, have only one cable franchise?

Yes, and it was the case back then as well. The majority of local governments often granted "exclusive franchises" in which only one cable company was permitted to operate in the community. There were various reasons for this. Most small communities did not have enough customers to support two cable companies. Also, smaller cable companies would not even make a bid for a franchise in many communities because they could not afford to compete with the established bigger cable companies. In any case, the result was a cable company with a monopoly on cable service in a community. That situation has changed today because cable companies now have more competition, mostly from satellite TV providers. However, in 1986, when cable was the "only game in town," the issue of exclusive local cable franchises made its way to the Supreme Court.

Franchises

Companies must use public utility poles to string cables across communities. Local and state governments have authority over these public structures, and governments are therefore allowed to exercise some control over the cable companies that use these poles. The local government thus acts as an LFA and has the power to give a cable system the right to operate in the community. (In some states, state public utility commissions oversee cable TV regulation.)

The major Supreme Court ruling concerning franchising is *City of Los Angeles v. Preferred.*[9] Cable operator Preferred Communications wanted to lease space on Los Angeles utility poles and underground conduits to run its TV cables. However, the city's Department of Water and Power said it could not lease any space unless Preferred had a franchise from the city. The city refused a franchise request because Preferred had not taken part in the city's franchise auction process. Preferred sued the city, saying it had a First Amendment right to operate a cable system in Los Angeles. Preferred argued there was "sufficient excess physical capacity" on poles and underground conduits and enough customer demand in the area to support a second cable company. Preferred also said the city's auction process was unfair, allowing only one cable company to operate based on which company the city considered "best." The city argued that there was limited economic demand for cable services in the community and that there was limited space on public utility structures. The city also expressed concerns that the installation process would create traffic problems and the extra cables on poles might be unattractive.

An appeals court agreed with Preferred and said the cable company had a First Amendment right to use these public rights of way. The U.S. Supreme Court generally agreed with the appeals court that cable operators have basic First Amendment rights, but the court also said that a city has the right to award a franchise to only one company. The Supreme Court remanded the case to a district court, where the judge ruled for Preferred because the city utility structures could handle more than one cable company and the city's rule about granting only one cable franchise was a violation of the First Amendment rights of cable operators.

FAQ

Did this ruling prohibit all exclusive cable franchises?

It certainly set the wheels in motion. In 1992, Congress gave some teeth to the judge's ruling when it banned communities from awarding exclusive franchises.

ACCESS CHANNEL RULES

The 1972 *Report and Order*[6,7] said that access channels would help increase citizen involvement in community affairs and give "third parties" access to the cable system. The FCC established four basic types of access channels to meet these needs and mandated that cable systems in the top 100 markets carry them. Cable systems were also required to provide facilities for access channel program production. If there was no public demand for all four types of channels, cable companies would be allowed to carry fewer than four.

---

[9]476 U.S. 488 (1986)

In 1976, the FCC expanded the access channel rule to include cable systems with more than 3500 subscribers, but these cable systems were still required to provide facilities for production of local access programs. In addition, the FCC required cable systems of this size to have a 20-channel capacity by 1986.

FAQ

Weren't these access channel rules another violation of cable operators' rights to make independent programming decisions?

Many cable operators thought so, and they argued that these rules were similar in nature to the antisiphoning rules, which the courts had struck down. Midwest Video Corporation challenged the access channel rules on First Amendment grounds, arguing that the FCC was trying to treat cable companies like broadcasting. In 1979, in *FCC v. Midwest Video* (also called *Midwest Video II*),[10] the Supreme Court ruled that the FCC had gone beyond the authority granted to it in the Communications Act of 1934. The FCC could not make cable systems carry public access channels or abide by channel capacity requirements. The court ruled that making cable systems carry original local programs turned CATV into a "common carrier" like a telephone system. The court said the FCC needed the permission of Congress to treat cable as a common carrier and to enforce such rules. In fact, Congress got involved in the matter 5 years later with the Cable Act of 1984.

PEG Channels No Longer Mandatory

Section 611 of the Cable Act says that a local franchising authority *may* require cable companies to set aside channels for public, educational, or governmental (PEG) use. Again, the Supreme Court, in *Midwest Video II,* said the FCC could not force cable companies to carry access channels. In 1984, however, Congress said that franchising authorities could require cable companies to do so. In this way, the decisions about access channels were placed in the hands of local governments instead of the FCC. Usually, the LFA and cable company negotiate over the types of access channels to be offered, or they may choose not to carry any PEG channels. The 1984 Cable Act allowed LFAs to determine their own policies for use of these channels.

FAQ

Does the 1984 Cable Act lay out any basic rules regarding PEG channels?

Yes. Some of the major rules from the 1984 act include the following:

▣ Franchising authorities may require cable companies to provide facilities, services, or equipment for use of PEG channels.

---

[10]440 U.S. 689 (1979)

- A cable company can require certain production standards for PEG programs.
- A cable company can require users to undergo training (how to operate cameras, how to do proper lighting, etc.).
- A cable company is not allowed to refuse a request for time on an access channel based simply on the content of the material.
- Access channels are designated for nonprofit activities, and therefore commercial programs of any sort are not allowed, except on leased access channels.
- Cable companies may grant time on these channels on a first-come-first-served basis.
- Cable companies are allowed to enforce age restrictions, such as requiring persons younger than 18 to have an adult cosign on requests for time.

FAQ

What are the differences between the four types of access channels?

Public Access. These channels are supposed to be open for free use by the general public, and the cable company may not censor content. Franchising authorities may designate a third party to oversee these channels. Public access channels were designed to allow free "first-come nondiscriminatory access," but cable operators may charge users for any costs involved in producing programs. The FCC originally said that public access channels should not allow any advertising, lottery information, obscenity, or indecent material. However, the rules against indecent material were overturned, which will be discussed in more detail in chapter 11.

Educational Access. These channels are set aside for educational institutions and are to be used solely for educational purposes. The franchising authority or cable operator works in conjunction with local schools and universities to allocate time on these channels. The FCC says that "educational authorities" are to control the content on these channels. Therefore, an educational access channel is not a "public" channel, and the general public does not have an automatic right to air programs on this channel. The same holds true for the next type of channel.

Governmental Access. In most cases, the franchising authority controls access to these channels to show local government programming, such as city council meetings. In 1972, the FCC said that local governments were allowed to control the content on these channels.

Leased Access. These are also called *commercial access* channels. They may be rented or "leased" by third parties who wish to air programming and, as the name indicates, the channels may be used for commercial purposes. The channels often air programming such as infomercials, local sports events, foreign language shows, real estate programs, and political shows.

Cable operators may not control content on these channels, but, at the same time, cable systems are not legally liable for access channel content. It is the program producers who are liable for such things as false advertising, obscenity, and libel. When these access channels are not being used by third parties, a cable system may use the channels for whatever purposes it wishes.

FAQ

May cable companies or LFAs regulate content on PEG channels?

No. The 1984 Cable Act says that cable companies are not allowed to censor any material on PEG channels. A 1989 case reaffirmed this concept in a public access channel controversy involving the Ku Klux Klan.

The KKK and Public Access

Congress intended for cable access channels to be open to all citizens, no matter what their viewpoints. Controversy arose in the late 1980s in Kansas City when a cable company allowed members of the Ku Klux Klan to use the public access channel. The KKK appearance on the channel created community outrage, and the cable company argued it had no choice—public access channels were designed to be open to anyone.

Soon after the KKK appearance, the LFA in Kansas City decided it would simply get rid of its public access channel to help avoid such controversies. The city argued that the *Midwest Video II* ruling made it clear that a cable system could not be forced to carry access channels. However, the KKK said the LFA was pulling the access channel to deny the Klan a future venue for its speech, so the KKK took the matter to court.

In 1989, in *Missouri Knights of the Ku Klux Klan v. Kansas City,*[11] a federal district court judge called access channels a "public forum." The judge said that an LFA did indeed have the right not to offer access channels. However, in this case, the judge said that the Kansas City LFA had pulled the channel because it did not like the Klan's message. An access channel is a "public forum," the judge said, and the city should not manipulate its use or nonuse to silence certain viewpoints.

The judge said the KKK had a legitimate argument here, and he refused to dismiss the complaint. To avoid more legal hassles, the Kansas City LFA and the cable company agreed to reinstate the public access channel and to pay the KKK's legal fees. This case did not establish any true legal precedent because the parties involved settled their differences out of court. Still, the ruling reinforced the 1984 Cable Act's prohibition on censorship on access channels.

FAQ

These rulings involved PEG channels. Are there any FCC rules regarding leased access channels?

Although the 1984 Cable Act made PEG channels an *option* for LFAs, leased access channels were made a *requirement* for many cable systems.

---

[11]723 F. Supp. 1347 (WD Mo. 1989)

Mandatory Leased Access

Congress felt that independent programmers should have some means of access to cable systems. To meet that need, the 1984 Cable Act mandated that cable systems with 36 to 54 activated channels had to set aside 10% of channel space for leased access. Systems with 55 or more activated channels must set aside 15%. (*Activated* means channels that are regularly available to customers, including PEG channels.) Cable systems with fewer than 36 channels do not have to provide leased access channels. Cable operators must charge "reasonable" rates for the use of leased access channels.

However, the 1984 Cable Act had more profound effects than just establishing access channel guidelines.

PRIVACY

FAQ

When I purchase programming from my cable system, does the cable company keep that information private?

A cable operator is supposed to keep information about customers' viewing habits confidential. The 1984 Cable Act established general privacy guidelines. For example, a cable company may only collect as much information as is needed to provide the requested programming (billing information, equipment needs such as a converter box, etc.) or to detect illegal reception of cable services. The cable company must tell you what information they have collected about you, why they are collecting it, for what reasons they may disclose it, and how long they intend to keep it. Customers have a right to see this information.

The cable company may disclose information about general viewing habits of all of its customers (for example, how many people subscribe to HBO). However, the company may not release any individual person's name. The cable company is only allowed to release information about a specific person's viewing habits if ordered to do so by a court or law enforcement. The release of this information must be relevant to a criminal investigation, and the person has a right to contest the release.

Cable companies must have the permission of customers before releasing any person's name, phone number, or address.

CABLE TV AND COPYRIGHT LAW

In 1968, the Supreme Court dealt with the issue of cable systems retransmitting copyrighted programs from broadcast stations. Should cable systems have to pay a royalty fee for the rights to redistribute these programs?

In *Fortnightly v. United Artists,*[12] the court said no. The justices said that when a cable system carries a TV station's signal, it is not "performing" the copyrighted shows appearing on those stations. CATV is simply strengthening the signals and retransmitting them to people's homes for a fee. The court said this was not a copyright violation, and cable systems were exempt from paying copyright fees.

In 1974, in *Teleprompter v. CBS,*[13] the court added that copyright fees still did not apply, even for cable systems that used microwave facilities to retransmit signals over larger distances. The court said the waiving of copyright fees applied only to "live" retransmissions. If the cable system taped programs for later transmission, then copyright fees would apply.

These rulings were common law. The Supreme Court established a set of rules because there were no specific federal laws providing guidance in this area. That would change a few years later in the Copyright Act of 1976, with the concept of compulsory licensing.

Compulsory Licensing

Fortnightly and *Teleprompter* exempted cable companies from many copyright fees, and others in the entertainment industry thought this was unfair. After all, cable systems could intercept copyrighted programming, retransmit it to paying customers, and pay no copyright fees. Cable operators, though, said it would be impossible to pay a royalty for each individual program carried on cable.

The 1976 Copyright Act provided a solution through what is called *compulsory licensing.* Just as radio stations pay ASCAP and BMI flat rates for the rights to play copyrighted music, cable companies are required to pay this compulsory licensing flat fee for the right to rebroadcast copyrighted programming. The fee is based on the size of the cable system and varies according to the number of channels and subscribers.

Important note: Compulsory licensing applies only to retransmission of broadcast signals. It does not apply to channels that are only available on cable, such as HBO, Lifetime, or ESPN. Therefore, compulsory licensing applies to local network affiliates, independent broadcast stations, public broadcast stations, and superstations such as WOR and WGN (WOR and WGN are licensed broadcast stations in New York City and Chicago, respectively, which are picked up by cable systems across the country).

FAQ

How do the owners of copyrighted TV programs get paid through this system?

The compulsory license fees are collected by the Copyright Royalty Tribunal, which is part of the federal Copyright Office. Owners of copyrighted programming on broadcast stations must file claims with the office, and the tribunal divides the collected fees among those who file claims.

---

[12]392 U.S. 390 (1968)

[13]415 U.S. 394 (1974)

"Must-Carry" Rules

In 1965, the FCC established its first broad-based "must-carry" rules. Must-carry meant that cable systems were required to carry every "local or significantly viewed" broadcast station in the area. In 1966, the rule was amended so that it applied only to cable systems that carried at least one local station. (In other words, if a cable system carried one local broadcast station, it had to carry all other local broadcast stations.) These rules were designed to prevent cable companies from "shutting out" local broadcasters and to help ensure "the financial viability of free, community-oriented television."

By 1984, the must-carry rules were modified and required cable systems to carry the signals of all television stations within a 35-mile radius of the community served by the cable company, as well as stations "significantly viewed in the community." Carriage of local stations was mandatory for most cable systems.

FAQ

Weren't the must-carry rules yet another attempt by the FCC to force programming rules on cable operators?

A cable company in Quincy, WA, certainly thought so and challenged the rules in *Quincy Cable TV, Inc. v. FCC.*[14] The cable company had refused to carry two television stations from nearby Spokane, choosing instead to carry selected cable channels. The FCC fined the cable company $5000 for violating the must-carry rules.

In 1985, a federal appeals court struck down the must-carry rules and said they were a violation of the First Amendment. The "scarcity rationale" cannot be applied to cable TV as a justification for content regulation, the court said. The rules are intrusive and force cable companies to carry certain stations they may not want to carry. Also, the rules "favor one group of speakers over another" because "local broadcasters are guaranteed the right to convey their messages over the cable system while cable programmers must vie for a pro-portionately diminished number of channels." (The Quincy cable system back then had a capacity of only 12 channels.)

The court said that the government's interest in protecting broadcast stations "is insufficient to justify the subordination of First Amendment freedoms" of cable opera-tors. It pointed out that the FCC had provided no real proof that the lack of must-carry rules would significantly harm local broadcast stations. The court felt that the must-carry rules were "overinclusive," forcing some cable systems to carry 20 local stations. The rules also required carriage of local stations even if those stations provided no local programming.

The FCC tried to reinstate must-carry rules in 1987, but a federal appeals court struck down the law that same year in *Century Communications v. FCC.*[15] However, must-carry rules in a new form would emerge 5 years later in the Cable Act of 1992.

---

[14]768 F.2d 1434 (D.C. Cir. 1985)

[15]835 F.2d 292 (D.C. Cir. 1987)

THE CABLE TELEVISION CONSUMER PROTECTION AND COMPETITION ACT OF 1992

If the 1984 Cable Act helped to deregulate cable, then the 1992 act was a major reregulation of the cable industry. There were several significant changes implemented by the 1992 Cable Act, and Congress showed that it was beginning to look at cable more as a multichannel service provider instead of as a direct threat to broadcasters. Still, Congress recognized a need to provide some protection to broadcasters.

As cable expanded rapidly in the 1980s, broadcasters continued to see their market share erode. In 1970, the major broadcasters drew 90% of viewers at any given time. By the early 1990s, that audience share had dropped to less than 60%. (In November 2003, ratings information from "sweeps" showed that the cable audience share exceeded the broadcast audience share for the first time in history.) The once dominant broadcasters were steadily losing audiences to cable. The 1992 Cable Act recognized this situation and introduced modified must-carry rules.

"Must-Carry" and "May-Carry"

For decades, cable companies carried local broadcast stations on their cable systems without paying those stations any fees. Many broadcasters said that the cable companies should pay the stations for the rights to carry their signals. Cable companies argued that the broadcasters should not complain because carriage on the cable system provided the broadcast station with a larger audience, and those audiences would usually get clearer reception than they would through an antenna.

The 1992 Cable Act addressed this issue by giving broadcast stations two options regarding carriage on a local cable system:

- ▣ *Must-Carry:* If a station chooses must-carry, then the cable system in its service area is required to carry that station. However, the cable system is not required to pay the station for the mandatory use of its signal.
- ▣ *May-Carry (or "Retransmission Consent"):* If the station chooses may-carry, or retransmission consent, then the cable system has to get permission from the station before carrying the station's signal and must usually pay the station in some way. A cable system is not permitted to carry a broadcast station's signal if a retransmission consent deal has not been reached. These deals are considered private and do not have to be divulged to the public.

The rules did provide relief for smaller cable companies. The smallest cable systems (with 12 or fewer channels) did not have to carry more than 3 commercial stations and one noncommercial station. Cable operators with more than 12 channels had to set aside up to one third of their channels for must-carry. The FCC provided an example: If a cable system has 60 channels, it must set aside up to 20 channels for must-carry. If there are 25 stations in the market that choose must-carry, the cable system may choose not to carry 5 of those stations. Of course, the company may carry all 25 if it wishes, but it is not a requirement. However, if there are only 15 stations electing must-carry, the cable system must carry all 15 stations in that market. (The FCC says a *market* for a television station is that station's designated market area [DMA] as determined by Nielsen Media Research.)

FAQ

The courts had recently struck down similar must-carry rules. Wouldn't these new rules suffer the same fate?

To the surprise of many, the Supreme Court upheld the new rules in *Turner Broadcasting v. FCC.*[16,17] There were actually two *Turner* rulings, one in 1994 and one in 1997. In *Turner I,*[16] the court ruled 5-4 that cable companies are still monopolies in most communities, and the FCC is justified in enforcing the must-carry rules.

In *Turner II,*[17] the Supreme Court looked at the must-carry rules again and, once again, ruled 5-4 in favor of the FCC's rules.

FAQ

Why did the court say that must-carry rules were now OK?

Remember, the previous must-carry rulings were in lower courts, and the Supreme Court simply chose to ignore those rulings. The court argued that there was substantial evidence to show that many local broadcast stations would go out of business without must-carry rules (thus upholding the FCC's concept of localism). Keeping local broadcast stations around is important in serving local communities and providing diverse viewpoints, the court said. Also, cable systems now have more channel capacity, so a requirement to carry local stations is not a great burden and does not shut out cable channels.

The bargaining for retransmission consent, or may-carry, has led to some situations in which cable companies "black out" local stations because agreements for payment have not been reached; however, these blackouts are usually brief. Probably the most famous of these blackouts occurred in May 2000, during ratings sweeps. Time Warner Cable and ABC could not reach a retransmission consent deal for the carriage of ABC affiliates in several large cities, so Time Warner began to black out those ABC signals. The FCC said the blackout was unjustified, and Time Warner and ABC eventually reached a retransmission consent deal. The blackout lasted for 36 hours.

Television stations and cable channels must renegotiate these contracts every 3 years. The contract renewal dates were established in the Telecomm Act of 1996. The next contract deadline is October 1, 2005, with the contracts becoming effective January 1, 2006.

Must-Carry and Radio Stations on Cable

Many cable systems will play a local radio station as background music for bulletin board services that run on access channels, or a system may offer local radio stations on

---

[16]512 U.S. 622 (1994)

[17]520 U.S. 180 (1997)

an "all-band" channel. The cable system must obtain consent to carry any radio stations within a 57-mile radius. For the most part, cable systems do not have to get permission from stations outside the 57-mile radius unless a particular station specifically asks for retransmission consent.

Rate Regulation . . . for a Time

Congress discovered that the deregulation of the 1980s had led not only to rapid growth of the cable industry but also to rapidly increasing cable rates, often at two or three times the rate of inflation. Consumers began to complain. LFAs had been allowed to regulate rates for basic cable service but, prior to 1992, the FCC did not regulate cable rates. The 1992 Cable Act instituted rate regulations that would last for several years.

Cable Equipment and Basic Cable Tier. "Basic cable" is the cheapest type of service available to cable customers. It usually includes local broadcast channels, access channels, and public television. In areas where there was no "effective competition" for the cable operator, the 1992 Cable Act said, local and state governments were allowed to regulate rates for cable equipment and basic cable.

FAQ

What is "effective competition"?

Effective competition means that there is at least one other cable system in the area or some other multichannel distribution system, such as satellite TV. At least half of the households in the area must have access to both systems, and the smallest system has to have a market share of at least 15%. Also, cable system subscribers must constitute fewer than 30% of households in the franchise area.

FAQ

Isn't the concept of effective competition now obsolete because of the widespread availability of satellite TV?

For the most part, yes. The 1996 Telecomm Act revisited the 1992 rate regulations and set most of them to expire in 1999. Any rate regulations that did remain applied only if there was "no effective competition." However, by 1999, most Americans had access to satellite TV services, which provided the effective competition. As a result, cable rate regulation is basically nonexistent now.

The 1992 Cable Act also regulated cable rates in other areas:

Cable Programming Service Tier: The 1992 Cable Act had allowed local governments to regulate rates on the cable service tier (which includes all cable channels and video programming not available on basic cable). However, the Telecommunications Act of 1996 mandated that local governments would no longer be allowed to regulate rates on the cable service tier as of March 31, 1999.

Per-Channel or Per-Program Tier: This includes "premium" cable channels, such as Showtime and pay-per-view channels, for which customers pay extra fees to receive the programming. Neither the FCC nor an LFA have the right to regulate rates for these channels.

Also, the FCC was no longer allowed to act on consumer complaints regarding rates on the cable service tier. In 1999, FCC chairman William Kennard defended the rate regulations. He announced that cable rate regulations in effect from 1993 to 1999 saved customers $3 billion to $5 billion. During that time, the FCC had also ordered cable companies to pay approximately $100 million in refunds to 40 million cable subscribers who had been overcharged.[18]

Rate Rollbacks

The Cable Act mandated that cable rates be reduced by about 17% over a 2-year period. Cable companies challenged these mandatory rate reductions, but in 1995 a federal appeals court ruled in *Time Warner Entertainment v. FCC*[19] that the FCC had a right to enforce the rate rollbacks.

Proportional Rates

Cable systems were required to charge rates that were directly proportional to their costs for the various kinds of programming offered. They were also told to distribute the costs of the system among the various basic and premium channels appropriately.

Channel Repositioning

Cable systems were informed that they were not allowed to move stations that were must-carry to a different channel without permission from that station. Broadcast stations should be allowed to occupy their actual channel number on the cable system, when possible.

Service Standards

Because of complaints from consumers about the poor quality of customer service at some cable companies, Congress developed minimum service standards for all cable systems. Those standards are broken down into four service areas, and it is the responsibility of each LFA to enforce them.

Telephone Calls and Office Hours. Each cable system must (a) maintain a 24-hour local, toll-free, or collect call telephone line 7 days a week; (b) have a real person answer the phone during normal business hours, with an answering system at all other times ("normal" business hours must include evening hours at least 1 night per week and/or some weekend

---

[18]Federal Communications Commission. (1999, March 31). *FCC Chairman Kennard launches cable consumer bill of rights campaign.* FCC Order: CS Docket No. 96-85, FCC 99-57.

[19]56 F.3d 151 (D.C. Cir. 1995)

hours); (c) answer all calls within 30 seconds after the connection is made, which includes any time the caller is put on hold (if a customer call is transferred, the transfer time must be made within 30 seconds); ensure that customers receive busy signals no more than 3% of the time; and meet these standards for telephone customer service 90% of the time.

Installation, Outages, Service Calls. Each cable system must (a) perform most standard installations of cable service within 7 days of the order; (b) work on service interruptions within 24 hours, unless there are severe circumstances (*service interruption* means picture or sound on one or more channels has been lost); (c) make appointments for cable service at a specific time or during a 4-hour time block during normal business hours (cable companies may schedule service calls outside of normal business hours if this is convenient for the customer); (d) not cancel a customer appointment after the close of business on the business day prior to the scheduled appointment; (e) require a cable technician or installer to call customers if he or she is going to be late for an appointment, and the appointment must be rescheduled at the convenience of the subscriber; (f) meet these standards 95% of the time during normal operating conditions.

Billing Practices. Each cable system must, (a) when possible, give customers at least 30 days advance notice regarding any changes in cable rates, channel positions, or programming services that are within the control of the cable company. This notice must be either in writing or through messages on the cable system. (b) Systems must provide customer bills that are "clear, concise and understandable, with full itemization of services and charges." Systems must (c) respond to written complaints about billing matters within 30 days and (d) provide any customer refunds by the customer's next billing cycle or 30 days after the complaint was settled, whichever is earlier.

Cable System–Customer Communications. The following information must be provided to customers yearly, at the time of installation or upon request: products and services available; installation and service maintenance policies; channel positions of cable system programming; prices and programming service options; instructions about how to use cable services; and billing and complaint procedures, including the address and phone number of the LFA.

FAQ

Aren't some of these rules difficult and costly for smaller cable companies?

The FCC recognizes this and says that cable systems with fewer than 1000 subscribers are "encouraged" to seek waivers for any of the standards that are too "burdensome."

SYNDICATED EXCLUSIVITY ("SYNDEX")

Part of the deregulation of the 1980s included getting rid of "Syndex," or the Syndicated Exclusivity Rule. This rule dealt with syndicated shows. Here is an example of how it worked:

A local broadcast station, WTZ, has negotiated for the *exclusive rights* to air *Wheel of Fortune* in its market, so that means that no other station in the market is allowed to air the show. WTZ is carried on the local cable system; however, the cable system carries an independent TV station from a city 70 miles away, and that independent station also carries *Wheel of Fortune*. Under Syndex, WTZ can demand that the cable system black out *Wheel of Fortune* on the independent station. Syndex also applied to nationally broadcast "superstations" (such as WTBS and WGN).

Local broadcasters liked Syndex. If a station was guaranteed exclusive rights to a show, the station would get more viewers for that show and be able to get more advertising revenue.

Syndex Reborn

The FCC reinstated Syndex in 1990, and there were some new guidelines. Local stations with exclusive rights to a show can still demand that cable systems black out the show being carried on a distant broadcast station or nationally broadcast superstation. This rule applies even if the program is carried at a different time or on a different day. Cable systems with fewer than 1000 subscribers are exempt from Syndex, and no cable system must black out a show on a distant station if local residents can pick up that station with a decent antenna (after all, if people can pick up the station with an antenna, that station is not really "distant").

NETWORK NONDUPLICATION RULES

These rules prohibit cable systems with more than 1000 subscribers from carrying distant network affiliates if the cable system already carries a local affiliate for that same network. The reasoning behind these rules is that if customers are given the choice of two CBS affiliates, the audience will be split for each CBS show. That will result in fewer viewers and less advertising revenue for the local affiliate. The rules are meant to support the doctrine of localism and protect the financial interests of local broadcasters.

The "zones of protection" are a 35-mile radius for the top 100 TV markets and a 55-mile radius for smaller TV markets. For example, a cable system may not carry a distant CBS affiliate from a city only 20 miles away when the cable system is already carrying the local CBS affiliate. However, a cable system in a top 100 market would be allowed to carry a distant station from a city 45 miles away.

CABLE DESCRAMBLERS

In the 1980s, many television sets were not "cable ready." As a result, a customer would need to purchase or lease a cable converter box from the cable company to receive basic cable service through channel 3 or 4 on a TV set. Back then, converter boxes were not available in stores, so cable customers had no choice but to pay whatever price the cable company asked for a converter box. The cable company would program converter boxes so customers would only receive cable channels they had paid for.

In 1986, the federal government ruled that other companies were allowed to manufacture cable boxes and sell them to the public. This is also included the sale of devices known as "descramblers." Cable descramblers act like converter boxes, but they will also restore the original sound and pictures from "scrambled" channels. That is why cable companies do not like the widespread availability of descramblers. The devices allow people to descramble cable programming they have not purchased.

FAQ

Is it legal to own and use a descrambler?

Yes, it is legal to own one, but it is *illegal* to use the descrambler to access channels you have not paid for. This is "theft of services," and persons face criminal penalties if caught. However, the law treats descramblers like CD burners. Both the 1992 Cable Act and the Telecomm Act of 1996 allow for the sale of descramblers, saying it is legal for cable customers to purchase their own cable equipment or "third-party" equipment. As is stated in the 1992 Cable Act, "Cable operators may not prevent customers from using their own equipment if such equipment is technically compatible with the cable system."

Persons are required to notify the cable company after purchasing a descrambler. Illegal use of descramblers can result in $50,000 in fines and up to 2 years in prison.

Cable companies use other methods to try to keep people from gaining illegal access to cable programming. For example, there are devices called "traps" that are placed on telephone poles to divert premium services away from nonsubscribers. Any person tampering with a trap is violating the law.

Public Inspection Files

Cable systems with 1000 or more subscribers must keep a public inspection file. It is similar to the contents of a broadcast station public file and must be available during regular business hours at the cable company office where customers come to pay bills or request service. The file must include sponsorship identification records, political files, commercial records for children's programming, records for leased access channels, ownership records, repair logs, proof-of-performance test data, and EEO documents.

The public file may be kept on computer or in a paper file. It must be readily accessible to the public.

Cable systems with 1000 or more subscribers are also required to keep an updated copy of Cable Television Rules and Regulations (47 C.F.R., Parts 76 and 78). It is the responsibility of each cable system to stay updated on new FCC cable rules and regulations.

Cable System Fines

The FCC has the authority to fine cable systems who violate rules and regulations. The commission may fine a cable system up to $25,000 per day for each violation. Each day of a continuing violation is considered a separate offense. However, total fines may not exceed $250,000 for any "notice of apparent liability" or hearing on a specific violation.

SATELLITE RADIO AND TV

One of the major roles of the FCC is to help coordinate the introduction of new technologies. We saw the importance of this FCC role in the 1940s when the commission saw that a new medium called television was developing too rapidly. The FCC wanted some time to establish some national technical standards for TV, and the its solution was to put a freeze on new TV licenses from 1948 to 1952.

We will now analyze how the FCC has dealt with some newer technologies that got their starts in the 1990s and beyond.

Satellite Radio

Satellite radio actually got its start in 1992, when the FCC allocated a spectrum in the "S" band for a national satellite radio service. In 1997, XM and Sirius each paid more than $80 million for the rights to use part of the S band for their satellite radio broadcast services.

Satellite radio offers numerous advantages over traditional analog radio, including digital sound, a display feature on the radio receiver that provides information such as song title, artist, and music format, many commercial-free channels, and the ability for customers to receive the service nationwide.

Briefly, here is how satellite radio works: XM, WorldSpace, and Sirius each have two or three satellites orbiting the earth. Each company beams its radio programming to the satellites, which then retransmit the signals to the ground, where receivers pick up the signals and unscramble the digital data. In cities, large buildings can block the satellite signals, so the companies often place transmitters in those areas to ensure that subscribers can receive the signals. Each company also has an extra satellite ready to launch in case one of their orbiting satellites fails.

In September 2001, satellite radio, or satellite digital audio radio service, made its debut in America. XM Satellite Radio went on the air, offering 100 different channels of radio programming and boasting that it had 1.5 million songs in its music library and more than 30 channels or "stations" that were commercial free. The company said it would have to get more than four million subscribers in the following 4 years just to break even. XM had a rather rough start. The company had planned to launch its service on September 12, 2001, but the September 11 terrorist attacks made the company push the launch date back to September 25. By November 2003, XM had one million subscribers, and only 8 months later in July 2004, it had doubled that number.

Sirius Satellite Radio launched a similar service in early 2002. By July 2004, Sirius was a distant second to XM, with fewer than 500,000 subscribers. A third company, called WorldSpace, broadcasts mostly in Asia and Africa but plans to expand its reach to South America.

All of these satellite radio services offer a wide variety of music formats, as well as channels with news, sports, and talk. Subscribers also have access to channels offering radio programming from sources such as CNN and the Weather Channel. Local broadcast stations are not available on satellite radio.

Satellite Radio Regulations

In 1997, the FCC said that satellite radio providers should abide by political broadcasting rules such as Section 315 and Section 312(a)(7). However, satellite radio would not be subject to FCC content regulations such as indecency. It was for this reason in 2004 that radio shock jock Howard Stern announced a deal with Sirius Satellite Radio. On Sirius, Stern can broadcast his material without fear of FCC indecency fines. The reason is that satellite radio does not operate on the "public airwaves" and is a subscription service similar to cable.

Also, the FCC does not require satellite radio stations to meet any public interest obligations.

These and other issues are sure to be debated as satellite radio becomes more popular.

FAQ

Is satellite radio's rising popularity seen as a threat to local radio stations?

The National Association of Broadcasters seems to think so and has taken steps to protect local radio stations from losing large numbers of listeners to satellite radio. In late 2003, satellite radio companies began to offer national channels that provided localized traffic and weather information for major cities. On XM, the service also provided weather and traffic updates for popular travel routes.

In 2004, the National Association of Broadcasters asked the FCC to prohibit such local services, arguing that satellite radio was authorized as a *national* service.[20] In fact, when the FCC allocated part of the spectrum to satellite radio, XM promised the commission it would not air any localized programming that would compete directly with local broadcast stations. The NAB said that these localized channels "compete directly with local broadcasters with local content without being subject to any public interest obligations." The NAB also asked the FCC to prohibit satellite radio services from using radios that can provide listeners with different local information as they travel from one area to another.

The NAB's actions are known as *regulatory capture*. This means that a government-regulated industry, such as broadcasting, is using a government agency to ward off competition. Economists argue that regulatory capture almost always harms consumers by denying them new products and services.

XM radio responded by calling the NAB a "bully." XM e-mailed all of its subscribers and encouraged them to file comments with the FCC in support of satellite radio. In the e-mail, XM said that the NAB and local broadcasters felt "threatened" by satellite radio's success, and "Instead of competing and improving their services, they want the government to protect their businesses by attacking satellite radio."[21] XM accused the NAB of

---

[20]Federal Communications Commission. (2004, April 27). *Request for comment on petition filed by the National Association of Broadcasters regarding programming carried by satellite digital audio radio services.* Public notice: DA 04-1096.

[21]*XM satellite radio.* (2004). Retrieved June 1, 2004, from http://www.xmradio.com

having used similar tactics in the 1940s when it tried to "squash" television to protect radio and in the 1970s when the trade group "tried to put the kibosh on FM stations" to protect AM radio. By the June 4, 2004 deadline, more than 27,000 XM listeners had sent comments to the FCC.

The NAB also persuaded some members of Congress to sponsor a resolution (HR 4026) that would prohibit localized programs on satellite radio. As of this writing, no action has been taken on the proposed legislation.

Satellite TV

The Satellite Home Viewer Improvement Act of 1999

Because of something called the 1988 Satellite Home Viewer Act, the cable industry had a huge competitive advantage over satellite TV providers. The satellite companies were not allowed to provide subscribers with signals from local TV stations. As a result, many potential satellite TV customers stayed with cable so they could receive their favorite local stations.

The situation changed, though, with the Satellite Home Viewer Improvement Act of 1999. Congress voted to allow satellite companies to provide "local-into-local" service. This meant satellite TV subscribers could now get local TV stations through their satellite dishes as long as those subscribers lived in the local TV station's DMA as defined by Nielsen Media Research.

It is important to note that the Satellite Home Viewer Improvement Act does not require that satellite TV providers offer local stations. It is simply an option. A satellite TV service still has to negotiate with local TV stations for the rights to carry their signals.

There are two basic types of satellite services. There is C-band, which uses a large dish. There is also direct broadcast satellite (DBS), which uses smaller dishes to receive the satellite TV signals.

Satellite TV Regulations

As noted in chapter 3, satellite TV providers must abide by political broadcasting rules, such as Section 315 and Section 312(a)(7).

The "Carry One, Carry All" Rule

As of January 1, 2002, if a satellite TV service has chosen to offer local-into-local service, it must also provide its subscribers with signals from all local TV stations in that particular DMA that have requested carriage on the satellite service. This includes all non-commercial educational stations as well.

The following rules apply to "carry one, carry all:" Just as with cable, local TV stations may choose mandatory carriage on the satellite system or may negotiate for retransmission consent. The satellite service may offer the local stations to subscribers as a package deal or "a la carte." The satellite provider may require subscribers to purchase additional equipment (such as an extra dish) to receive all of the local signals in a market. However, a satellite provider may NOT require the purchase of additional equipment for the reception of only *some* local stations. The satellite service is allowed to charge subscribers for carriage of local stations.

FAQ

What if my satellite service chooses not to provide local TV signals? Can I still get network programs?

Yes. There's always a roof-top antenna. However, if that type of antenna does not provide quality signals, you may qualify as an "unserved household." That means your household is unserved by local TV stations. Unserved households are allowed to receive up to two "distant" network station signals for each network. Satellite services are allowed to provide unserved households with up to two distant affiliates from each of the major networks (ABC, CBS, NBC, Fox). A "distant" signal comes from a station outside of a subscriber's DMA. People who have dishes permanently attached to commercial trucks or motor homes can also qualify as "unserved households."

To clarify, if you can receive local signals for CBS, NBC, and Fox through a rooftop antenna, you count as a "served" household for those local affiliates. If, however, you cannot receive a local ABC station via antenna, you are "unserved" for ABC. The satellite provider is required to offer you only the local CBS, NBC, and Fox affiliates but is permitted to offer you a "distant" ABC affiliate.

In 2000, the FCC voted that satellite TV must follow three rules that also apply to cable systems, with some modifications. These rules apply to both C-band (large dish) and DBS (small dish) systems.

The Network Nonduplication Rule. An example of this rule is a local CBS affiliate that requires a satellite service to black out CBS programs being carried on a nationally broadcast superstation. This rule applies even if the satellite service does not carry the local CBS affiliate.

The Syndicated Exclusivity Rule ("Syndex"). An example of this rule is a local TV station that has exclusive rights to air a syndicated show in the market. The station may require a satellite service to black out that same syndicated show when it airs on a national superstation. This rules applies even if the local station is not carried by the satellite service.

In regard to these two rules, the FCC says six broadcasters qualify as "national superstations": KTLA-TV (Los Angeles), KWGN-TV (Denver), WGN-TV (Chicago), WPIX-TV (New York), WSBK-TV (Boston), and WWOR-TV (New York).

The Sports Blackout Rule. This rule applies to satellite services and concerns sporting events carried on network stations and nationally distributed superstations. The rule gives protection to a sports team or league's exclusive distribution rights to a local sporting event or sports team. Therefore, the rule applies only if a local TV broadcast station is not carrying a local game. Then all other broadcasters' signals showing the game may not be shown in the protected local blackout zone.

These three rules do not apply to satellite services with fewer than 1000 subscribers in "zones of protection."

High Definition Television (HDTV)

A Brief History

For decades, American television stations have broadcast analog signals for television sets with 525 lines of resolution. This also known as standard definition television. In the late 1980s, the FCC started to look into the idea of having all American TV stations broadcasting digital TV (DTV) signals with as much as 1125 lines of resolution. This would also become known as high definition television (HDTV). In 1992, WRC-TV in Washington, DC, was the first station in the nation to broadcast a program in HDTV. The show was a 1-hour news program, and the signal was at 1050 lines of resolution.

In 1993, the FCC established a group called the Grand Alliance, made up of such companies as AT&T, Philips, and Zenith. The job of the Grand Alliance was to establish an industry standard for HDTV. The FCC did not want each manufacturer having different technical standards for HDTV sets. The Grand Alliance supports a system using 1080 lines of resolution.

In 1995, WCBS-TV in New York City got the first experimental HDTV license from the FCC. WCBS broadcast its programming with two signals: the standard analog signal and the new digital signal, with a 55-mile radius.

In 1997, the FCC mandated a gradual phase-in of HDTV across America. All TV stations would continue to broadcast their analog signals, but the FCC also gave each station a new channel for a digital signal. The FCC did not have any auctions on these new digital channels, so the stations got these channels for free. In 1998, several TV stations across the country began experimenting with DTV broadcasts. The FCC then ruled that all commercial stations in the top 10 TV markets had to be broadcasting digital signals by May 1999. Stations in markets 11 through 30 had until November 1999.

One top-ten market station, WFAA-TV in Dallas, made news in 1998 when its experimental HDTV signal began to interfere with 12 low-power heart monitors at nearby Baylor University Medical Center. No patients were harmed, but WFAA temporarily turned off its HDTV transmitter until Baylor corrected the problem. The problem was that the FCC for years had been allowing hospitals to use vacant TV frequencies for wireless medical devices. The Medical Center had been using older heart monitors, which operated on channel 9, the same channel the FCC gave to WFAA for its HDTV signal. The FCC said it is the responsibility of hospitals to find equipment that will not have interference problems with HDTV signals.

2009 Target Date

The FCC says that TV stations in all markets have until January 1, 2009 to convert *completely* to DTV. The FCC had originally set the deadline for 2006, but industry experts predicted that only about 30% to 40% of homes would have HDTV by that time. As a result, in October 2004, the FCC announced the new 2009 deadline to give stations more time to make the transition. At that time, all TV stations are supposed to cease their broadcasts of analog signals. There is a catch, though. Stations may continue to broadcast analog signals if fewer than 85% of homes in their markets have digital sets or sets with digital tuners.

Missed Deadlines

All commercial stations had until May 1, 2002 to construct digital facilities, but more than 650 stations (more than half of all commercial TV stations nationwide) told the FCC they could not meet that deadline. Many of those broadcasters argued that they just did not have the money to buy all of the necessary digital equipment. They said they needed more time to raise the necessary revenue. Other stations argued that they had trouble getting permission from local governments to build new TV towers. (For technical reasons, many stations are unable to use their old towers for the new digital transmitters.)

Noncommercial stations had a deadline of May 2003. The FCC has also given all broadcasters until December 2004 to have their digital signals equal the reach of their current analog broadcast areas.

Manufacturer Deadlines

In the summer of 2002, the FCC also announced a deadline for manufacturers of HDTV sets. After all, it is pointless to have TV stations broadcasting digital signals if there are not enough HDTV sets in the marketplace for consumers. The FCC has set 2007 as the deadline for manufacturers to include DTV tuners in *all* television sets. Some manufacturers say this will add roughly $300 to cost of a TV set. We will see if that holds true.

Overall, a Slow Start but Gaining Momentum

The slow start was largely because HDTV sets were very expensive at first. In 1998, industry trade shows featured HDTV sets from various companies, with prices from $6000 to $10,000. People were reluctant to invest in these new televisions when the vast majority of broadcast and cable signals were still in analog. Also, many consumers are unsure about what DTV has to offer.

DTV is also an expensive investment for TV stations. For example, KSTP-TV in Minneapolis–St. Paul, MN, spent roughly $1.5 million making the digital transition in 1999. That price tag includes not only new towers and digital transmitters but new digital studio equipment as well.

Three years later, in 2001, HDTV prices had come down, but the new digital televisions were not exactly flying off of the shelves. In fact, digital televisions accounted for less than 1% of all TV set sales. In 2001, Americans bought roughly 25 million analog sets and only about 150,000 HDTV sets. However, by 2003, 2.5 million HDTV sets were being sold annually in the United States.

FAQ

How is HDTV different from analog TV?

HDTV has better picture quality. Many broadcasters have announced that they will be using an HDTV signal with 1080 lines of resolution, compared with the 525 lines used in analog signals. Picture quality is greatly enhanced: It is more than five times sharper than analog. HDTV also uses digital sound, with six-channel surround sound, and has wider screens. Analog sets have a screen size with a ratio of 4:3. HDTV sets have a screen ratio of 16:9, the same that is used for many motion pictures.

HDTV sets have a variety of interactive features unavailable on analog sets, as well as the capability for "ancillary" channels. Unlike analog signals, a digital signal allows for separate "streams" of programming on the one digital channel. So, along with the TV programs, stations can send ancillary streams of data services, children's programs, and so on.

FAQ

What if I can't afford to buy one of these new HDTV sets? Will my old analog TV set be useless?

No. An old analog set will be able to receive these new signals through an adaptor box, which will be much cheaper than having to buy a new HDTV set. However, these adaptors have some drawbacks. The adaptor will not enable your old analog TV to deliver true HDTV-quality pictures. The adaptor will simply translate the digital signal into a higher quality analog signal. You will need to buy an actual HDTV set to receive the full benefits of the digital technology. It is still uncertain whether these adaptors will be compatible with all digital signals and analog sets.

Also, for many years to come, the analog sets will still be compatible with cable and home satellite services, as well as with VCRs and DVDs.

FAQ

Are cable companies and satellite services required to carry both the analog and digital signals from broadcast stations?

No. They are exempt from these DTV rules during the transition. Many cable operators have argued that they do not have the channel capacity to carry both signals.

FAQ

Will there be DTV must-carry rules for cable and satellite after the transition is complete?

It looks that way. The FCC seems to be leaning in the direction of requiring cable operators and satellite services to carry just the "primary video" stream from each broadcaster. Cable and satellite would not be required to carry any ancillary digital services from a broadcaster's signal. As a result, broadcasters would have to decide which stream should be considered primary video.

FAQ

What will happen to the old analog channels?

The FCC says the old analog TV channels will be auctioned off to the highest bidders.

Digital Radio

Digital radio is basically HDTV for radio, and many in the industry refer to it as "HD radio." Digital radio is also known as digital audio broadcasting (DAB). In 2004, FCC chairman Michael Powell urged the radio industry to begin the transition to HD radio so that it can have a hope of competing with services like satellite radio.

DAB, or HD radio, involves individual radio stations broadcasting digital signals to consumers who must own special digital radio receivers to pick up the signals. The concept is very similar to the technology used for compact discs. It would represent a vast improvement in sound quality for radio stations today on the AM and FM dials, which broadcast analog signals.

Developing a DAB Standard (IBOC)

Just as with HDTV, the FCC had to figure out which method would be best for delivering these new DAB signals. The FCC wanted to make sure than any new DAB signals would not interfere with existing broadcast stations and would provide the best service to the public.

In 1998, a company then called USA Digital Radio (later known as iBiquity Digital Corporation) pushed the FCC for the adoption of what is called in-band, on-channel (IBOC) technology. Much like HDTV, IBOC allows for the simultaneous broadcast of both analog and digital radio signals, also known as "hybrid mode." Once the transition is complete, it will then be known as "all-digital mode."

In November 2001, the National Radio Systems Committee (NRSC) gave its support to iBiquity's IBOC technology for FM broadcasting. In April 2002, the NRSC endorsed iBiquity's technology for daytime broadcasts on AM radio. The NRSC is an advisory panel sponsored by the Consumer Electronics Association and the National Association of Broadcasters. The NRSC's main purpose is to make recommendations regarding technical standards in the radio industry. The NRSC is currently urging the FCC to move forward with approval of IBOC for both FM and daytime AM radio service. iBiquity is the only company developing and licensing digital technology for AM and FM broadcasting. iBiquity's Web site says its numerous investors include some of America's top radio station owners, including Clear Channel, Viacom, and ABC.[22] In October 2002, the FCC gave the final go-ahead to the IBOC technology.

---

[22]*iBiquity digital.* (2003). Retrieved June 1, 2004, from http://www.ibiquity.com

---

FAQ

Exactly how is DAB different from analog radio?

Probably the easiest way to explain this new technology is to look at the major selling points for DAB and IBOC.

Digital Radio: Advantages for Listeners

The primary advantage is digital sound. AM digital radio would have the quality of FM radio today, and FM digital radio would have CD-quality sound. Digital radio has less "noise" than analog signals. There is practically no interference, static, or "signal echoes," which may occur because of the weather, driving under power lines, or from signal reflections off of buildings. The digital receivers filter out all interference. However, digital radio signal reception can be disrupted in larger tunnels.

Digital radio receivers monitor radio signals for strength. For example, if a person in a car is listening to a classical music station and that signal starts to fade, the receiver will automatically change from the fading signal to a stronger signal from a nearby station with the same format.

Digital radio receivers also have an advanced liquid crystal display (LCD) screen, which can provide weather updates, visual displays of weather maps, traffic information, news and sports updates, station call letters, or station names, as well as station music formats, names of songs and artists, song lyrics, stock market data, paging services, supplementary radio advertising, and radio station games and contests.

"Pay radio" is considered to be another advantage. This would be similar to pay-per-view on cable. A digital radio listener would pay for the rights to listen to exclusive programs (concerts, etc.).

Digital Radio: Advantages for Stations

Digital signal transmission requires much less electricity than analog signals. Up to six stations may be able to share one digital transmitter and one DAB channel. Also, stations can sell extra advertising on the data stream of their signal.

The transition from analog to digital will be cheap compared to TV stations' transition to HDTV; iBiquity says stations will pay somewhere between $30,000 and $200,000 to go digital. Most stations will be able to use their existing towers and facilities when making the digital transition.

IBOC would reduce confusion for consumers making the transition from analog to digital. IBOC technology means, for example, that 102.7 FM on an analog radio would also be 102.7 FM on the new digital radios. The IBOC receivers would also be compatible for both signals, allowing reception of a station's old analog signal and a new digital signal. This will make it easier for stations to keep their listeners during the transition period.

By 2004, roughly 300 stations were broadcasting in digital. Also in 2004, the Corporation for Public Broadcasting gave out more than $5 million in grants to help public radio stations made the transition to digital transmission. That same year, Clear Channel

Communications (the largest owner of radio stations) announced it would spend $100 million over the next decade to upgrade its 1200 stations to digital.

Summary

Because they are available to subscribers only, cable and satellite delivery systems are not considered the "public airwaves," and therefore the FCC and the courts place fewer content regulations on cable. However, the courts have upheld the FCC's right to regulate cable in a variety of areas, including rate regulations, franchising, and must-carry rules.

For many years, regulations on cable were justified by the fact that cable companies often had a monopoly on multichannel TV service in communities. However, many regulations regarding cable have been modified or dropped as the cable industry faces increasing competition from other media, especially satellite TV.

Satellite TV received a major boost when Congress voted to allow local channels on satellite TV, which made it possible for satellite to provide significant competition to the cable industry. The federal government has set deadlines for the transition to HDTV, but many stations in smaller markets have had trouble meeting those deadlines, mostly because of the costs involved.

Satellite radio has gained strength in recent years, and that has groups like the NAB concerned about the impact on traditional broadcast stations. One way for AM and FM stations to compete could be HD Radio. FCC chairman Michael Powell is urging traditional broadcast radio stations to make the transition to digital broadcasting in the new digital age.

5

MEDIA OWNERSHIP RULES

It is the purpose of this Act, among other things, to maintain control of the United States over all the channels of interstate and foreign radio transmission, and to provide for the use of such channels, but not the ownership thereof, by persons for limited periods of time, under licenses granted by Federal authority, and no such license shall be construed to create any right, beyond the terms, conditions, and periods of the license.

—Section 301, Communications Act of 1934

The Communications Act of 1934 reestablished the point that the public airwaves were "scarce." They were considered a limited and precious resource and therefore would be subject to government rules and regulations. As the Supreme Court would state in 1943, "The radio spectrum simply is not large enough to accommodate everybody. There is a fixed natural limitation upon the number of stations that can operate without interfering with one another."[1] In reality, the airwaves are infinite, but the government has made a limited number of positions available for use.

In the 1930s, the broadcast industry grew steadily, and the FCC had to grapple with the issue of broadcast station ownership. The FCC felt that a diversity of viewpoints on the airwaves served the public interest and was best achieved through diversity in station ownership. Therefore, to prevent individuals or companies from controlling too many broadcast stations in one area or across the country, the FCC eventually instituted ownership rules. These rules limit how many broadcast stations a person can own in a single market or nationwide.

HISTORY OF BROADCAST OWNERSHIP RULES

1940: The Duopoly Rule

This rule stated that no person or company could own more than one broadcast station (AM, FM, TV) in any one market. The rule was meant to prevent one person

---

[1]See *NBC v. U.S.*, 319 U.S. 198 (1943)

from having too much control over the airwaves in a given area. The Duopoly Rule was supposed to promote diversity and ensure that there were numerous "voices" or owners of broadcast stations within communities.

However, the FCC would often allow exceptions to these rules to keep as many stations on the air as possible. The FCC would, many times, permit one person to own an AM-FM combination in a market or to own a radio station and UHF TV station in the same market. For example, the FCC granted exceptions to companies that had already owned two broadcast stations in a market before this rule went into effect. This is called a *grandfather clause*. The FCC would also allow one entity to own multiple stations within a market if that was the only way to keep those stations on the air. Many times, existing stations were the only ones that had the interest or finances to acquire faltering broadcast stations and keep them on the air. The FCC also allowed existing stations to acquire or construct FM and TV stations (especially UHF) in the same market to encourage the growth of broadcast services.

As will be seen later in this chapter, the Duopoly Rule is no longer in effect in many situations.

1943: The Supreme Court Limits Broadcast Network Powers

In 1938, the FCC started doing research for its *Report on Chain Broadcasting* (or broadcast networks). By the end of the year, the FCC had discovered that there were 660 commercial radio stations in the United States, and more than half (341) were affiliated with one of four national networks. NBC actually operated two national networks, the Red and the Blue, for a total of 135 stations. CBS had 102 stations, and the Mutual Broadcasting System operated 74. Another 30 stations had "dual affiliations" with two of these networks.

The FCC found that the affiliates of these four networks made up 97% of the total nighttime broadcasting power of all the stations in America. (NBC and CBS controlled roughly 85%. Mutual owned a lot of low-power stations and was considered a very weak network in comparison.) The FCC was particularly disturbed by how much power the networks had over the programming on affiliate stations. For example, networks required affiliates to air all network programs and prohibited affiliates from airing another network's programs. The FCC felt that such network rules limited the ability of affiliate stations to air programming that served the interests of their local audiences.

In 1941, the FCC released its *Report on Chain Broadcasting*.[2] The report showed that CBS and NBC owned 18 stations in cities such as New York, Chicago, and Washington, and these stations were "the most powerful and desirable in the country, and were permanently inaccessible to competing networks." The FCC said this concentration of ownership "had a discouraging effect upon the creation and growth of new networks." Because of this, the FCC mandated an overhaul in how networks dealt with their affiliates: Networks could no longer prohibit an affiliate from airing programs from another network; network-affiliate contracts would now last for 2 years instead of 5 years; affiliates would now have the right to reject network programs for pretty much any reason; a

---

[2]Commission Order No. 37, Docket No. 5060, May 1941

network could not own another network; and networks could no longer set advertising rates for local affiliates.

FAQ

Weren't such rules a violation of the rights of networks?

NBC and CBS thought so, and they took the FCC to court over the new rules, saying that the commission was violating the First Amendment rights of the networks and that it did not have the authority to enforce such rules.

However, in 1943, in *NBC v. U.S.*,[3] the Supreme Court said the FCC did have such power: "The facilities of radio are limited and therefore precious; they cannot be left to wasteful use without detriment to the public interest." Therefore, the court said, the FCC had the right to limit the power of radio networks to "encourage the larger and more effective use of radio in the public interest."

As a result of this ruling, NBC was forced to sell the Blue network, which later became ABC (remember, the new FCC rules said a network could not own another network), and all the networks were forced to rework rules and contracts with their affiliates.

FAQ

Did this ruling give the FCC a lot more power to regulate networks?

No. It is important to note that the FCC was not given the authority to regulate the networks directly. The Supreme Court simply said the networks were not allowed to interfere with the local operations of their affiliates. The FCC had argued that it had a right to ensure *local* control of broadcast stations, and the court agreed with that argument. For example, the FCC had the right to deny a license renewal to a network-affiliated station if the network had too much control over the station's programming or if the network engaged in activities that prevented the affiliate from serving the public interest.

In 1946, the FCC began enforcing the Dual TV Network Ownership Prohibition. Any national TV broadcast network was now prohibited from owning another national TV broadcast network.

In 1948, the FCC imposed a "freeze" on new applications for TV licenses because there were more applications than there were channel spaces available. This lasted for 4 years and is known as the "Freeze of 1948-1952." During those 4 years, the number of TV sets in homes rose from 250,000 to more than 17 million. The freeze had no impact on network ownership rules but is mentioned in this discussion to show how rapidly the broadcast industry was growing at this time.

---

[3]319 U.S. 190 (1943)

From 1970 to 1995, networks' powers were limited further with the Financial Interest and Syndication Rule ("fin-syn"). The rule prohibited the major TV networks from having too much influence and financial interest in their own programming. Fin-syn placed strict limits on the networks owning, producing and syndicating their own shows. *Syndication* is the sale and distribution of a television series directly to individual TV stations instead of through a TV network. The basic reason for the fin-syn rule was to prevent the networks from gaining too much power and to allow smaller production companies to make a profit in Hollywood.

By the 1990s, cable TV was a much more powerful force, and many non-network production companies had become very successful. Also, the networks were losing audience shares. Lawmakers no longer saw a need to restrict the networks from profiting from their own shows, and the rule was officially eliminated in 1995.

Broadcast Station Ownership Limits: 7-7-7, 12-12-12, and Beyond

The FCC felt the public interest was best served by not having one person or company owning too many stations across the country. Therefore, the commission placed limits on how many broadcast stations could be owned by one entity. Until 1944, the FCC had allowed a party to own up to three TV stations nationwide. The commission increased that number to five in 1944.

In 1953, the FCC established the 7-7-7 Rule or the "Rule of Sevens." It stated that one party could not own more than seven AM, seven FM, and seven TV stations nationwide. (At least two of the TV stations had to be UHF. VHF is channels 2 through 13. UHF is channels 14 through 69.) Also, a single owner could not have stations in each medium reaching more than 25% of the national audience. Soon after, the FCC denied Storer Broadcasting Company a license for a sixth VHF station, and the company took the FCC to court. In 1956, the Supreme Court ruled that the FCC had the right to enforce ownership limits.[4]

FAQ

Why 7-7-7? Why 25%?

Critics of FCC ownership rules have frequently accused commissioners of picking such numbers "out of thin air." Critics ask, "Why 7-7-7 and not 8-8-8? Why 25% and not 20% or 30%?" The FCC sometimes lays out no clear justification for enacting such limits. As will be seen later in this chapter, when such numbers are challenged in court, judges often demand that the FCC provide concrete research and rationale to justify such limits.

In 1964, the FCC enacted the TV Duopoly Rule, which prohibited any entity from owning two or more TV stations in the same market. The FCC strictly enforced this rule until 1999. (In 2003, the FCC attempted to replace this rule with more liberal ownership limits, which will be discussed later in this chapter.)

---

[4]*U.S. v. Storer Broadcasting*, 351 U.S. 192 (1956)

In 1985, the 7-7-7 rule was dropped and became the 12-12-12 rule, or "Rule of Twelves." Now one party could own up to 12 AM, 12 FM, and 12 TV stations nationwide. The 25% rule for each medium still applied. These rules were strictly enforced. In 1985, Capital Cities and ABC merged. The merger meant ABC/Capital Cities had radio and TV stations reaching more than 28% of the U.S. population. The newly formed company had to sell off some of its stations to get below 25%. The FCC also noticed that very few minorities owned radio and TV stations. To increase diversity in ownership, the FCC in 1985 instituted a 14-14-14 minority rule to allow minorities to own up to 14 each of AM, FM, and TV stations. These stations would be allowed to reach up to 30% of the national audience.

In 1992, the 12-12-12 rule became the 18–18–12 rule. Now, a broadcast owner could have up to 18 AM, 18 FM, and 12 TV stations. Only 2 years later, in 1994, ownership limits were raised to 20-20-12.

FAQ

Why did the FCC raise ownership limits at these times?

The FCC was acknowledging increased competition in the electronic media and that the radio industry was struggling financially. The commission felt that relaxing ownership limits would allow bigger companies to buy smaller, struggling radio operations and keep those stations on the air. The FCC also said that the limits needed to be increased as the number of radio stations continued to increase.

CROSS-OWNERSHIP RULES

These rules were designed to prevent one electronic medium from having too much influence in other electronic media. Once again, it is the FCC's public interest standard that is the impetus for such rules, with the commission arguing that diversity in ownership is better than consolidation.

From 1970 to 2002, the FCC enforced the Cable/Broadcast Cross-Ownership (CBCO) Rule, which prohibited a cable system from owning broadcast TV stations in its own market. In 1970, the FCC dissolved all existing cable-broadcast cross-ownerships. However, an appeals court, in *Fox v. FCC*,[5] in 2002, struck down CBCO. The FCC had kept the CBCO Rule to avoid consolidation of media ownership and to promote diversity of ownership of cable systems and broadcast stations. The court, though, said the FCC had not considered "the increase in the number of competing television stations since it had promulgated the Rule in 1970." The court acknowledged that there might be some damage to diversity of ownership, "but we hardly think it could be substantial."

In 1970, the FCC also passed the Radio-TV Cross-Ownership Rule. This rule prohibited most companies from owning a radio station and a TV station in the same market, but the

---

[5]293 F.3d 537 (D.C. Cir. 2002)

FCC did not strictly enforce this rule. The commission allowed most existing radio-TV cross-ownerships to continue but prohibited any new combinations.

In 1999, the FCC issued new guidelines for radio-TV cross-ownership that allowed one party to own a television station and any of the following radio station combinations in the same market. Note how the FCC is concerned about the number of *independent voices* in a market:

- One AM or FM radio station, regardless of the number of independent voices in the market
- Up to four radio stations (any combination of AM or FM, as long as they are permitted under the local radio ownership rules) in any market where at least 10 independent voices would remain after the merger
- Up to six radio stations (any combination of AM or FM stations, as long as they are permitted under the local radio ownership rules) in any market where at least 20 independent voices would remain after the merger

A TV station could choose any of these four options and still own or purchase a second TV station if permitted by the updated TV Duopoly Rule (see page 113). In those markets where the revised rules allowed parties to own eight outlets in the form of two TV stations and six radio stations, a single party could also choose to own one TV station and seven radio stations. The FCC would allow waivers to these limits if one station was a failed station.

Independent Voices

The FCC said the term *independent voices* (in relation to the Radio-TV Cross-Ownership Rule) included radio stations, TV stations, newspapers, and cable systems that met the following criteria.

1. *All independently owned, full-power operational commercial and noncommercial television stations* licensed to a community in the DMA in which the TV station was located

2. *All independently owned operational commercial and noncommercial radio stations* licensed to, or with a reportable share in, the radio metro market where the TV station involved was located

3. *Daily newspapers* that were published in the DMA with a circulation exceeding 5% of the population in the DMA

4. *Wired cable systems*, provided cable service was generally available in the DMA

In 1975, the FCC announced the Newspaper-Broadcast Cross-Ownership Rule, which prohibited one party from owning both a broadcast station and a newspaper in the same market. Cable systems were exempt from this rule.

FAQ

Why was the FCC getting involved in newspaper ownership regulation?

The FCC may only regulate newspaper ownership when it involves broadcast ownership as well. The FCC felt that concentration of ownership of print and broadcast outlets would give a single entity too much control over the dissemination of information in a community.

In fact, the commission ordered the breakup of more than a dozen newspaper-broadcast cross-ownerships in smaller communities. These were situations in which the only broadcast station in town also owned the only newspaper in town or vice versa.

However, the FCC allowed all other existing newspaper-broadcast cross-ownerships to continue, but it would not allow any new mergers. Various members of the broadcast and print media filed lawsuits to stop the FCC from enforcing the rule. Some complained that the rules were too strict and others said the rules were not strict enough.

In 1978, in *FCC v. National Citizens Committee for Broadcasting*,[6] the Supreme Court upheld the newspaper-broadcast cross-ownership rule. The justices ruled unanimously that the FCC had given sufficient justification for the rule and had the right to enforce it. The FCC did enforce it in the next 15 years, rarely allowing such mergers. Then, in the early 1990s, with the growing number of media voices, especially in larger markets, lawmakers and the FCC relaxed these limits a bit. In 2003, as will soon be discussed, the FCC attempted to replace the rule with a more liberal rule.

In 1993, Congress passed a law allowing the FCC to permit radio-newspaper mergers in the top 25 markets, but there had to be at least 30 other independent radio and TV voices in that market after the merger.

TV-Newspaper Cross-Ownership Liberalized

The 1993 law still discouraged TV stations from owning newspapers in any market. In 1998, though, the FCC granted a waiver to the Tribune Company so it could own both a newspaper and a TV station in the Miami-Fort Lauderdale market. Then, in its 2000 biennial review of ownership rules, the FCC said it would continue to consider waivers for TV-newspaper mergers in larger markets with numerous independent voices.

FAQ

Are there any ownership rules involving satellite TV providers?

Satellite TV–Cable Cross-Ownership

The FCC has considered some restrictions on a cable system owning a direct broadcast satellite (DBS) service, such as the Dish Network, but there are no such rules in writing yet. If a cable company attempts to buy a satellite TV provider, then the FCC or the Department of Justice will step in to see if such a merger would violate antitrust laws and damage competition in the cable and satellite TV markets.

In 1998, such a situation arose with satellite TV provider Primestar, which was run by five of the nation's largest cable companies. Primestar had tried to acquire the DBS assets of MCI and News Corporation Limited (News Corp). The Department of Justice filed a civil lawsuit to stop the purchase, saying the merger would have allowed Primestar's owners to protect their existing cable monopolies and would discourage competition in the satellite

---

[6]436 U.S. 775 (1978)

TV market. Soon after, Primestar abandoned its proposed merger, and the lawsuit was dropped. In January 1999, the five cable companies that owned Primestar sold its 2.2 million subscribers to DirectTV.

That same year, though, FCC chairman William Kennard said he would oppose any regulation prohibiting cross-ownership of cable companies and DBS. In 2001, with Michael Powell as its new chairman, the FCC said it was looking at a possible cable-DBS cross-ownership ban.

THE TELECOMMUNICATIONS ACT OF 1996

This act was the most sweeping change in broadcast regulation since the Communications Act of 1934. Our concern in this chapter is how the act affected ownership regulations. Major changes occurred for all electronic media.

Radio Ownership Limits

The New Rules from the Telecommunications Act of 1996

1. No national limit on radio stations. Owners would no longer have to worry about reaching more than 25% of the national audience. There is now no national limit.

2. The Radio Duopoly Rule was dropped. Persons could now own more than one station in a market, depending on market size. Those limits are laid out in Table 5.1.

The FCC still has the right to reject requests for multiple ownerships of stations, even if the guidelines are met. In 2002, for example, Clear Channel wanted to purchase about half a dozen radio stations in several markets, but the FCC denied those requests, saying the new stations would give Clear Channel too much power in those markets.

FAQ

What impact did these new rules have on the radio industry?

These changes in ownership rules had a major impact. Within a year, there were more than 1000 radio mergers. Remember, under the 1994 rules, no party could own more than 40 radio stations in America. With the new rules, Clear Channel Communications in 2003 owned more than 1250 radio stations nationwide or approximately one of out of every nine stations in the country.

The new ownership rules, obviously, consolidated the industry. In 1996, there were roughly 5100 radio station owners in the country. By 2002, the FCC said the number of owners had dropped to approximately 3800. Whether this is a good thing or a bad thing continues to be a topic of debate.

FAQ

What are the main arguments in favor of these new rules?

Table 5.1 Radio Ownership Limits

Number of Commercial Stations in Market	Maximum Number of Stations	Maximum Number of Same-Service (AM or FM)
45 or more	8	5
30-44	7	4
15-29	6	4
14 or fewer	5[a]	3

NOTE: These limits are all still in effect.

a. A person or company is not allowed to own more than 50% of radio stations in a market with 14 or fewer commercial stations. In markets with only three stations, an entity may own two stations only if they are an AM-FM combination.

Radio station owners get to operate more like other business owners and compete more fully in a free market—with fewer government restrictions. The new rules also increase diversity in general and the number of different formats on the air. There are more stations, with a greater variety of program formats, than there were before 1996. The FCC reported a 7.1% increase in the number of commercial radio stations on the air between March 1996 and March 2001. One big benefit was for Spanish language stations, which increased from 400 in 1996 to more than 600 in 2003. The new ownership rules made it easier for existing station owners to expand.

Struggling stations survive. Big companies are now allowed to purchase struggling stations in various markets and keep them on the air. Without these new rules, the stations might have gone off the air. The rules are especially helpful to small markets. Under the old duopoly rules, an existing station owner was not allowed to start up a second or third station. Under the new rules, these owners have begun putting more stations on the air and have given listeners more formats to choose from. This is especially noticeable in smaller markets. In some markets, more stations mean more jobs (however, this is not true in most instances, as will be discussed in the next section).

Advertisers have more choices. With more stations, advertisers have more options and are better able to hit their target demographics.

Quality may improve. A station is likely to have a better overall sound because it is being controlled by a national company with higher professional standards. An offshoot of this is "collective contesting." Big companies buy radio stations in smaller markets, enabling these small stations to offer bigger contests with bigger prizes and thus attract more listeners.

The radio industry is less consolidated than other industries. An NAB fact sheet from 2003 said the top ten radio station owners accounted for 49% of industry revenues. The NAB compared this with figures showing that the top ten cable companies control 89% of the cable industry's revenues and the top five music labels account for 84% of all album sales.

FAQ

What are the main arguments against the new radio ownership rules?

Detractors say that radio is being transformed from a local medium to one controlled by national corporations. Corporate-owned radio stations are more concerned about profits instead of serving local communities ("profits over public"). Minority ownership suffers. Big company ownership of many radio stations greatly reduces the opportunity for minority ownership of stations. In February 2003, the National Association of Black Owned Broadcasters, Inc., reported to the FCC that minority-owned stations had decreased 14% since 1996.[7] Part of the reason for this could be found in a 2000 report by the Minority Telecommunications Development Program. It argued that many minority broadcasters own only one station, and that fact makes it "practically impossible to compete with media conglomerates."[8]

More stations are turning to automation systems to program their stations. The big companies often prefer to have a computer run a station. It is much cheaper than hiring a full-time staff to be on the air 24 hours a day. As a result, critics say the on-air sound is bland and uncreative.

This emphasis on automation means fewer jobs. Stations do not need to hire as many people when a computer can do the job. The Bureau of Labor Statistics reported that from June 2000 to June 2002, radio station jobs decreased by 7000, thus leaving the radio industry with fewer jobs than it had in 1982. Automation also means more stations are "unattended." Therefore, no one is "live" on the air at the station to alert listeners about breaking news or emergencies.

For example: Did a dangerous chemical spill go unnoticed on local radio stations? On January 18, 2002 at 1:30 a.m. in Minot, ND, a train derailed, and its cargo of deadly anhydrous ammonia fertilizer exploded and burned. City and emergency officials said they tried to contact the local radio stations to help alert the public about the toxic ammonia fumes, but officials claimed no one answered the phones at the stations. All six Minot radio stations were owned by Clear Channel, and all six stations were running on automation at the time of the accident. Officials complained there was no news person or DJ at any of the stations to get on the air and inform the community about the deadly ammonia cloud. According to the Federal Emergency Management Agency, one person died as a result of the spill and 13 others were hospitalized.

Critics of radio deregulation frequently use the Minot incident as an example of how the consolidation of the radio industry is harmful to the public. The incident received widespread attention, including mention in a joint resolution of the Vermont legislature in May 2002. The resolution called for the FCC to avoid relaxing media ownership rules any further, saying incidents like the North Dakota train derailment show that many local radio stations are no longer doing a good job of serving the public interest.[9]

In 2004, though, Clear Channel disputed the Minot accounts. The company said its news station was indeed staffed and that reporters were sent to the scene of the derailment. Clear Channel placed much of the blame on the city, saying that Minot officials had tried to contact the station using old Emergency Broadcast System equipment instead of updated Emergency Alert System (EAS) equipment. Clear Channel said it sent engineers to Minot

---

[7]National Association of Black Owned Broadcasters, Inc., & Rainbow/Push Coalition, Inc. (2003, February 3). *Matter of 2002 biennial review: Reply comments.* MB Docket No. 02-277.

[8]Rawls, D. (2002, December 12). Minorities and the media: Little ownership and even less control. *AlterNet.* Retrieved July 22, 2003, from http://www.alternet.org/story.html?StoryID=14751

[9]Lynn, A. S. (2002, May 15). Vermont takes FCC lead. *Addison County Independent*, p. 4.

and found that the city still had the new EAS equipment in boxes. The company said it helped the city install the EAS equipment and then trained officials on its proper use.

Another argument against the new rules is that stations will have less news. Big companies, to cut costs, have cut back on radio station newscasts and news staffs. The Minot incident is certainly one example of this. Several studies have shown that media consolidation has "led to a serious decline in the quality of local news as distant corporate media executives demand cuts in news budgets to boost profits."[10] A study released in 2002 by the Project for Excellence in Journalism claimed that radio stations owned by individuals or smaller groups produced higher quality local newscasts than stations owned by large corporations.

Allegations are that music playlists have become narrower, and music is less diverse. Big companies tend to emphasize a heavy rotation of a narrow list of popular songs. Critics say that companies such as Clear Channel "homogenize playlists in a relentless quest for profit."[11] The big companies use the same programming formula at most of their stations, so a lot of radio sounds the same as you travel across the country.

Antitrust issues are surfacing. In 2001, a Denver promotion company called Nobody In Particular Presents (NIPP) filed an antitrust lawsuit against Clear Channel. Clear Channel also is a major player in the concert industry through its Clear Channel Entertainment division. NIPP accused the media giant of using its radio stations and concert division to engage in "monopolistic and predatory practices." NIPP said these practices included Clear Channel Entertainment preventing other concert promoters from advertising their shows on Clear Channel stations. In April 2004, in *Nobody in Particular Presents, Inc., v. Clear Channel*,[12] a federal district judge ruled that the lawsuit could go to trial. However, the two sides settled out of court in June 2004. The terms were not disclosed, but Clear Channel said the settlement included no admission of wrongdoing on its part.

The number of station owners is declining. As mentioned earlier, station owners decreased from roughly 5100 in 1996 to an estimated 3800 by 2002, a decline of roughly 25%. This means that fewer stations are owned and operated by local people.

FAQ

Why is a decrease in local ownership considered such a bad thing?

Critics argue that local owners have a more sincere and vested interest in their local communities and, as a result, serve those communities better.

In the *Biennial Review of Broadcast Ownership Rules*, released on June 2, 2003, the FCC voted to maintain the current local radio ownership limits. The FCC also concluded that current local radio ownership limits "continue to be necessary in the public interest." The only major change was how radio markets would now be defined. Such markets are now to be

---

[10]AFL-CIO Executive Council. (2003, February 26). *Media monopolies: A threat to American democracy*. Retrieved June 15, 2004, from http://www.aflcio.org/aboutaflcio/ecouncil/ec02262003.cfm

[11]Sanders, E., & Leeds, J. (2003, January 30). Clear Channel is facing a lot of static inside the capitol. *Los Angeles Times*, p. C1.

[12]311 F. Supp.2d 1048 (D. Co. 2004)

determined by a geographic market approach established by Arbitron, the main company for collecting radio ratings data in America.

Other Major Changes From the Telecomm Act of 1996

Network-Cable Ownership Rule

Congress ordered the FCC to drop the prohibition on networks owning cable systems. However, it stated that network-owned cable systems must operate fairly and not discriminate against non-network affiliate stations. For example, a network cannot try to force a local independent TV station out of business by refusing to carry that station on the cable system.

Telephone-Cable Cross-Ownership Rule

Until 1996, telephone companies were banned from owning cable companies. The 1996 act lifted that ban. Local telephone companies were now free to own and operate cable systems. The local phone companies were also allowed to offer long-distance services and Internet access and to manufacture telephone equipment. At the same time, long-distance providers such as Sprint and AT&T were allowed to offer Internet access as well as local telephone services.

This new rule also allowed cable companies and phone companies to provide video services and programming through telephone lines.

New Network Ownership Rules

In the 1996 act, Congress directed the FCC to prohibit the "Big Four" TV networks (CBS, NBC, ABC, and Fox) from operating a smaller network as well. This also meant that other companies could not have dual ownership of a Big Four network and a smaller network. The Big Four networks were also prohibited from merging with each other. At the same time, companies were permitted to operate more than one TV network as long as it did not include any of the Big Four.

These rules soon created problems in 2000 for Viacom, Inc., when it acquired CBS in a merger deal. Viacom already owned the fledgling UPN network. The rules stated clearly that a company could not own two networks if one was a Big Four network. Viacom argued that it should be allowed to hold on to UPN because the fledgling network would not survive without support from a major company. Viacom also noted that UPN programs attracted large minority audiences, particularly black viewers. In 2001, the FCC agreed with both arguments and updated (or re-established) network ownership rules. A Big Four network is now allowed to merge with an emerging network (including any network that started up after 1996), and Big Four networks are allowed to start up their own, smaller networks. Big Four networks are allowed to purchase cable networks and may even convert the cable network to a broadcast network if they so desire. Smaller networks may also acquire other smaller networks.

The Big Four are still restricted from merging with each other.

Broadcast Ownership Rules and the Biennial Review

The Telecommunications Act of 1996 mandates that the FCC review all of its ownership rules every 2 years to determine if they are still applicable in a changing media environment.

The FCC is allowing more and more concentration of ownership of broadcast stations. The commission has argued that this is no real threat to the diversity of viewpoints available on the airwaves because there are so many other outlets for communication these days—cable, satellite, and the Internet, to name just a few.

TV Duopoly Rule Updated

In 1999, the FCC announced new rules,[13] saying it would consider duopolies if (a) the duopoly would result in keeping a "failed" or "failing" station on the air, and there were no other available buyers for that station; (b) it would result in the construction of a previously unbuilt station; or (c) only one of the two stations was among the top four-ranked stations in the market and there were at least eight full-power independent stations (commercial and noncommercial) within the market after the merger.

FAQ

What is a "failed" or "failing" station?

The FCC says a failed station is one that has been off the air for at least 4 months or is involved in involuntary bankruptcy or insolvency proceedings.

The definition for a failing station is a little less specific. This is a station that has had a low audience share in the market and has been "struggling financially" during the past several years.

The FCC said these new TV duopoly rules had several benefits. The rules would lead to increased news and public affairs reporting because joint ownership and operation leads to more efficient use of broadcast resources. The rules could ensure the survival of struggling stations and thus keep more stations on the air. To ensure such benefits, consolidation of ownership would only occur "where competition and diversity will not be unduly diminished."

Concerns about competition and diversity became the center of attention in 2003 when the FCC announced major changes to TV ownership and cross-ownership rules. Many lawmakers in Congress said the changes were the most controversial in the commission's history.

The New 2003 TV and Cross-Media Rules

In 2003, the FCC attempted to liberalize the TV and cross-media ownership rules even further, but the commission met with fierce resistance from lawmakers, media groups, the public, and the courts.

In the Telecomm Act of 1996, Congress gave the FCC authority to liberalize the 25% national audience reach limit. The FCC decided that entities could own TV stations that

---

[13]Report No. MM 99-8 MM, Docket No. 91-221 and 87-8

reached up to 35% of the national audience. However, in 2002, in *Fox Television v. FCC*,[14] the DC Court of Appeals ruled that the FCC had not provided good reasons for picking 35% for a limit on TV station ownership. The court called the 35% cap "arbitrary and capricious and contrary to the law." The court sent the issue back to the FCC for reconsideration.

On June 3, 2003, the FCC responded to the court's mandate with a new set of rules it said would "withstand future judicial scrutiny." The FCC voted 3-2 along party lines (3 Republicans, 2 Democrats) and threw out the 35% limit. Details are provided to show how the FCC tried to justify the changes.

1. Proposed 45% National TV Ownership Limit

The FCC said a company could now own TV stations that reached up to a *45% share of U.S. TV households. Share would be determined by counting the number of TV households in each market* in which the company owns a station. Ratings would not matter. The number would therefore be based on every *potential* TV household. The FCC pointed this out to show that a 45% share of TV household would *not* equal a 45% share of TV stations in the United States.

A 50% UHF discount would apply. Owners would have to count only 50% of their audiences for UHF stations when calculating the 45% limit. The FCC said it did this to promote the growth of UHF stations, which have smaller signal coverage areas than VHF stations. However, once the transition to digital TV is complete, the UHF discount would be eliminated for stations owned by the Big Four networks.

These new rules would not result in huge media consolidation. To prove this, the FCC noted that there were 1340 commercial TV stations in the United States as of March 31, 2003. Of those, the biggest owner, Viacom, owned only 39 (2.9%). Fox owned 37 (2.8%), NBC owned 29 (2.2%), and ABC owned 10 (0.8%).

In announcing the 45% limit, the FCC responded to the court in the *Fox* case and said the previous 35% cap "did not strike the right balance of promoting localism and preserving free over-the-air television." It said that establishing a cap of 45% would still "protect localism by allowing a body of network affiliates to negotiate collectively with the broadcast networks on network programming decisions."[15] The commission said that boosting the limit to 45% would encourage networks to keep costly and popular programming, such as sporting events, on "free, over-the-air television."

2. Local TV Multiple Ownership Limits

From 1964 until 1999, the FCC used the TV Duopoly Rule to effectively ban any TV station from owning another TV station in the same market. In 1999, though, the FCC loosened the rule to allow some companies to own two TV stations in the same market under certain conditions (based on market size and the number of stations within a market).

In June 2003, the FCC loosened the restrictions even further, only banning TV duopolies in the smallest markets.

---

[14]280 F.3d 1027 (D.C. Cir. 2002)

[15]Federal Communications Commission. (2003, June 2). FCC sets limits on media concentration (news release). *NEWS*, p. 5.

Proposed Local TV Multiple Ownership Limits

In markets with five or more TV stations, a company may own two stations as long as both stations are not in the top four in the ratings. In markets with 18 or more TV stations, a company may now own three TV stations, as long as only one of the stations is in the top four in the ratings. In markets with 11 or fewer stations, the FCC will institute a waiver process for companies wishing to own two top-four stations. The commission will decide such matters on a case-by-case basis to determine if such dual ownerships would better serve the community than if the stations remained separate.

Both commercial and noncommercial TV stations are counted when deciding the number of stations in a market.

FAQ

Why did the FCC settle on this "top-four rating" idea?

The commission said it chose to base the new rule on a "top-four rating" because each one of the top four stations in most markets usually produces an independent local newscast. As a result, the commission said people would still be able to get news and information from a number of independent voices in each market. The FCC said the ban on top-four mergers would "have the effect of preserving viewpoint diversity in local markets."

3. Cross-Media Limits Rule

The FCC announced that this new rule would replace the radio-TV cross-ownership rules and the broadcast-newspaper rules.

In markets with three or fewer TV stations, *no* cross-ownership is allowed between TV, radio, and newspapers. A company may get a waiver for this ban if it can show that the TV station does not serve the area served by the radio station or newspaper.

In markets with four to eight TV stations, only *one* of the following combinations is permitted: (a) A daily newspaper, one TV station, and up to half of the radio station limit for that market (e.g., if the radio station limit in a market is eight, the company can own up to four radio stations in this combination); (b) a daily newspaper and up to the limit for radio stations in that market (no ownership of a TV station would be permitted); *or* (c) two TV stations (if permissible under the new local TV multiple ownership limits mentioned earlier) and up to the limit for radio stations in that market (no daily newspaper ownership would be allowed).

For markets with nine or more TV stations, the FCC eliminated the TV-radio cross-ownership ban and the newspaper-broadcast cross-ownership ban.

The Diversity Index

The FCC said it established this three-tier system as part of what it called a Diversity Index. Their concern was for the number of independent media outlets delivering news and information in each market. The FCC said it wanted to ensure that there was a "diversity of viewpoints" available in local media. The commission explained the rationale behind each tier.

The smallest markets, those with three or fewer TV stations, are "sufficiently limited" in their media outlets. The FCC said any cross-ownership in these markets "would harm viewpoint diversity." Markets with four to eight TV stations are, obviously, less concentrated. The FCC felt that certain media combinations could occur without harming the diversity of viewpoints. The FCC said that the larger markets, those with nine or more TV stations, have enough media outlets to justify dropping old cross-ownership rules. The commission felt that current ownership limits for radio and TV "were more than sufficient to protect viewpoint diversity."

FCC chairman Michael Powell said that these new rules simply reflected the changing media landscape. For example, the commission said, "greater participation by newspaper publishers in the television and radio business would improve the quality and quantity of news available to the public."

4. Dual Network Ownership Prohibition

The FCC announced that it would continue to ban any mergers between the top four national broadcast networks.

5. Defining Radio Markets

The FCC ruled that noncommercial stations should be counted when determining the number of radio stations in a market. The commission also ruled that Arbitron Radio Metro numbers may be used to define, for ownership purposes, where one market starts and another ends.

2003 Ownership Changes Harshly Criticized

The sharpest criticism came from the two Democratic commissioners on the FCC, Michael Copps and Jonathan Adelstein. Adelstein was particularly harsh, calling the new rules "the most sweeping and destructive rollback of consumer protection rules in the history of American broadcasting." He added that "this Order simply makes it easier for existing media giants to gobble up more outlets and fortify their already massive market power."[16] Copps said he was "deeply saddened" by the "radical deregulation" created by the new rules and warned that the new rules gave "a handful of corporations awesome powers over our news, information, and entertainment."[17] Other critics joined in, saying these new rules would lead to the "Clear Channelization" of the TV industry.

The day after the new rules were announced, all five FCC commissioners appeared before the Senate Committee on Commerce, Science and Transportation. Most of the committee senators were highly critical of the new rules and sided with the

---

[16]Federal Communications Commission. (2003, June 2). Statement of Jonathan S. Adelstein, dissenting. *NEWS*, p. 1.

[17]Federal Communications Commission. (2003, June 2). Statement of Michael J. Copps, dissenting. *NEWS*, p. 1.

two dissenting Democratic commissioners. Commissioner Adelstein told the committee that the debate about changing the ownership rules resulted in a record number of Americans contacting the FCC. He said that 750,000 people had written, called, faxed and e-mailed the FCC and that "99.9% of them oppose further media consolidation." Adelstein added, "The public interest standard, if not dead, is mortally wounded."[18] A court would soon agree.

Court Blocks New Ownership Rules

In September 2003, the Third U.S. Circuit Court of Appeals blocked the new ownership rules from taking effect. Media groups that had been planning mergers under the new ownership rules were forced to put their plans on hold. In June 2004, a federal appeals court in Philadelphia sent the new rules back to the FCC, saying the commission had not provided sufficient justification for its numerical ownership limits in radio, TV, and cross-ownership. The court did uphold the FCC's inclusion of noncommercial stations in market counts, as well as the use of Arbitron Radio Metro for market definition.

NATIONAL CABLE OWNERSHIP RULES

To control the power of cable companies, the FCC has placed ownership restrictions on any multiple system operator (MSO). An MSO is a large company, such as Time Warner Cable, which operates cable systems across the country. Until October 1999, the FCC said that no MSO could serve more than 30% of all *cable* subscribers nationwide.

Then the rules changed. Starting in October 1999, the FCC said that no MSO would be allowed to serve more than 30% of all *multichannel video program distributors* (MVPDs) subscribers nationwide. MVPDs include cable systems *and* satellite TV services such as DBS. According to the FCC, roughly 22 million homes in 2001 received their TV programming through a DBS system, such as the Dish Network. Nearly 73 million were hooked up to cable that same year.

This new definition created problems for companies such as AT&T. AT&T was in the process of merging with Media One, but the merger would have given AT&T more than 30% of MVPD subscribers nationwide. AT&T and Time Warner called the 30% cap unconstitutional and took the FCC to court.

In *Time Warner v. FCC*,[19] a federal appeals court threw out the 30% cable ownership cap, saying the FCC had no justification for that limit. In fact, the court said the FCC's 30% limit appeared to have been "plucked . . . out of thin air." The court suggested that a 60% cap might be more reasonable and remanded the issue to the FCC for further consideration. So, for now, the 30% cap is gone, and the FCC is considering a 45% cap. It will be up to that same appeals court to determine whether the FCC can justify a new cable ownership cap.

---

[18]Adelstein, J. S. (2003, June 2). *Statement before the Senate Committee on Commerce, Science and Transportation hearing on FCC oversight.* p. 2. Retrieved June 10, 2003, from http://www.fcc.gov/Daily_Releases/Daily_Business/2003/db0602/DOC-235047A8.pdf

[19]240 F.3d 1126 (D.C. Cir. 2001)

ANTITRUST LAWS AND MEDIA MERGERS

Station owners must not only be aware of FCC rules but of possible violations of antitrust laws. The federal government, through the Department of Justice (DOJ), enforces antitrust laws, which prohibit unfair competition. This is also spelled out in Section 314 of the Communications Act of 1934, which prohibits broadcasters from engaging in any practice that "lessens competition or restrains commerce."[20]

The 1980s and 1990s saw a flurry of merger activity in the media, and some antitrust concerns arose as more and more media outlets were being owned by fewer and fewer companies. Merger activity was especially noticeable among the major TV networks. The once-dominant Big Three networks (ABC, CBS, and NBC) had seen their power and audience shares erode as cable and home video became more popular. The FCC was also becoming less opposed to mergers involving major broadcast companies. In 1986, the Big Three all changed hands. General Electric purchased RCA and, as a result, NBC. Capital Cities purchased ABC. Lawrence Tisch and his Loew's Inc. investment firm took control of CBS.

The ownership landscape for major TV networks continued to change dramatically in the 1990s. In 1995, Disney purchased Cap Cities (ABC), as well as cable sports giant ESPN. Also that year, Time Warner acquired Turner Broadcasting. Westinghouse bought CBS in 1996. Later that year, Westinghouse (CBS) merged with Infinity Broadcasting, which resulted in the creation of the second-largest radio group in the United States. In 1999, a merger with Viacom gave Westinghouse an additional 160 radio stations, 35 TV stations, several production companies, Blockbuster Video, MTV, Nickelodeon, Paramount Pictures, and the fledgling UPN network. As noted earlier in the chapter, one of the most controversial issues in this massive merger was that it gave the company control of two networks, CBS and UPN, a violation of network ownership rules. However, the FCC amended the rules in 2000 to allow dual network ownership as long as *both* networks are not among the Big Four.

The DOJ was also keeping its eye on the flurry of radio mergers after the passage of the Telecomm Act of 1996. That year, American Radio Systems proposed a $655 million dollar merger with EZ Communications. However, the DOJ only approved the merger after American Radio agreed to divest itself of two radio stations in Charlotte and Sacramento. For example, in Charlotte, the DOJ said the original merger would have given American Radio control of 55% of Charlotte's radio revenues, which the DOJ said was too much. By selling off a top-rated station, American Radio then owned seven stations and roughly 40% of Charlotte radio revenues. American radio had to amend a similar situation in Sacramento before the merger was approved.

Also in 1996, the DOJ put the brakes on a merger by Jacor Communications because it would have given the company control of 53% of Cincinnati radio ad revenues. Jacor was forced to sell a top-rated station before the DOJ finally approved the merger.

Australian media mogul Rupert Murdoch tested the limits of media ownership in the 1980s when he began purchasing American media companies. In 1985, Murdoch and his Australian-based company News Corp. purchased Twentieth Century Fox and bought seven TV stations from Metromedia for $2 billion. In 1986, Murdoch used those stations to launch

---

[20]Communication Act of 1934, 47 U.S.C. § 314 (1934)

the Fox Television Network. Murdoch had become a naturalized U.S. citizen in 1985 to comply with FCC rules prohibiting a foreigner from owning broadcast stations. At the same time, a foreign company was allowed to have up to a 25% interest in an American broadcast station.

FAQ

If Murdoch's company News Corp. was based in Australia, didn't this create other foreign ownership problems?

It did. In 1994, Murdoch was eager to turn Fox TV into a competitive fourth TV network, and he paid $500 million to New World Communications for 12 TV stations which then abandoned their affiliations with CBS, NBC, and ABC. In 1995, News Corp. announced another deal that would have led to more Big Three affiliates switching to Fox. Four of those stations were NBC affiliates, and NBC filed a complaint with the FCC, claiming that Murdoch and News Corp. may have been violating the commission's 25% limit on foreign ownership of broadcast stations.

After an investigation by the FCC's Mass Media Bureau, the commission ruled that News Corp. had indeed exceeded the 25% limit because, although Murdoch had 76% of the voting shares, Australian-based News Corp. had true control over Fox because it supplied 99% of the funds to purchase the stations. Still, the FCC was eager to see a fourth TV network emerge, feeling that it would benefit the public interest. As a result, the FCC urged Murdoch to seek a waiver of the 25% limit, and it was granted.

Low-Power FM Stations

As mentioned, the new radio ownership rules in the Telecomm Act of 1996 led to rapid consolidation in the radio industry in the late 1990s. Large companies began buying radio stations across the country, and the number of radio stations with local ownership was shrinking. Critics said radio stations were no longer focused on serving their local communities.

In response, the FCC decided to encourage the development of low-power radio stations that would be more focused on serving local communities. These stations would be called low-power FM (LPFM). In January 2000, the FCC approved this new class of radio stations, "designed to serve very localized communities or underrepresented groups within a community."[21] For LPFM guidelines, see Figure 5.1.

FAQ

You say that LPFM stations aren't allowed to act as "translators." What is a translator?

---

[21]Federal Communications Commission. (2000, January 20). *FCC approves new non-commercial low power FM radio service*. MM Docket No. 99-25.

1. Parties may apply for one of two classes of LPFM:
   a. LP10: power from 1-10 watts (service radius of 1-2 miles).
   b. LP100: power from 50-100 watts (service radius of about 3.5 miles).

2. Parties eligible for LPFM licenses
   a. Noncommercial educational institutions (government or private)
   b. Nonprofit groups with educational purposes
   c. Nonprofit or government groups providing local public safety or transportation services

3. Dial location
   a. LPFM stations are allowed to be located anywhere on the FM dial, provided that the LPFM signal does not interfere with any existing radio station's signal.

4. License term
   a. LPFM stations will be licensed for 8-year, renewable terms.

5. Ownership rules
   a. During the first 2 years, a party may operate only one LPFM station nationwide. After 2 years, a party may own up to five LPFMs. After 3 years, a party may own up to ten stations nationwide.
   b. No existing broadcaster or other media entity may own an LPFM or provide programming services to an LPFM.

6. LPFM broadcast programming rules
   a. LPFM stations must broadcast at least 36 hours per week.
   b. LPFM stations must air a station identification every hour. Call letters for the stations will consist of four letters followed by the letters LP.
   c. LPFM stations are required to follow certain FCC rules, including sponsorship identification, political programming, and prohibitions on indecent and obscene programming. They must take part in the national Emergency Alert System.
   d. LPFM stations are *not* required to keep a public file, file ownership reports, or adhere to the Main Studio Rule.
   e. LPFM stations may not operate as translators.

7. If there are competing applications for an LPFM license within a community, the following factors work in favor of an applicant:
   a. Pledging to operate at least 12 hours daily
   b. Pledging to air at least 8 hours of local programming daily
   c. Verifying an established community presence for at least 2 years before the application
   d. Having physical headquarters within 10 miles of the station the applicant plans to operate or having 75% of the station's board members living within 10 miles of the station.

8. Pirate broadcasters (someone who is broadcasting illegally, without an FCC license) are allowed to apply for LPFM licenses if they
   a. voluntarily stopped broadcasting illegally as of February 26, 1999
   b. stopped illegal broadcasts within 24 hours of an FCC order to do so

Figure 5.1   Low-Power FM Radio Guidelines

A translator is basically a radio station "repeater." Example: Jonesville is a small community with no radio stations, and it is surrounded by mountains. As a result, people there cannot not receive a popular FM station from Smithtown, 20 miles away. So Jonesville places a translator on top of one of the mountains. The translator is able to pick up the signal from the Smithtown FM station. The translator then rebroadcasts that Smithtown FM station signal clearly to the people in Jonesville. It is like a cable system for radio, without the cables.

The FCC does not want LPFMs operating as translators because the main goal of translator stations is to bring in a distant signal. LPFM stations are supposed to be local.

Competing Applications. The FCC says diversity and local ownership are encouraged when it gives preference to applicants who are physically headquartered within 10 miles of the station they plan to operate or who have 75% of their board members living within 10 miles of the station.

Pirate Broadcasting. According to the LPFM Guidelines, any person who continued pirate broadcasting after being ordered by the FCC to desist was ineligible for an LPFM license. In 2000, Congress made this provision a law when it passed the Radio Broadcasting Preservation Act.

In 2002, though, a federal appeals court found the provision unconstitutional. The court said the FCC could not deny an LPFM license to a person just because that person had engaged in pirate broadcasting. The court said the FCC could take a history of pirate broadcasting into account when considering LPFM licenses, but the commission could not give blanket denials to former "pirates."

As of June 2003, the FCC reported that 195 LPFM stations were on the air, and more than 2400 applications had been received. The largest numbers of LPFM applicants were from religious organizations. Programming on LPFM stations tends to include music, news, weather, information, local sports coverage, and community events. The stations are usually run by volunteers. It has to be stressed that LPFM stations *must* operate as non-commercial entities. In 2004, the FCC sent a letter of admonishment to WLFK-LP in Eau Claire, WI, for broadcasting underwriting announcements that sounded too much like advertisements.[22]

Opposition to LPFM

The National Association of Broadcasters and some large broadcast groups, such as National Public Radio, did not feel that the FCC had done enough to make sure that new LPFM stations would not interfere with the signals of existing broadcasters. The NAB was successful in lobbying Congress to pass the Third Adjacent Channel Requirement of the Radio Preservation Act in 2000. This act requires that LPFM stations not be located closer than three "channels" to an existing high-power broadcast station. On FM, a channel represents 0.2 MHz. So, for example, if a high-power station is broadcasting at 102.7 FM, an LPFM could only get as close as 102.1 FM or 103.3 FM.

---

[22]FCC cautions LPFM about airing ads. (2004, November 9). *Radio World Online.* Retrieved November 17, 2004, from http://rwonline.com/dailynews/one.php?id=6168

In 2004, the FCC urged that the restrictions in the 2000 act be dropped, citing a study that showed LPFMs had posed "no significant risk" to existing broadcasters. The FCC also argued that the "three channel" rule was keeping LPFMs off the air in some markets. The NAB responded by calling the FCC study "deeply flawed" and argued that the FCC drop its opposition to the 2000 act.

LOW-POWER TELEVISION (LPTV)

LPTV has been in existence since 1982. LPTV was devised by the FCC for reasons very similar to those for LPFM development. The FCC wanted to bring TV stations to smaller communities or certain sections of large urban areas. Two thirds of LPTV stations are in rural areas. The FCC says LPTV is designed to provide programming "tailored to the interests and self-expression of viewers."[23] LPTV stations are restricted to an effective radiated power of 150 kilowatts for UHF and 3 kilowatts for VHF. Depending on several factors, including antenna height and surrounding terrain, an LPTV signal can reach more than 20 miles. LPTV stations must not interfere with the signals of existing or future full-service TV stations, but they must accept interference from full-service stations.

FAQ

Does the FCC have fewer regulations for LPTV, just as it does for LPFM?

Yes. As with LPFM, the FCC places fewer regulations on LPTV. This makes it easier for people to start and maintain the stations. LPTV stations are not required to maintain public files, and there are no minimum hours of operation required. LPTV stations, unlike LPFM stations, may accept advertising or offer subscription programming to viewers. LPTV operators may create their own programming or purchase it from other sources. There are no limits on how many LPTV stations may be owned by one entity. National commercial networks and broadcast licensees may own and operate LPTV stations; LPTV stations are not included in the FCC cross-ownership rules.

As of 2001, there were more than 2000 LPTV stations, 250 of which made up a statewide network in Alaska. Most LPTV stations are operated by religious organizations, colleges, high schools, local governments, and private citizens. Persons may apply for LPTV licenses from the FCC during designated 2-month filing windows each year.

There are also 5000 TV translators in the United States. Most of these translators are in western states, rebroadcasting the signals of full-service stations.

LOCAL MARKETING AGREEMENTS (LMA)

An example of an LMA is a case in which one TV station assists a second TV station (or brokered station) in the same market with its day-to-day operations, but each TV station

---

[23]Federal Communications Commission. (2001, November). *FCC fact sheet: Low power television*. Retrieved August 7, 2002, from http://www.fcc.gov/mb/video/files/LPTVFactSheet.html

is owned by a different company. In 2000, the FCC said that "the majority of LMAs will become permissible under the new TV Duopoly rule or related waiver policies." The amount of time brokered must be more than 15% of the brokered station's weekly broadcast hours.

FCC chairman Michael Powell has commented numerous times that he believes LMAs are a dying breed. He says new ownership rules will eventually allow most LMAs to be owned outright by another station.

SUMMARY

As seen in this chapter, the trend is toward fewer ownership rules for the media.

Deregulation in 1996 led to a consolidation of the radio industry, the most prominent example being Clear Channel, which now owns roughly 1250 radio stations in America. Deregulation opponents say corporate-owned radio stations do not do as good of a job serving the public interest as do locally owned stations. The big media companies will argue, though, that it is just the free marketplace at work.

Critics will continue to argue that the newer rules are leading to fewer and fewer media companies gaining more and more power. In 2003, the FCC announced new ownership rules for TV, as well as cross-media rules affecting TV, radio, and newspaper ownership, but a federal court in 2004 struck down those new limits. Opponents of such changes argue that the public is being deprived of the opportunity to get news and information from a diversity of sources. The FCC, though, says the public has many other sources of information nowadays, with such options as cable, satellite, and the Internet.

One response to the ownership changes in the Telecomm Act of 1996 was the introduction of LPFM radio. These low-powered FM stations are designed to serve their immediate communities and bring back more local ownership in response to national companies buying up local broadcast stations.

6

BROADCAST STATION REGULATIONS

Through firm, fast, flexible and fair enforcement of the Communications Act and the FCC's rules, promote competition, protect consumers, and foster efficient use of the spectrum while furthering public safety goals.

—Mission statement, FCC Enforcement Bureau

P robably the biggest responsibility for a station owner is making sure the station is following FCC guidelines. This chapter provides an analysis of these rules, one by one.

BROADCAST IDENTIFICATIONS

Station Identification (or Legal Identification)

A broadcast station must identify itself at three different times.

Hourly. Station identification (ID) must be given "as close to the hour as feasible, at a natural break in program offerings."[1] Many radio stations instruct their staff to play the station ID within 2 minutes of the top of the hour. Stations often try to program their music so the ID comes as close to the top of the hour as possible. It is often easier for TV stations to play the ID at the exact time because of their more fixed programming schedules.

At the Beginning and End of Each Time of Operation. This rule applies to stations that are not on the air 24 hours a day.

After an Interruption in the Broadcast Signal. For example, if an electrical storm knocks a station off the air for 30 minutes, someone must broadcast the station ID as soon as the station is back on the air.

---

[1]See 47 C.F.R. § 73.1201 (as of Oct. 1, 2001)

Content

A station ID for a radio station *must* contain two elements: (a) call letters, followed by (b) community(s) specified in the station's license as its location. For television stations, the ID must contain the same two elements, as well as the station's channel number.

The Code of Federal Regulation states that other information *may* be "inserted between the call letters and station location"; specifically: name of the licensee and the station's frequency. The Code of Federal Regulation notes, "No other insertions are permitted." (The name of the licensee and the frequency may also be placed *before* the call letters.)

The names of additional or surrounding communities may be added after the station location is named. However, the community of origin must come *first*.

AM and FM stations that simulcast may do a joint station ID, provided the stations are owned by the same licensee.

FAQ

Is it legal to use promotional language or station names in a station ID?

The Code of Federal Regulation makes no mention of any other types of information being allowed in a legal ID. As a result, some communication attorneys advise their client stations to avoid using promotional language ("Your Hit Music Leader") or a station name ("Mix 99") in station IDs. However, other attorneys say such uses are fine as long as the call letters and city of origin are included. To be safe, though, it might be better to avoid any information not mentioned specifically in the Code of Federal Regulation.

For example, acceptable station IDs might include

"WIUS, Macomb."

"WMQZ, Macomb, Colchester, Blandinsville."

"WIUS, 88.3 FM, Macomb."

"WIGS, Scope Broadcasting, Smithtown."

"This is 88.3 FM, WIUS, Macomb."

Examples of unacceptable station IDs:

"WIUS, Colchester, Macomb." (The city of origin, Macomb, must come first.)

"88.3 FM, Macomb." (The ID must include the call letters.)

FAQ

Is it OK to use music and sound effects in a legal ID?

Yes. Just make sure the call letters and city of origin are understandable.

IMPORTANT STATION PAPERWORK

Logs

Station Logs

All stations must maintain and keep station operating (transmitter) logs. All station logs must include the following:

1. Entries concerning problems with any tower light, regardless of its position on the tower. (This rule does not apply to all stations. For example, some stations have their transmitters on the roofs of buildings instead of on towers.) Two important notes about tower lights: Tower lights must be monitored either by visual inspection at least *once every 24 hours* or by an automatic alarm system that constantly monitors the lights (these alarm systems must be inspected at least once every 3 months).

It is *recommended* that stations record the results of all tower light inspections in the station log. (This can be as simple as writing, "Tower lights on. Visual check 2:18 p.m.") Remember, this is only recommended, not required. If a steady-burning or flashing tower light is malfunctioning, the FCC requires the station to contact the Federal Aviation Administration (FAA) within 30 minutes. The station must contact the FAA again when the light is fixed. The station should post the phone number for the nearest FAA Flight Service Center where station personnel can find it easily.

2. Notation of weekly and monthly Emergency Alert System tests.

3. Entries concerning any transmitter problems and the amount of time the station was off the air.

FAQ

How long do stations have to keep these logs on file?

Station logs must be kept on file for 2 years. They are to be readily available for inspection or copying at the FCC's request. All station personnel should be aware of the location of the station logs file in case of an FCC inspection or a citizen request.

Program Logs

As of 1983, the FCC no longer requires that stations keep program logs. Today, the only stations required to keep program logs are *international* broadcast stations (stations based in the United States that broadcast to other countries). Their logs are similar to the program logs previously required for all U.S. broadcast stations.

Their logs must note the exact time a station ID was played. Also, the logs must have entries describing every program broadcast, including the title, sponsor(s), the time the program started and ended, the language in which the program was broadcast, and a brief description of the program type (music, news, drama, etc.).

POWER READINGS

FM stations stronger than 10 watts and all AM stations must maintain operating power between 90% and 105% of their authorized limit. Many stations today have their reading checked automatically by a computer. However, there are still stations where readings are checked manually in the studio or through a telephone system.

FAQ

How often do stations need to take power readings?

The FCC simply mandates that stations conduct "sufficient metering" of their power. This is rather ambiguous, but the standard practice at many stations today is to have on-air personnel check the readings every 3 hours and record the readings in the station log. Other stations have automated systems monitor their power readings.

MAIN STUDIO RULES

A station's main studio must be located within the community of license (within the principal community contour), or it may be located within 25 miles of the center of the community of license, whichever is the largest. (For many communities, the official center is the Post Office.) The main studio must be capable of originating programming and should be a fully functional facility.

The FCC says a person must be at the station's main studio for a total of 8 hours each weekday. Those 8 hours must fall between 8:00 a.m. and 6:00 p.m. Stations that have five or more full-time employees must make sure there is one management-level person and one full-time staff person assigned to the main studio. The FCC says that these persons must spend a "substantial amount of time" at the main studio each weekday. Stations with fewer than five full-time employees only need to have a management-level person "report" to the main studio each weekday.

In 2004, the FCC fined WMSR-AM in Manchester, TN, $7000 for failing to have a meaningful staff presence at its main studio during business hours. The fine resulted from a 2002 incident when an FCC field inspector found no staff members at the station's main studio and several phones calls led only to an answering machine message.

FAQ

What if a station can't afford to pay an FCC fine?

That is what WMSR argued in this case, saying the $7000 fine would be a "financial strain." The FCC does sometimes lower fines if such penalties would bankrupt a station. However, in this case, the FCC upheld the ruling when it determined that the fine represented a "small percentage" of the station's gross revenues.

THE EMERGENCY ALERT SYSTEM

As of July 1, 1996, all broadcast stations must have equipment capable of receiving and sending digital EAS signals. The deadline for all cable systems was 2002.

EAS, formerly the Emergency Broadcast System, is designed to inform the public about national or regional emergencies. It is a cooperative effort between the FCC and broadcasters, the National Weather Service, and the Federal Emergency Management Administration. Initially, the system was designed so that the president would be able to address the nation during a national crisis, although no president has used it.

The newer EAS system has several advantages over the old Emergency Broadcast System system. The digital technology allows state and local officials to send out emergency information to specific local areas. EAS can be programmed to interrupt programming automatically, even if no one is at the broadcast station (this is a great advantage for, e.g., automated radio stations). The EAS digital signal is identical to the signal used by the National Weather Service for its National Oceanic and Atmospheric Administration Weather Radio. This allows broadcasters to retransmit National Weather Service weather alerts immediately through the EAS system.

The new EAS tests are shorter and "less obtrusive," according to the FCC. Officials believe that listeners and viewers will thus take the messages more seriously. People were more likely to "tune out" during the older, longer tests. EAS digital messages can also be converted into any language used by the cable system or broadcast station.

Basic EAS Rules for Stations

First, stations must keep a copy of the most recent version of the *EAS Handbook* next to their EAS equipment. The handbook can be downloaded from the FCC's Web site at http://www.fcc.gov.

Required Weekly Tests (RWT)

To make sure each station's EAS equipment is functioning properly, the FCC requires broadcasters to test the equipment once a week. This is done in two ways.

1. Receiving Weekly Tests. Stations receive an RWT from two nearby broadcast stations that are required to send these tests. The stations are designated as "local primaries": LP1 and LP2. A station's EAS receiver must be tuned to receive both the LP1 and the LP2. These two stations are responsible for sending out weekly tests of the EAS two-tone attention signal to make sure it is transmitting properly. The weekly tests are to be done on *random days and times at any time of the day or night.*

When a station receives an RWT from the LP1 and LP2, the EAS unit will print out a receipt indicating that the station has received its weekly test. Stations are required to keep records of all EAS tests, so this receipt should be stapled or taped to the station's transmitter log. *These tests do not have to be broadcast.* However, the next test does have to be done over the air.

2. Sending Weekly Tests. A station also needs to broadcast an RWT, which consists of transmitting the EAS tones once a week. These tests should be done on different days at different times. Most stations conduct the test in a manner similar to the following: "This station [call letters] is conducting a test of the Emergency Alert System. The following tones would be heard in an emergency." The announcer then presses "Weekly Test" on the EAS unit, and the EAS tones transmit for at least 8 seconds. The announcer (or, more usually, a recording) then says: "These tones were a test of the Emergency Alert System. If this had been a real emergency, official messages would have followed these test tones, or you may have been instructed to tune to another broadcast station in our area for vital information. That concludes this test of the Emergency Alert System." The EAS unit will print out a receipt of the test, which should be attached to the station's transmitter log. If the printer on the EAS is not working, the date and time of the RWT should be written on the log.

Required Monthly Tests (RMT)

Stations must also receive and log a *monthly test* sent by the LP1 and LP2 stations. In odd-numbered months, the test is to be done between 8:30 a.m. and sunset. In even-numbered months, the test is done between sunset and 8:30 a.m. Monthly tests are coordinated by each state's Emergency Communications Committee.

In 2002, the FCC ruled that an RMT must be retransmitted by a station within 60 minutes of its receipt. Many stations set their EAS units to do this automatically. The EAS unit will print out a receipt of this test, and it should be attached to the transmitter log. If the printer unit of an EAS system is out of paper or malfunctioning, station personnel should simply write the date and time of the test on the transmitter log.

Note: During weeks in which there are monthly tests, stations are not required to do a weekly test.

If there are problems sending or receiving any EAS tests, the station must make notation of these problems in the transmitter log. This must include the date and time of any EAS equipment repairs or outages. Stations that violate EAS rules face a maximum fine of $32,500 per day and up to a total of $325,000 for a "continuing violation."

FAQ

Was EAS activated on September 11, 2001 during the terrorist attacks?

No. In fact, critics complained that the system had become obsolete because EAS was not activated during the September 11 terrorist attacks. Those critics charged that if there had ever been a reason that warranted a use of EAS, September 11 provided it.

However, the FCC said that all major radio and TV networks were covering the events that day, and no one knew the events were terrorist related until the second plane hit the World Trade Center on live television. Thus, an EAS message would have been unnecessary and annoying because it would have interrupted important news coverage of the events. The system was designed to alert people to a national emergency, and the national news media had already made the public aware of the situation that day.

FAQ

If EAS is not used for major events like 9/11, what is its major purpose today?

EAS is most often activated on the local level for weather emergencies, such as flash floods, severe thunderstorms, and tornadoes.

However, in 2004, the president of the Florida Association of Broadcasters, Pat Roberts, complained that the vast majority of local and state governments do not know how to access EAS in case of emergencies. One problem is that the FCC does not require state and local governments to be connected to EAS. Roberts said he could think of only "three or four states where EAS works."

EAS has been successful, however, in the search for missing children.

EAS and the "Amber Alert"

In the summer of 2002, the national news media gave prominent coverage to numerous cases involving the kidnappings and murders of children. As a result, the nation also became more aware of something known as America's Missing: Broadcast Emergency Response, usually called the Amber Plan or the Amber Alert System.

Initially, the Amber Plan was named in memory of 9-year-old Amber Hagerman, who had been riding her bike in Arlington, TX, in 1996 when she was kidnapped and murdered. Soon after, local residents called radio and TV stations suggesting a new broadcast alert system for child kidnappings. The idea involved having police contact local media immediately after the report of a kidnapping. Local broadcast stations would then air an "alert" about the missing child. The idea soon caught on nationwide but not as a coordinated national program. Instead, it was up to individual states to determine whether they wanted to adopt their own Amber Alert systems. As a result, in the summer of 2002, when child abductions were making national headlines, only 21 states had working Amber Alert systems in place.

Prior to this, in February 2002, the FCC had amended the Emergency Alert System rules to include a new Child Abduction Emergency Code that could be used to activate various state Amber Plans. Stations were not required to add this code to their existing EAS equipment. The FCC simply gave broadcast stations and cable systems permission to update their EAS equipment to make it capable of receiving and transmitting Amber Alerts from and to law enforcement officials. However, in an effort to get more states to adopt the Amber Alert system, the FCC said that any EAS equipment installed after February 1, 2004 must be capable of receiving and transmitting the new Amber codes.

In the autumn of 2002, both the U.S. House and Senate passed legislation to provide federal funding that would help states set up Amber Alert systems. President Bush signed the bill into law in 2003.

FAQ

Do Amber Alerts really work very well?

In September 2003, the National Center for Missing and Exploited Children announced that the Amber Alert system had helped rescue 100 children in 7 years. One famous example was in August 2002 in California, when a man kidnapped two teenage girls from their cars at a "lover's lane" area. Authorities issued an Amber Alert, and broadcasters provided the girls' descriptions, as well as a description of the kidnapper and the stolen truck he was driving. Electric roadside signs alerted motorists to tune to specific radio stations for details. Twelve hours later, a state Animal Control officer spotted the stolen truck in a remote area and recognized it from the Amber Alert details. Police converged on the scene, and the kidnapper was shot and killed. Police said the girls were probably 10 minutes away from being murdered by their abductor. The man apparently had taken the girls to the remote area to kill and bury them. Officials credited the Amber Alert System with saving the teenage girls' lives.

FAQ

Isn't there a potential for too many Amber Alerts to be issued, or even false alerts, thus reducing its effectiveness?

Officials foresaw the potential problems. That is why most states require that certain guidelines be met before an Amber Alert is issued. Law enforcement officials must have confirmed an abduction and must believe a child (under 16 years old) is in danger of serious injury or death. Also, there must be enough information about the child or the abductor so that an immediate broadcast would be helpful. The information could include a description of the child or the kidnapper or details about an abductor's vehicle. Many states also use electric roadside signs to notify motorists about current Amber Alerts.

FAQ

Are Amber Alerts usually broadcast nationally?

In most instances, an Amber Alert is not broadcast too far outside of the kidnapping area. Officials fear that issuing nationwide or statewide alerts too frequently would make the alerts lose their significance and urgency with the public. The state of Texas, for example, issues the alert within a 200-mile radius of the abduction.

As of January 2005, Hawaii was the only state without an Amber Alert plan.

CHIEF OPERATORS AND LOGS

Every station must specify a chief operator, a person responsible for ensuring that a broadcast station is following all FCC technological requirements.

Guidelines for Chief Operators

The station must notify the FCC in writing of the name of the chief operator, who must hold a commercial radio operator license or permit. The name of the chief operator must be in writing at the station. A copy of this document should be posted at the station or be readily available. All station personnel should know the name of the chief operator.

The chief operator is responsible for reviewing station logs at least once a week to determine if required entries are being made properly. The chief operator must then sign and date the logs each week. He or she must also oversee regular inspections of monitoring, metering, and transmitter systems.

FAQ

Who qualifies as a chief operator?

The chief operator should be someone with engineering and technical experience who has a working knowledge of broadcasting equipment.

PUBLIC INSPECTION FILE

The FCC requires that broadcast stations and operators of translators keep what is called a *public file*. The file is meant to provide the general public with basic information about such matters as broadcasting regulations, the responsibility that broadcasters have to the public, and how the public may file complaints against broadcasters. When the FCC does spot inspections of stations, an inspector often asks to see the public file as the first order of business. In October 2003, the FCC fined 28 radio stations $3000 each for not complying with some element of the public file requirements in the following list.

A radio station's public inspection file must contain these items:

1. Most current *FCC authorization* to construct or operate the station

2. All *FCC applications* and related materials

3. *Citizen agreements,* if any (usually for noncommercial purposes). These are written agreements between a licensee and local citizens regarding employment practices, programming, or community concerns

4. Current *contour maps* that show the main studio and transmitter locations (not all stations are required to have contour maps)

5. The most recent *FCC ownership reports* for the station and related materials

6. *Political file* (a record of all broadcasts made by politicians for any public office)

7. *Equal Employment Opportunity file,* which ensures that the station is not discriminatory in its hiring practices (the FCC is reevaluating its EEO rules to comply with recent court rulings)

8. The most recent version of the FCC manual *The Public and Broadcasting* (the updated edition may be downloaded from the FCC Web site)

9. *Letters and e-mails from the public* (noncommercial stations are excluded from this rule, but for commercial stations, all written comments and complaints from the public about the station must be kept for 3 years)

10. Noncommercial stations must keep *lists of donors* who support specific programs, and this list must remain in the file for 2 years after the program airs

11. Until the FCC says a station may discard it, the station must keep material related to any *FCC inquiry or investigation*

12. TV stations only—documentation showing compliance with Children's Programming Rules and commercial limits in children's programming. Also, documentation of any must-carry/retransmission consent agreements

13. Issues and Programs List

The final element in the public file, the *Issues and Programs List*, is the one that takes up the most space. Every quarter (every 3 months), the station must compile a list of programs that have served the public interest and given "significant treatment" to community issues during the previous 3 months. This list must be completed and placed in the public file within 10 days of the end of the quarter. The station must keep these lists for the entire license term (8 years). All descriptions of programs must include the title of each program, the length of the program, a brief narrative describing the issues discussed, and the date and time the program aired.

FAQ

What kinds of programs would qualify for this part of the file?

Operators of broadcast stations are often unsure about what types of programming qualify as serving the public interest. In a 1960 Programming Policy Statement,[2] the FCC enumerated 14 types of programs that contain elements necessary to serve the public interest: call-in, write-in, or interview shows on which local citizens can express opinions on important issues; opportunities for local self-expression (guest commentaries or editorials, etc.); public affairs shows that discuss important local issues; educational shows; religious programs; children's programs; political broadcasts; news programs; agricultural programs; programs that serve minority groups (including music shows); sports programs; station editorials about important issues; weather and market reports; and entertainment programming (for example, playing music that meets the needs of a certain audience).

In this 1960 report, the FCC gave stations guidelines for a minimum amount of news and public affairs programming that should be broadcast. By the 1980s, the FCC dropped these requirements because of increased competition from other media. The FCC said competition such as cable TV helped serve the public interest. Therefore, the FCC was much less strict about how broadcast stations could "serve the public interest."

Still, though, the FCC does require stations to serve the public interest and provide evidence of "significant treatment" of public issues. What is "significant?" Most stations try to air one longer public affairs show each week (30 minutes or an hour) or numerous short public affairs programs (5 minutes each) throughout the week. These shows, along with several other types of programming from the list, will usually demonstrate to the FCC that a station is meeting its public interest obligation.

FAQ

Where should the public file be kept?

If the main studio is located within its community of license, then the public file must be kept at that studio. All stations whose main studio is not located within their community of license must keep their file at any place easily accessible to the public within the

---

[2]*En Banc Programming Inquiry*, 44 F.C.C. 2303 (1960)

community of license. There are stations, for example, that have kept their public files at local convenience stores. The stations just have to make sure the employees at such places are aware of the file and the basic rules surrounding it. Also, all station personnel should know where to find the public file. The FCC expects station employees to know its location.

Wherever it is located, the public file must be readily available to the public or the FCC during regular business hours and be available for photocopying or other reproduction.

The Station Copy of FCC Rules and Regulations

Each broadcast station is required to maintain a current copy of FCC rules and regulations, as found in CFR-47, sections 11, 17, 25, 73, and 74. Stations must be able to produce these documents on request. Copies are available for purchase from the Federal Printing Service.

Telephone Rules

Recording Interstate Telephone Conversations. The laws regarding the recording of phone conversations vary from state to state. Some states require that only one party know the phone call is being recorded; other states require the consent of both parties. It is the responsibility of broadcasters to know the laws in their states. Every broadcaster needs to be aware of FCC regulations regarding *interstate* phone calls. In such instances, the caller must tell the other party the phone call is being recorded. This can be handled in three ways: you can get permission from all parties before calling, you can ask for permission at the start of the recording, or you can use a "beep tone" that is repeated at intervals throughout the call.[3]

Broadcasting Telephone Conversations. When broadcasting telephone calls, *the station must inform the caller beforehand that the call will be broadcast.* This rule applies to both live and recorded phone calls.

FAQ

But I hear DJs violate this rule all the time with such things as airing "surprise calls" to unsuspecting people. Is this wrong?

Yes. This type of gimmick is popular especially with radio morning show DJs, and it is a violation of the phone rule. Typically, the DJ makes a call to a person and broadcasts that person's "surprise" reaction to being on the air. This is illegal because the person on the phone did not give any prior consent for the phone conversation to be aired. Some people who are the targets of such pranks contact the FCC, and the commission does not hesitate to fine the station.

---

[3]Can we tape? (2000, Spring). *Reporter's Committee for the Freedom of the Press.* Retrieved June 28, 2002, from http://www.rcfp.org/taping/fcc.html

FAQ

What if the DJ obtains the person's consent on the air? Is this OK?

This also is not acceptable. Consider this situation. While on the air, a DJ calls a person at random and airs the sound of the phone ringing and the person picking up the phone to say "Hello?" The DJ says immediately, "This is All Hits 99. You're live on the air. You could win $1000 right now if you can answer two questions. May we continue to air this phone call?" The person then gives approval and tries to answer the questions. However, the FCC would say this is a violation of the telephone rule because the "Hello" was aired without prior consent. You must get consent from the person before *any* portion of the phone call is recorded or broadcast.

The FCC is very strict about prior consent. In 1993, a radio station in Utah got a $5000 fine when its DJs were doing a "remote" broadcast. They took an incoming phone call, assuming that people back in the studio had informed the caller the conversation would be broadcast. However, the caller had not been informed. The station said it was an innocent mistake, but the FCC fined the station anyway.[4]

FAQ

What about contests where the DJ takes phone calls live on the air as part of the contest?

This is legal because there is "implied consent" on the part of the caller. For example, radio stations frequently air contests that involve the DJ saying something like, "I'll take the first caller right now on our live phone line." Then the DJ takes the first call and says, "Hi. You're on the air, and you're the first caller. You've won. What's your name?" This is acceptable because the FCC says the telephone rule does not apply to "conversations whose broadcast can reasonably be presumed." The person knew that calling this phone number could result in the conversation being broadcast; therefore there was prior consent.

Implied consent also protects formats like news-talk where airing live phone calls is a regular and expected part of the programming. When people call these radio stations, they are calling with the intent of getting on the air. There is no deception by the station.

The "Live" Rule

Broadcast stations may not say or even insinuate that a broadcast is live when it is not.

---

[4]See 8 F.C.C.R. 6735 (1993)

Live Newscasts and Teasers

In 1992, a small radio station in upstate New York aired a teaser 5 minutes before a newscast. The teaser said, "Here are the stories we are working on for the top of the hour." However, the newsperson had recorded the newscast earlier. The FCC ruled that the teaser gave the impression the newscast was live. The resulting fine: $5000.

Live News Reports

The same rationale applies to live news reports. A typical example would be a radio station doing election night coverage, during which a reporter phones in a report from the county courthouse. A person at the station records the reporter's story. The recorded story airs 10 minutes later and begins with the reporter saying "I'm live at the courthouse." The station might argue that this situation is legitimate because the reporter was still at the courthouse when the report aired, so technically the reporter was still there live. The FCC does not see it that way. Although the reporter may still be there, "live," the recorded report that aired was not live. This would be a violation of the live rule.

Stations must apply this rule to other live remote broadcasts as well. The basic rule is this: *A broadcaster should never say he or she is "live" in a recording.*

FAQ

What about TV news reporters who record their reports but end those reports with a phrase like, "Now, back to you in the studio." Doesn't this falsely imply that the report is live?

No. In the news business, these types of reports are called "look lives." There is no direct insinuation that the reporter is live, so it is not a violation. Simply saying "back to you" or similar phrasing does not directly imply that the report is "live." The reporter must still avoid the word *live*, however.

The live rule is meant to keep broadcast stations from misrepresenting themselves to the public. The next form of misrepresentation can be much more serious, but the FCC, surprisingly, did not have any rules about it until the 1990s.

Broadcast Hoaxes

Section 325(a) of the Communication Act of 1934 states, "No person within the jurisdiction of the United States shall knowingly utter or transmit, or cause to be uttered or transmitted, any false or fraudulent signal of distress, or communication relating thereto."[5] The famous *War of the Worlds* radio broadcast in 1939 demonstrated the power of false messages over the airwaves. The broadcast was not intentionally false, but it did include a fake radio newscast announcing that Martians had invaded Earth. Many listeners who had not heard the disclaimer at the start of the show believed that the newscast was real and panicked. Frantic listeners clogged switchboards at police stations, and there were numerous traffic accidents reported as a result of people scrambling to escape the "alien invasion."

---

[5]47 U.S.C. § 325 (a) (1994)

In the early 1990s, the FCC suddenly realized it had no established guidelines about what constituted false or fraudulent distress signals. Several on-air hoaxes at radio stations forced the FCC to formulate new policies.

Volcano in Connecticut?

In 1990, WCCM-FM in Hartford, CT, falsely broadcast a report that a volcano had erupted in the area. Listeners took the joke seriously, jamming police phone lines to ask about the "natural disaster." The fake broadcast also led to traffic jams, as people tried to escape from the area.

The FCC said no specific rules had been broken by this fake announcement, and the FCC simply sent the station a Letter of Admonishment (such letters are a "slap on the wrist" to warn stations about a potentially bad activity). The next situation, though, was a definite violation of the rules.

Fake Nuclear Attack

In January 1991, two weeks after the beginning of the Persian Gulf War, disc jockey John Ulett at KSHE-FM in St. Louis broadcast a fake report about a nuclear attack on the United States during the Persian Gulf War. Ulett interrupted a song with a 10-second broadcast tone and then aired a different announcer saying, "Ladies and gentlemen, we are experiencing technical difficulties. Please stand b—" The sound of an air raid siren cut off the announcement, and another announcer said: "Attention! Attention! The United States is under nuclear attack!"

Ulett played sounds of explosions and screams, repeated the broadcast tone, had the first announcer say normal broadcasting would soon resume, and then music came back on.[6] Two hours later, Ulett got on the air and said the broadcast was a joke and that he wanted to make a statement about nuclear war. The station also aired several apologies throughout the day, and another apology was run the next day on a KSHE newscast.

The FCC said Ulett's broadcast "obviously had the potential to create widespread panic." The FCC fined KSHE $25,000 and said it was a "false distress signal" and an obvious violation of Section 325(a). The FCC was particularly disturbed by Ulett's use of the emergency broadcast tone to create the hoax. KSHE suspended Ulett for 1 week without pay, and the station created new guidelines for on-air staff regarding similar hoaxes. Ulett paid in other ways for his hoax. The St. Louis Cardinals fired Ulett as their public address announcer, a job he had held for 8 years.

The FCC had no problem labeling this broadcast as a false emergency broadcast. However, the FCC had trouble giving stiff punishments to several other on-air hoaxes because they did not qualify as "false distress signals."

"Confess Your Crime" Hoax

This highly publicized case began in June 1990 and was a major impetus for the FCC to create the antihoax rule. Two morning radio personalities, Kevin Ryder and Gene "Bean" Baxter, on KROQ-FM in Los Angeles, had a skit called "Confess Your Crime." The purpose of the skit was to have people call in and confess to minor law violations. On this day, an "anonymous" caller confessed on the air that he had badly beaten his girlfriend after he found her sleeping with another man.

---

[6]Searcy, D. R. (1991, April 24). *Letter to Emmis Broadcasting Co., licensee, KSHE (FM)*. 6 F.C.C.R. 2289 (1991)

DJ: Is there a chance, seriously, that you killed her?

Caller: Yeah, I know I did.

The caller then hung up. People called into the station to ask if it was a joke, but Baxter and Ryder said it was a "true confession." Local media reported the "confession," and the TV series "Unsolved Mysteries" did a segment on the alleged murder. The Los Angeles County Sheriff's Department spent 10 months investigating the "crime."

Almost a year later in April 1991, the two KROQ morning personalities revealed the call was a joke by another broadcaster named Doug Roberts. (KROQ actually hired Roberts shortly after the June 1990 broadcast, not realizing at the time that he had been part of the hoax.) After the revelation, the Los Angeles County Sheriff's Department said it was furious about the time it wasted investigating this "murder," and the department presented KROQ with a $12,000 bill to pay for its investigations. The station made the three DJs pay the bill, suspended the trio for 5 days without pay and made them each do 149 hours of community service.

Many were waiting for the FCC to take harsh action, hoping for a fine similar to the $25,000 given to KSHE in St. Louis. However, the FCC said this hoax did not violate Section 325(a) because a fake on-air murder confession did not constitute a "false distress signal." Therefore, the commission did not have the power to fine the station because no specific rule had been violated.

Some broadcasters suggested that the only proper punishment would be to revoke KROQ's license, but the FCC simply sent the station a Letter of Admonishment:

> Station KROQ-FM's broadcast of the hoax murder confession was a spontaneous, isolated event, orchestrated solely by certain on-air personnel, who subsequently engaged in a cover-up. Neither station management nor the licensee knew, or had any reason to suspect, that the broadcast was actually a hoax. Further, upon learning that the broadcast was a hoax, management promptly effectuated disciplinary and remedial action.[7]

Shortly after, another case demonstrated to the FCC that it needed a more clearly defined rule to punish these types of on-air hoaxes.

Dead Radio Host Hoax

In July 1991, WALE-AM talk show host Steve White had news director Thomas Moriarty play a "joke" on the air by announcing that White had been "shot in the head" just outside the station. Moriarty went on the air 10 minutes later to announce that the shooting story was false, but police by this time were already rushing to the station. Also, other media reporters were arriving at the station to investigate the "shooting." The station aired apologies for the rest of the day and then fired White and Moriarty. The station also agreed to reimburse police for any expenses.

Once again, with no concrete rule on the books, the FCC was limited in how it could punish the station. WALE received a simple Letter of Admonishment.[8]

---

[7]Searcy, D. R. (1991, December 4). *Letter to Lyle Reeb, General Manager, Radio Station KROQ-FM*. 6 F.C.C.R. 7262

[8]Wise, E. (1992, March 24). *Letter to Frank Battaglia, President, North American Broadcasting Co., Inc., licensee, radio station WALE-AM*. 7 F.C.C.R. 2345

FCC Creates Broadcast Hoax Rule

This rule became effective in June 1992. It allows the commission to fine stations up to $25,000 for violations. It also goes beyond "false distress" broadcasts and provides punishments for a wider range of hoaxes.[9]

Broadcast Hoax Rule

No licensee or permittee of any broadcast station shall broadcast false information concerning a *crime or catastrophe* if:

(a) The licensee knows the information is *false;*
(b) It is *foreseeable* that broadcast of the information will cause *substantial public harm,* and;
(c) Broadcast of the information does in fact *directly cause substantial public harm.*

Disclaimer rule: Any programming accompanied by a disclaimer will be presumed not to pose foreseeable harm if the disclaimer clearly characterizes the program as fiction and is presented in such a way that is reasonable under the circumstances.

FAQ

What types of events qualify as "foreseeable" or causing "public harm"?

Public harm. This can occur in two different ways: (a) The harm happens immediately and results in actual and direct damage to property or to the health or safety of the general public. (b) The hoax diverts health, safety, or law enforcement officials from their duties.

Foreseeable. This means that a broadcaster "could expect with a significant degree of certainty that public harm would occur."

Catastrophe. A violent or sudden event involving a disaster or approaching disaster that would affect the public.

If this 1992 rule had been in place a few years earlier, WALE, KROQ, and WCCM probably would have faced stiff fines.

BROADCAST CONTENT

News Content

Individual stations must be allowed to make news decisions free of interference from the federal government. The FCC may never censor a station's news programs or tell a station

---

[9] 47 C.F.R. § 73.1217

how to select its news material. The FCC cannot ban any type of editorial statement and is not allowed to set standards for who may become a news reporter, anchor, or commentator.

Drug Lyrics

Radio stations should avoid playing songs which endorse or appear to endorse illegal use of drugs. If a station has a history of playing songs with lyrics endorsing drug use, the FCC can use it against the station at license renewal time. The FCC also frowns on any on-air personalities endorsing illegal drugs. Thus on-air jokes or conversations about such things as "getting high" or "being stoned" should be avoided.

Contests

TV and radio stations frequently have contests and giveaways to help generate listener enthusiasm and develop long-term listener loyalty for a station. However, stations must be careful to follow FCC rules regarding over-the-air contests.

The FCC defines a *contest* as "a scheme in which a prize is offered or awarded, based upon chance, diligence, knowledge or skill, to members of the public." The contest must also not be misleading in any way, especially in regard to the prizes that may be won.

In general, radio stations should provide the following information, known as *material terms,* when conducting any contests: (a) how to enter or participate, (b) entry deadline dates, (c) eligibility restrictions, (d) prizes (if any) that can be won, (e) when those prizes can be won, (f) the nature and value of the prizes, (g) how prize value is determined, (h) time and means of selecting winners, and (i) how ties are broken.

Announcing the Rules

The FCC says "the time and manner of disclosure of the material terms of a contest are within the licensee's discretion." The FCC does say, however, that the station is obligated to announce the material terms of a contest from the date and time on which the contest is first announced until it is completed.

FAQ

How often are stations required to announce contest rules?

The vagueness of some FCC rules can be confusing and aggravating. The FCC says announcements of a contest's material terms should be made "periodically" in a "reasonable number of broadcast announcements." What does that mean? Many stations have a practice of announcing the material terms of a contest at least once during each "daypart" (the sections into which radio stations divide the day, such as morning drive time), or four or five times each day. That appears to be "reasonable" for the FCC. The FCC also encourages stations to announce the material terms in nonbroadcast ways, such as on a Web site or through contest guideline sheets that listeners can pick up at the station. A station is not obligated to enumerate the material terms every single time it announces or mentions the contest.

Contest Rules Exceptions

There are four types of contests in which these rules do not apply: (a) contests conducted by other businesses or groups, announced in broadcast ads; (b) in-station contests that are not broadcast or advertised to the general public (or to a substantial segment of the listening audience); (c) contests in which the general public is not invited or eligible to participate; and (d) contests conducted by a nonbroadcast company or division related to the licensee.

It is very important to note that a contest cannot be a *lottery*.

FAQ

What constitutes a "lottery"?

A lottery occurs when someone is required to purchase something or pay money to enter a radio or TV contest.[10] This is not allowed.

FAQ

What if it's nonprofit? For example, can a station accept advertising for a charity raffle? Church bingo games?

Check state law. Most states allow ads for nonprofit lottery ads, but some states still do not. Many states also do not allow advertisements for raffles or lotteries by commercial establishments.

FAQ

Can a station advertise a state lottery game? Casinos?

Yes, but if a station is in a state with no official state lottery or gambling, that state's laws may not allow the station to accept advertising for another state's lottery or casinos.

FCC Actions Against Station Contests

What is the value in U.S. dollars of 10,000 lira? A million lira?

In February, 2000, KPRR-FM in El Paso, TX, was fined $4000 by the FCC for not "fully and accurately disclosing the material terms of a contest."

Two DJs on the morning show said they were spoofing the TV show "Who Wants to Be a Millionaire" with a contest called "So You Want to Win 10,000." The rules stated that a

---

[10]47 C.F.R. § 73.1216

person had to answer ten questions correctly to win "10,000." A female listener correctly answered all ten questions, and she assumed she had won 10,000 *dollars.* The disc jockeys then told her the station had never said "10,000 dollars," just "10,000." She was then told she had actually won 10,000 *Italian lira,* worth about $53.

The woman complained to the FCC, saying the contest was misleading. The station argued that the "contest was just another silly bit on the KPRR morning show" and that its Web site clearly stated that the actual prize was 10,000 lira. However, the station admitted it never once *broadcast* that the prize was in lira rather than dollars.

In levying the $4000 fine against Clear Channel (the owners of KPRR), the FCC referred to Section 73.1216 of the Code of Federal Regulation: "No contest description shall be false, misleading or deceptive with respect to any material term." The FCC said the Web site announcement was not sufficient and was "not a substitute for broadcast announcements." The FCC pointed out another factor in its decision: Clear Channel admitted it intentionally did not broadcast the nature of the prize.[11]

A few months later, the FCC handed out a fine for a similar stunt at KITT-FM in Shreveport, LA. The station held a "Millionaire Monday" contest with a prize of "one million." Again, listeners assumed the prize was in dollars. The winning contestant was then told he had won "one million Turkish lira," or roughly $1.90. As with the KPRR case, the FCC fined KITT $4000. The FCC warned that broadcasters are "responsible for broadcasting accurate statements as to the nature and value of contest prizes."[12]

Attempting to deceive listeners even for comedy purposes will lead to FCC sanctions. The FCC is very strict about these guidelines, even when the station's motives may appear to be well-intentioned.

Give Away What You Promise

A radio station ran a contest in which the grand prize was a $2000 big screen TV.

The winner said the TV given as the prize was actually worth "less than $1100." The station agreed and awarded the listener other items to bring the total prize value to $2000. The listener told the FCC he was content with the new prize package.

However, the FCC was not content and fined the station $6250 for "failing to conduct the contest substantially as advertised."[13] Even though the station acted in good faith by awarding extra prizes, the FCC said the station emphasized a $2000 big screen TV in its promotions. Therefore, the station was obligated to give away that exact prize.

In 2004, the FCC levied a fine of $4000 against WDRQ-FM in Detroit for not clearly stating the terms of a contest. A man had won a ticket from WDRQ to see the movie *Spiderman* for a specific night. When the man arrived at the theater, he could not get in because the movie was sold out. The station then gave him tickets for another night, along with some station promotional items. WDRQ said it had told the man when he won the ticket that there was no guarantee he would get in. The station also said that it had told listeners afterward that it could not guarantee admission for movie ticket winners. However, the FCC ruled that the "nature and value of the prize" was not clearly stated because it obviously was not clear to the man that the movie might be sold out or that the station would offer substitute prizes.

---

[11]*Clear Channel Broadcasting Licensees, Inc.,* DA 00-238 (EB released February 10, 2000)

[12]*Citicasters Co.,* DA 00-1016 (EB released May 9, 2000)

[13]Cole, H. (1993, January 20). The FCC creates another fine mess. *Radio World,* p. 30.

In an effort to avoid future fines, WDRQ has instituted a disclaimer for its contests, telling listeners that the station "reserves the right to substitute a prize of equal or greater value" if the announced prize is not available.[14]

PAYOLA AND PLUGOLA

These are activities that could result in prison sentences for the personnel and licensees of radio stations. This is serious business.

Payola

In 1959, Congress announced that it was launching an investigation into record companies' bribing of radio stations to play music, also known as "pay to play," or payola. The first criminal indictment for payola involved radio DJ Alan Freed of WABC radio in New York City. The station had fired him in November 1959 after he refused to sign a statement that he had never taken gifts or money in return for playing music. Freed said he refused to sign based on principle and not because of any wrongdoing. A few weeks later, Freed admitted to taking money from record companies for "consultation" but denied it was payola.

In court, Freed was accused of taking $2500 from record companies to play certain songs. He eventually pleaded guilty, paid a $300 fine, and served a 6-month suspended sentence. After that, Freed could not get a job in the radio business, and he died in 1965 after apparently drinking himself to death.

The crime of payola involves three actions: (a) A radio station employee accepts money or anything of value in exchange for playing music or promoting businesses (or other material) on the air, (b) the employee does not notify station management before the broadcasting, and (c) the employee does not broadcast a sponsorship identification with the material.

Examples of Problem Situations

A local band asks a radio station's music director to play one of its new songs on the station. The music director says no. The band then calls a DJ at the station one night, offering the DJ free concert tickets if he will play the band's new song on the air. The DJ takes the concert tickets, plays the song on the air, and never tells station management.

Another DJ at the station is good friends with Joe, the owner of a local bar. During his on-air show, the DJ often makes casual mention of the bar by saying things like, "After my show tonight, I'm heading over to Joe's Bar for a few drinks. Drop by and see me." In return, Joe gives the DJ free drinks. The DJ does not tell station management.

These DJs just engaged in payola, and they are guilty of a crime.

FAQ

What are the penalties for payola?

---

[14]"Spidey" gets WDRQ fined. (2004, January 14). *Radio World*, p. 5.

Both the employee and the licensee face a fine of up to $10,000 and a year in prison. On top of that, the station may face additional sanctions from the FCC.

Independent Promoters: Payola in Disguise?

Consolidation in the radio industry has meant bigger companies, such as Clear Channel Communications, owning more radio stations. Critics charge that some of these companies are allowing their radio stations to practice payola through a "middleman."

The middleman they are talking about is called an *independent promoter.* Here is how the system has been working: Record companies hire the independent promoters, and the promoters lobby radio stations to play certain songs on the air. The promoters pay the stations a fixed monthly or annual fee to "encourage" the station to play certain songs ("pay to play"). Because the radio station is not receiving money *directly* from the record company, no laws are broken—provided the station reveals the name of the promoter.

Obviously, stations like this practice because they are getting money to play music. However, new music artists who are not affiliated with large record companies say it is now more difficult for them to get their music played on larger radio stations because the stations are now telling smaller artists that they have to "pay to play."

In 2002, Wisconsin Senator Russ Feingold sponsored the Competition in Radio and Concert Industries Act. It would prohibit radio stations from receiving money from independent promoters in return for airplay of certain songs. As of this writing, Feingold's bill does not even have a co-sponsor, and it appears doubtful the bill will go anywhere in the near future. In the summer of 2003, Clear Channel announced it was going to stop engaging in payola, but FCC Commissioner Jonathan Adelstein said it is not known yet if the company has truly stopped the practice in all its forms.

In November 2003, Adelstein publicly expressed concern about the new problems with payola and said the FCC should learn more about the issue. He said payola may also include artists and musicians being influenced to play at certain concerts or at certain venues (many of those venues are owned by Clear Channel or other radio companies). He said music companies paying thousands of dollars to have lunch or cocktail parties with radio programmers to influence airplay of songs could also be regarded as payola.

There is also concern about a payola practice emerging at some TV stations. What appear to be news interviews at some stations are actually turning out to be paid advertisements. During local newscasts, reporters will interview local business people in a "news story." In reality, the local business people have paid for the right to be interviewed for that segment. Critics say if the station does not disclose that the segment is purchased, it is a form of payola.

Plugola

Plugola means that a broadcast station employee is promoting nonbroadcast activities in which he or she has a financial interest.

Examples of Plugola

A DJ on a radio station also owns and operates a local restaurant. During his on-air show, he frequently mentions his business and some of the daily specials.

Another DJ consistently encourages listeners to buy the latest CD from a new music group. He never mentions that he is the drummer for this group.

Both of these situations are plugola, and they are illegal. The penalties are the same as those for payola.

FAQ

Is it all right for a broadcaster to mention the names of businesses in which he or she has no financial interest?

It is perfectly legal for a DJ to mention or "plug" a local business, as long as no payment is made. However, most radio stations frown upon this practice because it tends to make other advertisers angry.

OTHER LEGAL ISSUES

Sponsor Identification

Sponsor identification is very basic. A station must always identify the person or entity that is paying to deliver a message to the station's audience. This includes all types of *paid* announcements, from commercials to editorial ads. For ads, the mention of the business or product name is sufficient for identification.

This rule also applies to situations in which the station receives gifts or anything of value for broadcasting any kind of material. The station must identify the source of those gifts.

In any case, it should be easy for a station's listeners to identify the sponsor of an ad or other endorsement. This is especially important for political ads. Most stations make it a practice to have political ads end with something like "This message was paid for by the John Smith for Congress campaign."

Sponsors must be clearly identified on both commercial and noncommercial stations.[15]

Subliminal Advertising

Subliminal advertising supposedly affects people on a subconscious level. A popular example of subliminal advertising is a movie theater flashing a picture of popcorn on the screen for 1/100 of a second. Consciously, a person cannot recognize the image, but some say a person's subconscious can perceive it and make that person "unconsciously" crave popcorn.

Because the exact effects are unknown, the FCC says subliminal ads are "inconsistent with a station's obligation to serve the public interest because the broadcast is intended to be deceptive." Use of subliminal messages in ads or station promotions should be avoided. Use of such messages can hurt a station come license renewal time.

---

[15]See 47 C.F.R. 73.4242

Soliciting Funds

Whenever a station asks its listeners for money, that money must be used for legitimate radio station purposes. The money must go toward the purposes announced on the air. Asking listeners for money is done mostly by noncommercial stations, although the FCC says it is up to individual stations whether to allow "solicitations." It is perfectly legitimate for any station to ask for money to meet its operating expenses, for example. However, there must not be any kind of fraud in the way a station makes it money. Consider the following situation.

Be Careful What You Ask For. . . .

A severe storm had damaged a radio station's tower, so a DJ went on the air and jokingly asked listeners for donations to repair the tower. The DJ went on to joke that if the station didn't raise enough money, some DJs would lose their jobs. Listeners then "donated" $98, which the station gave to charity.

The FCC, though, was not charitable. It said the station had engaged in a "fraudulent" scheme to raise money. Why? The FCC said the station knew insurance was going to pay for the tower damage. The FCC fined the station $2500 for "obtaining money by false or fraudulent pretenses."[16]

Unattended or Automated Radio Stations

Many radio stations today are automated. An automated station is one in which a computer plays the music, commercials, promotional spots, legal IDs, and even prerecorded comments by DJs. To save money, many stations automate 24 hours a day. During the day, there are often people at the station to perform necessary FCC tasks, such as taking power readings and checking the tower lights.

At night and on weekends, though, many stations automate completely, and no one is in the station. The FCC calls it an *unattended operation,* and it is legal. To comply with FCC rules, an unattended operation has one of two options. It may install automatic transmission system (ATS) monitoring equipment to control the transmitter, or, if it has no ATS, station personnel must monitor the station for problems.

If a station is operating at excessive transmitting power, the problem must be corrected within 3 hours. If not, the station must be taken off the air until the transmitting problem is fixed. The ATS should be programmed to shut off the station automatically in such situations.

At unattended stations, the Emergency Alert System equipment needs to be up to date to allow for automatic broadcast of emergency announcements. The station must still conduct weekly and monthly tests, however.

Telephone Access

Each station is required to maintain a toll-free or local phone number within its community of license. If a station operates outside of the community of license, it must guarantee that community residents can access this number.

---

[16]See 18 U.S.C. § 1343

Non-FCC Legal Issues

The following pranks and miscues by radio stations wound up violating laws and fall outside of the FCC's jurisdiction. Although the pranks may not have violated any FCC regulations, these antics have led to other legal problems, such as disrupting traffic, fraud, and animal cruelty.

Radio Traffic Jam

On May 26, 1993, DJ Erich "Mancow" Muller created a traffic nightmare in the San Francisco Bay Area with a radio stunt, but he also wound up creating legal and financial nightmares for himself and for his station, KSOL-FM.

That morning, Muller had a station van block traffic on the westbound deck of the Bay Bridge while a KSOL employee got a haircut. (Muller performed the stunt to bring attention to reports that President Clinton had allegedly held up traffic at Los Angeles International Airport while sitting in Air Force One to get a $200 haircut.) Apparently, Muller did not foresee the public outrage that would follow over one of the worst traffic jams in the bridge's history. In court, Muller pleaded no contest to creating a public nuisance. He was fined $500 and was ordered to perform 100 hours of community service.

United Broadcasting, the owners of KSOL, faced a much more expensive civil lawsuit filed by the state. United wound up paying $1.5 million in damages, including $500,000 in bridge tolls. As a result, motorists did not have to pay any tolls on the Bay Bridge for 3 days in May 1997, courtesy of KSOL. Muller has since left the station and went on to become a successful radio DJ in Chicago.[17]

Radio Traffic Jam II

Radio stations not only need to be very careful about their DJs pulling stunts; they have to be careful about contests or promotions that ask listeners to do "crazy" or "outrageous" acts.

In 1997, WKQI-FM personality Danny Bonaduce ("Danny" of the "Partridge Family") created traffic problems in Detroit when two of his female listeners staged a minor car accident and fight during morning rush hour. It was the women's attempt to win a station contest called "How Low Can You Go?" Several passing motorists assumed the accident and brawl were real and called authorities. An ambulance and seven police cars responded before everyone realized it was a prank.

Police ticketed the two women for blocking traffic, but Bonaduce was not charged. Instead, he hand-delivered 30 bag lunches to police headquarters in Royal Oak and agreed to pay for emergency costs. Bonaduce realized he got off with a pretty light sentence: "Call it stupid radio. That's what it was. I guess I could be facing serious charges right now."[18]

---

[17]Schwartz, J. (2000, November 1). Of plummeting chickens, Britney hoaxes and Bay Bridge haircuts. *South Coast Today*. Retrieved October 19, 2004, from http://www.s-t.com/daily/11-00/11-01-00/b04ae116.htm

[18]People, places, and things in the news. (1997, February 23). *SouthCoast Today*, p. 1.

It Pays to Read

Sometimes, the most well-intentioned radio promotions can go horribly wrong. As with the Bonaduce incident, a DJ at a Texas station did not consider the possible legal consequences when asking listeners to participate in a contest.

In 1994, a DJ on KYNG-FM in Fort Worth, Texas had a noble cause—he wanted to promote reading. So he told his listeners he had hidden $100 in the Fort Worth Public Library. As a result, an estimated 800 listeners stormed the library, tearing up magazines and books while looking for the money. Adding to the mayhem was a rumor that the cash prize was as much as $10,000.

In the end, $10,000 is what KYNG wound up donating to the library to avoid potential lawsuits, and the station also agreed to pay for any damaged library books and materials. KYNG also made the library its "charity of the month," airing hourly ads to solicit donations. The station paid a lot of money for what was supposed to be a simple $100 promotion for reading.

Prank Phone Call to the White House

In October 2000, three employees at KISS-FM in Idaho had become annoyed with two teenage boys who repeatedly called the station to request a song. The employees decided to play a prank, telling the boys they would win a certain amount of money by calling an 800 number and saying the "phrase that pays." The 800 number was for the White House, and the phrase was "I'm going to kill the president." The boys called the number and repeated the phrase.

The U.S. Secret Service takes seriously any threats to the president, even ones that are "jokes." Authorities traced the phone call, and the boys told the Secret Service the radio station had set up the prank. KISS-FM fired the three employees involved, including the station's regional operations manager.[19]

Animal Cruelty Case

In January 2001, a Denver jury found a disc jockey guilty of animal cruelty for a radio stunt involving a chicken. A year earlier, DJ Steven Meade ("Willie B") had an intern drop a chicken from a second-story window and then again from the third story to see if the chicken would fly. A concerned listener drove to the station and took the chicken to a veterinarian. (The bird apparently suffered leg and foot injuries.)

A judge sentenced Meade to 1 year of probation, which included 100 hours of community service to any group that helped animals, and he had to pay nearly $1000 in fines and court fees. The judge also ordered Meade to attend counseling sessions designed for people who abuse animals.[20]

Wedding Announcement Prank

On April 1, 1994, a picture appeared in the *Watertown* [NY] *Daily Times* in the bridal announcements section. The "bride" in the picture was actually a man dressed in a wedding

---

[19]McKinnie, J. (2000, October 25). KISS FM radio fires 3 for prank. *Idaho Statesman*, p. 5.

[20]Denver DJ sentenced for cruelty to hen. (2001, Spring). *Poultry Press* (news release).

gown wearing a wig and makeup: Johnny Spezzano, morning personality at WBDR/ WBDI-FM in Watertown. The bridal announcement was an April Fool's Day prank by Spezzano, and the article contained all of the usual information about the wedding and the bride, including that the "bride" worked at a splatball company. WBDR's station secretary was also in on the prank. She pretended to be the "bride" when the *Times* called to confirm the bridal announcement.

The *Times* was not amused to find out it had been fooled and sued WBDR and the station secretary for "fraud, conspiracy, criminal impersonation, theft of services, unfair competition, and violation of the Latham Act and general business law."[21]

Some local citizens wrote to the paper to say "lighten up," but the *Times* wanted to discourage other people from submitting "jokes" and other false information to the newspaper. WBDR reached a settlement with the *Times* when the station promised never to pull such a stunt again. The station also had to pay for a $250 ad in the paper to apologize for the fake wedding announcement.

"Worthless Money" Prank

Spezzano also got himself in hot water in 1999 with the U.S. Secret Service for an on-air prank regarding U.S. currency. Spezzano told his listeners he had a letter from the U.S. Treasury department stating that $20 bills would have no value starting the next day. As a result, people flocked to local banks trying to "cash in" their $20 bills. The Secret Service immediately called WBDR to let the station know that "joking around" about U.S. currency was not a laughing matter. WBDR's station manager avoided punishment by promising that neither the DJ nor the station would ever again pull such a prank.

Honk If You Want a Lawsuit

A DJ was upset with a local motel owner and told listeners to honk as they drove by the motel. Needless to say, the motel owner soon became annoyed. He sued the radio station and the DJ for outrageous conduct, creating a public nuisance, and intentional infliction of emotional distress. The radio station settled out of court with the motel owner for roughly $25,000. (Defense lawyers wanted to avoid going to court because they did not think they could find a jury that would like the "obnoxious DJ.")

The station also forked over more than $50,000 in legal expenses.[22]

Radio "Terrorist"

In 2004, radio personality Dan Chappell of KHFI-FM in Austin, TX, allegedly wore a ski mask into a local convenience store. He allegedly walked around the store and used a phone to do a live broadcast about his experience. A store clerk, thinking Chappell was a would-be robber, pressed a silent alarm. Chappell then bought a pack of gum and left. Police arrested Chappell as he was walking away from the store and charged him with making a

---

[21]Dely, L. (2000, July 19). Station prank turns sour. *Radio World*, p. 34.

[22]First Media Insurance Specialists, Inc. of Kansas City. (2004). *Sample claims: Radio rancor.* Retrieved July 10, 2004, from http://firstmediainc.com

terrorist threat. If convicted, he could get a $4000 fine and up to a year in jail. Chappell was also suspended from the station, along with his on-air partner Bobby Bones.[23]

SUMMARY

This chapter covers some of the main rules of which broadcast stations need to be aware in their daily operations. Stations must be careful to follow these rules. Violations can lead to serious fines from the FCC. In extreme instances, violations could damage the licensee during license renewal time. Stations may also face civil lawsuits for actions that embarrass or harm individuals.

---

[23]Carter, K. (2004). Big dumb stunt guy alert. *Radio & Records.Com.* Retrieved July 14, 2004, from http://radio andrecords.com/Formats/News

7

LIBEL

A person's good name is priceless.

—Bezanson, Cranzberg, and Soloski[1] (p. 1)

LIBEL AND SLANDER

Generally, *libel* is written and *slander* is spoken. However, they both really mean the same thing. From this point on, *libel* will be used to refer to both libel and slander.

Six Elements of Libel

These six elements must be present for libel to have occurred:

1. *Defamation.* A statement has been made about a person that damages that person's reputation.

2. *Falsity.* The information was false.

3. *Communication.* The story or statement must have been broadcast or published where at least one person (besides the plaintiff and the defendant) has seen or heard it.

4. *Identification.* The story or statement identifies the individual either by name or in a way that clearly identifies the individual to others besides the individual.

5. *Fault.* In cases involving public issues, the media outlet knew the story was false or strongly suspected it was false but broadcast or printed it anyway. This is called *actual malice* or *reckless disregard for the truth.*

6. *Harm.* The story harmed the individual in some way (loss of reputation, embarrassment, out-of-pocket losses). In court, individuals have to prove this loss actually occurred. For example, an individual could bring in witnesses who said they stopped doing business with the individual because of a libelous story.

Direct and Indirect Libel

Sometimes you will see these two terms used: *libel per se* and *libel per quod.* Libel per se is direct accusation, such as "John Smith is an adulterer" or "Jane Brown is a thief." It is pretty

---

[1]Bezanson, R., Cranzberg, G., & Soloski, J. (1987). *Libel law and the press.* New York: Free Press.

straightforward. Libel per quod is more indirect, more like an insinuation: "Mrs. Jane Smith was frequently alone in her home with John Jones." To some readers, this might imply that Smith and Jones were having an affair, when in actuality the news reporter failed to mention that Jones was hired to paint the inside of Smith's house.

Media Defenses Against Libel

There are three basic ways a media outlet can defend itself against libel: truth, privilege, and fair comment and criticism.

If the media can prove a statement is true, then that statement is not libelous. The plaintiff (the person suing) has the burden of proving the statement is false. There are also certain "privileged" sources of information that are protected in libel cases. Most governmental meetings and court records are considered privileged. That means a reporter can include any information from these sources without fear of libel, even if these government sources contain libelous information. The reporter cannot be held responsible for errors in such documents.

"Fair comment and criticism" means that the media are allowed to analyze and critique performances of public persons (people who place themselves in the spotlight) and that the opinions expressed in the analyses and critiques are fine as long as they do not contain false statements of fact. Protected opinion: "The mayor is not very bright." Potentially libelous opinion: "The mayor is not very bright because of years of cocaine addiction."

DEFINING TRUTH

The Actual Malice Standard

Libel law today is based mostly on a landmark Supreme Court case from 1964, *New York Times v. Sullivan.*[2] At that time, there was no national standard for determining libel. States had varying laws about what constituted libel.

New York Times v. Sullivan

On March 29, 1960, the *New York Times* ran an editorial ad in its pages (see box for pertinent parts of ad). The ad was purchased by a civil rights group named the Committee to Defend Martin Luther King and the Struggle for Freedom in the South. The group paid $4800 for the ad, to express its displeasure with police treatment of demonstrators during a protest at Alabama State College (for text of ad, see box).

Heed Their Rising Voices

[Paragraph 1]

As the whole world knows by now, thousands of Southern Negro students are engaged in widespread non-violent demonstrations in positive affirmation of the right to live in human dignity as guaranteed by the U.S. Constitution and the Bill of Rights. In their efforts to uphold

---

[2]376 U.S. 254 (1964)

these guarantees, they are being met by an unprecedented wave of terror by those who would deny and negate that document which the whole world looks upon as setting the pattern for modern freedom.

[Paragraph 3]

In Montgomery, Alabama, after students sang "My Country, 'Tis of Thee" on the State Capitol steps, their leaders were expelled from school, and truckloads of police armed with shotguns and tear-gas ringed the Alabama State College Campus. When the entire student body protested to state authorities by refusing to re-register, their dining hall was padlocked in an attempt to starve them into submission.

[Paragraph 6]

Again and again the Southern violators have answered Dr. King's peaceful protests with intimidation and violence. They have bombed his home almost killing his wife and child. They have assaulted this person. They have arrested him seven times—for "speeding," "loitering" and similar "offenses." And now they have charged him with "perjury"—a *felony* under which they could imprison him for *ten years.*

Some of the claims in the ad in paragraphs 3 and 6 turned out to be inaccurate:

- Students sang *The Star Spangled Banner*, not *My Country 'Tis of Thee*.
- No students were expelled for demonstrating.
- Some students protested the expulsions by boycotting classes for 1 day, not by refusing to register for classes. The vast majority of students did register.
- Neither police nor the university padlocked the dining hall. A few students were barred from the dining hall because they had not paid appropriate bills.
- Many police showed up but not enough to form a "ring" around the campus.
- Police were not called to campus because of a protest on the capitol steps.
- Dr. King had been arrested four times, not seven.
- A police officer denied any assault on Dr. King during an arrest years before.
- Police were never implicated in the two bombings on Dr. King's house.

Obviously, the ad contained numerous factual errors, and this upset L. B. Sullivan, the commissioner of police in Montgomery. Sullivan's name did not appear in the ad, but he felt the negative comments about the police reflected directly on him. Sullivan, Alabama governor John Patterson, and three other Montgomery officials filed a libel lawsuit against the *New York Times* and four people whose names appeared at the bottom of the ad. Sullivan said the newspaper should have checked the ad to make sure it was accurate.

An Alabama jury awarded Sullivan $500,000 in damages, finding the *New York Times* guilty of violating Alabama's libel law. On appeal, the Alabama Supreme Court upheld the $500,000 judgment.

FAQ

But weren't a lot of the errors in the ad "innocent mistakes?" Should we punish the media for errors such as this?

The highest court in the land said we should not. In 1964, the U.S. Supreme Court voted 9-0 to overturn that judgment, and it ruled for the newspaper in *New York Times v. Sullivan.* Newspapers and other media must not be punished for "honest misstatements of fact," the court said, even if those misstatements cause embarrassment or humiliation for public officials. The court ruled that a person could only win a libel suit against a media outlet if the person was able to prove *actual malice.* Actual malice involves printing a statement "with knowledge that it was false" *and/or* printing a statement with a "reckless disregard of whether it was false or not" or with a "reckless disregard for the truth."

"With knowledge that it was false" is pretty straightforward. This means that a reporter or editor knew beforehand that information in an article or ad was not true, but the story was printed anyway. "Reckless disregard for the truth" means that a media outlet was reckless or careless in its newsgathering.

FAQ

What are some examples of reckless disregard?

Using unreliable sources. A reporter has information about a local politician soliciting prostitutes, but the only source is a prostitute who admitted to being on drugs during the interview. That is a fairly unreliable source.

The depth of the reporting. Did the media outlet do a good job verifying information? Was it professional in its investigation? Did the media have a tendency to jump to conclusions?

Media motives. Did the media outlet have any sort of "score to settle" with the people in the story? Was the media outlet more concerned about profits than about making sure the facts were correct?

Serious doubts. Did the reporter or editor have "serious doubts" about a story's truthfulness?

The media are expected to exercise good judgment when gathering and printing information. A lapse in judgment could be considered reckless. However, the Supreme Court wrote that "erroneous statement is inevitable in free debate, and that it must be protected if the freedoms of expression are to have the 'breathing space' that they 'need . . . to survive.'"[3] The court felt that the First Amendment was meant to protect the media from "honest little mistakes." All media—newspapers, magazines, radio, TV—make innocent mistakes every day. This is why newspapers have to print retractions so often. If we punished the media every time they made an unintentional factual error about a public official, the media would be swamped with libel lawsuits.

FAQ

At the same time, doesn't this give perhaps too much protection to the media?

---

[3]Taken in part from *NAACP v. Button,* 371 U.S. 415, 433 (1963)

Justice Brennan said in *Sullivan* that giving the media this kind of protection is based on "a profound national commitment to the principle that debate on public issues should be *uninhibited, robust, and wide-open*, and that it may well include vehement, caustic and sometimes unpleasant sharp attacks on government and public officials" (italics added).

Brennan said that allowing a libel judgment such as the $500,000 jury verdict in Alabama would create a chilling effect on the media. The media would be trapped in a "pall of fear and timidity" and would back away from controversial stories out of fear of libel lawsuits. Justice Black concurred: "I doubt that a country can live in freedom where its people can be made to suffer physically or financially for criticizing their government, its actions, or its officials."

FAQ

Does the Sullivan ruling make it easier for the media to win libel cases?

This actual malice standard provides great protection to the media. In fact, many libel cases (nearly 60% in 2003, according to one source[4]) are won by the media. It is difficult to prove that a reporter or editor acted with "actual malice." How does one prove that a reporter *knew* a story was false? It is often very difficult to present proof about what a reporter was thinking when he and she wrote a story.

As for reckless disregard for the truth, most media outlets are extremely careful these days about double- and triple-checking controversial information before they print or broadcast it. Most media today will have lawyers read over controversial stories before the stories are released to the public.

Also, if the media will simply print or broadcast a retraction, that will many times keep a public official from filing a lawsuit.

Actually Proving Actual Malice

The Supreme Court tackled this issue in 1979 in *Herbert v. Lando.*[5] The case involved a 1973 *60 Minutes* broadcast on CBS. Reporters interviewed retired Army Colonel Anthony Herbert, who said the government had covered up atrocities in Vietnam. Herbert says the show implied that he was just making up those charges to rationalize his lost command. In his lawsuit, Herbert agreed that, as a public figure, he would have to prove actual malice as established in *Sullivan.* But how to prove it?

Herbert's lawyers said it was necessary to look at two issues involving reporters and editors when the story was being written: (a) the media's state of mind and (b) the media's actions and conduct. Basically, the *Herbert* case argued that it was important to be able to

---

[4]Libel Defense Resource Center. (2001, August 27). *Annual study of media law trials shows 14 trials in 2003 with media winning 57 percent* (Press release). Retrieved October 22, 2004, from http://www.ldrc.com/Press_Releases/bull2004-1.html. The press release said that the media saw eventual victory "over 80 percent of the time in reported [actual malice] cases" involving a summary judgment.

[5]441 U.S. 153 (1979)

analyze reporters' thoughts and opinions when they were writing stories. For example, in this case, was it fair for Herbert's lawyers to ask if the *60 Minutes* reporter made negative comments about Herbert to a cameraperson or editor?

The Supreme Court ruled that such questions are permitted in libel cases. Justice White said that it is "essential" that public figures be allowed to ask reporters about their attitudes and actions in libel cases. Supporters of the media argued that such questions would create a chilling effect on investigative reporting, but the court said *not* allowing such questions would give the media too much power in libel cases.

PUBLIC FIGURES AND PRIVATE CITIZENS

A *public official* is anyone who is elected to a public office, from the president of the United States to a county clerk. These people's salaries come out of tax dollars, and therefore they are accountable to the taxpayers and are subject to public scrutiny. Public officials are also those who are appointed to public office, such as members of the president's cabinet. The Supreme Court says a public official is anyone who has a "substantial role" in governmental affairs.

Public figures are celebrities, people who voluntarily place themselves in the public spotlight. A public figure is someone who has attained special prominence in society. Corporations, because of their prominence in society, also count as public figures.

FAQ

Isn't it sometimes difficult to determine who qualifies as a public figure?

It can be very difficult. Controversy erupted over this issue in 1971 in *Rosenbloom v. Metromedia.*[6] This case concerned a man who distributed nudist magazines in Philadelphia and was arrested for possession of obscene material. A local radio station aired stories about Rosenbloom's arrest, saying the seized books were obscene instead of "allegedly obscene." (The station corrected the error and added "allegedly" in subsequent broadcasts.) Radio station stories also said people like Rosenbloom were "smut distributors" and "girlie book peddlers" involved in a "smut literature racket." Officials later ruled that the books were not obscene.

Rosenbloom sued for libel, saying the broadcasts defamed him. Did Rosenbloom have to prove actual malice on the part of the radio station? Pennsylvania state law at the time said that private citizens only had to prove the media did not exercise "reasonable care." With those guidelines, a district court jury awarded damages to Rosenbloom.

However, a federal court of appeals overturned the jury verdict, and the Supreme Court upheld that judgment. The Supreme Court said that Rosenbloom, a private citizen, had to prove actual malice by the radio station because he was involved "in a matter of public or general concern." Therefore, Rosenbloom was required to prove that the radio station knew the statements were false or that the station showed a reckless disregard for the truth. This is much harder to prove than a simple lack of "reasonable care," as mandated under Pennsylvania's law.

---

[6]403 U.S. 29 (1971)

Rosenbloom Rethought

The 1974 case *Gertz v. Welch*[7] effectively overturned *Rosenbloom* and made it easier for private citizens to win libel cases.

Gertz was a case about prominent Chicago civil rights lawyer, Elmer Gertz. A Chicago police officer had been convicted of killing a young boy, and Gertz represented the boy's parents in a civil rights lawsuit against the officer. The police officer was convicted of murder.

The magazine *American Opinion* disagreed with the murder conviction and ran an article accusing Gertz of "framing" the police officer. The article also called Gertz a "communist-fronter" and a "Leninist" who wanted to create a national police force under a communist government. The article also accused Gertz of having a substantial police record, which was not true. Gertz sued the magazine for libel.

Gertz was a lawyer in a case that received substantial media attention. Did this make him a public figure? Two lower courts basically said yes and ruled that Gertz was involved in an important public matter and thus had to prove actual malice.

The U.S. Supreme Court, though, voted 5-4 to overturn the lower court rulings. *The court said Gertz was a private citizen, and he only had to prove* negligence *or a lack of reasonable care.* This is much easier to prove than actual malice. However, *the court left it up to individual states* to determine whether private citizens need to prove mere negligence or the stricter standard of actual malice.

FAQ

What about the lawyers in the O. J. Simpson criminal trial? Wouldn't many of them be considered public figures?

In *Gertz*, Justice Lewis Powell tried to bring some clarity to questions like this. He listed two basic types of public figures:

1. *All-purpose public figures.* These are people who are widely known and recognized. They occupy prominent positions in government, entertainment, and society (e.g., politicians, celebrities, people who have general power and influence).

2. *Limited (or "vortex") public figures.* These are people who *voluntarily* enter the public spotlight to try to *change the outcome* of an important *public controversy.* All three of these elements (in italics) must be proven for a person to be considered a limited public figure. These people often return to being "private citizens" after leaving the spotlight.

So, according to these guidelines, was Gertz a private citizen or public figure? The Supreme Court said he remained a private citizen because he did not try to change public opinion during this trial. He simply was doing his job as a lawyer in a case that happened to get media attention. In 1982, a federal appeals court upheld a $400,000 damage award given to Gertz.

As for the lawyers in the O. J. Simpson case, someone like F. Lee Bailey might be considered a public figure because of his fame. However, that determination would be left to the

---

[7]418 U.S. 323 (1974)

courts. One of the prosecution lawyers, Marcia Clark, most likely would be considered a public figure because she sought the public spotlight after the trial (she hosted a cable show, for example). However, a person seeking the public spotlight does not automatically become a public figure, as shown by the circumstances in the next case.

Time v. Firestone

The courts grappled again with the definition of "public figure" in 1976 in *Time v. Firestone*.[8] Russell Firestone was an heir to the Firestone tire company fortune, and he had filed for divorce from his wife, Mary Alice Firestone. The divorce made headlines, and *Time* magazine ran an article mistakenly stating that Russell got the divorce based on Mary Alice's "extreme cruelty and adultery." Mrs. Firestone sued *Time* for libel for calling her an "adulteress."

Mary Alice Firestone is one of those people who walks the line between private citizen and public figure. She was not necessarily a celebrity, but she was a member of a wealthy prominent family. She was also actively involved in many prominent social activities and clubs. Almost 90 stories about the divorce appeared in Miami and Palm Beach newspapers. That extensive coverage was partly because Mrs. Firestone used the public spotlight when she held press conferences during the 17-month divorce proceedings.

In spite of this, the Supreme Court ruled that Mrs. Firestone was still a private citizen. She did not actively seek to change public opinion on any controversial issue, and she did not have any special prominence in society's affairs, other than in local Palm Beach society. Also, although divorce proceedings may be listed in public court records, a divorce is usually not a public controversy of public importance. The court also pointed out that Mrs. Firestone did not voluntarily seek the spotlight: She was required to go to court to settle the divorce. Her press conferences were a response to media reports, not an attempt to seek the spotlight or to resolve some "unrelated controversy."

Mrs. Firestone eventually chose not to pursue the lawsuit, and the case was dismissed. The case, however, provided important guidelines about private citizens and public figures.

FAQ

Is there a defined time limit on how long a private citizen remains a limited public figure?

There are no set limits. It is analyzed on a case-by-case basis.

Wolston v. Reader's Digest

In 1957, Jack and Myra Soble were arrested and later pleaded guilty to spying for the Soviet Union. The Sobles' nephew, Ilya Wolston, was issued a subpoena to testify before a grand jury in July 1958, but he did not appear. As a result, he was found in contempt and was given probation. The libel case at issue here arose more than 15 years later, when

---

[8]424 U.S. 448 (1976)

Reader's Digest published a book in 1974, *KGB: The Secret Works of Soviet Secret Agents*. The book included information about the Sobles and also called Wolston a "Soviet agent," based on the events in the 1950s. Wolston sued for libel.

Reader's Digest argued that Wolston was a limited-purpose public figure because of his failure to obey a federal subpoena in 1958. In *Wolston v. Reader's Digest*,[9] the Supreme Court ruled that Wolston was not a public figure because he did not try to change the outcome of any important public controversy. The court said that Wolston never sought the public spotlight and was drawn into a public controversy against his will.

In the next case, the courts found that a woman did voluntarily subject herself to the public spotlight, at least for a brief time.

The "Chicken Butt" Case

On February 15, 2000, on San Francisco radio station KLLC, talk show hosts Sarah Clark and Vincent Crackhorn were making jokes about a local woman named Jennifer Seelig, who had appeared on the TV show *Who Wants to Marry a Millionaire*. Fifty women competed for the right to win prizes and marry a man they had not known before the show. The radio station had invited Seelig to be a guest on KLLC's *Sarah and Vinnie Show*, but she declined. Then the two radio hosts went on the air and called Seelig a "chicken butt," "local loser," and "big skank." Seelig sued the station for libel.

In 2002, in *Seelig v. Infinity Broadcasting Corporation*,[10] a California superior court judge threw out the libel suit because Seelig chose to appear on a national TV show and thus "voluntarily subjected herself to inevitable scrutiny and potential ridicule by the public and the media." Also, the judge said, words such as "skank," "loser," and "chicken butt" are "too vague to be found true or false." Such words were simply "name-calling of the 'sticks and stones will break my bones' variety." (Consider this: For Seeling to have won this case, she would have needed to come up with a concrete definition for "chicken butt" and then prove to the court she was *not* one.)

The radio station was awarded trial costs and attorney fees.

RECKLESS DISREGARD FOR THE TRUTH

Attempted Assassinations Lead to a Radio Libel Suit

On September 5, 1975, former Charles Manson cult member Lynette "Squeaky" Fromme attempted to shoot President Gerald Ford in Sacramento, CA. Secret Service agent Larry Buendorf grabbed the gun from Fromme, saving the president's life. Then on September 25, 1975, President Ford was in San Francisco when Sara Jane Moore attempted to shoot him. However, a man named Oliver Sipple hit Moore's arm just before she fired, and the shot missed the president. In their coverage of the event, some prominent newspapers mentioned that Sipple was a "prominent figure" in San Francisco's gay community. (This case will be discussed in detail in the next chapter.)

---

[9] 443 U.S. 157 (1979)

[10] 02 C.D.O.S. 3262 (2002)

Many years later, on April 11, 1992, Daniel Schorr was discussing homosexuality and media privacy issues with another host on the National Public Radio program *Weekend Edition*. Schorr asked a research assistant to "get me the name of that guy who saved President Ford's life." The assistant only found the story on the first assassination attempt. Schorr went on the air and mistakenly said that Secret Service Agent Larry Buendorf, not Oliver Sipple, was "exposed as being a homosexual."

On August 6, 1992, Buendorf filed a lawsuit against National Public Radio for libel. He said the homosexual claim affected his job because "anyone in government with a secret clearance who is practicing homosexual sex is subject to being blackmailed or compromised for fear of disclosure." That same day, National Public Radio issued a press release to correct the error and apologize to Buendorf.

In *Buendorf v. National Public Radio,*[11] the court had to deal with the following issues:

- ◫ *Is Buendorf a public official?* Yes. The court said law enforcement officials such as Secret Service agents are public officials because of their "substantial responsibility" in government affairs.
- ◫ *Therefore, Buendorf must prove actual malice. Did he?* No. Schorr did not knowingly make the false statement. It was a mistake. Yes, Schorr could have done a better job making sure his research assistant had the right information, but the court said this did not qualify as "reckless disregard."

Deadline Pressure

News reporters face deadlines every day. Sometimes that pressure means a journalist may not take the necessary time to validate certain information. If the story turns out to contain libelous information, can a reporter use deadline pressure as a valid excuse for not checking sources? As you will see, it depends on the circumstances.

In 1967, the Supreme Court handed down two libel rulings simultaneously in *AP v. Walker* and *Curtis Publishing Co. v. Butts.*[12] The court dealt with the cases together because they each dealt with the issue of "serious doubt" and reckless disregard.

The *Walker* case involved an incident in which federal marshals were called in to protect a young African American man as he arrived for his first day of classes at the University of Mississippi. An Associated Press (AP) reporter on the scene wrote a story saying that a "mob" of white protesters was led by retired Major General Edwin Walker, a known segregationist. Other media carried similar stories about Walker's role, but the media stories were wrong. Walker said he did not act as a mob leader that day. Walker sued the AP and other media outlets for libel.

The Supreme Court ruled for the AP, saying there was no evidence of reckless disregard. For the AP editor in the office, the court said, the campus disturbance was a "breaking" news story. The editor felt a need to get the story out on the wires quickly. The AP reporter on the scene was relatively young but had a good record of reliability and trustworthiness. General Walker was known for being involved in public protests. The story about him leading a mob was not "out of place." There was no "serious doubt" here. The editor had no reason to be suspicious

---

[11]822 F. Supp. 6 (D.D.C. 1993)

[12]388 U.S. 130 (1967)

about the story's authenticity. The reporter was gathering the information in a rather chaotic atmosphere on campus. The atmosphere contributed to the unintentional reporting error.

FAQ

Doesn't this ruling allow the media to use deadline pressures and chaotic news scenes as excuses for sloppy and libelous reporting?

The Supreme Court did not think so in this case and said the main concern should be "serious doubt" when ruling on cases such as this. Because of the deadline pressure, there was not adequate time to double-check information. Also, as noted, there was nothing in the story that seemed out of the ordinary, considering General Walker's previous involvement in civil rights protests.

However, the lack of deadline pressure and some sloppy reporting led to a different ruling for the media in the second case. There should have been some "serious doubt" before publication took place here.

Football Fix

In *Curtis v. Butts,*[135] the case revolved around an article in the *Saturday Evening Post* and an alleged conversation between Wally Butts, the athletic director at the University of Georgia, and Paul "Bear" Bryant, the head football coach at the University of Alabama. During this conversation, the *Post* wrote that Butts and Bryant had conspired to "fix" an upcoming football game between Georgia and Alabama. The source of the *Post* story was George Burnett, a man with a criminal record. Burnett had claimed he was making a phone call when the phone company accidentally connected him to a phone call between Butts and Bryant. He said he took detailed notes of the conversation, and he then gave this information to the *Post.*

A lower court awarded Butts nearly $500,000 in damages. In *Curtis v. Butts,* the U.S. Supreme Court upheld the libel judgment against the *Post* for several reasons. For example, there was no deadline pressure, as in the *Walker* case. The *Post* published the story months after receiving the information. It had time to check the facts. Also, this story was pretty remarkable. The magazine's staff should have had someone with football expertise read the story to see if it was even credible, but the magazine did not perform even this simple task of double-checking information. In *Walker,* the main source was a respected journalist. In *Post,* the main source was a man with a criminal record who was on probation for writing bad checks. This should have created some "serious doubt" for the *Post.* The Supreme Court pointed out that other people were with Burnett when he allegedly overheard this phone conversation, but the *Post* never tried to contact them for verification. Before the story was published, some *Post* editors had said it needed to be investigated more thoroughly, but their advice was ignored, and the story was published anyway.

All of these actions showed the court that the *Post* had indeed exercised reckless disregard for the truth. The credibility of the source and the nature of that source's story should have raised "serious doubts" for the *Post*—doubts that should have led to the story never being published in the first place.

Defining *Privilege*

As noted earlier, the media cannot be held responsible for reporting material that turns out to be libelous if that libelous material was quoted from a "privileged" source, such as court records or a congressman speaking on the House floor.

FAQ

Can a media outlet be held responsible for libelous statements made by usually reliable news sources?

Consider this situation: You are interviewing a local sheriff for a TV news story about some possibly illegal conduct by your city's mayor. You have interviewed this sheriff before, and he has always been a reliable and honest source. The sheriff tells you that the mayor is facing corruption and embezzlement charges. You trust that the sheriff is giving you accurate information, you feel no need to double-check the sheriff's comments, and you include the sheriff's comments in your story. It turns out that the sheriff was given incorrect information—it is actually the *deputy* mayor who is facing these charges. The mayor sues the sheriff and your station for libel.

This example deals with the issue of whether the media can be held liable for repeating libelous statements in news stories when those statements were made by reliable, prominent people, such as a law enforcement official, a politician, or medical personnel. Are reporters expected to second-guess high-ranking officials like this? This takes us into an interesting and sometimes controversial area of libel law.

Neutral Reportage

This concept says the media are protected from libel claims when they write (a) accurate, unbiased, newsworthy stories (b) in which trustworthy prominent persons or organizations (c) make false accusations against public figures.

FAQ

How does actual malice apply in neutral reportage cases?

Because neutral reportage involves stories about public figures, persons bringing libel suits must prove actual malice.

FAQ

Does neutral reportage also cover false accusations made against private citizens?

It does not. That became a central issue in the following cases.

New York Times Wins Neutral Reportage Case

In the April 1972 edition of the Audubon Society's *American Birds,* the publication's editor, respected amateur ornithologist Robert Arbib, Jr., wrote about the controversy regarding the insecticide dichlorodiphenyltrichloroethane (DDT) and its effects on birds. He said pro-DDT scientists were "paid to lie" and that they "misused" Audubon Bird Count data to claim that bird populations were actually increasing despite the widespread use of DDT.

Nature reporter John Devlin of the *New York Times* phoned Arbib about his comments and asked Arbib to name some of the scientists he thought were being "paid to lie." Arbib talked with Audubon Society Vice President Ronald Clement, who provided the names of five scientists that the society said were "consistent misinterpretors of the information in *American Birds.*" He refused to call them liars, though. Devlin contacted three of the five scientists about Arbib's comments, and they all denied being "paid to lie." One of the scientists said Arbib's claims were "almost libelous." Two of the scientists sent Devlin "voluminous supporting materials" to bolster their arguments about DDT.

Devlin felt he had investigated both sides of the controversy well, and in the August 14, 1972 edition of the *Times,* Devlin's article appeared under the headline "Pesticide Spokesmen Accused of 'Lying' on Higher Bird Count." The article included Arbib's accusations about the scientists being "paid to lie."

Three of the five scientists sued the Audubon Society and the *Times* for libel. A jury ruled against the *Times* and Robert Clement, who had provided the scientists' names to Arbib. In awarding $61,000 in damages, the jury said Devlin had been "reckless" when writing the article because he did not investigate Arbib's claims more thoroughly.

The *Times* appealed, saying Devlin's report should be protected under the concept of neutral reportage. In *Edwards et al. v. Audubon and New York Times,*[13] a federal appeals court threw out the jury verdict and ruled for Devlin and the *Times*. The court said that the scientists named in the story were public figures. Therefore, the jury verdict could not be upheld unless there was proof of actual malice. Devlin's report was "fair and dispassionate," the court said, with no actual malice. There was also no evidence that Devlin had "serious doubts" about Arbib's claims.

Devlin's quotes from Arbib were protected under the rationale of neutral reportage: "The public interest in being fully informed about controversies that often rage around sensitive issues demands that the press be afforded the freedom to report such charges without assuming responsibility for them." The court concluded that the *Times* could not

---

[13]556 F.2d 113 (2d Cir. 1977)

be found guilty of libel "for the accurate reporting of newsworthy accusations made by a responsible and well-noted organization like the National Audubon Society."

The lesson here? A reporter should always double-check accusations made by a news source. If that source is a reliable person or group who is making charges against public figures, the concept of neutral reportage *may* protect the reporter. Many media outlets prefer to avoid "neutrally reported" accusations altogether. Even if the media outlet wins in the end, it has still spent a lot of time and money in court.

FAIR COMMENT AND CRITICISM

The media are supposed to be protected from libel suits if a reporter or columnist is simply engaging in commentary or criticism. For example, a restaurant critic who says a diner's food is "nauseating and disgusting" is not guilty of libel. Those are not fact-based comments that can be proven or disproven. They are simply one person's opinion. If the critic says the diner is "rat infested," that is potentially libelous because the critic is making a factual claim that can be proved or disproved.

The courts have ruled that fair comment and criticism is protected if it meets four criteria: (a) the published criticism is of legitimate public interest, (b) the criticism is based on clearly stated facts or on facts that are likely to be known by the reader, (c) the criticism represents the actual opinion of the critic, and (d) the critic's sole purpose was not to harm the person criticized.

We'll see these four principles applied in the following cases.

Marxist Professor?

In May 1978, a column by nationally syndicated columnists Rowland Evans and Robert Novak appeared in newspapers across the country, including the *Washington Post.* The column focused on Bertell Ollman, a political science professor at New York University, who had just been appointed as head of the University of Maryland's Department of Government and Politics. In the column, Evans and Novak criticized "the appointment of a Marxist to head the University of Maryland's department of politics and government." They also said, "His [Ollman's] candid writings avow his desire to use the classroom as an instrument for preparing what he calls 'the revolution.' . . . Amid the increasingly popular Marxist movement in university life, he is distinct from philosophical Marxists. Rather, he is an outspoken proponent of 'political Marxism.'" The columnists quoted an Ollman article in which the professor said, in reference to one political science class, that "the purpose of my course is to convert students to socialism."

Ollman sued. He did not accuse Evans and Novak of misquoting him; he was more upset by the conclusions the writers made. Ollman said the column "denies his reputation as a scholar and portrays him as a 'political activist' who seeks to use the classroom not for purposes of teaching but rather for ulterior purposes."

In *Ollman v. Evans,*[14] a federal appeals court ruled in favor of Evans and Novak, saying the column was protected opinion and contained no "underlying false or defamatory statements of fact."

---

[14]750 F.2d 970 (D.C. Cir. 1984)

FAQ

Isn't there a lot of gray area between what is fact and opinion?

There can be. That is why the court provided four guidelines for determining whether a statement is libel or protected opinion. Appropriately, these have become known as the Ollman Test.

1. Can the comment or statement be proven true or false? (This was discussed in the Ollman case.)

2. Are the damaging words in the commentary meant to be taken literally? A movie critic calling a film "a piece of garbage" does not mean the critic found the film in a trash can. The comment is not meant to be taken literally. However, saying the movie was "funded by gangsters" is a little more literal.

3. What was the journalistic use for the comments? Were the comments included in a news story or in an editorial? Commentary and criticism are expected to appear on the editorial page. Commentaries disguised as news stories may not receive as much protection from the courts.

4. What is the social context for the comment? Were the offending comments made in a place where you would expect to hear opinion, such as during a debate? Comments made in more "fact-based" settings (history lectures, scientific symposiums) may not receive protection under fair comment and criticism. In such a context, the audience is not expecting to hear criticisms of people.

The Wrestling Coach and Alleged Perjury

In January 1975, a sports column by Theodore Diadiun in the *News-Herald* in Willoughby, OH, focused on a brawl that had broken out after a Maple Heights High School wrestling match against Mentor High School. The Maple Heights wrestling team had been disqualified from competing in the Ohio state wrestling tournament because of the incident, in which seven people were injured. Soon after, wrestling coach Michael Milkovich was called to testify before a panel investigating the brawl.

Diadiun wrote in his column that anyone who was at the wrestling match that day "knows in his heart" that Milkovich "lied at the hearing . . . after having given his solemn oath to tell the truth." Diadiun also accused Milkovich of basically starting the brawl by encouraging people to attack students and fans from Mentor High School. Diadiun then wrote that Milkovich told his students, "If you get in jam, lie your way out."

Milkovich sued the newspaper for libel, saying the article accused him of a crime: perjury. In *Milkovich v. Lorain Journal Co.,*[15] the U.S. Supreme Court ruled that Diadiun's article went beyond "fair comment and criticism." That was because the writer made a claim that could be proven true or false—the claim that Milkovich had committed perjury.

FAQ

Didn't Diadiun's phrasing suggest that he was giving an opinion and not a factual statement?

---

[15]497 U.S. 1 (1991)

Diadiun wrote that any person at the wrestling match "knows in his heart" that Milkovich lied. The Supreme Court ruled that Diadiun was still directly implying that Milkovich had lied. In fact, Chief Justice Rehnquist wrote that even if Diadiun had written "I *think* Milkovich lied," it would still be an assertion of fact and not an opinion.

The Supreme Court remanded the case to an Ohio court. Eventually, the paper settled out of court with Milkovich for more than $100,000.

Radio Call-in Show Leads to Defamation Suit

Just as newspapers can be held liable for defamatory statements made in letters published in their letters to the editor section, radio stations can get into legal hot water over commentary and criticism made by listeners on interview or call-in shows.

In one case, a grade school student got through to a morning radio call-in show. The student told the listening audience that a teacher and the principal at his school were having an affair. The station should have taken the student off of the air at that point. Instead, the student was allowed to keep talking, and he then named the teacher, the principal, and the school on the air.

The teacher and principal sued the radio station for defamation and invasion of privacy. Legal expenses and an out-of-court settlement cost the radio station more than $100,000.[16]

Veggie Libel

Veggie libel or *product disparagement* involves cases in which the media have raised questions about the safety of certain foods. Such media reports can make the public fearful of buying certain foods, and the food producers lose money. As a result, some of those food producers file what are called veggie libel lawsuits.

In 1989, the CBS news magazine *60 Minutes* aired an investigative report suggesting that apples from Washington State were dangerous to eat because they had been sprayed with the chemical Alar. Alar was supposed to produce bigger apples, but *60 Minutes* reported that some scientists said it also might cause cancer, particularly in children.

Soon after the broadcast, apples sales dropped sharply. For example, many schools stopped ordering any fruit treated with Alar. The apple industry claimed it suffered $130 million in lost sales and filed a lawsuit against CBS.

In *Auvil v. 60 Minutes,*[17] a federal appeals court ruled in favor of CBS. The court said the apple industry did not prove the *60 Minutes* report was false. The court noted that the scientific community continued to debate the effects of Alar, so how could the apple industry say for certain that it was *not* harmful? There is an important note here. In libel cases, it is the responsibility of the plaintiff (the apple industry, in this case) to prove actual malice.

FAQ

If there was still much scientific debate about the main evidence in the Alar story, isn't it unfair for the media to present such information to the public as possible fact?

---

[16]First Media Insurance Agency. (2004). *Sample claims.* Retrieved July 2, 2004, from http://www.firstmediainc.com

[17]67 F.3d 816 (9th Cir. 1995)

That is why many states were uncomfortable with this ruling. In response to the Alar case, 13 states (as of 2002) have enacted veggie libel laws. (In Texas, for example, it is called the Texas False Defamation of Perishable Food Products Law.) These laws allow food producers to sue if the media falsely claim that a perishable food product is not safe. Many of the laws say the media must be "truthful" in their claims, using only "reliable scientific data." The media say this is unfair because, as we just read in the Alar lawsuit, the scientific community is not always in agreement on such issues.

So, do the media have a right to report scientific data that "may" be true? Should journalists be more cautious about reporting "questionable" data when it could lead to great economic damage for a food producer? The 13 states with veggie libel laws apparently want the media to exercise a little more discretion than *60 Minutes* did in its Alar story.[18] The media argue that such laws create a chilling effect on investigative reporting about unsafe foods.

Oprah Winfrey Versus the Beef Industry

On April 16, 1996, the nationally syndicated *Oprah Winfrey Show* focused on "dangerous foods." One of the topics was bovine encephalopathy ("mad cow") disease in the United States (there had been a recent outbreak in Europe). A guest on the show said American cattlemen often feed ground animal parts to their cattle, making mad cow disease more likely. Winfrey responded she was "stopped cold from eating another burger."

In 1998, Texas cattle ranchers sued Oprah Winfrey for her comments. In the 2 weeks after the show, beef prices fell. A group of Texas cattlemen claimed they lost $12 million after the episode aired.

In *Engler v. Winfrey,*[19] a federal appeals court upheld a lower court judgment and ruled for Winfrey based on two issues under Texas law: the cattlemen did not prove cattle were a "perishable food," and the cattlemen did not prove actual malice (that Winfrey made "knowingly false" statements). Winfrey was simply giving an *opinion* in reaction to the information presented on her show.

INTENTIONAL INFLICTION OF EMOTIONAL DISTRESS

Many libel suits now include other actions as well. Lawyers frequently "tack on" other claims, such as intentional infliction of emotional distress, in case the libel part of the suit is not successful.

One of the first famous cases to use this tactic resulted from a November 1983 edition of *Hustler* magazine that included an alcohol ad parody. It featured a picture of the Reverend Jerry Falwell and included a "mock" interview with Falwell. The parody made references to Falwell having sex with his mother and with a goat. It also insinuated that Falwell was drunk when he delivered sermons.

On the bottom of the page, the magazine printed "Ad parody not to be taken seriously," but Falwell took the ad very seriously. He did not appreciate being characterized as engaging in bestiality, incest, and drunkenness. He sued the magazine for libel, invasion of privacy, and intentional infliction of emotional distress. A lower court threw out the privacy claim because Falwell was a public figure and was fair game for public commentary and

---

[18]Those 13 states are Alabama, Arizona, Colorado, Florida, Georgia, Idaho, Louisiana, Mississippi, North Dakota, Ohio, Oklahoma, South Dakota, and Texas.

[19]201 F.3d 680 (5th Cir. 2000)

ridicule. The libel charge was also thrown out because the ad parody was not meant to be factual. It was obviously a joke and also qualified as political speech. Besides, to prove libel, Falwell would have to have proved the falsity of an ad parody that was *meant* to be false. However, the jury did find *Hustler* guilty of intentional infliction of emotional distress and awarded Falwell $200,000 in damages.

The magazine appealed and won on all three counts in *Hustler v. Falwell*.[20] The U.S. Supreme Court not only upheld the lower court rulings on the privacy and libel claims but also reversed the jury ruling on the emotional distress count. Chief Justice William Rehnquist wrote that the parody was "doubtless gross and repugnant in the eyes of most," but he compared the parody with political cartoons, which are "often calculated to injure the feelings of the subject." The court said that public figures have to expect "emotional distress" from public ridicule and commentary. It is part of being in the public spotlight.

Ugliest Bride

In 1996, two DJs on WPYX-FM in Albany, NY, had a routine called the "ugliest bride" contest, during which they would pick out pictures from the bridal announcements in local newspapers. They would make derogatory remarks about certain women's pictures and then invite listeners to call in and add commentary. The DJs' standard practice on the air was to use only the first names of the brides.

However, in the case of Annette Esposito-Hilder, the DJs announced her full name, as well as her job position and where she worked. (She happened to work for another broadcasting company in town.) The DJs also identified some of her supervisors and colleagues. The woman filed a $300,000 lawsuit against the station and the two DJs for intentional infliction of emotional distress. The Appellate Division of the New York State Supreme Court allowed the lawsuit to go forward, saying there was evidence to show the DJs had "an intent to injure" the woman with their comments.[21]

In its ruling to allow the suit to go forward, the appellate court did recognize that the DJs' speech was afforded some First Amendment protection because it was "pure, subjective opinion." However, the court also noted that "comedic expression does not receive absolute First Amendment protection." The court also cited the *Hustler* ruling and said that Esposito-Hilder's case was strengthened by the fact that she was a private citizen, not a public figure, and that the DJs' comments did not concern a matter of public interest and concern. Therefore, the court said, the DJs' speech might be "less stringently protected" and that the "State's relatively strong interest in compensating individuals for harm outweighs the relatively weak First Amendment protection to be accorded defendants."

However, before the case went to trial, the station settled the lawsuit by paying for the bride's honeymoon vacation. As a result, a trial court did not have a chance to determine if the DJs had gone "too far."

TAKING LIBERTIES WITH QUOTATIONS

Practically every print or broadcast journalist has had the following experience. The reporter gets a great story to cover and is imagining the wonderful quotations or sound bites that will be given by sources. However, for whatever reasons, the interviews are not as

---

[20]485 U.S. 46 (1988)

[21]*Esposito-Hilder v. SFX Broadcasting Inc.*, 236 A.D.2d 186 (1997)

great as was hoped. Those dynamic bites or quotations just are not there. The story is falling flat. There is the temptation for the broadcast reporter to use a sound bite slightly out of context because it makes the story sound more dramatic. The newspaper reporter gets the urge to alter a few quotations "ever so slightly" to help bring out some points that a source did not state clearly in the interview.

Are journalists crossing ethical and legal lines by engaging in such tactics? The landmark case in this area is *Masson v. New Yorker.*[22] The case involved Janet Malcolm of *New Yorker Magazine* and her 1984 story about a controversial psychoanalyst named Jeffrey Masson. In her article, Malcolm wrote that Masson called himself "the greatest analyst who ever lived" and an "intellectual gigolo."

Masson sued the *New Yorker,* arguing that he never used such words and that Malcolm deliberately made up the quotations. He said her misrepresentations damaged his professional reputation by making him appear arrogant and irresponsible.

Malcolm argued that the quotations were accurate. She had tape-recorded 40 hours of interviews with Masson, but the quotations in dispute could not be found on those tapes. However, Malcolm says she also did interviews with Masson that were not recorded and that she took detailed notes of those interviews. Masson claimed that Malcolm never took notes during the nontaped interviews. Malcolm says she took the disputed quotations from those notes, but she could not produce the notes when asked.

A federal district court and appeals court did not even allow the case to go to a jury trial. Both courts ruled for the *New Yorker,* saying that journalists must be allowed some "journalistic license" and that the disputed quotations were "reasonable interpretations" of what Masson had said on the tapes. The U.S. Supreme Court gave Masson a ray of hope by reinstating his case and remanding it to the federal appeals court to determine whether Masson had a right to a jury trial.

Masson was considered a public figure, and he would therefore be required to prove actual malice on Malcolm's part. The Supreme Court told the appeals court to look more closely at the evidence to determine whether the reporter's actions made her guilty of actual malice or reckless disregard for the truth. In the end, a federal appeals court in 1996 upheld a jury verdict against Masson. The jury said Masson did not prove that Malcolm had acted with actual malice or recklessness when writing the story.[23]

In 1995, Masson said she finally found those notes from the nontaped interviews and that the notes verified the "gigolo" comment, among other things. The magazine probably wishes she had found the notes back in 1984. During the 12 years that this case went through a variety of courts, legal expenses for Malcolm and *New Yorker Magazine* topped $2.5 million.

LIBEL AND STATUTES OF LIMITATIONS

FAQ

What are statutes of limitations?

---

[22]501 U.S. 496 (1991)

[23]85 F.3d 1394 (9th Cir. 1996)

A statute of limitations is a "law of time limits." For example: A state has a statute of limitations of 6 years for burglary. If a person burglarizes a house and is not arrested within 6 years, that person can no longer be prosecuted for that crime. The statute of limitations is up. States do this to provide some incentive for law enforcement officials to solve a crime within a certain time period. Mostly, though, statutes of limitations are meant to keep the court system from being clogged by old cases. The Constitution, after all, does guarantee every person a public and *speedy* trial. (There are no statutes of limitations on crimes such as kidnapping and murder. No matter how much time has gone by, a person can always be prosecuted for those crimes.)

Most states (44 of them) have statutes of limitations of 1 or 2 years for libel. In those states, a libel suit must be filed within 1 or 2 years of publication. However, six states have a 3-year statute of limitations for libel suits—Arkansas, Massachusetts, New Hampshire, New Mexico, Rhode Island, and Vermont.

These "laws of time limits" played a major role in 1984 in *Keeton v. Hustler.*[24] The case involved an executive at *Penthouse* magazine, Kathy Keeton. *Hustler* magazine had printed a cartoon implying *Penthouse* publisher Bob Guccione had given Keeton a venereal disease. Keeton planned to sue for libel in Ohio where *Hustler* was headquartered. However, the statute of limitations for libel in Ohio had expired, and Keeton was unable to file her case there.

Because *Hustler* was distributed nationally, Keeton decided to do what is called *forum shopping.* She looked for a state where the statute of limitations for libel had not expired. There was only one state—New Hampshire. At the time, the state had a 6-year statute of limitations on libel, so Keeton sued *Hustler* in New Hampshire. Keeton argued that roughly 10,000 copies of *Hustler* were sold in New Hampshire monthly and that she had been libeled there just as she had been libeled in Ohio or any other state.

A federal district court and a federal appeals court ruled that New Hampshire courts had no jurisdiction in this case because Keeton lived and worked in New York. However, the U.S. Supreme Court overturned those rulings and said Keeton had a right to sue for libel in New Hampshire because "There is no unfairness in calling [*Hustler*] to answer for the contents of that publication wherever a substantial number of copies are regularly sold and distributed."

Libel and Jurisdiction

Also in 1984, actress Shirley Jones and her husband Marty Ingels sued the *National Enquirer* for a story that claimed Jones became a "crying drunk" almost daily because of her husband's treatment. The couple chose to sue the tabloid in their home state of California. However, the story's writer, John South, and the tabloid's editor, Ian Calder, lived in Florida, where the *Enquirer* was headquartered. They argued that allowing the trial in California would lead to a chilling effect on journalists. Why? Journalists would be afraid to publish or broadcast stories out of fear of having to travel across the country to defend themselves in every single libel suit that came up. They said Jones and Ingels should come to Florida because that was where the tabloid was headquartered.

In *Calder v. Jones,*[25] the Supreme Court rejected the *Enquirer's* arguments and voted 9-0 that California was the proper jurisdiction for this case. Jones and Ingels were "injured" in

---

[24] 465 U.S. 770 (1984)

[25] 465 U.S. 783 (1984)

their home state of California, and that was where they would suffer the most harm to their reputations. At the time, the *Enquirer* sold 600,000 copies each week in California, nearly one eighth of its total national weekly sales of 5 million. The court rejected the chilling effects argument, saying that the editor and writer should have considered this issue before they wrote the story and opened themselves up to a libel suit in a distant state.

LIBEL AND LARGE GROUPS

At the beginning of the chapter, we discussed the point that identification is one of the six main factors that must be present for libel to occur. A person or group must be clearly identified if a libel suit is to have any chance of success. However, when the group is very large, libel is more difficult to prove. For example, if a student newspaper editorial claims that "all of the professors in the history department are racists" and the history department only has six professors, that's a small group, and each faculty member could suffer damage from the claim. However, if the editorial claimed that "all 800 faculty members at our university are racists," a court would most likely rule the claim is too broad to affect any one professor. It is difficult to libel large groups.

That is the issue in the following case.

The Guns of Autumn

A 1975 CBS news documentary, *The Guns of Autumn*, and a sequel, *Echoes of the Guns of Autumn*, painted a rather negative view of people who hunted for sport. For example, during one scene, a hunter talked about the joys of hunting while film was shown of men loading dead deer onto trucks.

A Michigan hunters' group, the Michigan United Conservation Club (MUCC), said the documentaries "emphasized the slaughter rather than the 'spirit of the hunt.'" One hunter said he suffered "personal humiliation and discredit" because of his appearance on the CBS broadcast. MUCC sued CBS for libel in *Michigan United Conservation Club v. CBS*.[26] In fact, MUCC said the CBS broadcasts defamed "*all* Michigan hunters." At the time, there were upwards of a million hunters in Michigan. The suit was claiming that more than a million people had been defamed by these two documentaries.

A federal appeals court ruled for CBS, saying some of the MUCC hunters claiming harm were not "shown, described, named, identified, or in any way mentioned in either of the films." Probably the court's most important statement was this: "Vague, general references to a comparatively large group do not constitute actionable defamation."

FAQ

So, what does qualify as a "comparatively large group"?

Obviously, a million hunters would qualify. However, a general cut-off point for the courts has been 25. Again, in *general,* groups larger than 25 people are considered to be "comparatively large," but it depends on the case and the libel issues involved.

---

[26]665 F.2d 110 (6th Cir. 1981)

The case of *Neiman-Marcus v. Lait*[27] in 1952 is a useful guide to the "numbers game" in libel cases. The book *U.S.A. Confidential,* written by two men named Lait and Mortimer, was highly critical of the Neiman-Marcus department store in Dallas. The authors said Neiman models were "call girls—the top babes in town . . . a hundred bucks a night." Neiman sales girls were called "cheaper—twenty bucks on the average." The authors added that most of Neiman's salesmen were "faggots" and "fairies."

The numbers of models, salesmen, and sales girls became a pivotal issue in deciding this case. There were 9 Neiman models, 25 salesmen, and 382 saleswomen. Each of the three groups sued for libel. In trying to determine whether each group had a legitimate case, a federal district court noted "the following propositions are rather widely accepted. . . . Where the group or class libeled is *large,* none can sue even though the language used is inclusive. . . . Where the group or class libeled is *small,* and each and every member of the group or class is referred to, then any individual member can sue."

With these guidelines, the court allowed the lawsuits to go forward for the 9 models and 25 salesmen. The court, though, dismissed the libel suit brought by the group of 382 saleswomen, ruling that there was no legal precedent to "support a cause of action by an individual member of any group of such magnitude."

SOME GOOD TIPS TO KEEP YOU AWAY FROM LIBEL CASES

1. *When in doubt, leave it out.* If you are not sure about something, do not air it or print it.

2. *Double-check your sources,* especially for controversial stories.

3. *Double-check your facts,* especially for controversial stories. Make sure names and other vital information are correct.

4. Be careful about using *unnamed sources* in controversial stories. This can create special problems if a libel case is brought against you. (If your sources will not come forward in a trial, how can the court determine whether your sources were credible?)

5. *Arrests.* Be very careful when writing stories about an arrest. Always remember that a person is innocent until proven guilty. *An arrest is not an indication of guilt.*

6. *Alleged.* Saying "alleged" or "allegedly" is not a foolproof safeguard against libel. *Avoid:* (a) "Police say Smith allegedly held up the bank." Instead, keep the crime and the name of the suspect separated. (b) "Police say a man held up the bank at 2:00 p.m. They later arrested 42-year-old Joe Smith." The arrest is a fact. Smith holding up the bank is not a fact. Thus (b) is better than (a). Follow the same logic when it comes to

7. *Convictions.* Once someone has been convicted of a crime, it is perfectly fine to call the person a "killer" or "convicted killer." However, some news directors and reporters are reluctant to use a term such as *killer* out of fear that someone could come back and sue if a conviction gets overturned. Some news stations use the policy of avoiding such wording as (a) "The jury convicted Jones. He killed an elderly Smithtown couple in 1998." Instead,

---

[27]107 F. Supp 96, 13 F.R.D. 311 (D.N.Y. 1952)

some stations prefer this: (b) "The jury convicted Jones for the 1998 double murder." The writing in (a) says Jones definitely killed the couple. The writing in (b) says he was *convicted* of killing them. We know the conviction is a fact. The murder may not be a fact because the jury may have reached an incorrect verdict. However, most stations feel comfortable labeling someone a "killer," "rapist," or "robber" after a conviction.

8. Be careful about using *language that infers* (a) involvement in crime or with criminal groups, (b) embarrassing financial problems (poverty, bankruptcy, foreclosures, etc.), (c) sexual matters (promiscuity, homosexuality, adultery), (d) intolerance (racism, religious bigotry, etc.), (e) lying, (f) involvement in scams, (g) "extreme" political views (Nazism, fascism, white supremacy, etc.), (h) horrible diseases (AIDS, venereal diseases, Alzheimer's), (i) alcohol problems (calling someone a drunk or a lush), (j) mental problems (use of the terms *insane, lunatic, unstable*), (k) references to stupidity (*moron, idiot, imbecile*), (l) negative references to character (*lazy, immoral, cowardly*), (m) involvement in Satanism or other religions considered questionable by community standards, (n) information about a person having an abortion, or (o) unprofessional behavior.

Summary

Six elements must be present for libel to have occurred: *defamation, falsity, communication, identification, fault,* and *harm.* Fault includes the important criteria of *actual malice* and *reckless disregard for the truth.* The three defenses against libel are *truth, privilege,* and *fair comment and criticism.*

The landmark case *New York Times v. Sullivan* established the actual malice standard and gave greater protection to media in libel cases. Under actual malice, a plaintiff must prove that the media knowingly printed defamatory material or did so with a reckless disregard for the truth.

In many states, it is much easier for a private citizen to win a libel suit. Whereas public figures must prove actual malice, private citizens may only have to prove negligence on the media's part, a less stringent standard.

8

PRIVACY

In short, it is the right to be let alone.

—*Gill v. Curtis*[1]

The right to be let alone. It is a right that people cherish. Technology, though, has altered the playing field, and Americans are finding more and more places where they are being "watched." It is now common for businesses to install security cameras in their stores to help prevent crime. Cities such as Washington, DC, have placed cameras at busy intersections to catch people who run red lights; and those people then get tickets in the mail soon after. Your picture is usually taken at an ATM. Businesses use devices to keep track of their employees' Internet use. The media are now capable of doing investigative reporting with cameras and microphones that can be hidden in a pocket or hat. Such technology has found its way into private homes, as some parents have installed cameras in bedrooms to monitor their children's behavior. Technology seems to be allowing greater intrusion into areas of our lives once considered private. Such concerns about technology, media, and privacy are nothing new.

HISTORY OF PRIVACY LAW

Two Boston attorneys recognized technology's threat to privacy in 1890. In the article "The Right of Privacy," published in the *Harvard Law Review,* Samuel Warren and future Supreme Court justice Louis Brandeis warned of the threats to individual privacy posed by new technologies such as instant photography: "Numerous mechanical devices threaten to make good the prediction that 'what is whispered in the closet shall be proclaimed from the housetops.'"[2] The authors said they were especially upset with newspapers printing sensational stories based on "gossip." They argued that these stories caused mental pain and distress that was greater than any physical pain.

---

[1] *Gill v. Curtis,* 38 Cal.2d 273, 239 P.2d 630 (1952)

[2] Warren, S., & Brandeis, L. (1890). The right of privacy. 4 *Harvard Law Review* 193.

The Constitution recognizes certain privacy rights. The Fourth Amendment prohibits the government from unwarranted searches and seizures within private homes. However, up until this time, U.S. courts had not recognized an individual right to privacy. Warren and Brandeis used their article to argue that all citizens are entitled to a legal right to privacy, similar to personal property rights and intellectual property rights.

The article received great attention in the legal and scholarly communities, but states were very slow to enact privacy laws. Twelve years after the article was published, the nation's highest court refused to recognize a legal right to privacy. In 1902, a New York court did not recognize a person's legal right to control the commercial use of a person's name or image. In *Roberson v. Rochester Folding Box Co.*,[3] a woman had discovered that her picture was being used on flour ads without her permission. She sued the company, but the court said there was only a "so-called right to privacy" and that this right had yet to be established in American law.

In 1903, the New York State legislature helped to establish that right by passing America's first misappropriation law.[4] It made illegal the use of a living person's name, picture, or portrait for commercial purposes unless the person had given written consent.

1905 saw the first court case upholding this right. In *Pavesich v. New England Life Insurance Company*,[5] an artist had sued an insurance company for using his picture without permission in an ad. The ad also included a fake "testimonial" from the artist, which said he recommended the insurance. The Georgia Supreme Court ruled that the artist's name and likeness had been "misappropriated," and he had a right to sue for damages. Since then, courts and the states slowly began to recognize an individual right to privacy.

Concerns about government use of private information led to the Privacy Act of 1974,[6] which attempted to regulate how the federal government collected and used personal data and records of citizens. (There will be more discussion on privacy and government records in the final chapter of this book.)

Privacy Law Torts

FAQ

What is a tort?

Privacy law involves *tort* actions, civil lawsuits in which someone sues another party. In this chapter, many of the lawsuits involve individuals suing the media for some form of invasion of privacy. Privacy law is similar to libel law in many ways because in both cases,

---

[3] 64 N.E. 442 (1902)

[4] 1903 N.Y. Laws § 132 1-2, codified as amended at N.Y. Civil Rights Law §§ 50-51

[5] 50 S.E. 68 (1905)

[6] 5 U.S.C. § 552a

people are seeking damages for "negative publicity." However, there are distinct differences between libel law and privacy law, as will be seen.

There are four basic areas or torts in privacy law.

Four Basic Torts of Privacy Law

The four basic torts of privacy law are (a) intrusion into a person's seclusion or private affairs, (b) public disclosure of embarrassing private facts, (c) "false light," and (d) misappropriation. As we discuss these four areas, it will become clear that a person's status as private citizen or public figure is an important factor in many cases.

Public figures or *officials* are people in the public spotlight. The media have more rights to discuss these people's private affairs in news stories. Public officials and public figures surrender many of their privacy rights when they enter the public arena. *Private citizens* have a greater "expectation of privacy" and more of a legal right to be "let alone." However, this right is not absolute.

The following examples help to explain the difference between a public official and a private citizen when considering privacy and news stories:

Situation 1: A married U.S. senator is having a sexual affair with a female staffer.

Situation 2: A married construction worker in Portland, OR, is having a romantic relationship with another woman.

Is it an invasion of the senator's privacy if the news media report the affair? In such cases, the courts have said no. The senator is an elected official. The media have a right to scrutinize his private life. It reflects on his "character" as an elected lawmaker.

In regard to the construction worker's affair, however, the courts have said that such a case would be an invasion of privacy. This man is a private citizen and is not in the public spotlight. There is no "newsworthiness" in reporting his infidelity. Revealing his affair would invade his privacy and be a "disclosure of embarrassing private facts."

With these examples in mind, we begin our analysis of privacy cases involving both private and public persons. We begin with the area of intrusion and a landmark case that helped to establish some limits on the rights of private persons in public places.

Intrusion and the Media

FAQ

What rights do the media have in regard to photographing private citizens in public places?

In general, the courts have been very protective of the media's rights in such matters. In 1947, John Gill and his wife were sitting at a table at an ice cream stand they operated at the Farmer's Market in Los Angeles. A photographer captured the Gills in "an affectionate pose" (the man was sitting close to wife with his arm around her). The picture appeared in the October 1947 *Harper's Bazaar* and in the May 1949 *Ladies Home Journal.* Both magazines used the picture in conjunction with articles about "love."

In *Gill v. Hearst,*[7] the Gills claimed that the picture invaded their privacy because neither one had consented to the photograph being taken or being used in a magazine. However, the California Supreme Court ruled that the Gills had no expectation of privacy. The couple was in a public place. They had "voluntarily exposed themselves to public gaze." Also, the picture did not offend "ordinary sensibilities." It showed a husband and wife being affectionate in public. It did not go beyond the limits of public decency.

If the Gills won this case, the court said, there would be a chilling effect. Magazines, newspapers, and TV stations would be fearful of publishing or broadcasting pictures from public events (parades, political rallies, etc.). The ruling thus established that a "private" act performed in public or within the public's view becomes a "public" act under the law. Much of the same reasoning applied in the next case, which was an important ruling for the news media.

TV Camera on a Sidewalk

On December 31, 1976, a camera crew from KING-TV in Seattle went to the home of pharmacist Albert Mark. The TV station was doing a news story about the pharmacist's having allegedly filled out $200,000 worth of false prescriptions for Medicaid patients. Mark was not at home, so the camera crew went to Mark's pharmacy. The pharmacy was closed, but Mark was inside talking on the phone. His wife and a friend were also there.

The cameraman walked up the driveway area of the pharmacy, stood on the sidewalk, pressed the lens of the camera against the window, turned on the camera light, and began filming. Mark turned away, and his friend tried to block the camera's view. The cameraman kept moving and getting film of the inside of the pharmacy. On January 7, 1977, KING ran a news story about the pharmacist and the charges of Medicaid fraud. The story included roughly 53 seconds of the film taken by the cameraman, including shots of the outside and inside of the pharmacy and a shot of Mark talking on the phone.

In June 1977, Mark was found guilty of forgery and grand larceny in connection with the false Medicaid prescriptions. About 1½ years later, in November 1978, Mark sued KING for invasion of privacy. He claimed the film clips used in the news broadcast invaded his privacy with "an unreasonable intrusion into his seclusion and physical solitude." Mark also said the TV station trespassed on his private property.

In *Mark v. KING,*[8] a Washington state appeals court ruled for the TV station. The cameraman was on a public sidewalk, "a place that was open to the public," the court pointed out. It would only have been invasion of privacy if the intrusion were "highly offensive to a reasonable person." The court said that Mark was not portrayed in an unreasonable manner. The film only showed what "any passerby would have seen passing the building." Also, the court said, "The filming was accomplished without ruse or subterfuge." There was no hidden camera. There was no trickery on the TV station's part. It was obvious what the cameraman was doing. KING was covering a news story of legitimate public interest.

---

[7] 40 Cal.2d 224; 253 P.2d 441 (1953)

[8] 618 P.2d 512 (1980)

FAQ

Would this ruling apply to persons in their private homes?

Yes. A person's actions are no longer "private" when they are performed within public view. This is an important case for news gatherers. It establishes that pictures of private property or actions on that property are usually not an invasion of privacy as long as those pictures are taken from a public place.

Journalists Airing Recorded Phone Conversations

If a person illegally records a phone conversation and, in pursuing a story, a journalist legally obtains the recording and airs it, is the journalist liable for invasion of privacy? That was a question the U.S. Supreme Court decided in 2001.

In *Bartnicki v. Vopper*,[9] Pennsylvania broadcaster Fred Vopper, through a third party, legally obtained a recording of a private cell phone conversation between two officials of a teacher's union. One official talked about "blowing off the front porches" of school board members who opposed teacher pay raises. The two officials sued Vopper for broadcasting the tape.

The Supreme Court ruled 6-3 that Vopper had a right to air the tape because it was a newsworthy story dealing with an important public issue. In a concurring opinion, Justices Breyer and O'Connor emphasized that the media may not broadcast such tapes if they include discussions of private or personal matters. Vopper was protected in this case because the conversations involved important public issues. The court added that even though the person who made the original recording broke the law, Vopper was not guilty of any offense because he obtained the tape legally and had no part in the illegal taping.

The ruling was different in the following case because of the journalist's activities surrounding the illegal taping.

Carver Dan Peavy, who was an elected trustee for Dallas, TX schools, had a neighbor, Charles Harman, with a police scanner. Harman was listening to the scanner one day when it picked up one of Peavy's cordless phone conversations. Harman said the conversations included "threats to his safety," discussions about Peavy wanting to sue the Harmans, and Peavy discussing involvement in an illegal school insurance kickback scheme. Harman said he began making recordings of the phone calls.

Harman soon after contacted WFAA-TV reporter Robert Riggs. WFAA did not air any of the tapes, but the station did use information from the tapes in several stories that suggested Peavy was engaged in wrongdoing. Peavy sued and a trial court ruled for the TV station. However, a federal appeals reinstated Peavy's lawsuit, saying that WFAA "knew or should have known the interceptions were illegal" and, most important, that the station "had some participation concerning the interceptions."[10]

Man Commits Suicide After Phone Conversation Airs on TV Station

During the Columbine High School shooting in 1999, in which 15 people died, a student called a local Colorado TV station to say that he was locked in a classroom and heard a lot

---

[9]532 U.S. 514 (2001)

[10]*Peavy v. WFAA-TV,* 221 F.3d 158 (5th Cir. 2000)

of crying and screaming in the hallway. The TV station aired part of the phone call, and there was much debate about the ethics of doing so. The student was unharmed, but there was debate about whether the broadcast could have potentially endangered the student's safety had the gunmen seen the coverage on a school TV.

In a 1996 case, it was the media who made the phone call to a man barricaded in his house. Police had surrounded Bruce Clift's house after he had called his wife at work and threatened suicide. A TV reporter called Clift at roughly 5:00 p.m., and he agreed to a recorded phone conversation. The reporter had not notified police or other officials about the phone call. At 6:04 p.m., TV station Channel 12 aired a story with excerpts from the phone call in which Clift said he was not giving up and "this is the final stand." At 6:07 p.m., Clift killed himself. Police entered the home and found TVs tuned to Channel 12.

His widow sued the station for numerous causes of action, but the Superior Court of Rhode Island ruled in favor of the TV station. However, in 1996, the Supreme Court of Rhode Island, in *Clift v. Narragansett TV*,[11] ruled that Clift's widow had a right to sue on four claims, including negligence. The court remanded the case to the Superior Court, with instructions that the lower court consider testimony from a medical expert who said the Channel 12 story might have been negligent and thus "exacerbated" the suicide.

Crime and Disaster Scenes

Fire at Private Home

Law enforcement and emergency officials do not have an automatic right to enter a private home without just cause. That is why police often have to obtain search warrants from a court before entering or searching a home. However, once these officials have legally entered a private home, it does not mean the media have a right to be there, too.

In this case, fire officials were at the scene of a fatal house fire in Florida. The fire marshal was taking pictures of the scene when he ran out of film, so he invited a newspaper photographer to enter the burned home and take pictures. One of the pictures taken was a silhouette of ashes left behind by a girl who had died in the fire. That photograph was published in the *Florida Times Union* newspaper. The parents of the girl sued the newspaper for invasion of privacy. The paper argued it had a right to use the photograph because it was taken with the fire marshal's approval. The parents argued that it was their private home, and they did not invite the photographer to take any pictures.

In *Florida Publishing Co. v. Fletcher*,[12] the court ruled for the newspaper because the fire marshal, whose goal was to have the media assist in evidence gathering, had invited the photographer to take the pictures; also, the fire was newsworthy.

FAQ

Does this ruling give the media a right to go on private property during newsworthy events?

---

[11]688 A.2d 805 (1996)

[12]340 So.2d 914 (Fla. 1976)

No. It is important to keep in mind that this ruling is unique. In most cases, the courts do *not* approve of the media intruding on private property even when invited by public officials. (The next chapter will deal with such cases in more detail.)

There is also a certain expectation of privacy for people in jails, but it depends on the specific circumstances.

Jails and Prisons

In Russelville, AR, police had arrested and jailed an attorney and former judge, Marvin Holman, for drunken driving. In jail, Holman banged on his cell door and was screaming and cursing while talking with his lawyer inside the cell. A radio reporter who had been granted access to the jail area made an audio recording of Holman's ranting and raving. A portion of that recording aired later in a news story on the radio station.

Holman sued, saying he had a right to privacy in his jail cell and a right to private conversations with his lawyer. In 1979, in *Holman v. Central Arkansas Broadcasting*,[13] a federal appeals court ruled for the radio station. Holman obviously did not intend for his conversation with his lawyer to be private, as he was talking loudly and could easily be heard by others in the jail. No confidential legal advice between Holman and his lawyer was recorded or broadcast by the radio station: The station acted in good faith. The court also pointed out that jail officials had given the TV reporter permission to be there, so there was no "malicious entry."

FAQ

Does this ruling mean that people have fewer privacy rights when in jail or prison?

No. There was no expectation of privacy here because Holman was obviously drawing attention to himself with his behavior. The next case, though, shows that prisoners do have certain expectations of privacy within prison.

Prisoner in a Prison Exercise Room

An NBC news crew from WMAQ-TV in Chicago had been granted access to a federal prison in Marion, IL to do a report on prison conditions. Officials told the news crew that it was a violation of federal regulations to take any pictures of inmates without their consent. NBC agreed to follow these regulations.

During their videotaping, the WMAQ cameraman took several minutes of video of prisoner Arnold Huskey working out in a small exercise room. Huskey was wearing only gym shorts, and several of his distinctive tattoos could be seen clearly. Huskey noticed the camera and told a guard he did not want to be filmed, but the guard did not stop the TV crew from videotaping. The tape of Huskey did not air, but Huskey did not want NBC to be able to use any of the videotape for future broadcasts, so he filed a lawsuit.

Huskey sued for invasion of privacy, saying he was "engaged in private activities in the most private environment available to him for those activities." NBC argued that Huskey

---

[13]610 F.2d 542 (8th Cir. 1979)

was in a "publicly visible area," that covering prison conditions was a newsworthy endeavor, and that Huskey was a limited public figure.

In 1986, in *Huskey v. NBC*,[14] a federal district court ruled for Huskey. NBC broke its promise not to videotape prisoners without their permission, the court said; also, a federal prisoner is not a public figure. Huskey had privacy rights. Just because Huskey was not in a "secluded area" did not mean he lost his privacy rights. The court said, "the mere fact a person can be seen by others does not mean that person cannot be legally 'secluded.'" The court added that people are "exposed" to guests and family members in their homes, "*but that does not mean they have opened the door to television cameras.*"

Unlike the situation in the *Holman* case, Huskey was not drawing attention to himself. NBC should have respected his privacy by getting his permission to videotape or by erasing the video afterward.

Public Figures and Privacy Rights

FAQ

Do public figures have any right to privacy?

Yes, but the law gives more protection to private citizens. However, public figures do have a right to their "personal space" and a right to be protected from excessive harassment. Probably no case explains this issue better than *Galella v. Onassis.*[15]

A freelance photographer, Donald Galella, was known as a *paparazzo* (*paparazzi* is the plural). Celebrities frequently refer to them as "stalkarazzi" because of their tendencies to stalk or follow famous people relentlessly. It can be a lucrative job because tabloid newspapers will sometimes pay huge amounts of money for paparazzi photographs. One of Galella's favorite subjects in the late 1960s and early 1970s was Jacqueline Kennedy Onassis, the widow of John F. Kennedy.

Within a short time, Secret Service agents felt Galella was becoming a danger to Onassis. and her children, John Jr. and Caroline. Agents reported that Galella once jumped into the path of John Jr. as the boy was riding a bike through Central Park, that he had sneaked into the children's private schools, and that he once drove a power boat "uncomfortably close" to Onassis when she was swimming. Galella also, on several occasions, physically touched Onassis and her daughter.

Onassis obtained restraining orders against Galella, but he ignored them. Three Secret Service agents finally arrested Galella, and he sued the government for false arrest. A district ruled that the Secret Service agents were justified in arresting Galella. The more interesting issue for our purposes is the lawsuit brought by Onassis against Galella for invasion of privacy, assault, intentional infliction of emotional distress, and harassment.

---

[14]632 F. Supp. 1282 (N.D. Ill.1986)

[15]487 F.2d 986 (2d Cir. 1973)

Onassis was a public figure, so she certainly could not expect a right to privacy when it came to people photographing her in public places. However, she did have a right to be protected from assault and harassment. That is why a district court ruled that Galella had to "keep his distance." The court said that he must stay 100 yards away from the children's schools, 75 yards away from the children, 50 yards away from Onassis, and 100 yards away from their home.

In 1973, in *Galella v. Onassis,*[163] a federal appeals court upheld the district court's ruling, with some modifications. The court ruled that Galella had to stay only 25 feet away from Onassis, must never touch her, and must stay only 30 feet away from the children. The court dropped the 100 yard "bubble zone" around the Onassis home and gave Galella no restrictions in this regard. Instead of staying 100 yards away from the schools, Galella was simply barred from entering the schools or play areas of the children.

A dissenting judge said the majority should have kept the more restrictive guidelines established by the district court. The judge said the new guidelines were too lenient and were "unworkable and ineffective."

FAQ

Was this ruling a win for either side?

The court struck a balance in this case. Members of the media have a right to take pictures of public figures in public places. However, public figures also have a right to a certain amount of personal space and a right to be protected from the tactics of overzealous photographers.

In 1982, Galella violated the bubble zone established by the appeals court. In what was called *Galella II,*[16] Galella was found in contempt, and he was given a choice: go to jail or stop following Onassis. He chose the latter, promising never to take another picture of Onassis. He kept that promise until 1994, when she died. Celebrities hailed the ruling in *Galella II* when the court said "systematic public surveillance" of a person could be considered an invasion of privacy.

Antipaparazzi Law Passed

After Princess Diana died in a car accident in Paris in 1997, many Hollywood celebrities spoke out against the intrusive tactics of the paparazzi who had been following Diana's car on motorcycles the night of the crash. The home state of many celebrities, California, passed an antipaparazzi law in 1998, largely in response to Diana's death.[17] The law says that it is a physical invasion of privacy if a media person trespasses to obtain pictures or audio of family or personal activities on private property where there is a reasonable expectation of privacy. The law then created a second form of trespass that it called a *constructive* invasion of privacy. A constructive invasion of privacy occurs when pictures or audio have been obtained through the use of telephoto lens, boom microphones, or other "visual or auditory enhancing devices" and could not have been obtained without these devices.

---

[16]533 F. Supp. 1076 (S.D.N.Y. 1982)

[17]See the *California Civil Code*, § 1708.8

However, the law also states, "Sale, transmission, publication, broadcast or use of any image . . . shall not in itself constitute a violation." Media may still face damages if they encouraged or enticed persons to get such images. The law stipulates that violators may face *treble* damages, or triple actual damages.

Critics of the law said it was redundant because California law already protected people from trespassing and invasion of privacy, as in the next case.

Actress Sues Tabloids Over Topless Photos

In July 2002, actress Jennifer Aniston reached a settlement with two magazine publishers who had printed pictures of her sunbathing topless in her backyard. Aniston is famous for her role on the popular NBC-TV show *Friends*. A photographer had taken the pictures in February 1999, and the photos later appeared in the magazines *High Society*, *Celebrity Sleuth*, *Celebrity Skin*, and several European magazines and newspapers.

The photos in question showed Aniston wearing only panties and lying on her stomach as she sunbathed behind her home in Malibu. Photographer François Navarre trespassed through a neighbor's yard, climbed an 8-foot wall, and then used a camera with a telephoto lens to snap the pictures. It was these tactics that led to a settlement in favor of Aniston. All citizens, including celebrities, have a certain expectation of privacy in their homes and on their property, especially if the home is surrounded by a high wall. The wall was built to provide privacy. The photographer violated that privacy by trespassing and then climbing the wall.

FAQ

What if there had been no security wall?

It would have been different if Aniston had been sunbathing in a backyard that was in plain view of a public sidewalk or highway. The photographer would not have been invading Aniston's privacy in such an instance because the celebrity chose to do this activity within plain public view. However, that was not the case here.

In a settlement, Navarre paid Aniston $550,000 in damages and admitted that he illegally distributed the photographs. However, Aniston accepted Navarre's claim that he did not trespass to get the photographs.[18]

SEXUAL ASSAULT VICTIMS

Publishing or Broadcasting Rape Victims' Names

In 1975, the Supreme Court handed down an important decision in this very controversial area of privacy law. Crime victim groups often argue that it is an invasion of privacy to release the names of any victim of rape or sexual assault. These groups argue that

---

[18]Cadorette, G. (2003, November 21). *Aniston settles topless photo suit, Spector pleads innocent, Ang Lee to helm gay western*. Retrieved October 24, 2004, from http://www.hollywood.com/news/detail/article/1733986

releasing the victim's name is another form of rape and may keep victims from reporting the crimes. With these concerns in mind, lawmakers have tried unsuccessfully to ban the media from releasing names of sexual assault victims.

Georgia was one state that had banned the publication or broadcast of names of sexual assault victims. A TV reporter for a station in Atlanta, GA, was present at the indictment of six men who were accused of gang-raping a young woman who then choked on her own vomit and died. The court indictment contained the young woman's name, and the reporter included her name in his TV report. The parents of the murdered woman sued the station for invasion of privacy.

Lower courts ruled for the parents. However, in a landmark decision in 1975, the U.S. Supreme Court overturned those rulings in *Cox Broadcasting v. Cohn*.[19] The court ruled 8-1 that the media cannot be punished for publishing or broadcasting material that was obtained legally from public documents, even if that information is considered embarrassing or harmful to the victims.

The Supreme Court reaffirmed this concept 14 years later in *Florida Star v. B.J.F.*[20] The newspaper printed the full name of a woman who had been robbed and sexually assaulted. A reporter had obtained the information from a report placed in the press room at the police station. However, the State of Florida had passed a law making it illegal to "print, publish, or broadcast" the name of any sexual crime victim "in any instrument of mass communication."

B.J.F. sued the newspaper for violating the Florida law and subjecting her to emotional distress. She said her mother received phone calls from a man who was threatening to rape B.J.F. again. She said she also had to move, change her phone number, get mental health counseling, and obtain police protection.

A jury sided with B.J.F. and awarded her $100,000 in damages. The U.S. Supreme Court, though, sided with the newspaper. In reiterating its reasoning from *Cohn,* the court said that the newspaper had lawfully obtained information about a matter of public significance. The court added that individual media outlets may develop their own policies about releasing names of sexual assault victims, but the state may not censor the material if it is obtained legally from government records. Similarly, in 2003, a federal appeals court ruled for the media in *Doe 2 v. Associated Press*.[21] The case involved a sexual assault victim who had testified in a hearing in which the judge ordered the media not to divulge any victim's name. In a news report the next day, the AP identified the victim by name. The court ruled there was no invasion of privacy because the AP had obtained the name legally in a public court proceeding.

FAQ

If reporting such information is legal, why do media outlets rarely use it?

---

[19]420 U.S. 469 (1975)

[20]109 S. Ct. 2603 (1989)

[21]331 F.3d 417 (4th Cir. 2003)

Most media feel that releasing such information can be damaging to the victims, and the release could also create a public backlash against the media outlet. For these reasons and others, the vast majority of media in this country have internal policies prohibiting the release of the names of victims of sexual assaults, as well as the names of juveniles who have been arrested. However, the Supreme Court says states cannot pass laws *requiring* the media to follow such policies. The court made a similar ruling regarding court proceedings involving sexual assault cases.

Media Coverage of Rape Trials

To protect the emotional well being of young women, the Commonwealth of Massachusetts made it illegal for the media or the public to have any access to the records of sexual assault or rape trials that involved victims younger than 18. The state argued that the law would make more young victims want to come forward to prosecute their attackers because the victims would feel more comfortable in doing so if the trials were not "public."

Newspapers sued, saying the law was a violation of their constitutional right to cover criminal trials. In *Globe Newspaper Co. v. Superior Court,*[22] the U.S. Supreme Court over-turned the Massachusetts law. The media and the public have a First Amendment right of access to criminal trials, and the court said that this right overrides the state's interest in protecting minors. The court also pointed out that under the state law, the public and press still would have had access to court records and transcripts of testimony; thus the law was not really achieving its goal of protecting these crime victims. The law was too broad, as well. It barred the public and media from *all* sexual assault trials, even when the victim, prosecutor, and defendant had no objections.

PUBLISHING THE NAMES OF JUVENILES

The media often have policies regarding the names of juveniles who have been charged with crimes. For example, a West Virginia law made it illegal for a newspaper to publish the name of any youth charged as a juvenile offender unless the newspaper had written approval from a juvenile court to do so. The law was designed to "protect the anonymity of juvenile offend-ers to further their rehabilitation." The state felt that the embarrassment and humiliation of publicity might make it harder to keep juvenile offenders from repeating their crimes.

In *Smith v. Daily Mail Publishing Co.,*[23] the issue involved newspaper stories about a 14-year-old boy who had killed another youth. Two newspapers had gotten the boy's name from various news sources, including police, witnesses, and an assistant prosecuting attor-ney at the crime scene; they had also monitored police radio frequencies. Using the same reasoning it had used for rape victims' names in *Cohn,* the U.S. Supreme Court ruled for the newspapers because the information was lawfully obtained. Also, the court noted that the law only restricted newspapers and not radio or TV. Therefore, the law did "not accom-plish its stated purpose."

---

[22]457 U.S. 596 (1982)

[23]443 U.S. 97 (1979)

DISCLOSURE OF EMBARRASSING PRIVATE FACTS

All people have "skeletons in the closet," or aspects of their private lives they would not want disclosed to the public. This area of privacy law is meant to protect persons from unnecessary or embarrassing disclosures of personal matters or behaviors.

FAQ

What if the embarrassment takes place in a public place?

It often depends on several factors:

- ▨ What were the actions of the media or other source?
- ▨ Did the person subject him- or herself to public exposure in some way?
- ▨ Was the location truly a public place, where there was no expectation of privacy?

Video Voyeurism

As stated earlier, technology has forced lawmakers and the courts to reevaluate privacy laws. For example, many gyms and sports clubs have banned all cell phones in public restrooms, locker rooms, and gym showers. The concern is not the phone itself but the cameras that now come on many cell phones. Some persons have used the cameras to take pictures of nude persons in these places, and those pictures can end up on the Internet within seconds. Such concerns led the National Basketball Association in 2004 to ban reporters from using cell phones to interview players in locker rooms. Courts say that even though people in such situations may be willfully naked in front of other people of the same gender, they are not consenting to their nudity being made available to others outside that situation or to persons of the other gender. Thus although a locker room at a community swimming pool is in one sense a public place supported by tax dollars, persons in that locker room still have certain expectations of privacy. Some persons are fighting the cell phone camera bans, saying they may need to take their phones into locker rooms or restrooms because they are expecting an important call or might need the cell phones for emergencies.

The whole issue of video voyeurism received widespread attention in 1999 when the *Chicago Tribune* reported that persons were marketing hidden-camera videotapes and Web sites that showed nude college athletes in showers and locker rooms during sports competitions at various universities. The cameras had apparently been hidden in gym bags between 1990 and 1999 and captured images of athletes from such places as Northwestern, Illinois State, and the University of Pennsylvania. The videotapes and Web sites had titles such as *Between the Lockers* and *Voyeur Time*. Forty-six college athletes from several universities sued the makers and distributors of the videos, and a federal judge in 2002 awarded the athletes $506 million dollars in damages.[24] The athletes then tried to sue GTE and other companies that provided the Internet access to the sellers. In 2003, in

---

[24]See *Doe v. Franco Productions*, 2000 U.S. Dist. LEXIS 8645 (N.D. Ill. June 21, 2000)

Doe v. GTE,[25] a federal appeals court ruled that the Internet service providers (ISPs) could not be held responsible for the actions of the defendants.

FAQ

What about recent controversies in which men on public streets or in stores have aimed these cameras up women's dresses to take pictures?

Even though the women may be walking on a public sidewalk, those women are not inviting people to gaze up their dresses. The photographers are taking extraordinary measures to disclose private facts about a person and are violating privacy law. Many states and communities have updated their voyeurism laws to deal with changing technology. In Wisconsin, for example, such a photographer could face felony charges for video voyeurism under a state law passed in 2001. In 2000, the Wisconsin Supreme Court found a previous video voyeurism law unconstitutional because it was too broad.

Accidental Public Exposures

In *Neff v. Time,*[26] in 1976, a Pittsburgh Steeler fan asked a photographer at a football game to take his picture. The photographer obliged, and the fan was excited to discover the picture was being published in *Sports Illustrated*—until the fan noticed that his fly was unzipped in the picture. He sued the publishers for invading his privacy with this "embarrassing" public display. However, the court said the exposure was not indecent, and the man should have checked his fly before the picture was snapped. The magazine could not be held accountable for the fan's mistake.

In a similar situation, a photographer from the *Brownsville Herald* in Texas took pictures at a local high school soccer game. In the newspaper the next day, one of the pictures was published along with a story about the soccer game. The picture showed a soccer player named McNamara and another player in full stride chasing the soccer ball. Neither the photographer nor anyone at the newspaper noticed that the picture revealed McNamara's genitals under his soccer shorts.

The father of the boy sued the newspaper for invasion of privacy, public disclosure of private facts, and publishing indecent material. The father said the paper should have had better safeguards to prevent "accidental" publication of these kinds of photographs.

In *McNamara v. Freedom Newspapers,*[27] a Texas appeals court ruled for the newspaper. The photograph was taken at a public event in connection with a newsworthy story, and the photograph accurately depicted that public event. It showed what anyone at the soccer game could have seen. McNamara was voluntarily participating in this public event (the court was implying that he should have worn underwear or a jockstrap). No one at the newspaper realized the young man was exposed in the picture. The newspaper should not be punished for an innocent mistake.

---

[25]347 F. 3d 655 (7th Cir. 2003)

[26]406 F. Supp. 858 (W.D. Pa. 1976)

[27]802 S.W.2d 901 (1991)

McNamara argued that the newspaper had many other photographs it could have used. The court said the existence of alternatives is not a justification for punishing a newspaper.

Sex Change Revealed

At the College of Alameda in California, Toni Ann Diaz became the first female to be elected student body president. Later, the *Oakland Tribune* did some investigating and discovered that Diaz had been born in Puerto Rico as Antony Diaz, a male.

Diaz sued the paper for invasion of privacy for disclosure of private facts. During the trial, the judge said the newspaper had to prove the story was newsworthy. The paper apparently did not make its case, because the jury awarded Diaz $775,000 in damages.

That judgment was overturned in 1983, however, by a state appeals court, in *Diaz v. Oakland Tribune.*[28] The appeals court ordered a new trial and said it was Diaz who had to prove the story was not newsworthy. Also, the court basically said that Diaz was a public figure as student body president because she was frequently in the news. Diaz did not want to endure another trial, so she dropped the case.

FAQ

A student body president is a public figure?

This case has created debate among legal scholars. Is the sex change newsworthy information? Is Diaz a public figure because she was elected student body president of a community college? Perhaps these questions would have been answered more directly had Diaz not dropped the case. Courts did give more direct answers in the next case, which also dealt with personal sexual matters.

Newspaper "Outing"

On September 22, 1975, President Gerald Ford was at Union Square in San Francisco when Sara Jane Moore attempted to assassinate him. A man in the crowd, Oliver Sipple, hit Moore's arm just before she fired, and the bullet was deflected. Sipple soon received extensive media attention for perhaps saving the president's life. Part of that media coverage included an article 2 days later in the *San Francisco Chronicle.* Reporter Herb Caen's story included the following details about Sipple's personal life:

> One of the heroes of the day, Oliver "Bill" Sipple, the ex-Marine who grabbed Sara Jane Moore's arm just as her gun was fired and thereby may have saved the President's life, was the center of midnight attention at the Red Lantern, a Golden Gate Ave. bar he favors. The Rev. Ray Broshears, head of Helping Hands, and Boy Politico, Harvey Milk, who claim to be among Sipple's close friends, describe themselves as "proud—maybe this will help break the stereotype." Sipple is among the workers in Milk's campaign for Supervisor.

Other newspapers, including the *Los Angeles Times,* ran the story and said Sipple was a "prominent figure" in San Francisco's gay community. The stories also suggested that

---

[28]139 C.A.3d 118 (1983)

Sipple had not yet been invited to the White House because he was gay. Sipple said the articles invaded his privacy because his family did not know about his sexual orientation. He said his family stopped speaking to him after the newspaper stories came out. Sipple sued the *Chronicle* for invasion of privacy, saying the exposure of his homosexuality caused him "great mental anguish, embarrassment, and humiliation."

FAQ

Why did the *Chronicle* even mention his homosexuality? It has nothing to do with the story.

Sipple agreed, saying that his homosexuality was not a legitimate public concern in relation to a story about an assassination attempt. However, in 1984, in *Sipple v. Chronicle*,[29] a California appeals court ruled in favor of the *Chronicle* for several reasons. For example, Sipple's homosexuality was not private. For years, Sipple had been actively involved in numerous gay public events, including parades. His homosexuality was "known by hundreds of people in a variety of cities." The court determined that the story was newsworthy. It involved an attempted assassination of the president and background on the "hero." The story was not meant to sensationalize Sipple's lifestyle. That was not the goal. Instead, the court noted that the story actually tried "to dispel the false opinion that gays were timid, weak and unheroic figures." The court pointed out that the story was not indecent or shocking, and said Sipple had to prove that the story was "so offensive as to shock the community notions of indecency." Because his homosexuality was out in the open, it could not be considered shocking or indecent.

FALSE LIGHT

False light is a mix of privacy and libel law. It involves cases in which the media place an individual in a "false light" before the public. Unlike libel, a person suing for false light does not need to prove defamation. Instead, the person must prove that (a) a broadcast or publication placed the person in a negative false light, (b) the false light would be offensive to a reasonable person, and (c) the broadcaster or publisher is guilty of actual malice.

Ten states do not recognize the concept of false light privacy cases. Persons can still bring false light cases in those states; they will just be suing for defamation under libel law.

The following cases make the concept of false light in privacy law a little more clear. The inappropriate use of photographs or video is frequently an issue in false light cases.

Pictures and False Light

In Alabama, in 1947, a 10-year-old girl named Eleanor Leverton was nearly run over by a car that had run a red light. A newspaper photographer happened to be nearby and took a photograph of a bystander lifting the crying girl to her feet. The dramatic picture appeared the next day in a Birmingham newspaper.

---

[29]154 Cal. App. 3d 1040 (1984)

Almost 2 years later, Curtis Publishing Company purchased a copy of the Leverton photograph for use with an article in the *Saturday Evening Post.* The article emphasized that careless pedestrians often cause traffic accidents. The article was entitled "They Ask to Be Killed." Leverton sued for invasion of privacy, saying the use of the photo with this article made it appear that she was a careless pedestrian. A district court jury awarded her $5000 in damages.

In *Leverton v. Curtis,*[30] a federal appeals court upheld the jury verdict, ruling that the *Post*'s use of the picture "invades her interest in being left alone" and "exceeds the bounds of privilege." The court said the use of the picture with the original accident story was fine. However, using the picture with the *Post* article gave the false impression that "this plaintiff narrowly escaped death because she was careless of her own safety." That was not true. The driver of the car had run a red light. The girl was not "careless."

News Reporter Embellishes a Story

It is a temptation most news reporters face at one time or another—that temptation to embellish a news story to make it more dramatic. However, such embellishments can lead to legal problems. Such is the case in this landmark false light ruling.

In December 1967, 44 people, including Marvin Cantrell, were killed in the collapse of the Silver Bridge in Point Pleasant, WV. Reporter Joseph Eszterhas from the *Cleveland Plain Dealer* did a story about Cantrell's funeral and how the family was coping with the tragedy. Five months later, Eszterhas returned to Point Pleasant with his photographer to do a follow-up story on the Cantrells. Eszterhas and the photographer were at the Cantrell home for 60 to 90 minutes, during which time they talked with the children and took 50 photographs. Mrs. Cantrell was not there at the time.

In the August 4, 1968 edition of the *Plain Dealer Sunday Magazine,* Eszterhas wrote the lead feature story about the Cantrell family. The article included numerous photographs and details that emphasized that the family was living in poverty, the children's clothes did not fit right, and the house was deteriorating. The reporter also wrote, "Margaret Cantrell will neither talk about what happened nor about how they are doing. She wears the same mask of non-expression she wore at the funeral. . . . She says that after it happened, the people in town offered to help them out with money and they refused to take it."

This description proved to be the most damaging to the newspaper because Mrs. Cantrell never saw or spoke with the reporter or photographer that day. Margaret Cantrell and four of her children filed a lawsuit against the newspaper for invasion of privacy for placing her family "in a false light before the public through its many inaccuracies and untruths." The family said the story made them the "objects of pity and ridicule" and caused them to suffer "outrage, mental distress, shame and humiliation."

In *Cantrell v. Forest City Publishing,*[31] the U.S. Supreme Court ruled for the Cantrells. The court said that newspaper had "published knowing or reckless falsehoods about the Cantrells." Mrs. Cantrell was not at the house, but the reporter implied she was there by describing such things as her "mask of non-expression." The court said these were obvious, "calculated falsehoods." As a result, the story placed the Cantrells in a false light.

Eszterhas apparently thought these were minor "embellishments" in the Cantrell story. The Cantrells and the courts did not agree.

---

[30]192 F.2d 974 (3d Cir. 1951)

[31]419 U.S. 245 (1974)

TV News Video and Herpes

TV news operations need to be especially careful about video that is placed with narrative. A 1984 lawsuit highlights this issue.

WJLA-TV in Washington, DC, was doing a story about a new treatment for genital herpes, and the station sent a photographer to get random shots of people on the street. One of those people was Linda Duncan. The reports about genital herpes aired on the 6:00 p.m. and 11:00 p.m. newscasts. During the 6:00 p.m. newscast, there was no narrative while a close-up shot of Duncan was shown. The video then cut from Duncan to a reporter saying, "For the 20 million Americans who have herpes, it's not a cure." During the 11:00 p.m. newscast, an edited version of the same story aired. As the anchor was saying, "20 million Americans who have herpes," viewers saw the close-up of Duncan. Duncan said the placement of her picture with that narrative put her in a false light by implying that she was one of the 20 million Americans with herpes.

FAQ

Duncan was on a public street, so isn't this similar to *Gill v. Hearst*? Doesn't the station have a right to use the video because Duncan was voluntarily subjecting herself to public gaze?

This case is different because of the context. The story was not about "love," as was the case in *Hearst.* This story concerned a sexually transmitted disease. In *Duncan v. WJLA-TV,*[32] a court allowed the lawsuit to proceed regarding the 11:00 p.m. newscast because of the timing of the picture with the narrative. The court said the 11:00 p.m. newscast gave Duncan a valid false light claim. The court dismissed the claim about the 6:00 p.m. newscast, because the narrative about "20 million" came *after* her picture appeared.

TV News Video and Drugs

The A&E Television Network aired a series called "Seized by the Law" as part of its *Investigative Reports* program. The program showed how federal officers seize property from people suspected of drug trafficking. Reporter Bill Kurtis pointed out that African American men are more likely to be targeted than white men.

During the report, Kurtis reported that officials were suspicious of anyone who was paying cash for a ticket, who was planning a short stay, or "most importantly, was a person of color." As Kurtis said this, video was shown of an African American man, Gregory Osby, walking through the airport. Osby is shown a second time in the program walking behind an African American man and woman while an interviewee on the show says, "If a minority citizen of this country is traveling through an airport. . . ."

Osby sued A&E, saying the narration coupled with the video placed him in a false light, making it appear that he was involved in illegal drug activity. In 1997, in *Osby v. A&E,*[33] a federal district court ruled for A&E. The court said the video did not place Osby in a false

---

[32]10 MLR 1385, 106 F.R.D. 4 (1984)

[33]Civil Action No. 96-7347, 1997 U.S. Dist LEXIS 8656

light because the narrative was stressing that average African American men who did not fit the "profile" were still in danger of being searched because of their race. If anything, the court said, the video made Osby appear to be innocent. Also, there was nothing in the video or narrative to connect Osby to drug trafficking. "No reasonable viewer . . . could have concluded Osby . . . was involved in criminal activity, or was suspected of criminal activity."

Man Harassed After Radio Station Airs His Phone Number

In 1995, two DJs on KRXO radio in Oklahoma City saw Web postings on America Online of t-shirts with offensive slogans about the bombing of the Murrah Federal Building in Oklahoma City (one slogan was "Visit Oklahoma—It's a Blast!"). The postings included a phone number and told persons to "Ask for Ken." In May 1995, the DJs read the slogans over the air and urged listeners to call the phone number to express their disgust. The phone number belonged to Kenneth Zeran of Seattle, and he received numerous phone calls, some including death threats. Zeran contacted local police and the FBI, fearing for his safety. He proved he had nothing to do with selling the t-shirts and that someone had posted his phone number and first name without his knowledge.

Zeran called the radio station and explained the situation. The station apologized and broadcast two retractions that day and one the following morning, stating that "Ken" had no connection to the t-shirts and that people should stop calling. Still, Zeran sued the radio station for false light invasion of privacy, defamation, and intentional infliction of emotional distress. Zeran said he had to get prescription medicine to deal with the anxiety and loss of sleep he suffered because of the phone calls.

In *Zeran v. Diamond Broadcasting Inc.*,[34] a federal district court ruled for the radio station on all counts. The court dismissed the false light claim by saying the station never broadcast Zeran's last name and "the plaintiff cannot identify a single person in the world who thinks less of him today than they did before the broadcast." To win the false light claim, Zeran needed to prove that the radio station was negligent and reckless in broadcasting the information. Zeran said the DJs should have investigated the truthfulness of the posting more carefully. However, the court said that there was no proof the DJs knew the information was fictitious. The court added that the DJs' "failure to investigate before [broadcasting] . . . is not sufficient to establish reckless disregard."

Zeran did not win the defamation claim because he did not provide any evidence that the broadcasts damaged him economically or professionally. (The court said that Zeran's medical expenses were "minimal.") Regarding the emotional distress claim, the court said there was no evidence that the DJs intentionally or recklessly "behaved in an extreme or outrageous manner" toward Zeran.

An Expensive Lesson From a "Sexy Teacher"

WXTB-FM in Clearwater, FL, ran a "sexy teacher" photo contest in 2001 through its Web site, offering a $1000 prize to the teacher who received the most votes. One of those pictures was of a local middle school Spanish teacher, Rosemary Geier-Scalzo. She says the photo was placed on the Web site without her permission. Geier-Scalzo sued the station

---

[34]19 F. Supp.2d 1249 (W.D. Okla.1997)

for invasion of privacy, placing her in a false light, and displaying her photo without her consent. However, it turned out that her husband had sent in the photo. Also, in a letter to her school district, she wrote that she had told students her picture was part of the contest, but she argued that she did not encourage them to go to the Web site.

The radio station's "sexy teacher" Web site included a picture of a topless woman with black squares hiding her nipples. The site also asked the question, "Did you ever have a teacher you wanted to have sex with?" Geier-Salzo said this material was not on the Web site when her husband sent in the photo, and its presence caused her "personal humiliation and mental anguish."

When school officials learned of the Web site's content, they suspended Geier-Scalzo for 3 days. She said the controversy could also damage her chances for promotion. Her lawyer said that damages in the lawsuit could exceed $1 million.[35]

MISAPPROPRIATION

Misappropriation means using a person's name, image, or likeness for commercial gain without the person's permission. This is also known as a person's *right of publicity* and *commercial appropriation.*

> ### FAQ
>
> Do most misappropriation cases involve famous people?

Yes. After all, celebrities' names and likenesses usually have more economic value than those of private citizens. That is why celebrity endorsements are an important part of advertising. Such endorsements can mean huge profits, not only for the celebrity but for any company whose product that celebrity chooses to endorse. However, if a celebrity allows his or her image to be used without permission or in numerous commercial settings, that image begins to lose its uniqueness and value. For these reasons, celebrities are often fiercely protective of their public personas.

> ### FAQ
>
> Why is misappropriation included in privacy law? It appears to involve economic concerns more than privacy concerns.

This part of privacy law involves personal rights but often focuses on damage done to a person's *economic* rights. It concerns the dollar value of a person's *public persona.* The use of that public persona without the person's permission is an invasion of privacy.

---

[35]Moore, B. (2001, July 18). Suspended teacher sues radio station. *St. Petersburg Times*. Retrieved October 24, 2004, from http://www.sptimes.com/News/071801/NorthPinellas/Suspended_teacher_sue.shtml

As mentioned at the beginning of the chapter, the courts did not always recognize such rights. A New York court in 1902 in *Roberson* rejected misappropriation claims from a woman whose face had been used without her permission on flour ads. The court declared that claim of privacy in this case was only a "so-called right" because no laws had been written acknowledging this right. However, in 1905, the Georgia Supreme Court ruled that a man could sue for the commercial misappropriation of his name and likeness. Still, the "right of publicity" was a slowly evolving concept in the 20th century.

Baseball Cards and Baseball Players

The term *right of publicity* was first used in 1953, when a federal appeals court ruled that baseball players had a right to profit from the use of their images and names on baseball trading cards. In *Haelen Laboratories v. Topps Chewing Gum,*[36] the court said that each baseball player under New York common law had more than just an individual right to privacy in this case: "A man has a right in the publicity value of his photograph, i.e., the right to grant the exclusive privilege of publishing his picture." The court called this a "right of publicity."

This case helped to solidify an important concept in privacy law. A person's name or image is personal property, is valuable, and should be protected. Twenty years later, the Supreme Court would issue a controversial ruling about news reporting and the protections afforded under a right of publicity.

Misappropriation and the News Media

The Human Cannonball Case

In 1972, Hugo Zacchini performed his "human cannonball" stunt at a county fair in Ohio. Zacchini would be shot out of a cannon, and then he would land in a net. At this fair, a TV news crew from a TV station owned by Scripps-Howard had shown up to film the circus, and it filmed Zacchini's entire 15-second act. Zacchini objected to the filming, but the station still aired the human cannonball act on one of its newscasts.

Zacchini sued the station for violating his right of publicity. He argued that airing his entire act on the news damaged his ability to make money because if people saw his act on TV, they would be less likely to pay to see it in person. Lower courts ruled in favor of Scripps-Howard, saying the TV station was simply covering a newsworthy public event.

However, in *Zacchini v. Scripps-Howard Broadcasting,*[37] the U.S. Supreme Court ruled 5-4 in favor of Zacchini. The court said that the TV station was not immune from such a lawsuit. The court then remanded the case to an Ohio court, where Zachinni was awarded damages. The court said that broadcasting Zacchini's entire act without his approval damaged his ability to profit from it. The economic value of his act had been diminished by the news story.

FAQ

Doesn't this ruling hinder news reporting on commercial events?

---

[36]202 F.2d 866 (2d Cir. 1953)

[37]433 U.S. 562 (1977)

Many journalists said this ruling made them fearful of doing news stories about people's professional activities. However, this was a rare decision against the media. The main problem here was that the newscast used Zacchini's *entire* act. True, it was only 15 seconds long, but those 15 seconds represented his livelihood.

Endorsement Claims

Celebrities not only have a right to protect their public personas, they have a right to protect themselves against false endorsement claims by the media. The media have their rights as well. In 1976, in *Namath v. Sports Illustrated,*[38] football legend Joe Namath had sued *Sports Illustrated* for using his picture without permission and violating his right of publicity. The sports magazine had numerous photographs of Namath in its archives. They used one file picture of Namath in a subscription ad that included the heading, "How to Get Close to Joe Namath." A court ruled for the magazine, saying that Namath had no right of publicity here. The magazine had a right to use its old photographs as long as there was no false claim that Namath endorsed the magazine.

The courts reached a similar conclusion in 1995 in *Montana v. Mercury News.*[39] The case involved star quarterback Joe Montana of the San Francisco 49ers. The *San Jose Mercury News* printed souvenir editions of its paper to commemorate the 49ers' Super Bowl victories. The paper then sold posters, which included reproductions of the souvenir section and drawings and archive photos of Montana. Montana sued the newspaper for misappropriation of his name, likeness, and photograph, but a California appeals court ruled that the newspaper had a right to promote itself "by reproducing its originally protected articles or photographs." The court also noted that the paper made no false claims of endorsement by Montana.

FAQ

Wasn't it wrong, though, for the paper to make money from this?

The fact that the *San Jose Mercury News* sold the posters is irrelevant. The court said that a newspaper or media outlet "does not lose its constitutional protection because [the activity] is undertaken for profit."

FAQ

Do these rulings cover similar uses in the electronic media?

Yes. Both rulings established that all media have a right to use archived news interview material, including video and audio, to promote their stations without worrying about misappropriation. However, the media need to make sure they do not falsely imply that a celebrity endorses them. Also, the image or name may not be used to promote something other than the station.

---

[38]352 N.E.2d 584 (1976)

[39]34 Cal. App. 4th 790 (1995)

A false endorsement claim led to a celebrity victory in 1982 in *Cher v. Forum International.*[40] A federal appeals court ruled that *Forum* magazine falsely implied that actress-singer Cher gave an exclusive interview to the magazine. *Forum*'s ads had claimed there were things Cher "would never tell *Us*" magazine, when in actuality she had originally done the interview so it would appear only in *Us*.

The court said that there must always be a balance between the right of publicity and the right to free expression. If persons are given too much protection under the right of publicity, then free expression suffers. That was the sentiment of a dissenting judge in the next case involving a TV game show hostess.

Striking a "Careful Balance"

Samsung Electronics had been running a TV ad that featured a female robot with a blonde wig, long gown, and large jewelry, and the robot was shown turning letters on a large game board. Samsung later admitted the ad was a parody of famous letter-turner Vanna White and the popular TV game show *Wheel of Fortune*. White sued Samsung, saying the ad violated her right of publicity. In 1993, in *White v. Samsung,*[41] a federal appeals court ruled that the ad created "confusion" about whether White was endorsing Samsung's products. The court allowed White's lawsuit to move forward, and Samsung eventually paid her $400,000 in damages.

Robot look-alikes were also the issue in another case involving Paramount's TV show *Cheers*. Host International had obtained permission from Paramount to reproduce the *Cheers* set in airport bars. However, the bars also included robot look-alikes of actors George Wendt and John Ratzenburger, who played the *Cheers* characters Norm and Cliff. Both actors sued, saying that Host had permission to do a mock-up of the *Cheers* set but did not have specific permission to use likenesses of the actors. Host argued that Paramount owned the copyright to the set *and* to the actors. In 1997, in *Wendt v. Host International,*[42] a federal appeals court ruled that Wendt's and Ratzenburger's rights of publicity had been violated. The court said that an actor does not lose the right to control commercial use of his image even if the copyright to his fictional character is owned by someone else. Both actors were eventually awarded damages.

FAQ

Don't these rulings make it difficult for advertisers or others to make fun of celebrities?

Rulings such as these had some legal experts concerned that the right of publicity was trumping the First Amendment in too many cases. In a strongly worded dissent in *White v. Samsung,* Judge Alex Kozinski argued for more protection of parodies. He said the court was taking the right of publicity too far and inhibiting artistic freedom: "Something very

---

[40]692 A.2d 634 (1982)

[41]989 F.2d 1512 (9th Cir. 1993)

[42]125 F.3d 860 (9th Cir. 1997)

dangerous is going on here. . . . Overprotecting intellectual property is as harmful as underprotecting it. Creativity is impossible without a rich public domain." This dissenting opinion laid the groundwork for an important 2001 decision about the extent of protecting intellectual property rights.

In *Hoffman v. Capital Cities/ABC*,[43] in 2001, the Ninth Circuit also had to strike a balance between the First Amendment and a right of publicity claim from actor Dustin Hoffman. Hoffman had starred in the 1982 movie *Tootsie*, in which he played a character who dressed as a woman to get a role on a soap opera. A famous still photograph from the movie showed Hoffman in a red dress and high heels, standing in front of an American flag. In 1997, *L.A. Magazine* used computer technology to alter stills from famous films to make it look like actors were wearing spring 1997 fashions. For the *Tootsie* still, *L.A. Magazine* kept the flag and Hoffman's head and then superimposed a hairy male body wearing a silk evening dress and high-heeled sandals. The picture also had a caption: "Dustin Hoffman isn't a drag in a butter-colored silk gown by Richard Tyler and Ralph Lauren heels."

Hoffman sued for commercial misappropriation of his name and likeness. The court acknowledged that it had to consider "the careful balance that courts have gradually constructed between the right of publicity and the First Amendment." With that in mind, the court said that *L.A. Magazine*'s altered pictures were not commercial speech. The article and pictures were a parody, a "combination of fashion photography, humor, and visual verbal editorial comment on classic films and famous actors." Also, there was no actual malice. *L.A. Magazine* was not trying to steal anyone's public persona to profit from it. The goal of using the photographs was for parody purposes only.

FAQ

According to the courts, parodies in some ads are OK and in others they are not. How is the line drawn?

A Right of Publicity Test

In 2001, the California Supreme Court established a test to help determine when artistic use of a celebrity image is protected by the First Amendment. The case of *Comedy III Production v. Saderup*[44] involved artist Gary Saderup, who was well known for his charcoal drawings of celebrities. In this instance, he had done charcoal sketches of the Three Stooges and sold the images on lithographs and tee shirts. Comedy III owns the rights to Three Stooges images and sued Saderup for violating the company's right of publicity. The California Supreme Court ruled for Comedy III and said that Saderup's works were not protected by the First Amendment. The court provided the following test for cases like this, borrowing elements of the fair use test in copyright law:

▣ *Does the artistic expression take the form of a literal depiction or imitation of a celebrity for commercial gain?* In this case, the court said yes because the economic value of Saderup's drawings was derived "primarily from the fame of the celebrities depicted."

---

[43]255 F.3d 1180 (9th Cir. 2001)

[44]21 P.3d 797 (2001)

▣ *Does the work contain "significant transformative elements"?* In other words, do the works add "significant expression" that goes beyond the use of the images themselves? Here, the court said no. Saderup's works did not "transform" the Three Stooges; instead, they were "literal, conventional depictions of the Three Stooges so as to exploit their fame."

FAQ

What's an example of a transformative work?

The judges pointed to the art of Andy Warhol as an example. Warhol often used celebrity images in his artwork, and the court said Warhol had created a form of social commentary about the dehumanizing of celebrities. His works had a distinct style and "transformed" the images of the celebrities. Thus, they became Warhol's images. When people see these works, they usually recognize them as Warhol works. However, Saderup's images of the Three Stooges had no such "transformative" value. The court warned that distinctions in this area of law would sometimes be subtle but said this was frequently the case in First Amendment disputes.

Courts often have to grapple with such gray areas in privacy law. For example, exactly what aspects of someone's public persona are protected under a right of publicity? The courts sometimes find that a right to publicity goes beyond a person's name or likeness.

Misappropriation of an Identifying Characteristic

A Trademark Phrase

From 1962 to 1992, Johnny Carson was the host of NBC's *Tonight Show*. Every night, sidekick Ed McMahon would introduce Carson by saying "And now, heeeeeere's Johnny." As a result, "Here's Johnny" became unmistakably associated with one Johnny and one Johnny only—Johnny Carson. In 1967, a chain of restaurants used the name "Here's Johnny Restaurants" only after obtaining Carson's permission.

In 1976, a portable toilet company decided a catchy name for its toilets would be "Here's Johnny." The company also used the slogan, "The World's Foremost Commodian." The company was obviously trying to use Carson's image to sell toilets.

Johnny Carson sued the toilet company for unfair competition, invasion of privacy, and violating his right to publicity. A federal appeals court ruled for the toilet company on the first two claims, but the court did rule in favor of Carson on the right of publicity claim. In *Carson v. Here's Johnny Portable Toilets*,[45] the court ruled "there was an appropriation of Carson's identity without using his name." The court ruled that a celebrity's identity is more than just the celebrity's name or likeness. That identity also includes "achievements, identifying characteristics or actual performances." The phrase "Here's Johnny" had become one of Carson's identifying characteristics. The court said this ruling would "prevent unjust enrichment by persons . . . who seek commercially to exploit the identity of celebrities without their consent."

---

[45]698 F.2d 831 (6th Cir. 1983)

The court said its ruling would encourage celebrities to seek achievement in their fields because celebrities would know their "public identity" had protection from unauthorized uses.

FAQ

What about the movie *The Shining*, in which Jack Nicholson screams "Here's Johnny" at another character? Isn't that misappropriation as well?

No. The phrase "Here's Johnny" may be used in other commercial settings as long as the goal is not to exploit Carson's image. Jack Nicholson's character in the movie *The Shining* has a famous scene in which he sticks his head through a hole in a door and screams "Here's Johnny!" This use was for dramatic purposes. Its goal was not to sell a product but to parody the famous phrase.

The courts have also ruled that the sound of a person's voice can be connected to a public persona.

Celebrity Sound-Alikes

Every person's voice is distinctive. For celebrities, especially singers, a distinctive voice can be a valuable commodity.

In 1985, Young & Rubicam produced ads for Ford Lincoln Mercury as part of a "Yuppie Campaign." The ads used popular 1970s songs, and the ad agency tried to get the original singers to perform the songs for the ads. Ten celebrities, including Bette Midler, refused, so Young & Rubicam hired "celebrity sound-alikes." The sound-alike for Midler was Ula Hedwig, who had been a backup singer for Midler in the 1970s. Hedwig recorded a version of "Do You Want to Dance," a song that Midler had recorded on a 1973 album. The ad agency told Hedwig to "sound as much as possible like the Bette Midler record." Hedwig did her best to sound like Midler, and Hedwig's version was used in TV ads.

Friends of both Midler and Hedwig said the song on the ad sounded "exactly" like Midler. Midler sued for misappropriation, saying the use of a "sound-alike" was a theft of her distinctive vocal style.

In *Midler v. Ford Motor Company*,[46] a federal appeals court ruled in favor of Midler for several reasons. A person's voice is one of the most distinct ways a person is identified, and as a result, the court said, "To impersonate her [Midler's] voice is to pirate her identity." The agency was obviously trying to make customers believe it was actually Midler singing in the ad. Midler's voice clearly had value to Ford; the ad agency otherwise would not have gone to the trouble of getting a sound-alike.

There were no copyright issues here because Young & Rubicam had obtained permission to use the song from the song's copyright holder.

---

[46]849 F.2d 460 (9th Cir. 1988)

FAQ

Comedians frequently imitate celebrities' singing voices for entertainment. Is that misappropriation as well?

No. That is a parody. As is discussed in the copyright chapter, parody is a protected form of humor or criticism. The purpose of the imitation on a comedy show is to entertain and make a commentary about a certain person's singing style. However, the purpose of the imitation in the Midler case was to use the person's singing style to sell a product. Parodies can work in ads, though. A similar case involving Nancy Sinatra had a different outcome because there was no attempt to use a sound-alike.

Not a Celebrity Sound-Alike

In the 1960s, Nancy Sinatra had a number-one hit: "These Boots Are Made for Walkin'." The song was also known for its video (rare in the 1960s), which showed Sinatra and some dancers dressed in boots and "mod" clothing. In 1967, Goodyear Tire and Rubber Company described some of its tires as having "wide boots," and Goodyear developed an ad campaign using the music and lyrics from the Nancy Sinatra hit. The ad agency tried to get Nancy Sinatra to sing on the ads, but she declined.

There were four TV ads and two radio ads. The radio ads included female voices singing "These Boots Are Made for Walkin'" while a male voice narrated. The TV ads included the same audio and also showed four women dressed in high boots and mod clothes next to rolling tires. Goodyear's ad agency, Young & Rubicam, had obtained the necessary copyright licenses to use the song in the ads.

Sinatra sued Goodyear for unfair competition, saying the tire company misappropriated a likeness of her voice "for the purpose of deceiving the public into believing that [Sinatra] was a participant in the commercials."

In *Sinatra v. Goodyear*,[47] a federal appeals court ruled for Goodyear. The difference between this case and the Midler case is that the singers hired for the Goodyear ads did not try to directly imitate Sinatra's style. The court said: "Defendants did not pass-off; that is, they did not mislead the public into thinking their commercials were the product of plaintiff [Sinatra] or anyone else."

GENERAL TIPS ABOUT PRIVACY

Danger Areas

Reporters should always be cautious about using the following types of information in a story because it could lead to invasion of privacy suits: (a) personal finances; (b) sexual relationships; (c) sexually transmitted diseases or other "embarrassing" illnesses, such as Alzheimer's; (d) reproductive problems (impotence, infertility); (e) income tax returns;

---

[47]435 F.2d 711 (9th Cir. 1970)

[48]486 U.S. 35 (1988)

(f) photographs taken on private property; (g) private letters or correspondence; (h) family disagreements and quarrels; and (i) details of someone's home life.

Safe Areas

All of the following are considered public facts. As long as the information is obtained legally, it is safe to use. Some of the main categories include (a) arrest reports, (b) crime reports, (c) court reports, (d) addresses, (e) publicly listed phone numbers, (f) information from lawsuits, (g) accident reports, (h) natural disasters, (i) fire and arson reports, (j) names of victims of crime, (k) a person's date or place of birth, (l) marital status (including divorce), (m) names of suicide victims, (n) a person's occupation, (o) a person's military record, (p) information included in legislative debates and records, and (q) items in people's garbage.

A 1988 ruling by the U.S. Supreme Court said that a person has no reasonable expectation of privacy once personal garbage is placed on a public sidewalk or street. The case of *California v. Greenwood*[48] stemmed from a police investigator not obtaining a search warrant before asking a garbage collector to give him trash bags left on a public street in front of a suspected drug dealer's house. The court said that when a person leaves a garbage container on the curb or sidewalk, that person is knowingly making the trash "readily accessible" to third parties such as animals, children, and scavengers. The court said that those third parties also include garbage collectors, who may choose to go through the garbage or make it available to others, such as the police. In 2003, the New Hampshire Supreme Court ruled that garbage is private. It said its state constitution grants more rights to privacy than the federal constitution. New Hampshire journalists complained about the ruling, saying that going through garbage is sometimes a valuable tool in investigative reporting when other methods of newsgathering have failed.

SUMMARY

The right to privacy is *the right to be let alone*. There are four basic torts of privacy law: intrusion, disclosure of embarrassing private facts, false light, and misappropriation.

Private citizens have a greater expectation of privacy, but public figures and officials also have privacy rights. The Galella case showed that celebrities have a right to be protected from overzealous media members who "cross the line" in pursuit of celebrity interviews and photographs. In 1998, California passed an antipaparazzi law to try to extend more privacy protection to celebrities.

When covering news events, the media must be careful not to disclose embarrassing private facts or place people in a false light. The media must also be aware of privacy law regarding "public" places such as prisons. Privacy law also covers the area of misappropriation, which protects a person's right to control public uses of his or her name, image, and likeness.

9

INTRUSIVE NEWSGATHERING METHODS

Hidden Cameras, Media Ride-Alongs, Ambush Interviews

The First Amendment is not a license to trespass.

—*Dietemann v. Time*[1]

When doing a news story, do the media have a right to record you secretly to get a better story? Do the media have a right to "ride along" with law enforcement officials and emergency workers? Do the media have a right to hound people to get a story? The following cases show that various factors play a role here, including where and how the camera footage was shot, as well as the newsworthiness of the story. Also, intrusive newsgathering cases often involve issues of privacy.

MIXED RULINGS ON HIDDEN CAMERAS AND MICROPHONES

One of the first cases to address hidden cameras and microphones in newsgathering showed that the courts are very uneasy with the media and law enforcement combining forces to uncover wrongdoing.

"Crackdown on Quackery"

This was the title of an article appearing in a 1963 edition of *Life* magazine, owned by Time, Inc. The article focused on a man named Dietemann who said he could heal people with such remedies as clay, minerals, and herbs. Reporters for *Life* worked out an agreement with the Los Angeles County District Attorney's Office to investigate Dietemann for practicing medicine without a license. Two *Life* reporters went to Dietemann's home

---

[1]*Dietemann v. Time*, 449 F.2d 245 (9th Cir. 1971)

posing as patients. The reporters had a hidden still camera as well as a hidden microphone. The microphone allowed three people in a nearby car to listen to the conversations. Those three people were another *Life* reporter (who took notes), a representative of the district attorney's office, and an investigator for the state health department.

The pictures taken inside and the audio from the hidden microphone were used as evidence by the authorities, and *Life* used two of the photographs in their story. One picture showed Dietemann's arrest. Dietemann sued for invasion of privacy. The magazine said it had a right to do an important newsworthy story about a "quack" doctor. However, a lower court awarded Dietemann $1000 in damages. In *Dietemann v. Time*[197] in 1971, a federal appeals court ruled that the media did indeed invade Dietemann's privacy. The court pointed out that Dietemann operated his business from his private home, "a sphere from which he could reasonably expect to exclude eavesdropping newsmen." The court also emphasized that hidden cameras and microphones are *not* "indispensable tools of investigative reporting," as Time had argued. The court pointed out that there is a history of excellent investigative reporting done before the invention of miniature cameras and other such devices.

The First Amendment is not a license to trespass. The court expressed its discomfort with police using the news media to gather information on crimes: "There is a risk that an intrusion from such an alliance between press and police would not further the public prosecution interest."

FAQ

Was the court saying that the magazine should not have covered this story?

No. *Life* had the right to cover this newsworthy story but should have used less intrusive methods. The courts are very cautious about law enforcement and the use of hidden microphones and cameras, especially in conjunction with the media.

In 1967, in *Katz v. U.S.,*[2] FBI agents were trying to catch criminals who were using pay phones to transmit illegal bets across state lines, so the FBI placed hidden cameras and microphones outside a phone booth from which the calls were being made. The U.S. Supreme Court ruled that this electronic surveillance was an invasion of privacy. The court said there is an expectation of privacy in a phone booth because a person "is entitled to assume that the words he utters into the mouthpiece will not be broadcast to the world." Such expectations of privacy also extend to certain elements of accident scenes.

Privacy, Car Accidents, and Ambulances

On June 24, 1990, Ruth Shulman and her son Wayne were injured in a car accident on Interstate 10 in Riverside County in California. Rescue workers had to use the "jaws of life" to free the Shulmans from the car.

---

[2]389 U.S. 347 (1967)

A rescue helicopter arrived with flight nurse Laura Carnahan and Joel Cooke, a TV cameraman from Group W Productions. Cooke videotaped rescue efforts at the accident scene. Cooke also attached a wireless microphone to Nurse Carnahan and recorded her conversations with Ruth Shulman and rescue workers. Cooke felt a "hidden" microphone would allow for more natural responses from the victims. Cooke continued to shoot video and record conversations inside a medical helicopter.

Cooke's footage aired September 29, 1990 on a television program called *On Scene: Emergency Response*. The video showed Ruth trapped in the car. Her face was hard to see because of an oxygen mask, but the microphone on Nurse Carnahan picked up Ruth's voice pretty clearly. Ruth appeared to be confused at points, asking the same questions repeatedly. She was also heard saying things like "I just want to die." In the helicopter, the nurse could be heard talking about Ruth's vital signs and that Ruth was unable to feel or move her feet. Ruth's face was seen under the oxygen mask. No video was shown of Wayne. Ruth Shulman was left a paraplegic.

Ruth was still in the hospital on September 29 when she saw the TV show. Ruth said she was "shocked" and felt "exploited." She said she had no idea the rescue was being recorded for TV and that she never consented to the videotaping or audiorecording. She and her son sued Group W Productions for invasion of privacy on two counts: unlawful intrusion in videotaping the rescue and public disclosure of private facts in the broadcast.

California law requires two factors be in place for a plaintiff to win an intrusion case: (a) The activity must have occurred in a private place or where there is an expectation of privacy and (b) the activity is "highly offensive" to the average person. In *Shulman v. Group W. Productions*,[3] the California Supreme Court gave the Shulmans a partial victory. Recording the video and audio of Ruth Shulman in a medical helicopter was an intrusion, the court said; persons have an expectation of privacy in an ambulance or rescue helicopter, just as they would in a hospital room. There is also a "reasonable expectation of privacy" when an accident victim is talking with medical personnel at an accident scene. Cooke should not have used a hidden microphone on the nurse to record private conversations between Shulman and Carnahan. These were not conversations that could have been heard by onlookers; thus they were not "public."

The court, though, could not reach a consensus about whether the media's conduct in this regard was "highly offensive." Some justices said the recorded conversations were an important part of the newsgathering process and contained mostly basic, nonoffensive material such as blood pressure readings and estimated hospital arrival times. However, other justices were unwilling to ignore the fact that the conversations did take place with a health-care provider and that patients should be able to expect privacy in such medical situations. The media saw a partial victory here, noting that a majority of the justices did not find the media conduct highly offensive. The court recognized that "a reporter's motive to discover socially important information may reduce the offensiveness of the intrusion." Still, the court did agree that the plaintiff's claim should *not* be dismissed.

FAQ

Wasn't the accident scene itself a public event because it occurred on the side of a public highway?

---

[3]955 P.2d 469 (1998)

Yes. The court ruled for Group W on the broadcast of private facts, saying the Shulmans could have had no *general* expectation of privacy at the accident scene. The scene was next to a busy public highway where there were numerous onlookers, the court pointed out. "Their statements or exclamations could be freely heard by all who passed by and were thus public, not private." Also, the car accident was newsworthy. The cameras had a right to cover this.

Later that year, a federal district court in Arizona used the *Shulman* reasoning to dismiss an intrusion claim against ABC. In *Medical Laboratory Management Consultants v. ABC*,[4] ABC was doing an investigative report about medical labs frequently making errors in pap smear tests. ABC employees used a hidden camera during conversations with the owner of a pap smear lab. The owner also took the two ABC employees on a tour of the facilities. Footage of the conversation and the tour aired on *PrimeTime Live*, and the reporter pointed out that the lab failed to detect cervical cancer on pretested pap smear slides that ABC had sent to the lab.

The lab sued ABC for numerous claims, including intrusion on seclusion. The court found that ABC's conduct was not highly offensive, emphasizing the newsworthiness of "reporting on potential laboratory errors in testing of pap smear information that was clearly in the public interest." The court also ruled that there was no invasion of the lab owner's privacy because ABC did not "intrude on his home or aspects of his private life."

Some Workplaces Are "Private"

A 1999 case showed that there are limitations about where TV stations can use hidden cameras. It was also the first time broadcasters were ordered by the court to pay out compensatory and punitive damages in an intrusion case.

In *Sanders v. ABC*,[5] TV reporter Stacy Lescht got a job as a "telepsychic" with the Psychic Marketing Group (PMG). Her job included sitting at a desk and giving psychic readings to people over the telephone. Lescht had concealed a small video camera in her hat and a microphone in her bra, and she secretly recorded conversations with her coworkers, including a man named Mark Sanders. Short segments of the recorded conversations appeared on an investigative report on *PrimeTime Live*.

Sanders sued ABC for recording confidential conversations and for invasion of privacy. It is important to note where these conversations involving Sanders were recorded: (a) in the aisle outside Lescht's cubicle, where Sanders was standing and talking in "moderate tones" with three other employees, and (b) in Sanders' cubicle, where Lescht was sitting and talking with Sanders about his personal goals. Lescht also gave Sanders a psychic reading.

A jury awarded Sanders $1.2 million in damages. A state appeals court threw out those damages, saying there was no reasonable expectation of privacy in this workplace area. The court said it was not a "secluded" area where one might expect privacy. However, the California Supreme Court disagreed and ruled for Sanders, saying: "An employee may, under some circumstances, have a reasonable expectation of visual or aural privacy against electronic intrusion by a stranger to the workplace." The court said this ruling would not place a chill on hidden camera reporting. The justices pointed out that PMG ran a nonpublic workplace. Their phone banks and cubicles were not regularly open to observation by the press or public. Therefore, PMG workers could have more of an expectation

---

[4]30 F. Supp.2d 1182 (U.S.D. Ariz. 1998)

[5]978 P.2d 67 (1999)

of privacy than someone working in a more public work setting, such as a department store. Employees at nonpublic workplaces do not lose privacy rights because "conversations and interactions at issue could be witnessed by coworkers or the employer."

The court then remanded the case to the appeals court, where the jury damage award and legal fees were reduced to $934,000, which ABC paid to Sanders in February 2000.

This was not the end of the story, though. Coworkers of Sanders also sued ABC for violating the federal wiretapping statute. One of the statute's provisions bans secret recordings that are used to commit "any criminal or tortious act in violation of the Constitution or laws of the United States or of any state." The coworkers claimed that ABC's actions violated this statute because the hidden cameras intruded on their seclusion. In 1999, in *Sussman v. ABC*,[6] the Ninth Circuit Court of Appeals dismissed the lawsuit, ruling that ABC had not engaged in any criminal or tortious act.

Hidden Cameras in Eye Clinic

On June 10, 1993, the ABC news magazine *PrimeTime Live* aired a hidden camera investigative report about an eye clinic's alleged misuse of auto-refractor machines to deceive older patients into wrongly believing they had cataracts.

Originally, an ABC producer had contacted Dr. James Desnick at the Desnick Eye Center in Chicago. The producer told Desnick the story would be about cataract surgery and would not involve undercover or "ambush" journalism. ABC was then allowed to interview medical staff and videotape a live cataract surgery. However, ABC had also hired seven people to pose as patients in Desnick clinics in Indiana and Wisconsin, and the "patients" were accompanied by persons with hidden cameras and microphones.

The show that aired featured the hidden camera footage, as well as an interview with a former Desnick employee named Paddy Kalish. Eye clinic personnel had told ABC that Kalish was "biased" and had previously lied about practices at Desnick Eye Centers. It was Kalish who claimed on camera that the eye clinic tampered with autorefractors.

In *Desnick v. ABC*,[7] Desnick sued ABC on six basic counts. A district court in 1994 ruled for ABC on five of those counts:

1. Trespass. Desnick said the undercover reporters were only allowed in the eye clinic because it was assumed they were real patients. The court said there was no trespass because the reporters were *invited in.* Trespass occurs when people are not invited. The *intentions* of the reporters do not matter when considering trespassing charges.

2. Invasion of Privacy. Desnick argued that doctors expect examination rooms to be private, and the intrusion by hidden cameras would make doctors nervous about other patients and hinder future doctor-patient relationships. The court ruled that hidden cameras were OK in this case because the "patients" did the recordings: "The privacy and privilege of the doctor-patient relationship is for the patient, not the doctor." If the doctors had been doing the recording, it would have been a privacy violation for the patients.

3. Defamation. The story defamed the two doctors who were alleged to have used the autorefractor deceitfully. Desnick said its reputation was damaged by one claim: that Desnick

---

[6] 186 F.3d 1200 (9th Cir. 1999)

[7] 851 F. Supp. 303 (N.D. Ill. 1994)

doctors misused autorefractors. However, the ABC report also contained numerous other facts damaging to Desnick. Therefore, the court said Desnick could not argue that this issue of autorefractors was the sole cause of damage. Desnick was already damaged by other information in the broadcast.

4. Fraud. The ABC producer lied about "no undercover" journalism. The injury to Desnick was not caused by the fraud of the ABC producer. Damage was caused by practices at the eye clinics. Also, the producer kept his promise about not using undercover cameras during the Chicago interviews. The hidden cameras were used in Indiana and Wisconsin.

5. Violation of Federal and State Wiretapping Laws. Desnick said doctors and staff were recorded on tape without consent. The court said ABC did not violate Wisconsin wiretapping laws (Indiana and Illinois' laws were not at issue here because the plaintiffs used only the Wisconsin statute in their case). The law says only one party needs to know a conversation is being recorded unless the communication is for criminal purposes. That was not the case here.

The court did rule for Desnick on one smaller count:

6. Breach of Contract. ABC had promised not to use undercover tactics and not to have the report focus solely on Desnick. ABC broke both promises. The court said, "The victim of a breach of contract is entitled to nominal damages, even if the plaintiff was not injured by the breach, because the breach itself is wrong."

In 1995, a federal appeals court gave total victory to ABC and dismissed all of Desnick's claims, including breach of contract.[8] The ruling was a major victory for hidden camera investigations.

Food Lion Case

This is one of the more famous hidden camera cases. It involved a *PrimeTime Live* investigative report about food handling practices at Food Lion supermarkets. In 1992, two ABC reporters used false resumes to get jobs at two Food Lion stores. Those reporters then worked for Food Lion while wearing hidden cameras and microphones.

The hidden camera footage appeared in a November 5, 1992 broadcast of *PrimeTime Live*. The videotape showed violations of food handling procedures such as workers taking chicken past its expiration date, covering it with barbecue sauce to hide any odors, and reselling it as "gourmet chicken." Other video included workers rewrapping and redating fish that had passed its expiration date and mixing old ground beef with new beef. The show also included interviews with former Food Lion employees who shared stories about employees climbing into dumpsters to retrieve expired meat or employees being told to put cauliflower back on the shelves after using brushes to scrape off the black spots. Obviously, the broadcast was not favorable to Food Lion, and the supermarket chain saw drops in sales following the broadcast.

FAQ

Wouldn't this be a good "veggie libel" case?

---

[8]44 F.3d 1345 (7th Cir. 1995)

Possibly, but Food Lion did not sue ABC for libel because the video plainly showed numerous food handling violations, and the video made it pretty difficult for Food Lion to prove actual malice or reporting of false information. Instead, Food Lion sued for (a) fraud (the ABC reporters filled out false job applications), (b) trespassing (the reporters obtained their jobs fraudulently, and therefore Food Lion said they had no right to be in "nonpublic" sections of the stores), (c) unfair trade practices (Food Lion said the use of hidden cameras was unfair and led to a story that damaged the grocery chain's profits), and (d) breach of the duty of loyalty (obviously, the ABC reporters did not act like loyal employees).

A jury found the tactics of the ABC reporters to be underhanded and deceitful, and they ruled in favor of Food Lion. Investigative reporters across the country were shocked to learn that the supermarket giant was awarded $1,402 in compensatory damages—compensation for the wages paid by Food Lion to the ABC reporters—and $5.5 million in punitive damages. The jury was telling ABC and all broadcasters that hidden camera investigations were going too far and trampling on the rights of businesses and their employees.

FAQ

Didn't this jury verdict put a serious chilling effect on hidden camera investigations?

Many in the news media said it did. However, in 1999, a federal appeals court overturned the jury verdict in *Food Lion v. ABC.*[9] The court still awarded Food Lion damages: $2.00. That is not a misprint. The court gave Food Lion $1.00 in damages for each reporter's trespassing and failure to be a loyal employee.

The court reasoned that the $2.00 in damages acknowledged that the reporters did commit fraud on their job applications and trespass. *However, ABC's goal was not to defraud Food Lion. The goal was to uncover wrongdoing and protect the public.* The reporters' deception did not harm Food Lion. It was Food Lion's food handling practices that harmed Food Lion.

This appeals court ruling was an important ruling for hidden camera investigations, although not a complete victory. The courts acknowledged that a certain amount of deceit is necessary for reporters to uncover dangerous or criminal behavior. If the media could be held liable for trespass and fraud in such instances, undercover reporting would be stifled. At the same time, the court did hold ABC liable for breach of contract, even though it was only $2.00 in damages. With this, the court acknowledged that hidden camera investigations can violate tort law.

FAQ

What if the story is NOT covering criminal or unethical behavior? Is there still protection?

---

[9] 194 F.3d 505 (4th Cir. 1999)

There can be. It depends on the newsworthiness of the story and how the hidden recording devices are used. It's also depends on the court issuing the ruling.

Is the Outside of Your Home Private?

On June 12, 1994, Nicole Brown Simpson and Ronald Goldman were murdered in Los Angeles. That same night, NFL legend O. J. Simpson (Ms. Simpson's ex-husband) flew on an American Airlines flight from Los Angeles to Chicago.

Soon after the murders, the media began speculating about O. J. Simpson's possible role in the murders. An ABC News producer, Anthony Radziwill, wanted to interview Beverly Deteresa, one of the flight attendants on Simpson's flight to Chicago. Radziwill went to Deteresa's home in Irvine, CA, and the two stood and talked in the doorway of her condominium. She declined to do an interview on camera, but she did tell Radziwill some details about the flight. For example, she said media rumors were untrue about Simpson hiding his hand in a bag during the flight.

Radziwill did not tell Deteresa he was wearing a hidden microphone or that there was an ABC cameraperson in a car across the street, secretly videotaping the scene.

Radziwill called Deteresa again the next morning, and she again said no to appearing on camera. Radziwill then told her about the hidden camera and microphone from the previous day. Deteresa hung up, told her husband, and he called ABC. He told ABC not to air any portion of the tape, but ABC argued that it did not need the Deteresas' consent. The next day, ABC aired a 5-second clip of the videotape on their show *Day One* while reading a story about how Deteresa said she did not see Simpson wrap his hand in a bag of ice. The show did not run any audio from Deteresa or mention her name.

The Deteresas sued ABC for intrusion into private affairs and unlawful eavesdropping, among other charges. In *Deteresa v. ABC*,[10] a federal appeals court ruled for ABC, saying Deteresa could have no expectation of privacy because she never told the reporter her statements were "off the record" or "in confidence." She never said he could not share the statements with anyone else. She was in full public view from the street when she was videotaped. A passerby could have seen what the camera had seen.

ABC did not air private facts such as Deteresa's address, license plate numbers, or even her name. ABC was not trying to intrude on Deteresa's privacy. As for the hidden microphone and audio recording, the court said, "Deteresa spoke voluntarily and freely with an individual who she knew was a reporter." The reporter did not trespass. Besides, ABC did not air any portions of the audiotape.

FAQ

But aren't there laws against "unlawful eavesdropping?" Wouldn't this situation qualify?

---

[10]121 F.3d 460 (9th Cir. 1997)

In this case, neither the video nor the audio recording was unlawful eavesdropping, because the reporter did not tape the conversation with the *intention* of invading Deteresa's privacy. The intention was to gather information on a newsworthy story. However, 2 years later, a federal appeals court did not provide protection for the media in a very similar situation.

The 1999 case of *Alpha Therapeutic Corporation v. Nippon Hoso Koikai* (NHK)[11] was nearly identical to the news media tactics used in *Deteresa.* NHK, a Japanese public broadcasting corporation, was doing an investigative report alleging that Alpha Therapeutic had been knowingly shipping AIDS-tainted blood products to Japan and had lied to the FDA about an infected blood donor. NHK sent a reporter to the home of Alpha's medical director, and the reporter interviewed the director outside of his front door. The reporter used a hidden microphone and a van across the street concealed a hidden camera. The director sued for several torts, including invasion of privacy.

In a surprising contrast to *Deteresa,* the Ninth Circuit Court of Appeals ruled that the plaintiff had a right to sue NHK for invasion of privacy. The court cited *Sanders* and ruled that even though the director "knew he was speaking with a reporter . . . a person may reasonably expect privacy against the electronic recording of a communication, even though he or she had no reasonable expectation of the confidentiality of the communication's contents." The court said that the case met the two standards required under California law for an actionable intrusion: (a) The action was highly offensive to a reasonable person, and (b) the action occurred in a private place. The case was remanded to a lower court for trial.

However, a California appellate court ruled that these two standards were not met in another 1999 decision, *Wilkins v. NBC.*[12] In this case, *Dateline NBC* was doing a story on businesses that charged for services on toll-free 800 numbers. Two reporters, using hidden microphones and cameras, posed as investors while listening to the pitches of two salesmen on a crowded restaurant patio. Portions of the interview aired on *Dateline NBC*, and the salesmen sued for invasion of privacy. The court dismissed the lawsuit, saying that the men spoke freely in a crowded public place and even spoke freely when waiters came to the table. Also, the court said that the recorded conversations did not deal with any personal matters but only with business matters. As a result, the court ruled that there was nothing highly offensive about the tapings.

Summary on Hidden Cameras and Microphones

Here are some general guidelines that journalists need to keep in mind before using hidden cameras and microphones.

Location

Private Property. As was seen in *Dietemann,* if you are *inside* a person's private residence, there is a greater likelihood the courts will view a hidden camera as a form of trespassing. However, if your hidden camera is on public property and shooting a scene that anyone else could see from a public area, you are most likely going to be protected.

---

[11]199 F.3d 1078 (9th Cir. 1999)

[12]71 Cal. App.4th 1066 (1999)

Workplaces. If a workplace is considered "nonpublic," as in *Sanders* (the psychic hotline business), hidden cameras face much tighter restrictions. If the workplace is a supermarket, as in the Food Lion case, this is considered more of a public environment and courts are more likely to protect hidden camera use.

Newsworthiness

Is there serious wrongdoing being uncovered? If you are covering issues such as unsafe food handling practices at a supermarket, the courts will see the hidden cameras as a necessary tool to inform and protect the public.

FAQ

Are hidden cameras legal across the country?

Legality

There are nine states where it is illegal to use hidden cameras (still or video) to record someone without that person's consent: Alabama, Delaware, Georgia, Hawaii, Maine, Michigan, New Hampshire, South Dakota, and Utah.

Media Ride-Alongs

Media Ride-Alongs With Paramedics

In October 1979, a news crew from KNBC-TV in Los Angeles was accompanying paramedics from the L.A. Fire Department as they performed their normal duties (this is a "ride-along"). The paramedics were summoned to the home of Dave Miller, who had suffered a heart attack in his bedroom.

The film crew (reporter, cameraman, soundman) followed the two paramedics inside and filmed the paramedics performing cardiopulmonary resuscitation on Miller. A police officer had taken Miller's wife Brownie to another room, so she did not see the TV crew come in with the paramedics. She did not ask anyone to leave, but the TV crew never asked for her permission to be there or to shoot film. Dave Miller died soon after at a hospital.

Several weeks later, Brownie Miller happened to see the KNBC news report with the film of paramedics working on her husband. Miller said she screamed and turned off the television. She filed a lawsuit against NBC and the city of Los Angeles for invasion of privacy and trespassing for the TV crew's "unauthorized entry" into her home. She also sued for intentional infliction of emotional distress.

NBC argued that their TV crew had a right to be in the Millers' apartment for two basic reasons: (a) Calling for paramedics meant the Millers gave "implied consent" for the NBC TV crew to come into their home, and (b) NBC's constitutional right to gather news overrode Mrs. Miller's right to privacy. A trial court ruled for NBC, saying that the TV crew did not enter the home maliciously. The court added that Brownie Miller suffered no "actual damages" because of the entry.

In *Miller v. NBC*,[13] a state appeals court overturned the trial court. In ruling for Brownie Miller, the court made some important clarifications about the rights of the media and the rights of private citizens. NBC argued that its crew had a right to be in the Millers' home because no one asked it to leave. The court said, though, that the TV station needed to consider the context of the events here. Brownie Miller was taken to another room by a police officer, and she was obviously in an emotional state. The TV crew should have asked for her permission to be there. The crew should not have "assumed" a right to be there. This was in a private home where people have an expectation of privacy. If the video had been shot on a public street, it would have been a different matter.

Brownie Miller eventually settled out of court with NBC.

FAQ

But the TV crew was given permission by the paramedics to be there. Doesn't that protect the media in this case?

The court said no. Persons seeking emergency help do not "open the door" for other persons who have no "justifiable official reason" to be there. In other words, when you call for paramedics, you do not expect to get a camera crew, too. NBC had a right to gather news but *not* to invade a person's solitude. "News gatherers cannot immunize their conduct by purporting to act jointly with public officials such as the police and paramedics."

Such media ride-alongs became a legal issue again in the 1990s as a series of popular reality TV shows put average citizens in unwanted spotlights.

Courts Limit Media Ride-Alongs With Police

In *Florida Publishing Co. v. Fletcher* (discussed in the previous chapter), the court ruled that it was all right for a photographer to enter the scene of a house fire because a fire official had invited the photographer. However, when police invite media cameras along on arrests, does this violate a suspect's right to privacy?

"A Search Warrant Is Simply Not a Press Pass"

In 1994, the courts began to give some hints about how they felt about TV cameras tagging along with police. The case of *Ayeni v. Mottola*[14] involved the CBS program *Street Stories*. In one episode, Secret Service agents had a warrant to search the home of a man suspected of credit card fraud, and a CBS *Street Stories* crew was invited to accompany the agents during their search. The man sued, saying the broadcast of the search violated his right to privacy. A federal appeals court agreed, saying the CBS camera's presence in a private home had no legitimate law enforcement purpose. The main purpose of the camera was to get video for an entertainment program, and the court objected to that: "A private

---

[13]232 Cal. Rptr. 668 (1986)

[14]35 F.3d 680 (2d Cir. 1994)

home is not a soundstage for law enforcement theatricals." To drive the point home, the court added: "A search warrant is simply not a press pass."

In 1996, a federal appeals court had a different opinion in *Parker v. Boyer*.[15] This court said, "most courts have rejected the argument that the United States Constitution forbids the media to encroach on a person's property while the police search it."

In 1999, though, the Supreme Court used the following two cases to echo the *Ayeni* ruling. The court basically told the media to curtail their practice of accompanying police officers during arrests on private property.

Wilson v. Layne

In April 1992, police officers from a Maryland county and from the U.S. Marshals Service allowed a newspaper reporter and a photographer from the *Washington Post* to ride along on an attempted arrest. The officers had warrants to arrest Dominic Wilson, who was "likely to be armed and to resist arrest." Things did not go as planned.

Police were incorrectly given the address of Wilson's parents, and officers burst into the home. Charles and Geraldine Wilson were still in bed. A startled Mr. Wilson ran into the living room wearing only his briefs, and he saw five men in plain clothes with guns. Wilson was scared and confused and demanded they leave, and he cursed at them repeatedly. The officers mistook Mr. Wilson for his son, and they wrestled him to the floor. Mrs. Wilson then ran into the living room wearing only her nightgown.

A photographer had followed police into the home and took photographs of the scuffle between officers and Mr. Wilson. The officers soon discovered Dominic Wilson was not in the home, and they left. The *Post* never published any of the photographs. The Wilsons sued the law enforcement officials for violating their privacy under the Fourth Amendment, which prohibits the government from subjecting citizens to any unreasonable search and seizure. The couple was also upset about the media's presence.

In *Wilson v. Layne*,[16] the U.S. Supreme Court sided with the Wilsons, saying that law enforcement had overstepped its bounds. Police violated the Wilson's Fourth Amendment rights by allowing the media to enter the home. "Third parties" such as the media do not aid police in executing an arrest warrant, so those third parties have no business being there.

The newspaper had argued that the ride-along was an important newsgathering method and allowed the media to act as "watchdogs" regarding police behavior during arrests. However, the court did not buy this argument. It said the media members were really there to report and take pictures "for their own private purposes, not for the purpose of protecting the police or the home's residents."

The Supreme Court was breaking new ground here, because prior to this case, "there were no judicial opinions holding that this practice [a media ride-along] became unlawful when it entered a home." Because the law had been unclear, the court did not allow the officers involved to be sued. From now on, though, the court said, the law would be clear: *Law enforcement officials face lawsuits in the future if they allow the media to ride along into private homes or onto private property.*

---

[15] 93 F.3d 445 (8th Cir. 1996)

[16] 526 U.S. 603 (1999)

> ## FAQ
>
> What if the photographer had taken the pictures from a public street outside the home?

It would have been fine. The decisions in *Wilson* and other cases indicate that recording of law enforcement activity is legal when it is done on public property. Photographers are free to take pictures of a driver being ticketed for speeding because the pictures are taken on a public highway where anyone passing by could see the ticket being issued. A person really has no "expectation of privacy" in such a situation. The media would also have the right to photograph police arresting and handcuffing a criminal in a public area such as a street or a park. Remember, the *Wilson* case stressed that the media are intruding only when they enter *private* areas with police.

> ## FAQ
>
> Why do many TV stations still blot out people's faces or license plate numbers when the arrests are made on public streets?

Many stations have policies prohibiting the broadcast of video from ride-alongs if it includes the faces or license plate numbers of people pulled over for speeding or other offenses. Also, many police departments will not allow the media to do ride-alongs unless there is a guarantee that people's identities, including license plate numbers, will be concealed. When people are pulled over for speeding, they are not expecting a camera crew to come along with the police officer.

However, if the media are not doing a ride along and simply shoot the video from a public place, there is no need to conceal identities. The Supreme Court would soon have another chance to express its discomfort with media ride-alongs on private property.

Hanlon v. Berger

In March 1993, federal agents from the Fish and Wildlife Service (FWS) had a search warrant for the Montana ranch of Paul and Erma Berger. The FWS had received tips that the Bergers had used poison to kill predators, including bald eagles, which is illegal.

A CNN camera crew had been given permission to accompany FWS and state agents during the search of the ranch. CNN had its cameras rolling when 20 agents entered the ranch. One FWS agent wore a hidden CNN microphone, which recorded agents questioning the Bergers. CNN used the footage in a news story about ranchers who kill predators. The Bergers said they did not know the cameras were news cameras. They had assumed they were government cameras being used to document evidence.

The Bergers sued, saying the use of news cameras during a law enforcement action violated their Fourth Amendment rights against unreasonable search and seizure. The Bergers also sued CNN and the government for trespassing and intentional infliction of emotional distress. Agents argued that the presence of the media was educational, and it would help the public understand the difficulties of law enforcement.

In *Hanlon v. Berger*,[17] the U.S. Supreme Court showed its discomfort once again with the media accompanying law enforcement officials into private homes. The court looked at the actions of both parties here.

Law Enforcement. Police were not liable for monetary damages in this case because this area of law (media ride-alongs) was still developing. However, the court said that the argument about cameras helping to "educate" the public did not "justify the ride-along into a private home." The court said the police should not have to pay for this mistake . . . this time. However, in the future, law enforcement could be sued for allowing media ride-alongs during arrests, searches, and similar events.

Media. The media were liable. The Supreme Court remanded this issue to the appeals court, which said that CNN could be held liable on all three counts: trespass, emotional distress, and violating the Bergers' Fourth Amendment rights.

It may seem unfair that the Supreme Court held the media liable in this case but not the police. After all, it was the police who allowed CNN and its cameras to ride along. The appeals court ruled in *Berger v. Hanlon*[18] that CNN's goal was not to aid police in an investigation but to get footage for "television entertainment." As a result, the court said CNN did not have the same "qualified immunity" as law enforcement officials. *The court sent a strong signal here that media ride-alongs into private homes were not going to be tolerated.* CNN settled out of court with the Bergers.

Chief Justice William Rehnquist summarized the sentiment of the Supreme Court:

> It is a violation of the Fourth Amendment for police to bring members of the media or other third parties into a home during the execution of a warrant when the presence of the third parties in the home was not in the aid of the execution of the warrant.[213]

Since the *Berger* decision, the television media have cut back significantly on ride-alongs with law enforcement. Both police and the media are now fearful of lawsuits and would just prefer to avoid the issue altogether.

FAQ

Aren't there still programs on television that feature "real-life ride-alongs" showing people being arrested in their homes?

The TV shows *COPS* is one example. Shortly after the Supreme Court rulings, the executive producer of *COPS*, John Langley, did an interview with the *Washington Post*. Langley told the paper that the Supreme Court decisions would not change how *COPS* was done. He told the *Post*, "As a so-called ride-along program, we are unaffected by the decision because we obtain releases from everyone involved in our program."[19] Langley emphasized that his show does not violate any person's right to privacy. When shows like *COPS* do not obtain

---

[17]526 U.S. 808 (1999)

[18]188 F.3d 1155 (9th Cir. 1999)

[19]Biskupic, J., & Kurtz, H. (1999, May 25). Police can be sued for letting media see raids. *Washington Post*, p. A8.

permission from individuals, the videotape is either not aired, or the person's face is blotted out using computer technology.

California Supreme Court Orders Ride-Along Case to Be "Depublished"

When a case is *depublished*, it means that a higher court has ruled that a lower court's opinion is not valid. This often means that the higher court found substantial errors in the lower court ruling and does not want those errors to be "on the record." Therefore, the case opinion is officially "not citable" and may not be used as precedent by other courts.

Such was the case in 1999 when the California Supreme Court ordered that a California Court of Appeal ruling, *Marich v. QRZ Media,*[20] be depublished. The case involved an episode of a TV show, *L.A.P.D.: Life on the Beat*, in which a camera crew accompanied police into an apartment where a drug overdose victim was found dead on the floor. The apartment building owner apparently gave the media permission to enter.

The camera crew recorded a police officer phoning the victim's parents, but only "unintelligible" sounds could be heard from the parents. When aired, the TV show blotted out the victim's face and did not reveal the names of the victim or his parents.

The parents sued for intrusion regarding the phone conversation. A lower court dismissed their lawsuit, but the California Court of Appeal reinstated it. The court said that even though the parents' words were unintelligible on the TV show, that did "not preclude the viewer from recognizing the anguish" in their voices. The court saw this as an invasion of privacy. The court also said that the parents had a reasonable expectation that a third party would not record the conversation for use on a TV program.

The court had used *Sanders* and *Shulman* as rationale for its ruling, but the state's highest court apparently felt that the lower court had misread those cases in this instance, which may have been a major factor in the ruling being depublished. A dissent by Court of Appeal Justice Vogel may have summed up the rationale behind the Supreme Court's depublishing order. Vogel said that all that could be heard on the tape was a "low volume, muffled emission of sound." Vogel argued that the "zone of privacy" for the parents was their actual conversation, but their words were unintelligible on the tape, thus "revealing nothing of their confidential communications to the officer." As a result, Vogel argued, there was no intrusion by the media.

AMBUSHING

The *ambush* is a style of newsgathering used most often by investigative reporters.

An example would be a TV news show investigating a doctor accused of insurance fraud. The doctor refuses to do a TV interview, so the TV reporter and cameraperson wait for the doctor outside of his office. When the doctor leaves work, the reporter follows the doctor down the sidewalk and asks him questions while the camera rolls. It is usually not much of an interview. The doctor will probably only say things like "no comment." The ambush tactic was used in the next case, and it backfired for the media.

---

[20]86 Cal. Rptr.2d 406 (1999) *not citable—ordered not published*

The Le Mistral Case

A CBS-TV news station was investigating health code violations at various New York City restaurants. The news crew decided it would use an ambush technique at the Le Mistral restaurant. With cameras rolling, the crew walked into the restaurant as the reporter shouted out directions. The bright camera lights and noisy reporter alarmed many customers, some of whom hid under tables, covered their faces with tablecloths and napkins, or left without paying. The owner of the restaurant asked the journalists to leave immediately, but they refused and kept filming until the owner had them physically removed. (Conflicting testimony at the jury trial had the CBS crew inside the restaurant for as little as 1 minute and as long as 10 minutes.)

The restaurant sued CBS for trespassing. CBS said it had a right to enter "a place of public accommodation" to investigate a newsworthy story. A jury ruled against CBS, and in *Le Mistral v. CBS*,[21] the court upheld the jury verdict for several reasons. For example, CBS "burst into the plaintiff's restaurant in a noisy and obtrusive fashion" and began filming customers. This was wrong, the court said, because "patronizing a restaurant does not carry with it an obligation to appear on television." Even some CBS employees admitted they were trespassing on private property. Reporters have no right to be on private property if the owner does not approve.

FAQ

Why wasn't newsworthiness more of a factor here in favor of the media? It was an important factor in the Food Lion case.

The court made it clear that the media do not have a license to go wherever they wish in the name of newsworthiness. Interestingly, if CBS had used hidden cameras in this case, it would have been considered less "intrusive." The abrasive tactics used by the CBS news crew created the problem here. Abrasive tactics were definitely the central issue in the following case, in which the media engaged in repeated harassment.

Inside Edition Gets Too Close

In 1996, the TV show *Inside Edition* was doing an investigative report on the high salaries paid to executives at U.S. Healthcare. Richard and Nancy Wolfson were department directors for the company, and Nancy Wolfson's father, Leonard Abramson, was chairman of the board for U.S. Healthcare. Two *Inside Edition* reporters requested interviews with Abramson, but he refused to go on camera. The reporters began to engage in ambush interview techniques, including waiting for the Wolfsons outside their home and following them to work; sitting in a Jeep with tinted windows and parking in the driveway of a vacant house across from the Wolfsons' home, waiting to get video of the Wolfsons; following the Wolfsons' car as it took their 3-year-old daughter to nursery school and when the Wolfsons were driving with their 11-month-old child in a car seat; walking about 4 feet up the Wolfsons' driveway to shoot

---

[21]61 A.D.2d 491, 402 N.Y.S.2d 815 (1978)

video; and anchoring a boat about 60 yards away from the Abramsons' home in Florida when the Wolfsons were visiting. In this instance, the reporters and cameraman used a "shotgun" microphone (to pick up sounds from distances) and cameras with zoom lenses. The boat remained anchored there for several hours in public waterways.

Prior to all of this, Leonard Abramson had received anonymous threats against himself and his family. The presence of the *Inside Edition* reporters made the Abramsons and Wolfsons afraid to leave their homes. The families said they often kept their drapes drawn, instructed their children to stay away from windows, and often changed their travel routes to avoid the ever-present cameras. Mrs. Wolfson later testified, "I felt like a prisoner in my own house. I couldn't leave the house, the kids couldn't go outside."

In *Wolfson v. Lewis*,[22] the family sued the reporters for stalking, harassment, trespass, intrusion, and invasion of privacy. A federal district judge ruled that the reporters had engaged in "hounding, harassing and ambushing," and he said the Wolfsons had a "reasonable likelihood of success" to win their invasion of privacy case before a jury. The court then ordered the reporters to stop following and harassing the family members. The judge said that this would not curtail *Inside Edition*'s ability to do newsgathering on the story; it would just curtail the "intruding, frightening, terrorizing" newsgathering tactics.

SUMMARY

Hidden cameras, media ride-alongs, and ambush interviews are all intrusive methods of gathering video for news or for simple entertainment. The media must always be aware of the laws involving these newsgathering methods to avoid potential invasions of privacy. The courts have recently taken issue with the media doing ride-alongs with law enforcement, stating that such tandems are often an invasion of privacy, especially when the incidents occur on private property.

---

[22]924 F. Supp. 1413 (E.D. Pa. 1996)

10

MEDIA LIABILITY LAWSUITS

DO NOT ATTEMPT this method.

—Herceg v. Hustler[1]

W arning labels have become more commonplace on many products as companies try to protect themselves from potential lawsuits. Years ago, for example, no one thought it necessary to place a warning on something as "harmless" as a box of garbage bags. However, that changed when children suffocated in plastic bags and their parents began suing the makers of the bags, not for making defective products but for not providing adequate warnings. Now, many plastic bags have written warnings such as, "This is not a toy. Danger of suffocation. Keep away from children."

Should the electronic media provide similar warnings about content that may lead to illegal or dangerous activities? Are the media liable for actions that are "inspired" by a movie or TV show? American history is filled with accounts of criminals claiming that something in the mass media inspired them to commit crimes. Charles Manson said the Beatles'"white album" and the song "Helter Skelter" in particular encouraged him to order the Tate-LaBianca murders in 1969. In 1980, Mark David Chapman murdered John Lennon and then claimed the character Holden Caulfield from the book *The Catcher in the Rye* was his motivation for pulling the trigger. (Hours before shooting Lennon, Chapman had asked the former Beatle to sign a copy of the book, and the book was in his possession when he was arrested.) In 1981, John Hinckley, Jr., said he tried to assassinate President Reagan to impress actress Jodie Foster, saying he was imitating a scene from the movie *Taxi Driver*.

Only recently, though, have more people been taking this "blame game" into the courtroom. In this era of litigation, the media are finding themselves more and more the targets of negligence lawsuits. If a media outlet produces material that in some way inspires a dangerous or illegal activity, the outlet could find itself in court fending off charges that it was negligent in distributing the material. Even though the media are found not to be liable in the majority of these cases, it still is a financial burden to fight these legal battles.

---

[1]814 F.2d 1017 (5th Cir. 1987)

It is not difficult to find news accounts of people being injured or killed when imitating actions that have been portrayed or discussed in the media:

▣ December 1994: An 18-year-old man in Stonesboro, PA, lay down on a double yellow line in the middle of a road just over the crest of a hill. He was imitating a scene from the movie *The Program*. He was killed when a truck hit him. Disney Studios removed the scene from the movie after the man's death.

▣ July 1999: A 7-year-old boy in Dallas, TX, was a big fan of professional wrestling on TV. Imitating what he had seen on TV, the boy performed a "clothesline" move on his 3-year-old brother. The 3-year-old died from severe head injuries.

▣ June 2003: Two teenage stepbrothers in Newport, TN, said they were imitating the video game *Grand Theft Auto* when they fired shotguns at cars on Interstate 40. A 45-year-old man was killed. His family sued the makers of the video game.

None of these cases resulted in a trial in which the media were held liable for their actions.

FAQ

Is it easy for people to win negligence lawsuits against the media?

The guidelines established in *Brandenburg v. Ohio*[2] make it difficult for people to win media liability cases. The plaintiff in such a case has a heavy burden and must prove that words or images in movies, books, TV shows, video games, musical recordings, and other media are likely to result in "imminent lawless action" and that the media outlet could "foresee" what would happen.

The courts will consider some or all of the following criteria in determining whether the media can be held accountable for a "copycat" crime.

COMMON CRITERIA IN COPYCAT CASES

▣ Did the media purposefully incite or encourage dangerous behavior or criminal activity?

▣ Did the media create "an undue risk of harm" with their speech?

▣ Was there "foreseeability?" In other words, did the media know there was a "clear and present danger" that injury might result from the media message?

▣ Did the media provide warnings or disclaimers about potentially harmful content?

▣ Will there be a future "chilling effect" on free speech if the media are held liable in a particular case?

▣ What other factors may have led to the crime? Can the media truly be blamed as the main instigator of this crime?

▣ Was this crime an isolated response to the media message? Were numerous others *not* affected by the message?

---

[2] 395 U.S. 444 (1969)

America's First Media Copycat Claim?

In 1881, 11-year-old Jesse Pomeroy of Boston (who became known as the "boy-fiend") began taking young children into remote areas where he would strip them, tie them up, and torture them. Eventually, Pomeroy's tortures turned into murder, and he was convicted at age 14 of the murders of two children. (He had apparently confessed to 27 murders.)

During Pomeroy's trial, social commentators and religious groups began to push for a ban on what were known as "dime novels." Many of these books contained graphic descriptions of various crimes, including murder, and the critics of the books said that Pomeroy's killings were caused by these novels. However, the argument lost steam during the trial when Pomeroy said he had never read these dime novels.

It was not until the 1970s that the courts began to grapple head-on with the issue of media liability. The ruling in a radio case showed that the First Amendment did not provide blanket protection to the media in liability cases.

Radio Station "Mad Scramble"

In July 1970, Los Angeles radio station KHJ ran a contest called "The Super Summer Spectacular." KHJ was the top-rated station in Los Angeles among teenage listeners, and this contest was geared toward that age group. The station said the contest was designed to make KHJ seem "more exciting" to its listeners.

On July 16, KHJ disc jockey "The Real Don Steele" drove around Los Angeles in a conspicuous red car while the station aired live updates about his location. The first person to find Steele won a cash prize. (Listeners also had to meet another contest condition, such as answering a question.) The following are excerpts from that day's broadcast:

The Real Don Steele is back on his feet again with some money, and he is headed for the Valley. Thought I would give you a warning so that you can get your kids out of the street.

The Real Don Steele is moving into Canoga Park, so be on the lookout for him. . . . He's got 25 dollars to give away, if you can get it.

The Real Don Steele is in the Valley near the intersection of Topanga and Roscoe Boulevard, right by the Loew's Holiday Theater—you know where that is at, and he's standing there with a little money he would like to give away to the first person to arrive and tell him what type car I helped Robert W. Morgan give away yesterday morning at KHJ. If you know that, split. Intersection of Topanga and Roscoe Boulevard—right nearby the Loew's Holiday Theater—you will find the Real Don Steele. Tell him and pick up the bread.

17-year-old Robert Sentner and 19-year-old Marsha Baime drove to the Holiday Theater only to discover that someone else had arrived there first and won the prize. Steele was already moving on to another location, and both teenage drivers reached speeds of 80 miles an hour as they tried to follow Steele's car on an expressway. (Steele was never accused of speeding, by the way.) During this time, the station aired the following update:

Be on the lookout, he may stop in Thousand Oaks and may stop along the way. Looks like it may be a good stop, Steele—drop some bread to those folks.

In an attempt to follow Steele's car onto an off-ramp, the erratic driving of either Baime's or Sentner's car forced a third car onto the expressway's center divider, where it crashed. The man driving the third car was killed. The man's widow and children filed a wrongful death suit against the two teenage drivers and KHJ. A jury found both KHJ and Baime liable for the man's death and awarded the man's family $300,000 in damages. (Sentner had earlier settled out of court with the widow.)

In *Weirum v. RKO,*[3] the Supreme Court of California upheld the jury's ruling, saying the radio station was liable for the man's death for several reasons. For example, the KHJ give-away was a "competitive scramble" on *public* streets. It was not a commonplace invitation. The live broadcasts with their repeated messages intensified the "thrill of the chase." Considering these two elements, the court said, the radio station should have seen that it was were creating "an undue risk of harm." The court also upheld the damages awarded by the jury.

FAQ

What effect did this ruling have on other radio stations?

As a result of this ruling, radio stations across the nation began to scrutinize any contest that might have encouraged listeners to "hurry up and get here." Stations realized that they must always think about *potential* lawsuits when conducting contests. Keep in mind, though, that the RKO case was unique. The station was encouraging listeners in their cars to chase a DJ around town and was intensifying the situation with live updates.

Within the next decade, others tried to use the *Weirum* ruling as a basis for winning incitement or copycat lawsuits against the media. In the following cases, though, the courts did not find that the media were actually encouraging or inciting particular behaviors. The courts were particularly concerned about a "chilling effect" that might result if the media were held liable in each case.

STIMULUS VERSUS ENCOURAGEMENT

In 1974, NBC aired the movie *Born Innocent*, which contained scene with four girls who entered a shower room and used the handle of a plunger (or plumber's helper) to rape another girl. Four days after the broadcast, a 9-year-old girl was attacked and raped with a bottle by a group of minors at a San Francisco beach. The attackers later said the movie's shower scene gave them the idea to commit the rape.

The family of the young girl blamed NBC for inspiring the crime and filed a lawsuit in *Olivia N. v. NBC.*[4] The lawsuit claimed NBC was responsible for this rape because the network had studies showing that children and susceptible people might imitate crimes seen on TV. The lawsuit also claimed that NBC did not give a proper warning about the movie's content. As a result, the family said NBC was negligent for airing the movie.

---

[3]15 Cal.3d 40; 539 P.2d 36 (1975)

[4]126 Cal. App.3d 488 (Cal. Ct. App. 1981), cert. denied, 458 U.S. 1108 (1982)

A California Court of Appeals ruled that NBC was not responsible for the girl's rape. Holding NBC liable in this case would create a "chilling effect" on all media, the court said. It would lead producers to self-censor all sorts of scenes, which would lead to movies and TV shows "only suitable for children." What if someone copied a crime described in a TV news story? Should society hold the newscast responsible for copycat crimes? The court said no.

The NBC film did not directly incite people to commit a crime. The film was simply a dramatization with no intent for people to imitate it.

FAQ

But wasn't this case similar to *Weirum* in that a program in the mass media was the main stimulus for the actions of these boys?

The family of the girl also argued that this case was similar to *Weirum v. RKO*, but the court rejected the comparison, saying the radio station in *Weirum* had been *directly* urging its listeners to act. The court made an important distinction here by saying the movie simply was a "stimulus," not an "encouragement." The movie was not directly encouraging its viewers to imitate any acts. The Supreme Court of California refused to hear an appeal.

In cases like these, the courts will also consider whether the copycat action was a common occurrence. Did a lot of people imitate this act, or was the copycat incident an isolated response to a media event? The court addressed this issue in the following case.

The *Mickey Mouse Club* Case—"One Out of 16 Million"

In February 1978, 11-year-old Craig Shannon of Georgia was watching the *Mickey Mouse Club* on TV. On this day, the show featured "magic you can create with sound effects." A person on the show demonstrated how to reproduce the sound of a tire coming off of a car. He placed a BB pellet inside a "large, round balloon," filled the balloon with air, and swirled the BB inside the balloon.

Young Craig tried to imitate the stunt at home and placed a piece of lead (about two times bigger than a BB) inside a "large, skinny balloon." When Craig inflated the balloon, the balloon popped, and the piece of lead flew into his eye. He was partially blinded. The young boy and his family filed a lawsuit against the *Mickey Mouse Club* show, Walt Disney Productions, and two other media companies.

A trial judge ruled in favor of Shannon, but the Supreme Court of Georgia eventually overturned the ruling in *Disney v. Shannon*[5] because, for one thing, what children were invited to do during this program did not present "a clear and present danger that injury would in fact result." Also, out of an estimated 16 million children watching the show that day, Craig Shannon was the only person known to have reported an injury. The court concluded that ruling for Shannon in this case would have "a seriously chilling effect on the flow of protected speech through society's medium's of communication."

---

[5]247 Ga. 402; 276 S.E.2d 580 (1981)

FAQ

What if a copycat act leads to a person's death? Are the media more likely to be held liable in such cases?

In the next case, the courts ruled that the flow of free speech must be protected even if the "copycat" actions are fatal.

"We Warned You. . . ."

It was, admittedly, a dangerous stunt. On May 23, 1979, NBC's *The Tonight Show*, starring Johnny Carson, had professional stuntman Dar Robinson as a guest. Carson announced early in the show that Robinson would "hang" Carson during a stunt later in the program. In what would become an important part of the case, Robinson warned the audience: "Believe me, it's not something that you would want to go and try. This is a stunt." Robinson later added, "I happen to know somebody who did something similar to it, just fooling around, and almost broke his neck."

During the stunt, Carson stood on some gallows with a noose by his side as Robinson and a "hangman" stood by. The men placed a hood on Carson's head and put the noose over the hood. The trapdoor was sprung, and Carson fell through. The stunt was successful, and Carson was not injured.

In Rhode Island, 13-year-old Nicholas "Nicky" DeFilippo was watching the show and attempted to imitate the hanging trick. Several hours after the broadcast, Nicky's parents found their dead son hanging from a noose in front of their TV, which was still tuned to NBC. The parents learned about the content of the program and filed a lawsuit in *DeFilippo v. NBC*,[6] suing for $10 million in damages. They made two basic claims: (a) NBC "failed to adequately warn and inform (viewers) of the dangers of this program," and (b) NBC intentionally and negligently aired the program "with malicious and reckless disregard of plaintiff's and Nicky's welfare" (the parents added that NBC was more concerned about profits than about their son's life).

As was done in *Olivia N.*, the plaintiffs in this case also tried to use the *Weirum* case as precedent. In the end, the Supreme Court of Rhode Island rejected that argument and ruled that NBC could not be held legally responsible for Nicky DeFilippo's death. The court provided reasoning very similar to previous cases described in this chapter. The TV show may have been a stimulus, but it did not contain incitement. The death was an isolated incident. "Nicky was, as far as we are aware, the only person who is alleged to have emulated the action" from the hanging stunt. Ruling for the DeFilippos would cause self-censorship by broadcasters who would feel pressured to "remove any matter that *may be* emulated and lead to a lawsuit."

NBC provided evidence of the repeated "warnings" given by Robinson on the show. "It appears that despite these warnings, Nicky felt encouraged to emulate the stunt." NBC could not be called "negligent" because it aired warnings.

---

[6]446 A.2d 1036 (1982)

FAQ

So, do warnings or disclaimers help to get the media off the hook in such cases?

Many times they can play an important role in protecting the media in copycat lawsuits. That is, as long as the disclaimers are sincere, with no ulterior motives. That was the case in 1987 in *Herceg v. Hustler.*[7] A federal appeals court ruled in favor of *Hustler* magazine in a lawsuit stemming from an article entitled "Orgasm of Death." The article described a practice called "autoerotic asphyxia" during which a person is supposed to heighten sexual pleasure by masturbating while "hanging" himself. A 14-year-old boy died as a result of attempting the practice. His mother sued *Hustler,* but the court ruled that the magazine could not be held liable for the boy's death because the article did not encourage the practice but actually contained numerous disclaimers about the dangers. The article explicitly stated "DO NOT ATTEMPT this method" and warned that people who attempted autoerotic asphyxia would most likely "end up in cold storage with a coroner's tag on your big toe."

These four copycat lawsuits demonstrated that the courts were developing a pattern of protecting the media from liability in copycat cases. The courts said the media were stimuli in these cases, but plaintiffs could win their cases only by proving direct incitement by the media, and that was not present in these cases. In the following case, the plaintiffs tried a broader approach, saying that television in *general* is a cause of violence. Their argument failed as well.

"TV Intoxication"

In June 1977, 15-year-old Ronny Zamora was convicted of killing his 83-year-old neighbor Elinor Haggart in Miami, FL. The young man claimed that he committed the murder because he had been "intoxicated" by television violence since he was 5 years old. Zamora and his parents then filed a lawsuit against CBS, NBC, and ABC. In *Zamora v. CBS,*[8] the Zamoras claimed that young Ronny had "become involuntarily addicted to and 'completely subliminally intoxicated' by the extensive viewing of television violence." As a result, they argued that Ronny developed a "sociopathic personality, became desensitized to violent behavior, and became a danger to himself and others."

The court dismissed the Zamora family's claims and ruled for the TV networks. The "cause" of the young Zamora's murderous urge and action was extremely vague. The family was trying to blame all of TV in general. That is a pretty big target. The networks cannot be expected to predict the violent behavior of people who watch their programs. In any case, Zamora watched the shows voluntarily. It was his choice. The court summed it up by saying that any restraints on the First Amendment "must be viewed with suspicion." The public has a right to receive "suitable access" to a variety of ideas and experiences through television.

---

[7]814 F.2d 1017 (5th Cir. 1987)

[8]480 F. Supp. 199 (S.D. Fla. 1979)

FAQ

Did the court see a possible chilling effect here?

Yes. The court said that a ruling against the media in this case would "place broadcasters in jeopardy for televising *Hamlet, Julius Caesar, Grimm's Fairy Tales . . . All Quiet on the Western Front,* and even the Holocaust." As a result of these rulings, the courts showed that the media were in no way negligent for airing such programming. There was no "foreseeable harm" from airing these shows.

Advertisements and "Foreseeable Harm"

In 1989, the Florida Supreme Court would extend similar protections to commercial speech. The case of *Sakon v. Pepsico*[9] involved a 14-year-old boy who had seriously injured himself after imitating a stunt he had seen in a TV soda commercial. The ad for Mountain Dew showed "lake jumping," which involved young people riding bikes down a hill and up a ramp, with the kids landing their bikes safely in the water. Michael Sakon attempted to copy the stunt in a creek that was only 3 feet deep. When his bike hit the water, he flew over the handle bars and landed head first in the water, breaking his neck. Sakon sued the soft drink maker for negligence, saying Pepsico glorified a dangerous activity in a commercial that was targeted to a young audience. Sakon said the commercial did not warn viewers about the dangers of "lake jumping" and that the ad was produced "in a manner likely to induce a young viewer to imitate the activity."

The Florida Supreme Court rejected those arguments and ruled in favor of Pepsico. The ad did not directly encourage any activity other than drinking Mountain Dew: "The product being advertised had nothing to do with the activity." The court cited the *Zamora* case and said that a verdict in favor of Sakon would subject the media to a flood of liability lawsuits that involved children imitating acts they had seen on TV shows and commercials.

The court also asked what kind of warning would have kept Sakon from mimicking this stunt: "For instance, should the ad specify the depth of the water? If too shallow, the actor might strike the bottom. If too deep, he might drown. Must the actor be warned he must be able to swim?" The court continued: "Should the operator of a ski area, when advertising and showing persons skiing, be required to warn viewers or readers they need to take lessons before trying to ski?" The court said the answer has to be no, to protect free expression.

The court concluded that Sakon's accident was not a "foreseeable consequence of Pepsico's advertisement."

Even though the media won this case, advertisers became nervous and began putting disclaimers on TV commercials that included any type of dangerous activity that might be imitated. For example, in an ad that shows a car speeding around dangerous curves, a disclaimer might read: "Do not attempt. Professional driver on closed course." The warnings are designed to fend off lawsuits as well as to protect the advertiser in the event of a copycat lawsuit.

---

[9]553 So.2d 163 (1989)

TABLOID TALK SHOWS

TV Talk Show Topic Leads to Murder

In the 1990s, the TV "tabloid talk" format was very popular. These shows became notorious for humiliating guests on national television by placing them in embarrassing situations. On March 6, 1995, the *Jenny Jones Show* taped an episode about "secret crushes." The show invited Jonathan Schmitz to be a guest, along with one of his female friends. The show's producers told Schmitz that during the show he would find out that one of his friends had a "secret crush" on him.

During the show, Jenny Jones brought out Schmitz's male friend Scott Amedure, who confessed that he had a crush on Schmitz. The show wanted to shock Schmitz by revealing that it was a male who had the crush on him. On the tape of the show (which never aired), Schmitz laughed when Amedure walked out on stage, and Schmitz laughingly said, "You lied to me!" Amedure later described a sexual fantasy with Schmitz involving whipped cream, strawberries, and champagne. Schmitz reacted by burying his face in his hands.

Three days later, Schmitz found an anonymous "suggestive" note on his doorstep and assumed Amedure wrote it. Schmitz went to Amedure's home and shot and killed him. Schmitz was convicted of murder in a criminal trial.

However, it was the civil trial that gathered intensive media attention. The family of Scott Amedure filed a wrongful death suit against the *Jenny Jones Show* and its owner Warner Brothers for $71.5 million. The family claimed that the TV show was ultimately responsible for Amedure's death because the show's producers invited a "mentally ill" Jonathan Schmitz onto their show (Schmitz had previously attempted suicide). They said the show intentionally "ambushed" and "humiliated" Schmitz and thus "incited" the murder. The family also said that *Jenny Jones* should have provided "post-show counseling" to make sure that Schmitz was all right.

The *Jenny Jones Show* said it had no liability for Schmitz's actions. It was Schmitz who purchased the shotgun at one store, drove to another store to buy ammunition, and then drove to Amedure's home to kill him. Schmitz was told before the show that his admirer could be a woman or a man. A producer claimed Schmitz did not appear to be upset after the taping. He and Amedure even "partied" together after the show. *Jenny Jones* speculated that Schmitz might have killed Amedure because the two had a sexual encounter of some sort.

In May 1999, a Michigan jury awarded more than $29 million in damages to the Amedure family, holding the *Jenny Jones Show* responsible for the murder. The jurors felt the show intentionally humiliated Schmitz and that it should have thought more carefully about possible reactions from embarrassed guests. Basically, the jury said that the murder would never have occurred if it had not been for that episode of the show. In March 2000, the judge who oversaw the trial upheld the $29 million jury verdict. Judge Gene Schneltz wrote, "Whether they like it or not, each side received a trial of its own making and neither has any cause to complain."

FAQ

Didn't this verdict create a chilling effect in the talk show world?

Yes. Lawyers were soon advising TV talk shows about what topics to air and *not* to air. The verdict sparked numerous debates in the legal and entertainment communities about "how far is too far?"

Verdict Overturned

In October 2002, in *Graves v. Warner Brothers*,[10] the Michigan Court of Appeals said the jury's verdict had gone too far. The appeals court threw out the jury award, ruling that "the defendants in this case had no duty to anticipate and prevent the act of murder committed by Schmitz." The case was remanded to the trial court, which was ordered to render a judgment in favor of Warner Brothers and the *Jenny Jones Show*. The appeals court said that such TV shows, even though they may embarrass and humiliate guests, could not be held responsible for the "homicidal acts of a third party." Once again, the courts ruled that there was no foreseeability in such cases and that the media were not legally liable.

MTV PUSHES THE ENVELOPE

Jackass

MTV's *Jackass* aired in 2000 and 2001 and was a show during which host Johnny Knoxville engaged in outrageous stunts for shock value. The popular show was then turned into a hit Hollywood film, *Jackass: The Movie*. However, MTV and the makers of *Jackass* soon found themselves fending off possible lawsuits from viewers who were injured while copying the show's stunts.

In one episode, Knoxville put on a flame-retardant suit and headgear. Under the watchful eye of experts (with fire extinguishers at the ready), Knoxville was set on fire. After a short time, the heat became too much for Knoxville and he was safely extinguished. In another episode, Knoxville became a "human barbecue" when he wore a fireproof suit with steaks attached to it. He then placed himself on a large grill while people sprayed the fire with lighter fluid.

In January 2001, 13-year-old Jason Lind of Connecticut tried to copy the fire stunts by soaking his feet and legs with gasoline. One of his friends then lit a match. Lind wound up in critical condition with second- and third-degree burns. The youth who lit the match was charged with first-degree reckless endangerment. Lind's father said MTV was at least partially responsible and that he was considering legal action.

A few months later, an 11-year-old boy from Connecticut suffered second-degree burns when he also tried to imitate the fire stunts from *Jackass*.

MTV defended the program, saying the show has a TV-MA rating, indicating that it is not suitable for people under 18. MTV also noted that the show has frequent warnings at the beginning of the show and throughout that state

> The following show features stunts performed by professionals and/or total idiots under very strict control and supervision. MTV and the producers insist that neither you or anyone else attempt to recreate or perform anything you have seen on this show.

---

[10]253 Mich. App. 486, 656 N.W.2d 195 (2002)

That disclaimer apparently did not discourage 21-year-old model Stephanie Hodges, a student at UCLA. In April 2001, Hodges broke her back and pelvis while trying to copy a stunt from *Jackass* that involved riding a mattress down a hill and catapulting off a snow bank. (She had actually appeared on the program before.) She said she had no intention of suing the program. That same month, a 16-year-old boy in Kentucky was injured after his friend drove a speeding car toward him, imitating yet another stunt from *Jackass*. The boy was supposed to dive out of the way "at the last minute," but he did not quite make it. (Another friend in the car was videotaping the failed stunt, hoping to send it to MTV.) The boy ended up with a broken leg and numerous cuts and bruises. The teens were charged with wanton endangerment, a felony in Kentucky.

In response to all of these copycat incidents, MTV moved the show from 9:00 p.m. to 10:00 p.m. on Sundays. The network also tried to discourage more copycats by adding wording to its disclaimer. The network now told viewers not to send in videotapes of stunts and that MTV would not even look at such tapes.

Lawsuits that have resulted have arisen either from the actual production of the show or from its spin-offs.

In October 2002, a woman sued MTV for injuries she suffered during the filming of a *Jackass* episode. She said she was "recruited" by the show to ask scripted questions of the cast. While at a podium, Wendy Linden said, she was surprised by another cast member who ran into a podium behind her by "using his body as a missile." The podium wound up hitting Linden. In her lawsuit, she claimed back and knee injuries and sued MTV for infliction of emotional distress, negligence, and battery.

Earlier in 2002, a couple had sued MTV in regard to a show called *Harassment*. The program involved hidden-camera pranks, and this one had involved a fake bloody corpse that had been placed in the couple's hotel room in Las Vegas. In 2001, two 14-year-old girls had sued MTV for negligence, battery, and infliction of emotional distress for an incident involving the *Jackass*-like show *Dude, This Sucks*. The girls were in the audience at a stage show featuring two men known as the "Shower Rangers." One of the men opened a flap on the back of his pants, spread his cheeks, and then sprayed fecal matter on the girls. MTV apologized for the incident and did not air the episode. The network said it would take steps to avoid such situations in the future.

MTV had previously been accused of instigating violent acts with its programming. In 1994, a 5-year-old boy in Florida had watched MTV's cartoon *Beavis and Butthead* during which the two animated characters talked about "fire, fire, fire." The boy then accidentally set his bed on fire, burning down his family's trailer and killing his 2-year-old sister.

In response, MTV put a disclaimer at the beginning of the show telling viewers not to imitate the program. MTV also moved the show to a later time slot and took out any references to fire in the program.

Movies

Natural Born Killers

In 1994, the Oliver Stone movie *Natural Born Killers* was released. The movie is about a couple's violent crime spree, during which they kill 52 people in 3 weeks. The movie received extensive publicity for its extremely violent and graphic depictions of the murders.

In March 1995, Sarah Edmonson robbed a convenience store in Ponchatoula, LA, and shot store employee Patsy Byers in the neck, leaving her paralyzed. Benjamin Darras drove the getaway car. After being arrested, both Edmonson and Darras admitted they had watched *Natural Born Killers* repeatedly and were inspired by it. Edmonson was convicted for shooting Byers, and Darras was convicted of murdering a Mississippi man during another part of their crime spree.

Byers sued Oliver Stone, saying his movie incited the shooting. Her lawsuit claimed that the movie's intent was for people like Darras and Edmonson to watch it over and over and then go on killing sprees. The lawsuit added that this was accomplished through "subliminal suggestion or glorification of violent acts."

A district judge said that the movie was protected by the First Amendment, but a Louisiana appeals court in May 1998 ruled that the First Amendment did not prevent Byers' family from having its day in court.[11] (Byers had died of cancer in November 1997, but her family continued with the lawsuit on her behalf.) Oliver Stone appealed to the U.S. Supreme Court, but the high court refused to hear the appeal, thus clearing the way for the Byers lawsuit to move forward. However, the case did not go far.

Lawsuit Thrown Out

In March 2001, a state judge in Louisiana threw out the lawsuit. He said Oliver Stone and Time Warner Entertainment did not make the movie with the intention of inciting violence. The movie was protected on First Amendment grounds.

FAQ

Why did the appeals court and U.S. Supreme Court allow such a lawsuit to go forward? Hadn't previous courts ruled that the media can't be held liable for such copycat crimes?

The courts were not taking sides in this case but were simply saying that the plaintiffs should have their day in court. As the appeals court judge put it, "Proof of intent in cases such as [this] . . . will be remote and even rare, but at this stage of the proceeding we find that Byers' cause of action is not barred by the First Amendment." The judge noted that the First Amendment would most likely protect Oliver Stone's movie in the end. However, citizens also have a right for their lawsuits to be given a fair hearing in court. That means people that like Stone may wind up spending time and money fighting off lawsuits, no matter how frivolous those lawsuits may be.

At about the same time, a variety of media were being blamed for a school shooting.

Paducah School Shooting Lawsuit

On December 1, 1997, 14-year-old Michael Carneal carried six guns into Heath High School in Paducah, KY, and opened fire on a student prayer meeting in the lobby. He killed three girls and injured five others. After the shooting, police discovered that Carneal was an avid fan of violent video games, as well as "a consumer of movies containing obscenity,

---

[11]*Byers v. Edmonson*, 712 So.2d 681, cert. denied, 526 U.S. 1005 (1999)

obscenity for minors, pornography, sexual violence, and/or violence." One movie in particular caught police attention: *The Basketball Diaries*. In the film, Leonardo DiCaprio portrays a student who, in a dream sequence, calmly walks into a school classroom and shoots fellow classmates (as other students cheer).

The parents of the three dead girls filed a $33 million lawsuit against the makers of *The Basketball Diaries* in *James v. Meow Media*.[12] The lawsuit did not stop with the filmmaker, though. The parents sued a total of 25 companies, and there were three basic categories: filmmakers, Web sites, and makers of violent video games.

The lawsuit claimed that all of the companies had contributed to making Carneal a violent and homicidal person. The parents hired adolescent psychologist Dr. Diane Schetky to analyze Carneal's behavior. She concluded, "The media's depiction of violence as a means of resolving conflict and a national culture which tends to glorify violence further condones his thinking."

The lawsuit outlined its complaints with each of the three media. *Movies* were accused of glorifying "senseless and gratuitous violence, hatred of religion, [and] disregard of authority." *Video games* were said to make "violence pleasurable and attractive, and disconnected the violence from the natural consequences thereof." *Internet sites* with sexual violence apparently "provoked violence in Carneal, and disconnected the violence from the natural consequences thereof."

In essence, the parents said the 25 media companies were at least partly responsible for their daughters' deaths for four reasons: (a) The media should have known that copycat crimes would result from people using their products; (b) the media products created a special risk for minors; (c) there was an issue of product liability, because the media should have known that their products were "unreasonably defective" and "likely to be dangerous"; and (d) the media did not "exercise reasonable care" to warn people about their products.

In April 2000, a U.S. district court judge in Kentucky threw out the lawsuit. The judge ruled that there was no issue with product liability laws because these media are not covered under such laws. The various media could not foresee what someone like Carneal might do, the judge said; the media cannot be expected to analyze the mental condition of every person who purchases a video game, rents a movie, or logs on to an Internet site. Carneal's murderous actions were "highly extraordinary" and "unforeseeable." His shooting spree was not a "normal response" to these media. The judge concluded that a ruling against the media would "allow the freaks and misfits of society to declare what the rest of the country can and cannot read, watch, and hear."

Carneal was found guilty of second-degree murder and sentenced to 25 years in prison without the possibility of parole.

MUSIC AND SUICIDE

"Suicide Solution"

Do certain "dark" and "depressing" rock music lyrics make people want to kill themselves? Rock artist Ozzy Osbourne and his lawyers had to answer this question in court in 1988 in *McCollum v. CBS*.[13]

---

[12]90 F. Supp.2d 798 (W.D. Ky. 2000)

[13]202 Cal. App.3d 989 (1988)

The case dealt with a 19-year-old John McCollum of California, who shot and killed himself in October 1984 as he was lying on his bed listening to Osbourne's music "over and over." He was found the next morning wearing headphones with an Osbourne's album *Speak of the Devil* still spinning on the turntable of his bedroom stereo. A year later, McCollum's family sued Osbourne and his music company, CBS Records, for negligence, intentional misconduct, and product liability.

However, their lawsuit targeted two of Osbourne's other albums, *Blizzard of Oz* and *Diary of a Madman*. John had listened to these albums on the family stereo before going to his room, where he listened to *Speak of the Devil* and then shot himself. The family said that Osbourne "was a cult figure who had a powerful influence on his young listeners." They claimed his music made suicide seem "not only acceptable, but desirable." The family made special note of Osbourne's song "Suicide Solution," from the album *Blizzard of Oz*. Some of the lyrics included "Suicide is the only way out" and "Get the gun and try it. Shoot, shoot, shoot."

A California appeals court threw out the lawsuit, ruling that Osbourne and CBS were not responsible for McCollum's death. The family attributed no blame to the album *Speak of the Devil*, the album to which John was listening when he killed himself. The court pointed out that themes of suicide and despair have "a long intellectual tradition" in such classic works as *Hamlet, Death of a Salesman*, and "Suicide is Painless" (the theme to the popular movie and TV show *M*A*S*H*). The lyrics on the albums could "easily be viewed as poetic device." The court said that "Suicide Solution" was not telling people to kill themselves. The song was about an alcoholic who used alcohol as a solution to problems; he knew alcohol would kill him in the end, and thus it became a "suicide solution."

FAQ

The court didn't see any direct incitement in these lyrics?

No. "Merely because art may evoke a mood of depression as it figuratively depicts the darker side of human nature does not mean that it constitutes a direct 'incitement to imminent violence,'" the court said. McCollum's suicide was an "irrational response to Osbourne's music." Artists cannot be forced to censor their material because of *possible* negative reactions by "emotionally troubled individuals." Finally, the court said the First Amendment gives protection "to all artistic and literary expression, whether in music, concerts, plays, pictures, or books."

Another famous music copycat case would try to argue that the danger from some "dark music" was more sinister because it used subliminal messages.

"The Music Made Me 'Do It'"

In December 1985, 20-year-old James Vance and 18-year-old Raymond Belknap took a sawed-off shotgun to a playground at a church in Sparks, NV. Belknap put the gun under his chin and pulled the trigger, killing himself. Vance also shot himself, but he survived, with critical injuries. He then rode his bicycle around town, "displaying" his rather grotesque injuries. (He died 4 years later from complications related to those injuries.)

Shortly after, Vance claimed that he and Belknap had been listening to heavy metal music for hours before the shootings, and it was the music that inspired them to form a suicide pact. Vance wrote a letter to Belknap's mother: "I believe that alcohol and heavy metal music, such as Judas Priest, led us or even 'mesmerized' us into believing that the answer to 'life was death.'" (He was quoting Judas Priest's lyrics.)

That letter soon led Vance and Belknap's mother to file a $6.2 million wrongful death lawsuit against the makers of the music—the British group Judas Priest. The suit focused on the group's 1978 album *Stained Class*. The lawsuit claimed that Judas Priest's music contained suggestive lyrics about death and suicide, along with hypnotic rhythms and beats that "aided, advised, and encouraged" personal harm or suicide. The suit claimed that the lyrics and rhythms were directed at a certain class of people "likely to follow such suggestions and imitate their heroes." Perhaps the most interesting claim was that the music had subliminal messages (allegedly recorded forward and backward), such as "Do it," "Sing my evil spirit," and "Try suicide."

Attorneys for Judas Priest then presented evidence to show that both boys were "dysfunctional" and that there were numerous personal and family issues that led to the shootings. Both youths had a history of drug use, including cocaine and amphetamines. Court records said Vance was a victim of child abuse by alcoholic parents. Hours before the shooting, Vance had argued with his mother. Also, both boys drank two six-packs of beer, smoked two or three marijuana joints, and decided to quit their jobs. At the age of 7 and 8 years, Vance had ripped out chunks of his hair during school, was labeled "self-destructive" by a school psychiatrist, had attacked his mother with a hammer, and had tried to choke her while she was driving the car. Vance had numerous "brushes with the law," including burglary, indecent exposure, and shoplifting.

Finally, Judas Priest's attorneys argued that it would make no sense for Judas Priest to encourage its "customers" to kill themselves. Why would a music group want to "kill off" the people who pay money for concerts and albums?

In 1990, a trial court judge ruled in favor of Judas Priest, and the Nevada Supreme Court upheld that ruling in 1993 in *Judas Priest v. Vance.*[14] The state's highest court upheld the following lower court findings: (a) The so-called subliminal messages, such as "Do it," were actually combinations of breath and instrument sounds; (a) even if there had been subliminal messages, the families did not prove that these messages incited the boys to commit suicide; and (c) it was obvious that other, personal factors contributed to the boys' deaths.

THE INTERNET

Antiabortion Web Site

This case has created controversy about where the line is drawn between confrontational political speech and incitement to violence.

In January 1997, an antiabortion group, American Coalition of Life Activists (ACLA), started a Web site called *The Nuremburg Files*. The Web site listed such information as

---

[14]104 Nev. 424; 760 P.2d 137 (1993)

the names and phone numbers of abortion doctors, or "baby butchers." The ACLA had also distributed "wanted" posters with the same information about abortion doctors. Some posters offered "$5000 rewards" for information about those doctors and sometimes included doctors' pictures.

The Web site and posters were especially controversial in the early 1990s because of the murders of three U.S. abortion doctors in 1993 and 1994. Before each of the murders, a wanted poster had been circulated for each doctor. A poster for one of the doctors killed, Dr. John Britton, described him as "armed and extremely dangerous, especially to women and children."

The Web site asked people to "Visualize Abortionists on Trial." The site listed hundreds of abortion doctors and asked people to send in personal information about the doctors, such as their home and work addresses, the names of their children, and car license plate numbers. The list included Dr. Britton's name. After he was killed, the Web site crossed off his name by putting a line through it. The same was done to the other doctors who had been killed.

An abortion clinic, abortion doctors, and Planned Parenthood sued the ACLA in *Planned Parenthood v. American Coalition of Life Activists.*[15] In 1999, a federal district court jury ruled for Planned Parenthood, saying the posters and Web site directly incited violence against abortion doctors and patients. The jury ordered the ACLA and other defendants to stop making the posters, to remove certain doctors' names from the Web site, and to pay $107 million in damages. Abortion doctors testified that they lived their lives in fear because of the Web site and posters.

In 2001, a three-judge panel of the Ninth Circuit U.S. Court of Appeals threw out the $107 million judgment and ruled that the Web site and posters were protected free speech. The judges said the Web site and posters did not authorize or directly incite violence and therefore did not constitute "true threats." They said such speech was not likely to cause "imminent lawless action." Instead, the court said the Web site was merely a list of information about clinics and doctors. It was not responsible for what people did with that information. Most important, the court said, was that the speech in this case involved the highly charged political issues involving abortion. "If political discourse is to rally public opinion and challenge conventional thinking, it cannot be subdued."

However, in 2002, in a controversial decision, the Ninth Circuit U.S. Court of Appeals reconsidered the case en banc, voted 6-5 to reinstate the compensatory damages, and ordered the trial court to reevaluate the punitive damages. The majority said the language on the Web site did indeed constitute true threats and a reasonable likelihood of "physical violence."[16]

Summary

The cases in this chapter demonstrate how the media are oftentimes protected by the legal system in copycat or incitement cases. For the most part, the media cannot be held accountable for the actions of disturbed or naive people who mimic actions they have seen or heard in the media.

However, if the media are perceived as directly or carelessly inciting illegal activities, the courts will not hesitate to put First Amendment protections aside and punish the media.

---

[15]244 F.3d 1007 (9th Cir. 2000)

[16]290 F.3d 1058 (9th Cir. 2002)

11

OBSCENITY

I know it when I see it.

—Supreme Court Justice Potter Stewart[1]

H ow about you? Do you know obscenity when you see it? Do you even have an idea about what kinds of material might qualify as "obscene"?

When people hear the word *obscenity*, many often associate it with pornography. This is a pretty accurate association, because obscenity deals with sexually explicit speech or material. However, not all obscenity cases deal with pornographic films or magazines. Songs, artwork, and literary novels are just some of the other forms of expression that have faced charges of obscenity. The U.S. Supreme Court has ruled that if material is found to be "obscene," it is not protected by the First Amendment. In other words, obscene speech may be considered illegal speech by the courts. As a result, that speech may be censored.

So, who decides what is obscene? What are the guidelines? To understand this issue better, it is important to look at a brief history of obscenity laws in the United States and analyze the more recent rulings regarding obscene speech. First, however, we need to understand the legal differences between obscenity and indecency. (Indecency will be covered in the next chapter.)

Obscenity. Material found to be legally obscene does not have First Amendment protection and may be censored by the government. The current definition for obscenity is taken from the 1973 case *Miller v. California*, discussed later in this chapter. Obscene material contains "patently offensive" descriptions of sexual conduct.

Indecency. Unlike obscenity, indecent material does have First Amendment protection. Indecent material also involves sexual matters, but it is not considered as graphic or as "offensive" as obscene material. The current definition for indecency is taken from the 1978 case *FCC v. Pacifica* (discussed in chapter 12). The goal of indecency laws is to protect children from getting access to sexually explicit material while allowing access to adults.

---

[1] *Jacobellis v. Ohio*, 378 U.S. 184 (1964)

OBSCENITY LAWS: A BRIEF HISTORY

In 1712, the colonial legislature in Massachusetts passed an obscenity and libel law that banned "any filthy, obscene, or profane song, pamphlet, libel or mock sermon." More often than not, a law such as this was used to punish blasphemy or ridiculing of religion.

Still, what would have qualified as "obscene" or "filthy"? The law did not say. It was pretty much up to colonial officials to "know it when they saw it." A century later, in 1821, Vermont became the first state to pass an obscenity law in the newly founded United States. It outlawed the publication and distribution of obscene material. Other states started adopting similar laws, and obscenity was illegal in much of America by the middle of the century.

Congress passed the Tariff Act of 1842, which banned the importing of "all indecent and obscene prints, paintings, lithographs, engravings, and transparencies." Once again, decisions about obscenity were often left in the hands of government officials, who would "know" if something was obscene "when they saw it." Basically, if the material violated the sexual mores of the day, it was considered obscene. In 1857, Congress rewrote the Tariff Act to include printed material.

The 1868 British case *Regina v. Hicklin*[2] had a large impact on American law. The case concerned a pamphlet that was critical of the Catholic Church, and Britain's chief justice said it violated English obscenity law. The Hicklin Test, as it came to be known, said a work could be labeled obscene based on two criteria: (a) looking at individual passages taken out of context and (b) looking at its effect on the most sensitive and susceptible people in society.

Therefore, if one sentence in an entire book was considered "damaging" to a 5-year-old, the Hicklin Test allowed the *entire* work to be labeled obscene.

In 1865, Congress had made it illegal to mail obscene material. In 1873, on the heels of the Hicklin Test, Congress passed the Comstock Act (or the Anti-Obscenity Act of 1873).[3] The act gave the Post Office authority to confiscate any mail in the form of an "obscene, lewd, lascivious, or filthy book, pamphlet, picture, paper, letter, writing, print, or other publication of an indecent character." The act also made it illegal to send contraceptives or any information about contraception or abortion through the mail.

FAQ

Who ultimately made the obscenity determinations in these cases?

It was up to the Post Office to determine what material was obscene, and Congress appointed Anthony Comstock as "postal censor." Comstock, years later, said he had destroyed 160 tons of obscene material and convicted 3600 people for obscenity. This number included pharmacists arrested for sharing contraception information.[4] It was not until 1936, in *United States v. One Package*,[5] that a federal appeals court ruled it was legal for

---

[2]L.R. 3 Q.B. 360 (1868)

[3]18 U.S.C. §1462

[4]Quarterman, J. (1996). *Definitions and decency.* Retrieved October 25, 2004, from http://www2.cddc.vt.edu/eff/pub/Censorship/Internet_censorship_bills/quarterman_cda_0396.article

[5]86 F.2d 737 (2d Cir. 1936)

doctors to distribute contraceptives and information about contraceptives and abortion across state lines, thus nullifying that aspect of the Comstock Act.

The 1930s saw the government battle against obscenity continue when U.S. customs agents confiscated copies of James Joyce's book *Ulysses*. The officials were enforcing the Tariff Act of 1930,[6] which continued the ban on the importation of obscene material.

In *One Book Entitled "Ulysses" v. U.S.* in 1934, a federal court ruled that *Ulysses* "as a whole is not pornographic."[7] The court established two new criteria for obscenity: (a) The work must be judged *as a whole*, and (b) the work must be judged by its effect on *the average person*.

The courts were beginning to show that they would no longer allow government officials to ban material based on such loose standards as those found in the Hicklin Test. However, it was more than 20 years later that the U.S. Supreme Court took its first stand on government regulation of obscenity.

"What Is Only Fit for Children. . . ."

The highest court in the land finally entered the obscenity arena in 1957 in *Butler v. Michigan*.[8] This case involved a Michigan statute that banned the sale of books that had the potential to corrupt the morals of children or that might inspire children to engage in depraved acts. The U.S. Supreme Court ruled that the Michigan law violated the First Amendment. The justices said the law's attempt to "shield juvenile innocence" would "reduce the adult population of Michigan to reading what is only fit for children." The court said that the government cannot keep adults from reading, viewing, or listening to certain material simply because children might get access to it and be harmed by it. (However, as will be discussed in the next chapter, the courts have not extended this "only fit for children" argument to the regulation of indecent material.)

FAQ

Did this case help to establish any definition for obscenity?

The Supreme Court gave no guidelines or definitions for obscenity. The court still considered the matter to be solely a state issue, but that would soon change.

The Roth Test

Later in 1957, the Supreme Court handed down a landmark decision in *Roth v. U.S.*,[9] in which it provided its first definition of *obscenity*. The case involved Samuel Roth, who was convicted for mailing obscene material. The court upheld Roth's conviction, saying that obscene speech had no value and therefore no place in a civilized society.

---

[6] 19 U.S.C. 1595a(c)

[7] 72 F.2d 705 (2d Cir. 1934)

[8] 352 U.S. 380 (1957)

[9] 354 U.S. 476 (1957)

The court ruled that states could still ban obscene material, but they would have to abide by the court's new definition, which became known as the Roth Test. The court said that juries must determine what materials qualified as obscene by applying the Roth Test.

This is the Roth Test. Material is obscene if (a) the average person, (b) applying contemporary community standards, (c) finds that the dominant theme of the material as a whole (d) appeals to the prurient interest.

FAQ

What does "prurient" mean?

Prurient refers to materials that promote lustful thoughts and urges.

FAQ

Aren't these guidelines rather vague?

Critics thought so and attacked the definition as unenforceable. After all, who qualifies as an "average person"? Who determines community standards? What counts as a "community"? What kinds of material appeal to "prurient interests"?

Two of the biggest critics of the *Roth* ruling were the case's dissenting justices. In dissenting opinions, justices Hugo Black and William O. Douglas argued for an *absolutist* view of the First Amendment. Absolutists believe there should be either no limits or, at least, very few limits on speech.

Black and Douglas wrote that the punishment of obscenity through the Roth Test created numerous First Amendment problems. It "gives the censor free reign over a vast domain." It would give juries the power to "censor, suppress, and punish what they don't like. . . . This is community censorship in one of worst forms." The community standards rationale was "too loose, too capricious, too destructive of freedom of expression to be squared with the First Amendment." The justices argued that "By these standards *punishment is inflicted for thoughts provoked,* not for overt acts nor antisocial conduct" (italics added).

Black and Douglas argued that *Roth* allowed the government to punish persons for mere thoughts, and the pair said that this violated the very essence of the First Amendment.

FAQ

How do courts define community standards?

The Supreme Court tried to answer the community standards question in 1964 in *Jacobellis v. Ohio.*[10] The case involved a theater owner who was convicted of violating Ohio's

---

[10]378 U.S. 184 (1964)

obscenity law for showing a French film called *Les Amants.* The court said that the movie was not obscene and threw out the conviction. This is the case where Justice Potter Stewart made his famous claim "I know it when I see it" because he was frustrated with the court's inability to agree on a clear-cut obscenity definition. In a plurality opinion, Justice William Brennan wrote that obscenity should be judged on a *national* standard, but other justices argued that the varying standards of individual communities should be taken into account.

The guidelines for obscenity became even more confusing in a ruling involving the book *Fanny Hill.* The real title of the book is *Memoirs of a Woman of Pleasure,* and it was originally published in 1748 in England by John Cleland. The book describes the activities of a London prostitute from her point of view. In 1821, Massachusetts convicted a man of obscenity for publishing a more explicit version of *Fanny Hill.* In the 1960s, Massachusetts' attorney general tried to have the book declared obscene, even though the book was in the Library of Congress and was available in libraries across the country. In 1966, in *Memoirs v. Massachusetts,*[11] the U.S. Supreme Court ruled that the book was not obscene. A plurality opinion provided a new three-pronged test for obscenity: (a) the material does not pass the Roth Test, (b) the material is "patently offensive," and (c) the material is "utterly without redeeming social value."

FAQ

What does the phrase "utterly without redeeming social value" really mean?

The third prong—"utterly without redeeming social value"—made prosecuting obscenity extremely difficult. Legally, there is virtually no material that is "utterly" or "totally" without some sort of "social value." Producers of porn films could argue that their works had social value because of the "sexual education value." Publishers of hard-core pornographic magazines argued about the value of information provided in articles and interviews. The Supreme Court later threw out this third prong of *Memoirs,* saying it was "a burden virtually impossible to discharge under our criminal standards of proof."[12]

Is It Legal to *Own* Obscene Material?

In the war against illegal drugs, our court systems often hand out much stiffer sentences to those who sell and transport illegal drugs than to those who buy the drugs. The same kind of reasoning applies in obscenity law.

In 1969's *Stanley v. Georgia,*[13] police had raided Robert Stanley's home looking for illegal gambling materials, but they stumbled across the man's stash of "adult films." After setting up the man's projector and viewing the films, police arrested him for violating Georgia's obscenity law. He was later convicted.

The U.S. Supreme Court overturned Stanley's conviction, saying that *people have the right to possess obscene material in the privacy of their homes.* The court wrote that the First

---

[11]383 U.S. 413 (1966)

[12]See *Miller v. California,* 413 U.S. 15 (1973)

[13]394 U.S. 557 (1969)

Amendment "means that a state has no business telling a man, sitting alone in his own house, what books he may read or what films he may watch."

FAQ

So it's not illegal to possess obscene material?

No. This case established an important precedent. The Supreme Court was saying it would not allow the punishment of people who owned obscene material. It was becoming clear that producers and distributors of obscenity would be the main targets for prosecution.

Transporting Obscene Material

Within the next few years, the Supreme Court clarified that *Stanley* did not protect the transport of obscene materials. In 1971, the court upheld the federal obscenity law banning the mailing of obscene materials, even to adults who request the material. The court also ruled that it is legal for U.S. Customs officials to confiscate obscene material from the luggage of international travelers.[14]

FAQ

Is it legal to own the mailed material once it reaches a person's home?

If obscene material makes it through the mail or through a U.S. Customs search and winds up in a person's home, *Stanley* would protect that individual's right to possess the material. However, an individual cannot transport it by mail or, internationally, in luggage.

Congress Calls for Study on Pornography

Presidential Commission on Obscenity and Pornography

In the late 1960s, Congress became concerned about court decisions such as *Stanley v. Georgia* that upheld the right of citizens to possess obscene material in the privacy of their homes. Many in Congress were worried that American society, with the permission of the courts, was becoming more "perverse." As a result, Congress approved $2 million for the Presidential Commission on Obscenity and Pornography (PCOP) to analyze the role of pornography in society.[15]

However, the commission in 1970 did not reach the conclusions that some in Congress might have desired. This commission instead *recommended that obscenity laws be repealed.*

---

[14]See *U.S. v. Reidel*, 402 U.S. 351 (1971), and *U.S. v. Thirty-Seven Photographs*, 402 U.S. 363 (1971).

[15]President's Commission on Obscenity and Pornography. (1970). *Report of the Commission on Obscenity and Pornography*. Washington, DC: U.S. Government Printing Office.

The PCOP report said that pornography could actually be "therapeutic" and "cathartic" for many individuals. PCOP, among other things, concluded that people who were exposed to various forms of pornography did not exhibit major changes in their attitudes toward women, showed no increased likelihood to commit sexual violence, did not become "sexual deviants" (the commission said that sexual deviants were already deviant when they sought out pornography), appeared to suffer no lasting detrimental effects, and experienced decreasing interest in pornography after repeated exposures to it.

PCOP also recommended that America engage in a "massive sex education campaign" and "open discussion, based on facts, of issues relating to obscenity and pornography."[16] PCOP said that adults should not be prohibited from viewing sexual material, but society should still protect children from seeing such matter. For these reasons and others, supporters of PCOP said the report was reasoned and balanced.

However, other critics said the report did not do enough to encourage protection of the "public morality." President Nixon was just one of many politicians who was upset with the commission's findings: "So long as I am in the White House, there will be no relaxation in the effort to control and eliminate smut from our national life."[17] Several months after the commission released its report, the U.S. Senate voted overwhelmingly to reject the commission's findings, but the report eventually did get published and was made available to the public.

A few years later, the debate over obscenity intensified when the Supreme Court once again ruled that obscene material was not protected by the First Amendment.

THE LANDMARK MILLER DECISION

In 1973, the Supreme Court handed down a ruling that is still used today as the standard for defining obscenity.

The case of *Miller v. California*[18] involved a man named Marvin Miller who was convicted of using mass mailings to try to sell obscene material. One of his books was titled *Sex Orgies Illustrated*. The brochures he mailed contained pictures "explicitly depicting men and women in groups of two or more engaging in a variety of sexual activities, with genitals often prominently displayed." Some brochures were mailed to a restaurant, and the owner complained to police. Miller was subsequently convicted of a misdemeanor under California's penal code for "knowingly distributing obscene matter."

In a 5-4 ruling, the Supreme Court upheld Miller's conviction, reestablishing that obscene material is not protected by the First Amendment. The court took some of the wording from obscenity rulings in *Roth* and *Memoirs* and crafted a new obscenity definition.

The Miller Test

A work is obscene if

1. The average person, applying contemporary community standards, finds that the work, taken as a whole, appeals to the prurient interest

---

[16]*Ibid.*, pp. 47-48.

[17]Critics: Censored! (1970, November 9). *Senior Scholastic*, p. 6.

[18]413 U.S. 15 (1973)

2. The work depicts or describes, in a patently offensive way, sexual conduct specifically defined by applicable state law

3. The work, taken as a whole, lacks serious literary, artistic, political, or scientific value (often called the LAPS test)

FAQ

What qualifies as "patently offensive"?

In defining the term, the Supreme Court used the term, thus leaving some flexibility for the types of material a state might consider patently offensive or obscene under a state law. The court said that *patently offensive* refers to patently offensive representations or descriptions of ultimate sexual acts, normal or perverted, actual or simulated, and patently offensive representations or descriptions of masturbation, excretory functions, and lewd exhibition of the genitals.

The Supreme Court explained that this new test for obscenity was meant to provide "concrete guidelines to isolate 'hard core' pornography from expression protected by the First Amendment." The court said that defining obscenity "may not be an easy road." However, the majority justices felt that if there were no limits placed on obscene speech, it would lead to "an absolutist, 'anything goes' view of the First Amendment."

The dissenting justices in *Miller* echoed the dissenters in *Roth* and said the court had overstepped its bounds. Justices Douglas and Brennan said the new obscenity definition from the court was "vague" and a "hodge-podge" and was impossible to enforce fairly. Both justices wrote that obscenity is not mentioned in the Constitution and the court had no justification for banning it.

> As is intimated by the Court's opinion, the material before us may be garbage. But so is much of what is said in political campaigns, in the daily press, on TV, or on the radio. By reason of the First Amendment—and solely because of it—speakers and publishers have not been threatened or subdued because their thoughts and ideas may be "offensive" to some.

These dissenters argued that the "vagueness" of the definition would lead to numerous problems when governments tried to prosecute obscenity. The next cases show some of the problems courts have encountered in this area. One of the more difficult questions is addressed here.

FAQ

How are community standards determined?

Local Standards, Not National

The Supreme Court in *Miller* ruled that trying to use a *national standard* to determine obscenity was an "exercise in futility." As a result, the court ruled that contemporary community standards must indeed be determined by a local community or by the state. The court stated that local juries should determine what is obscene because the legal system "has historically permitted triers of fact to draw on the standards of their community, guided always by limiting instructions on the law."

The Supreme Court further clarified this issue in 1978 in *Pinkus v. U.S.*[19] The court ruled that juries must also determine contemporary community standards based on the adults in the community. Children may *not* be included as part of the "community."

The courts have also ruled that community standards may play an important role in how cities and towns determine where "adult" businesses are allowed to set up shop.

TIME, PLACE, AND MANNER RESTRICTIONS AND PORNOGRAPHY

As discussed in chapter 2, a time, place, and manner (TPM) restriction involves the government regulating *how, when,* or *where* a speech or activity is performed but not banning the speech or activity itself. When the issue is pornography, the courts say there has to be a balance between free speech and various community concerns.

Zoning Ordinances

Detroit had success with zoning laws in 1976 in *Young v. American Mini-Theatres.*[20] The city ordinance prohibited adult theaters from locating within 1000 feet of other "regulated uses," including other adult theaters, hotels, bars, pool halls, pawn shops, and secondhand stores. (The city said it was worried about "problem" businesses all ending up in one section of town.) The ordinance also prohibited adult theaters from locating within 500 feet of a residential zone. The city said it wanted to protect the property values of private homes.

The Supreme Court upheld Detroit's zoning law because the law was not focused on the "adult" material itself and was not meant to ban the material. It was designed as a reasonable *time, place, and manner restriction.* Detroit was regulating only the location of adult theaters. There were many places in Detroit where adult theaters could operate and not violate the zoning law.

The city of Renton, WA, saw the success of Detroit in the *Young* case and passed a zoning ordinance banning adult movie theaters from locating within 1000 feet of any church, park, school, residential zone, or single- or multiple-family dwelling. Playtime Theaters sued the city of Renton, but in *Renton v. Playtime,*[21] the Supreme Court ruled that the zoning ordinance was reasonable and constitutional.

FAQ

What are the guidelines for determining reasonable zoning laws?

---

[19]436 U.S. 493 (1978)

[20]427 U.S. 50 (1976)

[21]475 U.S. 41 (1986)

In *Renton*, the Supreme Court provided four basic guidelines:

1. The ordinance does not try to significantly reduce or "ban adult theaters altogether."

2. The ordinance does not aim at the content of the films. It must be a time, place, and manner restriction.

3. The ordinance is designed "to serve a substantial government interest." The city was concerned about "secondary effects," such as lowered property values and the impact the adult bookstores could have on children. The court agreed that these were "admittedly serious problems."

4. The ordinance is not overly restrictive and "does not unreasonably limit alternative avenues of communication." The court noted that the ordinance left open 520 acres of "ample, accessible real estate" in the city for adult theaters. That was more than 5% of Renton. If this ordinance had resulted in, for example, only 10 acres being available, the court would probably have ruled against the city for being overly restrictive.

The Supreme Court said that the ordinance provided a good balance by making "some areas available for adult theaters and their patrons, while at the same time preserving the quality of life in the community at large by preventing those theaters from locating in other areas."

FAQ

How is "serious value" determined?

Material may violate community standards, appeal to the prurient interest, and be patently offensive, but it is still not obscene if it has serious literary, artistic, political or scientific value. However, how is such "value" determined?

The Supreme Court answered this question in 1987 in *Pope v. Illinois.*[22] Illinois authorities had prosecuted two clerks at an adult bookstore for selling obscene material.

During the initial trial, the judge instructed the jury to determine the value of the works based on the standards of ordinary adults in Illinois. The Supreme Court said this was the wrong instruction for the jury. The court made a fine distinction here: The first two parts of the Miller Test may be based on the "ordinary" person in a given community, but when it comes to the third part and determining "serious value," a jury must consider "whether a *reasonable* person would find such value in the material."

The Supreme Court ruled that serious LAPS value may not be determined by using local community standards. Instead, in determining "serious value," local juries must be instructed to use a *national standard* of a "reasonable" person. (However, the reality is that many juries will still use local standards, no matter how they are instructed.) The Supreme Court also ruled that defense lawyers in obscenity cases are allowed to call in "experts" from outside the community to help argue for the serious value of a work.

---

[22]107 S. Ct. 1918 (1987)

OBSCENITY AND DISCLAIMERS

Some movie theater owners across the country had argued that they should be allowed to show obscene material if they took precautions to keep children out of the theaters. The Supreme Court ruled that such safeguards were beside the point. The test case involved two adult movie theaters in Atlanta, GA, which had shown two hard-core pornographic films. State officials prosecuted the theaters' owner for violating Georgia's obscenity statute. Prosecutors said the films left "little to the imagination." A trial court ruled in favor of the theaters. The trial judge ruled the movies were "constitutionally permissible" because the theater had warning signs near its entrance. The signs said "Adult Theatre—You must be 21 and able to prove it. If viewing the nude body offends you, Please Do Not Enter."

The trial judge said this was sufficient notice to adults who did not want to view the material and also provided "reasonable protection against exposure of these films to minors." The Georgia Supreme Court overturned the trial judge's ruling. The U.S. Supreme Court agreed in *Paris Adult Theater v. Slaton*.[23] (The ruling came out on the same day as the *Miller* decision.) The Supreme Court gave the following reasoning: Obscene material is not protected by the First Amendment for *anyone*; therefore, obscene films are not legal "simply because they are exhibited for consenting adults only." Prohibiting obscenity is a legitimate state interest, protecting the public's "quality of life and the total community environment." The court quoted a government study that showed "at least an arguable correlation between obscene material and crime."

The courts frequently express concerns about "quality of life" or public morality in obscenity cases. It was similar concerns about "quality of life" that led President Reagan in the 1980s to order a study on the effects of pornography on society.

THE MEESE COMMISSION

In 1985, President Reagan set up the Attorney General's Commission on Pornography under the direction of Attorney General Edwin Meese. The Meese Commission's official task was to "determine the nature, extent, and impact on society of pornography in the United States, and to make specific recommendations to the Attorney General concerning more effective ways in which the spread of pornography could be contained, consistent with Constitutional guarantees."

The commission was made up of 11 members and included law enforcement officials, social science professors, and ministers. The commission held six large public hearings across the country between May 1985 and February 1986. The Meese Commission released its report in 1986 and reached far different conclusions than the 1970 PCOP.

Commission member James Dobson said the panel viewed a lot of "soft-core" material such as *Playboy* and *Penthouse* that would not qualify as legally obscene. Dobson and other panel members expressed their shock, however, at extremely graphic "hard-core" material "available in massive quantities today" that included practices such as bestiality, voluntary amputation, group sex, and simulated child pornography.[24] Today, authorities say, the

---

[23]413 U.S. 49 (1973)

[24]Dobson, J. C. (1987). Enough is enough. In T. Minnery (Ed.), *Pornography, a human tragedy*. Wheaton, IL: Tyndale House. p. 35.

Internet, videos, and magazines contain all of this kind of material and more. These types of material actually take us to the heart of the obscenity battle in our country because it is hard-core material that many times leads to obscenity cases. Juries and judges often have to view such material in obscenity cases.

FAQ

Didn't critics accuse this commission of being too "conservative"?

Critics said that President Reagan had stacked the panel with too many opponents of pornography. However, supporters argued that the commission backed up all of its conclusions with credible testimonials and research. In conclusion, the commission said it found strong links between pornography and "organized crime, sexual violence and degradation, civil injustice, and other societal harms." Unlike PCOP in 1970, the Meese commission strongly recommended that obscenity laws should be stricter.

There is considerably less controversy when it comes to protecting children from access to pornography or from their exploitation in its production.

CHILDREN AND OBSCENITY

Protecting Children From Accessing Pornography

The Supreme Court ruled in *Butler* that the government cannot ban pornography because children *might* get access to it. However, could the government punish people who knowingly make such material available to minors? The courts said yes in 1968 in *Ginsberg v. New York.*[25] The case involved a luncheonette owner had sold four "adult" magazines to a 16-year-old boy. The magazines contained erotic photos of nude women.

The state of New York prosecuted the restaurant owner for selling pornographic material to someone under the age of 18 years. The U.S. Supreme Court upheld the prosecution. States may enact variable obscenity laws, the court said. These laws can prohibit the sale of pornography to children but still allow adults access to the same material. Why? The court said that government has a legitimate interest in protecting "the welfare of children." Children, the court said, are not emotionally or psychologically prepared to deal with the material in certain "adult" works.

However, the following attempt to protect children from "adult" material did not receive approval from the courts.

1994: Variable Obscenity Law Shot Down Over Due Process Concerns

Washington State had passed a law prohibiting the sale of "erotic" recordings (CDs, tapes, records) to anyone under the age of 18. Here is how the law worked. A prosecutor would get a copy of a questionable recording from a music store. A local judge would then determine whether the material was erotic. If the material was determined to be erotic, the

---

[25]390 U.S. 51 (1968)

store owner had two choices—put an "adults only" label on the recording and sell it only to adults, or stop selling it altogether. If that owner or any other music store owner in Washington sold the recording to someone less than 18 years old or without the "adults only" label, he or she could be prosecuted.

In *Soundgarden v. Eikenberry,*[26] state courts struck down the law for several reasons. For example, if a court found a recording to be erotic, the law did not mandate that all music store owners be notified about this recording. As a result, these store owners could be prosecuted for selling this recording to a minor even though the owner did not know it had been declared illegal for minors. The courts said that the law should not have allowed determinations about whether recordings were erotic to be made by a judge. Such determinations should be made by a jury. The law created a chilling effect on sales of the material. People over the age of 18 years might be embarrassed to buy music labeled "adults only."

The court here was concerned about *due process.*

FAQ

What is due process?

Due process means that all laws and legal proceedings must be fair. Here, the court said it was not fair to have a single judge make a ruling about whether materials were erotic. That determination should be made by a jury. It was also not fair that music store owners were given no notification about potentially erotic materials. The court said store owners had to be given a chance to remove the materials from their stores.

CHILD PORNOGRAPHY

Child pornography is material that depicts children engaged in sexual activities, whether it is by themselves, with other children, or with adults. State and federal courts are in agreement that child pornography is illegal because its creation involves illegal sexual exploitation of children.

The case of *New York v. Ferber*[27] in 1982 concerned New York State outlawing child pornography. The law prohibited anyone from knowingly encouraging a child under the age of 16 to engage in a sexual act and then distributing photographic copies of the act. (The law was carefully crafted and provided details about prohibited acts.)

The Supreme Court upheld the New York child pornography law, saying there was a legitimate state interest involved: stopping the sexual exploitation of children.

A very important note from this case: *Child pornography does not have to be legally obscene under the Miller Test to be illegal.* In *Ferber,* the Supreme Court ruled that many parts of the Miller Test are not applicable to child pornography, thus making it easier to prosecute child pornographers:

---

[26]871 P.2d 1050 (1994)

[27]458 U.S. 747 (1982)

- Child pornography may be illegal even if it does not appeal to the prurient interest of the average person.
- Child pornography may be illegal even if it is not patently offensive.
- Child pornography does not have to be considered "as a whole."

The Supreme Court wanted to make sure that child pornographers could not use the Miller Test to justify the sexual exploitation of children.

FAQ

Does the Stanley ruling apply here? Is it legal to own child pornography?

The Supreme Court answered this question with a firm "no" in 1990 in *Osborne v. Ohio*[28] The *Stanley* ruling states that it is legal for adults to possess obscene material in the privacy of their homes, but *Stanley* does not apply to child pornography.

Ohio passed a law making it illegal simply to possess child pornography. The state was concerned that legalizing possession would lead to an increased demand for the material, which would then lead to increased production of child pornography. The U.S. Supreme Court upheld the law, ruling that Ohio was furthering a legitimate state interest: "It is reasonable for the state to conclude that it will decrease the production of child pornography if it penalizes those who possess and view the product."

As is the case in many areas of law, there is a gray area here as well. Should all nude depictions of children be banned? What about actors who portray children in sexual situations? As we will see, new technologies and concerns about artistic freedom can make answering these questions somewhat difficult.

1977 Protection of Children Against Exploitation Act

In the 1970s, lawmakers in Washington were becoming concerned about young actors in sexually explicit film roles. Stories surfaced about underage girls who lied about their ages to get roles in pornographic films. In response, Congress passed this act and made it a federal offense for anyone to produce or market sexually explicit materials that involved minors, even when film producers did not know an actor or actress was less than 18 years old.

FAQ

Wasn't this unfair to filmmakers who had been deceived by underage actors?

Film producers said so, arguing that they would never use underage actors on purpose in sex scenes. In 1994, in *U.S. v. X-Citement Video Inc.,*[29] the Supreme Court ruled that a film producer could be prosecuted under the 1977 act only if the producer *knowingly* used an

---

[28]495 U.S. 103 (1990)

[29]513 U.S. 64 (1994)

underage person in an adult film. However, Congress created some confusion in this area 2 years later when it passed a new child pornography law.

1996 Child Pornography Prevention Act (CPPA)

The age of computers brought with it an easier way for child pornographers to produce their material. Computer programs could create realistic computerized images of children engaged in sexual acts. Lawmakers said the material simply fed the urges of depraved persons and encouraged sexual exploitation of children. The producers of the material said the children in these productions were not real, and therefore no crime had been committed. Lawmakers also accused Hollywood of producing too many films in which minors appeared to be having sex.

In response to these new technologies and Hollywood films, Congress passed the Child Pornography Prevention Act. It banned images that "appear to depict a minor engaged in sexually explicit conduct," advertising that conveys the impression that a minor is involved in sexual activity, and the use of identifiable children in computer-altered sexual material (for example, taking the face of a real child and superimposing it on a nude body).

FAQ

Haven't all sorts of movies "appeared to depict minors" in sexual situations?

Hollywood immediately attacked the new law, saying it would lead to censorship of all sorts of movies. *Romeo and Juliet,* for example, involves two underage characters engaged in sexual activity. Would this new law prohibit television stations from airing movie versions of this classic love story? Would Hollywood be prohibited from producing a new version of this Shakespeare tale? The critics also pointed to popular movies such as *Porky's* and *Taxi Driver,* saying these motion pictures would be banned under the CPPA because of scenes with minor characters engaged in sexual activity.

The controversy over the CPPA came to a head in 1998 when production began in Hollywood on *Lolita,* a remake of a film about an older man who has a sexual relationship with an underage girl, played by a 15-year-old actress. Because the movie had nudity, the director had an actress of legal age stand in for the nude scenes. Apparently, even these scenes were cut because of concerns about the CPPA's ban on any production "appearing to depict a minor engaged in sexually explicit conduct."

In 2002, the Supreme Court struck down the first two components of the CPPA in *Ashcroft v. Free Speech Coalition.*[30] Justice Anthony Kennedy wrote for the 6-3 majority and addressed each area.

1. Movies With Images "Appearing to Depict" Minors Engaging in Sex. The Supreme Court ruled that these images could not be banned. Kennedy wrote, "Pictures of what appear to be a 17-year-old engaging in sexually explicit activity do not in every case contravene community standards." He added that teenagers having sex is a part of modern society "and has been a theme in art and literature for centuries." He made mention of Shakespeare's

---

[30]535 U.S. 234 (2002)

Romeo and Juliet, in which one of the lovers is just 13. Kennedy also pointed to recent motion pictures, such as *Traffic.* In that movie, the high school–age daughter of a national drug czar has sex in exchange for drugs. In *American Beauty,* Kennedy noted sex scenes between two teenagers and between an older man and a teenage girl. Both of these films had won Academy Awards. Kennedy said the CPPA would create a chilling effect on the production of such films.

2. Computerized Images of Children Engaging in Sex. The Supreme Court ruled that these images could not be banned. The court upheld a 1999 appeals court ruling that said the government had not proved a connection between computer-generated children engaging in sex and the sexual exploitation of real children.

In a dissent, Chief Justice William Rehnquist argued that these computer-generated images are indeed harmful because they "are virtually indistinguishable from real children engaged in sexually explicit conduct." Rehnquist also pointed out that *Traffic* and *American Beauty* were produced after the CPPA was adopted. Therefore, he argued, the law did not keep these movies from being made or from winning major awards, thus negating the chilling effect concern mentioned in the majority opinion.

3. Using Real Children in Computer-Altered Sexual Images. This part of the CPPA was left standing because the Free Speech Coalition (which brought the case) did not challenge this part of the law. Therefore, it is illegal to superimpose a real child's face on another nude body or on a computerized nude body.

FAQ

Must video stores and bookstores that sell pornography always know the content of what they sell?

In 1959, in *Smith v. California,*[31] the Supreme Court ruled that the state must prove a seller was *aware* that material was obscene before the state could prosecute the seller for obscenity. (This is called *scienter,* which means a person had foreknowledge of a crime.)

In 1974, in *Hamling v. U.S.,*[32] the Supreme Court clarified the issue of scienter when it ruled that the government only has to prove sellers had "general knowledge" about the contents of the materials they sell. If the cover of a magazine or video insinuated that there were explicit pictures of rape inside, the seller would have a difficult time arguing that he or she did not have a general knowledge of the magazine's contents.

OBSCENITY AND POPULAR MUSIC

Popular music has often been known for "pushing the envelope" when it comes to lyrics. However, it is rare for a music artist to face obscenity charges. In 1963, a rock band called

---

[31]361 U.S. 147 (1959)

[32]418 U.S. 87 (1974)

the Kingsmen had no idea that their recording of the song "Louie Louie" would lead to radio stations banning the song and federal obscenity investigations.

The Kingsmen said they were not very happy with how the final version of "Louie Louie" sounded. They felt lead singer Jack Ely's vocals were garbled and unintelligible, partly because Ely had been wearing braces on his teeth. However, the song soon began getting airplay on Boston radio, and rumors began to fly that Ely's garbled lead vocals actually contained obscenities. As a result, the song gained notoriety nationwide, and the song hit number two on Billboard's singles chart in December 1963.

In early 1964, the governor of Indiana banned the song from airplay on that state's radio stations. Meanwhile, parents had been sending letters to Washington alerting federal authorities to the possible obscene lyrics in "Louie Louie." The letters contained numerous versions of what people thought they heard in the song. One of those versions:

> Each night at ten I'll lay her again
> I'll fuck my girl all kinds of ways
> And on that chair I'll lay her there
> I felt my boner in her hair.

The actual lyrics for that part of the song are:

> Three nights and days we sailed the sea
> Me think of girl constantly
> On the ship, I dream she there
> I smell the rose in her hair.

The FBI and FCC opened investigations into the song's lyrics, investigations that could have led to federal obscenity charges against the Kingsmen. During the FBI investigation, audio technicians played the 45 rpm recording of "Louie Louie" at 33 1/3 rpm. The investigators said that the song played on the slower speed appeared to reveal the "hidden" obscene lyrics, but they admitted that the lyrics were difficult to interpret. The investigation continued for 30 months and even included FBI agents interviewing members of the Kingsmen. In 1966, the FBI reached the conclusion that Ely's rendition of the lyrics was unintelligible. The matter was dropped.[33]

In 1992, in *Luke Records Inc. v. Navarro,*[34] a recording by the rap group 2 Live Crew led to a landmark ruling. It was the first time a federal court of appeals had been asked to apply the Miller Test to a musical recording. The case focused on the group's album *As Nasty as They Wanna Be*. The album was brought to the attention of Nick Navarro, the sheriff of Broward County, FL. Navarro took the album to a district court judge, who listened to the recording and ruled that it was obscene. The lyrics contained frequent uses of the word *fuck* and other profanities, as well as graphic references to sex.

The case gained nationwide attention when police in Broward County arrested a music store owner for selling *As Nasty as They Wanna Be*. Because the album had just been declared obscene by a judge, it was therefore considered illegal in Broward County.

---

[33]The lascivious Louie Louie. (2004). *The Smoking Gun.* Retrieved October 26, 2004, from http://www.thesmoking gun.com/louie/louie.html

[34]960 F.2d 134 (11th Cir. 1992)

An appeals court overturned the district court ruling and ruled that *As Nasty as They Wanna Be* was not obscene. The only evidence Sheriff Navarro presented to the district judge was a cassette recording of the album. This is not sufficient in an obscenity case. Navarro called no witnesses concerning prurient interest, community standards, or serious artistic value. Also, the case was tried by a judge with no jury. The judge relied *only* on his own beliefs about community standards and artistic value. A jury should have helped make these determinations, based on expert testimony.

The U.S. Supreme Court declined to hear an appeal of the ruling.

THE INTERNET: A NEW BATTLEGROUND IN OBSCENITY LAW

In 1996, Congress amended federal obscenity laws (18 U.S.C. §1462 and §1465) to prohibit the use of a computer to transmit obscene material. The Supreme Court has made it clear that obscene speech is not protected by the First Amendment. However, the Internet poses some special problems when it comes to enforcing obscenity laws between the states. Those problems are highlighted in the following case.

In the 1990s, Robert and Carleen Thomas of Milipitas, CA, operated an "adult" bulletin board service (BBS) called Amateur Action Computer Bulletin Board (AACBB). Subscribers could exchange sexually explicit messages and photographs. Authorities in California had investigated the material on the Thomases' BBS and ruled that AACBB was not obscene according to community standards there.

It was a different story in Tennessee, though. A postal inspector in Memphis subscribed to AACBB and downloaded pornographic images he believed were obscene according to community standards in Tennessee. A Tennessee trial court convicted the Thomases of 10 counts of interstate transport of obscenity through telephone lines. In 1996, in *U.S. v. Thomas*,[35] a federal appeals court upheld the jury verdict. The Thomases appealed to the U.S. Supreme Court, but the high court refused to hear the appeal. Critics said that the ruling essentially made the community standards of Tennessee the standards for the entire country.

The basic lesson of this case is that sexual material may be legal where an Internet site is based, but the producers of this material may be subject to obscenity prosecutions in communities around the country. The same rationale applies to e-mails. The Communications Decency Act of 1996 (which will be discussed in more detail in the next chapter) banned obscene e-mails. In 1999, in *ApolloMedia Corp. v. Reno*,[36] the Supreme Court upheld this ban.

In August 2003, the U.S. attorney for the Western District of Pennsylvania, Mary Beth Buchanan, announced that a federal grand jury had indicted the owners of Extreme Associates on 10 counts of obscenity, the first major federal crackdown on obscenity since the *Thomas* case. Buchanan told a U.S. Senate committee in 2003 that Web sites owned by Extreme Associates sold videos and other material that were "vile, offensive and degrading."[37] One video, for example, portrayed the graphic rapes and murders of three women; another showed Jesus coming down from the cross to rape an angel.

---

[35]74 F.3d 701 (6th Cir. 1996)

[36]526 U.S. 1061 (1999)

[37]Buchanan, M. B. (2003, October 15). *Indecent exposure: Oversight of DOJ's efforts to protect pornography's victims* (Testimony before the U.S. Senate Committee on the Judiciary). Retrieved October 25, 2004, from http://judiciary .senate.gov/print_testimony.cfm?id=961&wit_id=2725

In her testimony before the committee, Buchanan said that the Internet had drastically changed the nature of obscenity cases: "The adult bookstore has largely been replaced by thousands of web sites advertising and selling pornography." She added that the "world's worst adult bookstore now operates on a personal computer in almost every home in America." Buchanan said that the government felt a need to prosecute a company like Extreme Associates to send a message: "If the law isn't enforced, the material is going to proliferate and become more violent, more degrading, and more disgusting." As a result, a heated debate has arisen over how to define "community standards" in cases dealing with online obscenity. Can you prosecute someone for making obscene material available to people in the privacy of their homes?

Extreme Associates president Rob Zicari said that the Internet has made the argument about community standards obsolete. In an interview aired on the CBS news program *60 Minutes* on September 5, 2004, Zicari (also known as Rob Black) argued that pornography sold over the Internet does not involve a community: "It's involving a private individual, who purchased these videos, and downloaded the images from the Internet into their home. So, where does that community standard apply?"[38] *60 Minutes* also interviewed lawyer and author Fred Lane, who said that the original goal of the community standards rationale in *Miller* was to give communities the power "to regulate what came into their borders, what was displayed on Main Street, what kids were actually seeing as they went around the community." Lane said the courts must now answer the question about whether private citizens downloading obscenity in their homes has a negative impact on the "community."[38] Such discussions ultimately lead back to *Stanley v. Georgia,* in which the court ruled that persons have the right to view obscene material in the privacy of their homes. (If convicted, Zicari and his wife Janet face $2.5 million in fines and 50 years in prison.)

Buchanan fired back, saying that the abundance of obscene material on the Internet means that more children are being exposed to it and that children "are susceptible to predators who view them as sexual objects." She said that, as a result, obscene material on the Internet does endanger the "community," and protecting children becomes a main justification for enforcement of obscenity laws in cyberspace.[37]

At the same time in August 2003, the federal government convicted a West Virginia couple of obscenity for using their Web site to sell videos with graphic depictions of women defecating. In an affidavit, the government said the tapes also showed women masturbating, spreading feces on their nude bodies, and drinking their own urine. The couple received jail sentences of 13 to 18 months, probation, and fines totaling $100,000.[39]

Thus with debate raging about the application of community standards to the Internet, federal prosecutors such as Mary Beth Buchanan say they will continue to find and punish those who violate obscenity laws on the World Wide Web.

Summary

The Supreme Court has ruled that obscenity has no First Amendment protection. Throughout history, societies have tried to regulate obscene material to protect the public

---

[38]CBSNews.com. (2004, September 5). Porn in the USA. *60 Minutes.* Retrieved October 28, 2004, from http://www.cbsnews.com/stories/2003/11/21/60minutes/main585049.shtml

[39]Svitek, T. W. (2003, March 25). *Affidavit.* Retrieved October 28, 2004, from http://www.thesmokinggun.com/archive/poopvid1.html

from its effects. In America, the current definition for obscenity comes from the *Miller* case and is determined by such criteria as contemporary community standards, the average person, applicable state laws, whether the material is patently offensive, and whether the material has serious value under the LAPS test. However, persons are allowed to have obscene material within the privacy of their homes. Obscenity laws usually target the makers and distributors of the material. Obscenity should not be confused with indecency, which the courts say does have First Amendment protection.

When a person faces obscenity charges, that person has a right to jury trial. A judge may not make solo determinations about obscenity, as was done in the 2 Live Crew case.

Child pornography is illegal because it involves criminal sexual exploitation of children. Possession of child pornography is illegal as well. The courts struck down an attempt by Congress to outlaw depictions of underage movie characters engaged in sexual acts. The courts also said that completely computerized images of child sexual acts are legal. Obscenity law is in its infancy regarding the Internet.

When it comes to sexual material, there will always be debate about what is and what is not acceptable under the law. The cases discussed in this chapter provide valuable insight into the never-ending public battle over pornography and obscenity.

12

INDECENCY AND VIOLENCE

Patently offensive, indecent material presented over the airwaves confronts the citizen, not only in public, but also in the privacy of the home, where the individual's right to be left alone plainly outweighs the First Amendment rights of an intruder.

—U.S. Supreme Court Justice John Paul Stevens[1]

Justice Stevens penned these words in the landmark 1978 case *FCC v. Pacifica*.[1] In this case, the Supreme Court ruled that the FCC had the legal authority to regulate indecent speech over the public airwaves. In the previous chapter, we learned that obscene speech is not protected by the First Amendment: The court has said that obscenity has no "societal value" and therefore may be prohibited. However, what about sexual speech that might be considered "vulgar" but not legally obscene? Such speech is often called *indecent*, and the Supreme Court has ruled that indecent speech has First Amendment protection. As Justice Stevens pointed out, it becomes a different legal matter when indecent speech is delivered over the public airwaves. In such instances, the nation's highest court has ruled that indecency has limited First Amendment protection. The court's main justification for these limits is to protect children from indecent material.

A HISTORY OF BROADCAST INDECENCY REGULATION

As early as 1932, the federal courts showed that they were willing to allow the federal government to regulate "inappropriate" or "indecent" material on the airwaves. In *Trinity Methodist Church South v. Federal Radio Commission*,[2] the U.S. Court of Appeals in Washington, DC, upheld the right of the Federal Radio Commission to deny license renewal to a radio station that had aired "words suggestive of sexual immorality." KGEF of Los Angeles had aired commentary from a minister who had criticized the Roman Catholic Church and made "sensational" references to "prostitutes" and "pimps." The court said that the First Amendment gave

---

[1] *FCC v. Pacifica*, 438 U.S. 726, 728 (1978)

[2] 62 F.2d 850 (D.C. Cir. 1932)

the minister the right to make these comments, but it did not give him protection from FRC punishments that resulted from those comments being broadcast on the public airwaves. The court upheld the FRC's denial of license renewal to KGEF because "the evidence abundantly sustains the conclusion of the Commission that the continuance of the broadcasting programs of appellant is not in the public interest."

Section 326 of the Communications Act of 1934 prohibited the use of "obscene or indecent language" on the airwaves. In 1948, these prohibitions were added to the criminal code in U.S.C.A. § 1464. This section mandated that use of obscene, profane, or indecent language on the airwaves could result in a fine of up to $10,000, a prison term of 2 years, or both.

In 1955, the FCC denied application for a TV license to a licensee who had broadcast "sexually vulgar and suggestive" songs on its radio station.[3] The FCC wanted to send the message that it would not tolerate "racy" song lyrics.

In 1962, the FCC denied license renewal to Palmetto Broadcasting Corporation because of programming on its radio station WDKD in South Carolina. During one of the station's programs several years earlier, a talk show host had used phrases like "let it all hang out" and "if the crotches in those britches could talk." WDKD appealed the denial of its license renewal, but the FCC upheld the denial and reminded WKDK that the language used on the talk show was "coarse, vulgar, and suggestive."[4]

In 1964, the FCC was considering the license renewal of stations belonging to the Pacifica Foundation. The commission had received complaints about five Pacifica programs, including a talk show where homosexuals discussed their lifestyles and problems. This show, along with three others, was broadcast late at night. The FCC did not deny any license renewals but did warn that some listeners might have been "offended" by the programs. However, the FCC was worried about banning such material because it would have meant that "only the wholly inoffensive, the bland, could gain access to the radio, microphone, or TV camera."[5]

In 1970, an interview with Jerry Garcia of the rock band The Grateful Dead got an FM station in Philadelphia into trouble. Garcia used phrases such as "all that shit" and "every fuckin' year" during a taped interview aired at 10:00 p.m. on WUHY-FM. The FCC fined the station $100 for indecency because the station did not edit out the vulgar language, which the FCC called "utterly without redeeming social value."[6]

"Topless Radio"

By the early 1970s, a phenomenon known as "topless radio" began to emerge. The format usually involved afternoon talk shows that contained discussions of intimate sexual material, and the FCC received many complaints about the popular format. FCC staff members began to record some of the shows as evidence.

---

[3] *WREC Broadcasting Service*, 19 F.C.C. 1082, 1113, 1115 (1955)

[4] *In re Palmetto Broadcasting Co.,* 33 F.C.C. 250 (1962)

[5] *Pacifica Foundation*, 36 F.C.C. 147, 1 R.R.2d 747 (1964)

[6] *Eastern Educational Radio (WUHY-FM),* 24 F.C.C.2d 408, 18 R.R.2d 860 (1970)

One of the first to feel the FCC's sting was Sonderling Broadcasting Corporation, owner of WGLD-FM in Oak Park, IL. The topless radio program in question aired in the afternoon and involved a conversation between the announcer and a female listener who described various techniques of oral sex, such as spreading peanut butter on her husband's private parts. The FCC fined Sonderling $2000 for airing "explicit" discussions of sexual issues.[7]

Two citizens groups urged the commission to reconsider the fine against Sonderling, saying that listeners had a right to hear discussions of sexual matters. The FCC held its ground, pointing to the "intrusive" nature of radio. The FCC added that the afternoon broadcast "was even more clearly unlawful when presented to an audience which included children."[8] One of the citizens groups appealed the ruling in *Illinois Citizens Committee for Broadcasting v. FCC*, but an appellate court upheld the FCC's decision, as well as the $2000 fine.[9]

FCC v. Pacifica

In 1973, Pacifica radio station WBAI-FM in New York City aired a 12-minute monologue entitled "Filthy Words" by comedian George Carlin. The theme was the "seven dirty words" no one could say on radio or TV. Those words were *shit, piss, fuck, cunt, cocksucker, motherfucker*, and *tits*.

Before airing the show at 2:00 p.m., WBAI broadcast a disclaimer stating that the program might be offensive to some listeners. A man was driving in his car with his 15-year-old son when he happened to tune in to the Carlin monologue. The man wrote a letter to the FCC complaining about the language in the program, stating that he could understand how the material might be sold for private use but saying that he did not approve of it being broadcast in the middle of the day when children could hear it.

The FCC forwarded the complaint to the radio station. Pacifica responded that the station had aired a disclaimer and argued that Carlin was a "significant social satirist . . . in the tradition of Mark Twain and Mort Sahl" who was "merely using words to satirize as harmless and essentially silly our attitudes toward those words."[10] The FCC did not agree with this assessment and ruled that the broadcast was in violation of U.S. Code § 1464.

The FCC did not fine Pacifica but put the matter on file in the event further complaints were received.

The FCC ruled that it had a right to prohibit indecent language during the day. However, the commission said indecent programs should be aired at a time of day when children were not likely to be in the audience. The commission said their ruling was "simply channeling behavior more than actually prohibiting it."[11] Pacifica appealed the ruling, saying that the FCC had no constitutional right to regulate speech on the airwaves.

In *Pacifica v. FCC*, the U.S. Court of Appeals in Washington called the FCC's ruling "censorship." One of the judges said the FCC indecency standard would ban reading certain

---

[7]*Sonderling Broadcasting Corp.*, 27 R.R.2d 285, *on reconsideration*, 41 F.C.C.2d 777 (1973)

[8]See 41 F.C.C.2d 777, 27 R.R.2d 1508 (1973)

[9]515 F.2d 397 (D.C. Cir. 1974)

[10]Gillmor & Barron, *op. cit.*, pp. 890, 899

[11]Carter, T., Franklin, M., & Wright, J. (1989). *The First Amendment and the Fourth Estate*. Westbury, NY: Foundation Press. p. 677

parts of the Bible on the air and said the FCC ruling was like "burning the house to roast the pig."[12]

The U.S. Supreme Court overturned the appeals court ruling in 1978 in *FCC v. Pacifica*.[13] Five justices said the FCC was justified in protecting children from indecent broadcasts and that such protections did not violate the First Amendment:

> Of all forms of communication, broadcasting has the most limited First Amendment protection. . . . Broadcasts extend into the privacy of the home and it is impossible completely to avoid those that are patently offensive. Broadcasting, moreover, is uniquely accessible to children.[14]

The Supreme Court then provided a definition of indecency which is still used today. Indecent material (a) depicts or describes, (b) in terms patently offensive (c) as measured by contemporary community standards for the broadcast medium, (d) sexual or excretory activities or organs (e) at times of day when there is a reasonable risk that children may be in the audience.[15]

FAQ

Why did the Supreme Court rule that indecency should be regulated on the broadcast airwaves but not in other forms of media?

The court pointed out that broadcast airwaves are "scarce" and therefore may be regulated. Broadcast airwaves also are "intrusive" and come into homes uninvited; people have a right to be "left alone" in their homes. Adults may not want to hear such material and may not always hear disclaimers at the start of a show. Children have easy access to broadcasting, and the government has an interest in protecting the well-being of its youth.

The Supreme Court said that adults do have a First Amendment right to hear or watch indecent material on radio and TV. However, the high court ruled that this is a "limited right"—which would be demonstrated through the "safe harbor."

The Safe Harbor: 10:00 p.m. to 6:00 a.m.

The "safe harbor" is a time of day when broadcasters can air indecent material without fear of FCC sanctions. The hours between 10:00 p.m. and 6:00 a.m. have been considered the traditional safe harbor by broadcasters. This safe harbor is a form of "channeling." Indecent material is channeled to a time of day (or night) when children are less likely to be listening or when their listening would be more likely to be monitored by adults. The safe harbor also was designed to protect nonconsenting adults who did not want to be confronted by indecent programming during regular listening and viewing hours.

---

[12]*Pacifica Foundation v. FCC*, 556 F.2d 9, 13 (D.C. Cir. 1977)

[13]438 U.S. 726 (1978)

[14]*Ibid.*, p. 728

[15]556 F.2d 9 (D.C. Cir. 1977)

With all of this in mind, broadcasters from 1978 to 1987 thought they had a good idea of exactly what the FCC considered indecent: any programming with the "seven dirty words" that was aired outside of the safe harbor.

Shock Radio

The mid-1980s brought some confusion about indecency regulation because of a new genre known as "shock radio." The most infamous shock radio DJ (or "shock jock") was Howard Stern. His style of broadcasting more or less came to define shock radio.

Stern had morning shows on stations in Philadelphia and New York City during which he used everything from racial slurs to explicit sexual humor. The material was meant to shock listeners with its vulgarity and, as a result, gain a large listening audience.

In 1986, the FCC claimed to have received roughly 20,000 letters complaining about the commission's lack of action against shock radio and other indecent programming.[16] Many in Congress were also complaining about the general amount of sex and violence in the media, and lawmakers were threatening to cut off FCC funding if the commission did not take some action against indecency. As a result, the FCC acted in 1987 and handed out fines to numerous radio stations for indecent programs, including fines for Howard Stern's broadcasts.[17]

FAQ

What qualified as indecency? Was it simply the seven dirty words?

Many broadcasters thought so. However, the FCC soon informed broadcasters that the "seven dirty words" would no longer be the benchmark for indecency regulation.

The Rules Start to Change

As of 1987, the FCC's new rules for indecency included the following:

1. Innuendo and double entendre can be indecent if intermingled with explicit references.

2. Deliberate and repetitive use of expletives can be indecent.

3. Contemporary community standards must be taken into account.

4. Stations must avoid airing such material when it is "likely" that children will be in the audience, but it is up to stations to determine those times.[17]

Many broadcasters and legal scholars claimed that the new guidelines were confusing, some calling them as "clear as mud."[18] Fifteen media outlets petitioned the FCC in June 1987, saying the new standards were vague and overly broad and should be thrown out.

---

[16]Indecency policy clear as mud. (1987, Summer). *News Media and the Law, 11(3),* 3.

[17]*New indecency enforcement standards,* 2 FCC Rcd. 2726 (1988)

[18]Indecency policy, *op. cit.,* p. 3

The FCC, though, stuck by its new guidelines. Then, several months later, the FCC threw some more gas on the fire.

A Smaller Harbor?

In December 1987, the FCC shortened the safe harbor by 2 hours. The FCC said the new safe harbor would be from midnight to 6:00 a.m. As noted earlier, the old safe harbor had been from 10:00 p.m. to 6:00 a.m. Media groups took the FCC to court over the sudden change.

In July 1988, an appeals court in *Action for Children's Television v. FCC* (*"ACT I"*) rejected the FCC's new safe harbor times, saying, "We are approving the concept but rejecting its execution."[19] In other words, the court said that the FCC had a right to regulate indecency, but the commission did not provide good reasoning for changing the safe harbor. The court ordered the FCC to restore the old safe harbor time.

At about the same time, though, Congress passed a law that provided *no* safe harbor, prohibiting indecent broadcasts 24 hours a day. President Reagan signed the bill into law in October 1988.

FAQ

Would the courts uphold a 24-hour indecency ban?

No. Media groups challenged the new law in courts. In January 1990, in what became known as *ACT II*, the DC Court of Appeals ordered a stay on the 24-hour ban.[20] The court ordered the FCC to conduct hearings on the constitutionality of the ban. The FCC gathered and presented its evidence, but the same appeals court in June 1991 ruled that the 24-hour ban was unconstitutional. The FCC then reinstated the 10:00 p.m. to 6:00 a.m. safe harbor.

Then in 1995, in *ACT III*, several media groups challenged the methods used by the FCC when it investigated and fined broadcasters who aired indecent material. The groups claimed that FCC enforcement and fining procedures "lack appropriate safeguards— including prompt judicial review—which forces broadcasters to conform with potential unconstitutional restrictions upon their speech."[21] The court rejected the media groups' claims and reaffirmed the FCC's right to regulate indecency on the airwaves. The court ruled that there was no evidence that the FCC was violating the First Amendment by restricting indecency on the airwaves outside of the safe harbor times.

Howard Stern Strikes Again—and the FCC Strikes Back

In 1995, Infinity Broadcasting paid a record $1.715 million in FCC indecency fines for material aired by Howard Stern on several Infinity radio stations. The FCC also gave out

---

[19]564 F.2d 458 (D.C. Cir. 1988)

[20]*ACT v. FCC (ACT II)*, 932 F.2d 1504 (D.C. Cir. 1989)

[21]*ACT v. FCC (ACT III)*, 58 F.3d 654 (D.C. Cir. 1995)

$50,000 fines to the individual Infinity stations airing Stern's show for "their apparent willful and repeated violations."[22]

The FCC, as it usually does in indecency matters, provided a transcript of the offending Howard Stern programs. None of the seven dirty words was present, but the commission pointed to the "patently offensive" discussion of sexual matters. On one program, Stern had been talking with another man about oral sex that the man had received from a woman the night before. Stern called the man a "monster" and made repeated references to the woman "gagging."[23]

The indecency fines continued to pile up for radio stations airing Stern's show. Another example is WBZU-FM in Richmond, VA, which was fined $10,000 in 1996. One of the offending Stern programs (aired on October 23, 1995) involved a man looking at six pictures of women's genitals. Stern then asked the man if he could pick out the picture of his daughter's sexual organs. The father apparently chose the correct picture as he referred to "Daddy's little girl."[24]

In an effort to inform broadcasters about the types of material that the FCC would often consider indecent, the commission issued a directive to lay out some guidelines. It said stations should avoid "explicit references" to the following: ejaculation, masturbation, penis size, breast size, sexual intercourse, nudity, urination, genitals, oral-genital contact, erections, sodomy, bestiality, menstruation, and testicles.

2001: The FCC Issues New Guidelines on Indecency Regulation

Even with these guidelines, some broadcasters said they were still unsure about the FCC's definition of indecency. In April 2001, the FCC released a policy statement to "provide guidance to the broadcast industry regarding . . . our enforcement policies with respect to broadcast indecency."[25] The commission reiterated the indecency definition from *Pacifica,* reminding broadcasters of two fundamentals: Indecent material describes or depicts sexual or excretory activities or organs, and it is patently offensive according to contemporary community standards for the broadcast medium (for more details, see box).

Three Factors to Help Determine Indecency

1. The *explicitness or graphic nature* of the sexual/excretory material
2. Whether the material *dwells on or repeats at length* the descriptions of sexual or excretory activities or organs
3. Whether the material *appears to pander or titillate* or *appears to have been presented for its shock value*[25]

---

[22]*Notice of apparent liability*, FCC 94-121, released May 20, 1994. The stations fined were WJFK-AM, Baltimore; WXRX-FM, New York City; WYSP-FM, Philadelphia; and WJFK-FM, Manassas, VA.

[23]*Ibid.*, pp. 3-4

[24]*Notice of apparent liability*, FCC 97-1286, released June 24, 1997.

[25]*Industry guidance on the commission's case law interpreting 18 U.S.C. § 1464 and enforcement policies regarding broadcast indecency*, FCC 01-90, released April 6, 2001 (File No. EB-00-IH-0089)

The FCC made special mention of the third factor (pandering, titillation, and presentation), saying that *context* is very important. If explicit sexual language is used during an educational radio talk show, the FCC will often say that this is not indecent because the context is "informational." However, if that same explicit sexual language is used by a radio personality to shock an audience, it is more likely to be considered indecent.

FAQ

Has the FCC provided examples of the types of material it considers indecent?

Yes. In its April 2001 policy statement on broadcast indecency, the FCC provided transcripts of material that had led to indecency fines. Examples included sexual innuendo and double entendre in which "the sexual or excretory import is unmistakable," such as in the "Candy Wrapper Song," which used the names of candy bars as sexual references. There was also a DJ making reference to genital size when discussing "a big organ for a big cathedral." Repetition of slang terms for genitals, extended discussions about "farting" and other bodily functions, and crude DJ jokes about sex with children fell under the definition of *indecency*, as did deliberate and repeated uses of the any of the seven "filthy words." The FCC noted that airing phone calls from listeners who talked in graphic detail about their sex lives would be considered indecent, and mentioned the case of an on-air person reading an article from *Playboy* in which Jessica Hahn described her famous affair with televangelist Jim Bakker, including graphic descriptions of an alleged rape.

FAQ

Has the FCC explained why certain types of material are not considered to be indecent?

Yes. The FCC provided examples of this in its 2001 policy statement and explained why the broadcasters were not fined. The commission looked specifically at *context*. For example, an on-air guest said "fuck" and the DJ apologized immediately. The FCC said this was not intentional and constituted a "fleeting and isolated utterance within the context of live and spontaneous programming." In another instance, a "filthy word" went over the air by accident because a person did not realize a microphone was on. Again, the FCC saw this as "fleeting and isolated." When a TV station aired portions of a sex education class from a local high school that showed, among other things, realistic models of sexual organs, the FCC said the context was educational and therefore not indecent.

In an NPR news story that included an unedited recording of organized crime figure John Gotti, a wiretapped phone conversation in which Gotti says "fuck" ten times, the station aired a disclaimer before the broadcast. The FCC said it was not actionably indecent because it was within the context of an important news story. On one episode of the *Oprah Winfrey Show,* sex experts talked about topics such as orgasms and masturbation. The FCC said the goal was to educate viewers and not to shock them. The show aired a disclaimer at the start, as well. When the film *Schindler's List* (an R-rated movie) was aired unedited on network television, stations aired a disclaimer before and during the film warning viewers about "adult" subject matter, including nudity. The film depicted atrocities in Nazi prison camps in World War II, and it contained scenes of adult frontal nudity. The FCC ruled "full adult frontal nudity is not *per se* indecent." The commission said the full context was important here. Considering "the subject matter of the film, the manner of its presentation, and the warnings that accompanied the broadcast," the nudity in this film was "not actionably indecent."

Eminem and "The [Edited] Real Slim Shady"

In June 2001, the FCC fined KKMG-FM in Pueblo, CO, $7000 for playing the song "The Real Slim Shady" by popular rap artist Eminem. The song was a number one hit and had been played repeatedly on Top 40 stations across America.

What was most interesting about this case was that KKMG had played the "radio edit" of the song, a version with the profanities bleeped out. The $7000 fine scared a lot of programmers at radio stations that frequently played edited songs on the air. The FCC ruled, "The edited version of the song contains unmistakable offensive sexual references" and "that the licensee failed to purge a number of indecent references."[26]

Then, in January 2002, the FCC reversed itself and dropped the $7000 fine against Citadel Broadcasting, the owners of KKMG. After an appeal from Citadel, the FCC decided that the bleeps were adequate and that the sexual references in the edited version of the song were "not expressed in terms sufficiently explicit or graphic enough to be found patently offensive."[27] Broadcasters nationwide who frequently played "radio edits" breathed a sigh of relief.

At about the same time, the FCC considered punishing a radio station for playing a song that condemned graphic lyrics in rap music.

A Song Denouncing "Indecent" Hip-Hop Lyrics Is Called Indecent

Feminist black performer Sarah Jones wrote and recorded the song "Your Revolution." She wrote the song (which was originally a poem) to criticize what she saw as the sexual exploitation of women in pop music, particularly in rap songs. What offended the FCC were lyrics such as "Your revolution will not happen between these thighs" and "Your notorious revolution will never allow you to lace no lyrical douche in my bush." In May 2001, the FCC fined KBOO-FM in Portland, OR, $7000 for playing the song. The commission said "the sexual references appear to be designed to pander and shock and are patently offensive."[28]

Jones then staged a revolution against the FCC, filing a historic lawsuit against the commission in January 2002. She said the FCC violated her First Amendment rights when it fined KBOO for airing "Your Revolution." This marked the first time a person had sued the FCC over an indecency action. Jones' lawsuit sought to prevent the FCC from collecting the $7000 fine from the station. The lawsuit also claimed that the FCC's indecency ruling harmed her reputation as a singer and limited the "reach" of her song. She said the FCC fine

[26]*Notice of apparent liability*, DA 01-1334, released June 1, 2001.

[27]*Memorandum opinion and order*, DA 02-23, released January 8, 2002.

[28]*Notice of apparent liability for forfeiture*, DA 01-1212, released May 17, 2001.

created a chilling effect, making other radio stations afraid to play a song that had been labeled indecent by the commission. A federal district court in New York dismissed the lawsuit, saying it had no jurisdiction in an FCC indecency claim. Jones appealed that dismissal to the U.S. Court of Appeals in Washington.

Shortly before her case was to be heard in court in February 2003, the FCC reversed itself and dropped the fine against KBOO.

2003: Public Outrage Builds Over Indecent Broadcasts—and FCC Rulings

2003 set the stage for some major changes in indecency enforcement that would come about in 2004.

Controversial Ruling on the Word Fuck

For decades, most broadcasters had assumed that any use of *fuck* outside of the safe harbor constituted an automatic violation of indecency rules. However, in 2003, the FCC enforcement bureau issued a controversial ruling when it announced that some uses of *fuck* could be permissible, depending on the context. The ruling stemmed from a complaint about a live January 2003 broadcast of the Golden Globe awards on NBC. During an acceptance speech, rock singer Bono of the group U2 said, "This is really, really fucking brilliant." NBC did not edit out the expletive.

In dismissing the complaint about the use of "fucking," the enforcement bureau said that the context of Bono's use of the word was such that the word "did not describe sexual or excretory activities or organs" but was instead used "as an adjective or expletive to emphasize an exclamation." The bureau also noted that when similar offensive language is used as an insult (calling someone a "fucking idiot," for example), it would also not be considered indecent. The Parent's Television Council, which had filed the complaint, said the ruling showed that the FCC was a "toothless lion" and did not take broadcast indecency seriously. Members of Congress also expressed disgust over the ruling.[29]

Critics argued that indecency continued to flourish on the airwaves because of the FCC's history of handing out relatively small indecency fines to broadcasters. For example, a $5000 or $10,000 indecency fine was not a huge financial blow for most broadcast stations in larger markets. The FCC had the power to fine stations as much as $27,500 for each indecency incident, but the commission rarely issued this maximum fine. Also, the FCC did not usually fine stations for each individual indecent "utterance" but would instead issue a general fine for an entire indecent broadcast. As a result, stations that frequently aired indecent material looked at FCC fines as one of the "costs of doing business." The fines obviously were not a deterrent for these stations. The FCC recognized this fact, and the commission in 2003 began to hand out much harsher fines for broadcast indecency.

---

[29]*In the matter of complaints against various broadcast licensees regarding the airing of "The Golden Globes" program* (Petition for reconsideration before the Federal Communications Commission, file no. EB-03-IH-0110). (2004, April 19). Retrieved October 28, 2004, from http://www.fcc.gov/eb/broadcast/Pleadings/Indecent_Recon.pdf

Stiff Fines for Broadcast Indecency

One of the most talked-about stunts in the history of radio indecency is a stunt that was done as part of the *Opie and Anthony Show* on WNEW-FM in New York City in August 2002. The syndicated show also aired in 17 other markets. The stunt involved a promotion for "54 risky locations for people to have sex." A Virginia couple picked St. Patrick's Cathedral in New York as a "risky" site, and the couple allegedly had sex in a vestibule, which was just feet away from worshippers. The *Opie and Anthony Show* then broadcast a live "eyewitness report" via cell phone from the show's producer, who was inside the church.

Catholic groups were outraged that a church had been desecrated and immediately filed a complaint with the FCC, demanding not only a fine but a revocation of WNEW's license. WNEW's owner Infinity Broadcasting responded by firing Opie and Anthony (Greg Hughes and Anthony Cumia) and canceling the popular show. Catholic groups said WNEW acted responsibly by firing the duo and said they would not push for revocation of the station's license. (The Virginia couple was arrested for public lewdness. Their lawyer claimed the couple was only simulating sex.)

In a record fine for a single broadcast incident, the FCC in October 2003 announced that it was fining Infinity Broadcasting $357,500 for the *Opie and Anthony* stunt. In November 2003, Infinity asked for a reduction in the fine, saying the stunt contained only "oblique references and innuendo." The FCC rejected the appeal.[30]

Wanting to show that it was serious about stricter enforcement of indecency regulations, the FCC levied a $715,000 fine against Clear Channel for six stations that aired a program hosted by "Bubba the Love Sponge." The FCC reached this total by assessing the maximum fine of $27,500 for each of 26 individual indecency violations.

FAQ

How do commissioners ultimately determine what qualifies as indecent?

Although the FCC says it has specific guidelines regarding indecency, critics charge that the process is too subjective and allows fines to be assessed based on the sensitivities and subjectivity of individual commissioners. For example, in the "Bubba" case, commissioner Kevin Martin wanted a fine exceeding $1.3 million. His interpretation of indecency rules led him to find 49 individual indecency violations, not 26.[31] Such differences of opinion occur frequently among commissioners in indecency cases.

Critics of the FCC's new indecency crackdown came from across the political spectrum. It was hardly surprising when radio personalities such as Howard Stern accused the FCC of engaging in censorship. However, many analysts were surprised when conservative talk radio host Rush Limbaugh said the FCC's crackdown had him a "little frightened" as well. He said, "I am in the free speech business. It's one thing for a company to determine if they

---

[30]*Notice of apparent liability for forfeiture*, FCC 03-234, released October 2, 2003.

[31]*In the matter of Clear Channel Broadcasting Licenses, Inc., notice of apparent liability for forfeiture*, FCC 04-17, January 27, 2004, separate statement of Commissioner Kevin J. Martin.

are going to be a party to it. It's another thing for the government to do it." Limbaugh also complained that the FCC is stricter with radio than with TV: "Smut on TV gets praised. Smut on TV wins Emmys. On radio, there seems to be different standards."[32]

> # FAQ
>
> Are fines the only way the FCC can punish stations for indecency?

No. The commission has the power under Section 312(a)(6) of the Communications Act to revoke (or take away) a broadcaster's license. That is what Commissioner Michael Copps wanted in the Bubba case. In a dissenting opinion, Copps said these large fines were not enough. He said that the $715,000 fine would be "easily absorbed" by a media giant like Clear Channel. Copps pointed out that "Bubba the Love Sponge" had previously been fined three times by the FCC, but the fines did not dissuade stations from airing indecent material on future segments of the show. Copps asked, "How many strikes are we going to give them?" He said the FCC should have seriously considered revoking the licenses of each of the four stations. The majority was not ready to take such action in this case but did say that future violations "may well lead to license revocation proceedings." Copps said license revocation was the only sure way to "stop the media's slide to the bottom."[33]

Many in Congress and the public felt that broadcasters truly hit bottom with an incident during the half-time show of the 2004 Super Bowl. It would prove to be an impetus for major changes in FCC indecency regulation.

NEW CRACKDOWN ON INDECENCY

The 2004 Super Bowl "Wardrobe Malfunction"

It was a brief glimpse of a woman's breast on CBS, but it sparked national outrage about what was seen as declining morality on the broadcast airwaves. The outrage resulted largely from the fact that the incident occurred during the Super Bowl, one of the top-rated programs each year and a program that many parents watch with their children. It is usually considered a "safe" show for all ages.

During the live half-time show, produced by MTV, singer Justin Timberlake walked toward singer Janet Jackson as he sang, "I'm gonna have you naked by the end of this song." He then reached over and ripped away a portion of Jackson's costume, revealing one of Jackson's breasts. Jackson quickly covered her breast with her hand, and CBS immediately cut away from the shot. Soon after, CBS and the FCC received numerous complaints about the incident.

Timberlake blamed the episode on a "wardrobe malfunction," saying there was supposed to be another garment underneath Jackson's costume to cover her breast. In spite of

---

[32]Comments made on the *Rush Limbaugh Radio Show*, February 26, 2004.

[33]*In the matter of Clear Channel, op. cit.*, separate statement of Commissioner Michael J. Copps.

this explanation, FCC chairman Michael Powell called it "a classless, crass and deplorable stunt." CBS said it did not know about the stunt before broadcast.

In September 2004, the FCC fined Viacom $550,000, representing $27,500 fines for each of the 20 stations owned and operated directly by CBS.[34] More than 200 other CBS affiliates were not fined because the FCC reasoned that those affiliates could not have predicted what happened and had no part in planning the half-time show. Of course, none of the owned and operated CBS stations could have predicted the event either, but FCC rules prohibit the commission from fining a parent network for the actions of individual stations it does not directly own. Therefore, fining the owned and operated stations was the only way the commission could punish the CBS network.

Public outrage over the Jackson-Timberlake episode gave the FCC and Congress renewed vigor in cracking down on broadcast indecency, and the radio industry took notice. In February 2004, Clear Channel announced a new "zero tolerance" policy for broadcast indecency. The policy said that as soon as the company learned about an indecency investigation by the FCC, the company would remove the offending personality from the air and begin an internal investigation. Clear Channel did just that by firing "Bubba the Love Sponge" after the FCC announced its investigation. Clear Channel also took Howard Stern's radio show off six of its major market stations. (A few months later, Stern has his show back on the air in many of those markets on other stations.) In October 2004, Stern said that he had had enough with FCC indecency regulation and announced a $500 million, 5-year deal with Sirius Satellite Radio. Because Sirius is a subscriber-based system and is not broadcast on the public airwaves, Sirius radio channels are not subject to FCC indecency regulations. Stern is scheduled to begin airing his program on Sirius in January 2006.[35]

Other major radio companies announced similar new indecency policies. That same month, Clear Channel president John Hogan appeared before the House Committee on Energy and Commerce to try to assure Congress that his company had "cleaned up its act." Hogan testified that his stations were "wrong to air that material" and that Clear Channel would no longer tolerate indecency programming by people like Howard Stern and "Bubba."[36]

The television industry also became more fearful about increased indecency enforcement. In January 2004, the FCC fined KRON-TV in San Francisco the maximum $27,500 for a 2002 broadcast involving a performance called *Puppetry of the Penis*. One of the performers exposed his penis for less than a second, but the FCC said it was still "graphic" and "explicit" and worthy of a fine.[37] In spring 2004, the NBC series *ER* decided to delete an emergency room shot of an elderly woman's breast, not knowing if the FCC would find it "artistic" or "indecent." The show had aired partial nudity in previous episodes, but the

---

[34]*Notice of apparent liability for forfeiture,* FCC 04-209, released September 22, 2004.

[35]*Howard Stern and Sirius announce the most important deal in radio history.* (2004, October 6). Retrieved October 8, 2004, from http://www.siriusradio.com/servlet/ContentServer?pagename=Sirius/CachedPage&c=PresRele Asset&cid=1097008921509

[36]House Committee on Energy and Commerce. (2004, February 26). *Prepared witness testimony.* Retrieved March 17, 2004, from http://energycommerce.house.gov/108/Hearings/02262004hearing1216/Hogan1866.htm

[37]*Notice of apparent liability for forfeiture,* FCC 04-16, released January 27, 2004.

show's producers were unsure of how the FCC would view such content now.[38] In October 2004, the FCC continued to target the television industry when it announced a $1.2 million fine against Fox for its reality TV show *Married by America*. It was the largest indecency penalty ever levied against a TV network, representing $7000 fine for each of the 169 Fox affiliates that aired the program (one affiliate, in North Carolina, chose not to air the program and was not fined). The FCC pointed to one scene in the show where two topless female strippers were spanking a man in his underwear. Fox had pixilated the strippers' breasts, but the commission said that the covering of the nudity was not sufficient because "even a child would have known the strippers were topless and that sexual activity was being shown."[39]

Bono Ruling Overturned

In March 2004, with pressure from Congress and the outrage over the Super Bowl stunt very fresh in people's minds, FCC commissioners reversed the enforcement bureau's ruling on broadcasts of the word *fuck*. The FCC said that virtually any use of *fuck* would be considered indecent on the broadcast airwaves, calling the word "one of the most vulgar, graphic and explicit descriptions of sexual activity in the English language." The FCC said this rule would apply to unintentional airings, such as the Bono incident. NBC was not fined for Bono's use, but the commission warned that there would be fines for future infractions on live broadcasts. The commission said that broadcasters should use "delay" technology when airing live events to edit out such language in the future.[40]

Congress Reacts With Tough New Fines

Also in March 2004, the House passed a bill raising the maximum indecency fine from $27,500 to $500,000, topping the $275,000 maximum fine just passed by the Senate. The House bill also stipulated that three violations by the same broadcaster would lead to license revocation hearings before the FCC.[41]

Fining Individuals?

The House bill also gave the FCC the power to levy fines of up to $500,000 against individual performers such as Howard Stern. FCC chairman Michael Powell said fining individuals had serious First Amendment implications and was a "very touchy area for the FCC."[42] Many in the broadcasting industry expressed their discomfort over this provision as well. The FCC had already had the power to fine individual performers up to $11,000 for

---

[38]NBC won't air ER breast shot. (2004, February 5). *CNN/Money*. Retrieved October 29, 2004 from http://money.cnn.com/2004/02/05/news/companies/nbc_er/

[39]*Notice of apparent liability*, FCC 04-242, released October 12, 2004.

[40]*In the matter of complaints against various broadcast licensees regarding the airing of "The Golden Globes" program, op. cit.*

[41]Broadcast decency enforcement act, H.R. 3717, 108th Cong. (2004).

[42]Boliek, B. (2004, April 1). FCC brass uneasy over artist fines. *Hollywood Reporter*. Retrieved August 21, 2004, from http://www.hollywoodreporter.com/thr/article_display.jsp?vnu_content_id=1000476554

an indecent broadcast if the performer had been warned, but the commission had never used that power.

Another Record Indecency Fine

In June 2004, Clear Channel Communications agreed to pay $1.75 million in "voluntary contributions" to the U.S. Treasury to settle all pending and existing indecency cases against the company. This topped the previous record indecency fine of $1.715 million paid by Infinity in 1995. In return, the FCC agreed to wipe the record clean for Clear Channel, which would help the company when it renewed station licenses or if it wanted to buy more stations. The record payout represented a combination of fines for programs by Howard Stern and Elliot Segal and included the $715,000 fine for "Bubba the Love Sponge" (Todd Clem).[43]

In July 2004, the indecency battle saw another milestone when Clear Channel became the first broadcaster ever to sue a radio personality over FCC indecency fines. The radio giant said it was suing Howard Stern for $10 million for violating his contract.[44] In that contract, Stern had agreed not to engage in on-air activities that would violate any laws or regulations.

FAQ

Don't these large fines represent a major shift in how the FCC punishes broadcasters for indecency?

Most definitely. As Commissioner Copps mentioned in his statement in the "Bubba" ruling, the FCC feels these much larger fines will deter more broadcasters from airing "questionable" material. It appears to have worked with companies like Clear Channel, who are creating new "zero tolerance" policies for indecency.

FAQ

Does the FCC monitor the airwaves for indecency, or do they rely solely on complaints?

The FCC does not have staff members drive around the country listening to radio stations searching for indecent programs; it has neither the time nor the resources to do that. Instead, the commission relies on the public to document complaints about indecent broadcasts. All it takes is one citizen to contact the FCC and complain about an "indecent" radio or TV program.

---

[43] Ahrens, F. (2004, June 9). Radio giant in record indecency settlement. *Washington Post,* p. A01.

[44] Grossberg, J. (2004, July 21). Clear Channel countersues Stern. *E! Online News.* Retrieved August 15, 2004, from http://www.eonline.com/News/Items/0,1,14559,00.html?newsrellink

FAQ

Does the FCC require indecency complaints to come with proof of any kind?

The FCC prefers that an indecency complaint include three items: (a) a full or partial tape or transcript of or significant excerpts from the program, (b) the date and time of the broadcast, and (c) the call letters of the station involved.

The FCC, if it decides to act, may then take the following actions. The commission will issue a letter of inquiry to the licensee explaining the complaint or seeking further information about the broadcast. If the broadcast is found to be indecent, the commission issues the licensee a notice of apparent liability, which details the amount of the fine. The licensee then has a legal right to respond to or appeal the notice.

After this, the case is formally referred to the full commission for consideration and action. The FCC has found this method to be problematic at times because tapes and transcripts are not always available as proof of an indecent broadcast. That is why, in July 2004, the FCC proposed that all TV and AM and FM radio stations be required to keep recordings of all broadcasts of the previous 60 to 90 days, to help with indecency investigations. The proposal said that the recordings would be done daily, from 6:00 a.m. to 10:00 p.m. Some commissioners commented that the FCC should place less burden on citizens to prove indecency violations. The commission noted that it frequently has to dismiss indecency complaints because of a lack of tapes or transcripts. Almost immediately, the National Association of Broadcasters criticized the proposal as unneeded and burdensome, noting that only about 1% of indecency complaints are dismissed due to a lack of evidence.[45]

Indecency and Other Electronic Media

Cable TV

A Miami, FL, ordinance in the early 1980s prohibited cable TV systems from airing indecent material. The ordinance read, in part: "No person shall by means of a cable television system knowingly distribute by wire or cable any obscene or indecent material." The ordinance included a definition of indecency similar to the one in *Pacifica*.

In 1985, in *Cruz v. Ferre*,[46] an appeals court struck down the ordinance. The court ruled that the city could not prohibit indecent material on cable for several reasons. Cable TV "does not 'intrude' into the home" like broadcasting, the court said. "Cable programming is available only to those who have the cable attached to their television sets." Subscribers must make monthly decisions about cable service coming into their homes, and they may cancel their cable service if unhappy. Also, cable subscribers must make "the additional affirmative decision whether to purchase any 'extra' programming services, such as HBO."

[45]Associated Press. (2004, June 23). *Senate OKs higher fines for indecency*. Retrieved September 7, 2004, from http://www.firstamendmentcenter.org/news.aspx?id=13556

[46]*Cruz v. Ferre*, 755 F.2d 1415 (11th Cir. 1985)

The court also pointed out that, unlike broadcasting, cable TV is not as easily accessible by children. Parents choose to have the cable come into the home, and those parents may obtain "lockboxes" to keep children from viewing indecent programs.

The court made an important distinction here. *Pacifica* allows the FCC to regulate indecency on broadcast stations but not on cable TV. The court did uphold the city's right to prohibit *obscene* material on cable. That is because obscenity in any medium is not protected by the First Amendment (see *Miller v. California*).

Renewed Efforts to Regulate Indecency on Cable

In 2004, in the wake of the Super Bowl "wardrobe malfunction," the U.S. Senate Commerce Committee came within one vote of giving the FCC more power to regulate content on basic cable channels such as MTV, USA Network, and Lifetime. It would not have applied to pay channels such as HBO and The Movie Channel (TMC).[47] It is questionable whether such an amendment would survive judicial scrutiny.

Adult Cable Channels and "Signal Bleed"

The Telecommunications Act of 1996 sought to prevent another form of indecency that was coming into people's homes through cable. *Signal bleed* occurs when a cable company offers an "adult" movie channel on a leased access channel. The cable company scrambles the audio and video for nonpaying customers. However, the scrambling may not be thorough, and audio and video from the adult movies may "bleed through" to nonpaying customers.

There was a solution for parents. In Section 504 of the Telecomm Act, Congress required cable companies to fully scramble or completely block any cable channel at the customer's request. A cable company could not charge for this service. Still, lawmakers knew that many people would not take advantage of Section 504, and children would still have easy access to adult programming by watching signal bleeds.

Congress reacted to those concerns in Section 505 of the Telecomm Act of 1996. Section 505 mandated the following rules regarding signal bleed: (a) Cable systems offering channels dedicated primarily to sexually explicit "adult" programming must *fully scramble* the audio and video from those channels so nonsubscribers cannot receive the signals. (b) If the cable operator does not fully scramble these signals, the sexually explicit programming may be shown only between 10:00 p.m. and 6:00 a.m., when children are less likely to view the bleed through.

Playboy Entertainment Group, which operates sexually explicit cable channels, said that Section 505 was unconstitutional. In 2000, in *U.S. v. Playboy,*[48] the Supreme Court ruled 5-4 in favor of Playboy and overturned Section 505. Requiring complete blocking of these channels placed economic burdens on some cable systems, the court pointed out. Complete blocking is not always available and can be expensive. Also, forcing some cable companies to offer sexually explicit channels only between 10:00 p.m. and 6:00 a.m. meant that there were 18 hours each day when the material was not available to consenting adults who wished to view it.

---

[47]Wallenstein, A. (2004, March 26). Cable industry on high alert in rush to legislation. *Hollywood Reporter.* Retrieved October 28, 2004, from http://www.hollywoodreporter.com/thr/article_display.jsp? vnu_content_id= 1000473849

[48]529 U.S. 803 (2000)

Playboy presented studies that showed that as many as 50% of customers would purchase the adult programming prior to 10 p.m. The Supreme Court agreed that it was unfair to make companies like Playboy lose revenue because of Section 505. Section 504 (giving parents the option to fully block these channels for free) is the "less restrictive" way to protect children. Besides, the court said, "Section 504 would provide as much protection against unwanted programming as would Section 505."

The government did not prove that signal bleed was a significant problem or concern for many children or parents. Studies in 1996 and 1997 showed that fewer than 0.5% of cable customers had taken advantage of blocking options under Section 504. The court said this showed that the public greeted the problem of bleed through "with a collective yawn."

FAQ

Don't many cable companies do this signal bleed on purpose?

Many cable companies will not admit to it, but adult channel signal bleed is often intentional. Cable operators know that many people will sit and watch the signal bleed, trying to discern the scrambled images. As a result, people become frustrated and wind up purchasing the adult programming so they can "see what they are missing."

CABLE ACCESS CHANNELS

In the 1992 Cable Act, Section 10 stated that a cable operator could refuse to carry programs on PEG channels if those programs contained "obscene material, sexually explicit conduct, or material soliciting or promoting unlawful conduct." Section 506 of the Telecommunications Act of 1996 had similar provisions regarding "obscenity, indecency or nudity."

The Supreme Court overturned parts of these rules in *Denver Area Educational Telecommunications Consortium v. FCC.*[49] The court's ruling here is a bit confusing, but the justices basically ruled that PEG channels should be treated as limited public forums, and therefore cable companies may not censor material on them. (Keep in mind that LFAs usually give educational authorities and governmental bodies the power to choose the programming that appears on educational and government access channels, respectively. These types of officials are very unlikely to use these channels to air indecent programming. Indecency is usually an issue on *public* access channels, which are supposed to be open to everyone.)

Cable companies do have the right to censor material that is believed to be legally obscene. Also, cable companies may choose not to carry indecent programming on *leased access* or pay-per-view channels. The Supreme Court said that cable companies are allowed to make private business decisions about the commercial channels they carry. For example, if a cable company does not want to carry an "adult" movie channel, the government cannot force the cable company to do so.

---

[49]518 U.S. 727 (1996)

Indecency Regulations on "Pay-per-View"

The 1992 Cable Act required cable operators who offered sexually oriented material on leased access channels (or pay-per-view) to place it all on a single channel. The cable operator then had to block that channel to everyone except subscribers, and those subscribers had to request the program 30 days ahead of time.

The Supreme Court struck down this part of the act for two reasons: (a) It did not allow anyone to subscribe to such channels on the spur of the moment, and (b) it created a chilling effect—people might be afraid to request a channel 30 days in advance for fear of appearing on a list of persons who wanted to watch "dirty movies."

However, the court ruled that it was all right for a cable operator simply to refuse to air any leased access channels featuring "indecent" material. The court said that cable operators have a First Amendment right to carry or *not* to carry certain channels. In other words, the government cannot force a cable operator to carry an "indecent" or "adult" channel if the cable operator does not want to. However, once a cable operator chooses to offer these channels, it may not censor material on those channels.

FAQ

Are cable companies allowed to set up a safe harbor for indecent material on public access channels?

There are no court rulings on cable companies channeling indecent programming to late night on access channels. However, many cable companies and franchising authorities have such channeling rules in place and will only air "indecent" programming late at night on public access channels. When people are applying to air shows on cable access, the cable company often requires people to indicate whether a program has "adult" content: nudity, explicit sexual discussions, foul language, and so on. Thus, for now, many cable companies are only airing indecent material after 10:00 p.m. on public access channels.

This is one reason why many cable companies have government and educational access channels but not public access channels. Many franchising authorities want to avoid the hassles that often come with public access channels, so they choose to offer only educational and governmental access channels, where issues of indecency are rare or nonexistent.

The "openness" of public access channels has led to interesting controversies and some bizarre programming across the country. Some residents in Holland, MI, for example, became upset in 2001 with some of the risqué material appearing on their cable system's public access channel. One video produced by a group known as Crackhead Productions aired at 2:00 a.m. and included "simulated sex with stuffed animals, faked masturbation, and plenty of swear words."[50] The video also showed three young men running through a wooded area trying to keep away from a "twig" that was trying to "rape" them. In a story from the *Holland Sentinel,* the nonprofit agency that

---

[50]Jesse, D. (2002, January 4). Public access channel says it can't bar offensive video. *Holland Sentinel.* Retrieved June 15, 2002, from http://www.thehollandsentinel.net/stories/010402/loc_010402.shtml

runs the public access channel said it does not "censor or review anything" because the agency is "not allowed to" by law.[51] However, the agency only allows "indecent" programs to air between 11:00 p.m. and 6:00 a.m.

INDECENT PHONE SERVICES

In the 1980s, Congress became concerned about the number of "dial-a-porn" services and especially about how easily children were accessing these services. These phone services offered "adult" material: People could call in to hear sexually explicit discussions or advice. These were usually 900 area code numbers for which the caller would pay by the minute. Across the country, parents began getting phone bills in the thousands of dollars because their children had been secretly calling "dial-a-porn" numbers and listening for hours, at rates like $4.95 a minute. (At that rate, a one-hour phone call costs $297.) On top of the cost, parents were outraged that children could have such easy access to sexually explicit material over the telephone.

Congress Tries to Ban "Dial-a-Porn" and Fails

In response, Congress passed a law banning sexually oriented telephone messages. In 1989, the Supreme Court struck down the law in *Sable Communications v. FCC*.[52] The court said that these phone messages for adults might be indecent, but they are not legally obscene; therefore, they cannot be banned. It pointed out that there are feasible methods for keeping children from accessing these services (e.g., blocks on 900 numbers, age-verification measures at the dial-a-porn site). Also, the phone, unlike broadcasting, requires the listener to take affirmative steps to receive the communication.

Congress Passes Another "Dial-a-Porn" Law

After the *Sable* ruling, Congress rewrote the law so it would stand up in court. The new dial-a-porn law contains the following guidelines to help limit access by children and nonconsenting adults without violating the rights of consenting adults.

If a phone company handles the billing for these calls, it must offer what is called *reverse blocking*. This means the phone company may only connect a person with a dial-a-porn service if that person or telephone subscriber has requested *in writing* that they be given access to such services.

Dial-a-porn services may not "start the meter" with a customer unless the service has taken measures to ensure that the caller is an adult. This would include (a) asking in advance for a credit card number or (b) asking for a special code given only to verified adult customers.

FAQ

Can't minors still get around these safeguards?

---

[51]*Ibid.*, p. 1.

[52]492 U.S. 115 (1989)

Yes. However, the courts said the new law struck an appropriate balance between providing at least some safeguards for children and protecting the rights of dial-a-porn providers. In 1991, a court of appeals upheld this newer dial-a-porn law as a "narrowly tailored effort to serve the compelling interest of preventing minors from being exposed to indecent telephone messages."[53]

INDECENCY AND THE INTERNET

By the mid-1990s, the Internet had become a fairly commonplace communication tool in the United States, with approximately 40 million people hooked up to the Information Superhighway. Fewer people were sending letters through the mail and more were using e-mail, a much faster and cheaper means of contacting persons. People were also discovering the vast amount of information available out there on the World Wide Web.

People soon also discovered that there were a lot of sexually oriented Web sites in cyberspace. Parents were shocked to find out how easy it was for their children to access "adult" Web sites, either accidentally or intentionally. The concerns of these parents were soon communicated to lawmakers in Washington, who decided that something needed to be done to try to protect children from pornographic material in cyberspace.

Communications Decency Act

The Communications Decency Act (CDA) was the result. It was part of the Telecommunications Act of 1996. The CDA made it illegal to "knowingly" make available to minors any "obscene, lewd, lascivious, filthy or indecent" material.[54] The CDA then clarified the definition of *indecent*. It said it would be illegal for any person to "knowingly" use the Internet to make accessible or to send to minors any material that "depicts or describes, in terms patently offensive as measured by contemporary community standards, sexual or excretory activities or organs."[55]

FAQ

Isn't this the indecency definition from *Pacifica*?

Yes. However, the *Pacifica* definition applied only to the public airwaves or to broadcasters. Attempts to apply *Pacifica* to the telephone or to cable TV failed. The courts ruled that telephone and cable lines were not as "intrusive" as the public airwaves and were not subject to indecency regulation.

---

[53] *Information Providers' Coalition for Defense of the First Amendment v. FCC*, 928 F.2d 866 (9th Cir. 1991)

[54] U.S.C. § 223 (a) (1) (A-B)

[55] 47 U.S.C. § 223 (d)

FAQ

Should we treat the Internet like the public airwaves or like cable?

Some argued that the Internet is like cable because it must be "invited" into a person's home. On the other hand, some argued that the Internet is more like the public airwaves because it has become so pervasive in our society. The courts would soon rule that the Internet is indeed more like cable.

Soon after the passage of the CDA, many operators of adult Web sites cried censorship. They said that the CDA was a violation of their First Amendment rights to provide legal pornographic material to consenting adults. They said that there was no way to ensure that children would not access these sites, but the CDA would hold those sites responsible *if* children accessed them. Many adult Web sites, to make their customers aware of the new law, simply shut down and would often post a message such as this:

> Because of a new law passed by Congress called the Communications Decency Act, this Web site has been forced to shut down or face criminal prosecution. Contact your member of Congress to let him or her know how you feel about this new form of censorship.

President Clinton signed the CDA, making it a law, and he directed the Justice Department, under Attorney General Janet Reno, to enforce it. The American Civil Liberties Union (ACLU) filed suit against the government, saying the CDA violated the First Amendment.

In 1997, in *Reno v. ACLU*,[56] the U.S. Supreme Court threw out the CDA, saying the Internet could not be treated like the public airwaves. The Internet is unlike radio and TV. It is "invited into the home," much like cable TV. The government cannot use a "scarcity rationale" like it uses to support regulation of broadcasters. Justice John Paul Stevens pointed out that 200 million people were expected to be using the Internet by 1999, and that would hardly make the Internet a "scarce" resource.

The Internet should have "the highest protection from government intrusion," the Supreme Court said, because "government regulation of the content of speech is more likely to interfere with the free exchange of ideas than to encourage it." Also, in this case, the definitions for such words as *lewd* and *lascivious* were too vague. The court said the CDA could possibly lead to prosecutions of people using the Internet to discuss "birth control practices, homosexuality . . . the consequences of prison rape." The court said the CDA had not been "carefully tailored." The desire to protect children from sexually explicit Web sites was understandable, the court said, but the CDA was "unnecessarily broad." The court suggested other remedies, such as filters or blocks, to help limit children's access to such sites.

The Supreme Court *did* uphold one portion of the CDA: the ban on obscene material. The Court ruled that obscenity is not protected in any form, including via the Internet. This includes child pornography.

In essence, the court ruled that the Internet should be treated like books and newspapers and given the "highest protection" from government regulation.

---

[56]521 U.S. 844 (1997)

Child Online Protection Act (CDA Part II?)

In 1998, Congress continued to receive complaints from citizens about the vast array of adult Web sites that were easily accessed by children. Congress responded with the Child Online Protection Act (COPA).[57] Congress knew from *Reno* that it could not use indecency rules to try to regulate the Internet. However, Congress had seen success in the courts with its safeguards for children regarding dial-a-porn. So, in COPA, Congress required Web site operators to use credit card numbers or other screening methods to prevent children from accessing sexually explicit material.

Under COPA, persons could face $50,000 fines and/or 6 months in prison for "knowingly" using the Internet with "any communication for commercial purposes that is available to any minor and that includes any material that is harmful to minors" (minor in this case referred to a person less than 17 years old). COPA also used a Miller Test for children:

> The term "material that is harmful to minors" means any communication, picture, image, graphic image file, article, recording, writing, other matter of any kind that is obscene or that—
>
> A. the average person, applying contemporary community standards, would find, taking the material as a whole and *with respect to minors,* is designed to appeal to, or is designed to pander to, the prurient interest.
>
> B. depicts, describes, or represents, in a manner patently offensive with respect to minors, an actual or simulated sexual act or sexual contact, an actual or simulated normal or perverted sexual act, or a lewd exhibition of the genitals or post-pubescent female breast; and
>
> C. taken as a whole, lacks serious literary, artistic, political or scientific value for *minors.* (Italics added.)

The ACLU and other groups immediately filed suit, saying that COPA was similar to the CDA. They argued that the definition "harmful to minors" was vague and created a chilling effect, leading many Web sites to censor themselves out of fear of prosecution.

A federal judge granted an injunction against COPA, not allowing the law to go into effect until after a trial on the act's constitutionality. A federal appeals court upheld that injunction in 2000.[58]

In May 2002, in *Ashcroft v. ACLU,*[59] the U.S. Supreme Court remanded the case to the appeals court for a more "comprehensive analysis" of several issues.

- ▣ *Community standards:* The Supreme Court asked for more clarification on how to apply "community standards" under COPA, wondering whether "the [national] variation in community standards renders the act substantially overbroad."
- ▣ *Venue:* What would be the venue or location of trials that handled violations of COPA? The court assumed it would be local courts, and the justices suggested that would create problems: "The more venues the Government has to choose from, the more speech will be chilled by variation across the communities."
- ▣ *Material as a whole:* The court said that this definition created another problem. COPA would appear to punish large Web sites "which include only a small amount of the material that might run afoul of the act."

---

[57] 47 U.S.C. § 231

[58] *ACLU v. Reno,* 217 F.3d 162 (D.C. Cir. 2000)

[59] 122 S. Ct. 1700 (2002)

In March 2003, the appeals court found COPA unconstitutional, saying it was too vague and broad and would force Web site operators to engage in self-censorship. In October 2003, the U.S. Supreme Court agreed to hear an appeal of that ruling from the U.S. Justice Department. COPA has never been enforced.

FAQ

Are there any other ways that the government can protect children from pornography on the Internet?

Congress was successful in its next attempt.

Children's Internet Protection Act

By 2000, libraries across the country had connected to the Internet, providing patrons with access to the Information Superhighway. Many of those patrons were children, and some parents became alarmed that libraries had no filtering systems to prevent children from downloading pornography on these computers.

In December 2000, Congress reacted to concerns of these parents and passed the Children's Internet Protection Act (CIPA).

At first, CIPA applied only to schools and public libraries that received certain government funding (such as Universal Service Discounts or funds made available through the Library Services and Technology Act). The libraries had to use blocks or filters to prevent children from seeing any visual images considered "harmful to minors." They were also required to install filters to prevent all patrons, regardless of age, from viewing obscene material or any child pornography. The act did not require the use of any specific type of filtering software. Libraries just had to prove that they were using effective blocking mechanisms. They would be allowed to disable the filters for "bona fide research or other lawful purposes."

Libraries not following these guidelines would lose federal funding.

The American Library Association and other groups charged that CIPA was a violation of the First Amendment. In May 2002, in *American Library Association v. U.S.,*[60] a federal district court ruled that CIPA violated the First Amendment by violating the rights of adults. The court said that much of the blocking software available had problems and would "deny patrons access to constitutionally protected speech that libraries would otherwise provide to patrons." Shortly after the ruling, in an interview on CNN's *Larry King Live*, Attorney General John Ashcroft said he would fight to uphold CIPA. He said, "We've got a major problem in our culture, especially as it relates to the Internet and pornography and child pornography." He added, "I think the courts need to find a way to respect the Constitution and defend our children."[61]

---

[60]2002 U.S. Dist. LEXIS 9537

[61]Friedan, T. (2002, May 31). *Justice reviewing Internet screening ruling, may appeal*. Retrieved June 13, 2002, from http://www.cnn.com/2002/LAW/05/31/justice.internet.screening/index.html

In June 2003, the U.S. Supreme Court echoed Ashcroft's sentiments when it voted 6-3 to overturn the appeals court decision and reinstate CIPA. In *U.S. v. American Library Association,*[62] the court ruled that the government has a substantial interest in protecting children from inappropriate material and, at the same time, protecting the First Amendment rights of adults. In a plurality opinion, Chief Justice Rehnquist wrote that public libraries had traditionally excluded pornography from their print collections, so the libraries should not find it burdensome to restrict access to Internet pornography as well. Pornography in libraries is a problem in America, and the government has a legitimate right to take steps to prevent children from accessing it. The use of filtering software did not violate adult patrons' First Amendment rights; if a patron had to ask for help to disable a filter, this was a minimal burden, outweighed by the need to protect children.

In a concurring opinion, Justice Kennedy agreed that there is a substantial government interest in protecting children from inappropriate material. However, although he supported CIPA "on its face" in this case, he said he might rule differently in the future if it were proven that many libraries could not disengage filtering software adequately or if "it is shown that adult users' election to view Constitutionally protected Internet material is burdened in some other substantial way."

FAQ

Isn't this law basically redundant? Don't most libraries already take measures to keep children away from Internet pornography?

Many libraries argued that they do not need government to tell them how to address the issue of children viewing pornography on library computers. Many libraries allow children to use the Internet only if their parents have signed a permission form. Also, many libraries only allow minors to use computers in the children's section of the library, and those computers are usually set up with filtering software.

Violence

The Supreme Court has often recognized the government's right to protect children from certain harms. The government, for example, prohibits children from using alcohol and cigarettes. Child pornography is illegal. The government may remove children from abusive home situations. Many lawmakers say children also need to be protected from certain kinds of broadcasting content, such as sex and violence. This section of the chapter focuses on just how much power the government should have in controlling violent media content to protect children.

We have already seen one example of this in *FCC v. Pacifica,* which gives the FCC the power to regulate indecent material on the broadcast airwaves. The main rationale is to

---

[62]539 U.S. 194 (2003)

protect children. Broadcasters face fines if they air indecent programming "at a time of day when children are likely to be in the audience."

FAQ

Can extremely violent programming also lead to indecency fines?

Note that the definition for indecency focuses solely on "sexual and excretory activities or organs." Violent material does not fall under this definition. Unless the violence is *sexually* graphic, the FCC has no jurisdiction under indecency guidelines to punish excessively violent material.

Violent Music Lyrics Spark Controversy

In 1991, rap artist Ice-T and his new band Body Count recorded a song called "Cop Killer," which appeared on the group's self-titled debut album. The album was released in the spring of 1992. One month later, Los Angeles experienced racial riots in the aftermath of the acquittal of four police officers accused of beating Rodney King.

Not much later, in Texas, the Combined Law Enforcement Associations of Texas (CLEAT) became aware of the song "Cop Killer." CLEAT said the song was not only offensive, but advocated the murder of police officers with lyrics such as "I'm 'bout to dust some cops off," "tonight we get even," and "Die Pig Die!"

The song had been released on Warner Brothers records, so CLEAT decided to go after the Time-Warner company. CLEAT asked the public to boycott any products or media owned by Time-Warner. This included *Time* magazine, HBO, and movies such as *Batman* and *Lethal Weapon*. President George H. W. Bush and Vice President Dan Quayle spoke out publicly against the song. Police picketed outside of Time-Warner headquarters. The controversy received heavy media coverage.

Sales of the *Body Count* album tripled as a result. In July 1992, CLEAT discovered that Time-Warner had been marketing the Body Count album by distributing it in little black "body bags." Shortly after, Time-Warner shareholders met for their annual meeting and criticized the company for marketing the song. A police officer who had been blinded by a criminal's shotgun blast told his story to the shareholders, and actor Charlton Heston also spoke at the meeting, which drew even more media attention.

Twelve days later, Ice-T held a press conference to announce he was taking "Cop Killer" off the album. Ice-T said he took this action to prove he was not trying to make money from a song that appeared to promote killing police officers. The *Body Count* album was rereleased in October 1992 without "Cop Killer." Time-Warner refused to release Ice-T's next album, *Home Invasion*, and the rap artist moved to another label.

What was seen as too much violence and sexuality in the media would soon lead lawmakers to pass a rating system for TV shows.

The V-Chip and the TV Rating System

For decades, the motion picture industry in America has been rating its movies. Today, the five basic ratings are G, PG, PG-13, R, and NC-17. The PG-13 rating came about in the

1980s because of a concern about violence and sexuality in movies. Some PG movies, such as *Gremlins* and *Indiana Jones and the Temple of Doom*, had graphic violence. This upset many parents who had believed that the PG rating meant the movie was relatively safe for their children. Those parents argued that although they believed the movie did not deserve an R rating, they did not think "PG" provided enough warning. As a result, the movie industry developed the PG-13 rating as a middle ground between PG and R.

In the 1990s, parents began asking lawmakers to come up with a similar rating system for TV. Parents expressed frustration about sitting down to watch a TV sitcom that they thought was safe to watch with their kids, only to find out that the show contained rather explicit sexual dialogue.

In Section 551(a) of the Telecommunications Act of 1996, Congress echoed those parents' concerns:

> Congress finds that American children watch a significant amount of television, much of which contains acts of violence and casual treatment of sexual matters. Congress also finds that studies have shown children are negatively affected by exposure to sex and violence on television. Therefore, Congress finds that there is a compelling governmental interest in empowering parents to limit the negative influences of programming containing sex and violence.

This "empowerment" for parents came in the form of the V-chip. This electronic chip, when placed in televisions, would allow viewers to block any programs with a certain rating. Section 551 mandated that the FCC set up an advisory committee to develop a TV rating system that would label shows according to violent, sexual, or other indecent content. Also, television manufacturers were required to place a V-chip in all TV sets with picture screens 13 inches or larger.

Eventually, the FCC gathered input from various groups (broadcasters, filmmakers, parents' groups) and announced the new rating system. There are six basic ratings for TV shows. The first two are for children's programs, and the other four for all other shows.

Children's Programming

TV-Y means "this program is suitable for all children." However, the elements and themes in a TV-Y show are specifically created for children from 2 to 6 years old. There should be no elements of this show that would frighten children. *TV-Y7* means "this program is targeted to older children" (7 years old and older). Children watching a TV-Y7 program are expected to be able to distinguish between make-believe and reality. Parents are cautioned that this programming might contain comedic or fantasy violence that could frighten children younger than 7. *TV-Y7-FV* means "this program contains fantasy violence," which may be more intense than the violence or fantasy in regular TV-Y7 shows.

General Programming

TV-G means "general audience." These programs are considered suitable for all ages. TV-G shows are not designed specifically for children; however, parents will probably feel comfortable letting younger children watch this program without supervision. TV-G shows should contain few or no sexual situations or language, no strong language, and little or no violence.

TV-PG means "parental guidance suggested." This kind of program may be inappropriate for younger children. Parents will probably want to watch this show with their younger children. The program will contain one or more of the following: moderate violence (V), infrequent coarse language (L), some sexual situations (S), and some suggestive dialogue (D).

TV-14 means "parents strongly cautioned." These programs may be inappropriate for children younger than 14. Parents are strongly cautioned about program content, which will contain one or more of the following: intense violence (V), strong coarse language (L), intense sexual situations (S), and intensely suggestive dialogue (D).

TV-MA means "mature audience only." Programs with this rating are designed specifically for adults and may be inappropriate for children younger than 17. Parents are urged to exercise extreme caution because these programs contains one or more of the following: graphic violence (V), crude indecent language (L), explicit sexual content (S), and explicit sexual dialogue (D).

FAQ

Are all types of programs rated?

No. The following programs are not rated: news programs and news interview shows, sports shows and sporting events (pseudosports such as professional wrestling do get ratings for violence, dialogue, and sexual situations), and movies on premium cable channels (these movies have been rated already by the Motion Picture Association of America, so one of the following ratings will appear: G, PG, PG-13, R, NC-17). However, movies or shows produced specifically for a premium pay channel will get a TV rating.

FAQ

Is this rating system mandatory?

The rating system is purely voluntary. However, as of 2002, all of the major TV networks and the majority of cable channels use the rating system. Cable channels that are not using the rating system include news channels, Black Entertainment Television (BET), the Home Shopping Network (HSN), and the TV Guide Channel.

TV show producers or the networks decide the rating for each show. Having a government agency doing the ratings would lead to accusations of government censorship of certain programs. Besides, no government agency would have the time and resources to monitor and rate all of the TV shows that are aired every day.

How the V-Chip Works

The V-chip electronically detects the rating for a program. The rating appears in the upper left portion of the TV screen during the first 15 seconds of a program. For programs longer than an hour, the symbol will reappear at the beginning of each hour.

Viewers may program the V-chip to block any programs with certain ratings. TV sets should include instructions about how to program the V-chip. You will usually be asked to enter a personal identification number (PIN).

The V-chip in most televisions should allow you to block, for example, a TV-14-S show while allowing a TV-14-V show to come through. Some sets may also allow you to block a certain show at a certain time. You can also usually block an entire channel, if you wish.

Arguments Against the V-Chip

Although the V-chip looks like a good idea on paper and in principle, a lot of media critics and parents say the V-chip is not living up to expectations.

One problem, they say, is that the fox is guarding the henhouse. The producers or networks determine the ratings. In recent years, parents' groups have complained that shows do not get the ratings they deserve. A show may be given a TV-PG rating, but that is a judgment call. Others may watch that show and say it deserved a TV-14 rating. Did the show's producer purposely give the show a lesser rating so fewer parents would try to block it?

Complainants say the descriptors are vague. What is the difference between "intense" violence and "graphic" violence? Exactly what kinds of sexual humor make a show a TV-14 instead of a TV-PG? What are the specific guidelines for determining these ratings?

The V-chip is ineffective in that most parents are not using it. A 2001 Kaiser Family Foundation study found that only 36% of parents who owned a TV with a V-chip have used it to block a program, and only 17% use it on a regular basis. Those same studies show most parents either do not understand the ratings or do not even know the ratings exist.

Critics say that show ratings may actually entice a child to watch a program to see why the show got, for example, a TV-14 or TV-MA rating. The same child might ignore such a program if it had no rating.

The V-chip may lead to self-censorship. Are producers editing certain content to avoid a rating such as TV-MA?

Critics say it is not fair to exempt news and sports. Hockey and other sports sometimes contain brutal and bloody fights. Newscasts sometimes contain graphic pictures. Doesn't the rating system basically imply that although *fake* violence in movies and shows must be monitored, there is no need to monitor *real* violence in news and sports?

Even so, many parents claim that the V-chip and the rating system are better than nothing at all. They claim that these at least provide them with some sort of guideline regarding the content of shows and allow for better control of what their children are viewing.

BROADCAST TV AND CHILDREN'S PROGRAMMING RULES

Action for Children's Television (ACT) was a consumer group that lobbied Congress about issues relating to children and broadcasting. In public hearings in 1971, ACT urged the FCC to require commercial TV stations to air at least 14 hours of children's programs each week. ACT also wanted these shows to be targeted toward certain age groups, not just "children" in general. The FCC did not adopt these guidelines. Instead, the commission suggested that broadcasters try to follow the ACT guidelines voluntarily.

Children's TV in the 1980s

Until 1984, the government had limits on advertising in children's programming. A children's TV show could not have more than 12 minutes of commercials during weekdays and 9.5 minutes on weekends. In 1984, the FCC dropped these limits. The FCC said the marketplace would determine how much advertising was acceptable in children's television. The commission also noted that cable channels and other outlets were providing children's programming, so there was no longer a need for the government to mandate that all broadcasters carry educational programming.

The TV industry saw a chance to make lots of money. Children's shows soon had many more commercials. TV also was soon flooded with cartoons that were basically 30-minute ads for toys. The first show of this type was *Masters of the Universe*, created to market He-Man toys. Other toy manufacturers saw the money-making possibilities, and TV quickly had other cartoons that were basically designed as advertisements for toys (*GI Joe, Care Bears, Transformers*).

Sales of toys related to TV shows doubled from 1983 to 1989. Also, nearly 80% of all toy sales by 1989 had a tie-in to a TV show. In 1987, toy makers financed 80% of children's programming.

The Children's Television Act of 1990

Lawmakers in Washington soon started hearing complaints from citizens about the commercialization of children's television. Congress responded with the Children's Television Act (CTA) of 1990. This act gave broadcasters some distinct rules to follow regarding children's shows. For example, there were now limitations on commercials. TV broadcasters must limit advertising in children's shows to 12 minutes per hour on weekdays and 10½ minutes on weekends. In March 2004, the FCC voted that satellite TV providers such as DIRECTV and Dish Network must also abide by these rules. Also, no "program-length commercials" were allowed. This meant that broadcasters were prohibited from airing commercials for a toy during or directly adjacent to a show featuring that toy. For example, a broadcaster could not air an ad for a GI Joe action figure during the *GI Joe* program. Some people had argued that the *GI Joe* show itself was nothing more than an ad for GI Joe products. However, the FCC ruled that a 30-minute show based on a toy or other product is *not* in itself a program-length commercial.

Broadcast license renewals would be reviewed according to "the extent to which the licensee . . . has served the educational and informational needs of children through the licensee's overall programming." This included a requirement that TV broadcasters must "air some standard-length programming specifically designed to serve the educational and informational needs of children."

FAQ

Aren't some of these guidelines rather vague? For example, what does "some" children's programming mean? What counts as "educational"?

The FCC began enforcing these guidelines in October 1991 but soon ran into problems with its vague definitions of "some" and "educational." "Some" apparently meant at least one 30-minute show each week, but the guidelines were never clearly established. Also, some broadcasters argued that the following shows should count as "educational and informational": *Mighty Morphin Power Rangers, The Flintstones, The Jetsons, Biker Mice From Mars, America's Funniest Home Videos, X-Men, Yogi Bear, Saved by the Bell,* and *Woody Woodpecker.*

The FCC also discovered that among those stations that were indeed airing truly educational programs, many aired the shows early in the morning. A 1993 study of the top 20 TV markets found that 44% of truly educational children's shows were airing at 6:30 a.m. or earlier, times when many children were still asleep. Many educational shows get low ratings, so broadcasters put them in these less desirable time slots.

Another trick of broadcasters was to schedule children's shows in what are called "preemptible" time slots. An example: A TV station schedules a children's show for 2:00 p.m. on Saturday afternoons, but the station knows that it will often air network sporting events during that time. Thus the children's show is constantly preempted.

By 1993, Congress and the president began warning broadcasters to take the CTA seriously. TV stations across the country began a mad scramble, looking for legitimate, quality children's programming. Still, Congress realized it had to close some of the gaping loopholes in the CTA.

New CTA Guidelines

In 1996, Congress updated the CTA and mandated the following rules regarding children's TV programs.

"Core programs" will (a) be aired between 7:00 a.m. and 10:00 p.m. (these programs must be identified as educational and informational for children when they are aired), (b) have education as a significant goal, (c) have a clear objective and target age group, (d) be regularly scheduled (so no more preemptible time slots), (e) be at least 30 minutes in length, and (f) be aired at least 3 hours each week.

During license renewal, TV stations must provide proof that they have followed these new rules.

MUSIC WARNING LABELS

The early 1980s saw an increased public awareness of lyrics in popular music. Parents' groups and politicians were increasingly concerned about the sexuality, violence, and crude language in many popular songs.

1984: The Music Industry Takes Some Heat

In May 1984, Surgeon General C. Everett Koop condemned music videos for their sexual imagery. He claimed that people who watched too many music videos would "have trouble having satisfying relationships with the opposite sex . . . when you're raised with rock music that uses both pornography and violence." Around the country, citizens began to pressure local cable companies to stop carrying MTV.

Also that year, Wal-Mart said it would not sell the album *Love at First Sting* by the Scorpions because the album cover showed a partially nude couple, with the man tattooing the woman's thigh. PolyGram Records changed the cover, and Wal-Mart agreed to sell the album.

In December of that year, the National Coalition on Television Violence reported that music videos contained unnecessary and sometimes graphic violence. The coalition analyzed 900 music videos that had aired on MTV and WTBS, and its study found 17.9 "violent acts" per hour. The authors of the study said "the intense sadistic and sexual violence of a large number of rock videos is overwhelming." The coalition suggested that the government develop regulations for music videos.

That attempt at government regulation came partly in the form of a group of prominent political women. In 1984, they formed the Parents Music Resource Center (PMRC). The group's most famous member was Tipper Gore, the wife of Senator and future Vice President Al Gore. The PMRC said it was concerned about increasing references to violence, sex, drugs, and alcohol in popular music.

In 1985, the PMRC convinced the U.S. Senate Commerce Committee to conduct public hearings concerning the "alarming trends" in popular music. The hearings got a lot of media attention because of the subject matter and because of some of the famous musicians who testified including John Denver, Frank Zappa, and Dee Snider, the lead singer of the rock group Twisted Sister. The hearings were also controversial because the PMRC comprised many politicians' wives, including Tipper Gore, Susan Baker (wife of Treasury Secretary James Baker), Georgie Packwood (wife of Oregon Senator Bob Packwood), and Nancy Thurmond (wife of South Carolina Senator Strom Thurmond). Could senators on the committee be objective when grilling the wives of their fellow senators?

FAQ

Did the PMRC's efforts really have any impact?

Yes. The efforts of the PMRC were soon felt outside of the congressional hearing rooms. In 1985 alone, the TV show *American Bandstand* would not allow Sheena Easton to sing her song "Sugar Walls" because the PMRC had criticized the song's sexual references. The album *Dreams of a Lifetime* by Marvin Gaye originally had a song entitled "Sanctified Pussy." Fearing a backlash against the album, the record company had the song's title changed to "Sanctified Lady." San Antonio, TX, banned anyone 13 and younger from going to rock concerts on city-owned property. The head of the National Association of Broadcasters asked 45 major record companies to print lyric sheets for all songs sent to radio stations.

One of the PMRC's main goals was to convince the Senate to require music companies to put ratings or warning labels on recordings containing graphic lyrics. The PMRC succeeded. In November 1985, the Recording Industry Association of America (RIAA) agreed to place parental warning labels on any album containing graphic references to violence, sex, or drug use. This was part of an agreement reached between the PMRC, the national PTA, and the RIAA.

Many music artists claim the labels are a form of censorship. They say some people will be too embarrassed to purchase music with a label reading "explicit lyrics." Others would argue the opposite and say the music becomes more appealing because it appears "forbidden." Other arguments:

- ▣ *The wrong music gets labeled.* For example, Frank Zappa's 1986 album *Jazz from Hell* got an explicit lyrics label. The album is completely instrumental.
- ▣ *Self-censorship.* The RIAA admits that record companies will ask artists to rewrite songs or sometimes delete a song from an album to avoid getting the label.
- ▣ *Some stores refuse to sell labeled albums.* Probably the most famous example of this practice is Wal-Mart, the nation's largest music retailer. Kmart has a similar policy. The record companies often send "clean" versions of albums to Wal-Mart and Kmart, but the artists say this is censorship.
- ▣ *Radio stations avoid labeled songs.* Program directors are more likely to disregard songs with "explicit lyrics" labels. Artists say the label creates a stigma.
- ▣ *An album gets a stigma for one "bad" song.* Is it fair to call an album "explicit" when there is just one song on it that led to the parental advisory label?

Studies of music stores have shown that less than 1% (about 0.5%) of music gets labeled. The RIAA says that the average retail music store has roughly 110,000 different albums for sale, and only about 500 of those albums will have an advisory label.

FAQ

Who determines what albums get the label?

The record companies and the artists make the determination. If the record company has problems with any songs, the artist has two choices: change some lyrics or release the album with an explicit content label. The pressure from the record company to avoid a label may be a little more intense if the album is seen as having great mainstream appeal.

SUMMARY

Indecency, unlike obscenity, has First Amendment protection. However, it is a limited protection. The courts have given the FCC the right to punish broadcasters who air indecent material outside of the safe harbor times of 10:00 p.m. to 6:00 a.m. Those punishments are usually in the form of fines.

However, the FCC and the government do not have the right to regulate indecency on cable, cable access channels, or the Internet. The courts have upheld limited government restrictions on indecent messages provided over the telephone ("dial-a-porn").

The government has mandated tools such as the V-chip in an effort to help parents control what content their children see on TV. Studies show that only small numbers of parents actually use the devices. The government also instituted a TV rating system to help inform viewers about program content. Congress passed the Children's Television Act to mandate that TV stations air certain amounts of educational programming each week.

13

Copyright: The Basics

What's Mine Is Mine

The Constitution of the United States, Article I, § 8, grants Congress the power "to promote the progress of science and useful arts by securing for limited times to authors and inventors the exclusive right to their respective writings and discoveries."

That exclusive right mentioned in the Constitution is called *copyright*. The framers of the Constitution wanted persons to have legal possession of their creations. Copyright is a legal protection for a variety of creative works and is also one of many "intellectual property" rights. The federal government has jurisdiction in all copyright cases.

In 1790, Congress passed the first federal Copyright Act. It allowed the creators of maps and books to get federal copyright protection for their works for 14-year periods. In the years to come, the federal government would extend copyright protection to other kinds of creative works, often in response to changing technology. For example, photographs became copyrightable in 1865.

In the early 1900s, the federal government dealt with copyright issues on newer technologies in the 1909 Copyright Act. The most recent sweeping federal change in copyright laws came in the Copyright Act of 1976,[1] which gave the federal government sole jurisdiction on copyright issues. Today, the federal government continues to draft new laws to deal with newer technologies, such as the Internet and digital recordings.

Copyright law can seem very confusing. The book you are reading right now is copyrighted. It is a creative work, and the author has a right to profit from its use. The publisher of this book also has a legal right to control publications and first sales of this book. You have a right to read information here and share it verbally with friends. You even have a right to sell this book to someone else. However, you do not have a right to photocopy this text and sell the photocopied version. You also do not have a right to make this entire book available on the Internet on your personal Web site. The reasons for these restrictions will be discussed shortly.

The U.S. Copyright Office lists eight types of works that may be copyrighted: (a) literary works, including books, poetry, and computer programs; (b) musical works, including any accompanying spoken words; (c) dramatic works, including any accompanying

---

[1] 17 U.S.C. §§ 101-810

music; (d) choreographic works and pantomimes; (e) sound recordings; (f) motion pictures and other audiovisual works; (g) pictorial, graphic, and sculptural works; and (h) architectural works. *Important:* To be copyrightable, the work must be *fixed in a tangible medium of expression.* This means the work must be written down or recorded in some tangible way.

The U.S. Copyright Office also says there are many types of works that do *not* qualify for federal copyright protection: (a) noncreative compilations of facts and general information (including tape measures and rulers, calendars, telephone listings, height and weight charts, or any basic information taken from common sources such as public documents); (b) works not "fixed in a tangible medium of expression" (including improvised speeches and performances that have not been written down or recorded—for example, a pantomime not written down or recorded); (c) titles, names, short phrases, slogans, familiar symbols and designs, simple listings of ingredients or contents, and simple variations of typographic lettering, coloring, or ornamentation (however, many of the preceding may be protected as trademarks, which will be discussed later in this chapter); and (d) ideas, methods, concepts, principles, historical facts, procedures, systems, processes, discoveries, or devices (not including descriptions, explanations, or illustrations). In other words, copyright protects how you express a certain idea, but not the idea itself. Joe Smith may copyright his book about the Civil War, but that does not give him exclusive rights to that part of history. Others may also write books about the Civil War because the facts of the war cannot be copyrighted. However, copyright does protect such aspects as Smith's style, language, and arrangement of information. Therefore, copyright law does not protect a concept itself, but the tangible expression.

The Six Basic Rights of Copyright Holders

The 1976 Copyright Act gives copyright owners the following rights:

- ▣ *Reproduction.* The copyright holder may make audio recordings, copies, and so on.
- ▣ *Distribution.* The copyright holder may distribute recordings or copies of a work to the public. This includes sales of the work or any other transfer of ownership. It also includes rentals, leasing, and lending.
- ▣ *Derivative Works.* The copyright holder may make derivative works based on the original. An example would be a movie based on a novel. The movie is "derived" from the novel. Anyone else must have the permission of the copyright holder to make the movie. Another example of a derivative work is a musician doing a "cover" of a popular 1950s song.
- ▣ *Public Performance.* Permission from the copyright holder is needed to use the following copyrighted works in a public performance: musical works, literary works, choreographic works, dramatic works, pantomimes, motion pictures, and any other audiovisual works.
- ▣ *Public Display.* Permission from the copyright holder is needed to display these types of copyrighted works: musical, literary, choreographic, dramatic, graphic, pictorial, and sculptural works. This includes single images from motion pictures and other audiovisual works.

A sixth right was added in 1995 to cover sound recordings:

- ▣ *Public Digital Performance of a Sound Recording.* A 1995 law allows those who hold copyright to sound recordings to collect royalties when their work is "performed publicly by means of a digital audio transmission," such as through the Internet.

First Sale Doctrine

The U.S. Supreme Court first applied this doctrine in 1908 in *Bobbs-Merrill Co. v. Straus.*[2] The doctrine places a restriction on a copyright holder's right to distribute a work. The doctrine says a copyright holder has the right to profit from the *first sale* of a copy of a recording. If a person buys a CD, for example, the copyright owner makes money from that sale, but he or she surrenders control of what happens to that particular copy, including any rights to profit from future sales of that copy. Thus, if a person sells the CD a year later to a "used music" store, that person does not owe the copyright holder any money. The same rule applies if the store sells that used CD.

The first sale doctrine applies to video stores as well. Retailers can purchase videotapes and rent them to the public without the consent of the copyright holder. The law assumes that people are renting videotapes to view them and not to make illegal copies of them.

The law makes a different assumption, however, when it comes to the renting of records or compact discs. The first sale doctrine does not apply to the renting of recorded music because it is assumed that people's main purpose for the rental would be to make illegal copies of sound recordings. This was codified (put into law) with an amendment to the Copyright Act in 1984. The amendment says that phonograph records (and now other recordings, such as compact discs) cannot be rented without permission of the copyright holder. *Nonprofit libraries and educational institutions are exempt from this law.*

Works for Hire

Copyright law says that if a person creates a work as part of his or her job, the copyright for that work belongs to the employer. For example, the copyright for a TV reporter's story belongs to the station, unless the reporter has a contract that says otherwise.

A "work made for hire" is broken into two categories, as defined in Section 101 of the Copyright Act: (a) It is a work created by the employee as a result of that employee's regular job duties, or (b) it is a work specifically commissioned or ordered by the employer, in which there is a written agreement signed by all parties that the work is to be for hire. This includes nine categories of works: compilations, tests, answer materials for tests, instructional texts, atlases, supplementary works, transitions, parts of a motion picture or other audiovisual works, and contributions to a collective work.

However, for an independent contractor, or freelancer, the copyright for the work usually belongs to the individual and not the business that contracted the work. If there is a dispute, the courts will look at whether a person is truly an "independent" worker or more like an employee. If it is the latter, the creative work might belong to the company.

The Internet age has made copyright law more complicated in all areas, including works for hire. In the early 1990s, magazines and newspapers would frequently take articles written by freelance writers and place those articles on Web sites and electronic databases without getting the freelancer's permission. The freelancers argued for "electronic rights," or the right to be paid for the use of their works in electronic media. The publishers argued that the authors had already been paid for their work and that the Web site articles were simple reproductions, similar to a library transferring an article to microfiche, which is legal.

---

[2]210 U.S. 339 (1908)

The U.S. Supreme Court said this was a different type of copying and ruled for the freelancers in 2001 in *New York Times v. Tasini.*[3] The court said that electronic distribution resulted in the creation of new works, to which the freelancers had additional copyright protection. As a result of this ruling, most publishers now include special contract clauses to cover the electronic rights of freelancers.

Work for hire copyright law can be very complicated, and persons should investigate the intricacies of the law before entering into a creative endeavor with an employer. A work for hire copyright is good for 95 years after publication or 120 years after creation, whichever comes first.

OBTAINING A COPYRIGHT

Many people believe that a person must register with the U.S. Copyright Office to secure a copyright. This is not true. However, registering a copyright with the U.S. Copyright Office does have benefits. The registration provides a public record of the copyright, and the registration is helpful if the creator ever files a copyright infringement case in court.

As of this writing, a creator may register a work with the Register of Copyrights in Washington, DC, by filling out the necessary form and paying a $30 fee. This should be done within 3 months of creation or publication.

It is important to remember that even when a work is not registered, a copyright is secured *automatically* as soon as the work is created or "fixed in a tangible medium," such as in a book or sound recording. For example, a TV show's copyright is secured when the show is recorded on tape or film. A song's copyright is secured when the song is either written down (sheet music) or recorded (CD, cassette).

For "works in progress," whatever part of the work is completed and fixed in a tangible medium by a certain date is considered copyrighted as of that date.

Labeling your copyrighted work is simple. It must include three elements:

▣ The symbol © and the word *Copyright* or the abbreviation *Copr.*
▣ The year of first publication of the work (this may be omitted for works such as jewelry, stationery, toys, etc.)
▣ The name of the copyright owner, or a recognizable abbreviation of the owner's name

Examples: © 2004 W.I.U. Dept. of Communication *or* Copr. 2004 Western Illinois University *or* Copyright 2004 Roger Lee Sadler.

The format is similar for sound recordings (CD, cassette, phonograph record, etc.). Performance rights are indicated by the letter P in a circle: ℗ 2001 Heritage Music Inc.

The copyright notice should be easy to locate on the work. In books, the notice is often placed after the title page. Television shows often place a copyright notice in the closing credits. Radio programs often provide a verbal copyright notice in a show intro or outro. A photographer may choose to put the notice on the back of a picture because it would detract from the work to place the notice on the front.

---

[3]533 U.S. 483 (2001)

DURATION OF COPYRIGHT

The 1909 Copyright Act made copyrights good for up to 56 years (Copyright terms were 28 years, and those same copyrights could be renewed for a second 28-year period.) The 1976 Copyright Act gave copyrighted works protection for the life of the creator plus 50 years. For any works covered under the 1909 Act, the 1976 Act extended the copyright protection for another 75 years.

In 1998, the Sonny Bono Copyright Extension Act (also known as the 1998 Copyright Term Extension Act) made a copyright good for the life of the creator plus 70 years. A copyright holder can "bequeath" a copyright to survivors for 70 years after his or her death. If there are two or more creators who own the copyright, then the copyright is good for 70 years after the last creator dies. This 70-year rule applies to works created since January 1, 1978.

For pre-1978 works (that had a valid copyright when the 1998 law took effect), the copyright is now good for 95 years past the original copyright date. Works owned by corporations are also protected for 95 years.

However, in early 2002, a variety of groups filed suit against the U.S. Attorney General to overturn the Bono Act. The groups, including businesses and associations that use a lot of work in the public domain, argued that Congress did not have the legal authority to pass the 20-year copyright extension in the Bono Act.

In January 2003 in *Eldred v. Ashcroft*,[4] the U.S. Supreme Court upheld the Bono Act. The court ruled that the Constitution gives Congress "wide leeway to prescribe 'limited times' for copyright protection."

PUBLIC DOMAIN

When a copyright expires, the work becomes part of the *public domain*. That means the work can now be used by anyone for any purpose without having to pay royalties to the copyright owners. Examples of works in the public domain today would be many old church hymns, classical music by Bach and Mozart, or writings by someone like Plato. Many of these works were written before copyright law existed and have always been in the public domain, so these works can be used or copied by anyone.

However, a person can still copyright *versions or arrangements* of these works. Thus there can be a copyright on particular recordings of old musical works; the copyright holder just can not claim a copyright on the songs themselves. These old musical works, in essence, belong to us all. That is why it is called *public* domain. For example, government publications and materials are not copyrightable and are considered public domain.

Public domain was a major issue with the Bono Act. Many groups opposed to the act wanted to see creative works become part of the public domain more quickly because then they would be more accessible to the public on, say, the Internet. If it were not for the 1998 law, movies such as *The Wizard of Oz* and *Gone with the Wind* and books such as *The Great Gatsby* would all be part of the public domain right now.

---

[4] 239 F.3d 372, affirmed (D.C. Cir. 2001)

Confusion About Public Domain

"Happy Birthday" Is Copyrighted

Some works that are assumed to be in the public domain are actually copyrighted, and you must have permission to use them in public or in a commercial setting.

Consider the following scene for a TV soap opera. A character is having a birthday party, and the other characters in the scene begin singing the well-known "Happy Birthday to You." The soap opera producers must pay for the right to use this song because it is copyrighted.

Sisters Mildred Hill and Patty Smith Hill wrote this famous tune in 1893. A lawsuit led to the sisters copyrighting the song in 1935, and the copyright was renewed in 1963. In 1998, Warner Communications bought the rights to "Happy Birthday" for approximately $25 million.[5] The song continues to bring in millions of dollars in royalties each year. By the way, the copyright for "Happy Birthday" expires in 2030.

It is not a violation of copyright law for individuals to sing "Happy Birthday" to friends or relatives at a private home or even in a commercial setting, such as a restaurant. Problems can result, though, if the restaurant instigates the singing. Waiters and waitresses singing "Happy Birthday" to a customer technically would be a violation of copyright law because a commercial establishment is using the song in a profit-making setting. This is why many restaurants create their own birthday songs with different lyrics and melodies to avoid any potential copyright problems.

If this all seems rather petty and intrusive, consider the next situation.

The Girl Scouts and Campfire Songs

In 1996, ASCAP got into a public battle with the Girl Scouts of America over young girls singing copyrighted songs at Girl Scout meetings and campouts. ASCAP reminded the Girl Scouts that songs like "Happy Birthday" and "God Bless America" are still copyrighted and not in the public domain. In what turned out to be a public relations nightmare, ASCAP demanded the Girl Scouts pay a licensing fee to sing such songs at camps.

Out of fear of lawsuits, many Girl Scout camps put a halt to all singing for several months. Then news shows, radio talk shows, and newspapers got a hold of the story and harshly criticized ASCAP for threatening to sue the Girl Scouts just for singing songs around a campfire. The negative publicity forced ASCAP to back down. ASCAP, however, said it would still consider filing suits against camps that play recorded background music at their campgrounds. It sounds harsh, but the law does favor ASCAP.

Just who is this ASCAP, anyway?

MUSIC LICENSING

The American Society of Composers, Authors, and Publishers (ASCAP); Broadcast Music, Inc. (BMI); and the Society of European Stage Authors and Composers (SESAC) are music licensing organizations that simply make sure their members, who are *copyright owners*

---

[5]Happy birthday, we'll sue. (2002, August 11). *Snopes.com*. Retrieved October 29, 2004, from http://www.snopes .com/music/songs/birthday.htm

and songwriters, get paid when someone uses their songs publicly. BMI and ASCAP each control about 45% of copyrighted music in America; SESAC controls roughly 10%. It would be impossible for copyright owners to keep track of all of the public uses of their songs, so these music licensers monitor uses of copyrighted music and collect fees from broadcasters and businesses who use their music. BMI, ASCAP, and SESAC then redistribute the money to their members, based on the amount of airplay or other uses that a song gets. These three licensing agencies control the performing rights to more than 6 million songs; ASCAP alone collects close to $500 million each year in licensing fees.

Music licensing is actually a matter of contract law, not specifically copyright law. A music licenser grants performing rights, and there are two kinds of performances: *dramatic* and *nondramatic.* ASCAP/BMI/SESAC only handle licensing of nondramatic public performances of music, which includes occurrences of a song being played on radio or TV or being performed live on stage. ASCAP/BMI/SESAC do not handle licensing for dramatic works, which include musicals, plays, and TV and movie scripts. Licensing for dramatic uses is handled directly by writers, composers, or their agents.

It is hard to find a musical artist in America who is *not* affiliated with ASCAP, BMI, or SESAC. Here are the credits for two songs from a CD compilation of 1970s rock songs:

Some Kind of Wonderful—Grand Funk Railroad
(John Ellison) Dandelion Music Co./Crash Music Co. (BMI)
℗ 1974 Capitol Records, Inc.

Show Me the Way—Peter Frampton
(Peter Frampton) Almo Music Corp./Nuage Artists Music, Ltd. (ASCAP)
℗ 1975 A&M Records

Peter Frampton composed "Show Me the Way." He relies on ASCAP to pay him royalties when that song is played for commercial purposes, such as on a radio station. However, ASCAP and BMI must determine how often a song is played to pay people like Frampton accordingly. Here is how the system works for radio stations.

The radio station purchases a *blanket license* from ASCAP/BMI/SESAC which allows the station to *perform* all of the music in the ASCAP/BMI/SESAC libraries. Playing a song over the air is considered a "performance" of the song. A blanket license from both ASCAP/BMI/SESAC will cost a station a little more than 3% of their yearly gross station revenue. Noncommercial stations pay a flat fee. ASCAP/BMI/SESAC send out music logs to member stations. The DJs or other station personnel must then fill out the log, writing down the name of every song that was played in a specified time period (usually at least several days). The DJ must also write down the name of the song's *writer or composer.* This is important because ASCAP/BMI/SESAC pay the *writers* of songs, not the performers. (Many stations have their playlists in a database and simply mail copies to ASCAP/BMI/SESAC to avoid having to fill out the logs.)

Stations mail the logs to ASCAP/BMI/SESAC who then pay the songwriters and composers based on the amount of airplay their songs have received.

BMI, ASCAP, and SESAC keep track of music use on TV stations mostly through "cue sheets" from program producers, which list the music each show contains. For private businesses, a combination of logs and commercial music service lists are used to track music use. Businesses that use commercial music frequently often have licenses from all three of these music licensing organizations.

THE THREE BASIC RIGHTS

As noted, obtaining performing rights for music does not allow for all kinds of uses. There are other basic rights inherent in a music copyright that must be considered before using a copyrighted work:

- ▣ *Performance rights.* As discussed, this is the right to perform copyrighted music in public. ASCAP, BMI, and SESAC handle the licensing fees for the rights to "perform" music publicly for nondramatic uses.
- ▣ *Mechanical rights.* This is the right to make copies (CDs, cassettes, records, videotapes) of a work. You must have the permission from the copyright holder to make a mechanical reproduction of copyrighted music.
- ▣ *Synchronization rights.* This is the right to re-record copyrighted music and use it in conjunction with video or other audio. You must have permission from the copyright holder to "synchronize" music with visual images or other sounds.

Public Performance

The following are just *some* of the instances that require payment of music licensing fees because they are each a *public performance* and involve obtaining performance rights: concerts by live bands in bars, concerts by high school or college orchestras and bands, and choral groups. For these kinds of performance, renting or purchasing sheet music for a song does *not* authorize its public performance, except in religious services. Public schools and universities must sign licensing agreements with BMI, ASCAP, and SESAC to cover the performances of copyrighted music (live or recorded) on their campuses. Anyone wishing to make a video or audio recording of their band's or choir's performance must also contact the copyright holder of the song and pay for *recording rights.* ASCAP/BMI/SESAC do not license recording rights.

Here are more instances of public performance that require payment of music licensing fees: music played on nonprofit student radio and TV stations, broadcast or cable; telephone "on hold" music for a business; recorded music played at high school and college athletic events; recorded music played at school-sponsored dances and parties; recorded music played at any type of business; a radio station being played in ceiling speakers in a large department store; recorded music played in a school cafeteria; music played from a juke box in a business; a "mobile DJ" playing music at a wedding or a party; recorded music played at a political rally; recorded music played in a doctor or dentist's office; recorded music used at commercial conventions or training seminars; and recorded music played during an aerobics class at a health club.

The basic rule here: If you want to play, you have to pay.

Situations that are *not* considered public performances (no licensing fees required) include music played for a small circle of family members, music played for a small circle of friends, "Music played or sung as part of a worship service unless that service is transmitted beyond where it takes place"[6] (for example, through a radio or television broadcast), and music played as part of the learning process in a classroom at nonprofit educational institutions.

---

[6]The American Society of Composers, Authors and Publishers. (2004). *Frequently asked questions about licensing.* Retrieved October 28, 2004, from http://ascap.com/licensing/licensingfaq.html

Copyrighted Songs at Political Rallies

In 2000, the George W. Bush presidential campaign played Tom Petty's song "I Won't Back Down" at campaign events. Petty's music publisher sent a cease-and-desist letter to the Bush campaign saying, "Please be advised that this use has not been approved." The letter added, "Any use made by you or your campaign creates, either intentionally or unintentionally, the impression that you and your campaign have been endorsed by Tom Petty, which is not true."[7] The Bush campaign immediately stopped using the song, acknowledging that it had not paid the necessary music licensing fees.

In 1996, Bob Dole's presidential campaign had been energizing crowds at campaign rallies by playing "I'm a Dole Man," a take-off of the 1967 Motown hit "Soul Man." The Dole campaign stopped using the song after the owners of the Motown tune, Rondor Music International, threatened to sue Dole for up to $100,000 for each time the song was played at a campaign event. In a letter to the Dole campaign, Rondor said that the campaign's altering of the lyrics resulted in an "unauthorized derivative work" and required direct permission from the music publisher.[8]

In 2004, the George W. Bush presidential campaign was once again asked to stop using a popular song at its campaign rallies, this time the 1970s hit "Still the One" by Orleans. John Hall, one of the writers of the song, said he did not support Bush's reelection and that the Bush campaign had not obtained his permission to use the song. The campaign said it had paid the appropriate music licensing fees to play the song in public, but said it would stop using the song out of respect for Hall's wishes. Hall said he objected to the political use of the song, fearing it would harm the song's commercial appeal. The song had already been used in restaurant commercials for Burger King and Applebee's.[9]

To avoid situations such as these, songwriters sometimes have provisions in their publishing contracts that prevent their songs from being used for political purposes. If no such provision exists, political campaigns are allowed to play the songs, in spite of a songwriter's objections, as long as the appropriate music licensing fees have been paid to ASCAP, BMI, or SESAC.

FAQ

Does this same reasoning apply to political talk radio shows? For example, Rush Limbaugh uses parts of popular songs as theme music or as "bumper" music when coming out of commercial breaks.

The *Rush Limbaugh Show*, through its Excellence In Broadcasting Network, pays music licensing fees to ASCAP, BMI, and SESAC, which gives Limbaugh the right to use any of

---

[7]Vineyard, J. (2000, September 20). Tom Petty makes George W. Bush back down. *Rolling Stone.* Retrieved October 15, 2000, from http://www.rollingstone.com

[8]Ryan, M. L. (1996, August 29). Re: Soul Man. *Court TV online legal documents.* Retrieved October 31, 2004, from http://www.courttv.com/archive/legaldocs/misc/doleman.html

[9]Cohen, J. (2004, October 29). Bush stops using Orleans "Still the One." *Billboard.* Retrieved October 31, 2004, from http://www.billboard.com/bb/daily/article_display.jsp?vnu_content_id=1000694581

their licensed music in his program. For years, Limbaugh has used as his theme song the opening riff from the Pretenders' song "My City Was Gone." Pretenders lead singer Chrissie Hynde objected to Limbaugh's politics and to his use of the song, but Limbaugh's producer Kit Carson noted that payment of the "umbrella" licensing fees allows their network to use whatever music it chooses.[10]

Mechanical Rights

Making Copies With Home Recording Equipment

In the 1970s, a big concern for the recording industry was the popularity of the cassette tape. Cassette recording equipment made it easy for people to borrow music records from a friend and make cassette copies.

In the 1980s, compact discs began to displace records as Americans' preferred medium for recorded music. At the time, the only way to copy compact discs was through analog media, such as cassette tapes. However, the recording industry no longer saw tapes as being a serious threat because CDs lost considerable sound quality when dubbed to analog cassettes.

By the 1990s, though, media such as digital audiotape and minidiscs were allowing consumers to make *digital* copies of recorded music. The recording industry asked for some restrictions, and Congress responded with the Audio Home Recording Act of 1992 (AHRA).

AHRA had three main purposes: (a) to protect the rights of consumers to use home audio recording equipment, (b) to protect the rights of manufacturers to produce and sell audio home recording devices, and (c) to give some protection to creators of copyrighted music.

Here are the most important sections of AHRA.

Section 1002: Protections Against Copying. All digital audio recording devices have to contain *one* of the following: (a) a serial copy management system (SCMS). This device allows first-generation recordings, such as copying a music CD to minidisc. However, SCMS would not allow the copying of that minidisc to digital audiotape. Second-generation recordings, or serial copies, are thus blocked. If a device has no SCMS, it must have either (b) a system very similar to SCMS, with the same blocking capabilities, or (c) any system certified by the Secretary of Commerce that would block serial copying. It is illegal to produce a device with the ability to circumvent SCMS.

Sections 1003 and 1004: Royalty Payments. Any American company producing or importing digital recording devices must make the following royalty payments: (a) 3% of the wholesale price of any digital audio recording media (tapes, discs, etc.) and (b) 2% of the wholesale price of any digital recording unit (minidisc recorders, CD burners, etc.). The royalty minimum is $1, and the maximum is $8 per unit. Devices containing more than one digital recording device have a maximum royalty of $12 per unit. These royalties are only required of the first person to produce and distribute the recording devices. The royalties also apply to the first person to import and distribute the devices.

---

[10]Hochman, S. (1996, March 17). Pop music: Rock, country, R&B, rap, Latin jazz: Rush to judgment. *Los Angeles Times.* Retrieved October 29, 2004, from http://www.pretenders.org/arrush.htm

---

FAQ

Who collects these royalties? What is done with the money?

The Library of Congress and the Register of Copyrights collect the royalties. They then distribute the royalties to musicians, artists, songwriters, music publishers, and record companies. The royalties are based on sales of recorded music and radio station airplay during specified time periods. The money is meant to reimburse copyright holders with some portion of the royalties that are lost from illegal copying done with digital recording devices.

Section 1008: Consumers' Rights to Copy. Consumers have a right to use analog and digital home recording devices to make copies of copyrighted music for *noncommercial use.* The recording industry or artists may not file lawsuits over these types of home recordings. However, if a person makes copies of prerecorded music and tries to *sell* those copies, then there is a case for copyright infringement.

Section 1008 also prohibits copyright lawsuits against any company involved in the manufacture, distribution, or sale of analog and digital recording devices and media.

FAQ

What if I use my CD burner to make a copy of a CD and then give that CD to a friend? Is this a "noncommercial use" under AHRA?

Some legal experts have argued AHRA makes this kind of copying legal because the CD is not being sold and is therefore a "noncommercial" recording. Other legal experts disagree and say the act only applies to copies of music a person makes for personal use.

There is no known case of a person ever being prosecuted for burning CDs or making copies of music for friends. However, the music industry argues that such recordings are a violation of *mechanical rights* because, when someone copies a CD for a friend, that friend will not then go to a store and purchase a copy of the CD. As a result, music artists lose out on income from royalties. Take away that income, the industry says, and you take away an artist's incentive to create new music.

Basically, though, the music industry is not going to go after individuals making a few copies in their homes. The industry focuses most of its efforts on people who are trying to sell and distribute pirated music in the larger marketplace.

FAQ

I have lots of CDs, but I would like all of my favorite songs together on one CD. Does the law allow me to make a "favorites" CD from my own CD collection?

This is also known as *space-shifting*, and even the recording industry agrees that such copying is legal. Burning a "favorites" CD for personal use is just a rearrangement or compilation. The copyright owners of these songs have already made their money from the person who bought the CDs. Unlike copying music for a friend, the goal here is not to "get it for free." The goal is convenience, not theft. In this case, the mechanical rights of the copyright owner are suspended. At the same time, a person does not have a right to *sell* this compilation CD. That would *not* be a "noncommercial" use.

Synchronization Rights

Broadcast Station Uses

FAQ

If I pay for a blanket license, does this allow me to use parts of songs in radio station jingles and other promotional spots?

Yes. ASCAP and BMI say these are legal uses.

FAQ

So does paying for a blanket license give a station the right to change the lyrics of copyrighted songs for station jingles or other promotional purposes?

No. Persons must get permission from the copyright owners to, first, record their music and, second, to change one of their songs.

Copyrighted Music in Radio or TV Commercials

FAQ

Does paying for a blanket license from ASCAP or BMI give a station permission to use copyrighted music in radio or TV commercials?

A blanket license gives a station *performance rights,* or the right to play the song over the air for entertainment purposes. That blanket license does *not* give a broadcast station *synchronization rights,* or the right to use a song in conjunction with other audio or video, such as in an advertisement. (The use of the song in the ad might also wrongly imply that an artist endorses a certain product or business.)

This can be confusing. The ASCAP Web site actually states that a blanket license gives a broadcaster "the right to perform music in commercials."[11] There is a higher power, though, which says this is not so. That higher power is United States Copyright Law, which overrules ASCAP by stating clearly that *blanket licenses do not allow the use of a song in any type of radio or TV commercial.* That is the law, plain and simple.

If an advertiser insists on using a copyrighted song in an ad, the station must obtain *synchronization rights.* These rights guarantee that the composer receives royalties when his or her work is "synchronized" with video or other audio.

Types of situations that require *synchronization rights* include (a) using a song in a radio or TV ad, (b) making a music video for a popular song, (c) using a song in a movie, (d) using a song for an interactive CD-ROM, (e) using a song as background in a TV news story, and (f) any situation in which a song is "synchronized" with video or audio.

Obtaining synchronization rights can be a difficult task. The best place to start is the Harry Fox Agency, a huge licensing agency. Fox will let you know if they are in charge of the rights for a particular song you want to use and how much it would cost you. They may also point you to another agency that handles the synchronization rights to the song you want to use.

The Bonanza *Theme: An Adventure in Pursuing Synchronization Rights*

The following story is a good example of the legalities involved in obtaining synchronization rights. It is taken from an article in the May 29, 1996 issue of *Radio World.*[12] Craig Johnston, the production director at KDRV-TV in Medford, OR, was working with a local barbecue rib restaurant owner who wanted to produce a TV ad showing a local county map burning away, mimicking the opening segment of the TV show *Bonanza.* The owner of the restaurant was supposed to ride up on a horse with the *Bonanza* theme playing. The TV station shot the commercial, the client apparently "loved it," and Johnston attempted to get clearance to use the music. The following are the steps that Johnston took, *and you should take,* to secure synchronization rights:

> The CD listed the *Bonanza* theme as an ASCAP piece, so I called the company. ASCAP quickly steered me to the Harry Fox Agency that handles all sync rights. . . . The Harry Fox agency explained that it represented 50 percent of the music rights fee. The other 50 percent was represented, in the *Bonanza* music's case, by MCA.
>
> Of course, I called the MCA music licensing department . . . faxed my request and was told MCA would get back in touch with me.
>
> The decision was that the *Bonanza* theme was not available, at any price, for any local commercial. It seems there is still a lot of national interest in that music, especially by restaurant chains, and our use of it in Medford, Ore., might scare the big guys off.
>
> A couple of weeks later, I heard the music in a national commercial playing behind a shot of Shaquille O'Neal riding through a burning map. That certainly lent credence to the MCA "national interest" assertion.
>
> Realizing that the *Bonanza* theme was not available for a local commercial, what would a piece of music of similar age and fame cost me to license for a local spot in Medford, I asked.

---

[11]ASCAP, *op. cit.*, "What does the ASCAP radio or television license give you?"

[12]Johnston, C. (1996, May 29). The legal aspects of commercial music. *Radio World*, p. 67. Used with permission from the author.

The answer: $15,000.

As if anything over a couple hundred dollars was in the ballpark for such a local commercial, I asked if the $15,000 would be for the life of the commercial or just one year.

"Clean the wax out of your ear," was the reply. "It would be $15,000 for a year. We don't license anything for life."

The commercial in question now runs with original music ($150 dollars for lifetime rights), which imparts the original flavor desired without stepping on the *Bonanza* theme. What would happen if we went ahead and used the *Bonanza* theme? Let them catch us if they can. Would they come to Medford, Ore.?

As the old Magic Eight Ball used to reply, my sources say yes.

I mean, if music licensing folks can come after my friend the aerobics instructor for using unlicensed music (not the *Bonanza* theme) to bounce to, coming after a real business would seem a natural. It would be easy to prove the music was actually used in a commercial. All they would have to do is tape it off the air.

The potential cost? Throw out the $15,000 figure. That was only for the local spot we were told we could not make.

As there had been no price established, and because their lawyer is going to insist that the music's exposure in Medford has scared off national clients who were lined up around the block . . . well, it's going to cost a bundle.[12]

FAQ

I hear local radio stations using popular music in local ads all the time. Aren't they violating copyright law?

Many times, they are. Unlike Johnston, many broadcast station personnel are unaware of the details of copyright law. Stations often get away with illegal synchronizations because copyright owners do not have the time to "police" every station in the country to see if songs are being used illegally. Stations that do get caught may get a cease-and-desist order from a copyright owner, or the copyright owner could sue.

That's what happened in 1995 when the Spin Doctors sued Miller Brewing Company over a TV ad for Miller Lite Ice Beer. The ad centered on a bar scene with background music that was "substantially similar" to the Spin Doctors' song "Two Princes." A federal jury in 1996 ruled in favor of the Spin Doctors, saying that the song in the ad was a "knockoff" or "ripoff" of the Spin Doctors' song and was a copyright infringement.[13] Miller paid an out of court settlement for damages, reportedly in the millions of dollars.

FAQ

So what should stations use for music in radio and TV ads?

---

[13]*Spin Doctors v. Miller Brewing Co. et al.*, Case No. 95-6336 HLH (Mcx) (CD CA).

There are basically three options when it comes to using music in ads or some other form of synchronization: (a) Have a musician or firm compose and record original music for your station, (b) pay the sometimes hefty licensing fees for using copyrighted songs, or (c) purchase an instrumental production music library.

Production libraries usually come with three types of licenses or payment options: (a) laserdrop or needle-drop license, which is "pay-per-use" (you pay a set fee each time you use music from the company's library; (b) blanket license, in which you pay an annual fee for unlimited use of the music for a year, or (c) buy-out license, in which you purchase a collection of instrumental music CDs outright. The purchase price includes the right to use the music for as long as you wish (or until you get sick of the same old music used over and over and over in your commercial spots).

FAQ

I'm a TV sports anchor. I'm doing a 2-minute story on a high school basketball team winning a state championship. I want to use "We are the Champions" by Queen as background music for the video highlights of their season. Is this legal?

It depends. Check with your station to see if it has purchased a blanket license from ASCAP and BMI. If so, that license allows for the television performance of all music licensed by these organizations. If that Queen song is licensed by BMI or ASCAP, you are free to use it in your story. (As in radio, the licensing fee for TV is based on a percentage of the station's annual gross revenues.)

There are three classifications for use of licensed music on television: (a) background—as in the "Champions" example, you use music as background for a story; (b) theme—music is played at the start or end of a show to help "identify" the show; and (c) feature—music is the main attraction, such as a band performing a song on a show.

If your station does not have a blanket license, you would need to get permission from the owners of the copyright to "We are the Champions." You would have to pay for synchronization rights.

FAIRNESS IN MUSIC LICENSING ACT

For years, many businesses in America thought nothing about piping music from a radio station through the store intercom to entertain customers. Music licensers, though, said the playing of copyrighted music in a commercial setting was a "public performance," and those businesses should pay music licensing fees.

The businesses would often use arguments such as, "The radio stations are already paying their ASCAP fees. That should cover my use as well." Copyright owners said they deserved to be paid because their music was being used for commercial purposes to create a "pleasant business atmosphere." Until the late 1990s, most businesses had to pay licensing fees for the right to play copyrighted music in their establishments.

That changed in 1998 when Congress passed the Fairness in Music Licensing Act.[14] The act infuriated music licensers, but it pleased many restaurant and business owners. That was because the Congressional Research Service estimated that the act would wind up exempting more than 70% of restaurants and bars from paying music licensing fees.

Here is what the act stipulated. If you own a business and you want to play a radio station or recorded music during business hours, you must take two criteria into account: (a) the size of your business (square footage) and (b) *how* the music is being broadcast to customers. Businesses wishing to be exempt from music licensing fees must follow three rules. They must (a) play music only from licensed broadcast, cable, or satellite sources; (b) agree not to transmit the music beyond their establishment; and (c) not charge admission.

Once these conditions are met, the following businesses are exempt from licensing fees: (a) restaurants, bars, and grills smaller than 3750 square feet and (b) retail businesses smaller than 2000 square feet (that do not serve food or drink). Businesses exceeding these square footages also qualify for exemption if (a) they use six or fewer speakers, not exceeding four speakers in any room (these speaker limits apply to both radio and TV broadcasts); (b) they use no more than four TVs, having no more than one TV in any room; and (c) they have no TV screen larger than 55 inches (measured diagonally).

Music licensers and musicians were angered by the new rules. A lot of restaurants and businesses that had been paying music licensing fees before were now suddenly exempt. ASCAP argued that these new exemptions would result in losses of "millions of dollars annually for music creators and copyright owners."[15]

FAQ

So does this mean that, for example, a large department store or supermarket has to pay for the rights to play a radio station in the store?

Yes, larger stores still have to pay licensing fees. That is why most large stores avoid this problem altogether and purchase a music library. The purchase price includes performance rights fees.

However, the store *does not* have to pay licensing fees when the radio station is heard in only a small section of the store. Examples of this would be a clerk at the jewelry counter who has a radio on beside the cash register, or a radio turned on for demonstration purposes in the store's electronics section.

Special Exemption for Music Stores

Record and CD stores have always been allowed to play music in their establishments without paying licensing fees. That is because their purpose for playing it is to promote retail sales of the music and not just to provide a "pleasing commercial atmosphere."

---

[14]17 U.S.C. §110

[15]Fairness in music licensing legislation Q & A. (1999, February). *ASCAP Legislative Matters*. Retrieved November 21, 2003, from http://www.ascap.com/legislation/legis_qa.html

The 1998 act expanded this music store exemption to include other retail businesses that played the music for the purpose of increasing music sales, as well as for promoting sales of playback devices, such as CD players, stereos, and radios.

Live Bands and Juke Boxes in Businesses

In 1986, Bruce Springsteen and other music copyright owners sued a New Hampshire restaurant chain for the playing hit recordings of songs such as "Born in the USA" and "Abracadabra" on juke boxes. Many songs were also performed live by bands. The restaurant chain owner, Peter Yee, had refused to pay for the rights to play the music because he felt ASCAP music licensing fees were "unreasonably high." ASCAP had approached Yee on numerous occasions about obtaining a license, but Yee never paid. As a result, Springsteen and the other copyright owners filed suit.

The Federal District Court looked at several factors in its decision: (a) Yee's obvious refusal on numerous occasions to pay licensing fees, (b) Yee's imposition of cover charges for nights on which live musical groups were featured, and (c) the fact that the music had become a vital component of Yee's business.[16]

The court ruled against Yee, saying that restaurants must pay licensing fees for juke boxes and live bands. When a band performs in a bar or a restaurant, it is the responsibility of the business and not the band to take care of the licensing fees for public performances. Licensing fees are *not* required for juke boxes in private homes. In those cases, a juke box is the same as a personal stereo. It is not a public performance and is not being used for business purposes.

Compulsory Licensing

This is a basic but vital component of the music licensing business. *Compulsory licensing* means that once a song has been publicly performed, the copyright holder cannot deny one person the rights to record a song but grant the rights to others.

Say a well-known singer wants to record a country version of "Smooth" by Santana. However, Santana is not thrilled about their song becoming a country hit. That does not matter. Santana cannot prohibit the recording as long as the country artist pays the proper fees. That is what compulsory licensing is all about.

When the country artist sells copies of this new version of "Smooth," the artist will owe Santana the appropriate royalties for each recorded copy that is sold.

MUSIC PLAGIARISM

Subconscious Copyright Violation

The following cases deal with someone stealing or plagiarizing a copyrighted musical work. In such cases, a plaintiff must prove that an infringer violated one of the basic rights of the copyright holder. Also, the copyright owner must prove the infringing work is *substantially similar* to the original work and must also show that the infringer had access to

---

[16]*Sailor Music v. Mai Kai of Concord, Inc.,* 640 F. Supp. 629 (D.N.H. 1986)

the work. However, this area of law can be murky because popular songs often use the same basic chords, and many new songs may sound similar but not "substantially" similar to previously recorded songs. In plagiarism cases, the question often becomes, "How close is too close?"

In 1970, former Beatle George Harrison had a number-one hit with "My Sweet Lord." However, some people thought the song sounded very similar to "He's So Fine," a number-one hit for the Chiffons in 1963. The owners of "He's So Fine" sued, saying Harrison's song stole the main melody or "hook" of the song. Harrison claimed he had heard of the song, but he said he did not copy it. In 1976, a court ruled that Harrison did not deliberately copy the song.

However, in one of the more bizarre rulings in copyright law, the court still found Harrison guilty of copyright infringement. The judge ruled, "'My Sweet Lord' is the very same song as 'He's So Fine' with different words." He then added that Harrison did indeed copy the song, "a song his conscious mind did not remember," but "his subconscious knew."[17] The judge actually ruled that Harrison subconsciously (unconsciously?) engaged in copyright infringement. Many songwriters and publishers viewed this ruling as an alarming precedent in copyright law. The court said that unintentional copyright infringement is the same as an intentional infringement.

In an interesting twist, Harrison's former manager wound up purchasing the rights to "He's So Fine" before the end of the trial. The court ruled that this was a conflict of interest.

Harrison later had to pay a small fine. The court then gave Harrison ownership rights to both "He's So Fine" and "My Sweet Lord" in some other countries. However, the initial ruling remained.

John Fogerty v. John Fogerty?

Many times, musical artists may no longer have the rights to songs they have written. Sometimes this is by choice, as when the artist needs some quick cash and sells the rights to someone else. Sometimes a legal wrangling leads to a manager or other publisher getting the rights to an artist's songs.

John Fogerty is an accomplished solo artist but may best be known for his work with the rock group Creedence Clearwater Revival (CCR). The group had a string of top ten hits in the late 1960s and early 1970s. Fogerty wrote and produced most of CCR's songs. However, CCR's former manager and music publisher (under the name Fantasy, Inc.) came to own the copyrights to the group's songs. As a result, Fogerty now had to get permission from Fantasy to record or perform songs that he had written.

To avoid legal hassles, Fogerty focused on writing new music. In 1985, Fogerty released a solo album, which included the top ten hit "The Old Man Down the Road." However, Fantasy claimed that "Old Man" was a copy of the old CCR hit "Run Through the Jungle," for which Fantasy now owned the rights. Fantasy said Fogerty had simply copied the music of "Jungle," changed the lyrics, and released it as "Old Man." Fantasy sued Fogerty for copyright infringement.

Fogerty argued that all of his songs, old and new, had a distinctive "Swamp Rock" style and said it was just natural that all of his music would have a similar "flavor." In 1988, a jury

---

[17]*Bright Tunes Music Corp. v. Harrisongs Music, Ltd.*, 420 F. Supp. 177, 180 (S.D.N.Y. 1976)

sided with Fogerty, ruling that although there was similarity between the two songs, there was not enough of a "substantial similarity" to warrant a copyright infringement.

In 1994, the U.S. Supreme Court upheld the ruling.[18] It also upheld a district court's judgment that Fantasy had to pay for Fogerty's legal fees. The court remanded the case to the district court to determine just how much Fantasy would have to pay. Fantasy eventually wound up paying more than $1.3 million to Fogerty.[19]

Summary

Copyright law gives persons legal protection for their creative works or intellectual property. Various types of creative works may be copyrighted, including songs, books, motion pictures, and computer programs. Such works must be fixed in a tangible medium of expression. However, facts and general ideas may not be copyrighted, including such things as historical facts, telephone listings, and listings of ingredients. All copyright holders have basic rights to protect their works from being copied or used without permission. Works with no copyright or expired copyright are part of the public domain and may be used by anyone. The Bono Act makes most copyrights good for the life of the creator plus 70 years.

Music licensing companies, such as ASCAP and BMI, pay composers and songwriters for the public uses of their works. However, the Fairness in Music Licensing Act exempts many restaurants and other businesses from payment of music licensing fees.

---

[18]*Fogerty v. Fantasy,* 510 U.S. 517 (1994)

[19]*Fogerty v. Fantasy*, 94 F.3d 553 (9th Cir. 1996)

14

COPYRIGHT: FAIR USE

What's Fair Is Fair

air use doctrine is fairly self-explanatory. It deals with copyright issues involving the question: When is it *fair* for someone to *use* a copyrighted work without having to get permission from the copyright holder?

Issues of fair use arise frequently in all sorts of cases. Should a student have to get permission to use quotations from a copyrighted book to write a book report? Should a news reporter get copyright clearance before using short film clips from a copyrighted movie in a news report? Is it legal for a teacher to play copyrighted music in a classroom for educational purposes? Shouldn't the law allow for "reasonable" or "fair" uses of copyrighted material in such cases? If not, many people, such as teachers and news reporters, will have a more difficult time doing their jobs.

The Fair Use Doctrine was officially recognized in the 1976 Copyright Act. It outlined four criteria for determining fair use.

1. The Nature of the Work. Is it in the public domain? Is it out of print or no longer available for purchase? If any one of these is the case, you are often free to use the work. However, if the work *is* copyrighted, you must consider the next three criteria.

2. The Purpose of the Use. This factor looks at how the copyrighted work is being used. First, is it being used for commercial or noncommercial purposes? A ruling for fair use is considered much more likely for noncommercial uses, but many commercial uses are protected as well. Second, Section 107 of the Copyright Act provides "favored" protection to copyrighted works that are used for the purposes of criticism, comment, research, scholarship, teaching, and news reporting. In many instances, these are considered fair uses, but not always. Third, is the use transformative? Does the new work have a different character or purpose than the original? This point is critical in parody cases.

3. The Amount of the Work Used. For the most part, it is not considered fair to use most or all of a copyrighted work. Also, it may not be fair to use a *significant* or *vital* part of a work, even if the part you are using is a very small percentage of the whole work. At the same time, though, many uses of small portions of copyrighted works are considered a fair use, and that often depends on the next criteria.

4. The Effect of the Use on the Value or Marketability of the Copyrighted Work. Will your use of a copyrighted work damage the copyright holder's ability to profit from his or her work? The Supreme Court has called this "undoubtedly the single most important element in determining fair use."[1]

The wording of the fair use doctrine is purposefully vague. For example, in the third prong, it provides no specifics about what percentage of a work would be considered appropriate for a fair use. Some critics charge that this creates confusion and results in unfair application of the law. Others argue that rigid guidelines would unfairly restrict many uses of copyrighted works and that the vague guidelines allow for more fair use decisions to be made on a case-by-case basis.

FAIR USE AND THE VCR

One of the first major tests involving fair use concerned a new technology that was becoming very popular in the early 1980s: the videocassette recorder (VCR). SONY had marketed its Betamax VCR, the forerunner to VHS recorders. Major entertainment companies Universal and Disney sued, arguing that SONY's Betamax was contributing to copyright infringement because it was encouraging private citizens to make illegal copies of copyrighted television programming. (Universal and Disney decided that suing SONY would be much easier than trying to sue a group of individual VCR users.)

In a 5-4 decision in *Sony v. Universal,*[2] the U.S. Supreme Court in 1984 ruled for SONY after applying each of the four criteria for fair use:

- ▣ *The nature of the work:* The vast majority of the TV programming being recorded on VCRs was indeed copyrighted. The Supreme Court on this point agreed with Universal and thus moved to the second criterion.
- ▣ *The purpose of the use:* The court said that most private citizens were not engaged in commercial uses, such as making "pirate" copies of TV shows to sell to others. Instead, most people were engaging in "time shifting," or recording a show to watch it at a later time. The court ruled that such copying was a fair use in this regard because most of the copying was for "noncommercial, nonprofit activity." This point went to SONY.
- ▣ *Amount of the work used:* The court agreed that persons often used VCRs to record entire copyrighted programs. This aspect worked in Universal's favor because the use of an entire copyrighted work is often considered not to be a fair use. However, there was still the important fourth prong.
- ▣ *The effect on the work's value and marketability:* The ruling on this point helped to swing the decision in SONY's favor. The court said that private home recordings would do little damage to the value of copyrighted programs. These private home recordings would not deter other citizens from watching the same shows, and Universal could prove no harm on this point.

As is seen in this case, a person does not have to win all four points of the fair use test to win the case. Winning on a single major point can result in overall victory.

One of the major issues with the dissenting justices was the application of the third criterion—the amount of the work used. Justice Blackmun said copying of an entire work

---

[1] See *Harper & Row v. Nation,* 471 U.S. 539 (1985)

[2] *SONY Corp. of America v. Universal City Studios Inc.,* 464 U.S. 417 (1984)

for no productive use should never be considered a fair use. Blackmun said in his dissent that such copying results in "depriving authors of control over their works and consequently of their incentive to create."[3] He also argued that VCR usage created a *potential harm* to the value of copyrighted TV programs and that copyright owners should not have to prove *actual* harm. Blackmun saw a great potential harm from the practice of time shifting: If people kept copies of recorded TV show episodes on tape, they would be less likely to watch reruns of those episodes and that would reduce ratings for the reruns. Lower ratings would mean less advertising revenue for show producers, and Blackmun said that presented a foreseeable harm. Blackmun said the court needed to provide clearer rationale for its application of fair use criteria.

Fair Use and Sampling

FAQ

Is it illegal to sample a copyrighted song without the owner's permission?

Yes. Sampling involves one musician taking a recognizable portion of a copyrighted song (such as a melody or a bass line) and using it as part of a new recording. One famous sampling case involved the number one hit "Ice Ice Baby" by Vanilla Ice. The hit single, which sold 5 million copies in 5 months in 1990, sampled the bass line from "Under Pressure" by Queen and David Bowie. The song was also on Vanilla Ice's album *To the Extreme*. The album itself sold more than 15 million copies worldwide.

Vanilla Ice did not ask for permission to sample the song. He did not even give credit to Queen and David Bowie on the album. The copyright holders of "Under Pressure" threatened a lawsuit. Sensing he would lose in court, Vanilla Ice reached an out-of-court settlement with the owners, reportedly in the millions of dollars.

The courts again addressed the issue of sampling in 1991 in *Grand Upright Music v. Warner Bros.*[4] The case involved a song by Biz Markie entitled "Alone Again," which sampled the number one 1972 hit "Alone Again (Naturally)" by Gilbert O'Sullivan. Markie had already recorded his version when he tried to obtain permission to sample O'Sullivan's song, but he was denied. Markie released the recording anyway.

In ruling against Markie, the judge quoted the Seventh Commandment, "Thou shalt not steal." Markie's lawyers had argued that "stealing was rampant in the music business" and that Markie's "conduct here should be excused." The judge called that reasoning "totally specious."[5] He then referred the case to U.S. Attorney's office for possible criminal charges. This case established the precedent that unlicensed sampling is illegal.

---

[3]*Ibid.*, p. 422.

[4]780 F. Supp. 182 (S.D.N.Y. 1991)

[5]*Ibid.*, p. 184.

Fair Use and Broadcast News

FAQ

I'm doing a TV news story on a concert. My concert video includes natural sound of the orchestra playing copyrighted songs. Is it a fair use to include clips of the concert music in my news story?

Yes. A landmark case regarding this issue is from 1978. WABC-TV in New York City had aired footage of a parade, which included a high school marching band playing "Dove sta Zaza," a copyrighted song. Italian Book Corporation, which owned the rights to the song, sued WABC for copyright infringement, claiming the use of the song in a news story on a commercial television station was not a fair use.

The court, though, applied the fair use test and ruled for WABC[6]:

- *The nature of the work:* The song here was copyrighted, and not in the public domain. There might be an unfair use here. To help determine the fairness issue, the court moved on to the second criterion.
- *The nature of the use:* The use was in a commercial television newscast. The station makes money by selling advertising for its newscast. Does the Italian Book Corporation deserve a cut of the profits because its song was a part of this money-making newscast? Another important consideration here is that the use was part of TV coverage of a newsworthy event. Therefore, the station would argue that the nature of the use was to inform the public, not to profit from using the song. The court then considered the next two criteria.
- *The amount of the work used:* The court said the station used only a brief portion of the song as part of the news story. It was a small percentage of the entire work. The arguments were beginning to go in favor of the TV station, so the final concern became:
- *The effect of the use on the value or marketability of the work:* Would the use of a small portion of this song in a TV newscast lead to fewer people buying the work? No. Did the use somehow make the work less valuable to the public? No. The court said the song was merely "incidental" to the news story. The news story did not focus on the song. The story was about a parade, and the station simply aired a brief portion of a band playing the song at a public event.

Therefore, the use of this brief portion of a copyrighted song was considered fair use.

Using Movie Clips in Broadcast News Stories

FAQ

I'm doing a TV feature story about a local man who has appeared in several major motion pictures. I want to show examples of his acting from two of his movies. I go to a local video store, rent the movie, and use several short clips in my story. A reporter at a radio station across town rents the same movie and uses a 10-second clip of the actor's dialogue in a radio news story. Would these be fair uses?

---

[6]*Italian Book Corp. v. ABC*, 458 F. Supp. 65 (S.D.N.Y. 1978).

In recent cases, the courts have ruled that limited uses of movie clips in news stories are fair. One case began in July 1997 when Cable News Network (CNN) did a news story on the death of actor Robert Mitchum. The story on Mitchum's life lasted 2 minutes and 50 seconds and included 20 seconds of footage and dialogue from the 1945 movie *The Story of G.I. Joe*, for which Mitchum earned an Oscar nomination. CBS News and ABC News also used footage from Mitchum films in their televised obituaries. The copyright holder to the movie filed suit against the three news outlets, saying each network owed him $5,000 to $10,000 for the use of these clips (ranging from 6 to 22 seconds).[7] CNN, CBS, and ABC claimed the clips were a fair use.

The district court in this case ruled for the networks for a number of reasons, all based on the doctrine of fair use. For example, the nature of the use was "informative." The networks were not looking to profit from using these movie clips. Instead, the clips were used to inform viewers about the acting career of Robert Mitchum. The court also said the use was "transformative." The purpose of the original film was to detail the horrors of war. The court said the networks' uses "transformed" the original and had a different purpose. The networks simply wanted to chronicle an actor's life. The amount of the work used was minimal. Out of a 108-minute movie, the longest clip used by the networks was 22 seconds. As a result, use of these brief clips would not harm the marketability of the whole film. Therefore, the use of the movie clips was a fair use.

In a similar case, Detroit radio station WJR did a tribute to J. P. McCarthy, a station on-air personality. The tribute used a song written by one of McCarthy's friends, Bobby Laurel. The tribute also contained a line of dialogue from *Rosary Murders*, a movie produced by Laurel. The copyright owners of the song and movie sued the station for copyright infringement.

A federal appeals court ruled for the radio station. The court said the company, because of a technicality, did not have ownership of the version of the song that was used. More important was the ruling regarding the use of the movie clip. The court said that the use of a short clip from a movie on a radio program is a fair use in most instances. The court explained, "When a single line of a larger copyrighted work is appropriated by an alleged infringer, the test [for infringement] is whether the work is recognizable by an ordinary observer as having been taken from the copyrighted source."[8]

What would be a recognizable line? Obvious examples would be "Frankly, my dear, I don't give a damn" from *Gone With the Wind* or "I'm the king of the world!" from *Titanic*. The radio show on WJR had used a piece of dialogue that was simply an "incidental part of the [movie] background." As a result, it was "a phrase or slogan not worthy of copyright protection in its own right."[9]

Movie Sound Clips in Radio

FAQ

So it's OK to use short audio clips from movies in my radio show, as in a recorded intro or "liner"? I do this, and I hear other DJs do it, too.

---

[7]See *Video-Cinema Films, Inc., v. Cable News Network, Inc.*, 31 Med. L. Rep. 1634 (S.D.N.Y. March 30, 2003)

[8]*Murray Hill Publications v. ABC Communications*, 264 F.3d 622 (6th Cir. 2001)

[9]*Ibid.*, p. 624

The WJR case does appear to clear the way for such uses. There are many Internet sites that make a variety of movie clips available for radio people. The basic rule is to make sure you are not using recognizable or famous clips from movies. To be safe, only use movie dialogue clips that are "incidental"—that the average person would not be able to identify as being from the movie from which the clip came. Also, DJs should avoid using recognizable audio clips from commercials.

A "liner" (or "sweeper") is often a short, recorded promo for a radio station. Many stations today include a movie clip as part of a liner. If the dialogue clip from a movie is, "Oh, I love it!" A station might use it this way in a liner: "We play today's best rock. *'Oh, I love it!'* Modern rock 98.7."

Using "Newsworthy" Video in a TV News Story

FAQ

I'm doing a story about the September 11 terrorist attacks for my university's student station. I want to show some video of the planes hitting the World Trade Center. I recorded some of the video off of a cable news network. Am I allowed to use it? After all, isn't this video in the public domain because it has been shown so many times and because of its newsworthiness?

There are two major copyright concerns in your question.

1. Recording Other Stations' Newscasts. Simply because a piece of video is considered newsworthy does not mean it is free for anyone to use in any newscast. *Never* record any television newscast's video for use in a story unless you get the permission of that TV station. That is the station's copyrighted broadcast. Even if that newscast is using video that has been seen on every other news station, it is still that station's copyrighted newscast. Also, you do not know if that station had to pay for the rights to use that video. You had better check to see if you need to pay, too.

The issue of fair use and video clipping services came up in the 1980s with the rise of this service industry. These businesses would often record television newscasts and sell videotape copies of the newscasts (or particular stories) for profit. In 1993, a federal appeals court ruled that such recordings and sales are a copyright infringement. The court said the clipping services violated TV stations' rights to reproduce and distribute their copyrighted newscasts.[10] Now, many broadcast stations work out special licensing agreement with clipping services.

2. Using "Famous" News Video. As mentioned, not every piece of "famous" news footage is free for anyone to use. In the case of the World Trade Center attacks footage, on September 11, 2001, French filmmaker Jules Naudet happened to be shooting a documentary on New York City firefighters when he heard a plane roar overhead. Naudet instinctively pointed his camera skyward and captured the only pictures of the first plane hitting the

---

[10]*Georgia Television Company v. Television News Clips of Atlanta,* 983 F.2d 238 (11th Cir. 1993)

north tower. Naudet then shot footage of the firefighters as they went into the north tower. He also filmed the aftermath of the towers collapsing.

In March 2002, CBS-TV paid Naudet for the rights to use his video in a 2-hour documentary about the World Trade Center attacks. Naudet had already copyrighted his videotape from September 11, and he agreed to give proceeds from the tape to a scholarship fund for children of firefighters who were killed in the line of duty. However, Naudet became concerned about people making bootleg copies of his tape. He sent a letter to the firefighters' union, asking its 8500 members to help prevent "widespread distribution" of the tape, which "decreases the value of the footage and will therefore reduce the revenue that the fund will receive."[11]

Naudet's video is famous. It contains newsworthy events. But it is copyrighted. It is Naudet's property. Persons must pay or get permission to use it.

Another case of famous footage is that of the Rodney King video and the trial aftermath.

George Holliday shot one of the most famous pieces of home video in American history: the beating of Rodney King, a black man, by Los Angeles police in March 1991. Holliday gave permission to KTLA-TV in Los Angeles to air the video, and KTLA apparently paid him $500 for it. The famous video soon made its way onto the national networks and stations around the country. Three months later, Holliday sent cease-and-desist letters to 800 stations in North America, telling them to stop playing the video or face legal action. When that did not work, Holliday sued CBS, ABC, NBC, CNN, and KTLA for copyright infringement.

However, KTLA said it had Holliday on videotape granting KTLA "unlimited rights," including distributing the tape to other TV stations. In 1993, a federal judge dismissed Holliday's lawsuit. Holliday had indeed granted KTLA permission to use and distribute the tape. The tape was newsworthy, and the First Amendment allows for public use of material "of great importance to democratic debate." Holliday had already earned $150,000 for the "licensing of other derivative rights in the video," so there was obviously no damage to the marketability of his tape; therefore, the use of the tape by the TV stations was a "fair use."[12]

Not long after, another famous videotape led to a copyright suit in *Los Angeles News Service v. KCAL-TV.*[13] The Los Angeles News Service (LANS) was covering the riots that followed the verdict in the first Rodney King trial. From a helicopter, LANS shot the famous video of black rioters pulling white truck driver Reginald Denny out of his rig and beating him. LANS made the tape available to several stations with which it had licensing agreements but refused to give permission to KCAL-TV. KCAL, though, got the tape from another station and aired it without LANS' permission.

LANS sued for copyright infringement. KCAL argued that airing the tape qualified as a fair use because the events on the video were newsworthy. But a federal appeals court said newsworthiness was not the only issue here. The court said KCAL "rode LANS' copyrighted coattails" by not getting its own helicopter or paying for the tape. The court also noted that KCAL aired the tape with its own station logo and did not give any credit to LANS on the air. These actions all worked against KCAL's fair use argument. In 1997, the U.S. Supreme Court allowed the case to go to trial to determine damages.

---

[11]FF union upset over bootleg 9/11 video. (2002, January 24). *Newsday*. Retrieved March 20, 2002, from http://www.newsday.com

[12]*Holliday v. Cable News Network,* cv 92-3287 1H (C.D. Cal., 6/11/93)

[13]108 F.3d 1119 (9th Cir. 1997)

In a related case in 1998, LANS was awarded $60,000 in damages for unlicensed use of the Reginald Denny tape in Europe and Africa by Visnews (owned by Reuters, NBC, and the BBC).[14] The court ruled that the Visnews broadcast of the video was not a fair use because the tape had been copied illegally in the United States.

Writing Broadcast News Stories From Newspaper Articles

FAQ

I'm a radio news reporter. I missed a city council meeting last night, but I want to do a story on the meeting for a newscast today. I get the facts about the meeting from a local newspaper article. From that same article, I use two quotes from the mayor. I don't need to mention the local newspaper as my source, do I?

In this situation, you do. Most newspaper stories are copyrighted. Many broadcast news reporters lift information from newspaper stories all of the time, but there are certain parts of that story that are basically public domain and other parts that are the property of the newspaper.

When "borrowing" information from this story, the broadcast journalist needs to keep a few legal issues in mind. First, the broadcast journalist needs to attribute the mayor's quotations because those may be comments the mayor gave only to the newspaper reporter, making them, in a sense, "exclusive." After using the mayor's quotations in a broadcast news story, the broadcaster should also add, "The mayor made those comments in a copyrighted story printed in the April 3, 2002 edition of the *Muddtown Daily News*" or "According to the *Muddtown Daily News. . . .*"

As for the details about the meeting—the results of certain votes, issues discussed, the length of the meeting—those are basic facts that cannot be copyrighted. Anyone is free to borrow those facts from the newspaper article without attribution. Those facts, once reported, become "public." The broadcast reporter should just make sure those facts are not quoted verbatim from the newspaper article. Those facts should be described in the reporter's *own words*. The newspaper reporter's written version of the story (writing style, phrasing) is copyrightable. The broadcast journalist should also double-check the facts, in case the newspaper reporter got something wrong.

FAQ

Have radio or TV stations ever been sued for lifting information from a newspaper story?

---

[14]*Los Angeles News Service v. Reuters Television,* 149 F.3d 987 (9th Cir. 1998)

Yes. In 1963, a Pennsylvania radio station, WPAZ, was found guilty of the frequent pirating of news from a local newspaper; the radio station made it appear as its own staff had gathered the information and written the stories.[15] In copyright law, this is called *misappropriation, plagiarism,* or *unfair competition.* Misappropriation means that you are trying to pass off someone else's work as your own, and that is illegal.

In 1994, the publisher of the *Reading Eagle* newspaper in Pennsylvania sued Reading radio station WIOV for using its news stories verbatim on the air without the newspaper's permission. The *Eagle* originally sought $50,000 in damages. In 1995, a federal judge approved an out-of-court settlement after ruling that the radio station did not dispute the charges.[16] The final settlement amount was not disclosed.

COPYRIGHT AND SPORTS SCORES

FAQ

A radio station in my town has exclusive rights to air a local college's sporting events. I work at a competing radio station. Is it legal for me during my radio show to monitor that other station's sports coverage and give my listeners updates on the score?

This is legal. Sports scores are facts and cannot be copyrighted.

The courts dealt with this issue in the 1997 case *NBA v. Motorola.*[17] Motorola had produced a handheld pager called "SportsTrax" that provided subscribers with updates on professional basketball scores. Subscribers also got other game information, such as the time remaining in a quarter and what team was in possession of the ball. Motorola worked in conjunction with a firm called STATS, which hired people to monitor the games on radio or TV and then feed the game information into a computer. The information was then relayed to subscribers.

The National Basketball Association sued Motorola for misappropriation and unfair competition. The court ruled for Motorola, saying that providing simple game statistics is not unfair competition, nor is it a violation of copyright law.

The courts have consistently ruled that facts are not copyrightable. In 1991, the Supreme Court ruled in *Feist v. Rural Telephone* that the simple listing of names and phone numbers in a telephone directory is not copyrightable. The court ruled that gathering phone numbers and alphabetizing names is not a "creative process" worthy of copyright protection.[18]

---

[15] *Pottstown Daily News Publishing v. Pottstown Broadcasting,* 192 A.2d 657 (1963)

[16] Judge approves settlement in copyright lawsuit. (1995, March 15). *Legal Intelligencer,* p. 11.

[17] *NBA v. Motorola,* 105 F.3d 841 (2d Cir. 1997)

[18] *Feist Publications v. Rural Telephone Service Co.,* 499 U.S. 340 (1991)

That same year, though, an appeals court ruled in *Key Publications v. Chinatown Today* that a New York City business directory was copyrightable because it was more than just a list of facts. The court said the person who compiled the directory engaged in a creative process. That was because the directory was similar to the *Yellow Pages* in that it categorized businesses according to the services they provided. Therefore, the directory was more than a mere alphabetical or chronological listing.[19]

Simple, basic facts are not copyrightable. However, a creative arrangement of facts is copyrightable. That is why the audio and video recordings of sporting events are often copyrighted. Therefore, you must get permission to use another station's or network's sports video or audio in your sportscast.

PARODIES

FAQ

Is it legal to use copyrighted material for comedic purposes?

Yes, if your purpose is to make fun of the copyrighted work. Such humorous works are called parodies. Weird Al Yankovich is probably today's most famous parodist. Weird Al pokes fun at other artists' songs by making up humorous lyrics to go along with the artists' original music. There was "Eat It," a parody of Michael Jackson's hit "Beat It," as well as "Fat," a parody of Jackson's "Bad." Weird Al says he gets permission from the writers of songs before he does parodies of them.

But Weird Al got a bit of negative publicity with "Amish Paradise," his parody of Coolio's "Gangsta's Paradise." There had been some confusion about whether Weird Al's record label had asked for Coolio's "blessing" to do the parody. Coolio said that he had never given the OK for the parody and that he was offended by "Amish Paradise." Weird Al sent out a letter of apology to Coolio, saying it was his policy to ask for an artist's permission, if for no other reason than to be courteous.

However, *legally*, did Weird Al need to get that permission? According to Weird Al's Web site, "The law supports his ability to parody without permission."[20] The following cases show us that Weird Al's Web site is basically correct. The courts have ruled that legitimate parodies are a protected form of humor and criticism. If the courts did not allow people to use copyrighted works to make *fun* of those works, the public would be deprived of various kinds of humor and public commentary, from that of radio disc jockeys to political cartoons to TV comedy shows. At the same time, though, there is no guarantee that every parody will be given protection by the courts.

A case involving a popular late-night TV comedy show helped to set a standard for how the courts would apply fair use doctrine in parody cases.

---

[19] *Key Publications Inc. v. Chinatown Today*, 945 F.2d 509 (2d Cir. 1991)

[20] *"Weird Al" Yankovic FAQ*. (2004). Retrieved November 2, 2004, from http://www.weirdal.com/faq.htm

Saturday Night Live Parody

The NBC-TV show "*Saturday Night Live*" (*SNL*) is famous for how it mocks anything and everything in our culture. The show has done parodies of other TV shows, movies, and commercials, among other things. In the late 1970s, *SNL* aired a skit that ended with people singing "I Love Sodom" to the tune of "I Love New York." The song "I Love New York" was part of a famous promotional campaign for New York City. The city, which had commissioned the writing of "I Love New York," sued. It said the use of the song, even with the altered lyrics, was a copyright infringement. A U.S. Court of Appeals ruled for *SNL* and gave us an important precedent regarding parodies. The court ruled that a parody is simply "using the original as a known element of modern culture and contributing something new for humorous effect or commentary."[21] The court made two important points here: (a) The parody must build upon the original work, and (b) *using even a large amount of the original work is a fair use, as long as your goal is to* criticize *or* make fun of *the original work.*

FAQ

So parodies or other humorous uses of copyrighted material are always legal?

No. Parodists should not count on automatic protection for their parodies simply because their works are humorous. Using large amounts of a copyrighted work in a parody can lead to problems with other parts of the fair use test. In 1979, a company named Showcase Atlanta produced a three-act play entitled *Scarlett Fever*, a spoof of the book and MGM film classic *Gone With the Wind*. Their spoof called the plantation "Tiara" instead of "Tara," and the main character was "Shady Charlotte O'Mara" instead of Scarlett O'Hara. In *MGM v. Showcase Atlanta*,[22] a federal district court found that this spoof had crossed the line between parody and copyright infringement, even though the court found the play to be "humorous" and "entertaining."

The court looked at the purpose of the use and said that the play's purpose was neither parody nor critical commentary. The court found that the play created too much of its own comedy without mocking or criticizing the original book or movie, and this was an important element in defining a parody. As a result, the court said the play was merely a "derivative" work to which the copyright holders had legal rights.

As for the amount of the original work used, the court said the play was too literal and "incorporated more material from the film . . . and novel . . . than fair use allows." The play contained numerous scenes that lifted dialogue word-for-word from the movie and novel. The court said such extensive copying was not necessary to help the audience "recall" or "conjure up" the original work.

Showcase Atlanta had also argued that their play would enhance demand for the original works. The court disagreed, saying that the play "could harm a potential market for or value of a stage version of 'Gone With the Wind.'" The court said this point was speculative but felt a need to protect the derivative rights of the copyright holders.

---

[21] *Elsmere Music v. NBC*, 623 F.2d 252 (2d Cir.1980)

[22] 479 F. Supp. 351 (N.D. Ga. 1979)

The "criticism" factor would become a critical point in future parody cases. Parodists had to prove to the courts that their works were indeed mocking or criticizing the original work. Famous DJ Rick Dees was taken to court over a parody he recorded for a 1984 album. The song was called "When Sonny Sniffs Glue," a parody of the 1950s Johnny Mathis hit "When Sunny Gets Blue." The original song included the lyrics "When Sonny gets blue, her eyes get grey and cloudy, then the rain begins to fall."

Dees' version: "When Sonny sniffs glue, her eyes get red and bulgy, then her hair begins to fall."

In *Fisher v. Dees*[23], a U.S. Court of Appeals ruled for Dees, saying "When Sonny Sniffs Glue" was an obvious parody worthy of legal protection. The court applied the fair use doctrine here and determined, among other things, that Dees' main objective was humor. The court wrote that the parody's intent was "to poke fun at the composers' song and at Mr. Mathis' rather singular vocal range." This is an important point. The intent was to *criticize,* not to copy.

Copyright law says the copyright owner has the right to make copies. However, for parodies, the court said we have to allow for exact or near-exact copying of the original. Otherwise, the humor will not work. Finally, the parody did not damage the "marketability" of the original. In other words, people who want the original will purchase the original. People who like the parody will purchase the parody. They are two distinct markets. One will not affect the other. Therefore, Dees did not infringe on the copyright of the original.

FAQ

Aren't there parodies that could indeed damage the image or value of the original work? Would this still be a fair use?

In 1994, the Supreme Court addressed this issue in a landmark parody case.

THE RAP ON "(OH) PRETTY WOMAN"

In 1989, the rap group 2 Live Crew released the song "Pretty Woman," which the group said was a parody of Roy Orbison's 1964 classic "(Oh) Pretty Woman." 2 Live Crew had asked the owners of the song, Acuff-Rose Music, for permission to record the song, but Acuff-Rose refused. The group went ahead and used the basic melody, the first two lines from the song, and the opening bass notes, but they changed the rest of the lyrics to make fun of the song, with lines such as "Two timin' woman you's out with my boy last night."

Acuff-Rose Music filed suit against 2 Live Crew and its lead singer Luther R. Campbell. A U.S. Appeals Court ruled for Acuff-Rose, saying it is *never* a fair use to do a commercial parody.[24] But in 1994, in *Campbell v. Acuff-Rose Music, Inc.,*[25] the U.S. Supreme Court overturned the appellate court, ruling that 2 Live Crew's parody was a fair use, for several reasons.

---

[23]794 F.2d 432 (9th Cir. 1986)

[24]*Acuff-Rose v. Campbell*, 972 F.2d 1429 (6th Cir. 1992)

[25]510 U.S. 569 (1994)

Nature of the work: "(Oh) Pretty Woman" is a copyrighted published song, and this factor weighs in favor of Acuff-Rose. *Purpose of the use:* The Supreme Court saw that 2 Live Crew had three possible purposes here: commercial gain, social commentary, and parody. The court said that just because this parody was "commercial" did not automatically make it an "unfair use." Second, the court saw some deeper meanings in this song; it said that 2 Live Crew had used the original song to make a social commentary as well as a parody. Justice Souter wrote, "The later words can be taken as a comment on the naivete of the original of an earlier day."[26] Third, Acuff-Rose tried to argue that the song was *not* a parody, but the court said the song's lyrics proved "convincingly" that it was a parody. Justice Souter added that the free flow of information would be hindered if we did not allow for the use of copyrighted works in commercial endeavors such as newscasts, commentaries, research—and parodies. Souter acknowledged that parodies do not receive automatic protection, so the next two criteria needed to be addressed.

Amount of the work used: Souter wrote that 2 Live Crew copied the "heart" of the original work, but at the same time, the group's version "departed markedly" from the original lyrics. Souter said that 2 Live Crew "appropriates no more from the original than is necessary to accomplish reasonably its parodic purpose." *Effect on the market:* The Supreme Court ruled that this factor favored Campbell because it was "extremely unlikely that 2 Live Crew's song could adversely affect the market for the original. The intended audience for the two songs is entirely different." The court added that it is a violation of copyright when a copy *replaces* the original but not when the copy *mocks* the original. 2 Live Crew was definitely mocking here.

However, when an artist uses a copyrighted work to mock something *other* than the copyrighted work, the courts tend to see a violation of fair use.

Satire

Parody means using elements of a copyrighted work to make fun of that copyrighted work. *Satire* means using elements of a copyrighted work to make fun of *something else.* Satire does not receive the same protection as parody in copyright law. The best example of this is *Dr. Seuss Enterprises v. Penguin Books.*[27] In 1995, two authors made fun of the publicity surrounding the O. J. Simpson murder trial. Their "poetic" summary of the trial, titled *The Cat NOT in the Hat! A Parody by Dr. Juice* clearly mimicked the rhyme scheme used in Dr. Seuss' famous book *The Cat in the Hat.*

A U.S. Appeals Court ruled for Dr. Seuss Enterprises. The court pointed out that *Dr. Juice* was not written to make fun of *The Cat in the Hat.* Instead, *Dr. Juice* used the copyrighted style of *The Cat in the Hat* to make fun of something else—the O. J. Simpson trial. The court said that such a use was a *satire,* not a parody.

As a satire, the court said, *The Cat NOT in the Hat* basically stole a copyrighted style to ridicule a famous murder trial. That, unlike a parody, is illegal. The court ordered an immediate halt to the distribution of *The Cat NOT in the Hat!*

Movie Poster Cases

Two 1998 rulings also help to clarify the legal line drawn between a protected parody and an unprotected satire. The first case involved a poster for the Paramount movie *Naked*

---

[26]*Ibid.*, p. 583.

[27]109 F.3d 1394 (9th Cir.1997)

Gun 33 1/3: The Final Insult. The poster showed actor Leslie Nielsen's head superimposed on a nude pregnant woman, a spoof of a similar photograph of pregnant actress Demi Moore featured on a 1991 cover of *Vanity Fair.* Annie Leibovitz had shot the cover photo of Moore, and she sued for copyright infringement. In 1998, in *Leibovitz v. Paramount Pictures,*[28] the court ruled that the movie poster was a protected parody. The poster featured Nielsen smirking, and the court said this was in contrast to the serious look of Moore in her photo. The court said the poster "may reasonably be perceived as commenting on the seriousness, even the pretentiousness, of the original."

However, in *Columbia Pictures v. Miramax,*[29] the court did not see a parody in a movie poster for a Michael Moore documentary *The Big One.* The poster showed Moore dressed and posed like Tommy Lee Jones and Will Smith as they appeared on posters for the movie *Men in Black.* Moore was grinning, carrying large weapons, and standing in front of the New York City skyline at night, very similar to the layout of the *Men in Black* poster. Moore's poster read "Protecting the Earth from the Scum of Corporate America." The *Men in Black* poster reads, "Protecting the Earth from the Scum of the Universe." The court ruled that the Moore poster was not poking fun at *Men in Black* but was simply taking images from a copyrighted poster to ridicule corporate America. Moore tried to argue that his grin on the poster was a parody of the serious looks of Smith and Jones on their poster. The court, though, said this element was not enough to find for a fair use of the original. Too much of the poster was devoted to attacking something other than the original work.

COPYRIGHT AND THE INTERNET

With everything from illegal music download sites to the online pirating of commercial motion pictures, the Internet has provided numerous challenges in regard to copyright law. Many factors, including its widespread use and relative ease of access, have made the Internet difficult to police. However, in spite of these difficulties, lawmakers and copyright holders are striving to make sure that copyright laws are followed in cyberspace.

In 1995, a federal task force studied copyright issues regarding the Internet. The task force recommendations included outlawing devices that override anticopying technologies and eliminating the first sale doctrine. In 1998, without even addressing the task force's recommendation, the U.S. Supreme Court upheld the first sale doctrine in *Quality King Distributors v. L'Anza Research International.*[30]

Digital Millennium Copyright Act (DMCA)

Congress passed this act in 1998 to ensure that copyright laws protected new digital technologies as well as the Internet. However, librarians, broadcasters, teachers, and others complained that the DMCA limited some freedoms on the Web.[31]

---

[28] 137 F.3d 109 (2d Cir. 1998)

[29] 11 F. Supp. 1179 (C.D. Cal. 1998)

[30] 523 U.S. 135 (1998)

[31] 17 U.S.C. §1201

DMCA Main Elements

According to the DMCA, makers of digital recording equipment and VCRs must install technological protection measures (TPM) or a content scramble system (CSS) to help prevent people from making illegal copies of copyrighted works. For example, a VCR with TPM will not allow consumers to make illegal copies of movie rentals or pay-per-view programs. It is illegal to produce equipment that would help circumvent or "get around" a TPM or CSS.

Internet service providers (ISPs) cannot be held liable for copyright infringements when users upload material to their sites. However, the ISP must prove that it had no actual knowledge of the infringement and that it took quick action to eliminate the copyrighted material. Nonprofit libraries are allowed to make digital copies of some materials for archiving and replacement purposes.

Digital versions of graphics, sound recordings, movies, photographs, and videos have copyright protection.

Regarding people who Webcast music, the DMCA (a) does not allow the playing of more than three songs from one album in a 3-hour period, and no more than two consecutively; (b) prohibits Webcasters from publishing playlists of upcoming music; (c) prohibits Webcasters from using bootleg copies of music; (d) does not allow the playing of four songs from a boxed set or the same artist in a 3-hour period and no more than three consecutively. All of these rules were designed to help reduce the likelihood of people making illegal copies of music.

FAQ

Is it legal to record copyrighted songs off of the Internet?

Yes, as long as you have done so through a legitimate file-sharing site that has obtained permission from copyright holders. However, many of the first music-sharing sites were found to have violated copyright laws.

MP3s

One of the biggest controversies involves "music swapping" through the use of MP3 files. MP3 technology allows for the rapid copying of music from the Internet. In fact, the Recording Industry Association of America (RIAA) sued to stop manufacture of the MP3. The RIAA said the main purpose of MP3 technology was to make illegal copies of copyrighted music. In 1999, in *RIAA v. Diamond Multimedia Systems,*[32] a federal appeals court ruled that MP3 recorders also provide for various legal uses, and the technology could not be banned just because some people might use it illegally.

$53 Million Settlement for MP3.com

In August 2000, in *UMG Recordings et al. v. MP3.com,*[33] a federal district court judge ruled that the music-sharing Web site MP3.com would have to pay numerous music companies,

---

[32]180 F.3d 1072 (9th Cir. 1999)

[33]109 F. Supp.2d 223 (S.D.N.Y. 2000)

including Universal Music Group, Sony Music Group, and Warner Music Group, $25,000 for each illegally copied CD on the MP3.com Web site. Some experts estimated that would cost MP3.com as much as $250 million. Judge Jed Rakoff said the Web site had illegally stored copyrighted CDs on its Web site and then made 80,000 songs from those CDs available for illegal copying by its customers. MP3.com had not secured licensing deals with music companies before making the music available.

In November 2000, MP3.com reached an out-of-court settlement with Universal Music Group, agreeing to pay them $53.4 million to end the copyright suits. MP3.com had also reached earlier settlements with four other music companies, paying them $20 million each. At the same time, a much more prominent Internet copyright case was winding its way through the courts.

Napster

By the year 2000, the music-swapping Web site Napster had an estimated 70 million users worldwide. There were numerous smaller Web sites that allowed similar sharing, but Napster was by far the biggest and most popular. The recording industry saw a substantial threat here. If people were allowed to get copyrighted music for free through a computer, that would mean fewer paying customers at music stores.

The recording industry took action and filed suit against Napster in 1999 for copyright infringement. In July 2000, U.S. District Court Judge Marilyn Hall Patel, calling Napster "a monster," ruled that the Web site was guilty of copyright infringement. The Napster site violated the rights of the music companies to reproduce and distribute their works, damaging the music companies' ability to profit from their copyrighted works. "The more music . . . sampling users download, the less likely they are to eventually purchase the recordings on audio CD." Judge Patel also said that the trading of music files via Napster was not a fair use of copyrighted material. People often copied entire pieces of music, not just small portions. She ordered Napster to shut down and prohibited the Web site from doing any "copying, downloading, uploading, transmitting, or distributing" of music.

Napster appealed Judge Patel's ruling, and a federal appeals court stayed the shutdown order until the appeal could be heard. In February 2001, in *A&M Records et al. v. Napster*,[34] the federal appeals court ruled that a complete shutdown of Napster was unnecessary. That was partly because some of the music files on Napster were not copyrighted and there were some files that Napster had the copyright owner's permission to use.

The appeals court sent the case back to Patel for revision. Patel's new ruling said that Napster must only stop the downloading and uploading of copyrighted songs when a copyright owner requested that Napster do so. The copyright owner must provide Napster with the name of the artist, song title, and the names of these files in the Napster system.

Users of Napster tried to get around this law by making slight changes in the names of artists and songs ("Madonna" might become "Modanna," for example). The court, though, said that Napster also needed to weed out files with these name changes and spelling variations.

Napster tried to settle the lawsuit out of court by offering to pay the music companies $1 billion if those companies would license all of their music to Napster. The companies refused. In July 2001, Napster shut itself down to do some restructuring to figure out how it would comply with the order to eliminate copyrighted music from its site.

---

[34]239 F.3d 1004 (9th Cir. 2001)

Napster Goes Bankrupt and Then Reemerges

In June 2002, after being plagued by lawsuits and a large reduction in people using its Web site, Napster filed for Chapter 11 bankruptcy. However, that did not mean an automatic end for Napster. Chapter 11 allows companies to get back on their financial feet and reorganize. At the time, Napster said it had more than $100 million in liabilities and debts but only about $8 million in the bank. By 2003, Napster reappeared on the Web with a legal music downloading service that charged users a monthly fee. Numerous other pay sites emerged, including iTunes, which claims it sold more than 70 million songs during its first year.[35]

FAQ

Is there any proof that music file sharing has harmed the music industry?

The recording industry points to numerous studies that blame file sharing and other forms of music copying for decreases in recorded music sales. In 2002, the International Federation of the Phonographic Industry reported that sales for recorded music had decreased by 10% in the United States. In 2004, the federation announced that global music sales had declined for the fourth consecutive year, resulting in losses of thousands of jobs in the music industry. The recording industry in America looked at these numbers and decided to take action.

The Recording Industry Strikes Back

In 2003, the music industry continued its legal battle against pirated music on the Internet when the RIAA filed lawsuits against 261 individuals who had engaged in large-scale music file sharing. The lawsuits targeted "egregious uploaders" and included everyone from a 12-year-old girl in New York to a 71-year-old grandfather in Texas. (The RIAA eventually dropped one case against a 66-year-old Boston woman who said she did not even own file-sharing software. The RIAA had threatened to sue her for as much as $150,000 per song, claiming she had illegally shared more than 2000 songs.) The RIAA said file sharing was a main reason for a 31% drop in CD music sales since mid-2000 and that the lawsuits were designed to show Americans that the illegal downloading and sharing of music would no longer be tolerated. At the same time, the RIAA announced an amnesty program for users who admitted they had shared illegal music files via the Internet, but those users had to agree not to engage in the practice in the future.

To find violators more easily, the RIAA said it had subpoena power through the DMCA to force ISPs such as Verizon to reveal the identities of illegal file sharers. However, in December 2003, in *RIAA v. Verizon*,[36] a federal appeals court ruled that the RIAA could only obtain such information from ISPs through court-approved subpoenas. That way, accused file sharers would be allowed to challenge the subpoenas before having their names disclosed. However, the court said that this did not affect the RIAA's right to file lawsuits against file sharers.

---

[35]*iPod + iTunes for Mac and Windows.* (2004). Retrieved July 9, 2004, from http://www.apple.com/itunes/

[36]351 F.3d 1229 (D.C. Cir. 2003)

In the following months, the RIAA continued to file lawsuits. By March 2004, it had sued a total of nearly 2000 people. The RIAA's tactics appear to have worked to a large degree. A study by the research company NPD found that in August 2003, 1.4 million households deleted all music files on their computers. The NPD said that was up significantly from May, when 600,000 households had deleted music files. NPD also found an 11% decrease in the number of households engaging in peer-to-peer sharing of music files via the Internet. The NPD said that most of the deletions and decreases could be attributed to public fear resulting from the RIAA lawsuits.[37]

RADIO STATION WEBCASTING

By the late 1990s, radio stations across the country were broadcasting or "Webcasting" their signals through the Internet. Suddenly, a radio station in a small town could be heard around the world simply by streaming its audio onto the World Wide Web. However, the music industry argued that radio station Webcasting constituted another "use" of copyrighted music, and therefore, it argued, radio stations should pay extra copyright fees.[38]

In February 2002, under guidelines established through the DMCA, the Copyright Arbitration Royalties Panel (CARP) released a proposal that disheartened and frightened Internet broadcasters.[39] CARP proposed that anyone using copyrighted music on the Internet pay an annual $500 license fee. On top of that, commercial broadcasters who streamed their on-air signals would pay 7/100 cents "per performance" (which means "per song per listener").

FAQ

That's not that much to pay, is it—7/100 cents per performance?

It does not appear like much on the surface, but after doing some math, broadcasters went into a panic. If 200 people listened to 20 songs through a radio station's Web site, it would count as 4000 performances. For playing just those 20 songs over the Internet, the station would owe $280 in royalties. Many stations estimated that they would be paying tens of thousands of dollars each month in royalty fees. CARP also said that the rates would be retroactive to October 1998. Noncommercial broadcasters would pay 2/100 cents per song per listener. Internet-only Webcasters would pay 14/100 cents per performance. In June 2002, the Library of Congress rejected CARP's varied rate plan and said that all music Webcasting would cost 7/100 cents per performance. Faced with prohibitive costs, most

---

[37]NPD Group, Inc. (2003, November 5). *Consumers delete large numbers of digital music files from PC hard drives, the NPD group reports.* Retrieved November 3, 2004, from http://www.npd.com/press/releases/press_031105.htm

[38]Wired News. (2002, February 21). *Webcasters learn cost of music.* Retrieved March 28, 2002, from http://www.wired.com/news/mp3/0,1285,50551,00.html?tw=wn_story_related

[39]U.S. Copyright Office. (2002, February 20). *Webcasting rates.* Retrieved March 28, 2002, from http://www.copyright.gov/carp/

music radio stations across the country stopped broadcasting over the Internet, and many small music Webcasters shut down.

In October 2002, Congress passed the Small Webcaster Settlement Act[40] to allow small Webcasters to bypass the Library of Congress fees and negotiate individual royalty rates with the recording industry. The act did not define who qualifies as a "small" Webcaster, and it did not address the issue of retroactive royalties. In 2003, the recording industry provided discounted rates to noncommercial Webcasters and college radio stations.

Movie Bootlegs, the Internet, and CSS

In 2004, the Motion Picture Association of America (MPAA) said, 92% of pirated copies of movies ("bootlegs") were the result of a person sneaking a camcorder into a theater. The recordings are usually poor quality, with dark, grainy pictures and distorted audio. The tapes often include distractions, such as people walking in front of the camera or the sounds of others in the theater. Copies of these tapes are circulated on the black market through street vendors, disreputable video stores, and, more recently, the Web.[41]

In the 1990s, downloading a pirated movie off of the Internet was usually a time-consuming process that involved countless hours and viewing on a small computer screen, but technology would soon change that. By the new millennium, computers and Internet connections had become faster, and computers came with DVD burners. As a result, a full-length feature film could be downloaded in as little as an hour, and the person could watch the DVD copy on a TV. The quality had also improved, as some bootleggers were providing clean digital copies of movies.

FAQ

How do pirates obtain perfect copies of these films?

There are numerous methods. Before a film is released to the public, movie companies will send out DVDs of the movie to ad agencies and reviewers, and pirates find ways to get hold of them. Sometimes pirates will pay "insiders"—people who work in and around movie sets—and these insiders steal copies of the movie.

Filmmakers began to see a potential major threat to their livelihoods. In 2002, a pirated copy of the hit movie *Signs*, starring Mel Gibson, was available on the Internet weeks before the movie appeared in theaters. These bootlegs are, of course, a major threat to the home video and DVD market from which many films make the majority of their profits.

The movie industry has struck back. The MPAA lobbied to pass a law in California, where, as of January 1, 2004, it became illegal to use a camcorder to record a feature film in a theater. Violators face up to 1 year in jail and $2500 in fines. The MPAA is lobbying to get similar laws passed in other states. The MPAA also offers rewards of up to $500 for any

---

[40]116 Stat. 2780

[41]Techzonez. (2004, January 7). *Spiderman pirate caught red handed.* Retrieved November 3, 2004, from http://www.techzonez.com/forums/archive/index.php/t-10574.html

theater employee who catches a person with a camcorder. In summer 2004, a teenager in California was arrested at the premiere of *Spiderman 2* after he was found with a camcorder. A projectionist wearing night-vision goggles had spotted the young man.

In 2004, Congress passed two bills making such camcorder use in theaters a federal offense. Under the proposed laws, people who secretly videotape movies in theaters could face up to 3 years in prison for a first offense and up to 10 years for repeat offenses. People who secretly videotape for profit would face stiffer penalties. The bills also allow the copyright holders to sue for damages.

In November 2004, the Motion Picture Association of America announced a wave of lawsuits against individuals who distributed pirated movies through peer-to-peer sharing programs on the Internet. Copyright law allows penalties of up to $150,000 for each pirated movie that is traded.[42]

File-Sharing Software Ruled Legal

The motion picture and recording industries also took their battle to the courts in *MGM, Inc. v. Grokster,*[43] filing lawsuits against Streamcast Networks and Grokster, two companies that made video and audio file-sharing software. In April 2003, federal district court judge Stephen Wilson ruled that Streamcast and Grokster were not liable for illegal copying done with their software. Wilson wrote that these companies were not like Napster because they had no direct control over files shared on their networks. That ruling was upheld in August 2004 by the Ninth Circuit Court of Appeals.[44]

DVD-Copying Software Faces Legal Challenges

In February 2004, a federal district court judge did find a DVD-copying software to be a violation of the DMCA. In *321 Studios v. MGM Studios,*[45] the judge ruled that the software made by 321 Studios infringed on the copyrights of moviemakers. The argument of 321 was that the software provided fair uses, such as a person making extra copies of movies in case the original got scratched or broken. The judge, though, ruled that the software was still a bypass of CSS and prohibited by the DMCA.

In 2002, the Directors Guild of America sued CleanFlicks, a Colorado video store that was renting "clean" DVD copies of popular movies with objectionable material edited out. The Directors Guild also sued ClearPlay of Salt Lake City for creating software that allowed people to edit objectionable material from movies. The Directors Guild said both companies were illegally altering copyrighted motion pictures.

In 2004, the lawsuit had not been resolved, and RCA began selling a "family friendly" DVD player using the ClearPlay software. ClearPlay employees watch movies, keep track of objectionable material, and then create a "filter" for each movie. RCA said its DVD players would include ClearPlay filters for 100 popular Hollywood films. The lawsuit is pending.

---

[42]Gentile, G. (2004, November 16). *Film industry files anti-piracy lawsuits.* Retrieved November 17, 2004, from http://apnews.myway.com/article/20041116/D86D4AR01.html

[43]259 F. Supp.2d 1029 (S.D. Cal. 2003)

[44]*MGM, Inc. v. Grokster*, 380 F.3d 1154 (9th Cir.)

[45]307 F. Supp.2d 1085 (N.D. Cal. 2004)

BBS Sites

An Internet bulletin board service (BBS) is a site on which people can post information or pictures to exchange with other BBS users. However, the BBS owners can find themselves in legal trouble when users post copyrighted materials on the sites.

In *Playboy v. Frena*[46] in 1993, George Frena had operated a BBS site called Techs Warehouse, on which paid subscribers often posted pictures. In this case, the BBS users had posted 170 copyrighted photographs from *Playboy* magazine, and other users were able to download those images.

Playboy sued Frena for (a) *copyright infringement,* saying that Frena knowingly allowed the pictures to be used; (b) *trademark infringement* because the BBS site often described the pictures using the trademarked words *Playboy* and *Playmate;* and (c) *unfair competition* because Frena removed the trademarked words from the pictures and placed his site's name, "Techs Warehouse," and his phone number on the Web site pictures.

Frena argued that he was not guilty of copyright violations because, he said, he immediately removed all copyrighted *Playboy* pictures from the site when he was served with the summons and then more closely monitored the BBS to make sure no more copyrighted pictures were on the site. He added that he personally did not upload any images, only his users did.

The court found that Frena was guilty of copyright and trademark infringement, as well as unfair competition, because Frena supplied a product (the BBS) that contained unauthorized reproductions of copyrighted material, and the Copyright Act of 1976 says that copyright holders have various rights regarding their works, including the rights to reproduce, to distribute copies, and to display publicly. As a result, Frena's BBS violated *Playboy's* right to distribute copies of their works and to display those works publicly.

It did not matter that Frena did not upload the pictures to the site. He knew about them.

Copyright law allows for distribution of copyrighted material to a "small circle of family and friends." The subscribers to the Web site were outside of this small circle. The pictures were not a "fair use." Techs Warehouse was a commercial site, the works were copyrighted, Frena used the pictures in their entirety, and the posting of the pictures damaged *Playboy's* ability to profit from them.

Frena was also guilty of trademark infringement because using the trademarked names "falsely suggested affiliation with the trademark owner in a manner likely to cause confusion." The court said Frena gave the false impression that *Playboy* endorsed the use of the photographs on the BBS site. Frena was guilty of unfair competition, as well, when he put his name on some pictures in place of the *Playboy* name. The court said this denied *Playboy* the right to receive public credit for its works.

In a similar suit in 1998, *Playboy Enterprises v. Sanfilippo,*[47] a federal district court awarded Playboy $3.74 million in a suit against a Web site owner who had distributed nearly 7500 copyrighted Playboy photographs.

---

[46]839 F. Supp 1552 (M.D. Fla. 1993)

[47]1998 U.S. Dist. Lexis 4773

TRADEMARKS

A trademark is an "identifying symbol" for a product. The Federal Trademark Act of 1946,[48] also known as the Lanham Act, is the main governing law for trademarks. There is also something called a service mark, which is a symbol identifying a service. In essence, the law recognizes a trademark and a service mark as basically the same thing. *Trademark* is most often used to refer to both. As the Lanham Act points out, a trademark is an important protection for a businessperson with which he or she can "identify and distinguish his or her goods . . . from those manufactured and sold by others."[47]

A trademark is like a copyright. It protects a creative work. Whereas copyrights protect longer works, such as books, movies, and sound recordings, a trademark is a protection for a solitary symbol, such as a word, a name, a slogan, or a logo. Trademarks are all around us. Examples include the names and logos for Burger King, Coca-Cola, Kleenex, Tabasco Sauce, M&M's, Jell-O, *TV Guide*, and Kool Aid.

Sounds can also be trademarked, such as the familiar three-note refrain that accompanies the NBC peacock on TV, the roar of the MGM lion, or the four notes that play at the end of an ad for the Intel Pentium Processor.

Trademarks in News Stories

FAQ

Am I allowed to use a trademark as part of a news story?

Yes, as long as you are not exploiting for trademark for commercial gain.

The singing group New Kids on the Block brought a lawsuit in the 1980s against two publications, *USA Today* and *Star* magazine. Both publications had used the New Kids' trademark in print to promote a 900-number phone survey to find out which New Kid was most popular.

New Kids argued that the use of their trademark implied that the singing group endorsed the survey. The singing group also said there was commercial misappropriation because the newspapers made money from the 900 calls. A federal court rejected those arguments and ruled for the newspapers. The court said there is First Amendment protection for the use of a trademark in legitimate newsgathering. The court said news organizations should be allowed to use trademarks in stories to avoid "the danger of restricting newsgathering and dissemination."[49]

On the other hand, in broadcast news stories and other on-air material, stations often prefer to avoid using a trademark or brand name to identify a generic product. Using the brand name makes it appear like stations are giving free advertising to a certain item. So instead of saying, "The woman grabbed a Kleenex," say "The woman grabbed a tissue." Instead of saying, "He Xeroxed the report," say "He photocopied the report."

---

[48]15 U.S.C.A. § 1127 (West Supp. 1996)

[49]*New Kids on the Block v. News America Publishing, Inc.*, 745 F. Supp. 1540 (C.D. Cal. 1990)

Slogans such as "I'm Lovin' It" (McDonald's) are also protected as trademarks. Do not use any famous slogan in any type of broadcast station promotions. Although listeners may "love" a radio station, the station should not promote itself with "I'm Lovin' It."

Broadcasters also need to be careful about using slogans or trademarks in names of local programming. Although it would be OK to refer to the NBC show *Saturday Night Live* in a news report, it would not be OK to call a weekend radio show *Saturday Night Live*. It is a trademarked name.

These examples may seem rather obvious, but broadcasters inappropriately use trademarked names and phrases frequently.

Abandoned Trademarks

Some words that used to be trademarks have lost their trademark protection because a company abandons the words or the company allows the words to become part of everyday usage. Words such as *aspirin, thermos*, and *yo-yo* used to be registered trademarks until their generic usage placed them in the public domain.

Radio Station Trademarks

Broadcast stations are allowed to protect their call letters as trademarks.

In 1984, two radio stations in Indiana got into a legal battle over this issue. WMEE-FM in Fort Wayne covered some of the same listening area as WADM-FM of Decatur. When WADM changed its call letters to WMCZ, the problems started. "WMCZ" sounded very similar to "WMEE" when said on the air. A federal judge ruled that WMCZ was "overwhelmingly phonetically and rhythmically similar" to WMEE. Because WMEE had established its call letters first, the judge ordered the Decatur station to stop using the call letters WMCZ. The judge also told WMCZ to air a disclaimer to tell listeners that the station was *not* WMEE.[50]

Stations today are also identifying themselves by a name or slogan, such as "Classic 103," "The Blaze," "The Edge," and a radio station in St. Louis calling itself simply "Alice." Stations will often trademark their names, so be careful when trying to come up with a name for your station. The name may be taken already.

In Illinois in August 2000, a new station, WBZM-FM, hit the airwaves in Bloomington-Normal. It called itself "Modern Rock, The Buzz" and "107.7 The Buzz." Later that year, two other radio stations in Illinois had the same idea. In Macomb, the new station WNLF-FM called itself "Modern Rock 95.9 The Buzz." WNLF had spent thousands of dollars printing promotional items like tee shirts and bumper stickers with the station name emblazoned on them. At about the same time, an active rock station, WBZG-FM, in Lasalle-Peru, was also calling itself "The Buzz."

The Cromwell Group, owners of the *first* "Buzz," WBZM, threatened legal action against both stations. Unknown to those two stations, Cromwell had trademarked the name "The Buzz" for the entire state of Illinois. Soon, the Illinois Secretary of State's office got involved, sending cease-and-desist letters to both stations. The letter stated that no other Illinois radio station could call itself "The Buzz," even if its signal did not overlap with WBZM. To avoid lawsuits, both WBZG and WNLF agreed to stop calling themselves "The Buzz."

---

[50]*Pathfinder Communications Corp. v. Midwest Communications Co.* 593 F.Supp 281 (N.D. Ind. 1984)

TV Show Trademarks

In 1999, PBS viewers were becoming acquainted with a show called *Antiques Roadshow*, on which experts gave appraisals of people's heirlooms and antiques.

Also that year, the International Toy Collector's Association (ITCA) was traveling around the country with its "Antique Toy Roadshow." Their experts would appraise the value of toys and then try to purchase them.

The producer of PBS's *Antiques Roadshow*, WGBH-TV in Boston, brought a copyright lawsuit against the ITCA, saying the similarity in the names of the shows created confusion. An article in the July 1999 edition of *Maine Antique Digest* reported that "Antique Toy Roadshow" had allegedly bought some toys at "thousands of dollars under market value."[51] As a result, WGBH said this kind of behavior and a similar name brought an "unwanted comparison" with PBS's *Antiques Roadshow*. WGBH's attorney argued, "We have to defend that licensed trademark against anything that could cause a diversion of business or create confusion about our trademarked name."[52]

In December 1999, the two sides reached an undisclosed "mutually satisfactory agreement." That agreement appears to have included a name change, because ITCA dropped the word *antique* from its traveling show, which is now just called "The Toy Roadshow."[53]

The Federal Trademark Dilution Act of 1995

Owners of trademarks had become upset about people "parodying" their trademarks, whether it was to make fun of the product itself or to make fun of something else. The courts have defined *dilution* as "the gradual 'whittling away' of a trademark's value."[54] Basically, this is the negative use of a trademark that "tarnishes" that trademark's image. The 1995 act[55] gives more protection to owners of "famous" trademarks, whether registered or unregistered.

A famous dilution case in 1972 involved the use of the Coca-Cola trademark. A company had printed satirical posters reading "Enjoy cocaine" with lettering and coloring identical to the Coca-Cola logo. A court ruled for Coca-Cola, saying the association of the soft drink with an illegal drug could "dilute" the value of Coke's trademark. The court said that the posters could give people the wrong impression that the Coca-Cola Company was treating illegal drug use as something humorous.[56]

A recent example occurred in a 1997 case involving the retail chain Toys "R" Us. The company did not approve of a pornographic Web site calling itself "Adults R Us." A federal judge agreed that this was a dilution of the Toys "R" Us trademark, and the judge ordered the Web site to change its name.[57]

---

[51]Hewett, D. (1999, July). What distinguishes a *Roadshow* from the *Antiques Roadshow? Maine Antique Digest*. Retrieved November 2, 2004, from http://www.maineantiquedigest.com/articles/itca0799.htm

[52]*Ibid.*, p. 2

[53]Scheiber, D. (2002, January 8). Do you have this toy in your attic? *St. Petersburg Times*. Retrieved June 2, 2003, from http://www.sptimes.com/2002/01/08/news_pf/Floridian/Do_you_have_this_toy_.shtml

[54]See *Academy of Motion Picture Arts and Sciences v. Creative House Promotions, Inc.,* 944 F.2d 1446 (9th Cir. 1991) (citing McCarthy, J. [1984]. *Trademarks and unfair competition* [2nd ed., § 24, p. 13]).

[55]15 U.S.C. 1125(c)

[56]*Coca-Cola Co. v. Gemini Rising, Inc.,* 346 F. Supp. 1183 (E.D.N.Y. 1972)

[57]*Toys "R" Us, Inc., v. Akkaoui,* 40 U.S.P.Q.2d (BNA) 1836 (N.D. Cal. 1996)

In 2001, in *Playboy v. Welles*,[58] the case focused on *Playboy's* 1981 "Playmate of the Year" Terri Welles. Welles was running her own Web site in the 1990s, and she used the titles "Playmate of the Year" and "Playmate of the Month" to promote herself. She also used the abbreviation "PMOY" on the wallpaper (or background) of her site.

Playboy sued Welles for *trademark dilution.* Of course, Playboy also said she did not have permission to use the trademarked names. After the suit was filed, Welles put the following message on her Web site: "This site is neither endorsed, nor sponsored, nor affiliated with Playboy Enterprise, Inc. PLAYBOY™ PLAYMATE OF THE YEAR™ PLAYMATE OF THE MONTH™ are registered trademarks of Playboy Enterprise, Inc."

A federal appeals court upheld a lower court ruling in favor of Welles, saying that the uses of the trademarked names were "nominative." In other words, Welles only used the names to describe herself and not to identify the source. She earned such titles as "Playmate of the Year," and they had become a part of her public identity. Also, the uses of the titles by Welles were fair because they "imply no current sponsorship or endorsement" by *Playboy.* The court said that Welles did not "dilute" or unfairly use *Playboy* trademarks "any more than Michael Jordan would dilute the name 'Chicago Bulls' by referring to himself as a former member of that team." The same logic applies to winners of an Academy Award or a Super Bowl MVP.

Summary

Fair use of copyrighted works is governed by four criteria: the nature of the work, the purpose of the use, the amount of the work used, and the effect on the marketability of the work. Fair use doctrine has been used in various types of cases, including VCR recordings, sampling, and parodies.

The Internet has brought about numerous copyright challenges, most notably cases involving the sharing of music files. The court in the Napster case ruled that the unauthorized sharing of copyrighted music via the Internet is a violation of copyright laws.

---

[58] 279 F.3d 796 (9th Cir. 2001)

15

ADVERTISING LAW

The government may ban forms of communication more likely to deceive the public than to inform it.

—*Central Hudson v. Public Service Commission of New York*[1]

A dvertising is also known as *commercial speech*. The obvious goal of this type of speech is to sell something. The Federal Trade Commission is the federal agency overseeing advertising. Before looking at the role of the FTC, we will look at a brief history of how lawmakers and the courts have viewed commercial speech.

EARLY ADVERTISING LAW

No First Amendment Protection for Advertising?

The Supreme Court had basically never dealt with the issue of commercial speech until 1942, in *Valentine v. Chrestensen*.[2] A man named Chrestensen wanted to make money in New York City by offering tours of a surplus Navy submarine. He printed leaflets to advertise the tours, but a city antilittering ordinance banned distribution of nonpolitical leaflets. So Chrestensen wrote a message criticizing city officials on the back of the leaflets to make them "political." Chrestensen then filed a lawsuit against the city for violating his First Amendment right to distribute literature.

The Supreme Court ruled against Chrestensen. The court stated that purely commercial speech has *no* First Amendment protection. The leaflet's main goal was advertising. The message on the back was simply a ruse meant to distract from the leaflet's true intention—commercial speech.

---

[1]447 U.S. 557 (1980)

[2]316 U.S. 52 (1942)

FAQ

Why would the Supreme Court rule that advertising has no constitutional protection?

The court felt that the First Amendment was designed mainly to protect the exchange of information, thoughts, and ideas. The justices recognized that commercial speech was a means of conveying information, but they also recognized that its main goal was to separate people from their money. Therefore, the courts were more willing to allow restrictions on advertising to protect the public from being "taken" by dishonest advertisers.

Other Early Advertising Cases

Newspaper Want Ads

A Pittsburgh newspaper had been categorizing jobs in its want ads section according to "Male Interest" and "Female Interest." Thus a job for a construction worker would be listed under "Male Interest" and a job for a nurse would appear under "Female Interest." The city's Human Relations Commission said the categories were discriminatory and ordered the paper to stop the practice. The newspaper said it had a First Amendment right to create such categories.

However, in 1973, in *Pittsburgh Press v. Pittsburgh Commission on Human Relations*[3] (or *Pittsburgh Press I*), the Supreme Court ruled against the paper. The court pointed out that want ads are commercial speech, which has less First Amendment protection. This commercial speech was encouraging an illegal practice—job discrimination—and the city had a right to outlaw such advertising.

FAQ

What if the newspaper had printed an editorial praising the idea that only women should be nurses and only men should be construction workers?

That would be protected opinion. However, that opinion is not protected when the newspaper communicates it through commercial speech.

Newspaper Want Ads Part II

In *Pittsburgh Press II*,[4] the newspaper had printed ads with wording such as "Christian seeks work in Christian business" or "white woman seeks domestic work." Once again, the Human Relations Commission went after the paper, telling the *Press* to stop printing ads from people who were using race, sex, age, or religion in the descriptions. Pennsylvania's

---

[3]413 U.S. 376 (1973)

[4]*Commonwealth v. Pittsburgh Press Co.,* 396 A.2d 1187 (1979)

Supreme Court ruled for the paper. People looking for jobs have a constitutional right to use such descriptions, the court said. Also, the newspaper was not creating any categories like it did in the first case. It could not be held accountable for the words used within the want ads.

The Courts Give Commercial Speech More Protection

Abortion Ads

Abortion had just been legalized in New York in 1971. However, abortion and advertising for abortion was illegal in Virginia at the time. Jeffrey Bigelow of the *Virginia Weekly* published an ad from an abortion provider in New York City. Bigelow was convicted for illegally advertising abortion services in Virginia. In *Bigelow v. Virginia*,[5] the U.S. Supreme Court struck down the Virginia law against abortion ads.

The strict ruling from *Valentine* no longer applied, the court said. Speech should not lose its First Amendment protection just because it is for commercial purposes. Also, even though abortion was illegal in Virginia, it was legal in New York, and people in Virginia had a right to receive this information. From now on, the court said, states could not restrict commercial speech unless there was a legitimate reason for doing so.

A year later, the Supreme Court continued to show it was giving more protection to commercial speech.

Advertising the Price of Prescription Drugs

A Virginia statute made it illegal for pharmacists to advertise any price information about prescription drugs. This included any references to discounts, rebates, or credit terms. The state argued the law was good because (a) price competition would lead to pharmacists focusing on profits instead of on professional services; (b) price competition would actually lead to higher drug costs, as pharmacists would increase prices to pay for advertising expenses; and (c) the professional image of the pharmacist would be damaged.

In 1976, in *Virginia State Board of Pharmacy v. Virginia Citizens Consumer Council*,[6] the U.S. Supreme Court struck down the Virginia law, saying that "speech does not lose its First Amendment protection because money is spent to project it, as in a paid advertisement." The court pointed out several important factors in its decision. For example, drug prices varied greatly in Virginia pharmacies, sometimes even within communities. People had a right to know about this through advertising. Also, censoring drug price information had the most impact on the poor, elderly, and the sick, who often did not have the time to go from pharmacy to pharmacy to check prices. It was much easier to compare prices through advertisements.

FAQ

Were the courts now more willing to look at advertising as a legitimate means of exchanging information?

---

[5]421 U.S. 809 (1975)

[6]425 U.S. 748 (1976)

Yes. As the Supreme Court put it, advertising is dissemination of information protected by the First Amendment, allowing consumers to make informed purchasing decisions.

THE LANDMARK *CENTRAL HUDSON* CASE

In 1973, the United States was experiencing an "energy crisis." Many northern states, such as New York, were worried that they might not have enough energy supplies to meet electrical demands for the upcoming 1973-1974 winter.

In an effort to reduce energy consumption, New York's Public Service Commission prohibited electric utilities from running advertisements that "promote the use of energy."

Three years later, the advertising ban was still in effect, even though the energy crisis was easing. Still, the commission voted to extend the ban. Utility companies were allowed to run ads that were considered informational, but they were still banned from running ads that promoted or encouraged energy use because "all promotional advertising [is] contrary to the national policy of conserving energy." At the same time, though, the commission admitted that the ad ban would lead to only "piecemeal conservationism."

The Central Hudson Gas & Electric Company filed a lawsuit against the commission, saying the ad ban violated the First Amendment. In *Central Hudson Gas & Electric v. Public Service Commission of New York*,[1] the Supreme Court struck down the ad ban, saying the state had no right to censor truthful commercial speech.

The court then laid out the now famous "Central Hudson Test." If a state is considering restricting commercial speech, it must use the following four-part test:

1. *The commercial speech involved must concern lawful activity and not be misleading.* (In other words, the Central Hudson Test should not be used in cases involving advertising of illegal activities or false advertising. There are other legal ways to deal with those issues.)

2. *Is there a substantial* (or important) *government interest being served* with this particular regulation of commercial speech? In other words, does the government have a legitimate reason for this regulation? If the answer is no, the test stops here and the advertising restriction would be thrown out.

3. If the answer is yes to the first two questions, then a court must decide *whether the regulation directly advances the government interest.*

4. Then the court asks, *Is the regulation more excessive than is needed to serve that government interest?*

This legal jargon may be a little confusing, so let's apply this test to the Central Hudson utility ad.

1. The speech in the utility company's ads was *neither misleading nor supporting illegal activity.* On to step 2.

2. *The substantial government interest* here was energy conservation. The Supreme Court agreed that conserving energy was an important and substantial government interest. Because the answer is yes to parts 1 and 2, we move to step 3.

3. Did the commission's ban on utility ads *directly advance the state's interest?* The court said yes, agreeing with the state that there was "an immediate connection between advertising and demand for electricity." So far, the state is winning. However, it must also win in the fourth part of the test.

4. *Is this ban on utility ads more restrictive than is necessary to serve the state interest?* Here, the state loses. The court ruled that the ad ban was "excessive" because it also banned utility companies from *all* promotional advertising, even ads about items such as heat pumps, which would *save* energy. The court added that the commission could have achieved its energy conservation goals with a less restrictive regulation.

False Advertising

Concerns about misleading advertisements and other forms of unfair competition prompted Congress in 1946 to pass a federal trademark law, part of which included the *Lanham Act*.[7] Section 43(a) of this act allows businesses to file civil lawsuits against a competitor who engages in misleading or false advertising. Because this is a federal law, it deals only with products sold in interstate commerce.

Under the Lanham Act, a false advertisement has five basic components:

1. There was deception or false statements of fact by the advertiser about its product or a competitor's product.

2. The ad had the capacity to deceive a substantial segment of the target audience.

3. The deception is "material." (This means the advertiser was trying to fool consumers about an important selling point or attribute of the product. It would unfairly make a consumer want or not want to buy a product.)

4. The false ad caused "injury." (Simple deception can be considered an injury.)

5. The false statement became part of interstate commerce. (The Lanham Act is a federal law, so it is only concerned with national advertising. States must deal with local and state advertising issues.)

Federal Agencies Overseeing Advertising

Federal Trade Commission. The FTC was created in the Federal Trade Commission Act of 1914. Its responsibilities are to prevent companies from using unfair business practices and to take action against false and misleading advertising.

Food and Drug Administration. The FDA was formed in the Food, Drug and Cosmetic Act of 1938. Its responsibilities are to make sure foods, drugs, and cosmetics are pure and safe and to take action against false labeling of consumer goods.

FAQ

Do the FTC and FDA work separately on cases or together?

The FTC and the FDA often work together on cases, with the FTC handling the advertising aspects and the FDA dealing with labeling issues.

---

[7]15 U.S.C. §§ 1051-1127

Important Terms

Before we look at how false advertising cases are handled, we need to define some of the more common terms and practices used in the advertising industry.

Bait-and-Switch Advertising. A store advertises that it is having a sale on computer printers for $99. When customers arrive at the store, they are told that the $99 printers are sold out. A sales clerk then tries to sell them a "better" printer for $199. In other words, the store used the "bait" of a cheap printer to lure customers, but the real intention was to get them to "switch" to a more expensive product. This is illegal.

Comparative Advertising. One company advertises that its product is better than another company's product.

Express Claim. This is straightforward. "X Mouthwash stops gum disease" is an express claim. It makes a specific claim. Such claims need to be supported by reliable scientific evidence.

Implied Claim. Not as straightforward. "X Mouthwash kills the germs that cause gum disease." The ad does not claim directly that the mouthwash will stop gum disease, but the ad implies to many people that the mouthwash will do just that. Such claims also need to be backed up by reliable evidence.

Material Claim. This kind of claim is important to a consumer's decision to use or buy the product. Material claims include statements about a product's safety, performance, price, effectiveness, ingredients, and features. Such claims need to be true and backed up by reliable evidence. A material claim usually qualifies as an express claim as well.

Mock-Ups. These are also called *undisclosed simulations* or *undisclosed demonstrations.* This often occurs in TV ads. An example would be a TV ad for apples. While shooting the ad, the apples are sprayed with a clear coating to make the fruit glisten on camera. Is this misleading? The FTC would say such a mock-up is legal as long as the ad does not say something like "Our apples are the shiniest." If a mock-up is done for cosmetic purposes and does not mislead about a material aspect of the product, then it is fine.

Puffery. "Our pizza is the best in town." "Our service will make you smile." Puffery is the use of opinion or exaggeration in advertising, but no provable factual claims are made. This pizza is the best? That is an opinion. The service will *always* make you smile? That is an exaggeration. The FTC says such puffery, also called hyperbole, is legal. Puffery cannot be proven true or false.

Testimonial. This may involve a famous person or expert endorsing a product. It may also involve a "satisfied customer" endorsement. The FTC expects that the audience understands that the famous person is being paid to promote this product.

FAQ

What criteria are used to determine whether an ad is misleading?

The FTC relies on criteria established in the Lanham Act. The FTC usually does not deal with local ads and allows problems with them to be handled by state, county, or city agencies. These criteria apply to national or interstate advertising:

1. How does the ad affect the *reasonable consumer?*

2. What is the *entire context* of the ad? The FTC prefers not to focus on a few words but on the whole ad—pictures, phrases, and individual words.

3. The FTC looks at both *implied and express claims.* In either case, advertisers must have verifiable proof that the claims are accurate.

4. *What does the ad* not *say?* Leaving out important information can also mislead consumers. For example, an ad says a bike is on sale for $100. However, the ad fails to mention that the price is good only if you also purchase a $20 service agreement. The ad obviously misleads.

5. Is the advertising claim *material?*

6. Does the advertiser have *proof* that the claims are true? The law says advertisers must have objective or scientific evidence of its claims before the ad is run.

The FTC Web site (http://www.ftc.gov) says the agency pays closest attention to two types of advertisements for misleading claims: (a) ads making claims about *safety or health* (drugs, bike helmets, water filters, etc.) and (b) ads for which most consumers would be unlikely or unable to verify the claims themselves. Examples might be "XYZ Oil reduces engine wear," or "Our detergent won't pollute the environment," or "Our water heater uses 30% less energy."

FAQ

What are the punishments for false advertising?

The FTC and the courts employ three basic punishments or remedies for false advertising:

▣ *Cease-and-desist orders:* The FTC or courts order a company to stop running a deceptive ad or engaging in a deceptive practice. The FTC may also impose fines for violations of a cease-and-desist order.

▣ *Corrective advertising:* This includes running new ads to correct the misleading information. The company may also be required to inform customers about the misleading claims.

▣ *Civil damages:* This may include punitive damages. It may also include paying refunds to customers.

Some Famous False Advertising Cases

Implied Claims

Aspirin Is as Good as . . . Aspirin. Claim: "Anacin delivers the same headache relief as the leading pain relief medication."

Well, Anacin is aspirin. Aspirin is also the leading pain relief medication. So, basically, all the ad was saying was that "*aspirin* delivers the same headache relief as *aspirin.*" The FTC ruled that this cleverly veiled double-speak was misleading. The ad implied that the leading pain relief medication was something other than aspirin.

Hair Loss Drug. Claim: "You need not face the fear of more hair loss."

Ads for Propecia used this phrase to imply that the drug could *stop* hair loss. The FDA in 1998 ruled that such wording was misleading because tests showed Propecia could only *slow* hair loss, not stop it.

Tropicana Orange Juice. Claim: "It's pure pasteurized juice as it comes from the orange."

In February 1982, a Tropicana Orange Juice ad began airing on national TV that showed Olympic decathlon champion Bruce Jenner squeezing an orange and saying, "It's pure pasteurized juice as it comes from the orange." Jenner then poured the fresh-squeezed juice into a Tropicana Premium Pack carton. A narrator then said, "It's the only leading brand not made with concentrate and water."

The Coca-Cola Company is the maker of Minute Maid orange juice, and Coke sued Tropicana for false advertising. Coke said the ad falsely implied that every carton of Tropicana Premium Pack orange juice was made directly from fresh-squeezed oranges, with no processing steps. In *Coca-Cola v. Tropicana,*[8] a federal appeals court agreed that the Tropicana ad was misleading.

The court said that the visual of the fresh-squeezed juice being poured into the carton was "false on its face." The visual implied that this was how the juice was made and packaged. However, Tropicana Premium Pack orange juice was actually heated to 200 degrees Fahrenheit (pasteurization) and sometimes frozen before it was packaged. The statement "pasteurized juice as it comes from the orange" implied that juice can be pasteurized *before* it comes out of the orange. This was blatantly misleading. Juice can only be pasteurized *after* it comes out of the orange. The court felt that consumers were likely to be misled by the ad and " it is likely Coke will lose a portion of the chilled juice market and thus suffer irreparable injury."

Express Claims

Listerine. Claim: Listerine can "help prevent colds and relieve sore throats."

Listerine mouthwash included this claim in its ads for nearly 100 years. No one challenged this claim until the 1970s, and Listerine could not provide any scientific evidence to back it up. The FTC ordered Listerine's parent company, Warner-Lambert, to run $10 million worth of corrective print and broadcast advertising that included the words "contrary to prior advertising."

The company appealed, but in *Warner-Lambert Co. v. FTC,*[9] a federal appeals court in 1977 upheld the FTC order. However, the court did allow Warner-Lambert to drop the words "contrary to prior advertising" from its corrective ads.

In 2005, Listerine was once again found guilty of false advertising for claiming its mouthwash was "just as effective as floss at reducing plaque and gingivitis between teeth." A federal judge ruled there was no proof that the mouthwash could replace the benefits of flossing and ordered Listerine to stop running the ads.

Doan's Pills. Claim: Doan's Pills are more effective on back pain than other pain relievers.

The FTC ruled that Doan's Pills did alleviate back pain, but there was no evidence that the pills did this better than other pain relievers. The FTC in 1999 ordered the makers of Doan's Pills to run $8 million in corrective advertising and include the phrase "there is no evidence that Doan's is more effective than other pain relievers for back pain." A federal appeals court in 2000 upheld the FTC ruling.[10]

---

[8]690 F.2d 312 (2d Cir. 1982)

[9]562 F.2d 749 (D.C. Cir. 1977)

[10]*Novartis Corp. v. FTC,* 223 F.3d 783 (D.C. Cir. 2000)

FAQ

Can advertisers be punished for leaving out important information?

Yes.

Bayer. Claim: Taking Bayer Aspirin daily helps prevent strokes and heart attacks.

The FTC was concerned with what this ad did *not* say. The ad did not point out that a daily aspirin intake can be harmful to some people or that some people may not benefit at all. In 2000, Bayer spent $1 million on corrective advertising. This included giving free brochures to customers to explain the benefits and risks of daily aspirin use.

Roach Killers. Claim: Maxattrax roach bait boxes kill roaches in 24 hours.

Maxattrax used a TV ad called "Side by Side" to show the effectiveness of its roach bait box. The 15-second ad shows a dark kitchen and the Maxattrax box next to a generic box that looks somewhat like the packaging for the Combat brand sold by Clorox. An announcer asks, "Can you guess which bait kills roaches in 24 hours?"

The lights then come up showing a clean, roach-free kitchen on the Maxattrax side. The other side of the kitchen is a mess, the apparent result of roaches. At the bottom of the screen in small print appears "Based on lab tests." Some computer-animated roaches then kick over the generic box and dance on it. The ad ends with a shot of the Maxattrax box and the announcer saying, "To kill roaches in 24 hours, it's hot-shot Maxattrax. Maxattrax. It's the no-wait roach bait."

Clorox filed suit, claiming the ads were false regarding the 24-hour claim and the comparisons to Combat's effectiveness. In *United Industries v. Clorox,*[11] a federal appeals court ruled the Maxattrax ads were not misleading. Maxattrax's claim that it kills roaches within 24 hours "based on lab tests" is true. The court said that United Industries used "reliable" scientific tests proving that when roaches came in contact with the toxin in Maxattrax, the roaches died within 24 hours. The court ruled that the ad "did not convey a literally false message" by using the visuals of the clean kitchen accompanied by the animated roaches in the dirty kitchen. Clorox said this implied Maxattrax could rid a house of *all* roaches within 24 hours, but the court said these visuals were not misleading because the ad never mentioned that its product would result in *complete* roach control.

Rental Trucks. Claim: Jartran rental trucks are safer, less costly, and more fuel efficient than U-Haul trucks.

In its ads, Jartran said it was cheaper to travel to certain places when using their trucks instead of U-Haul's. Jartran's advertised prices were actually limited-time promotional "sale" prices, but the ads did not mention that. Other Jartran ads said its trucks were safer, more stable, more fuel efficient, and better designed than all of U-Haul's trucks and trailers.

In 1986, in *U-Haul International v. Jartran,*[12] an appeals court awarded U-Haul $40 million in damages, a record judgment in a false advertising case. U-Haul was able to prove

---

[11]140 F.3d 1175 (8th Cir. 1998)

[12]793 F.2d 1034 (9th Cir. 1986)

that the ads were misleading and that they led to a $73 million increase in revenues for Jartran from 1979 to 1980.

<hr>

FAQ

Is economic damage often a factor in false advertising rulings?

<hr>

Yes. That same year, U-Haul saw its first-ever annual decline in revenues—a loss of $17 million. In reaching his decision, the judge considered the revenue figures as well as the money U-Haul spent to counteract the misleading Jartran ads. The misleading advertising had an obvious, detrimental impact on U-Haul.

The judge prohibited Jartran from making any references to U-Haul in future ads regarding prices, safety, stability, fuel efficiency, or design.

Home Shopping Network Vitamin Sprays. Claim: The vitamin sprays were supposed to be able to treat various ailments, including hangovers and cold sores. Another spray was said to be able to help people stop smoking.

In March 1995, the FTC charged the Home Shopping Network and Life Way Health Products with making unproven claims about numerous spray products, including Life Way Antioxidant Spray and Smoke-Less Nutrient Spray. In a civil suit, HSN was ordered to pay $1.1 million dollars in penalties for the misleading ads. The ads made a number of unsubstantiated claims. The various vitamin sprays were said to be able to heal cold sores, mouth lesions, and cracked lip corners; relieve hangovers, prevent facial lines, and prevent colds; and reduce the risk of getting infectious diseases. The antismoking spray was said to be able to get rid of the weight gain and anxiety experienced by people who were trying to quit smoking, eliminate withdrawal symptoms, and easily help smokers to stop smoking.

The FTC said that the claims for these sprays were not supported by scientific evidence. In September 1996, the FTC gave HSN a cease-and-desist order, stopping the current ads and prohibiting the cable shopping network from making any further product claims it could not substantiate. However, HSN ignored this order, as is shown in the next case.

Home Shopping Network II. Less than a month after the September 1996 FTC order prohibiting HSN from airing unproven product claims, HSN began airing ads for the following products:

- ▣ *Serious Skin Care Products.* These included treatments for such problems as acne and dark skin patches.
- ▣ *Target Fat Loss System.* The promoters claimed that the vitamins and minerals in this system could help women lose 30 to 60 pounds.
- ▣ *Life Way Changes.* The promoters of this product claimed that it could relieve numerous problems associated with PMS and menopause, including hot flashes, water retention, and breast tenderness.

These ads aired frequently between 1996 and 1998. In 1999, a federal district court found HSN guilty of violating the FTC order to cease the advertising of unproven product claims. In *U.S. v. Home Shopping Network,* the court ruled that HSN had once again aired claims for products "without possessing and relying upon competent and reliable scientific evidence."[13] The court ruled that the FTC could fine HSN up to $11,000 for each broadcast containing the false claims.

Puffery

The FTC and the courts often use these three criteria to separate puffery from factual claims:

1. *Is the statement general or specific?* Specific statements are more likely to be considered factual; general statements are more likely to be puffery.

2. *Is the statement measurable?* If so, it is more likely to be a factual claim. If it is hard to measure, it is more likely to be puffery.

3. *Is the statement more of an opinion or fact?* Obviously, opinions are more likely to be considered puffery.

Notice how these criteria are applied in the following cases.

Papa John's and Pizza Hut. Claim: Papa John's has "Better Ingredients Better Pizza."

The TV ad showed Papa John's workers using fresh tomato sauce, also showing that Pizza Hut used canned sauce. Pizza Hut sued, saying Papa John's also used canned sauce and tomato paste.

A trial jury ordered Papa John's to pay $468,000 in damages to Pizza Hut and to remove the slogan "Better Ingredients Better Pizza" from its ads and boxes. The trial judge also banned Papa John's from running any ads with the word "better," and the ads could no longer include comparisons to Pizza Hut. The jury said that the Papa John's ads made claims that were not factual. Papa John's claimed it used "fresh, not frozen, dough," but Pizza Hut's lawyers were able to convince the jury that freezing the dough had no effect on its taste.

FAQ

Don't advertisers frequently use puffery such as "better" or "best?" Why was it wrong in this case?

An appeals court did not think it was wrong. Papa John's appealed, saying the phrase "Better Ingredients Better Pizza" was simple puffery. In 2000, in *Pizza Hut Inc. v. Papa John's International Inc.,*[14] an appeals court agreed and overturned the trial jury ruling. The court said that Pizza Hut did not prove the ads were likely to deceive people or affect their purchasing decisions. Pizza Hut appealed, but the U.S. Supreme Court refused to hear the case and let the appeals court ruling stand.

Ace Detergent. Claim: With Ace detergent, "Whiter is not possible."

In Puerto Rico, Proctor & Gamble sold laundry detergent named "Ace con Blanqueador" (Ace with Whitener). Ads for Ace included the phrase "Mas blanco no se puede" or "Whiter

---

[13]Civil Action No. 99-897-CIV-T-25C (U.S. District Court, M.D. Fla. 1999)

[14]227 F.3d 489 (5th Cir. 2000)

is not possible." Was this merely puffery or a factual claim? The wording implied that Ace whitened better than chlorine bleach.

The makers of Clorox Bleach sued Proctor & Gamble for false advertising. Clorox was able to convince the court that nothing is better at whitening clothes than chlorine bleach when used with detergent. In *Clorox Company Puerto Rico v. Proctor & Gamble,*[15] the court ruled that the Ace ad was "by necessary implication a superiority claim for Ace over chlorine bleach."

FAQ

Wasn't this similar to the Papa John's case in that Ace was simply using the word "whiter" as puffery?

There is a substantial difference in this case. *Better* is a fairly vague term because a lot of things can make one pizza "better" than another in people's minds. However, the term *whiter* refers directly to the main reason that people buy bleach—to get things whiter. Proctor & Gamble argued that "Whiter is not possible" was just simple puffery. The court, though, said the ad went beyond puffery because it "invites consumers to compare Ace's whitening power against either other detergents acting alone or detergents used with chlorine bleach."

Attorney Ad. Claim: "We're the low-cost commercial collection experts."

In 1988, the Northern California Collection Service (NCC) placed the following ad in a San Francisco credit information publication:

> *Do You Pay For An Attorney To Do Your Collection Work?*
> And pay. And pay. And pay! Were you quoted a really low "collection fee" only to find that "costs" are eating you alive? Do you find that you are doing all the "leg work" for your lawyer? Then call us—we're the low cost commercial collection experts.
> NORTHERN CALIFORNIA COLLECTION SERVICE, INC.
> SACRAMENTO VALLEY BOARD OF TRADE, INC.
> 700 Leisure Lane, Sacramento, CA 95815 (916) 929-7811
> Lawrence H. Cassidy, President

Another northern California law firm, Cook, Perkiss and Liehe, Inc., accused NCC of false advertising, as well as unfair competition, libel, defamation, and product disparagement. Cook said the ad was false for implying that NCC offers the same collection services as lawyers but at a lower price. In *Cook v. Northern California Collection Service,*[16] a federal appeals court ruled for NCC.

The court determined that the ad contained puffery and no direct factual claims. The court said the phrase, "we're the low cost commercial collection experts" was a general claim about price and not a factual representation. (If NCC had said something like "we're 20% cheaper," that would have been a factual claim.) Implications that NCC had similar services to attorneys, at lower prices, "were *general* assertions of superiority." Again, this is puffery.

---

[15] 228 F.3d 24 (1st Cir. 2000)

[16] 911 F..2d 242 (9th Cir. 1990)

Therefore, the court said, no "reasonable consumer would interpret this as a factual claim upon which he or she could rely."

Testimonial

A testimonial, whether by a celebrity or an average citizen, must follow certain guidelines established by the FTC:

1. If the ad implies that the endorser uses the product, then the endorser is required to be a regular user of the product for as long as the ad runs.

2. Testimonials must not contain any deceptive claims.

3. An endorser's claims about a product must be supported by reliable evidence or scientific proof.

4. The endorser's claims must be honest and current reflections of his or her experiences or beliefs.

5. Testimonials must not make implied or express claims about preventing, curing, or treating a disease (unless the endorser has specific qualifications and scientific evidence to support such claims).

The FTC has not enforced these guidelines very strictly. In fact, a case in 2000 marked the first time in nearly 20 years that the FTC had gone after a celebrity endorser for participating in allegedly false advertising.

Steve Garvey and The Enforma System

In April 2000, the makers of the "Enforma System" dieting program agreed to pay $10 million in fines for false advertising claims. Enforma had claimed its Fat Trapper product could "block fats from foods" and that its product Exercise in a Bottle could help people burn calories while they were resting. The FTC found that Enforma had no scientific evidence to support its claims and ordered that future Enforma ads tell people that exercise and dieting are needed to lose weight. A nutritionist who had made unsubstantiated claims in Enforma infomercials reached a separate settlement with the FTC. However, the FTC also targeted a celebrity who had endorsed Enforma.

Baseball legend Steve Garvey had appeared in Enforma TV advertisements and infomercials. Garvey had also endorsed Enforma through radio, print, and Internet ads.

The FTC decided that Garvey should also be held liable for the unsubstantiated claims about the Enforma System. The following statements by Garvey in an Enforma infomercial were considered problematic by the FTC: (a) Garvey talked about his baseball career and claimed that he had personal knowledge about exercise and physical fitness. (b) Garvey claimed that Enforma would help people burn more calories and lose weight. (c) Garvey said people could eat "forbidden foods," such as pizza and cheeseburgers, and still lose weight. (d) Garvey also claimed that Enforma could lower cholesterol levels "by simply taking a pill."

FAQ

Was Garvey under any obligation to find out if these claims were true?

The FTC said that Garvey, as an endorser, should have investigated to see if these product claims were supported by reliable scientific evidence. Also, the FTC said that simply being a former athlete did not make Garvey an expert on health and diet matters. The FTC sought $1.1 million dollars in damages (the amount that Enforma had paid Garvey to endorse their products). However, in September 2004, in *FTC v. Garvey,*[17] a federal appeals court ruled that Garvey did not have any knowledge about Life Way's false claims and therefore he could not be held liable. In fact, the court noted that Garvey and his wife had used the products and both had lost weight. Garvey had also met with other people who had used the products and who had positive results. As a result, the court said that there was no proof that Garvey had intentionally made false statements because he believed in what he was selling. The court said that Garvey's claims, as well as his personal success with the product, "clearly pass any substantiation requirement for celebrity endorsers."

Pat Boone and Acne-Statin

This case was pretty straightforward. In the 1970s, actor Pat Boone and his company, Cooga Mooga, were paid to endorse an antipimple cream named Acne-Statin, which people could purchase by calling a phone number. Boone received royalties based on the sales of the cream. In the ads, Boone claimed that all of his daughters used the cream and that it worked well for them. The FTC discovered that the claim was false—Boone's daughters never used Acne-Statin. As a result, the FTC ordered Boone to cease and desist from making the untrue claims about his daughters. It also required Boone and his company to pay money to people who had purchased Acne-Statin during the time when Boone's endorsements appeared on the air and required that Boone, in any future endorsements, announce his financial connections with the advertiser, such as the payment of royalties based on sales.

Mock-Ups

One of the few false advertising cases to reach the U.S. Supreme Court was *FTC v. Colgate-Palmolive,*[18] in 1965. This case showed that the high court was willing to let the FTC handle most decisions regarding false ads.

The case deals with *undisclosed simulations* (also called *undisclosed demonstrations*) in advertising. A classic example of an undisclosed simulation is a TV ad for ice cream. Ice cream tends to melt very quickly under hot TV lights. Therefore, to make production go more smoothly, a scoop of mashed potatoes is substituted for the ice cream. On camera, the potatoes look like ice cream, and the problem of constantly melting ice cream is eliminated. The FTC today would say this type of undisclosed simulation is legal because the ad's producers are not using the potatoes to deceive consumers about the ice cream itself. The potatoes are simply used for production purposes. The FTC, however, did have a problem with an undisclosed simulation in a 1961 TV advertisement for Rapid Shave shaving cream. The ad implied that Rapid Shave was so effective that it could even pass the "sandpaper test."

---

[17]383 F.3d 891 (9th Cir. 2004)

[18]380 U.S. 374 (1965)

In three separate 1-minute spots, Rapid Shave was put on something that looked like sandpaper. An announcer said, "To prove Rapid Shave's super-moisturizing power, we put it right from the can onto this tough, dry sandpaper. It was apply . . . soak . . . and off in a stroke." A razor was shown shaving the "sandpaper" clean.

Here is the truth about the "sandpaper test." The ad showed the Rapid Shave softening the "sandpaper" immediately, but tests showed that the "sandpaper" had to be soaked for 80 minutes before it could be shaved. The ad also used an undisclosed simulation. The "sandpaper" was actually a piece of plexiglass with sand on it.

An FTC hearing examiner said the misrepresentations regarding the time element and the use of plexiglass were not false advertising. The examiner said the timing element could not be adequately handled in a 60-second ad, and real sandpaper on TV did not look good and "appear[ed] to viewers to be nothing more than plain, colored paper." The examiner added that these two undisclosed simulations were justified because of the "inadequacies of television transmission."

FAQ

But wasn't the ad still misleading on key elements?

The FTC said yes and overturned the examiner's findings. The commission ruled that both tactics were *material misrepresentations.* First, it said, the ad was deceptive because "Rapid Shave could not shave sandpaper within the depicted time in the commercials." If the ad had announced that the actual soaking time was 80 minutes, the ad would not have been deceptive. Second, the plexiglass mock-up was deceptive. The FTC ruled that viewers were "misled into believing they had seen it done with their own eyes."

The FTC gave Colgate-Palmolive a cease-and-desist order, banning the Rapid Shave commercials from the airwaves. The FTC also banned the future use of undisclosed simulations in all TV ads.

The Supreme Court upheld the FTC's findings. The court also granted the FTC power to handle these cases because "the Commission is often in a better position than are courts to determine when a practice is 'deceptive.'"

But the Supreme Court ruled that the FTC could not ban all undisclosed simulations. The court made specific reference to the example at the start of this chapter—mashed potatoes substituted for ice cream. The court said that such undisclosed simulations do not make material misrepresentations about the product and are not deceptive.

Regulating Ads for Harmful Products

Gambling

Gambling Ads

One of the most controversial court decisions about commercial speech came from the Supreme Court in 1986 in *Posadas v. Tourism Co. of Puerto Rico.*[19] In 1948, Puerto Rico

---

[19]478 U.S. 328 (1986)

legalized some forms of casino gambling to attract foreign tourists. However, Puerto Rican lawmakers were worried about the effects of gambling on the island's citizens, so Puerto Rico made it illegal for the casinos to advertise to the citizens of Puerto Rico. (Residents were also not allowed to enter the casinos.) The casinos could still advertise to foreign tourists as they arrived by plane or ship.

In 1978, the Puerto Rico Tourism Company twice fined Posadas de Puerto Rico Associates when the company's casinos violated the ban on advertising to island residents. Posadas was fined again in 1981, and Posadas filed a lawsuit saying its commercial speech rights were being violated. In its ruling against Posadas, the U.S. Supreme Court applied the Central Hudson Test.

The court agreed that the ads *were for a legal activity* in Puerto Rico, and the ads were *not misleading.* The regulation against the ads did *serve a substantial government interest.* The court agreed with Puerto Rico's argument that "excessive casino gambling among local residents" would lead to increased local crime, corruption, prostitution, and organized crime. The court agreed that this was a legitimate concern because most U.S. states at the time outlawed casinos for similar reasons. The regulation *did directly advance this state interest.* Advertising aimed at local residents would obviously increase demand for the "product." Therefore, a ban on the ads would lead to decreased demand for casino gambling. The regulation *was not more restrictive than needed.* The Supreme Court said that the law did not ban all casino ads. It allowed ads aimed at tourists, just not ads aimed at residents.

FAQ

Doesn't this ruling take us back to the *Valentine* decision, in which the courts saw commercial speech as having less First Amendment protection?

Not necessarily, although opponents of the ruling saw it that way. The Supreme Court recognized that the Puerto Rico legislature has the power to outlaw casino gambling if it wishes to do so. If the legislature has that power, the court said, it must surely have the power to ban certain ads for those casinos.

Broadcast Lottery Ads

Title 18, Section 1304 of the U.S. Code banned broadcasters from advertising any form of lottery. These same restrictions are listed in the Code of Federal Regulation at 47 C.F.R. § 73.121. Broadcasters were forbidden from airing advertisements or programming that promoted

> any lottery, gift enterprise, or similar scheme, offering prizes dependent in whole or in part upon lot or chance, or any list of the prizes drawn or awarded by means of any such lottery, gift, enterprise, or scheme, whether said list contains any part or all of such prizes.

However, the law prohibiting gambling ads did not apply to state lotteries, certain non-profit fishing contests, or lotteries run by nonprofit groups and Native American tribes.

The FCC enforced this "lottery rule" strictly and had certain guidelines for the ads that did air. Acceptable lottery ads could not mention words such as *gambling, games,* or *chance.*

TV ads for casinos were not supposed to show people playing actual games. To follow FCC guidelines, casino ads would show people eating, drinking, laughing, and having a good time. The ads would not show people sitting at a slot machine, though. What was the reason for such rules? The FCC and courts had said gambling had a "demoralizing influence" on society, and advertisements for gambling should be restricted.

The FCC frequently handed out fines for violations of these rules. For example, a Wisconsin radio station had aired an ad for a casino operated by a Native American tribe. The ad said people could enjoy "Las Vegas–style games." The FCC said this wording was illegal, and the ad should have said something like "Las Vegas–style *fun.*" For using the word *games,* the station received a $6250 fine from the FCC.

In 1993, the U.S. Supreme Court upheld the broadcast lottery rules regarding broadcasters advertising *another* state's lottery. The case involved a North Carolina radio station airing ads for the state lottery in Virginia. North Carolina did not have a state lottery. In *United States v. Edge,*[20] the Supreme Court ruled that North Carolina could prohibit broadcast stations within its borders from advertising other states' lotteries.

FAQ

This seems like a contradiction of the *Bigelow* case, in which the court ruled that it was legal to advertise legal abortion services in another state. Why doesn't the same reasoning apply to advertising another state's legal lottery?

The Supreme Court felt that there were legitimate reasons for a state to want to discourage gambling among its citizens (see the *Posadas* case).

Still, for decades, broadcasters had argued that the rules and fines were unfair. In 1999, the U.S. Supreme Court agreed. In *Greater New Orleans Broadcasting Association v. United States,*[21] the issue was broadcasters in Louisiana who had aired advertisements for private casinos. However, the broadcasters' signals reached into Arkansas and Texas, where private casinos were not legal. The broadcasters filed suit, saying radio and TV stations had a First Amendment right to air ads for a legal activity. The Supreme Court threw out 18 U.S.C. § 1304 by applying the Central Hudson Test.

The court determined that the casino ads were not misleading and concerned legal activity. The federal government's interest in restricting gambling is "substantial," but the court said it is not necessarily vital in this instance. In answer to the question, Does this regulation directly advance the state interest of reducing gambling? The court said no. It said that the ads would not necessarily result in more people gambling but "would merely channel gamblers to one casino rather than another." On the other hand, when considering whether the regulation was more excessive than was necessary, the court said yes. It said the government did not prove its case that there is a "direct link between broadcast casino ads and compulsive gambling at casinos." The court said that the government should not restrict broadcast ads to discourage compulsive gambling. It said there are better ways to achieve this goal—betting limits, location restrictions, and limiting cash machine use at

---

[20]509 U.S. 418 (1993)

[21]527 U.S. 173 (1999)

casinos. "Because Section 1304 permits the advertising of commercial lotteries by not-for-profit organizations, governmental organizations, and Indian Tribes, it is impossible for it materially to discourage public participation in commercial lotteries."

In conclusion, the court said, "the speaker and the audience, not the Government, should be left to assess the value of accurate and non-misleading information about lawful conduct."

In states where gambling is legal, the FCC can no longer prohibit advertising for those gambling activities.

FAQ

Does the Edge ruling still apply?

Yes. Nonlottery states can still prohibit radio and TV stations from advertising other states' lotteries or casinos.

Gambling and the Internet

There is no federal law specifically banning Internet gambling, but the U.S. Justice Department has maintained that the 1961 Wire Act bans the use of all wire communications for interstate gambling. Still, in 2004, gambling Web sites took in an estimated $7 billion in bets. These sites are foreign-based and outside U.S. jurisdiction, so the Justice Department has used the Wire Act to go after American companies that carry ads for the sites. Because gambling is usually a state issue, individuals need to be aware of any laws in their own states regarding online betting.

Cigarettes

Cigarettes Ads Banned on Radio and TV

In 1970, Congress passed the Public Health Cigarette Smoking Act (Public Law 91-222) *banning the advertising of cigarettes on radio and TV as of January 1, 1971.* The FCC, as well as the Department of Justice and the Federal Trade Commission, are responsible for enforcing the act.

In 1971, six companies that operated radio stations tried to get the act overturned in *Capital Broadcasting v. Mitchell.*[22] The broadcasters argued that the ban unfairly censored speech about a legal product. But a federal district court upheld the act for several reasons. The court pointed out that advertising or commercial speech has less First Amendment protection than other forms of speech. Also, "The unique characteristics of electronic communication make it especially subject to regulation in the public interest." The court said that Congress had the right to ban broadcast cigarette ads as "an exercise of its power to regulate interstate commerce." Finally, nothing in the act prohibits broadcasters from airing points of view about cigarette smoking. These broadcasters did not lose their right to speak—only a way of making money from *others* wishing to broadcast advertisements.

---

[22]333 F. Supp. 582 (D.D.C. 1971)

Not all tobacco products are banned from the public airwaves, however. Cigarettes, little cigars, and smokeless tobacco (chewing tobacco, snuff) are not allowed in broadcast advertisements. Cigars, pipe tobacco, and smoking accessories (lighters, cigarette papers, pipes, etc.) are permitted in broadcast advertisements.

FAQ

Why are cigar ads permitted?

It is a health issue. Cigar smoke is normally not inhaled, and therefore cigars have been considered less of a health risk than cigarettes. However, the federal government's attitude toward cigars is changing. In 2000, the FTC reached an agreement with seven of the nation's biggest cigar companies and mandated that all cigar products and advertisements carry health warnings. Five different warnings must appear on a rotating basis. One of those warnings reads: "SURGEON GENERAL'S WARNING: Cigar Smoking Can Cause Cancers Of The Mouth And Throat, Even If You Do Not Inhale."

The other four labels warn that cigar smoking can cause lung cancer, heart disease, and infertility. There are also warnings that cigar smoking among women can lead to stillbirths and low birth weights. Another label says "Cigars Are Not A Safe Alternative To Cigarettes."

It appears that the government is starting to consider cigars as much of a health risk as cigarettes. Will that mean a ban on broadcast cigar ads? It would not be a surprise.

FAQ

This seems confusing. Can a radio station accept advertising from a tobacco shop that sells both cigars and cigarettes?

Because of confusion over questions like this, many broadcasters avoid any type of tobacco ads for fear of violating the law. Here are some good tips from a legal counsel memo from the National Association of Broadcasters:

Not Acceptable:

1. Do not mention any products that are prohibited—cigarettes, little cigars, and smokeless tobacco.

2. Do not mention any business name that includes the prohibited products. For example, an ad for "Joe's Cigarette Shop" would not be permitted.

Acceptable:

1. It is all right to air ads that include references to cigars, pipe tobacco, and smoking accessories.

2. In general, broadcasters may air ads for a store whose legal business name may include either the word "tobacco" or references to permitted smoking products. Thus the following business names would be acceptable in a radio or TV ad: "Barney's House of Tobacco," "Sam's Cigar Shop."

The NAB memo also recommends that broadcasters research a business to see if it sells mostly products that are permissible for advertising. A broadcast ad *might* not be acceptable if the tobacco business sells mostly items that are not permissible, even if the broadcast ad does not mention those products!

It can be confusing, and that is why many broadcasters refuse advertising from businesses wanting to promote any type of tobacco products.

Joe Camel

In 1988, R.J. Reynolds introduced a new ad campaign for Camel cigarettes. The central figure in the campaign was a cartoon character named Joe Camel. The use of a cartoon in cigarette advertising greatly concerned antismoking groups, who said that R.J. Reynolds was using the cartoon figure to appeal to younger audiences and to get kids smoking at a younger age.

FAQ

Did Joe Camel ads really have any impact on kids smoking?

Antismoking groups pointed to government studies showing that smoking rates among American youth had been declining in the 1980s. However, smoking among teenagers began to rise again in 1988, the year Joe Camel started appearing on billboards, on t-shirts, and in magazine ads. The government study also showed that between 1988 and 1996, the number of American youths who smoked daily jumped 73%. The Centers for Disease Control and Prevention said cartoon characters such as Joe Camel were a big reason for the increase in teen smoking. State and federal lawmakers began to consider legal action against R.J. Reynolds for intentionally marketing cigarettes to youths.

The End of Joe Camel. In 1994, the Federal Trade Commission said it was not going to pursue any action against Joe Camel ads. That decision infuriated antismoking advocates. However, the California Supreme Court ruled that communities could sue R.J. Reynolds for illegally targeting minors with the Joe Camel ads. (It is a violation of federal law to market cigarettes to children.) The communities responded. In 1997, the tobacco giant settled a lawsuit with California communities that had accused R.J. Reynolds of using Joe Camel to get kids hooked on cigarettes. The terms of the settlement included a payment by R.J. Reynolds of $10 million to fund youth antismoking programs in California. Also, Joe Camel could no longer be shown in cigarette ads in the state.

At about the same time, under pressure from antismoking groups and lawmakers, the FTC was moving toward a ban of Joe Camel. The FTC used numerous studies to show that Joe Camel's target audience was children. One Canadian study showed that 90% of 6-year-olds could identify Joe Camel with cigarettes. R.J. Reynolds realized that Joe Camel was becoming a liability, and the company dropped the cartoon character as a marketing tool in 1997. The company argued that Joe Camel was never meant to target teens but adults in their 20s.

Cigarette Ad Shams

A 1989 study of the TV coverage of the Marlboro Grand Prix showed that the name "Marlboro" appeared 5933 times, totaling 46 minutes of airtime. The Marlboro logo appeared frequently on the sides of race cars, on billboards, and on race drivers' jackets. Antitobacco groups call this tactic a *sham:* cigarette companies using sporting events or other TV programs to "sneak in" cigarette ads through visuals.

FAQ

Weren't these kinds of "shams" fairly commonplace on TV?

Yes. There were numerous examples, including the Virginia Slims Tennis Tournament, during which the Virginia Slims name was mentioned frequently by announcers and Virginia Slims ads were placed all around the tennis courts and were constantly seen on camera. The same situation occurred at other sporting events, such as baseball games, where cigarette billboards in the stadium would appear frequently on TV screens.

Crackdown on Shams. In 1995, the U.S. Department of Justice began to crack down on what it saw as shams and accused Madison Square Garden in New York of violating the Public Health Cigarette Smoking Act. The DOJ discovered that during New York Knicks basketball games, the Garden would display large Marlboro Cigarette signs in front of the scorers' table. As a result, the Marlboro sign was seen frequently on TV during the game. The DOJ was concerned about similar shams at other sporting events.

The DOJ worked out two important agreements in 1995:

- ▣ Madison Square Garden agreed that it would no longer place cigarette signs at locations "regularly in a camera's focus." This included areas around the basketball court and walkways to the locker rooms.
- ▣ The DOJ also worked out an agreement with Philip Morris to prohibit cigarette billboards next to playing fields or sports stadiums where TV cameras could see the ads.

At about this time, many major league baseball parks decided on their own to ban cigarette ads within ballparks. Other professional sports adopted similar policies, prohibiting tobacco ads in places normally seen by TV cameras. Shortly after in 1996, the Food and Drug Administration proposed a ban on all brand-name sponsorships of sporting events, such as Winston Cup Racing.

The 1998 Tobacco Settlement

Before the federal government passed any laws on these shams, cigarette companies in 1998 reached a settlement with 36 states regarding the marketing of cigarettes.

As of November 23, 2001, each tobacco company was allowed to have *only one brand-name sponsorship* of an event or series of events per year, such as the Kool Jazz Festival or Virginia Slims Tennis. No cigarette placards were allowed in *shopping malls, video game arcades, stadiums,* or *arenas.* No stadiums or arenas could be named after tobacco brands. There could be no *brand name sponsorship of team sports events* or events with significant youth audiences. No more *paid tobacco product placement in movies or TV shows* was allowed. This ended the practice of cigarette companies paying movie and TV producers to have a cigarette brand used by a character or displayed in a scene. Such paid placements were also prohibited in *videos, theater productions, musical recordings, musical performances,* and *video games.* No *cartoon characters* could be used in cigarette advertising. No more *outdoor advertising on billboards.* Cigarette ads were also prohibited on *mass transit buses and trains.*

FAQ

What about actors whose characters smoke cigarettes in TV shows and movies?

Antismoking groups also raised concerns about this issue, but the Department of Justice says such uses are legal. The laws are designed to ban *advertising* of cigarettes on radio and TV. As long as the characters or DJ are not promoting a certain brand, the references to smoking are legal. If the actor or DJ is being *paid* to smoke and talk about a certain brand, then it becomes advertising, and it would be a sham, as laid out in the 1998 Tobacco Settlement.

Other Cigarette Advertising Issues

The Public Health Cigarette Smoking Act required that cigarette packages carry the following label: WARNING: The Surgeon General Has Determined That Cigarette Smoking Is Dangerous To Your Health.

The act also requires the Surgeon General to produce annual reports about scientific studies relating to smoking and health. In 1981, the FTC told Congress that these warning labels were having little effect on people's smoking habits. In response, Congress passed the *Comprehensive Smoking Education Act of 1984* (Public Law 98-474). Labels saying smoking was "dangerous" apparently were not reducing the number of smokers. The act required that all cigarette packages and advertising carry four labels with more specific warnings:

- ▣ SURGEON GENERAL'S WARNING: Smoking Causes Lung Cancer, Heart Disease, Emphysema, and May Complicate Pregnancy.
- ▣ SURGEON GENERAL'S WARNING: Quitting Smoking Now Greatly Reduces Serious Risks to Your Health.
- ▣ SURGEON GENERAL'S WARNING: Cigarette Smoke Contains Carbon Monoxide.
- ▣ SURGEON GENERAL'S WARNING: Smoking By Pregnant Women May Result in Fetal Injury, Premature Birth, and Low Birth Weight.

In summary, the trend in the courts appears to be more regulation on tobacco advertising, not less.

Alcohol

Alcohol Price Ads

In the 1990s, the state of Rhode Island had three laws banning the advertisement of retail alcohol prices. The state said that these laws were designed to discourage alcohol abuse and promote "temperance." The laws stated that licensed dealers and out-of-state manufacturers could not advertise any alcohol prices. All media were banned from carrying alcohol ads from other states if those ads contained price information. The media also were not allowed to make any references to alcohol sales in other states. Signs inside package stores that advertised prices were not permitted if they could be seen from outside the store.

Liquor stores in Rhode Island and neighboring Massachusetts took the state of Rhode Island to court over the laws. In *44 Liquormart v. Rhode Island*,[23] the U.S. Supreme Court applied the Central Hudson Test and struck down the laws. The court said that the state was prohibiting the flow of truthful advertising. The laws "did not directly advance the state's substantial interest in promoting temperance" and were more restrictive than necessary to serve the state interest. Also, the laws damaged price competition in a free market society.

In 1995, the Supreme Court struck down a federal law that prohibited beer labels from disclosing alcohol content. The law's aim was to discourage alcoholism, but in *Rubin v. Coors*,[24] the court said that the government could not ban "factual, verifiable and nonmisleading factual information" about alcohol content.

Hard Liquor Ads

The broadcasting industry has always regulated itself in regard to alcohol ads. The first self-regulation came in 1937 in the National Association of Broadcasters Radio Code. Under "Acceptability of Advertisers and Products," the NAB advocated the following practices for broadcasters:

In general, because radio broadcasting is designed for the home and the entire family, the following principles shall govern the business classification:

1. The advertising of hard liquor shall not be accepted.

2. The advertising of beer and wines is acceptable when presented in the best of good taste and discretion.[25]

The code was adapted for TV, and for decades broadcasters have followed these guidelines. Again, these are just guidelines from the NAB. No broadcaster was required by law to follow these advertising suggestions. The NAB had only mild punishments for stations that violated the guidelines. The NAB codes are no longer in effect because the federal government said the code violated antitrust laws.

Still, many stations adopted the NAB Code as a general code of conduct. However, near the end of the century, attitudes started to change.

In June 1996, KRIS-TV in Corpus Christi, TX, became the first TV station to accept hard liquor ads (for Seagram's Crown Royal Canadian Whiskey). President Clinton asked broadcasters to adhere to the voluntary ban on hard liquor ads. In November, the Distilled Spirits Council of America voted to amend its code of practices and allow hard liquor advertising on TV. One month later, the FTC announced a first-ever investigation into alcohol ads on TV. The FTC's main goal was to look at the impact of hard liquor ads on underage viewers.

In April 1997, President Clinton asked the FCC to take action against hard liquor ads on radio and TV. In July, FCC chairman Reed Hundt asked broadcasters to bring back the voluntary ban on hard liquor ads. The four major TV networks agreed to abide by the voluntary

[23]517 U.S. 484 (1996)

[24]514 U.S. 476 (1995)

[25]National Association of Broadcasters. (1971, March). *The radio code* (16th ed.). Washington, DC: Author.

ban. By December 2000, however, hard liquor ads had become more commonplace on TV. More than 100 TV stations across the country had accepted ads from Seagram's. Ads for Jack Daniel's and Bacardi were also running on dozens of stations and cable systems throughout the United States.

In December 2001, NBC announced that it would soon begin to air hard liquor ads. First, though, the network would air "social responsibility" ads from Guinness UDV for its Smirnoff brand of vodka. These ads were meant as preparation for full-fledged ads to be aired later for Smirnoff, but those ads never aired. In March 2002, NBC canceled its plans to air hard liquor ads after pressure from lawmakers and public interest groups. The Distilled Spirits Council said it would continue to push for hard liquor ads on radio and TV.

Hard liquor ads had already gotten significant radio airplay. The Distilled Spirits Council of the United States said that between 1996 and 2001, more than 2000 radio stations in 250 markets had aired hard liquor ads. Thus, despite protests from lawmakers and public interest groups, hard liquor ads appear to be gaining acceptance on the broadcast airwaves, especially with such ads appearing more often on cable TV. By the end of 2003, more than 20 national cable networks were airing hard liquor ads.

UNDERWRITING RULES

The FCC prohibits noncommercial stations (also known as "public stations") from airing commercial advertising for products or services. Public stations are supposed to focus on educating and informing the public, and the federal government feels that having standard advertising on public stations detracts from a station's educational mission. Therefore, when a business pays to sponsor a program on a public station, that station may acknowledge the business through what is called *underwriting*.

Underwriting announcements should contain only the most basic information about a business or product. The FCC says the following types of information are permitted:

1. Slogans or "logograms" that identify and do *not* promote. Acceptable slogans include such things as "Clip Joint—the Hair Professionals," "The Ice Cream Hut—The Hut of 100 Flavors," and "Earl's Electronics—50 Years Serving Smithtown."

2. Location information and phone numbers. Give only the facts. Keep it simple. Acceptable language includes such phrases as "Tony's Barber Shop is located at 133 Clinton Street"; "Arnie's Clothing, 1589 South Elm, Jonesville"; and "their phone number is 555-9654."

3. Value-neutral descriptions of a product line or service. Acceptable examples: "Bailey's Garage also fixes foreign cars"; "Brady's Jewelry sells class rings for high school and college"; and "All dinners at the Roma include potato, salad, and drink."

4. Brand and trade names and product or service listings, such as "The Jean Scene sells Wrangler Jeans," "The Coffee Shoppe uses only Colombian beans," and "The Corner Café accepts Visa and MasterCard."

What to Avoid

The FCC has strict guidelines about underwriting language that must be avoided:

1. *Calls to action.* A station may not use language that encourages listeners to buy a product or contact a business. Examples of unacceptable calls to action: "Call them at 555-1466," "Stop by our store at 12 Main Street and see the new models," and "Try out a Jiffy mower today."

2. *References to price or value.* This includes information about interest rates or other references to savings. Unacceptable price and value references: "Midtown Bank has checking with 3% interest," "You'll save big by shopping at Joe's Market," and "Tickets are $20 at the door."

3. *Statements of Quality.* Avoid use of superlatives. Such language must also be avoided if it appears in a company slogan or logogram. Examples include "We have the *best* hamburgers," "Jiffy Mowers—A *Cut Above* the Rest," and "For the *finest* in jewelry."

4. *Comparisons.* Avoid comparisons with other products or businesses, such as "We're rated #1 in customer satisfaction for local restaurants," "Recent taste tests show our soda is preferred 2 to 1," and "No other dealership sells more cars."

5. *Encouragements to buy, rent, sell, or lease.* You may not entice listeners with special bargains or incentives. Examples: "Free car wash with 10-dollar gas purchase"; "Prizes for the first 100 customers"; "Buy one, get the second for half off!"

6. *Use of the words* you, your, our, we, *and* us. It is best to avoid these words in underwriting copy because they almost always result in a promotion of some sort: "Your #1 Car Dealer," "We give you better deals," "Our service makes it worth the drive."

Examples of Unacceptable Underwriting

In May 2000, the FCC fined Southern Rhode Island Public Radio Broadcasting $1000 for five instances of "impermissible donor and underwriting announcements" on WBLQ-FM. Here are two of the offending announcements. See if you can find the "impermissible" language in these spots:

1. The summer months are unofficially here. Just picture yourself driving along Atlantic Avenue on a beautiful summer's night, sunroof down, talking on your car phone, and cranking out the tunes in your superb sound system without a care in the world. Sounds nice, but a common concern for this scenario is—"Can I afford all of this?"

MP's of Westerly, the car phone store next to AutoZone on Granite Street, makes it easy. Craig can help you find a sound system and fix you up with a sunroof that will fit your budget. The cell phones have a fixed monthly rate, in both Connecticut and Rhode Island, with digital choice and choice single-rate plans. MP's of Westerly, the car phone store next to AutoZone on Granite Street, 348-3071. Another proud contributor to programming on WBLQ.

2. *Steven:* Hi. I am Steven King from King's Cyclery in Spindrift Village, Dunn's Corner. The warm weather is here, and we are ready with the latest in bicycles, gear, and accessories. One of our newest recumbent bicycles is "Bikee." In my opinion, it's a very relaxing and comfortable bike, in which one sits on a soft-padded chair with handlebars and peddles in front. The other new recumbent which WBLQ's own Chris DiPaulo experienced is "Vision." Chris, how did you like it?

Chris: Oh, Steve I loved it. Like Bikee, it's relaxing and comfortable. But, as you know, Steve, I could stand to lose a few pounds. Vision is perfect for me because it's also good exercise. You can adjust tension, and the handlebars are uniquely placed right next to where I sit, and the pedals are out in front.

Steven: Well, there you have it. You can find these recumbent bikes and all other kinds of bicycles, gear, and accessories, as well as a model train department, at King's Cyclery in the Spindrift Village in Dunn's Corner. And I am proud to be supporting local community radio on 88.1 WBLQ.

Chris: Steve, what is your phone number?

Steven: It's funny you should ask, Chris. It's 322-6005.[26]

---

[26]*Southern Rhode Island Public Radio Broadcasting, Inc.,* DA 00-1011 (EB released May 9, 2000)

Promoting Nonprofit Events

FAQ

What about a noncommercial station promoting a nonprofit event? Is it OK for the station to encourage listeners to take action?

It is perfectly all right for noncommercial stations to promote or broadcast calls to action for charities and other nonprofit activities and organizations. For example, it is acceptable for a noncommercial station to encourage persons to seek out a Red Cross bloodmobile and to "get out there and give blood."

Stations may also announce calls to action, use qualitative wording, or mention prices in non-underwriting announcements. For example, it is legal to announce the ticket prices for an upcoming concert or other event in a community calendar segment.

REGULATING TELEMARKETING

In the 1990s, the telemarketing industry exploded. Businesses realized they could sell products cheaply and easily by calling people at their homes and delivering sales pitches over the phone. However, many citizens became aggravated with the number of unwanted phone calls they were receiving from telemarketers.

Several states had passed laws restricting telemarketers. In 2003, Congress gave the FTC permission to establish a "do-not-call" registry. In September 2003, citizens were told they could sign up for list on the FTC's Web site or through a toll-free phone number. Within a short time, more than 53 million people had registered. Once a phone number is on the list, it is illegal for commercial telemarketers to call that number. However, telemarketers from charities and nonprofit organizations such as universities and political organizations may still call. Companies may also call individuals with whom they have recently done business. Officials estimated that the list would help block 80% of telemarketing calls. Telemarketers immediately challenged the law in court, saying it violated their First Amendment rights and that the law discriminated between commercial and noncommercial telemarketers. One lower court put a temporary stop to the do-not-call list, but in February 2004, the 10th U.S. Circuit Court of Appeals upheld the government's right to enforce the no-call registry. The government has punished violators. In November 2003, the FCC announced a fine of $10,000 against AT&T for 78 phone calls it made to 29 customers who were on the list.

REGULATING "SPAM" E-MAIL

At the same time citizens were complaining to lawmakers about unwanted telemarketing calls, there were loud cries going up about massive volumes of unsolicited messages from advertisers in people's e-mail boxes. Such unwanted messages are called *junk e-mail* or *spam*, and in 2003 it was estimated that they made up 50% of e-mail messages. In December 2003, President Bush signed the Can-Spam Act, the first legislation to outlaw spam. The law requires spammers to label pornographic messages and to give people a way to opt out of receiving future spam. It also prohibits spammers from using false return addresses. Spammers are also banned from harvesting e-mail addresses from other Web sites. Violators can face fines in the millions of dollars and up to 5 years in prison. Critics say the measure is weak because it cannot regulate spam from outside the United States, and businesses can still send spam to people until those people opt out. Opponents of the law say it means people will be spending more time opting out of spam than they used to spend deleting spam.

As of May 2004, spam containing sexually explicit material must be labeled "Sexually Explicit" in the subject line. Also, graphic images may not appear in the opening body of the message. Such images must only be visible by scrolling down or through a link. Violators may face imprisonment and fines of up to $500,000.

SUMMARY

In 1942, the U.S. Supreme Court ruled that commercial speech had no First Amendment protection. However, as the years passed, the courts began to give commercial speech more protection, striking down laws that banned the advertising of alcohol and prescription drug prices, for example. Eventually, the Supreme Court would establish the Central Hudson Test to use in determining whether a commercial speech restriction is permissible.

The government is permitted to place certain restrictions on the advertising of products considered to be harmful, such as tobacco and gambling. In 1971, Congress banned the advertising of most tobacco products on radio and TV.

The Federal Trade Commission punishes those who engage in false and misleading advertising and the Food and Drug Administration oversees food and drug safety, as well as ensuring the accurate labeling of products.

[1]*Problem phrases:* "picture yourself" "superb sound system" "Can I afford all this?" "makes it easy" "Craig can help you find" "fix you up" "will fit your budget" "fixed monthly rate" "choice single-rate plans."

[2]*Problem phrases:* "In my opinion, it's a very relaxing and comfortable bike" "WBLQ's own Chris DiPaulo experienced" "Chris, how do you like it?" "I loved it" "It's relaxing and comfortable" "perfect for me" "You can find these recumbent bikes and all other kinds. . . ."

16

Media and the Courts

In all criminal prosecutions, the accused shall enjoy the right to a speedy and public trial.

—Sixth Amendment

Cameras in the Courtroom

It's the First Amendment versus the Sixth Amendment—the right of the media to gather information about criminal and civil trials versus the right of the accused to receive a fair and speedy public trial. Does the presence of the media, specifically the broadcast media, somehow interfere with courtroom proceedings and not allow for a fair trial? The American Bar Association certainly believed so in 1937 when it drafted Canon 35[1]:

> Proceedings in court should be conducted with fitting dignity and decorum. The taking of photographs in the courtroom, during sessions of the court or recesses between sessions, and the broadcasting of court proceedings are calculated to detract from the essential dignity of the proceedings, degrade the court and create misconceptions with respect thereto in the mind of the public and should not be permitted.

Canon 35 was partly in response to the famous Lindbergh kidnapping trial in 1935. Bruno Hauptmann had been charged with kidnapping and killing the infant son of famous aviator Charles Lindbergh. Because of Lindbergh's celebrity status, Hauptmann's trial became a media circus. Photographers and reporters crammed into the courtroom every day, often disrupting proceedings. Hauptmann was found guilty and sentenced to death.

Soon after the trial, the federal government established a Special Committee on Cooperation between Press, Radio and Bar. It called the Hauptmann trial a "depressing example of improper publicity and professional misconduct."[2] The committee recommended standards of media conduct in court. The American Bar Association's Canon 35 soon followed.

---

[1]McElroy, D., Turner, K. (2004, August). Cameras in the courtroom. *Online Media Center.* Retrieved November 8, 2004, from http://www.flabar.org/DIVCOM/PI/RHandbook01.nsf/0/5192d3660a0dd573852569cb004c8e15? OpenDocument

[2]American Bar Association. (1937). Report of the Special Committee on Cooperation Between Press, Radio and Bar, as to publicity interfering with fair trial of judicial and quasi-judicial proceedings. In *Annual report* (pp. 851-866). Chicago: Author.

FAQ

Was Canon 35 enforced strictly?

Keep in mind that Canon 35 was not a law. It was simply a strong recommendation from the American Bar Association regarding courtroom cameras. The vast majority of states in the following decades did follow the recommendation and banned most electronic media from courtrooms. In 1946, all photography and radio broadcasts were banned in federal courts. TV cameras were later added to the ban.

The U.S. Supreme Court in 1965 agreed that cameras in courtrooms created unneeded distractions. In *Estes v. Texas,*[3] Billie Sol Estes had been convicted of swindling investors. TV cameras were present, and stations broadcast portions of the trial and preliminary hearing. The judge restricted cameras to a booth at the rear of the courtroom. However, these were large film cameras, which required numerous technicians, bright lights, and bulky cables. Estes appealed the conviction, saying that the cameras interfered with his Sixth Amendment rights. In a 5-4 decision, the U.S. Supreme Court ruled for Estes, saying that the *mere presence* of media cameras and recording devices at a trial can have "an adverse psychological impact" on the jury, witnesses, and other participants.

However, the Supreme Court acknowledged that future cameras might not be as bulky and therefore might be more suitable for courtrooms. The court was right.

Cameras No Longer "Intrusive"

In 1976, the Florida Supreme Court began a 1-year experimental program of allowing TV cameras to cover all court proceedings in Florida, even if the parties involved objected. Ten other states had been doing similar experiments. After the 1-year period, the Florida Supreme Court ruled that there was "more to be gained than lost" by having cameras in court. It said that electronic media coverage of trials provided "wider public acceptance and understanding of decisions" and gave the public more confidence in the legal process.

The court then drafted Canon 3A (7), which dictated that the judge controls conduct in the courtroom. Therefore, the judge was responsible for maintaining civility and preventing distractions. As a result, to ensure a fair trial, a judge was allowed to place restrictions on electronic and print media in the courtroom as long as those restrictions were in accordance with Florida Supreme Court guidelines.

Canon 3A (7) Challenged

The first challenge came in 1977, during a trial for two police officers charged with breaking and entering a Miami Beach restaurant. The officers had talked on their walkie-talkie radios during the burglary, and an amateur radio operator had recorded their conversation. The case made headlines, and TV stations wanted to have cameras in the courtroom. Lawyers for the police officers tried to keep the cameras out, to no avail.

---

[3]381 U.S. 532 (1965)

A TV camera recorded the testimony of the amateur radio operator, testimony that was very damning to the police officers. The station broadcast nearly 3 minutes of testimony and arguments, all from the prosecution's point of view. No broadcast time was given to the defense arguments. The jury found the police officers guilty on all counts. The officers appealed, arguing that the TV coverage denied them a fair trial. In *Chandler v. Florida,*[4] the U.S. Supreme Court upheld the convictions.

The court pointed out that there is no solid evidence to prove that cameras *inherently* create an unfair trial. The *Estes* ruling no longer applied because cameras had become "less obtrusive." The Florida law was reasonable, providing special rules to protect certain witnesses, such as children, sex crime victims, and informants. The court noted that jurors in this case were not allowed to watch TV, so they were not influenced by the TV coverage. *The ultimate decision,* the court said, *is in the hands of individual states,* which "must be free to experiment" with cameras in courtrooms.

FAQ

Won't there be some cases in which cameras do lead to an unfair trial?

The Supreme Court recognized that possibility and said that persons may still challenge convictions if they feel media coverage created an unfair trial atmosphere, as in the next case.

TV NEWS AND VIDEOTAPED CONFESSIONS

In February 1961, police in Lake Charles, LA, arrested Wilbert Rideau for robbery, kidnapping, and murder. Rideau confessed to the crimes during a 20-minute filmed interrogation with a local sheriff. There was no lawyer present to advise Rideau that he had a right to remain silent. Lake Charles TV stations aired the film over the next several days. When Rideau was arraigned, his lawyers asked for a change of venue because of the local TV coverage. The trial court denied the change of venue, and 2 months later Rideau was found guilty of murder and sentenced to death. Three jury members admitted they had seen Rideau's confession on TV.

Rideau's lawyers appealed, saying that the filmed confession made the public think Rideau was guilty. The lawyers said the majority of the community was exposed to Rideau's confession. The area population was 150,000, and an estimated 100,000 people saw the TV coverage. In *Rideau v. Louisiana,*[5] the U.S. Supreme Court ruled that Rideau should have been granted a change of venue.

The Supreme Court said that the jury should have been taken "from a community of people who had not seen and heard Rideau's televised 'interview.'" The court proceedings

---

[4]449 U.S. 560 (1981)

[5]373 U.S. 723 (1963)

were "a hollow formality" as a result of the TV coverage. Rideau's real trial appeared to have been the filmed interview with the sheriff, during which Rideau had no lawyer present. Persons have a right to a trial in a courtroom presided over by a judge, the right to a lawyer, and the right to plead not guilty. Rideau did not get these rights in the filmed interview.

Rideau was later retried in another courtroom and again found guilty. Several years later, the Supreme Court once again found the media could affect the outcome of a trial.

THE FAMOUS SAM SHEPPARD MURDER TRIAL

The TV series and movie *The Fugitive* were based on this murder case. Marilyn Sheppard, the wife of a well-known Cleveland osteopath, Dr. Sam Sheppard, was murdered in her home in 1954. The doctor said he was asleep on a downstairs sofa when his wife's screams awakened him. Sheppard said he was running up the stairs when an intruder attacked him from behind and knocked him unconscious. The local media openly questioned the doctor's account. Sheppard's murder trial became a media circus.

Many papers carried editorials saying that Sheppard should be convicted of murder. Lawyers spoke openly with the media about evidence and testimony. The judge placed no restrictions on what they could or could not say. The judge also allowed reporters to interview prospective witnesses. During the trial, the media packed the courtroom, and their frequent movements often made it difficult to hear testimony. News reporters were allowed to handle and photograph trial exhibits. Radio broadcasts were done from a room right next to the room where the jury took breaks and deliberated. Some reporters were allowed to sit "inside the bar," near evidence tables, lawyers' tables, and the witness stand. Before the trial, one newspaper published the names and phone numbers of jury members, basically telling the public to call and encourage a guilty verdict.

The jury found Sheppard guilty of murder.

FAQ

As mentioned in *Chandler,* weren't these the kinds of media actions that would lead to an unfair trial atmosphere?

Yes. In 1966, the U.S. Supreme Court overturned Sheppard's conviction in *Sheppard v. Maxwell.*[6] The court said that the media had stepped over the line, noting that "unfair and prejudicial news comment on pending trials has become increasingly prevalent." The court pointed to the "massive, pervasive and prejudicial publicity and disruptive influences" in the Sheppard trial and said that the judge "should have more closely regulated the conduct of the media in the courtroom" and "should have made some effort to control the release of prejudicial matters to the press." Sheppard was granted a new trial, and he was found not guilty. Sheppard died 4 years later at age 46.

---

[6]384 U.S. 333 (1966)

FAQ

What are some steps that can be taken to protect the rights of the media and at the same time protect a person's right to a fair trial?

The Supreme Court provided *six guidelines* for judges to follow to protect this often delicate balance between the First Amendment and the Sixth Amendment:

1. *The judge controls the courtroom.* Judges may adopt rules to regulate the media in the courtroom (including rules for personal behavior, placement of cameras, and the number of reporters allowed in the courtroom).

2. *Sequestering the jury.* For example, jury members may be placed in motel rooms and be prohibited from accessing any media accounts of the trial.

3. *Admonishing the jury.* The judge may tell jury members to disregard media accounts of the trial. Admonishment may also include questioning jurors to make sure they have not been influenced by news coverage of the case.

4. *Postpone the trial.* This is also called a "continuance." Delaying proceedings may help a community and the media "calm down" regarding certain trials.

5. *Gag orders.* The judge can prohibit or "gag" lawyers or witnesses, prohibiting them from talking with the media about certain aspects of a trial.

6. *Change of venue.* The judge may move the trial to another city or county, where there is less publicity about a case.

Problems With the Sheppard Guidelines

1. *The judge controls the courtroom.* The media claim that this gives the judge too much power in some cases and can restrict the First Amendment rights of the press.

2. *Sequestering the jury.* This can be a real problem, especially in longer trials. Jury members become frustrated with having to live in a motel room for weeks or months, away from their families and jobs.

3. *Admonishing the jury.* Does this really work? How can a judge guarantee that jury members have not seen media accounts of the trial or have not heard about those media accounts from friends and relatives?

4. *Postpone the trial.* The Sixth Amendment guarantees a "speedy" trial. Doesn't a delay violate a defendant's rights?

5. *Gag orders.* The media often accuse judges of enforcing gag orders that are far too restrictive.

6. *Change of venue.* Getting a trial in a new location may cause a delay, hindering a person's right to a speedy trial. The media also claim they cannot cover the trial as well when it is at a distant location.

The guidelines were designed to control some of the behaviors of the media and the possible effects those behaviors might have on juries, witnesses, and lawyers. However, the answer to one question remained a little cloudy:

FAQ

Does the Sheppard ruling recognize a basic right of the media to cover trials?

RIGHT OF ACCESS TO TRIALS

In 1979, the Supreme Court shocked the media and answered the above question with a *no*. In *Gannett v. DePasquale*,[7] the U.S. Supreme Court, in a narrow 5-4 ruling, upheld the closing of a trial in New York. A judge had barred the media and the public from a pretrial hearing for two men accused of killing a former police officer. In upholding the trial closing, the Supreme Court wrote that, in this case, "an open proceeding would pose a reasonable probability of prejudice to these defendants." The court added that the right to a public trial belongs "to the defendant and not to the public."

FAQ

Doesn't this ruling violate the basic essence of the Sixth Amendment regarding "public" trials?

The four dissenting justices in this case said yes, and they provided the following warning: "Secret hearings . . . are suspect by nature."

Trials Should Be Open to the Public

Only a year later in *Richmond Newspapers v. Virginia,* the Supreme Court showed that it was not willing to allow closure of most criminal trials. (The *Gannett* ruling affected *pretrial* proceedings.) The court ruled that there is a First Amendment right of access to trials for the media and the public.

The case involved a man who had four different trials in Virginia for the killing of a hotel manager. In the first trial, the man's conviction was thrown out on a technicality. The next two trials resulted in mistrials, one time because jurors were given information about the man's overturned conviction from the first trial. Before the start of the fourth trial, the defense asked that the judge close the trial to the public and the media. The defense was using a Virginia law that said a judge could remove "any persons whose presence would impair the conduct of a fair trial." The Virginia Supreme Court upheld the closing of the trial. The U.S. Supreme Court overturned that ruling:

> We hold that the right to attend criminal trials is implicit in the guarantees of the First Amendment; without the freedom to attend such trials, which people have exercised for centuries, important aspects of freedom of speech and of the press could be eviscerated.[8]

---

[7]443 U.S. 368 (1979)

[8]448 U.S. 555 (1980)

However, *some* trials can still be closed. The Supreme Court said that there may be circumstances in which judges have legitimate reasons or "overriding interests" to close trials.

FAQ

What would be considered "overriding interests"?

One example was provided in the next case, but lawmakers and judges must make such determinations carefully.

Closing Trials Involving Young Sex Victims

Massachusetts wanted to make it easier for juvenile victims of sex crimes to testify in court, so the state passed a law that trials be closed when juveniles testified about sexual assaults. The *Boston Globe* sued the state for the right to cover a rape trial in which three of the victims were younger than 18 years. In *Globe Newspaper v. Superior Court*,[9] the U.S. Supreme Court ruled that the state law was noble but too broad and sweeping in mandating that *every* case of this type be closed. The court said that a trial may be closed only if (a) there is a "compelling governmental interest," and (b) the law demanding closure "is narrowly tailored to serve that interest."

The Supreme Court said that the judge in each case should make the decision about closure based on the nature of the charges. The judge could then adequately determine whether closure was needed to protect any juveniles. That is exactly what judges did in the following cases.

In Ohio, in 1990, a judge closed a juvenile court hearing, and the Ohio Supreme Court upheld the closure, saying that such hearings may involve issues such as abuse, neglect, and custody. The court ruled that media coverage might be emotionally traumatic for the juveniles involved.[10] In the District of Columbia in 1991, journalists were allowed to cover the murder trial of a 14-year-old as long as they promised not to reveal the young suspect's identity in any way. However, one journalist broke that promise, so the judge banned all reporters from the rest of the trial.[11] In New Mexico in 2001, the state's supreme court ruled that the media did not have an absolute right to attend proceedings involving child neglect or abuse. In *Albuquerque Journal v. Jewell*,[12] the court felt that media coverage would inevitably lead to the release of the children's names and invade the privacy of these young victims.

FAQ

Are cameras allowed in the U.S. Supreme Court?

As of this writing, no.

---

[9]457 U.S. 596 (1982)

[10]In re *T.R.*, 52 Ohio St.3d 6 (1990)

[11]In re *J.D.C.*, 594 A.2d 70 (1991)

[12]18 P.3d 334 (2001)

Federal Courts and Cameras

When it comes to the issue of allowing cameras in federal courts, it is hard to forget the words of Supreme Court Justice David Souter in 1996 when he was asked if cameras should be allowed in the nation's highest court. His terse response: "When they roll them over my dead body." However, in 1990, Chief Justice William Rehnquist said he was not "averse to the idea" of cameras in federal courts. The next year, the idea was tried.

In 1991, federal courts began a 3-year experiment with cameras. Two federal appeals courts and six federal trial courts allowed cameras, but only for civil and appeals proceedings. No cameras were allowed in criminal trials. In most cases, the courts allowed only one photographer or videographer in the courtroom. The experiment ended in 1994, with no indication that such practices would become permanent.

In 1996, the Judicial Conference (a federal agency responsible for establishing policies for the federal courts) wrote new rules that allowed federal courts to make up their own minds about cameras in their courtrooms. As of 2002, only two federal appeals courts allow any cameras—the Second Circuit in New York City and the Ninth Circuit in San Francisco.

The Oklahoma City Bomber Trial

The trial of Timothy McVeigh was held in Denver for fear that McVeigh would not be able to receive a fair trial in Oklahoma. Families of the victims, though, felt it was unfair that they had to travel to Denver to watch the trial. Congress stepped in and allowed for the federal trial in Denver to be fed live to Oklahoma City via closed circuit television.

As was just mentioned, the experiments from 1991 to 1994 in federal courts did not allow cameras in criminal trials. In this case, cameras were allowed in a criminal trial even though the broadcasts were not meant for the public or the news media. Still, those in favor of courtroom cameras saw it as a "crack in the door."

Supreme Court Allows Audio Transcripts

In 2000, in *Bush v. Gore*,[13] the nation's highest court had to try to make sense out of the election nightmare in the state of Florida, where George W. Bush and Al Gore were separated by only a few hundred votes. The Florida Supreme Court had allowed television coverage of its proceedings in the case. When the case reached the nation's highest court, the justices allowed audio recordings of this Supreme Court case to be released immediately after the case was argued. This had never been done before. These "audio transcripts" allowed the media and the public to hear for themselves how Supreme Court proceedings are conducted. Since then, the court has been allowing more frequent use of audio recordings and release of transcripts, usually in high-profile cases.

The Sunshine in the Courtroom Act

In June 2001, encouraged by the landmark Supreme Court release of audio transcripts in *Bush v. Gore,* Senators Charles Grassley and Chuck Schumer introduced the Sunshine in the Courtroom Act. This act would allow federal trial and appellate judges to permit cameras in their courtrooms and would even extend the option to the U.S. Supreme Court. The

---

[13]531 U.S. 98 (2000)

act failed to make it through Congress but was reintroduced by the senators in 2003. The act failed once again.

Cameras Denied for Trial of "20th Hijacker"

Zacarias Moussaoui was dubbed by the media the "20th Hijacker" from the September 11 terrorist attacks. Before his trial on conspiracy charges, Court TV and C-SPAN asked that they be allowed to broadcast all proceedings related to the Moussaoui trial. In January 2002, in *U.S. v. Moussaoui*,[14] a federal district court judge banned cameras from the proceedings.

The judge cited Federal Rule of Criminal Procedure 53: "The taking of photographs . . . or radio broadcasting of judicial proceedings from the court room shall not be permitted by the court." The judge said the purpose of the trial was not to "educate the world about the American legal system. Instead, the purpose is to determine the innocence or guilt of this defendant."

Excluding cameras would help ensure anonymity for jurors. The media had agreed not to reveal jurors' faces on camera, but Judge Brinkema worried about media "mistakes." She pointed out that the case involved a person linked with a terrorist group. "Accidental" release of jurors' identities could put those jurors in danger. The judge added that "the faces of attorneys, court staff, and security officers would be exposed," subjecting them to possible retaliation from terrorist groups. Witnesses would be intimidated just knowing they would be on worldwide TV. This could lead to foreign witnesses refusing to testify for safety reasons.

The judge also expressed concerns about Moussaoui's "unorthodox and unpredictable" behavior in previous courtroom proceedings. "World-wide broadcasting of these proceedings, either by television, radio, or the Internet, would be an open invitation to any trial participant to engage in showmanship or make a public spectacle for the world to see."

States and Cameras in Court

FAQ

How many states allow cameras in court?

All 50 (the District of Columbia bans coverage of all appellate and trial courts). In 2001, Mississippi and South Dakota became the last two states to allow cameras in the courtroom. However, the laws vary from state to state. Perhaps the best way to explain this is just to provide a summary from the Radio-Television News Directors Association. The RTNDA breaks down state laws into three categories, based on the amount of coverage allowed in state courts.[15]

---

[14]205 F.R.D. 183 (2002)

[15]Radio-Television News Directors Association and Foundation. (2003). *Freedom of Information. Cameras in the Court: A State-by-State Guide.* Retrieved November 5, 2004, from http://www.rtndf.org/foi/scc.html. Check out this Web site for more specific details on each state's laws regarding cameras in the court.

Tier One: States That Allow the Most Coverage:

Alaska—must get consent for trials involving sex offense victims

Arizona—no coverage allowed of juvenile or adoption proceedings

California—presiding judge has broad discretion

Colorado—presiding judge has broad discretion

Connecticut—no coverage allowed of "family" and trade secret cases

Florida—must prove electronic media coverage would adversely affect trial

Georgia—presiding judge has broad discretion

Idaho—presiding judge has broad discretion

Iowa—must have consent of victims and witnesses in sexual abuse cases

Kentucky—presiding judge has broad discretion

Massachusetts—coverage of certain proceedings banned (e.g., jury selection hearings)

Michigan—judge may prohibit coverage of certain witnesses

Montana—presiding judge has broad discretion

Nevada—presiding judge has broad discretion

New Hampshire—presiding judge has broad discretion

New Mexico—judge may prohibit coverage of certain witnesses

North Carolina—judge may prohibit coverage of certain witnesses and cases

North Dakota—presiding judge has broad discretion

Rhode Island—presiding judge has broad discretion; judge may prohibit coverage of certain proceedings

South Carolina—presiding judge has broad discretion

Tennessee—presiding judge has broad discretion; coverage of minors restricted

Washington—presiding judge has broad discretion

West Virginia—presiding judge has broad discretion

Wisconsin—presiding judge has broad discretion

Wyoming—presiding judge has broad discretion

Tier Two: States With Moderate Restrictions

Hawaii—ban on coverage of certain cases and witnesses

Kansas—many types of witnesses may object

Missouri—many types of witnesses may object

New Jersey—coverage of sexual penetration cases banned

Ohio—victim or witness may object to coverage

Oregon—witnesses may object to coverage of certain cases

Texas—no rules for criminal trial coverage, but such coverage is becoming more commonplace

Virginia—ban on coverage of sex offense cases

Tier Three: States With the Strictest Limitations

Alabama—consent of all parties and their attorneys required

Arkansas—coverage stops when any party or attorney objects

Delaware—appellate coverage only

Illinois—appellate coverage only

Indiana—appellate coverage only

Louisiana—appellate coverage only

Maine—appellate coverage, civil trials, arraignments, and sentencings and other nontestimonial proceedings in criminal matters

Maryland—appellate coverage; civil trials only

Minnesota—appellate coverage; trial coverage requires consent of all parties

Mississippi—appellate coverage only via the Internet

Nebraska—appellate coverage; audio trial coverage only

New York—appellate coverage only

Oklahoma—consent of criminal defendant required

Pennsylvania—any witness who objects will not be covered; civil trials only without a jury

South Dakota—Supreme Court coverage only

Utah—appellate coverage; for trial coverage, still photography only

Vermont—presiding judge has broad discretion

FAQ

Are there some basic rules that all states follow regarding cameras in court?

Yes.

- Limits on the number of cameras allowed in the courtroom. Several states allow a maximum of two TV cameras and two still cameras.
- Flash bulbs and artificial lights are not allowed.
- Any photography of jurors is prohibited, in most states.
- Media wishing to cover proceedings must usually submit advance requests in writing to the court. Time limits vary. Louisiana requires 20 days advance notice for many proceedings. New Mexico requires only 24 hours. Other states, such as Massachusetts, just require a "reasonable" advance notice.
- Media pool arrangements must be made by the media, not the courts.

- ▣ No audio recordings may be made of attorney-client conferences or conferences at the bench. Video should be avoided if a person's lips can be read.
- ▣ Some states do not allow cameras or their operators to "bear the insignia or marking of any media agency or network."

FAQ

What are the main arguments for cameras in court?

Cameras help to educate the public about the legal system. Courtroom cameras let people come to their own conclusions about the verdict. Cameras enhance the Sixth Amendment and allow for a truly "public" trial. The camera becomes just another spectator and does not influence the behavior of anyone involved in the trial, but cameras can also act as a watchdog, allowing the public to monitor the judicial conduct of lawyers and judges.

FAQ

What are the main arguments against cameras in court?

Cameras create a "media circus." Critics point to the O. J. Simpson trial and what they called the excessive media coverage of the trial. Cameras can scare away witnesses. Some people become afraid to testify if they know the proceedings are being broadcast. Lawyers and judges "ham it up" for the cameras. Some studies have shown a marked difference in lawyers' behaviors when there is a camera in the court. As a result, some critics say these courtroom antics make trials last longer and that cameras detract from the general "dignity" of court proceedings.

Trial participants can become more focused on their "media presence" than on the case. (Remember the amount of attention given to Marcia Clark's hairstyle changes during the O. J. Simpson trial?) Juries can feel pressured to reach a certain verdict because of excessive media exposure (again, think back to the O. J. Simpson criminal trial). Excessive media presence leads to more of a need to sequester juries. Critics say the result is similar to the attitudes of the jury in the O. J. Simpson case. Afterward, several jurors admitted they were tired of being sequestered and were "anxious" to reach a verdict and go home.

Gag Orders

When a judge prohibits the media from reporting on all or some aspects of a criminal proceeding, this is a *gag order* (also called a *restrictive order*). A judge may also place gag orders on lawyers and witnesses that bar them from talking with the media about certain aspects of a trial.

In 1975, in the small town of Sutherland, NE, someone killed six members of the Kellie family. One day after the killings, a neighbor confessed to police that he was the killer. The murder trial of Erwin Simants attracted national media attention, but the local courts were not accustomed to such massive media coverage. A county judge became worried that the intense media coverage would make it difficult to find an impartial jury. Four days after the killings, and just as pretrial hearings were about to begin, the judge issued a gag order. It prohibited anyone at the pretrial hearing from "releasing or authorizing the release for public dissemination in any form or manner whatsoever any testimony given or evidence adduced." The gag order said that only after a jury was in place would the media be allowed to report on the court proceedings.

This gag order barred the media from reporting specifically on five subjects: Simants' confession, statements that Simants had made to others, contents of notes he had written on the night of the murders, certain medical evidence presented during the pretrial, and the names of victims who might have been sexually assaulted. (These five restrictions were based on the Nebraska Bar-Press Guidelines, which the media and lawyers had drafted years earlier as "voluntary measures" to help ensure fair trials.)

The county judge's gag order was upheld by District Judge Hugh Stuart, who said "there is a clear and present danger that pre-trial publicity could impinge upon the defendant's right to a fair trial."

FAQ

Did the judge go too far in gagging the media?

Many in the media certainly thought he went too far, calling the gag order a prior restraint, and they filed suit for a right to report on the pretrial hearings. In *Nebraska Press Association v. Stuart*,[16] the U.S. Supreme Court ruled unanimously for the media, saying that the gag order violated the Constitution: "Pretrial publicity—even pervasive, adverse publicity—does not inevitably lead to an unfair trial." The court said it respected the judge's efforts to ensure a fair trial, but "prior restraints on speech and publication are the most serious and the least tolerable infringement on First Amendment rights."

The Supreme Court said that it was difficult here balancing between the First and Sixth Amendments. However, the court said, "It is nonetheless clear that the barriers to prior restraint remain high." Four justices said such gag orders should *never* be permitted. However, a five-member majority said that gag orders may be permitted in exceptional circumstances. The five justices, including Chief Justice Warren Burger, laid out three guidelines to be considered before a judge bars the media from a pretrial hearing, now called the Nebraska Press Test.

1. What is the extent and nature of pretrial media coverage?

2. Is there another way besides a gag order? Can we minimize the effects of damaging pretrial publicity in some other way that does not gag the press?

3. Will this gag order really achieve its goal? For example, will it truly make it easier to find or keep an impartial jury?

---

[16]427 U.S. 539 (1976)

The Supreme Court said that a gag order should be issued rarely and only when there is a "clear and present danger" that pretrial publicity will damage a person's right to a fair trial.

FAQ

What effect did this ruling have on other cases?

It is interesting to see how the courts dealt with gag orders after the *Nebraska Press* decision. Whether a gag order is upheld depends on the media coverage and the nature of the trial. In most cases, gag orders are overturned on appeal.

Media Gag Orders Struck Down

KUTV v. Conder.[17] In the 1970s, Ronald Easthope had been convicted of several rapes in the Sugarhouse section of Salt Lake City. In 1981, he was on trial again for rape. The trial judge issued a gag order, telling Salt Lake City media not to refer to Easthope as the "Sugarhouse rapist" because the name might imply guilt in the current rape charge. The Utah Supreme Court overturned the gag order, saying the trial court did not consider any of the three elements from the *Nebraska Press* case.

CBS v. U.S. District Court.[18] In 1984, CBS News had obtained copies of government surveillance videotapes that contained damaging evidence against auto industry executive John DeLorean. DeLorean was about to go on trial for drug charges, and the trial judge placed a gag order on CBS, telling the network not to broadcast any part of the tapes. A federal appeals court ruled for CBS and dissolved the gag order the next day. That court ruled that there was no compelling reason to bar the tapes from being broadcast.

Media Gag Orders Upheld

KUTV v. Wilkinson.[19] In a trial involving felony theft charges, the judge told the jury members to ignore media accounts of the trial. However, four jurors in the case learned of media reports that said the defendant had close ties with the Mafia. The judge did not want to declare a mistrial or sequester the entire jury, so he gave the media a "narrowed" gag order. Until the jury started deliberations, the media were barred from talking about the defendant's alleged connections to organized crime. The Utah Supreme Court upheld the gag order, saying it satisfied the three-prong test from the *Nebraska Press* case.

U.S. v. CNN.[20] In 1990, Panama dictator Manual Noriega was about to go on trial in Florida for drug trafficking charges. CNN had obtained tape recordings of Noriega talking on the phone with his lawyers. A federal judge ordered CNN not to broadcast the tapes and to

---

[17] 668 P.2d 513 (1983)

[18] 729 F.2d 1174 (9th Cir. 1984)

[19] 686 P.2d 456 (1984)

[20] 865 F. Supp. 1549 (S.D. Fla. 1994)

hand over the tapes to the court. CNN disobeyed the gag order and broadcast parts of the tapes, at the same time appealing the gag order to the U.S. Supreme Court. However, the Supreme Court refused to hear the case. CNN then handed over the tapes to the lower court. Upon hearing the tapes, the judge determined that they would not damage Noriega's right to a fair trial. CNN was now free to air the tapes. The story does not end there. In 1994, the U.S. Attorney's office in Miami had not forgotten that CNN had broadcast portions of the tape before the Supreme Court decision came out. A federal judge fined CNN for disobeying an active gag order.

OPENING PRETRIAL PROCEEDINGS

Jury Selection Process

The U.S. Supreme Court ruled in 1984 that jury selection processes must be open to the media and the public. In 1981, a man was on trial for raping and killing a 13-year-old girl. The judge felt that the jury selection process should be closed because of the sensitive nature of the trial, but a local newspaper said the judge violated its First Amendment rights to cover the jury selection. In *Press-Enterprise v. Superior Court*[21] (later called *Press-Enterprise I* or *P-E I*), the Supreme Court unanimously overturned the judge's closure of jury selection. The court said that most jury selection processes must be open to the public so citizens will know jurors are "fairly and openly selected."

FAQ

Aren't there times when the jury selection process should be closed?

Yes. The Supreme Court said that there are some times when barring the public from jury selection is appropriate. The court then established a four-part test to determine whether jury selection processes may be closed. This test was later adapted to cover closures of all pretrial proceedings.

Press-Enterprise Test for Closing Pretrial Proceedings

Whoever is seeking closure must prove that there is a *substantial likelihood* that open proceedings would damage *overriding interests* (the defendant's right to a fair trial, a juror's right to privacy, etc.). The judge must not be able to find any *reasonable alternatives* to closure, must *clearly articulate the reasons* for closure, and must put these reasons in writing in the court record.

Any closure must be narrowly tailored to serve the overriding interest. Closing a pretrial hearing for two hours to protect the privacy of a certain witness would most likely be considered "narrowly tailored" and permissible. Closing the *entire* hearing for this one witness would be considered too broad and impermissible.

---

[21]464 U.S. 501 (1984)

Pretrial Hearings

It is important to remember that in the *Nebraska Press* case, reporters were still allowed to attend the pretrial hearings, although they were barred from reporting what they had heard.

FAQ

Can a judge simply avoid the gag order issue by barring the media from pretrial hearings?

That is what some judges did after the *Nebraska Press* case. In 1986, in *Press-Enterprise v. Superior Court*[22] (or *P-E II*), the U.S. Supreme Court put a stop to the practice. The court ruled that most pretrial and preliminary hearings must be open to the public. This case involved a preliminary hearing for a nurse accused of killing 12 of her patients by giving them lethal amounts of a heart drug. The case had already attracted national attention, and the nurse's attorneys asked the judge to close the pretrial hearings. The judge obliged and closed the hearings, which lasted 41 days. The judge said he feared that the media would pronounce the nurse guilty before she had a fair trial.

The California Supreme Court upheld the judge's ruling, but the U.S. Supreme Court ruled that the closure was a violation of the Constitution. A pretrial hearing is "often the final and most important in the criminal proceeding," the court said. It allows the public to see the criminal justice system at work. Open pretrial hearings allow the public and the media to act as watchdogs on lawyers and judges. Secret trials create suspicion and detract from "the appearance of fairness so essential to public confidence in the system." Also, the court said, the lower court judge did not meet the standards set forth in the four-prong test from *P-E I* when he failed to consider alternatives to complete closure.

FAQ

So far, we've discussed only criminal proceedings. What are the rules about cameras in court for lawsuits and other civil proceedings?

Civil Trials and Cameras

This issue often reminds people of the O. J. Simpson case. His criminal trial was televised; however, the judge in the later civil trial did not allow cameras. The media circus surrounding Simpson's criminal trial certainly played a part in the closure.

Several years later, the California Supreme Court ruled that most civil trials should be open to the public. In *NBC Subsidiary v. Superior Court*,[23] a case involving actor Clint Eastwood, the California Supreme Court ruled that "the public has an interest, in all civil

---

[22]478 U.S. 1 (1986)

[23]980 P.2d 337 (1999)

cases, in observing and assessing the performance of its public judicial system." This is a California ruling. It does not affect the rest of the country. It might begin to set a precedent in civil trials in other states, however.

FAQ

Do I as a reporter have a right to get important documents from the court during a trial?

Court Documents

For the most part, the media and the public have historically had easy access to most court documents. Some recent cases have reaffirmed this access. The 1983 case of *Associated Press v. District Court*[24] is important because the Ninth Circuit Court of Appeals ruled that the public has a right to see court documents. The case involved drug charges against auto executive John DeLorean, and a federal judge decided to close part of the pretrial hearings and seal numerous court documents. The appeals court overturned the judge's rulings and said that court documents should only be sealed for three reasons:

1. There is a "substantial probability" that opening the documents would do "irreparable damage" to a person's right to a fair trial.

2. There is a "substantial probability" that sealing the documents will prevent damage to a person's right to a fair trial.

3. The court has exhausted all other measures to ensure a fair trial.

The same court of appeals reaffirmed this principle in two 1998 decisions. *U.S. v. Kaczynski*[25] involved the case of the "Unabomber," Ted Kaczynski, who was convicted of using letter bombs to kill and injure numerous people. Kaczynski wanted his psychiatric competency reports sealed, saying such records are private. The appeals court ruled that most parts of the psychiatric reports should be made available under common law right of access, saying "the media's need for disclosure outweighed Kaczynski's privacy rights."

In *Phoenix Newspapers v. District Court*,[26] the case revolved around charges of jury tampering during the trial of former Arizona governor Fife Symington. A lower court judge had sealed transcripts from two hearings dealing with the charges. The appeals court ruled that judges may not simply seal documents without warning. The court "must provide sufficient notice to the public and the press to afford them the opportunity to object or offer alternatives" to sealing documents. If there are objections to a sealing, a hearing on those objections "must be held as soon as possible." In this case, some jurors had received threatening phone calls during the trial, and the media and the public had a right to know this. The judge provided no substantial reasons for sealing these documents.

---

[24]705 F.2d 1143 (9th Cir. 1983)

[25]154 F.3d 930 (9th Cir. 1998)

[26]156 F.3d 940 (9th Cir. 1998)

Access to Audio and Video Evidence

When a lawyer uses audio- or videotapes as evidence, do the media have a right to make copies of them? In 1978, the Supreme Court said no. *Nixon v. Warner Communications*[27] involved some of President Nixon's famous audiotapes from the Watergate trials. Radio and TV stations wanted copies of the tapes, but the court refused. The Supreme Court upheld that decision and ruled against the media, saying there is not an "absolute right" to copy these kinds of evidence. However, the court said such decisions must be made on a case-by-case basis "in light of the relevant facts and circumstances of the particular case." Times are changing, though, and more courts are allowing media access to taped evidence, depending on the circumstances.

During the trial of a mafia leader in Las Vegas, KVBC-TV wanted copies of taped evidence. The judge said no, fearing the tapes might be lost or damaged during copying. He also felt the broadcast of the tapes might prejudice the jury and hinder a fair trial. In 1986, in *Valley Broadcasting v. District Court*,[28] a federal appeals court ruled that the trial judge needed to reevaluate his ruling, based on the TV station's right of access based on common law precedent. (This means there is no concrete constitutional law on the issue, but the court is recognizing that previous court rulings have allowed open access to court documents, and that access would include taped evidence.) The appeals court voiced its support for allowing the media to copy audio and video evidence.

The court ruled that there is a "strong presumption" that the media are allowed to make copies of such evidence, based on common law. The taped evidence in this trial consisted of *copies* of FBI master tapes. If the TV station damaged the tapes during copying, the court would have the FBI master tapes as a backup. However, the court said, judges may deny access to original documents if there is "a reasonable possibility of the destruction of the original exhibits." Still, the court should make every effort possible to make copies available.

The court determined that broadcasting most of the tapes would not damage a fair trial. The TV station was allowed to copy the tapes except for one part that was possibly "prejudicial."

When Broadcast Would Damage Fair Trial

In 1993, in *Group W Television v. Maryland*,[29] a murder trial involved a home video that showed a woman putting her daughter in a car before driving to a nursery school. Shortly after, two men carjacked the vehicle and killed the woman. In the background on the tape were two men that police charged with the murder. The tape was shown during the trial of the first man (Miller), and a TV station asked for permission to air it. The court said no because the second suspect (Soloman) had not had his trial yet. The court said the TV station could air the tape only *after* the second trial.

The TV station appealed, but a state appeals court in Maryland ruled the media did not have a First Amendment right to copy the tape. The court said it "began by acknowledging a presumption in favor of access" and also acknowledged a limited *common law* right to copy the tapes. However, the court agreed that the broadcast of the home video would have damaged the second suspect's right to a fair trial. All of the media, including broadcasters, were

---

[27]434 U.S. 591 (1978)

[28]798 F.2d 1289 (9th 1986)

[29]626 A.2d 1032 (1993)

"permitted to listen to the tapes and report on what was heard." The court did not censor the material.

The court pointed out that the public had never had physical access to these tapes, so why should the media? The court cited *Estes:* "[A] reporter's constitutional rights are no greater than those of any member of the public." The Sixth Amendment right to a public trial does not guarantee "that the trial—or any part of it—be broadcast live or on tape to the public." Because of prior media coverage, the trial court said it was already having significant problems finding impartial jurors. The trial judge's ruling was proper and narrowly tailored. The media were still allowed to view the tapes; they were just not allowed to copy them until both trials had ended.

SUMMARY

It is probably safe to say that cameras in courtrooms are here to stay. It is hard to imagine state and federal courts reversing recent trends toward more openness of judicial proceedings. However, as we have seen, there will always be instances in which cameras are considered intrusive and seen as a threat to a person's right to a fair trial. Most states allow judges to close judicial proceedings if there are probable dangers to a defendant's Sixth Amendment rights.

The U.S. Supreme Court does not allow cameras but has allowed audio transcripts for major cases, including *Bush v. Gore.* Most federal courts still do not allow cameras, but federal lawmakers are trying to pass laws to open up more federal courts to cameras.

17

NEWS SOURCES

The crimes of news sources are no less reprehensible and threatening to the public interest when witnessed by a reporter than when they are not.

—*Branzburg v. Hayes*[1]

CONFIDENTIAL SOURCES

Shield laws are laws designed to protect journalists from divulging the names of confidential sources to courts or law enforcement officials.

Probably the most famous use of confidential sources by news reporters was when the *Washington Post's* Woodward and Bernstein used the source who called himself "Deep Throat" in their investigative reports during the Watergate scandal in the early 1970s. However, what happens when a judge demands that a reporter divulge the name of a confidential source? Reporters who refuse to divulge a source can be held in contempt of court.

The Landmark *Branzburg v. Hayes* Case

Branzburg v. Hayes[1] is actually four cases in one, but they all concern the rights of journalists to keep sources confidential. Two of the cases involved a reporter named Branzburg, of the *Louisville Courier-Journal.* He had used anonymous sources in stories about illegal drugs. In two separate cases, grand juries demanded that Branzburg reveal the names of his sources. He refused, but a state court ruled that Branzburg must supply the information to both grand juries. He appealed to the U.S. Supreme Court.

The other two cases involved reporters from a newspaper and TV station who both had done stories on the black militant group the Black Panthers. A grand jury asked a TV reporter to divulge names of confidential sources; another grand jury asked a newspaper reporter to hand over notes and tape recordings of interviews with Black Panthers. The newspaper reporter refused even to appear before the grand jury. A federal appeals court

---

[1]408 U.S. 665 (1972)

eventually ruled in the reporter's favor, saying journalists have a right to keep confidential sources secret. The government appealed the ruling.

The appeals for all four cases were consolidated in *Branzburg v. Hayes*. In a 5-4 ruling, the U.S. Supreme Court in 1972 ruled that the three journalists had to provide the information requested by the grand juries.

FAQ

Why was the Supreme Court not willing to give journalists an absolute right to protect confidential sources?

The court said, "[It] is the obligation of reporters to respond to grand jury subpoenas as other citizens do and to answer questions relevant to an investigation into the commission of a crime." The court said it could not "grant newsmen a testimonial privilege that other citizens do not enjoy." Reporters may not conceal criminal conduct of sources based "on the theory that it is better to write about a crime than to do something about it." The court added, *"The crimes of news sources are no less reprehensible and threatening to the public interest when witnessed by a reporter than when they are not"* (italics added). Public safety (catching criminals) must take precedence over news reporting.

The Supreme Court pointed out that the media have done well without protection for confidential sources. "From the beginning of our country the press has operated without constitutional protection for press informants, and the press has flourished." Ultimately, the court said that journalists do have a limited right to protect confidential sources and said that *Congress and the states must be free to fashion their own shield laws.*

The *Branzburg* ruling is controversial, and somewhat confusing, because one of the five majority justices—Lewis Powell—wrote a concurring opinion that actually supports arguments for the minority. Powell wrote that journalists testifying before grand juries do possess "constitutional rights with respect to the gathering of news or in safeguarding their sources." Powell did not join the minority in this case because he felt this right of journalists was not an *absolute* right. He said the right should be evaluated case by case.

FAQ

Couldn't this ruling have a chilling effect on investigative reporting?

In a strongly worded dissent, Justice Stewart, along with Justices Brennan and Marshall, said the majority ruling in *Branzburg* showed a "disturbing insensitivity to the critical role of an independent press in our society." They made three points: (a) Newsmen need informants to write stories, (b) confidentiality is critical to creating and maintaining relationships with sources, and (c) unchecked grand jury subpoena powers will discourage confidential sources from talking and discourage reporters from covering important stories. This will create a chilling effect on investigative news reporting.

Justice Stewart then suggested three criteria the government should consider before forcing a journalist to divulge a source, now referred to as the "Stewart Test":

1. There is a high likelihood that the journalist has information relating to a specific crime.

2. The government has no other way to get the information than through the journalist.

3. The government proves it has a "compelling and overriding interest in the information." (This third prong is sometimes applied with the question, "Is the information 'necessary and critical' to the case?")

The Stewart Test has been adopted in numerous state and federal shield law cases since 1972, in spite of the fact that it came from a *dissenting* opinion. In the 6 years after the *Branzburg* ruling, the House and Senate presented 99 proposals for a federal shield law. Not one passed. There is still no federal shield law on the books because federal lawmakers cannot seem to agree on how much protection the law should provide. Also, many lawmakers feel the issue is better handled by the states.

FAQ

Why do journalists say they need shield laws to protect the identities of confidential sources?

Journalists claim that it is one of their rights under the First Amendment to use confidential sources. Many news sources simply will not talk if their names are used. They may fear arrest, loss of a job, or retribution from the people they are "ratting on." However, confidential sources help to uncover wrongdoing, which in turn can aid law enforcement in solving certain crimes. If a journalist divulges the name of even one confidential source, that journalist will have trouble getting confidential sources in the future.

Journalists feel that law enforcement should develop its own sources; then the courts would not have to pressure journalists to divulge confidential sources. Journalists should have the same rights as physicians, lawyers, and psychiatrists to keep certain information confidential.

FAQ

What are the arguments against shield laws for journalists?

Physicians, lawyers, and psychiatrists are licensed and required to have certain educational degrees. Journalists are not licensed professionals and are not required to have a college degree. Journalists should be treated like all other citizens in a courtroom and face contempt charges for refusing a judge's order. The First Amendment does not provide a blanket right to use unnamed sources. Journalists should work with law enforcement, not against it. Revealing a confidential source can help police catch a criminal and perhaps prevent future crimes—maybe even save a life. Finally, much great investigative reporting in our history has been done without confidential sources.

State Shield Laws

As of 2002, *31 states* (see note for list) plus the District of Columbia have shield laws.[2] The laws vary from state to state, and some laws provide more protection than others.

FAQ

What can happen to a journalist who refuses to divulge a source to a court?

A judge can hold a journalist in *contempt of court*. This is a serious charge and can result in fines or jail time. In some instances, a judge has ruled that if a journalist will not divulge a source, then, *legally,* that source does not exist. (In other words, the court is saying that the reporter made up the source and if the source is false, then the reporter's story must be false, too. This can lead to another problem for the reporter—a libel suit.)

In any case, the reporter has engaged in *direct contempt* or *criminal contempt.* This can be refusing to obey a judge's order. It may also involve behavior in a courtroom that disrupts court proceedings. As will be seen throughout this chapter, journalists can be held in contempt of court for refusing to divulge a confidential source or refusing to obey a subpoena to testify.

Another good example of criminal or direct contempt is from 1985, when two reporters from the *Boulder Daily Camera* in Colorado disobeyed court rules and interviewed jurors during a murder trial. The court had to dismiss the jurors and repeat the jury selection process. Criminal contempt charges against the reporters and the newspaper were upheld on appeal. The newspaper and reporters also had to pay court costs resulting from the new jury selection which added four days to the trial.[3]

CIVIL CONTEMPT

The Reporters Committee for the Freedom of the Press keeps track of journalists who have had to spend time in jail for defying a judge's order. The judges in these instances are using a legal tactic called *civil contempt.* A judge uses a civil contempt citation to coerce a journalist or source to divulge information. Basically, the judge uses a fine or jail time (or the threat of either one) to persuade a person to obey a court order. Some examples:

---

[2]The 31 states with shield laws as of 2004: Alabama, Alaska, Arizona, Arkansas, California, Colorado, Delaware, Florida, Georgia, Illinois, Indiana, Kentucky, Louisiana, Maryland, Michigan, Minnesota, Montana, Nebraska, Nevada, New Jersey, New Mexico, New York, North Carolina, North Dakota, Ohio, Oklahoma, Oregon, Pennsylvania, Rhode Island, South Carolina, and Tennessee.

[3]*In re Michael Stone, Robert Knaus, and the Boulder Daily Camera,* 703 P.2d 1319 (1985)

- ▣ 1998, WCNC-TV, Charlotte, NC: A reporter was sentenced to 30 days in jail for refusing to testify about comments made by the attorney of a murder suspect. The reporter wound up only spending about 2 hours in jail because the attorney decided to provide the information that the court had sought from the reporter.
- ▣ 1996, *Miami Herald,* Palm Beach County, FL: A reporter spent 14 days in jail for refusing to testify about an interview with a jail prisoner. (He had originally been sentenced to 70 days.)
- ▣ 1996, *Anderson Valley Independent,* California: The newspaper's editor refused to give a judge a letter to the editor written by a prison inmate. After a week in jail, the editor turned over the letter, but the judge thought it was a fake. The editor spent another 6 days in jail before the judge accepted the letter as genuine.[4]

IMPORTANT POST-*BRANZBURG* CASES

There are a large number of cases dealing with shield laws. The following cases represent some of the more important decisions handed down regarding journalists trying to protect sources or information.

Reporters' Sources Protected

Baker v. F&F Investment[5]: *Civil Lawsuits Are Different*

This ruling was handed down in 1972, about 6 months after *Branzburg.* The case involved a 1962 story called "Confessions of a Block-buster" in the *Saturday Evening Post.* Writer Alfred Balk's story focused on real estate discrimination in Chicago. Balk used one anonymous source, whom he called "Norris Vitcheck." "Vitcheck" claimed he got white residents to sell him their houses at cheap prices by making them fearful of living near black neighborhoods. "Vitcheck" said he then sold those houses to blacks at inflated prices. Years later, a group of black residents sued real estate firms and landlords for engaging in these kinds of practices, and the group wanted Balk to reveal the identity of "Norris Vitcheck." Balk refused, saying his source worked in the real estate business and that revealing his identity could cause the source to lose his job, among other problems.

A federal appeals court ruled for Balk, saying this was a different case than *Branzburg* because it was a *civil lawsuit* and not a grand jury investigation. In civil lawsuits, the court said journalists have many more rights in protecting their confidential sources because the journalists are not a "party" to the lawsuit. The court also said that the plaintiffs in the civil suit had not even attempted to find the information through other sources.

Zerilli v. Smith[6]

This 1981 case upheld the principles established in *Baker* regarding journalists' privilege in *civil* suits. The case involved the U.S. Justice Department apparently leaking information to the *Detroit News* about wiretapped phone conversations between some Detroit underworld figures. These people brought a lawsuit against the Justice Department and asked that the *Detroit News* reporter be forced to reveal the sources for the story.

---

[4]Sidebar. (2001, Fall). *News Media and the Law, 25*(4), 28.

[5]470 F.2d 778 (2d Cir. 1972)

[6]656 F.2d 705 (D.C. Cir. 1981)

A federal appeals court ruled that the reporter did not have to divulge the sources, mostly because the underworld leaders could have obtained the information through other sources, such as other employees of the Justice Department.

The court reiterated the reasoning from *Baker,* saying that a reporter is not required to reveal sources in *civil lawsuits* in which the reporter is *not a party* in the lawsuit. The court said that there should only be rare exceptions to this rule. The court pointed out what it considered "exceptional" circumstances: (a) The lawsuit is legitimate and not frivolous, (b) the plaintiffs (or defendants, depending on the case) have exhausted all other sources of information, (c) the information sought from the journalist is relevant to the case.

U.S. v. Hubbard[7]: *Other Sources Available*

This case is pretty straightforward. In 1979, the *Washington Post* covered an FBI investigation of the Church of Scientology. The church asked that the newspaper hand over the reporter's notes about the FBI-Scientology story. The *Post* refused. A federal district court ruled that the reporter had a *qualified privilege* to keep the sources confidential. Besides, the court said, the church could obtain the information it was seeking directly from the FBI.

FAQ

What is meant by qualified privilege?

Qualified privilege is a privilege that is not absolute. It is "qualified." The judge here is giving the journalist the benefit of the doubt. The judge is trusting that the journalist has been truthful and is using genuine, reliable sources. If the journalist has been dishonest, the judge can revoke this privilege. In the same sense, having a driver's license is a qualified privilege. A judge may revoke your license if you are arrested for drinking and driving, for example.

Riley v. Chester[8]: *Modified Stewart Test*

This 1979 case involved a police officer suing his police chief. The officer wanted to know where *Delaware County Daily Times* reporter Geraldine Oliver got her information for a story related to the lawsuit. The officer subpoenaed Oliver, but she refused to name the source of her story. A lower court found her in contempt, but a federal appeals court ruled that Oliver had a right to keep the source confidential. In this case, the court used a modified version of the Stewart Test: (a) Was an effort made to get the information from other sources? If so, (b) it must be proven that the information was not obtainable from those sources. (c) Also, the information held by the journalist must be "clearly relevant" to the case. The court said the source's identity was not relevant to this case.

---

[7]493 F. Supp. 202 (D.D.C. 1979)

[8]612 F.2d 708 (3d Cir. 1979)

U.S. v. Burke[9]: *Stewart Test Standards Not Met*

This 1983 case involved allegations of point shaving and the Boston College basketball team. *Sports Illustrated* writer Douglas Looney had written an article on the scandal titled "How I Put the Fix In." The article was coauthored by a career criminal, Henry Hill, who named James Burke as the man running the point-shaving scheme. Burke was convicted, and during his appeal he said that *Sports Illustrated* should be required to turn over all notes and tapes concerning the article.

A federal appeals court used the three-part test devised by Justice Stewart in *Branzburg* and said Burke only met the first part. Yes, the notes and tapes had information related to the case. However, there were ways in which Burke could have tried to get this information other than through the media (e.g., he could have called other witnesses to make his case). Finally, Burke did not prove that the notes and tapes were "necessary and critical" to his case.

Shoen v. Shoen[10]: *Investigative Book Authors*

This 1993 case involved a yet-to-be-published book, *Birthright,* by Ronald Watkins. The book was going to focus on long-time feuds within the Shoen family, owners of the U-Haul rental company. One of the book's main topics was a murder mystery involving Eva Berg Shoen, the daughter-in-law of U-Haul founder Leonard Shoen. Eva was the wife of Sam Shoen, and she had been brutally murdered at a family log cabin Colorado.

Leonard Shoen agreed to provide information to Watkins for the book in return for a share of future royalties. Watkins did several interviews with Shoen, some of which were tape recorded. Watkins did not promise Shoen confidentiality, and this became an important factor for a shield law case.

In the meantime, Shoen had also made at least 29 public statements accusing his two sons Edward and Mark of having something to do with their sister-in-law's murder. In newspaper and TV interviews, he called his two sons "mentally ill." He appeared on the TV show *Hard Copy* and claimed, "I don't know this for a fact, but I am convinced these sons, either one or both of them, are directly responsible for this." Shoen also claimed his two sons meant to kill their brother Sam as well.

Edward and Mark Shoen sued their father for defamation. They knew their father had talked with Watkins, so the sons subpoenaed Watkins as a witness. They asked him to testify and to turn over all printed and recorded materials "relating to the death of Eva Berg Shoen." Watkins appeared in court, but he refused to release any of the information from his interviews with Leonard Shoen. Watkins said he was an investigative journalist, and he had a right to keep his information confidential. A district court in Arizona ordered Watkins to testify, but he disobeyed the court's order and was held in contempt.

A federal appeals court overturned the district court's judgment and ruled for Watkins. The court addressed three important issues:

- ▣ *Investigative book authors are journalists.* Therefore, Arizona's shield applied to Watkins in this case.
- ▣ *Confidentiality question.* Watkins did not promise Leonard Shoen confidentiality. Does a shield law protect information that was gathered where there was no expectation of confidentiality? The court said yes. "We hold that the journalist's privilege applies to a journalist's resource materials even in the absence of the element of confidentiality."

---

[9]700 F.2d 70 (2d Cir. 1983)

[10]5 F.3d 1289 (9th Cir. 1993)

◫ *Was there a compelling need for Watkins' materials?* No, because the sons had not "exhausted" other sources for this material. They had not even tried to get it directly from their father. Remember, the courts only want journalists to be used in these cases as a "last resort."

Shoen II

A few years later, the sons did subpoena their father to testify, and they once again asked for Watkins to reveal his interview materials. In 1995, in *Shoen v. Shoen,*[11] a federal appeals court again ruled for Watkins. The court applied two parts of the Stewart Test: The information the sons sought from Watkins was not relevant to the case, and the sons had still not exhausted all other sources. The court then added a third prong of its own: Is the material sought "repetitive" or "cumulative?" Yes, it said. In other words, Watkins' interview materials would simply repeat information that the sons had from other sources.

Many in the media cheered both of the *Shoen* decisions for their strong support of reporters being able to protect confidential *information.* Of course, book authors were encouraged because they were being treated like journalists and afforded the protection of shield laws.

Sealed Court Documents

In 2000, a reporter for the *Morning Star* newspaper in Wilmington, NC, Cory Reiss, was covering a trial involving Conoco and allegations that it had knowingly contaminated the water supply for a trailer park. Conoco settled out of court for an undisclosed amount of money, and the court agreed to seal the documents stating the amount of the settlement.

A few months later, Reiss wrote a story revealing that Conoco had paid $36 million in damages. Reiss said he got the information from two anonymous sources and "a clerk in the federal courthouse in Raleigh." Conoco was upset, saying that the court had promised the settlement amounts would remain legally sealed. Conoco asked that Reiss, an assisting reporter, and the newspaper be held in contempt for illegally revealing information from sealed court records. Conoco also asked that Reiss be forced to divulge the names of his anonymous sources. A district court held Reiss in contempt when he refused reveal his sources.

However, a federal appeals court in *Ashcraft v. Conoco*[12] overturned the district court and ruled that Reiss was protected by a qualified privilege. The appeals court said that the trial court had not followed proper procedures in sealing the original documents. Therefore, the seal was invalid. Because the seal was invalid, there was no "compelling interest" in having the journalist divulge his sources.

FAQ

What if the seal had been valid?

If that had been the case, the court might have ordered Reiss to reveal his sources.

---

[11]48 F.3d 412 (9th Cir. 1995)

[12]218 F.3d 282 (4th Cir. 2000)

Reporters' Sources *Not* Protected

U.S. v. Criden[13]: *Applying the Stewart Test*

Philadelphia Inquirer reporter Jan Schaffer had been covering a trial related to the FBI's Abscam investigation in the late 1970s (FBI agents posed as Arab sheiks and got some Philadelphia officials to take illegal bribes). During the trial, one of the government's prosecutors admitted giving some information to Schaffer over the telephone. The defendants in the trial wanted Schaffer to testify to see whether the prosecutor had released "sensational and prejudicial" information that might prevent a fair trial.

Schaffer refused to tell whether she had even talked with the prosecutor, saying she had a right to protect her sources. However, a federal appeals court ruled in 1980 that Schaffer was required to testify. The court said the defendants satisfied the requirements of the three-part Stewart Test: (a) Schaffer's testimony would be relevant to the defendant's case, (b) the defendants had proved that they had tried to get the information from other sources, and (c) Schaffer's testimony was "necessary and critical" in helping to determine the credibility of the prosecutor.

U.S. v. Cuthbertson[14]: *Pretrial Subpoenas*

This 1980 case dealt with the CBS news magazine *60 Minutes* and a report called "From Burgers to Bankruptcy," about a fast-food chain called Wild Bill's Family Restaurants. A grand jury later indicted the restaurant chain for some of its franchising activities. The restaurant's lawyers subpoenaed CBS before the trial, asking the network to hand over tapes and other materials related to the "Burgers" story. The judge in the trial wanted to determine whether the CBS material was relevant, so he ordered CBS to give him the requested information so he could examine it before the trial. CBS said no, and the judge held the network in contempt.

CBS appealed, but a federal appeals court upheld the contempt ruling. It said that the judge had a right to see the materials to determine whether they contained any information pertinent to the defendants' case. The U.S. Supreme Court refused to hear an appeal by CBS News, and the network eventually provided the trial judge with the requested information.

Nonconfidential Materials

Gonzales v. NBC[15]: *A Mixed Blessing for Nonconfidential Materials*

In 1997, the NBC news magazine *Dateline* aired a story involving allegations that Louisiana police unfairly targeted minorities and out-of-state travelers for traffic violations. Some citizens complained of unnecessary harassment and seizure of property. *Dateline* did a hidden camera investigation, with one of its employees, Pat Weiland, driving in a car with out-of-state plates. Weiland got pulled over by Louisiana police deputy Darrel

---

[13] 633 F.2d 346 (3d Cir. 1980)

[14] 630 F.2d 139 (3d Cir. 1980)

[15] 194 F.3d 29 (2d Cir. 1999)

Pierce, and *Dateline* said there was no apparent reason for the traffic stop other than the car had out-of-state plates.

Also in 1997, a Hispanic couple, Albert and Mary Gonzales, sued the police for another traffic stop by the same Deputy Pierce, and the couple needed corroborating evidence. The couple subpoenaed NBC for the original, unedited camera footage of Weiland being pulled over by Pierce. The couple also asked that NBC personnel testify about what they had seen on the tape. Soon after, Deputy Pierce served NBC with a similar subpoena.

NBC argued that it should be protected by a journalist's qualified privilege in such instances. The Second Circuit Court of Appeals at first said that NBC had no privilege but then decided that a privilege did apply to nonconfidential materials. Unfortunately for NBC, the court then ruled that the network did not qualify for privilege in this instance because (a) the NBC video outtakes were clearly relevant to the case; (b) the outtakes related to a "significant" issue in the case—whether the deputy had engaged in a pattern of harassing minorities and out-of-state drivers—and (c) the material in the outtakes was not available from other sources.

Journalists were encouraged by this case even though NBC was ordered to hand over the materials. That is because the Second Circuit Court of Appeals includes New York City, home to many major news operations. The court also said in this ruling, "NBC's videotapes are protected by a qualified journalist's privilege applicable to nonconfidential press materials." This important federal court had said it did indeed recognize a journalist's privilege for confidential and nonconfidential materials; it was just that in this case, the journalist's material could not be found elsewhere.

However, protection for nonconfidential materials is not guaranteed. Following are examples from two states where state courts have a different take on this matter.

Marketos v. American Employers Insurance[16]: *Unpublished Nonconfidential Photos*

A photographer for a Michigan newspaper, the *Ann Arbor News,* had taken photographs at the scene of a suspicious business fire. The business owner, George Marketos, filed a claim with his insurance company, but the company denied the claim, saying the fire was deliberately set. The fire marshal had taken photographs as well but was not able to determine the cause of the fire.

The newspaper had published several pictures of the fire, but the insurance company subpoenaed the newspaper to supply 20 unpublished photographs to see if they revealed any evidence of arson. The newspaper moved to quash the subpoena, saying the photographs would simply duplicate the fire marshal's photos. The insurance company said that it could not know that until it saw the actual photographs.

A circuit judge ordered the newspaper to release the photographs, asking the newspaper, "What are you protecting here? . . . You're not protecting any reporter's confidential sources or anything." A state appeals court, in 1990, said the Michigan shield law did not apply because it "provides no protection for a request in a civil case for nonconfidential materials." (The photographs were not confidential because the photographer snapped the shot from a public street in full view of bystanders.)

---

[16] 460 N.W.2d 272 (1990)

Idaho v. Salsbury[17]: *Nonconfidential TV News Video*

A reporter for KMVT-TV in Twin Falls, ID, had videotaped events at the scene of a fatal car accident in September 1993. The video included footage of newspaper reporter Michael Salsbury being arrested at the accident scene for obstructing a police officer and resisting arrest. The local county prosecutor handling Salsbury's case subpoenaed KMVT for a copy of the original unedited videotape. The TV station had thrown the videotape in the garbage but retrieved it when they received the subpoena. KMVT then handed the tape over to a local magistrate for an *in camera* inspection. ("In camera" means that the magistrate viewed the tape privately in his chambers.)

The magistrate made the following rulings, which were later upheld by a state appeals court. The videotaping act was not confidential. It took place on the side of a public highway and was "observable by anyone present." There were no confidential sources or information on the videotape itself. Salsbury could be seen at least three times on the tape, so it obviously was relevant to the case. The magistrate said that the "matters contained in the videotape are unique and unavailable from other sources" and also that requiring the station to hand over the videotape would not create a "chilling effect" on news reporting: "Credibility balks at the idea that a TV station might stop covering fatal automobile accidents if a consequence is that the station may be required to produce the videotape in a criminal prosecution."

FAQ

Why wasn't the Stewart Test applied here?

The court said that the three-pronged Stewart Test was not applicable in this case because it did not deal with confidential information before a grand jury, as was the case in *Branzburg*. However, the court said that even had it applied the test, the TV station still would have been required to turn over the tape because the criteria in the three prongs would have been met.

It is important to note how shield law applications vary from state to state. In both of these cases, Idaho and Michigan courts said their states' shield laws provided protection only for confidential sources and materials. The courts refused to extend that protection to nonconfidential materials and sources.

Federal Court Ruling on Nonconfidential Sources

In 2003, in *McKevitt v. Pallasch*,[18] a federal appeals court ruled that reporters had no privilege in federal law for nonconfidential information. The case involved Michael McKevitt, who was facing trial in Ireland for belonging to a terrorist group. A key witness against him was David Rupert. A group of journalists had been working on a biography about Rupert, and McKevitt wanted access to the journalists' taped interviews of Rupert. A district court

---

[17]924 P.2d 208 (1996)

[18]339 F.3d 530 (7th Cir. 2003)

ordered the journalists to supply the tapes to McKevitt for his defense. The journalists appealed but lost. The court said that the Rupert tapes had no protection as a nonconfidential source because Rupert actually wanted the tapes released but "it is the reporters, paradoxically, who want it secreted." The court appeared to be unwilling to recognize a federal privilege for nonconfidential information, writing that compelling the journalists to release the tapes did not violate their First Amendment rights.

The Leggett Shield Law Case

The issue of shield laws received national attention in 2002 because of a prominent case involving an author who spent almost half a year in jail for not revealing her sources. Vanessa Leggett was working on a book, *The Murder of a Bookie's Wife*, which detailed the investigation into the 1997 murder of Doris Angleton. Angleton's husband, Robert, was accused of hiring his brother to kill her. In the course of writing her book, Leggett interviewed Angleton and his brother on tape and did other in-depth research into the murder.

A grand jury subpoenaed Leggett to discuss what she knew about the murder. Leggett refused to reveal her confidential sources, and she wound up spending more than 5 months (168 days) in the Federal Detention Center in Houston. She was released from jail in January 2002. Robert Angleton was acquitted of murder charges.

FAQ

This is a federal case. Is there a shield law for such cases?

No. The Leggett case reinvigorated the debate about the necessity for a *federal* shield law. Look back at the ruling from *Branzburg* and you will see that the Supreme Court ruled that reporters have no special rights to refuse to testify before a state or federal grand jury. The *Branzburg* ruling also said that Congress is free to "fashion standards and rules as narrow or broad as deemed necessary." Many journalists would like to see Congress use the Leggett case as motivation for passing a federal shield law to protect journalists in federal court settings.

Defining *Journalist*

Shield laws are designed to protect the rights of journalists, but should anyone who "disseminates information" be labeled a journalist? That definition would allow a wide range of people to be called journalists, including teachers, newsstand operators, and designers of Web sites.

There is one court case that gives us guidance in this area, *Titan Sports v. Turner Broadcasting*.[19] The case involved Mark Madden, a well-known commentator for professional wrestling. World Championship Wrestling (WCW) paid Madden to deliver his comments through a 900 telephone number. One of Madden's phone commentaries said that the World

---

[19]967 F. Supp. 142 (W.D. Pa. 1997)

Wrestling Federation (WWF) was having severe financial problems. (The WWF is now World Wrestling Entertainment [WWE]. The name change was the result of a trademark dispute with the World Wildlife Fund, which claimed it had the rights to the acronym WWF.)

The WWF and the WCW sued each other for unfair competition, and a court ordered Madden to divulge where he got his information about the WWF's financial woes. Madden refused, saying he was a journalist who did not have to reveal his confidential sources. A federal district court ruled for Madden, but a federal appeals court said Madden did not qualify as a journalist worthy of shield law protections. In *Titan Sports v. Turner Broadcasting (in re Madden),*[20] the appeals court said that very few cases had outlined the exact qualifications for a "journalist" in regard to shield laws.

The court then provided its own definition: Journalists (a) "are engaged in investigative reporting," (b) "are gathering news," and (c) "possess at the inception of the newsgathering process the intention to disseminate the news to the public."

The court said that Madden did not meet this three-prong standard: "By his own admission, he is an entertainer, not a reporter, disseminating hype, not news." The court added that just because Madden called himself "Pro Wrestling's only real journalist," that did not mean he *was* a journalist.

JOURNALISTS AS EYEWITNESSES TO CRIME

"Generally, the more confidential the information sought, the greater the First Amendment protection."[21]

> ## FAQ
>
> What if a journalist is covering a story and happens to be an eyewitness to a drug deal or bank hold-up? Do shield laws protect reporters if they're called to testify about what they've seen?

No, in most cases. As a witness to a bank robbery, for example, the journalist was not engaging in investigative reporting, and the journalist certainly could not claim that the bank robber or drug dealer was a "confidential source" in such a situation.

The courts have ruled on similar occurrences, such as in the case of *Dillon v. San Francisco,*[22] in 1990. A man named Patrick Dillon, whose house had just burned, had returned to his home to retrieve belongings. As he was leaving, Dillon apparently walked through a roped-off area and police approached him. Dillon got into a scuffle with officers, and Dillon claimed the officers hit him in the face with a bullhorn and struck him in the back of the head. Dillon was arrested. Cameraman Gerald McEowen of KRON-TV witnessed the scuffle, but McEowen did not get any video of the event because he said his camera malfunctioned at that moment.

---

[20]151 F.3d 125 (3d Cir. 1998)

[21]See *Pinkard v. Johnson,* 118 F.R.D. 517 (1987)

[22]748 F. Supp. 722 (N.D. Cal.1990)

Dillon later sued the police for violating his civil rights through the use of excessive force during the arrest. Dillon subpoenaed McEowen to testify about what he had witnessed during the altercation with police. McEowen claimed California's shield law gave him immunity from testifying.

However, a federal district court ruled that McEowen was required to testify because this was a federal civil rights case, and the state shield law did not apply in federal courts. Also, McEowen's testimony was crucial to Dillon's case because it went to the "very heart" of Dillon's claim that the police had used excessive force.

Dillon had claimed that firefighters at the scene tried to prevent McEowen from videotaping the scuffle. McEowen was the only person who could testify about the truthfulness of these important charges. Finally, the charges brought by Dillon in this case were "substantial ones that rise to a constitutional level." That made McEowen's testimony even more important.

NEWSROOM SEARCHES

Most journalists see their newsrooms as an "inner sanctum" where they are free to do their jobs without government interference, but do authorities have the right to search a newsroom when a journalist refuses to hand over subpoenaed materials? This issue ignited emotions in 1971 when the *Stanford Daily* newspaper covered a demonstration during which people occupied administration offices at Stanford University Hospital. Police forcibly entered a hall near the offices, and some demonstrators attacked the officers with clubs. The paper ran a story on the confrontation and included several photographs.

The police wanted to look at all of the photographs taken by the newspaper to try to identify the attackers. The police showed up at the *Daily* offices with a search warrant and began combing through desks, cabinets, trash cans, and the photo lab. The search yielded only the pictures which had appeared in the newspaper.

The newspaper sued police officials, saying the search, even with a warrant, violated the First Amendment. However, in *Zurcher v. Stanford Daily,*[23] the U.S. Supreme Court ruled the search was legal. The court said that the Constitution allows for police to search private homes and businesses without warning, even if those people are not criminal suspects. The court said that the same reasoning applied to newsrooms. However, the court said, Congress and the states were free to pass laws forbidding newsroom searches.

FAQ

Did lawmakers respond and pass such laws?

Two years later, Congress passed such a law.

---

[23]436 U.S. 547 (1978)

The Privacy Protection Act of 1980 and Newsroom Searches

Congress was not pleased with the Supreme Court's ruling in *Zurcher* and did something about it. In the Privacy Protection Act of 1980,[24] Congress prohibited federal, state, and local authorities from conducting searches of newsrooms except under the following circumstances.

For "work products" (interview notes, videotapes, audiotapes, etc.), authorities may search a newsroom only if the journalist is suspected of a crime and the work products pertain to that crime or if there is a strong likelihood that seizure of the work products will help prevent a person's serious injury or death. For "documentary materials" (original government documents, court manuscripts, etc.), either of those conditions must be met, or authorities may obtain a search warrant (instead of a subpoena) for the element of surprise. (The concern is that notice of a subpoena might compel the journalist to hide, destroy, or change the materials.) A search warrant would also be needed when a journalist has already defied a subpoena and authorities have exhausted all other means to get the material. (The material must be critical in a court case or in a law enforcement investigation.)

Again, the Privacy Protection Act of 1980 is a federal law that covers law enforcement at all levels—local, state, and federal.

PROMISES OF CONFIDENTIALITY—KEEP YOUR PROMISES!

FAQ

If a journalist breaks a promise of confidentiality with a source, does that source have any legal rights?

In a narrow 5-4 ruling in 1991, the U.S. Supreme Court ruled that the media open themselves to lawsuits when such confidentiality pledges are broken.

The case of *Cohen v. Cowles Media*[25] involved two stories that appeared in the St. Paul *Pioneer Press Dispatch* and the Minneapolis *Star and Tribune* in 1982 just before an election for governor. The stories were based on information from Dan Cohen, who had been working with the Republican candidate for governor, Wheelock Whitney. Cohen told the *Press* and *Tribune* that court records showed that the Democratic candidate for lieutenant governor, Marlene Johnson, had a criminal conviction and several criminal charges in her past. Both of the reporters promised Cohen confidentiality.

The reporters soon discovered that Johnson's infractions were fairly minor. Both newspapers decided that the source of this information should be included in the stories because of the political implications and because of the nearness of election day. The Whitney campaign fired Cohen.

---

[24]42 U.S.C. § 2000aa (1988)

[25]501 U.S. 663 (1991)

Cohen then sued both newspapers, based on the legal doctrine of *promissory estoppel.* This doctrine says that people have a right to recover damages if they are harmed by the breaking of unwritten contracts or verbal promises. A jury ruled for Cohen and gave him $200,000 in compensatory damages and $500,000 in punitive damages. The Minnesota Supreme Court overturned those damages and ruled for the newspapers. It said that the legal doctrine of promissory estoppel did not apply to a news story in "these particular circumstances" because the breaking of the promise was part of an important newsworthy story. The U.S. Supreme Court, though, reversed and ruled for Cohen.

The court said that promissory estoppel *did* apply to the newspapers: "The publisher of a newspaper has no special immunity from the application of general laws. He has no special privilege to invade the rights and liberties of others." The newspapers argued that they should be protected from prosecution because they gained the information lawfully. The court rejected that argument, saying that "the First Amendment does not confer on the press a constitutional right to disregard promises that could otherwise be enforced under state law."

The newspapers argued that a ruling for Cohen would create a chilling effect on investigative reporters. The Supreme Court rejected this claim, saying that the press was simply having to follow "a generally applicable law that requires those who make certain kinds of promises to keep them." The court pointed out that the press is not chilled by having to follow other laws (copyright, trespass, etc.), so the press should not feel chilled by a law that requires promises to be kept.

The Supreme Court remanded the case to the Minnesota Supreme Court, which reinstated the $200,000 in compensatory damages for Cohen. Cohen was able to prove to the court that he satisfied the three requirements set forth in the common law doctrine of promissory estoppel: (a) He had *proof* that the reporters promised confidentiality, (b) he *suffered damage* as a result of the broken promise (he lost his job), and (c) the broken promise led to an *injustice that deserved remedy.* The remedy in this case was $200,000.[26]

The decision stirred a lot of debate in the media. Many agreed with the Supreme Court ruling that reporters should either make promises with the intention of keeping them or not make the promises in the first place. However, many also disagreed with the majority ruling and agreed with justice David Souter's dissent: "I believe the State's interest in enforcing a newspaper's promise of confidentiality insufficient to outweigh the interest in unfettered publication of the information revealed in this case."

INDIRECT CONTEMPT

Indirect contempt (also called *contempt by publication*) often involves a journalist or editorial writer writing negative comments about a judge. Judges used to charge the media with indirect contempt frequently, but Supreme Court cases in the 1940s changed that. The landmark case in the area of indirect contempt is *Bridges v. California,* which is actually two cases in one.[27] One case involved the *Los Angeles Times* using an editorial to urge a judge not to give probation to two men. A man named Bridges had telegrammed the U.S.

---

[26]479 N.W.2d 387 (1992)

[27]314 U.S. 252 (1941)

Secretary of Labor to say that a judge's ruling in a labor matter was "outrageous," and Bridges threatened to shut down West Coast docks if the judge did not rule a certain way. The judges in both cases handed out indirect contempt citations, saying that Bridges and the *Times* were attempting to unduly influence court proceedings. The California Supreme Court upheld the judges' actions, but the U.S. Supreme Court overturned the ruling, saying that these indirect contempt citations violated the First Amendment. The Supreme Court said that such citations could only be upheld if there were a *clear and present danger* to the justice system or to a particular case.

The court reinforced the *Bridges* ruling several years later in *Pennekamp v. Florida*[28] and *Craig v. Harney.*[29] In each case, a newspaper made factual errors when criticizing a judge's ruling. Initially, both papers were found guilty of indirect contempt, but the U.S. Supreme Court overturned both rulings, saying that errors were common in news reporting and there was no clear and present danger. These three cases significantly reduced the number of indirect contempt citations by judges. Judges were no longer allowed to "silence their critics" in the press.

Summary

Shield laws are designed to give legal protection to reporters who do not wish to divulge confidential sources used in news stories. The landmark *Branzburg* ruling said that there was no absolute right to protect confidential sources, but the Supreme Court left most decisions about shield laws to the states. The *Branzburg* case is also famous for its dissent by Justice Stewart, which produced what became known as the Stewart Test. This test would be applied in future shield law cases.

Shield laws vary from state to state, and there is currently no federal shield law. Journalists may face jail time and fines for disobeying a judge's order to divulge a source. Controversies regarding shield laws also include issues such as nonconfidential materials, newsroom searches, the definition of *journalist*, and journalists who witness crimes.

Journalists argue that shield laws are necessary if they are to do quality investigative reporting, but critics charge that great journalism has been achieved throughout history without shield law protections.

---

[28]328 U.S. 331 (1946)

[29]331 U.S. 367 (1947)

18

MEDIA ACCESS TO GOVERNMENT SOURCES

Secrecy in government is fundamentally anti-democratic.

—*New York Times Co. v. United States*[1]

ACCESS TO GOVERNMENT RECORDS AND DOCUMENTS

The Freedom of Information Act

In the 1960s, the media became increasingly concerned about the government keeping too many documents secret. Journalists said that a democracy could not survive unless the public was allowed to analyze the inner workings of its government. This concern led to Congress passing the Freedom of Information Act (FOIA) in 1966.[2] This law said that the public had a right of access to most existing government documents.

Agencies included under the FOIA are the executive branch of the government and its departments; all regulatory agencies, such as the FCC and the FTC; cabinet-level agencies, such as the Defense Department and the FBI; and government-controlled corporations, such as the U.S. Postal Service. Congress (the legislative branch of government), the courts (judicial), and the president and his immediate staff are not subject to the FOIA.

There are nine categories of material that cannot be obtained through the FOIA. These will be discussed a little later in the chapter. The government each year continues to classify millions of federal documents as "secret." Still, the majority of government documents are available to the public. These documents are supposed to be relatively easy to obtain, and fees for copying the documents are supposed to be reasonable. Each agency is supposed to print a list of their copying fees and make it available to the public. An agency may make the document available at a lesser fee or at no charge if it feels that the public would benefit from the document's release.

Some of the fees were getting expensive, and some argued that the costs were resulting in fewer people making FOIA requests. As a result, the FOIA's fee structure was amended by Congress in 1986. Lawmakers said that journalists, scientific organizations, and nonprofit

---

[1] *New York Times Co. v. United States*, 403 U.S. 713 (1971)

[2] 5 U.S.C. § 552

educational institutions should pay reduced fees for FOIA requests. Fees were increased for commercial businesses.

FAQ

How do I make an FOIA request?

Some records may already be available online at the agency's Web site. A person may also phone the agency, go to the agency in person, or send a written request via the U.S. mail, e-mail, Internet, or fax.

The head of each agency is required to make an "FOIA handbook" available for that particular agency to assist people in making FOIA requests. The sample request letter and fee schedule shown here are taken from the FTC Web site at http://www.ftc.gov/foia/foiarequest.htm.

Sample FOIA Request Letter

Freedom of Information Act Request
Office of General Counsel
Federal Trade Commission
600 Pennsylvania Avenue, N.W.
Washington, D.C. 29580

Dear Sir/Madam:

This is a request under the Freedom of Information Act. I request that a copy of the following document(s) be provided to me: [*identify the documents as specifically as possible, e.g., "all investigative documents concerning ABC company, located at 555 Main Street, City, State, from the years 1997-1999. This company offers franchises to sell widgets."*]

In order to help determine fees, you should know that I am a [*insert description of requester, e.g., individual, attorney, company, news organization*].

[*Optional*]

I am willing to pay fees up to $_____. If you expect the fees will exceed this, please contact me before proceeding.

[*Optional*]

I request a waiver of all fees for this request. Disclosure of the requested information to me is in the public interest because it is likely to contribute significantly to public understanding of the operations or activities of the government and is not primarily in my commercial interest. [*Include a specific explanation.*]

If you need to discuss this request, I can be reached at [*daytime phone number*]. Thank you for your consideration of my request.

Sincerely,

Name

Address

City, State, Zip

Telephone Number

FAQ

What are some of the fees I may encounter?

An example of the fees you may encounter when making an FOIA request is shown in Table 18.1, which represents a portion of the fee schedule taken from the FTC Web site in July 2003.

An FOIA request, depending on its size, may involve a lot of copying or extra staff time. That is why federal agencies are allowed to charge fees if necessary.

FAQ

How long will it take to get my materials?

As of 1996, federal agencies have *20 working days* to reply to an FOIA request. However, agencies are not always able to meet this deadline. An agency may ask for a 10-day extension of the FOIA time limit for any of three reasons: (A) the FOIA request contains a large number of documents, (b) the request requires two or more agency departments or offices to confer, or (c) the requested documents are located outside of the agency's offices.

The agency is supposed to notify individuals if there is a need for an extension beyond the 20-day limit.

FAQ

What if I need the materials immediately?

You may request a rush on your FOIA request if you can prove to the agency: (a) that there is an immediate threat to a person's life or safety if the records are not obtained quickly or (b) that your main job is disseminating information (you are a journalist, etc.) and there is an urgent need to tell the public about alleged or actual federal government activity.

Under the FOIA, agencies are not required to answer written questions, conduct investigations, analyze data, do research, or create records. The FOIA act says that an agency is just supposed to provide the documents and is not required to provide commentary or analysis of those documents. That would create too much extra work for the agencies.

Table 18.1   Sample Freedom of Information Act Fee Schedule

Requester fee categories

Requester Category	Searching	Reviewing	Copying
Commercial (including law firms)	Fee	Fee	None
Educational institutions	No charge	No charge	No charge for first 100 pages
News media	No charge	No charge	No charge for first 100 pages
Other (general public)	No charge for first 2 hours	No charge	No charge for first 100 pages

Search and review fees (per quarter hour)

Clerical	$4.50
Other professional	$8.00
Attorney or economist	$12.00
Minimum charge	$14.00

Paper fees

Paper copy (up to 8.5 × 14 inches)

Reproduced by commission	$0.14
Reproduced by requestor	$0.05
Computer paper	$0.14

Microfiche fees

Film copy—Paper to 16 mm film (per frame)	$0.04
Fiche copy—Paper to 105 mm fiche (per frame)	$0.08
Film copy—Duplication of existing 100 ft. roll of 16 mm film	$9.50
Fiche copy—Duplication of existing 105 mm fiche	$0.26

Paper copy—Converting existing 16 mm film to paper

Conversion by commission staff	$0.26

Paper copy—Converting existing 105 mm fiche to paper

Conversion by commission staff	$0.23
Film cassettes	$2.00

Electronic services

Converting paper into electronic format (scanning), per page	$2.50
Computer programming, per quarter hour	$8.00

Other fees

Computer tape	$18.50
Certification	$10.35
Express mail (first pound)	$3.50
Each additional pound, up to $15.00	$3.67

FAQ

What if I have an unusually large FOIA request?

Usually, the courts have said that an agency may not use cost or time as an excuse to deny an FOIA request. In the late 1970s, the IRS complained that one large request from Philip and Susan Long would cost the agency $160,000, so the IRS refused to honor the request. A district court ruled for the IRS, but a federal appeals court, in *Long v. IRS*,[3] said that the Longs had a right to get the large amount of information. The court said that "the costs and inconvenience in this case are not alone sufficient to require nondisclosure." The court added that Congress, when it passed the FOIA, showed a "willingness to impose substantial costs on agencies in the interest of public access to information."

If an agency denies a request or does not meet the 20-day deadline, persons can file suit in federal district court. The court then determines whether the agency wrongfully withheld documents and may order the agency to pay court and attorney fees. The FOIA used to require that such suits take precedence over most other cases in court, but in 1996, Congress threw out that provision because it was too burdensome for Washington courts.

FAQ

What can I do if I'm turned down for an FOIA request?

The Vaughn Index

If an agency turns down your FOIA request, you are entitled to a legal explanation. This explanation is called a *Vaughn Index*, taken from a 1973 case, *Vaughn v. Rosen*.[4] The federal appeals court in this case said that agencies are supposed to provide persons with legal reasons for *each* document that is withheld.

During his first term, President Clinton had noticed that certain government agencies were keeping some very old records secret, without good reason. In 1995, Clinton signed an executive order that required all federal agencies to be more open with their records. The executive order required federal agencies to, by the year 2000, open up most classified records more than 25 years old. (Some agencies, like the CIA, were exempt from this rule. However, a special panel has to approve all CIA exemptions.) The executive order dictated that agencies should have a "presumption of openness." Agencies should consistently strive to make documents public instead of "secret." Also, an agency must provide valid legal reasons for keeping any document secret.

---

[3]596 F.2d 362 (9th Cir. 1980)

[4]484 F.2d 820 (D.C. Cir. 1973)

ELECTRONIC FREEDOM OF INFORMATION ACT OF 1996

To keep up with the times and changing technologies, Congress amended the FOIA in 1996. These amendments became known as the Electronic Freedom of Information Act of 1996 (EFOIA). The major elements of the EFOIA:

- ▣ *Online records:* All agencies must have all records created on or after November 1, 1996, available online within a year. If this is not possible for some reason, the agency has to make the records available by "other electronic means," such as CD-ROM or computer disk.
- ▣ *Format choices:* The EFOIA requires that requesters get their documents in the format they choose. Before, agencies had been allowed to choose the format.
- ▣ *Electronic format preferred:* The EFOIA says the agency "shall make reasonable efforts to search for the records in electronic form or format."[5]
- ▣ *Yearly review:* The EFOIA requires that each agency submit a report to the Attorney General by February 1 every year. The reports must contain the number of times the agency denied FOIA requests, the number of persons appealed those denials, and the reasons for the denials; the number of FOIA requests in the previous fiscal year; the number of those FOIA requests that were actually processed; total FOIA fees collected; the amount of staff and money spent processing FOIA requests; and the median number of days it took the agency to process different types of requests.

Exemptions

There are nine types of information that are not available under the FOIA: top secret and classified documents, federal agency housekeeping materials, materials exempted by other laws, trade secrets and other commercial and financial information, internal memos and policy discussions within or between agencies, private personal information and files, certain law enforcement files and records, bank and financial materials, and oil and gas well exploration data.

1. Top Secret Documents

The government has a right to keep certain matters of national security secret or "classified." Many of these are documents related to the military, intelligence agencies (FBI, CIA), and foreign affairs. The president, through an executive order, can declare a document classified. There are three levels of classification: *confidential, secret,* and *top secret.* Top secret is the highest classification, and it means that the document contains material that could cause serious damage to national security if it were released.

FAQ

Isn't there great potential for abuse here by powerful people?

Probably the most famous abuse of this power was by President Nixon. In 1974, Congress amended the FOIA to allow courts to do a *camera review:* Judges, in private, could

---

[5]*Freedom of Information Act,* 5 U.S.C. § 552, as amended by Pub. L. No. 104-231, 110 Stat. 3048

inspect classified documents to make sure the president properly applied the criteria for classification. This does not give the courts much power, though, because a judge may not question the criteria—only whether the criteria were applied properly.

2. Housekeeping Materials

These are documents related to internal personnel matters of various federal agencies. They include individual agencies' rules for lunch breaks, parking regulations, and telephone usage. The concern is not secrecy. If this information were made available under FOIA, every agency would have to keep public records of the information. By exempting such housekeeping materials from FOI, it saves federal agencies time and paper.

3. Matters Exempted by Other Laws

This exemption "covers the bases." It makes sure documents and records not covered by the FOIA are protected. For example, the IRS is required by federal law to keep people's income tax returns private.

4. Trade Secrets and Financial Information

An example of a trade secret is the recipe for Kentucky Fried Chicken, which has been kept confidential for decades. If competitors got the recipe, or if people were able to make the chicken themselves, Kentucky Fried Chicken would obviously be harmed financially. Companies have a right to protect these secrets. Certain financial information of private companies and government agencies is also exempt.

5. Internal Agency Memos and Discussions

There are two basic categories here: *Attorney-client privilege* (any communication between an agency and its attorneys) and *executive privilege.* Executive privilege includes draft reports and working papers. It is information compiled by agency employees in decision-making processes (everything from writing a project report to working on a special committee within an agency).

Nixon Tries to Use Executive Privilege—and Fails. In 1974, the special Watergate prosecutor ordered President Nixon to hand over the famous White House tapes. Of course, the media were interested in hearing these tapes as well. Nixon refused, claiming the tapes were protected by Exemption 6 of the FOIA and contained "privileged" discussions with his staff. In *United States v. Nixon,*[6] the U.S. Supreme Court ordered Nixon to release the tapes. The court said that executive privilege was "not absolute." Besides, these tapes were needed for a criminal investigation, and that was more important than Nixon's claim to executive privilege here.

6. Private Personal Files

These include various personal material, such as medical files, agency personnel files (which contain personal employment data), and other private files.

---

[6]418 U.S. 683 (1974)

Personal Medical Records and HIPAA. News stories frequently contain information about persons' medical conditions. Congress passed the Health Insurance Portability and Accountability Act (HIPAA) in 1996 to protect the privacy of each person's "protected health information." HIPAA became a major issue for the news media in April 2003 when doctor's offices and hospitals were required to meet the privacy standards it established. HIPAA restricts the amount of information that may be released from a patient's protected health information to the public or placed in the hospital's directory.

When a request *specifically identifies the patient by name,* hospitals may confirm the patient's name, general condition (fair, serious, critical, etc.), and the patient's location in the hospital (e.g., "intensive care unit"). Hospitals and health care providers may not release this information if a request does not include a specific name. Hospitals may not disclose any of this information if the patient has requested that it not be released. The hospital or doctor must give the patient this option. The media may interview or photograph hospital patients only with the patient's prior written consent or with the written permission of a legal representative or guardian. These policies apply to all patients, whether they are private citizens or public figures or officials.

The Challenger *Recording and Privacy.* A famous case involving "other private files" concerned the explosion of the space shuttle *Challenger* in January 1986. The seven crew members of *Challenger* were killed in an explosion shortly after lift-off, but an audio recorder in the cockpit recorded the conversations of the astronauts in their last minutes. That taped recording was discovered when NASA found the *Challenger* cockpit on the ocean floor.

The *New York Times* made an FOIA request for a copy of the recording, but NASA would only provide a written transcript. NASA felt that releasing the recording would be an invasion of privacy for family members of the *Challenger* crew. In 1991, in *New York Times v. NASA,*[7] a federal district court ruled that the audio recordings should be treated like medical or personnel files and should not be released. The court said that playing the tapes in public would invade the privacy of *Challenger* families and worsen their grief. The court said those privacy concerns outweighed any need for the media to have these tapes.

7. Law Enforcement Files

This exemption protects police and government entities from having to release information that might jeopardize a criminal investigation, deny a person a fair trial, endanger a person's life, reveal certain investigative techniques, divulge the identity of confidential sources, or invade personal privacy.

Post Office Massacre. In August 1986, former postal employee Patrick Sherrill walked into the post office in Edmond, OK, and shot and killed 14 people and then himself. The U.S. Post Office eventually compiled a 4700-page report on the murders. Oklahoma City TV station WTVY asked for a copy of the complete report, but the Post Office would release only 2145 pages. The Post Office said releasing the other portions of the report would invade the privacy of people who spoke with postal investigators. (Those people had been promised confidentiality.) WTVY argued that the public had a right to know the details of the incident as well as what the post office could have done to prevent the shootings.

---

[7]782 F. Supp. 628 (D.D.C. 1991)

In *WTVY v. U. S. Postal Service*,[8] a federal appeals court ruled for the Post Office. The court said that the persons interviewed for the report "have a legitimate privacy interest in not being harassed or embarrassed by other persons." Releasing the names of these people had no news value. Their names and confidential remarks would not help the TV station determine whether the post office could have prevented the shootings.

However, in 1993, in *Outlaw v. U.S. Department of the Army*,[9] a federal district court ruled that the FOIA privacy exemption could not be used in relation to a 25-year-old murder case. An Army sergeant convicted of the murder wanted graphic crime-scene photographs of the victim to be released to the public. He said the photographs could help prove his innocence. The Army objected, citing privacy concerns for the victim's surviving relatives. However, the court ruled that the Army did not prove there were any relatives still alive who might be harmed by the photographs' release. The court added that any privacy concerns were outweighed by a public interest in seeing how the Army investigated the murder.

Dale Earnhardt Autopsy Photos. NASCAR racing legend Dale Earnhardt was killed on February 18, 2001, when his car hit a wall during the final lap of the Daytona 500. Under a barrage of media attention, Earnhardt's family obtained a court order to seal the photographs from the autopsy. However, the *Orlando Sentinel* was doing a story on the dangers of NASCAR, and the newspaper sued for the right to see Earnhardt's autopsy photographs under the state's freedom of information laws. Among other things, the paper wanted to hire medical experts to look over the photographs to try to determine whether head and neck restraints might have saved Earnhardt's life. The paper said that it had no intention of publishing the photographs. However, family members were fearful that the photographs might get "leaked" to other publications or to Internet sites.

In March 2001, both houses of the Florida legislature responded quickly to public sympathy for the Earnhardts and passed the Earnhardt Family Relief Act. The act amended the state's open records laws and said that autopsy photographs would now only be available to the public with a judge's approval. The *Sentinel* then reached a personal agreement with the Earnhardt family to have an independent medical examiner look over the autopsy photographs and write a report about how the NASCAR legend died.

The *Independent Florida Alligator*, the student newspaper at the University of Florida, had also asked to see the photographs, but a circuit judge in June 2001 denied the paper access, saying that the new Earnhardt Act was constitutional. The paper, though, argued that it had asked to see the photographs *before* the Earnhardt Act was passed and that the judge was applying the law retroactively. The *Orlando Sentinel* and the *Fort Lauderdale Sun-Sentinel* filed a lawsuit to challenge the constitutionality of the Earnhardt Act, but both papers dropped the suit in 2004.

Their incentive to drop the suits came largely from a 2004 Supreme Court ruling in *National Archives and Records Administration v. Favish*.[10] That case concerned 10 death-scene photographs of Clinton White House counsel Vince Foster, who was found dead in a Washington, DC, park in 1993. The Supreme Court ruled unanimously that the photos should not be released, based on the law enforcement exemption in FOIA, and that any public interest in release of the pictures was outweighed by the privacy concerns of Foster's relatives.

---

[8]919 F.2d 1465 (10th Cir. 1990)

[9]815 F. Supp. 505 (D.D.C. 1993)

[10]124 S. Ct. 1570 (2004)

FAQ

Have the media ever used autopsy photographs to uncover important information?

Yes. Autopsy photographs can be vital in investigative reporting. Reporters point to cases such as that of Florida death row inmate Frank Valdes in 1999. Guards said Valdes had died from self-inflicted injuries by throwing himself off of a bunk bed and "thrashing around" a room. Autopsy photographs, though, showed several boot prints on Valdes' skin, indicating he had been kicked and punched. This proof led some guards to confess that Valdes had indeed been beaten to death.[11]

8. Bank and Financial Data

This exemption is meant to prevent the release of information that could lead to a loss of public confidence in our nation's banking system. The exemption not only covers banks but agencies involved with financial matters.

9. Oil and Gas Well Exploration Data

Private companies give the federal government detailed information about oil and gas wells, including maps. This exemption allows the companies to keep the information secret and to be protected from "unscrupulous" competitors.

FOIA and September 11 Detainees

After the September 11 terrorist attacks, federal authorities arrested and jailed nearly 1000 individuals who were suspected of having ties to the attacks or to terrorist organizations. These arrests had taken place by October 25, 2001. Soon, various groups, including the media, civil liberties groups, and members of Congress, demanded that the names of the detainees be released under the Freedom of Information Act. The federal government refused, arguing that releasing the names would jeopardize ongoing investigations, including grand jury proceedings, and would give terrorists valuable insight into how the government was conducting its investigations. The government also argued that releasing such information could endanger the lives of detainees.

In August 2002, in *Center for National Security Studies v. U.S. Department of Justice*,[12] Judge Gladys Kessler of the United States District Court in the District of Columbia ordered that the government release the names of all who had been arrested. However, in June 2003, a federal appeals court handed the government a victory when it reversed major parts of Kessler's ruling. The court wrote that "neither the First Amendment nor federal common law requires the government to disclose the information sought by plaintiffs."[13] The U.S. Supreme Court refused to hear an appeal of the ruling.

---

[11]Autopsy photos are often used to refute official conclusions. (2001, Spring). *News Media and the Law, 25*(2), 9.

[12]2002 U.S. Dist. LEXIS 14168

[13]*Center for National Security Studies v. U.S. Department of Justice*, 331 F.3d 918 (2003)

ACCESS TO GOVERNMENT MEETINGS

All 50 states, as well as the federal government, have what are called *open meeting laws*. These laws require that government meetings be open to the public and to the media. First, let's look at the federal opening meetings act.

The Sunshine Act

The federal open meetings act was established in 1976 and is called the *Sunshine Act*.[14] The full name is actually "The Government in the Sunshine Act," reflecting the sentiment that government proceedings should be "in the light," for everyone to see.

The Sunshine Act mandates that approximately 50 federal administrative agencies conduct their meetings following three basic guidelines: (a) Meetings must be open to the public; (b) agencies must give public notice of these meetings at least 1 week in advance; and (c) agencies must maintain accurate, detailed minutes of the meetings.

The Sunshine Act applies only to federal regulatory agencies or commissions whose members were appointed by the President. Specifically, agencies for which the president has appointed the *majority* of the members, the Senate has approved the president's committee appointments, and that are composed of two or more individual members.

FAQ

What agencies have to abide by this act?

The regulatory agencies include the Federal Communications Commission, the Federal Trade Commission, the National Transportation Safety Board, the Federal Reserve Board, the Interstate Commerce Commission, the Consumer Product Safety Commission, the Nuclear Regulatory Commission, and the Equal Employment Opportunity Commission. The Sunshine Act does not affect the majority of government agencies or commissions, but it does cover many of the more important bodies.

FAQ

Are there ever legitimate reasons for an agency to close a meeting to the public?

Closed Meetings

There are 10 reasons why an agency may choose not to have certain meetings open to the public. When an agency or commission wants to hold a closed session, it must be able to justify that the meeting involves at least one of the following sensitive topics. Note that these are very similar to the exemptions from the FOIA: (a) discussions involving foreign policy secrets or national defense, (b) trade secrets of private businesses, (c) accusations

---

[14]5 U.S.C. § 552b

of crime, (d) internal agency personnel matters, (e) specific information exempted by federal law, (f) information that would invade a person's privacy, (g) the agency being involved in legal matters (lawsuits, issuing subpoenas), (h) reports on banks and financial institutions or government regulation of such, (i) information that might threaten the economy, and (j) information gathered for law enforcement actions.

FAQ

What counts as a "meeting" of a government agency?

The act defines a meeting as "the deliberations of at least the number of individual agency members required to take action on behalf of the agency where such deliberations determine or result in the joint conduct or disposition of official business." This means pretty much any meeting in which a quorum is present and the members are discussing official government business.

FAQ

Does Congress have to abide by the Sunshine Act?

No. However, our democratic system pretty much demands that House and Senate sessions be open to the public. Congress does have the power to close sessions to the public, but this is rarely done. Today, C-SPAN provides extensive coverage of the House and Senate, so our society has come to expect open sessions of both houses of Congress.

Sunshine Laws and September 11

After the September 11 terrorist attacks, government officials discovered that our nation's Sunshine Act made it very easy for terrorists to obtain sensitive information, such as detailed maps of some of our nation's nuclear power plants and major dams. As a result, many federal and state lawmakers feared that our government records were a little too open. As of May 2002, legislatures in at least 22 states had either considered or passed laws placing new limits on public access to government records.[15] Critics, including journalists and civil liberties groups, said the new limits would wind up hurting average Americans instead of preventing terrorism.

MEDIA CREDENTIALS

In the months following the terrorist attacks, the nation was still very nervous about any possible threats of terrorism. This nervousness was apparent in our law enforcement officials as

---

[15]Kennedy, D. (2002, May 2). Sunshine laws may be headed for twilight. *Fox News.* Retrieved May 2, 2002, from http://www.foxnews.com

well. In Omaha, NE, in November 2001, police officials suggested possible background checks for members of the media. Only after a reporter passed this background check would he or she be allowed to cover stories and news conferences with the police. The media were able to convince the police not to go through with the plans.

The Illinois News Broadcasters Association expressed concern over a similar plan in Chicago.[16] Media credentials with the Chicago Police Department were set to expire on March 31, 2002. In previous years, renewal of press credentials had been an easy process. However, in early 2002, with threats of terrorism on the minds of law enforcement officials, the deputy director of the Chicago Police Office of News Affairs announced a new system for issuing press credentials. Media members would now be required to undergo background checks, to be fingerprinted, and to have mug shots taken. The police wanted to make sure that reporters were who they said they were.

This new plan did not go over well with reporters, who felt they were being treated like criminals. Reporters wondered if something like a drunk driving conviction from 20 years ago would keep a reporter from being credentialed.

STATE FOI LAWS AND SUNSHINE LAWS

It is most important for journalists to be educated on state laws regarding open meetings and public documents. The laws vary from state to state, but here are some general guidelines that most states have in common.

State Sunshine Laws: Some Common Principles

State definitions of a "meeting" often require that a quorum be present. The laws apply to state, city, and county government meetings. This includes school boards or any board dealing with taxpayer money. Government bodies must provide public notice of meeting times and places.

States have special laws for "executive" sessions, which may be closed to the public for specific reasons (discussions of legal matters, personnel matters, etc.). States require public bodies to keep detailed minutes of all meetings. Many states allow citizens to sue for violations of opening meetings laws.

Any emergency or special meeting must be publicly announced, often at least 24 hours in advance.

State FOI Laws: Some Common Principles

Most laws affect all state, city, and county records. Many states have exemptions similar to federal exemptions—no access to personal tax returns, trade secrets, state agency personnel matters, and so on. There are often separate laws affecting access to court records.

You have a right to copy public documents in most states. Most laws allow "general access." You do not have to provide a reason for seeing these documents.

Police reports are open to the public. However, many law enforcement records (e.g., those providing details of investigations) are not open to the public.

---

[16]Roberts, B. (2002, March). Chicago police and media credentials. *Tune In,* pp. 2, 5.

FAQ

What are the punishments for officials who violate state FOI or sunshine laws?

Many states impose jail time and fines. For example, in Texas, any officer of public information who, with criminal negligence, "fails or refuses to give access to, or to permit or provide copying of, public information" could be guilty of a misdemeanor and face a fine of up to $1000 fine and 6 months in jail. The person also faces removal from office. Other states, such as Oklahoma, allow the officer of public information to be sued for civil damages. The officer, if found in violation, may also be forced to pay the plaintiff's attorney's fees.

There are also states such as Tennessee in which violations of state FOI laws are not a criminal offense. However, officials there may still face lawsuits.

FAQ

Are these fines and jail terms ever enforced?

Yes. A good example is from Florida, in 2003, when two Escambia County commissioners were found guilty of violating the state's sunshine law. Both men were accused of discussing public matters in private with other commissioners. One man was W. D. Childers, former president of the Florida Senate. He was sentenced to 60 days in jail, fined $500, and ordered to pay $3600 in court costs. The other commissioner escaped jail time but paid more than $4100 in fines and court costs. Childers received the stiffer sentence because he ignored warnings from the county attorney.

SUNSHINE LAWS AND SENSITIVE INFORMATION

FAQ

Don't the media have to be careful about releasing some information from police records, out of concern for certain individuals' safety?

Yes. In fact, many state sunshine laws prohibit the release of a crime victim's identity when there is a reasonable risk that releasing such information could endanger the victim. One case in Missouri demonstrated why states have such restrictions and highlighted the sometimes delicate balance between freedom of information and individual safety.

In 1980, Sandra Hyde was walking along a street in Columbia, MO, late at night when a car pulled up beside her. The male driver pointed a sawed-off shotgun at Hyde and forced her into the car. Within a short time, she was able to jump out of the car and run for help.

The *Columbia Daily Tribune* did a story about Hyde's abduction, and the paper provided information from the police report including Hyde's name and address.

Soon after, the man began stalking Hyde at her home and at work. He also made threatening phone calls, with messages such as, "I want to refresh your memory of who I am before I kill you tonight." Hyde blamed the city of Columbia and the *Tribune* for revealing her identity and address, and she sued them in *Hyde v. City of Columbia*.[17] She said the city and paper were negligent for not foreseeing the dangers of releasing the information. The city and the newspaper said they had a right to release the information under the state's public records law (a sunshine law), and a trial court ruled against Hyde. The jury agreed that the crime report was a public record, and the city and paper had a legal right to release information contained in it, even if it did bring harm to Hyde.

Much to the surprise of many in the media, though, a state appeals court overturned that verdict and ruled that Hyde indeed had a right to sue for negligence. The appeals court said that the sunshine law should not automatically mean that *anyone* should have a right to *all* information from criminal investigations. The court said such a reading of the law was an "absurdity." The court added that police and the media should have foreseen that releasing Hyde's personal information might lead the perpetrator "to intimidate the victim as a witness or commit other injury."

In closing, the court reiterated that it is not legal under the Missouri sunshine law to release the name and address of a crime victim when the perpetrator is still on the loose and poses a "foreseeable risk" to the victim. The City of Columbia appealed the ruling, but the U.S. Supreme Court declined to hear the case.

The *Hyde* ruling helped a woman win a similar case against the *Los Angeles Times* in 1988. The woman had came home one night to find that her roommate had been beaten, raped, and strangled to death. An intern for the *Times* obtained information about the crime from the coroner's office, and the *Times* story on the murder included the name of the woman who found her roommate's body. The woman feared that the killer might come after her. In *Times Mirror Co. v. Superior Court of San Diego County*,[18] a California appeals court used *Hyde* as a precedent and ruled that the woman had a right to sue for negligence and that the state's public records law did not protect the newspaper.

FAQ

Don't the courts usually protect the media when they obtain the information legally from public records?

Yes. In similar public records cases, courts have consistently ruled in favor of the media, striking down state laws that prohibited the release of sensitive crime information, such as the names of rape victims or the names of juveniles who have committed crimes. For ethical reasons, and to avoid potential lawsuits, most media outlets have internal policies

---

[17]637 S.W.2d 251 (Mo. App. 1982)

[18]198 Cal. App. 3d 1420, 244 Cal. Rptr. 16 (1988)

prohibiting the release of such information. In these two cases, though, the courts warned that the news media need to make sure that reporting certain crime victim information does not constitute a foreseeable risk to that victim.

PRISONS

The News Media and Access to Prisons

Jails and prisons are funded by taxpayers, but that does not mean that these facilities are open to the public. However, what are the rights of the media when it comes to these correctional facilities?

No Right of Media Access to Prisons

In 1974, the U.S. Supreme Court handed down two important decisions on the same day regarding the media and prisons. One case involved the *Washington Post*, which had asked for permission to interview inmates at two federal prisons in Connecticut and Pennsylvania. However, a federal law only allowed news interviews with inmates at minimum security prisons. News reporters were banned from interviewing prisoners at any other federal prisons. The newspaper sued, saying it had a First Amendment right of access to jails and prisons.

In California, state prisons had allowed the media to do face-to-face interviews with certain prisoners. However, prison officials soon discovered the media coverage turned those prisoners into "celebrities," with "disproportionate notoriety and influence among their fellow inmates." Officials said that this notoriety played a role in a prison incident during which several prisoners were killed. As a result, officials decided they would no longer allow the news media to do face-to-face interviews with prisoners. The media, as well as the inmates, sued.

In *Saxbe v. Washington Post*[19] and *Pell v. Procunier*[20] in 1974, the issue was not general access to prisons or prisoners. In fact, the media could write letters to inmates, and the media were free to do short interviews with prisoners during prison tours. However, in these two cases, the media argued that they should also have a First Amendment right to interview specific prisoners one-on-one.

The U.S. Supreme Court, in both cases, said that the media do not have a right to interview particular inmates. In *Pell,* the court said: "Newsmen have no constitutional right of access to prisons or their inmates beyond that afforded to the general public." The court added that the government is not required to provide the media with any and all information. That sentiment was reinforced in the next case.

Court Reaffirms Prison Restrictions for the Media

In March 1975, KQED-TV in San Francisco aired a story about a prisoner who had committed suicide in the Greystone section of the Santa Rita jail. The station wanted to follow up on the suicide and do a story about the conditions inside that section of the jail.

---

[19]417 U.S. 843 (1974)

[20]417 U.S. 817 (1974)

KQED asked Sheriff Houchins of Alameda County for permission to go inside the jail to take pictures and inspect the facilities. Houchins said no.

KQED filed suit against the sheriff and the county, saying the TV station had a First Amendment right to do "full and accurate news coverage of the conditions" in Greystone.

Greystone had been in the news before because of allegedly poor living conditions, as well as alleged beatings and rapes. The station argued that conditions inside the jail were "of great public importance." In July, the sheriff started limited public tours of the jail, but people were not allowed in certain areas, including Greystone.

KQED argued that jails and prisons are funded by taxpayers. They should be open to inspection. After all, the mission of penal institutions is crucial in the criminal justice system. The First Amendment gives the media the right to act as eyes and ears for the public, and the media can be a powerful force in bringing about needed change in such places.

Both a federal district court and appeals court ruled for the TV station, saying that KQED had a constitutional right of access to prisons and jails. The media should have a right to "government-controlled sources of information."

The U.S. Supreme Court, though, ruled for the sheriff in *Houchins v. KQED.*[21] The court said that the media do *not* have an absolute right of access to jails and prisons. The court pointed out that it is the job of state and federal lawmakers to deal with problems in prisons. The media are "ill-equipped" to deal with these problems. "The media are not a substitute for or an adjunct of government."

The Supreme Court said that the First Amendment does not give a right of access to *all* government-controlled sources of information. The First Amendment also does not *compel* anyone—private person or government—to give out information. The presence of the public or media in prisons can be disruptive to operations. Therefore, access by the public or media is left to the discretion of the prison operators. This rationale also applies to hospitals and mental institutions.

ACCESS TO RAP SHEETS

Do the media have a right to see a police record ("rap sheet") that shows you were arrested 15 years ago for disorderly conduct at a public rally? Should police only report the most recent crimes committed by a person? Should a detailed rap sheet be considered private?

In 1976, the Law Enforcement Assistance Administration issued federal guidelines about rap sheets. Any local or state police departments receiving federal funds were required to create policies regarding the release of information about anyone who was arrested. The guidelines were established for individual privacy reasons.

States have various laws about rap sheets, and many states restrict access to certain parts of individuals' rap sheets. However, many journalists say it is important to know, for example, about a politician's criminal past when doing campaign stories. Employers often say they need to know whether a prospective employee has a record of violent behavior. Many states now have laws requiring convicted sex offenders to register with local authorities. That way, local citizens can be made aware of sex offenders living in their neighborhoods.

Civil libertarians, though, argue that most rap sheet information should be kept private. They argue that "dredging up" past offenses will stigmatize a person and not allow him or

---

[21]438 U.S. 1 (1978)

her to move on with life. Journalists need to be aware of the laws in their state regarding rap sheet information.

IMPORTANT FEDERAL PRIVACY STATUTES

Privacy Act of 1974

This act gives citizens the right of access to their own files within the government. The 1974 Privacy Act[22] also gives people the right to correct any errors in those files. Federal agencies are prohibited from releasing certain types of personal information contained in these files. The person's consent is required before the files can be released. The Privacy Act covers any files about you that may be kept by agencies such as the Internal Revenue Service, the Social Security Administration, and even the FBI.

In 1984, Congress passed a law that said federal agencies could not use the Privacy Act as an excuse to deny an FOIA request. In situations where there is an apparent conflict between the FOIA and the Privacy Act, the FOIA is supposed to take precedence. However, agencies say the law is difficult to implement. Persons have the right to sue federal agencies who use FOIA to release "private" information.

Access to School and University Records

The Family Educational Rights and Privacy Act (FERPA)

Also known as the *Buckley Amendment,* FERPA is a 1974 federal law that protects the privacy of student education records. FERPA applies to schools that receive federal funds "under an applicable program" of the U.S. Department of Education. That includes almost all publicly funded schools and colleges. Schools violating FERPA may be denied federal funds.

Some of the major components of FERPA include parents' rights to see their child's education records until the child is 18. Once a person is 18 years old, he or she is considered an "eligible student" and is not obligated to disclose educational records to his or her parents. This includes college records. Parents and eligible students have a right to inspect the records and request corrections for any errors.

Schools may release "directory information," such as a student's name, address, phone number, date and place of birth, awards, honors, and dates of attendance. However, schools must let parents and eligible students know about the directory information. The school must provide a "reasonable amount of time" for parents and eligible students to request that directory information not be released.

FAQ

Do the media have a right to this information when doing news stories?

---

[22]5 U.S.C. § 552 (a)

Schools may not release educational records to journalists or the public without written permission from a parent or eligible student. This includes information about grades and school health records.

University Grades. A college student's grades are supposed to be kept confidential. FERPA says that schools are only in danger of losing federal funds when they exhibit consistent patterns of deliberately releasing educational records.

FERPA Problems. Out of fear of losing federal funds, many universities have used FERPA to deny release of information about student judicial proceedings, campus police records, and the academic standing of athletes.

This began to frustrate many reporters at college newspapers and broadcast stations. They discovered that they could get information about arrests from local police agencies, but campus police would not release the information for fear of violating FERPA. Also, colleges often would use FERPA to withhold information about violent crimes on their campuses. After all, too much reporting about campus crime can make a university appear "unsafe" and may scare away prospective students.

Campus Police Records. The basic rule here is that *access to campus crime records is governed by state laws.* The courts have ruled in several cases that if a state law requires such records to be open to the public, that state law overrides FERPA, and the media have a right to see those records.

The editor of the campus newspaper at Southwest Missouri State University decided to take one such matter to court. *Standard* editor Traci Bauer was frustrated with the lack of access to campus crime records. State law said she had a right to see the records, but the campus police said federal law under FERPA superseded the state law. In 1991, in *Bauer v. Kincaid,*[23] a district court ruled in Bauer's favor, saying the university did not have a right to withhold campus crime records that state law required to be open.

In 1998, the U.S. Department of Education filed a lawsuit to try to prevent universities from having to release campus crime information. Congress did not like this move and took action.

1998 Higher Education Act (The Clery Act)

The actual name of the act is the *Jeanne Clery Disclosure of Campus Security Policy and Campus Crime Statistics Act.* Clery was a student at Lehigh University who was murdered in her dorm room. University officials had forbidden the release of information about recent violent crimes on campus. Critics said the university's secrecy gave students the false impression that the campus was a safe place. They said that "illusion of safety" led Clery to leave a dorm security door ajar one night, which allowed someone to gain access to her room and kill her.

Congress passed the Clery Act to say that universities could not use FERPA as an excuse to keep certain campus crimes secret. The Clery Act reinforced the ruling in *Bauer,* which said that state laws override FERPA when it comes to campus police records and crime reports.

---

[23]759 F. Supp. 575 (W.D. Mo. 1991)

Universities Must Keep Public Crime Logs. The Clery Act said that any college receiving federal funds must keep a public log of all criminal occurrences reported to campus law enforcement officials. The logs must contain the following information about each complaint: date, time, nature of the complaint, location, and action taken by authorities. Law enforcement officials have 2 business days to make these records available to the public. Any new information about a previous complaint must also be made available to the public within 2 days. Also, universities are required to compile and publish annual reports about campus crime statistics.

FAQ

Does the Clery Act apply to private colleges?

Usually it does. The act says that any private university that takes money from the federal student loan program must abide by the Clery Act. The majority of private universities have students paying for school with federally insured student loans.

Campus Disciplinary Proceedings

A 2000 federal court ruling says that reporters and others do not have a right of access to information from campus disciplinary proceedings. In *U.S. v. Miami University,*[24] a federal district court judge ruled that records of student disciplinary bodies are considered "educational records," and FERPA does not allow their release. The judge also ruled that the U.S. Department of Education has a right to file lawsuits against schools to ensure that FERPA guidelines are being followed in such matters.

Access to Driving Records

In 1994, Congress passed the Driver's Privacy Protection Act (DPPA). This law says that people's driving records and motor vehicle registrations should not be considered public documents. Therefore, the public and the media are not allowed to access such records, which often contain a person's name, address, social security number, and telephone number. Criminals were using such data to commit identity fraud, to stalk people, and to commit other crimes, and the law was designed to curb such abuses of people's personal data.

The DPPA does have some exemptions. People from law enforcement, insurance companies, and other appropriate agencies may see these records when legally necessary. The DPPA also allows for the release of data regarding driving violations, accidents, and whether a certain driver has had a license revoked.

The law requires each state to abide by the DPPA. States may pass laws to avoid the blanket federal requirements, but that is only if the states include clauses that allow citizens to choose whether their records should be kept private.

---

[24]91 F. Supp. 2d 1132 (S.D. Ohio 2000)

FAQ

Doesn't the DPPA take away an important investigative tool for journalists?

For that reason and others, some states challenged the DPPA, but the Supreme Court upheld the law in 2000 in *Reno v. Condon*.[25] Journalists have criticized the DPPA, saying it takes away an important tool for investigative reporters. In the 1980s, the oil tanker Exxon Valdez ran aground off the coast of Alaska and spilled millions of gallons of crude oil into the ocean. Journalists were able to look at the driving records of the ship's captain, and they discovered he had been arrested several times for drunk driving. Today, the DPPA would restrict journalists from uncovering such information from driving records.

ACCESS TO GOVERNMENT OR PUBLIC PROPERTY

In the chapter on privacy, we discussed the point that reporters do not have an automatic right to go on private property even when covering newsworthy events. If permission is not granted for access to this property, reporters can be charged with trespassing.

However, there is often confusion about what constitutes a *public* area and what journalists' rights are regarding these areas. There are three basic types of *public arenas* or *public forums*.

1. Traditional Public Forums

There are really only three categories of these: public parks, public streets, and public sidewalks. These are public places where people have a right to congregate and engage in free speech, as long as they do not create unnecessary disturbances or violate laws. For example, you cannot use a public street for a parade unless you get a parade permit from the city first. The city has a right to regulate traffic and avoid nuisances. However, reporters are free to interview people and take pictures in any of these public places.

Traditional public forums may also extend to places such as the steps in front of a state capitol building or the lobby of a university union.

2. Limited Public Forums

These forums are open to the public as well, but time, place, and manner restrictions apply. Examples include city or school auditoriums, town meeting halls, city or county fairgrounds, a campus newspaper, public library meeting rooms, civic centers, stadiums, public schools, and government buildings. In general, all of these are "open" to the public. However, people must often get permission to use them. Let's look at a few of the venues in detail.

---

[25]528 U.S. 141 (2000)

Campus Newspapers. A student paper is a forum for free speech, but the paper is not obligated to print every letter to the editor nor to let anyone write a column.

Schools. Always check with school officials before taking pictures or interviewing students in public schools. Many schools require parents to sign permission forms before allowing students to talk with the media or appear on camera. Some schools even have rules that bar the media from big events, such as graduations. Check with the school first! Photographers have actually been arrested for taking unauthorized pictures at high school graduations.

Government Buildings. The rules vary here. Check with officials in the buildings before doing any interviews or taking pictures. There are also restrictions on protests or demonstrations in and around government buildings. Such protests might interfere with normal government operations.

Airports. Again, check with airport officials before trying to do any kind of reporting or photography at an airport. Case law is mixed here, so get permission first.

Civic Centers and Stadiums. The media do not have automatic rights of access here. A good example is from July 1987, when the Communications Workers of America were having a convention at the Miami Beach convention center. Some presidential candidates were scheduled to speak at the convention. NBC demanded access to the convention, but the CWA refused, saying it was a private convention. NBC argued that CWA was using a public forum and was required to let NBC in. In *NBC v. CWA*,[26] an appeals court ruled that NBC did not have a right of access to a limited public forum that was leased out to a private group. Groups that rent or lease limited public forums are not obligated to open their meetings to the public or the media.

3. Nonpublic Forums

These types of public property are not open to the general public and have great restrictions for public access: airport boarding areas (especially after September 11), military bases, and prisons and jails.

PUBLIC ACCESS TO EXECUTIONS

As of this writing, at least 37 states have the death penalty. The federal government also executes certain criminals, but very rarely. Most states allow limited access to executions. Many times, a certain number of media representatives are allowed to view an execution; however, no states allow the media to take pictures or video. In fact, the U.S. Supreme Court denied a request by a death row inmate to allow talk show host Phil Donahue and a cameraman to videotape his execution in a North Carolina gas chamber. The prison's warden refused to allow the videotaping because it would disrupt the operations of the prison. In *Lawson v. Dixon*,[27] the Supreme Court upheld lower court rulings supporting the warden's ban on the videotaping.

---

[26]860 F.2d 1022 (11th Cir. 1988)

[27]512 U.S. 1215 (1994)

ACCESS TO MILITARY INFORMATION

The government, throughout history, has tried to limit the power of the media in times of war, not only through sedition laws but by restricting how the press may cover military operations. The government argues that it is a matter of national security. The history of media wartime restrictions shows how technology and changing attitudes have resulted in more—and less—freedom for journalists when covering military conflicts.

World War I

This war began in 1914, with the U.S. entering the conflict in 1917. President Wilson set up the Committee on Public Information, whose basic job was to release only positive information about American involvement in the war. The Departments of War, State, and the Navy banned media reports about troop or weapon locations, American military weaknesses that could be exploited by enemies, planned military operations and tactics, and locations of missing ships or troops that could still be rescued.

Americans often saw films of the war in movie theaters. Most of the films were produced by the Army Signal Corps and were usually propaganda, showing the Germans as evil and the American troops as heroic. The public was not allowed to see large numbers of dead U.S. troops, but the government did release film of dead German soldiers and of villages burned by Germans.

World War II

In 1942, the government established the Office of War Information to control the kinds of government and military information that were made available to the public.

World War II press restrictions were similar to those of WWI, including prohibitions on reports of military operations, troop locations, and film of dead American troops. Censors were allowed to edit stories by journalists who traveled with the military.

Also, the media were warned not to release any weather information that might aid the enemy. (The FBI in 1942 arrested a German spy traveling to New York. He was carrying a copy of the *Farmer's Almanac*, which the FBI said he was using to gather weather information. The *Almanac* was not charged with violating any law, though.)

The Vietnam War

Compared to other wars up to this point, the Vietnam War had the least amount of government censorship. War reporters were allowed to travel with military personnel. This is known as *embedded* reporting or journalism. Reporters were pretty much allowed to wander freely throughout the country (at their own risk), and an estimated 75 reporters and other media employees were killed during the 13-year conflict. The military and the media had an unwritten agreement—officials would tell the media about planned operations and the media would promise not to release the information until battles had actually started. Most of the time, the media complied.

However, with so little military censorship, TV newscasts began to show more and more bloody battles and more stories about how the American effort there was not succeeding. The government blamed the media for eroding public support for the war.

Grenada and Press Pools

On October 25, 1983, President Reagan sent U.S. troops to the small Caribbean island of Grenada after a military coup resulted in the killing of the country's prime minister. Many in the media were upset because journalists were not allowed to accompany the military during the first 2 days of the conflict. The treatment of the media in Grenada led to the *Sidle Commission*, which produced a list of recommendations for the use of *press pools* in future American war efforts.

A press pool is made up of a select number of journalists from different news organizations. A lottery system may determine which reporters will be in the pool, or news organizations may pick which reporter will belong to a pool. Only members of the pool are allowed to travel with the military or to interview troops. This makes it easier for the military to protect and keep track of journalists. It also allows the troops to focus on their missions. Upon return from a battle or mission, the pool reporters must then share their information, pictures, and video with nonpool reporters. The military are responsible for transporting media members. Nonpool reporters are often prohibited from interviewing soldiers or from going into war zones. Depending on the length of the war, the military may rotate the membership of pools every several weeks. Pools should be implemented only during the early stages of a military conflict.

Media Lawsuit

Eight months after the Grenada conflict ended, *Hustler* magazine publisher Larry Flynt filed a lawsuit against Defense Secretary Caspar Weinberger for the press restrictions enacted during the first days of the Grenada invasion. The Pentagon moved to dismiss the case, saying that the access demanded by Flynt was granted to all of the media on November 7, 1983. A district judge agreed with the Pentagon and ruled that the case was moot (no longer significant). In *Flynt v. Weinberger*,[28] the district judge supported the right of the military to impose restrictions on the press during conflicts, saying that Flynt's lawsuit sought to "limit the range of options available to the commanders in the field in the future, possibly jeopardizing the success of military operations and the lives of military personnel and thereby gravely damaging the national interest."

A federal appeals court in 1985 agreed the matter was moot but also said the district failed to follow some necessary procedures to reach its mootness ruling.[29] The case was remanded to the district court, and that lower court once again deemed the matter moot.

The 1991 Persian Gulf War

Media Lawsuit

Before the Gulf War even began, a group of media outlets brought a lawsuit on January 10, 1991 against the Department of Defense for its policies regarding media coverage of foreign conflicts. The media wanted to establish what the rules would be *before* the war actually began. Some of the media bringing the lawsuit included magazines such as *Harper's, The Nation,* and *The Village Voice.* The media claimed they had a "First Amendment right to unlimited access to a foreign arena in which American military forces are engaged."

---

[28]558 F. Supp. 57 (S.D.N.Y. 1984)

[29]*Flynt v. Weinberger*, 762 F.2d 134 (D.C. Cir. 1985)

In *Nation Magazine v. Department of Defense*,[30] a district court dismissed the case. The court said that the media could not bring a case against the government for press restrictions that dated back to Vietnam and that the Department of Defense was in the process of revising: *"The court should not be evaluating a set of regulations that are currently being reviewed for probable revision, to determine their reasonableness in the context of a conflict that does not exist and the precise contours of which are unknown and unknowable."*

After the end of the Gulf War, journalists had complained about some of the restrictions placed on the media during the conflict. Members of the news media and the Pentagon devised a statement of principles in 1992 to be followed in future combat situations involving American troops (see box).

1992 Statement of Principles for Combat News Coverage

1. *Open and independent reporting* will be the principal means of coverage of U.S. military operations.
2. *Press pools should be limited* and are not to serve as the standard means of covering U.S. military operations.
   - ▣ Pools should be used mostly during the very early stages of a conflict.
   - ▣ The pools should then be disbanded as quickly as possible.
   - ▣ Pools should be as large as possible.
   - ▣ If journalists are already in the area before the military arrive, military press pools should not affect those journalists.
3. *Special press pools.* Even under conditions of open coverage, pools may be appropriate for specific events, such as those at extremely remote locations or where space is limited.
4. *Media credentials and ground rules.* Journalists in a U.S. combat area will be credentialed by the U.S. military. Journalists will also be required to follow a clear set of military security ground rules that protect U.S. forces and their operations. Violation of the ground rules can result in suspension of credentials and expulsion of the journalist from the combat zone. News organizations will make their best efforts to assign experienced journalists to combat operations and to make them familiar with U.S. military operations.
5. *General media access.* Journalists will be given access to all major military units. Special operations restrictions may limit access in some cases.
6. *Military public relations.* Military public affairs officers should act as liaisons but should not interfere with the reporting process.
7. *Media access to military aircraft and vehicles.* Under conditions of open coverage, field commanders should permit journalists to ride on military vehicles and aircraft whenever feasible. The military will be responsible for the transportation of pools.
8. *Media communications systems.* Consistent with its capabilities, the military will supply Public Affairs Officers (PAOs) with facilities to enable timely, secure, compatible transmission of pool material and will make these facilities available whenever possible for filing independent coverage. In cases when government facilities are unavailable, journalists will, as always, file by any other means available. The military will not ban communications systems operated by news organizations, but electromagnetic operational security in battlefield situations may require limited restrictions on the use of such systems.
9. *Application.* These principles will apply as well to the operations of the standing Department of Defense National Media Pool system.

---

[30]762 F. Supp. 1558 (S.D.N.Y. 1991)

> 10. *Military screening of words and pictures.* The media and the Pentagon could not agree on this 10th principle, so each came up with their own versions:
>
> *Military: "Military operational security may require review of news materials for conformance to reporting ground rules."* The Pentagon wanted this provision to keep the media from releasing any information or pictures that could aid the enemy and endanger U.S. soldiers.
>
> *Media: "News material, words, and pictures will not be subject to security review."* The media said they have done responsible coverage in previous wars, avoiding material that would endanger U.S. troops, and that the Pentagon should not be allowed to censor any media reports.

The War in Afghanistan

Flynt II

After the terrorist attacks of September 11, 2001, the United States attacked Afghanistan. In the early stages of the war, the Pentagon said it needed to place certain restrictions on the media to ensure a good start to the war effort. For example, media members were not allowed to accompany troops on combat missions in the mountainous terrain of Afghanistan, and most reporters had to rely on Pentagon briefings for information. The military did allow 40 journalists on three Navy ships, but none of the ships was playing a major role in the war. Some in the press complained they had only limited access to conduct interviews with military personnel.

Just as he had done after the Grenada invasion, publisher Larry Flynt and others filed suit against Defense Secretary Donald Rumsfeld and the Defense Department for these press restrictions. Once again, the courts ruled in favor of the Pentagon. In *Flynt v. Rumsfeld,*[31] a federal district court said that Flynt "was not likely to suffer irreparable harm" from the press restrictions.

The court said the media basically had not tried hard enough. "It does not appear that plaintiffs have in fact been denied the access they seek or that they necessarily would have been denied such access if they had pursued the matter fully through available military channels."

By the time the court heard this case in late 2001, the military had begun allowing the press to accompany U.S. troops on the ground in Afghanistan. Flynt and the other plaintiffs could not prove that the military "now would deny access to them," nor could they deny that "the media in fact has enjoyed increased access since this lawsuit was filed."

As we have seen, the courts are generally supportive of the military's right to be more restrictive with the media at the *start* of the war. The court in this case praised the military for its openness with the media as the war progressed.

The War in Iraq: Historic Media Access

This war has been one of the most open wars in history when it comes to media coverage. In early 2003, the United States, along with coalition forces, invaded Iraq, and the American military granted the media historic access to troops and information. Exceptional media access was allowed throughout the conflict, including during the very

---

[31]180 F. Supp.2d 174 (D.D.C. 2002)

early stages of the war, unlike the situation in Afghanistan. Technology allowed *embedded journalism* to take on a new meaning, as at least 500 journalists were allowed to ride with troops into combat areas and to broadcast live reports via satellite from most locations. Satellite broadcasts in the Gulf War, for example, required the use of large dishes mounted on trucks. By the time of the Iraq War, technology allowed reporters to carry satellite equipment in a backpack and communicate immediately via cell phone.

The media had agreed to abide by the following guidelines, revealed in a Pentagon memo, very similar to the 1992 guidelines: (a) Reporters had to be *properly credentialed* and approved by the military. (b) Reporters had to promise not to report any information that might jeopardize military operations or aid the enemy. This included information such as troop locations and future military operations. (c) The military would not censor, delay, or "review" media content unless the Pentagon suspected there might be sensitive material involved. (d) Reporters could divulge the number of *battlefield casualties,* but a dead soldier's identity could be not be revealed for at least 72 hours, or until all appropriate family members had been notified. (e) The military was not allowed to confiscate any reporter's property, including cameras, notebooks, or tape recorders. The military said it would instead contact the reporter's news organization if there were any problems. (f) The military had to provide media members with transportation, food, lodging, and with any necessary safety equipment, such as gas masks and helmets.

One reporter who got in trouble for violating these guidelines was Fox News Channel's Geraldo Rivera. In March 2003, Rivera was embedded with the 101st Airborne in Iraq. During a live report, Rivera used his finger to draw a map of Iraq in the sand, showing the location of Baghdad, the location of the 101st, and where the 101st would be going next. Fox News voluntarily removed Rivera from Iraq after the Pentagon announced it was going to expel him. Soon, Fox had Rivera back on the air doing reports from Kuwait.

Also in March 2003, a TV network fired a reporter for comments made during an interview with Iraqi TV. MSNBC's Peter Arnett said the U.S. war plan was failing because of Iraqi resistance. Arnett made some other "questionable" comments as well, and NBC said it was wrong for Arnett to grant a broadcast interview on an enemy's state-controlled media during a war. Public opinion polls at the time showed Americans strongly supporting the American military in Iraq, and NBC apparently did not want to keep a reporter on the air who appeared to be "anti-American."

Overall, though, the Iraq war will be remembered for the great amount of freedom granted to journalists in covering the conflict. This freedom came with a price, though, as at least 15 journalists were killed during the first year of the war.

The Media and Military Bases

Pictures at a Military Mortuary

Bodies of soldiers killed overseas are typically flown to Dover Air Force Base in Delaware. Until the start of Operation Desert Storm in the Persian Gulf in 1991, the media had been allowed to take pictures of soldiers' caskets as they were taken off the planes. Shortly before the start of Desert Storm in 1991, the Department of Defense (DOD) changed its guidelines and banned the media from taking pictures of the caskets. The DOD said the old policy created unnecessary emotional and economic hardship for some families, who felt obliged to travel to Dover to see a loved one's casket in person so they would not have to see it first on TV or in newspapers.

The DOD presented a new policy:

> Therefore, it is the military departments' policy that ceremonies/services be held at the service
> member's duty or home station and/or the interment site, rather than at the port of entry. Media cov-
> erage of the arrival of the remains at the port of entry or at interim stops will not be permitted, but
> may be permitted at the service member's duty or home station or at the internment site, if the family
> so desires.

Several media groups and veterans' organizations challenged the new regulation on First
Amendment grounds, saying they had a right to cover such events because they were newsworthy. In 1996, in *JB Pictures, Inc., v. Department of Defense*,[32] a federal appeals court ruled
for the government. The court said the DOD allowed for coverage of ceremonies with family
permission, and that although this was not a "perfect substitute for general access to Dover,"
it was sufficient and reasonable. The government was justified in protecting the privacy and
emotions of families who "may be upset at public display of the caskets of their loved ones."

This policy became an issue during the Iraq War. In 2004, a man named Russ Kick used
a Freedom of Information Act request to obtain dozens of photographs of flag-draped
coffins arriving at Dover Air Force Base, and he posted the pictures on the Internet. Other
media outlets soon published the photos as well. The Defense Department had not realized
that the photographs were available and said it would use the ruling in *JB Pictures* to prevent any further release of such photographs. Kick and others argued that the public
should see the pictures to understand the "cost of war." President Bush said the privacy of
military families should come first.

One final quotation from this case summarizes this entire section of the chapter very
nicely: "There is no right of access to government property or activities simply because
such access might lead to more thorough and better reporting."

Summary

The Freedom of Information Act is designed to give the public access to most existing
government documents. However, there are nine categories of material that cannot be
obtained through the FOIA, and these include top secret documents and certain law
enforcement information. Government agencies are supposed to respond to FOIA requests
within 20 working days, and agencies may charge reasonable fees for requests.

The Sunshine Act is designed to ensure openness of federal governmental meetings.
Agencies may only close meetings to the public for specific legitimate reasons. States also
have their own open meetings laws.

Some openness of government records leads to controversy, such as in the cases involving the Challenger audio recordings and the Dale Earnhardt autopsy photographs.

The courts have ruled that the media and the public do not have an automatic right of
access to certain government institutions, such as jails, military bases, and prisons. Also,
under FERPA, parents no longer have a right to see their children's educational records
once that child turns 18. Congress later passed the Clery Act, to prevent universities from
using FERPA to deny the release of campus crime information.

The media should be aware of the differences between traditional, limited, and nonpublic forums.

---

[32]86 F.3d 236 (D.C. Cir. 1996)

Table of Cases and FCC Rulings

A&M Records v. Napster	322
Abrams v. U.S.	19
Academy of Motion Picture Arts and Sciences v. Creative House Promotions, Inc.	330
Action for Children's Television v. FCC (ACT I)	260
Action for Children's Television v. FCC (ACT II)	260
Action for Children's Television v. FCC (ACT III)	260
Adarand v. Pena	41
Acuff-Rose v. Campbell	318
Albuquerque Journal v. Jewell	365
Alpha Therapeutic Corporation v. Nippon Hoso Koikai	210
American Library Association v. U.S.	279
AP v. District Court	375
AP v. Walker	160
ApolloMedia Corp. v. Reno	252
Arkansas Educational Television Commission v. Forbes	55
Ashcraft v. Conoco	385
Ashcroft v. Free Speech Coalition	249
Ashcroft v. ACLU	278
In re Aspen Institute and CBS	55
Auvil v. Minutes	166
Ayeni v. Mottola	212
Baker v. F&F Investment	382
Barron v. Baltimore	20
Bartnicki v. Vopper	178
Bauer v. Kincaid	413
Becker v. FCC	51
Berger v. Hanlon	251
Bigelow v. Virginia	334
Bobbs-Merrill Co. v. Straus	290
Branch v. FCC	49
Brandenburg v. Ohio	22
Branzburg v. Hayes	378
Bridges v. California	393

Brigham v. FCC   47
Bright Tunes Music Corp. v. Harrisongs Music, Ltd.   305
Buendorf v. NPR   160
Bush v. Gore   366
Butler v. Michigan   237
Byers v. Edmonson   230

Calder v. Jones   170
California v. Greenwood   201
Campbell v. Acuff-Rose Music   318
Cantrell v. Forest City Publishing   190
Capital Broadcasting v. Mitchell   349
Carson v. Here's Johnny Portable Toilets   198
Carter Mountain Transmission Corporation v. FCC   71
CBS, Inc., v. FCC   56
CBS v. U.S. District Court   372
Center for National Security Studies v. U.S. Dept. of Justice   404
Central Hudson Gas & Electric v. Public Service Commission of New York   335
Century Communications v. FCC   83
Chandler v. Florida   361
Chaplinsky v. New Hampshire   23
Cher v. Forum   196
Chisholm v. FCC   55
City of Los Angeles v. Preferred   77
Clear Channel Broadcasting Licensees, Inc.   265
Clift v. Narragansett TV   179
Clorox Company Puerto Rico v. Proctor & Gamble   343
Coca-Cola Co. v. Gemini Rising, Inc.   330
Coca-Cola v. Tropicana   339
Cohen v. California   23
Cohen v. Cowles Media   392
Columbia Pictures v. Miramax   320
Comedy III Production v. Saderup   197
Commonwealth v. Pittsburgh Press Co.   333
Cook v. Northern California Collection Service   343
Cox Broadcasting v. Cohn   184
Craig v. Harney   13
Cruz v. Ferre   270
Curtis Publishing Co. v. Butts   160

DeFilippo v. NBC   224
Dennis v. U.S.   21
Denver Area Educational Telecommunications Consortium v. FCC   272
Desnick v. ABC   206
Deteresa v. ABC   209
Diaz v. Oakland Tribune   188
Dietemann v. Time   202

Dillon v. San Francisco — 390
Disney v. Shannon — 223
Doe v. Franco Productions — 186
Doe v. GTE — 187
Doe v. University of Michigan — 27
Doe 2 v. Associated Press — 184
Dr. Seuss Enterprises v. Penguin Books — 319
Duncan v. WJLA-TV — 191

Eastern Educational Radio (WUHY-FM) — 256
Edwards v. Audubon and New York Times — 163
Eldred v. Ashcroft — 292
Elsmere Music v. NBC — 317
Engler v. Winfrey — 167
Esposito-Hilder v. SFX Broadcasting Inc. — 168
Estes v. Texas — 360

Farmers Educ. and Coop. Union of Am. v. WDAY — 50
FCC v. Midwest Video (Midwest Video II) — 78
FCC v. National Citizens Committee for Broadcasting — 107
FCC v. Pacifica — 235
Feist v. Rural Telephone — 315
Fisher v. Dees — 318
Florida Publishing Co. v. Fletcher — 179
Florida Star v. B.J.F. — 184
Flynt v. Rumsfeld — 420
Flynt v. Weinberger — 418
Fogerty v. Fantasy — 306
Food Lion v. ABC — 208
Fortnightly v. United Artists — 82
Liquormart v. Rhode Island — 354
Fox Television v. FCC — 114
FTC v. Colgate-Palmolive — 345
FTC v. Garvey — 345

Galella v. Onassis — 182
Gannett v. DePasquale — 364
Georgia Television Company v. Television News Clips of Atlanta — 312
Gertz v. Welch — 157
Gill v. Curtis — 174
Gill v. Hearst — 177
Gillett Communications of Atlanta, Inc. v. Becker — 51
Ginsberg v. New York — 246
Gitlow v. New York — 20
Globe Newspaper Co. v. Superior Court — 185
Gonzalez v. NBC — 386
Gooding v. Wilson — 23

Grand Upright Music v. Warner Brothers 309
Graves v. Warner Brothers 228
Greater New Orleans Broadcasting Association v. U.S. 348
Group W Television v. Maryland 376

Haelen Laboratories v. Topps Chewing Gum 194
Hamling v. U.S. 250
Hanlon v. Berger 215
Harper & Row v. Nation 308
Heffron v. Krishna 32
Herbert v. Lando 155
Herceg v. Hustler 225
Hess v. Indiana 22
Hoffman v. Capital Cities/ABC 197
Holliday v. CNN 313
Holman v. Central Arkansas Broadcasting 180
Home Box Office (HBO) v. FCC 75
Houchins v. KQED 411
Huskey v. NBC 181
Hustler v. Falwell 168
Hyde v. City of Columbia 409

Idaho v. Salsbury 388
Ignatow v. Commonwealth of Kentucky 12
Illinois Citizens Committee for Broadcasting v. FCC 257
In re Michael Stone, Robert Knaus, and the Boulder Daily Camera 381
In the matter of complaints against various broadcast
     licensees regarding the airing of The Golden Globes program 264
Information Providers' Coalition for Defense of the First Amendment v. FCC 275
Italian Book Corp. v. ABC 310

Jacobellis v. Ohio 235
James v. Meow Media 231
JB Pictures, Inc., v. Department of Defense 422
in re J.D.C. 365
Johnny Carson v. Here's Johnny Portable Toilets 198
Judas Priest v. Vance 233

Katz v. U.S. 203
Keeton v. Hustler 170
Kennedy for President Committee v. FCC 56
Key Publications v. Chinatown Today 316
King Broadcasting Co. v. FCC 57
KUTV v. Conder 372
KUTV v. Wilkinson 372

Lamprecht v. FCC 41
Lawson v. Dixon 416

Le Mistral v. CBS | 217
Leibovitz v. Paramount Pictures | 320
Leverton v. Curtis | 190
Long v. IRS | 399
Los Angeles News Service v. KCAL-TV | 313
Los Angeles News Service v. Reuters | 314
Luke Records Inc. v. Navarro | 251
Lutheran Church-Missouri Synod v. FCC | 40

Marbury v. Madison | 7
Marich v. QRZ Media | 216
Mark v. KING | 177
Marketos v. American Employers Insurance | 387
Masson v. New Yorker | 169
McCollum v. CBS | 231
McConnell v. FEC | 59
McKevitt v. Pallasch | 388
McNamara v. Freedom Newspapers | 187
MD/DC/DE Broadcasters Association v. FCC | 40
Medical Laboratory Management Consultants v. ABC | 205
Memoirs v. Massachusetts | 239
Meredith Corporation v. FCC | 67
Metro Broadcasting v. FCC | 41
MGM v. Grokster | 326
MGM v. Showcase Atlanta | 317
Michigan United Conservation Club v. CBS | 171
Miami Herald v. Tornillo | 63
Midler v. Ford Motor Co. | 199
Milkovich v. Lorain Journal Co. | 165
Miller v. California | 235
Miller v. NBC | 212
Missouri Knights of the Ku Klux Klan v. Kansas City | 80
Montana v. Mercury News | 195
Murray Hill Publications v. ABC Communications | 311

NAACP v. Button | 154
Namath v. Sports Illustrated | 195
Nation Magazine v. Department of Defense | 419
National Archives and Records Administration v. Favish | 403
NBA v. Motorola | 315
NBC v. CWA | 416
NBC v. U.S. | 101
NBC Subsidiary v. Superior Court | 374
Near v. Minnesota | 28
Nebraska Press Association v. Stuart | 371
Neff v. Time | 187
Neiman-Marcus v. Lait | 172
New Kids on the Block v. News America Publishing, Inc. | 328

New York v. Ferber   247
New York Times v. NASA   402
New York Times v. Sullivan   152
New York Times v. Tasini   291
New York Times v. U.S.   30
Nixon v. Warner Communications   376
Nobody in Particular Presents, Inc., v. Clear Channel   111
Novartis Corp. v. FTC   339

Olivia N. v. NBC   222
Ollman v. Evans   164
One Book Entitled 'Ulysses' v. U.S.   237
Osbourne v. Ohio   248
Osby v. A&E   191

Pacifica v. FCC   257
In re Palmetto Broadcasting Co.   256
Paris Adult Theater v. Slaton   245
Parker v. Boyer   213
Pathfinder Communications Corp. v. Midwest Communications Co.   329
Paulsen v. FCC   47
Pavesich v. New England Life Insurance Co.   175
Peavy v. WFAA-TV   178
Pell v. Procunier   410
Pennekamp v. Florida   394
Phoenix Newspapers v. District Court   375
Pinkard v. Johnson   390
Pinkus v. U.S.   243
Pittsburgh Press v. Pittsburgh Commission on Human Relations   333
Pittsburgh Press II   333
Pizza Hut v. Papa John's   342
Planned Parenthood v. American Coalition of Life Activists   234
Playboy v. Frena   327
Playboy v. Welles   331
Playboy Enterprises v. Sanfilippo   327
Posadas v. Tourism Co. of Puerto Rico   346
Pottstown Daily News Publishing v. Pottstown Broadcasting   315
Press-Enterprise v. Superior Court (P-E I)   373
Press-Enterprise v. Superior Court (P-E II)   374

Quality King Distributors v. L'Anza Research International   320
Quincy Cable v. FCC   70

R.A.V. v. St. Paul   25
Red Lion Broadcasting v. FCC   67
Regina v. Hicklin   236
Reno v. ACLU   276

Reno v. Condon 415
Renton v. Playtime 243
RIAA v. Diamond Multimedia Systems 321
RIAA v. Verizon 322
Richmond Newspapers v. Virginia 364
Rideau v. Louisiana 361
Riley v. Chester 383
Roberson v. Rochester Folding Box Co. 175
Rosenbloom v. Metromedia 156
Roth v. U.S. 237
RTNDA v. FCC 67
Rubin v. Coors 354

Sable Communications v. FCC 274
Sailor Music v. Mai Kai of Concord, Inc. 304
Sakon v. Pepsico 226
Sanders v. ABC 205
Saxbe v. Washington Post 410
Schenck v. U.S. 19
Seelig v. Infinity Broadcasting 159
Sheppard v. Maxwell 362
Shoen v. Shoen 384
Shulman v. Group W. Productions 204
Sinatra v. Goodyear 200
Sipple v. Chronicle 189
Smith v. California 205
Smith v. Daily Mail Publishing Co. 185
Sonderling Broadcasting Corp. 257
SONY Corp. of America v. Universal Cities Studios Inc. 308
Soundgarden v. Eikenberry 247
Southern Rhode Island Public Radio Broadcasting, Inc. 356
Spin Doctors v. Miller Brewing Co. 301
Stanley v. Georgia 239
Sussman v. ABC 206
Syracuse Peace Council v. FCC 68

Telecommunications Research Action Committee v. FCC 67
Teleprompter v. U.S. 82
Texas v. Johnson 27
321 Studios v. MGM Studios 326
Time v. Firestone 158
Time Warner v. FCC 117
Time Warner Entertainment v. FCC 87
Times Mirror Co. v. Superior Court of San Diego County 409
Titan Sports v. Turner Broadcasting 389
Titan Sports v. Turner Broadcasting (in re Madden) 309
Toys "R" Us, Inc. v. Akkaoui 330

Trinity Methodist Church South v. Federal Radio Commission 225
In re T.R. 365
Turner Broadcasting v. FCC (Turner I) 85
Turner Broadcasting v. FCC (Turner II) 85

U-Haul International v. Jartran 340
Ulysses v. U.S. 237
UMG Recordings v. MP.com 12
U.S. v. American Library Association 279
U.S. v. Burke 384
U.S. v. CNN 372
U.S. v. Cooper 18
U.S. v. Criden 386
U.S. v. Cuthbertson 386
U.S. v. Cutler 000
U.S. v. Edge 348
U.S. v. Eichman 28
U.S. v. Home Shopping Network 28
U.S. v. Hubbard 383
U.S. v. Kaczynski 375
U.S. v. Miami University 414
U.S. v. Midwest Video 73
U.S. v. Moussaoui 73
U.S. v. Nelson Brothers 37
U.S. v. Nixon 376
U.S. v. One Package 236
U.S. v. Playboy 245
U.S. v. Progressive 271
U.S. v. Reidel 31
U.S. v. Southwestern Cable 240
U.S. v. Storer Broadcasting 72
U.S. v. Thirty-Seven Photographs 240
U.S. v. Thomas 252
U.S. v. X-Citement Video Inc. 248
U.S. v. Zenith Radio Corporation 36

Valentine v. Chrestensen 332
Valley Broadcasting v. District Court 376
Vaughn v. Rosen 399
Video-Cinema Films, Inc., v. CNN 311
Village of Skokie v. National Socialist Party 24
Virginia v. Black 25
Virginia State Board of Pharmacy v. Virginia Citizens Consumer Council 334

Ward v. Rock Against Racism 33
Warner-Lambert Co. v. FTC 339
Weirum v. RKO 222

Wendt v. Host International 196
White v. Samsung Electronics America, Inc. 196
Whitney v. California 20
Wilkins v. NBC 210
Wilson v. Layne 213
Wisconsin v. Mitchell 26
Wolfson v. Lewis 218
Wolston v. Reader's Digest 159
WREC Broadcasting Services 256
WTVY v. United States Postal Service 403

Yates v. U.S. 22
Young v. American Mini-Theatres 243

Zachinni v. Scripps-Howard Broadcasting 194
Zamora v. CBS 225
Zeran v. Diamond Broadcasting Inc. 192
Zerilli v. Smith 382
Zurcher v. Stanford Daily 391

Appendix

The FCC Inspection

The following checklist is provided by the FCC and reprinted here as a guide for broadcast stations. Read through this checklist and see if your station would pass an FCC inspection. As we have seen throughout this book, the FCC is serious about handing out fines for violations of its rules.

Federal Communications Commission's Self-Inspection Checklist

Developed by Ronald Ramage
Kansas City Office
Compliance and Information Bureau

March 1997

Y = *Yes*. The station is in compliance with this item.

P = The station is not in compliance with this item. Corrective action is *pending*.

N/A = *Not applicable* to this station. If this response is not provided, then this question is applicable to all FM stations.

1. Y P   *Authorizations:* Are current station authorizations posted or readily available at the principal control point for the station?

2. Y P   *Logs/Records:* Are required station logs retained for a period of 2 years? (See 73.1840[a].)

3. Y P   *Availability:* Are station logs/records readily available for inspection and/or duplication at the request of the FCC or its representatives? (See 73.1225 and 73.1226.)

4. Y P N/A   *Equipment Performance Measurements:* Are the latest Equipment Performance Measurements maintained and readily available? (See 73.1590 [a].)

5. Y P   *Chief Operator Designation:* Has the licensee designated a person to serve as the station chief operator? (See 73.1870 [a & b].)

6. Y P   *Designation Posting:* Is the designation in writing with a copy of the document posted or readily available? (See 73.1870 [b].)

7. Y P   *Station Log Review:* Does the station's chief operator review the station logs *at least once each week* to determine if required entries are being made? (See 73.1870 [c].)

8. Y P   *Signing Station Logs:* Does the chief operator or a designee date and sign the logs upon completion of the weekly review of these documents? (See 73.1870 [c].)

9. Y P   *Identification:* Is the station identification made in accordance with 73.1201?

10. Y P   *Telephone Access:* Does the station maintain a local or toll-free telephone number in its community of license? (See 73.1125 [c].)

11. Y P   *File Maintained:* Does the station maintain a public inspection file in accordance with 73.3526 (d) or 73.3527 (d)?

12. Y P   *Availability:* Is the file available for public inspection at any time during regular business hours? (See 73.3526 [d] or 73.3527 [d].)

13. Y P   *Location:* Would a member of the public be correctly informed of the location of the public file upon contacting the station personnel at the main studio? (See 73.3526 [d] or 73.3527 [d].)

14. Y P   *Photocopying:* Are copies of any material required to be in the public file available for machine reproduction upon request made in person? (See 73.3526 [f] or 73.3527 [f].)

15. Y P   *Applications:* Does the public file contain copies of all applications, exhibits, letters, initial and final decisions in hearing cases, and other documents pertaining to the station which were filed with the Commission and which are open for public inspection at the FCC? (See 73.3526 [a] or 73.3527 [a].)

16. Y P N/A   *Ownership Reports:* For station licensees who are not sole proprietorships, does the public file contain copies of annual ownership reports and supplemental ownership reports filed with the Commission, including all exhibits, letters, and other documents associated with these filings? (See 73.3526 [a] [3] and 73.3527 [a] [3].)

17. Y P N/A   *Ownership Information:* For noncommercial stations, does the ownership information on file with the Commission reflect the current ownership (board members, officers, etc.) of this station? (See 73.3527 [a] [3] and 73.3615 [e & f].)

18. Y P N/A   *Retention of Ownership Reports:* Are ownership reports retained for the Term of the License? (See 73.3526 [e] or 73.3527 [e].)

19. Y P N/A   *Political:* Does the licensee have a complete record of all requests for broadcast time made by or on behalf of candidates for public office, together with an appropriate notation showing the disposition made by the licensee of such requests, and the charges made, if any, if the request was granted? (See 73.1943 and either 73.3526 [a] [4] or 73.3527 [a] [4].)

20. Y P N/A   *Free Political Time:* If free time was provided for use by or on behalf of such candidates, has a record of the free time that was provided been placed into the file? (See 73.1943 and either 73.3526 [a] [4] or 73.3527 [a] [4].)

21. Y P N/A *Retention of Political Records:* Are these records retained for a period of 2 years? (See 73.3526 [e] or 73.3527 [e].)

22. Y P N/A *Employment Reports:* For stations employing five or more full-time employees, has the licensee filed an annual employment report on FCC Form 395 on or before May 31st of each year and placed copies of each report in the public file? (See 73.3526 [a] [5] or 73.3527 [a] [5] and 73.3612.)

23. Y P N/A *Retention of Employment Reports:* Are employment reports retained for the Term of the License? (See 73.3526 [e] or 73.3527 [e].)

24. Y P N/A *Letters From the Public:* For commercial stations, does the licensee retain all written comments and suggestions received from the public regarding operation of their station unless the writer requested that the correspondence not be made public or the licensee felt that it must be excluded because of the nature of its content, such as a defamatory or obscene letter? (See 73.1202 and 73.3526 [a] [7].)

25. Y P N/A Retention of Letters: For commercial stations, are all letters retained for 3 years from the date received? (See 73.3526 [e].)

26. Y P *Issues-Program Lists:* Has the licensee maintained a list of programs that have provided the station's most significant treatment of community issues during the *preceding* calendar quarter? (See 73.3526 [a] [9] or 73.3527 [a] [7].)

27. Y P *Filed Quarterly:* Was the issues-programs list filed by the 10th day of the succeeding calendar quarter (e.g., January 10, April 10, July 10, or October 10)? (See 73.3526 [a] [9] or 73.3527 [a] [7].)

28. Y P *Narratives:* Do the issues-programs lists include a brief narrative describing what issues were given significant treatment and the programming that provided this treatment? (See 73.35265 [a] [9] or 73.3527 [a] [7].)

29. Y P *Descriptions:* Does the description of the programs include at a minimum the *time, date, duration,* and *title* of each program in which the issue was treated? (See 73.3526 [a] [9] or 73.3527 [a] [7].)

30. Y P *Retention of Issues-Programs Lists:* Are the issues-programs lists retained for the term of the license? (See 73.3526 [e] or 73.3527 [e].)

31. Y P N/A *Donor Lists:* For noncommercial stations, does the licensee maintain a list of donors supporting specific programs? (See 73.3527 [a] [8].)

32. Y P N/A *Retention of Donor Lists:* For noncommercial stations, does the licensee retain such donor list(s) for a period of 2 years? (See 73.3527 [e].)

33. Y P N/A *Time Brokerage Agreements:* Does the public file contain a copy of every agreement or contract involving time brokerage of the licensee's station, or of another station, by the licensee? Confidential or proprietary information may be removed. (See 73.3526 [a] [12].)

34. Y P N/A *Retention of Time Brokerage Agreements:* Are these records maintained as long as the contract or agreement is in force? (See 73.3526.)

35. Y P N/A *SCA Agreements:* Are all subchannel leasing agreements maintained and available at the station? (See 73.1226 [c] [2].)

36. Y P N/A *Registration:* Has the owner of the tower on which the station antenna is mounted obtained registration for the structure?

37. Y P N/A *Posting of Number:* Has the registration number been posted in an easily viewed location at the tower site?

38. Y P *Overall Height:* Does the overall height of the structure match that specified in the station authorization?

39. Y P *Antenna:* Does the number and height of the antenna bays match that specified in the station authorization?

40. Y P *Location:* Does the street address and geographical coordinates of the station transmitter/tower location match exactly with the information shown on the station authorization?

41. Y P N/A *Observations:* Is the lighting on the tower(s) observed at least once every 24 hours, either visually or by observing an automatic indicating device; or, alternatively, has the licensee/tower owner provided and maintained an automatic alarm system? (See 17.47.)

42. Y P N/A *Alarm Maintenance Checks:* If utilizing an automatic alarm system, have all automatic or mechanical control devices, indicators, and alarm systems been inspected within the last 3 months? (See 17.47.)

43. Y P N/A *Paint Specifications:* Does the painting on the tower structure(s) match the specifications in the station authorization?

44. Y P N/A *Paint Bands:* Does the structure have the correct number of bands, and are the top and bottom bands painted orange? (See Part 17.)

45. Y P N/A *Lighting Specifications:* Does the lighting on the tower structure match exactly with the specifications in the station authorization?

46. Y P N/A *FAA Notification:* Is the licensee and all station operators aware of the requirement to notify the nearest FAA Flight Service Station within 30 minutes of the observation of an outage *and* to notify the FAA again once the outage is corrected? (See 17.48.)

47. Y P N/A *Station Logs:* Does the licensee/tower owner maintain a station log containing entries concerning *any* observed or otherwise known extinguishment or improper functioning of *any* tower light? (See 17.49, 73.1213, and 73.1820 [a] [1] [i].)

48. Y P *Participating:* Does the management of this station know whether the station is a participating or nonparticipating EAS station?

49. Y P *Handbook/Authenticator List:* Does the station have an EAS Operating Handbook *and* a current authenticator word list posted or available at *each* EAS control point utilized during any portion of the broadcast day? (See 11.15 and 11.17.)

50. Y P *Certified Equipment:* Does the station use only certified equipment at each location utilized for EAS monitoring? (See 11.34.)

51. Y P *Equipment Status:* Is the required EAS decoding/receiving equipment currently installed and in operational condition? (See 11.35.)

52. Y P N/A *Instantaneous Alert Reception:* For manually operated EAS decoding equipment, is the decoder installed in a way that enables broadcast station staff to be alerted *instantaneously* upon receipt of an activation occurring during *any portion of your broadcast operation?* (See 11.52.)

53. Y P *Monitoring Assigned Station:* Is the EAS decoder/monitor tuned to receive EAS activations from the monitoring priorities named in the EAS Operating Handbook or State EAS plan? (See 11.52 and the EAS Operating Handbook.)

54. Y P N/A *Certified Equipment:* Does the station maintain certified equipment capable of generating the EAS protocol to modulate the transmitter so that the signal may be broadcast to other receiving stations? (See 11.34.)

55. Y P N/A *Equipment Status:* Is the required EAS encoding/generating equipment currently installed and operational at this station? (See 11.35.)

56. Y P N/A *Location:* For manually operated equipment, is the equipment positioned where responsible broadcast staff can initiate an activation during any portion of the broadcast day? (See 11.51.)

57. Y P N/A *Conduct EAS Tests:* Does the station conduct RWT/RMT transmission tests of the EAS header and EOM codes a minimum of once a week at random days and times? (See 11.61 [a].)

58. Y P N/A *Receipt of EAS Tests:* Did the station receive two EAS test activations during the last full calendar week from its two assigned EAS monitoring sources? (See 11.61 [a].)

59. Y P *Station Logs Maintained:* Does the licensee maintain a station log containing an entry of each test (both sent and received) of the Emergency Alert System? (See 11.51 [j], 11.52 [e], and 73.1820 [a] [1] [iii].)

60. Y P *Failure to Receive EAS Test:* Does the station log contain appropriate entries indicating the reasons why required EAS Weekly/Monthly Test Transmissions were not received? If all tests have been received and logged during the last 2-year period, then the appropriate response is yes (Y). (See 11.35 [a].)

61. Y P *Equipment Outage:* Does the station log contain appropriate entries documenting the date and time any EAS equipment was removed and/or restored to service? If there have been no such outages in the last 2 years, then the appropriate response is yes (Y). (See 11.35 [b].)

62. Y P N/A *Operating Power:* Is the station's operating power between 90% and 105% of the authorized? (See 73.1560.)

63. Y P N/A *Efficiency Factor:* Is the efficiency factor known for each transmitter used and a record kept as to its value, along with the source from which this value was determined? (See 73.267 [c].)

64. Y P *Frequency:* Is the station in compliance with the frequency tolerance specified in 73.1545?

65. Y P *Modulation:* Is the station in compliance with the modulation limits specified in 73.1570 (b)?

66. Y P *Control:* Does the equipment at this station allow transmitter control of turning off the transmitter at any time the station is in operation? (See 73.1350 [b] [2].)

67. Y P   *Operating Parameters:* Does the licensee maintain necessary metering to determine compliance with power and modulation? (See 73.1350 [c].)

68. Y P   *Schedules:* Has the licensee established procedures and schedules for monitoring the power and modulation at this station? (See 73.1350 [c] [1].)

69. Y P   *Calibration:* Has the licensee established procedures and schedules for conducting periodic inspection of the transmitting system and all monitors and to periodically calibrate these devices? (See 73.1350 [c] and 73.1580.)

70. Y P   *Logging:* Are the results of such calibration entered into the station log? (See 73.1820 [a] [2] [iii].)

71. Y N/A   *Unattended:* Does the station utilize self-monitoring or ATS type equipment that will take the station off the air within 3 hours of any technical malfunction capable of interference? (See 73.1400 [b].)

72. Y P N/A   *Attended:* If the station is not utilizing self-monitoring or ATS type equipment that will take the station off the air within 3 hours of a malfunction, then is there a person on duty at a fixed location during all periods that the station is on the air where they can either control the station themselves or be contacted by the automated equipment?

73. Y P N/A   *Notification:* Has the licensee notified the Mass Media Bureau in writing of the location of all transmission system control points other than the main studio or transmitter location? (See 73.1350 [g].)

74. Y P N/A   *Station Records:* Is a copy of this notification available in the station records?

75. Y   N/A   *LMA Status:* Has this station been engaged in a time brokerage agreement during any portion of the current term of the station authorization?

76. Y P N/A   *Filing:* Has the licensee submitted a copy of the LMA to the FCC within 30 days of execution of the agreement?

77. Y P N/A   *Lists:* Has the licensee provided a list of all contracts in effect along with the annual ownership report?

78. Y P   *Control:* Has the licensee maintained control over the station?

79. Y P   *Presence:* Does the licensee maintain full-time managerial and staff personnel at the station during normal business hours when the station is brokered?

Index

A&E Networks, 191-192
Abortion
  and advertising law, 334
  political ads, 51-52
  Web site, copycat case, 233-234
Action for Children's Television, 260
Adams, John, 18
Administrative law, 3-4
Advertising law, 332-358
  abortion ads, 234
  alcohol ads, 353-355
  broadcast lottery ads, 347-349
  Central Hudson case, 335-336
  cigarettes, 349-353
  false advertising, 336-346
  Federal Trade Commission, role, 336
  Food and Drug Administration, role, 336
  gambling, 346-349
  hard liquor ads, 354
  newspaper want ads, 333-334
  prescription drug ads, 334
  spam e-mail, 357-358
  telemarketing, 357
  tobacco settlement of 1998, 352-353
  underwriting, 355-356
Afghanistan war, 420
ALA. See American Library Association
Alcohol advertising, 353-355
Alien and Sedition Acts of 1798, 18
Amber alert, 130-131
Ambulances and privacy, 203-205
Ambush interviews, 216-218
Amendments to Constitution, 2-3
American legal system, 1-15
  courts, 5-9
  civil law, 10-12
  criminal law, 9-10
American Library Association (ALA), 279
American Society of Composers,
  Authors and Publishers (ASCAP), 293-294

Amicus curiae, 8
Aniston, Jennifer, 183
Anti-siphoning rules, cable, 74-75
Anti-trust law, 118-119
Appeals courts, federal, 6-7
Appellant, 6, 11
Arnett, Peter, 421
ASCAP. See American Society of
  Composers, Authors and Publishers
Aspen Rule, 54-57
Attorney General's Commission on Pornography
  (Meese Commission), 245-246
Audio Home Recording Act (AHRA), 297-299
Automated stations, 146
Autopsy photographs, media access, 403-404

Basketball Diaries, movie, 231
BCRA. See Bipartisan Campaign Reform
  Act of 2002
Bipartisan Campaign Reform Act of 2002
  (BCRA), 58-61
Black Panthers, 378
BMI. See Broadcast Music, Inc.
Bonaduce, Danny, 147
Bonanza theme and copyright, 300-301
Bono (U2), 264
Boone, Pat, 345
Bootleg movies, 325-326
Bork, Robert, 7
Born Innocent, TV movie, 222
Broadcast hoax rule, 136-139
Broadcast Music, Inc. (BMI), 293-296
Bubba the Love Sponge, indecency, 269
Buckley Amendment, 412
Bush, George H. W., 7
Bush, George W., 61, 296

Cable access channels, 77-81, 272
Cable Communications Policy Act of 1984, 75-76
Cable News Network (CNN), 214-215

Cable regulation, 70-90
    access channels, 77-81
    anti-siphoning rules, 74-75
    compulsory licensing, 82
    copyright, 81-82
    descramblers, 89-90
    franchising, 76-77
    indecency, 270-274
    leapfrogging, 72
    localism, 71
    may carry rules, 84
    must carry rules, 83-84
    network non-duplication rule, 89
    privacy, 81
    public inspection files, 90
    rate regulation, 86-87
    service standards, 87-88
    syndicated exclusivity, 88-89
    "signal bleed," 271-272
Cable Television Consumer Protection and
    Competition Act of 1992, 84-88
Cable Television Report and Order (1972), 74
Cameras in court, 359-375
    audio/video evidence, 376
    civil trials, 374-375
    court documents, 375
    gag orders, 370-373
    jury selection, 373
    pretrial proceedings, 373-374
    Sheppard guidelines, 363
    states, 360-361
    Supreme Court, 365-366
Campus disciplinary proceedings, 414
Campus police records, 413
Campus speech codes, 26-27
Carlin, George, 257
CARP. See Copyright Arbitration Royalties Panel
Carry one, carry all rule, 93
Carson, Johnny
    copycat case, 224
    misappropriation case, 198-199
Carter, Jimmy
    press conferences and Section 315, 56-57
    reasonable access for political ads, 64-65
Case citations, 12-14
Certificate of compliance, cable, 74
Challenger disaster, privacy, 402
Cheers TV show, 196
Cher, 196
Chief operators (broadcast stations), 131-132
Child Online Protection Act (COPA), 277-278
Child pornography, 247-248
Child Pornography Prevention Act (CPPA), 249-250
Children's Internet Protection Act (CIPA), 278-279
Children's Television Act of 1990, 284-285

Cigarette ads, 349-353
    broadcast guidelines, 350-351
    Joe Camel controversy, 351
    shams, 351-352
    Surgeon General's warnings, 350, 353
CIPA. See Children's Internet Protection Act
Citation styles for cases. See case citations
Civil contempt, 381-382
Civil law, 10-11
Clear and present danger, 19, 22
Clery Act (1998 Higher Education Act), 413-414
Clinton, Bill, 399
CNN. See Cable News Network
Code of Federal Regulations (CFR), 3
Common carrier, 38-39
Common law, 4
Communications Act of 1934, 36-37, 44, 101
Communications Decency Act (CDA), 275-277
Comparative hearings, 38
Compensatory damages, 10
Compulsory licensing (cable), 82
Compulsory licensing (music), 304
Comstock Act, 236
Confessions (videotaped), 361-362
Confidential sources, 378-391
Constitutional law, 1-3
"Content neutral," definition, 32
Contest rules (broadcast stations), 140-143
"Cop Killer" song, 280-281
COPA. See Child Online Protection Act
COPS (TV show), 215
Copycat cases, 219-234
Copyright Arbitration Royalties Panel (CARP), 324
Copyright law, 288-327
    Audio Home Recording Act (AHRA), 297-299
    basic rights, 289
    compulsory licensing (cable), 82
    compulsory licensing (music), 304
    Copyright Act of 1909, 288
    Copyright Act of 1976, 288
    copyrightable works, 288-289
    duration, 292
    fair use, 307-327
    Fairness in Music Licensing Act, 302-304
    first sale doctrine, 290
    juke boxes, 304
    mechanical rights, 295, 297-299
    music licensing, 293-304
    obtaining a copyright, 291
    performance rights, 295-297
    plagiarism, 304-305
    political rallies and copyrighted music, 296
    public domain, 292-293
    public performances, 295-296
    Sonny Bono Copyright Extension Act, 292

synchronization rights, 295, 299-302
works for hire, 290-291
See also fair use
Court system, 5-9
CPPA. *See* Child Pornography Prevention Act
Criminal law, 9-10

Dateline NBC, 210, 386-387
Dees, Rick, 318
Defamation. *See* libel
Defendant, 9, 10
Denny, Reginald, 313
Denver, John, 286
Depublishing of a court decision, 216
Descramblers (cable), 89-90
Dial-a-porn, 274-275
Digital Audio Broadcasting (DAB), 98-100
Digital Millennium Copyright Act, 320-321
Digital Radio (HD Radio), 98-100
Direct Broadcast Satellite (DBS), 93
Direct contempt, 151-152
District courts, federal, 5-6
Dole, Bob, 296
Double jeopardy, 11-12
DPPA. *See* Driver's Privacy Protection Act
Dr. Seuss, 319
Driver's Privacy Protection Act (DPPA), 414-415
Drug lyrics (broadcast stations), 140
Due process, 20
Duopoly rules, 102
DVD-copying software, 327

Earnhardt, Dale, 403
EAS. *See* Emergency Alert System
EEO rules. *See* Equal Employment
     Opportunity rules
EFOIA. *See* Electronic Freedom of Information Act
Electronic Freedom of Information Act, 400
Emergency Alert System (EAS), 128-131
     Amber alert, 130-131
Eminem, 263
en banc, definition, 6
Equal Employment Opportunity (EEO) rules, 39-43
Equal Time rule. *See* Section 315
Equity law, 4
Espionage Act of 1917, 18
Executions, media access to, 416
Executive powers, 4-5

Fahrenheit 9/11, 61
Failed/failing station, 113
Fair comment and criticism, 164-165
Fair Use, copyright, 307-327
     BBS sites, 327
     bootleg movies, 325-326

criteria, 307-308
DVD-copying software, 327
file-sharing software, 327
Internet issues, 320-327
movie clips, use in radio and
     TV segments, 310-312
Napster, 322-323
news reports, 310-315
newspaper stories used in broadcasts, 314-315
parodies, 316-319
RIAA lawsuits, 323-324
sampling of music, 309
satire, 319-320
sports scores, 315
VCRs, 308-309
video clipping services, 312
Webcasting, 324-325
Fairness Doctrine, 67-68
Fairness in Music Licensing Act, 302-304
False advertising, 336-346
False light, privacy law, 189-193
Falwell, Jerry, 167-168
Family Educational Rights and Privacy
     Act (FERPA), 412-414
Fanny Hill, 239
FECA (Federal Election Campaign Act), 58-61
Federal Communications Commission (FCC)
     adjudicating powers, 4
     auctions, 38
     bureaus, 39
     commissioners, 37-38
     construction permit, 39
     inspections. *See* appendix
     licensing, 39-43
     rule-making powers, 3
Federal Radio Commission, 36
Federal Register, 3, 38
Federal Trade Commission, role, 336
Federal Trademark Act of 1946 (Lanham Act), 328
Federal Trademark Dilution Act, 330
FERPA. *See* Family Educational
     Rights and Privacy Act
Fighting words, 23-25
"Filthy Words" monologue, 257
Financial Interest and Syndication
     Rule (Fin-syn), 104
First Amendment to the U. S. Constitution, 16
     and states, 20
Flag desecration/flag burning, 27-28
Flag Protection Act of 1989, 28
Flynt, Larry, 418, 420
Fogerty, John, 305
Food Lion, 207-208
Ford, Gerald, 159, 188
Foster, Vince, 403

Franchises, cable, 76-77
Freedom of Information Act (FOIA), 395-404
    deadline for requests, 397
    electronic FOIA, 400
    emergency requests, 397
    exemptions, 400-404
    fees, 397, 398
    Privacy Act of 1974, 412
    requests, 396
    state laws, 407-408
    Vaughn Index, 399
Freeze of 1948-1952, 103

Gag orders, 370-373
Gambling ads, 346-349
Garbage, privacy law, 201
Garvey, Steve, 344-345
Girl Scouts, copyright issue, 293
Gore, Tipper, 286
Gotti, John, 262
Grand Alliance, HDTV, 95
Grand Theft Auto, video game, 220
Grand jury, 9
Grenada conflict, 418

H-bomb case, 31
"Happy Birthday" song and copyright, 293
Harrison, George, 305
Hate Speech, 25-27
HDTV. *See* High Definition Television
HD Radio. *See* Digital Radio
Health Insurance Portability and
        Accountability Act (HIPAA), 402
Helter Skelter, song, 219
Hicklin Test (obscenity), 236
Hidden cameras and microphones, 202-211
High Definition Television (HDTV), 95-98
    deadlines, 95-96
    Grand Alliance, 95
Higher Education Act of 1998 (Clery Act), 413-414
Hill, Anita, 7
HIPAA. *See* Health Insurance Portability and
        Accountability Act
Hoaxes (broadcast stations), 136-139
Hoffman, Dustin, 196
Home Shopping Network, 341-342
Hung jury, 6
Hustler magazine
    copycat case, 225
    Falwell case, 167-168

IBOC (In-Band On-Channel),
        digital radio, 98
Ice-T, rap artist, 280-281
Illinois News Broadcasters Association, 407

Indecency, 255-279
    cable TV, 270-274
    Child Online Protection Act (COPA), 277-278
    Children's Internet Protection Act
            (CIPA), 278-279
    citizen complaints, procedure, 269-270
    Communications Decency Act (CDA), 275-277
    context, 262
    definition, 258
    fines, increased in 2004, 268-269
    Internet, 275-279
    Pacifica case, 257-258
    pay-per-view, 273
    safe harbor, 258-259, 260
    seven dirty words, 257
    shock radio, 259
    "signal bleed" on cable, 271-272
    Super Bowl 2004's "wardrobe
            malfunction," 266-267
    telephone (dial-a-porn), 274-275
    topless radio, 256-257
    2001 indecency guidelines, 261
Independent promoters, 144
Independent Regulatory Agencies (IRAs), 3
Indictment, 9
Indirect contempt, 393-394
Injunction, 4
Inside Edition, 217-218
Intentional infliction of emotional distress, 167-168
Internet
    BBS sites, 327
    Communications Decency Act (CDA), 275-277
    copyright issues, 320-327
    libraries, 278-279
    obscenity, 252-253
    trademark cases, 330-331
Iraq war, 421-422
    See also Persian Gulf War

Jackass, MTV, 228-229
Jackson, Janet, 266-267
Jails, media access, 180-181
Jefferson, Thomas, 18
Jenny Jones Show, 227-228
Joe Camel cigarette ads, 351
Jones, Sarah, 263-264
Jones, Shirley, 170
Journalist, definition of, 389-390
Judas Priest, rock group, 232-233
Jury trial, 11

Kennedy, Edward, 56-57
King, Rodney, 313
Kingsmen, "Louie, Louie" case, 251
Krishna case, 32

Ku Klux Klan
   cable access channel case, 80
   "call to action" case, 22

Lanham Act, 328
Leapfrogging, cable, 72
Legal ID, broadcast stations, 124-125
Legal reference guide, 14 (table)
Libel law, defamation, 151-173
   actual malice, 154
   deadline pressure, 160-162
   defenses against libel, 152
   direct and indirect libel, 151-152
   fair comment and criticism, 164-165
   group libel, 171-172
   intentional infliction of emotional
      distress, 167-168
   libel per quod, libel per se, 151-152
   neutral reportage, 162-164
   New York Times v. Sullivan, 152-154
   Ollman test, 165
   private citizens, 156-160
   privilege, 162-164
   public figures/officials, 156-160
   quotations, 168-169
   reckless disregard for the truth, 154, 159-160
   six elements of libel, 151
   statutes of limitations, 169-170
   tips to avoid libel, 172-173
   veggie libel, 166-167
Licenses for broadcast stations, 39-43
   EEO rules, 40-41
   minority preferences, 41
   qualifications for licensees, 39-40
   prefiling/postfiling guidelines, 42-43
   renewals, 41-42
   women preferences, 41
Life magazine, 202-203
Limbaugh, Rush, 68, 265-266, 296-297
Limited public forums, 415-416
Lindbergh kidnapping, media coverage, 359
"Live" rule (broadcast stations), 135-136
Local franchising authority (LFA), 76-77
Local-into-local service (satellite TV), 93
Local marketing agreement (LMA), 122-123
Localism. *See* cable regulation
Locke, John, 17
Logs. *See* station logs
Lotteries, broadcast, 347-349
"Louie Louie" obscenity case, 251
Low Power FM (LPFM), 119-122
Low Power TV (LPTV), 110-111
Lowest unit charge (LUC). *See* lowest unit rate
Lowest unit rate (LUR), 52-54
LUC/LUR. *See* lowest unit rate

Main studio rule (broadcast stations), 127
"Mancow" Muller, 147
McDonalds coffee case, 10
Mechanical rights (copyright), 295, 297-299
Media liability cases, 219-234
Meese Commission on obscenity, 245-246
Mickey Mouse Club, 223
Midler, Bette, 199
Military bases, media access, 421-422
Milton, John, 17
Minot, ND, train derailment, 110
Misappropriation, 193-200
Mississippi Burning, 26
Mistrial, 6
Mitchum, Robert, 311
Montana, Joe, 195
Moore, Michael, 61
Mountain Dew ad, 226
MP3 files, 321-322
MTV, 228-229
Murdoch, Rupert, 118-119
Music licensing, 293-304
Music lyrics
   "Louie Louie" case, 251
   suicide, copycat cases, 231-233
   warning labels, 285-287
Muslim mosque loudspeakers, 33-34
Must-carry rules. *See* cable regulation

Namath, Joe, 195
Napster, 322-323
National Public Radio, 160
Natural Born Killers, movie, 229-230
Nazi parade case, 24
Network Non-Duplication Rule, 64-65, 80, 94
Network ownership rules, 102-103, 112
Neutral reportage, 162-164
Newsroom searches, 391-392
Nixon, Richard, 30, 401
Nonconfidential sources, shield laws, 386-389
Nonpublic forums, 416
Notice of Inquiry, 38
Notice of Proposed Rulemaking, 38

Obscenity, 235-254
   child pornography, 247-248
   Child Pornography Prevention
      Act (1996), 249-250
   colonial laws, 236
   community standards, 238-239, 242-243
   Comstock Act, 236
   disclaimers, 245
   Hicklin Test, 236
   Internet, 252-253
   "Louie Louie" case, 251

Meese Commission, 245-246
Miller Test, 241-242
patently offensive, definition, 242
Presidential Commission on Obscenity
    and Pornography (PCOP), 240-241
Roth Test, 238
serious value, definition, 244
variable obscenity laws, 246-247
zoning laws, 243-244
See also pornography
Oklahoma City bombing, 192, 366
Onassis, Jacqueline, 181-182
Open meetings laws, 405-408
Orlando Sentinel, 403
Osbourne, Ozzy, 231-232
Ownership rules, 101-123
    anti-trust laws, 118-119
    biennial review, 112
    cable ownership (national rules), 116
    cable/broadcast cross-ownership rule, 105
    duopoly rules, 102
    freeze of 1948, 103
    minority ownership, 105
    network rules, 112
    network-cable ownership, 112
    newspaper-broadcast cross-ownership, 106-107
    radio ownership limits (1996), 108-112
    radio-TV cross-ownership, 105-106
    Report on Chain Broadcasting (1941), 102
    rule of sevens, 104
    rule of twelves, 105
    satellite TV-cable cross-ownership, 107-108
    telephone-cable cross-ownership, 112
    TV duopoly rule, 104
    2003 rules revisions, 113-117

Paducah school shooting, 230-231
Paparazzi, 182-183
    Parents Music Resource Center (PMRC), 286
Parodies (copyright), 316-319
Payola, 143-144
PCOP. *See* Presidential Commission
    on Pornography
Pentagon Papers, 29-30
Performance rights (copyright), 295-297
Persian Gulf War, 418-419
Personal attack rule, 66-67
Pied piper lawsuits. *See* copycat cases
Petition of certiorari, 8
Pirate broadcasting, 121
Plaintiff, 10
Planned Parenthood, 234
Playboy magazine, 327, 331
Plugola, 144-145
PMRC. *See* Parents Music Resource Center

Political broadcasting rules. *See* Section 315
Political editorial rule, 66-67
Political file, broadcast stations, 62
Pornography
    child pornography, 247-248
    Child Pornography Prevention
        Act (1996), 249-250
    Children's Internet Protection
        Act (CIPA), 278-279
    colonial laws, 236
    Internet, 252-253, 275-279
    Meese Commission, 245-246
    Presidential Commission on Obscenity and
        Pornography (PCOP), 240-241
Postfiling guidelines, broadcast stations, 42-43
Power readings (broadcast stations), 127
Precedents, 4
Prefiling guidelines, broadcast stations, 42-43
Preliminary hearing, 10
Presidential Commission on Obscenity and
    Pornography (PCOP), 240-241
Press pools, 418-421
PrimeTime Live, 207-208
Princess Diana, 182
Prior restraint, 28-30
Prisons, media access, 180-181, 410-411
Privacy Act of 1974, 175, 412
Privacy law, 174-201
    crime and disaster scenes, 179-180
    disclosure of embarrassing private
        facts, 186-189
    false light, 189-193
    intrusion, 176-185
    jails/prisons, 180-181
    juveniles' names, 185
    misappropriation, 193-200
    public figures, 181-183
    right of publicity test, 197
    sexual assault/rape victims' names, 183-185
    tips about privacy law, 200-201
    video voyeurism, 186-187
Privacy Protection Act of 1980, 392
Privilege, libel, 162-164
Program, The, movie, 220
Progressive magazine, 31
Promissory estoppel, 393
Protection of Children Against Exploitation Act, 247
Public airwaves, definition, 36-37
Public inspection file
    broadcast stations, 132-134
    cable operators, 90
Public forums, 415-416
Public Health Cigarette Smoking Act, 349
Public interest standard, 36
Public interest, convenience, and necessity, 36-37

Puffery, 337, 342-344
Punitive damages, 10

Qualified privilege, 383

Radio Act of 1912, 35
Radio Act of 1927, 35, 36, 44
Radio spectrum, 35
Rap sheets, media access, 411-412
Rape victims and privacy, 183-185
Rating system, TV, 281-283
Reader's Digest, 158-159
Reagan, Ronald, 7, 219, 418
Real Don Steele, DJ, 221-222
Reasonable Access Rule. *See* Section 312 (a) (7)
Reasonable doubt, 10
Reckless disregard for the truth. *See* libel
Regulatory capture, 92
Report and Order, FCC, 38
Report on Chain Broadcasting (1941), 102
Respondent, 6, 11
Restrictive orders. *See* gag orders
RIAA (Recording Industry Association of America)
    lawsuits, 323-324
Ride-alongs and newsgathering, 211-216
Rivera, Geraldo, 421
Roth Test for obscenity, 238
Rule of Sevens, Rule of Twelves, 104-105
Rumsfeld, Donald, 420

Safe harbor, indecency, 258-259, 260
Sampling of music, 309
Satellite Home Viewer Act of 1988, 93
Satellite Home Viewer Improvement
    Act of 1999 (SHVIA), 93-94
Satellite radio, 91-93
Satellite TV, 93-94
    carry one, carry all, 93
    sports blackout rule, 94
    syndicated exclusivity, 94
satire, copyright law, 319-320
Saturday Night Live, 317
Scarcity rationale, 37
Schwarzenegger, Arnold, 48
Scienter, obscenity, 250
SCMS. *See* Serial Copy Management System
Section 312 (a) (7)(Reasonable Access Rule), 63-66
    campaign season, signs it has begun, 65
    Carter-Mondale campaign, 64-65
Section 315 (Equal Time Rule), 43-63
    abortion ads, 51-52
    Aspen Rule, 54-57
    ballot issues, 62-63
    celebrity candidates, 47-49
    censorship of political ads, 50-52

deadlines, 45
debates, 54-57
equal time/equal opportunities, 45
legally qualified candidates, 46
libel in political ads, 50-51
lowest unit rate (LUR), 52-54
news exemptions, 44, 54
newspapers, 63
political file, 62
press conferences, 56-57
primaries, 49-50
satellite broadcasts, 45
sponsorship ID, 58
talk shows, 57-58
uses, 46-50
Zapple rule, 46
Sedition, 16-19
Sedition Act of 1918, 18-19
September 11 terrorist attacks
    airplane video copyright, 312-313
    detainees' names, 404
    media credentials, 406-407
    Moussaoui trial, 367
    sunshine laws, 406
Serial Copy Management System (SCMS), 297
SESAC. *See* Society of European
    Stage Authors and Composers
Seven Dirty Words, 257
7-7-7 rule, 94
Sheppard, Sam, murder trial, 362-364
Shield laws, 378-391
Sidle Commission press guidelines for wartime, 418
Simpson, O. J., 9, 10, 209, 319
Sinatra, Nancy, 200
Sirius satellite radio, 91-93, 267
60 Minutes, TV program, 155-156, 386
Slander, definition, 151
Smith Act, 21-22
Society of European Stage Authors and Composers
    (SESAC), 293-296
Soliciting of funds (broadcast stations), 146
Sonny Bono Copyright Extension Act, 292
Spam e-mail, 357-358
Spezzano, Johnny, DJ, 149
Sponsorship identification, 145
Sports blackout rules, 94
Sports Illustrated, *187*
"Stand by your ad" disclaimer, BCRA, 59-60
Stanford Daily, 391
Stare decisis, 4
Station ID, 124-125
Station logs, 126-127
Statutory law, 3
Stern, Howard, 260-261, 269
Stewart Test for shield laws, 380

Stone, Oliver, 229-230
Subliminal ads, 145
Subpoena, 11
Suicide, and music lyrics, 231-233
Summary judgment, 11
Sunshine Act, federal, 405
Sunshine laws, 405-410
   agencies affected, federal, 395
   closed meetings, 405-406
   Congress, 395
   exemptions, 405-406
   "meeting" defined, 407
   state laws, 407-408
Superstations, 94
Supreme Court, U.S., structure of, 7-9
Synchronization rights, 295, 299-303
Syndicated exclusivity rule (Syndex), 88-89, 94
   satellite TV, 94
Syndication, 104
Syracuse Peace Council, 68

Taxi Driver, movie, 219
Telecommunications Act of 1996,
   108-113, 243-245, 249
   Communications Decency Act, 275-277
Telemarketing, 357
Telephone booths and privacy, 203
Telephone rules (broadcast stations), 134-135, 146
Testimonials (advertising), 302, 308-309
Thomas, Clarence, 7
Three Stooges, 197-198
Timberlake, Justin, 266-267
Time, Place and Manner restrictions,
   31-34, 243-244
Titanic sinking and radio, 35
Title 47, Federal Register, 38
Tobacco settlement of 1998, 352-353
Topless radio, 256-257
Tort law, 10-12
Toys "R" Us, 330
Trademark law, 328-331
   abandoned trademarks, 329
   dilution, 330-331
   radio station names, 329
   TV show names, 230
Traditional public forums, 415

Transformative work, defined, 198
TV intoxication, 225-226
TV ratings system, 281-282
12-12-12 rule, 94
2 LiveCrew
   obscenity case, 251-252
   parody case, 318-319

Ulysses, book, 237
Unattended broadcast stations, 146
Underwriting, 355-356
University grades, media access, 413
University police records, 413

Vanilla Ice, 309
Variable obscenity laws, 246-247
Vaughn Index (FOIA), 399
V-Chip, 281-283
VCR use, copyright, 308-309
Veggie libel, 166-167
Video voyeurism, 186-187
Videotaped evidence, media access to, 376
Vietnam War, 417
Violence in the media, regulation of, 280-283

War coverage, 417-422
Warhol, Andy, 198
Warning labels, music, 285-287
WCW (World Championship Wrestling), 389
Webcasting, 324-325
White, Vanna, 196
Winfrey, Oprah, 167
Workplaces and privacy, 205-206
World War I, 18, 417
World War II, 21-22, 417
World Wide Web. *See* Internet
Writ of certiorari, 7

XM Satellite radio, 91-93

Yankovich, Weird Al, 316

Zappa, Frank, 286, 287
Zapple rule, 46
Zenger, John Peter, 17
Zoning laws, pornography, 243-244

ABOUT THE AUTHOR

Dr. Roger L. Sadler is Full Professor in the Department of Communication–Broadcasting at Western Illinois University in Macomb. He has been at WIU since 1990. Before that, he was an associate instructor at Indiana University and an instructor at the University of Central Oklahoma. He has a BA in Communications/English from the State University of New York at Plattsburgh, an MA in Journalism from the University of Missouri, and a PhD in Mass Communication from Indiana University. He has worked in the broadcasting field since 1979, when he got his first on-air job at his hometown radio station in Gouverneur, New York. Since then, he has worked as a DJ, producer, news reporter, news anchor, and faculty adviser at more than a dozen radio and TV stations in New York, Missouri, Oklahoma, Indiana, and Illinois. Presently, he is a weekend DJ on WJEQ-FM in Macomb, IL, and works during the summer months as a news reporter for WQAD-TV in Moline, IL.